**THE WORDS THAT DEFINED
OUR PLACE IN HISTORY.
THE WORDS THAT OPENED OUR EYE
AND ROUSED OUR EMOTIONS.**

IN OUR OWN WORDS
Extraordinary Speeches
of the
American Century

"Settle down for a fabulous journey through ten decades of American history. Let your imagination carry you beyond the words on the page so that you can hear the music in the speaker's delivery—the pitch of the voice, the inflection, the cadence, the changing rhythm, the alliteration, the pulse, the sense of movement—and most of all, the passion that stirred the heart of an audience and left an indelible mark on history."

—from the foreword by Doris Kearns Goodwin

★ ★ ★ ★ ★

"Uniquely textured. . . . There is no comparable one-volume collection of twentieth-century commentary that evokes such a diversity of viewpoints."

—*Library Journal*

"A fine snapshot. . . . All of the great moral and social debates can be found here."

—*New York Post*

"Just amazing. . . . It really is a history of our time."

—Charlie Rose

In Our Own Words

Extraordinary Speeches of the American Century

EDITED BY
SENATOR ROBERT TORRICELLI
AND ANDREW CARROLL
FOREWORD BY DORIS KEARNS GOODWIN

WASHINGTON SQUARE PRESS
PUBLISHED BY POCKET BOOKS

New York   London   Toronto   Sydney

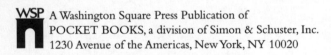

WSP A Washington Square Press Publication of
POCKET BOOKS, a division of Simon & Schuster, Inc.
1230 Avenue of the Americas, New York, NY 10020

ISBN: 0-7434-1052-1

First Washington Square Press trade paperback printing October 2000

10 9 8 7

Cover design by Brigid Pearson
Cover photo by Michael Barraud/Tony Stone Images

Printed in the U.S.A.

To Betty Lotz Torricelli
Mother, Teacher, Friend

CONTENTS

1950–1959

1960–1969

1970–1979

1980–1989

1990–1999

FOREWORD

A T A TIME WHEN THE OCCASIONS CALLING FOR GREAT ORATORY SEEM to be diminishing, this fascinating collection of celebrated American speeches delivered through the course of the twentieth century may appear at first blush an exercise in nostalgia. Yet, as Senator Robert Torricelli makes clear, while oratory today is different from what it was in the past, having shifted over time to accommodate the shifting forms of media, it is a mistake to conclude that its flame has been permanently extinguished.

As far back as ancient Rome, Tacitus lamented that all the great orators were gone. At the turn of the twentieth century, similar warnings were issued, as observers feared that the rise of the tabloid press with its emphasis on pictures would forever destroy the art of oratory. The memorable speeches collected here from the beginning to the end of this century prove these predictions wrong. For here in this single volume are thousands of spoken words which, taken together, uplifted, rallied, healed, led, taught, infuriated, and ennobled our fellow Americans through the extraordinary events of an extraordinary century.

The shifting style of oratory over time provides an interesting subtext to the collection. In the nineteenth century, when public speaking was a primary form of both communication and entertainment, families were willing to walk for miles to stand in an open field or sit on a hilltop in order to listen to dramatic speeches and fiery debates that often lasted for five or six hours. When most major newspapers still routinely printed the full texts of speeches, the literary quality of the speech was considered essential. With the coming of radio and television, however, speeches tended to take on a more conversational tone, as speakers looked for everyday words, concrete examples, and homely analogies they might use in an informal talk with one or two of their friends. Orators who successfully adapted to these changes were successful, those who did not were left behind, in much the same way as were the silent screen actors who could not make the shift to the talkies.

The collection opens in the progressive era, when an aroused populace was moved to action by the powerful exhortations of reformers, populists, progressives, socialists, and suffragettes. In our mind's eye, we can see Jane Addams standing before a cheering audience as she decried the spirit of materialism, "an inordinate desire to win wealth" and "to please those who are the possessors of wealth." We can hear Theodore Roosevelt and imagine the volume of his voice as he spoke with fervor of the "struggle of free men to gain and hold the right of self-government against the special interests." We can

hear the burning defiance in the voice of Rose Schneiderman as she exhorted unorganized workers to join the labor movement, and we can feel the
emotion Eugene Debs projected as he railed against wage slavery and called
on the toiling masses to rise. These were passionate times which called for
passionate oratory. The great principles of justice, equality, and freedom were
commonly invoked as orators strove to provide a voice for people who did
not have access to power—the poor, the disinherited, the oppressed.

The prevailing tone shifts during World War I and its aftermath, becoming more somber, more reflective, and then shifts again with the coming of
the Depression and World War II. Included here are several of Franklin Roosevelt's most eloquent speeches, beginning with his first inaugural delivered
at the height of the Depression in March 1933. We all remember the phrase
"the only thing we have to fear is fear itself," but what becomes evident upon
rereading the entire speech is not simply the president's judicious use of particular words, but the overall mood of confidence he was able to project to a
badly frightened people. By this single speech, White House aide Sam
Rosenman observed, Roosevelt had accomplished one of the most significant achievements of his presidency, "the renewal of the courage and hope
and faith of the American people."

At the end of the 1930s, as Hitler began his murderous conquest of Europe, Roosevelt's speeches became essential tools in moving an isolationist
country to a greater and greater commitment to the Allied cause. Included in
this collection are both Roosevelt's Lend-Lease speech which rallied the
American people to support England's lonely stand against the Nazis and his
address to the Congress the day after Pearl Harbor, a brief but powerful
speech that burned with anger and indignation. What makes this collection
so interesting to read, however, is that along with Roosevelt's call for intervention, we hear the champion of isolationism, Charles Lindbergh, as he de-
livers a passionate argument against becoming involved in the quarrels of the
European nations. So upset was Roosevelt by Lindbergh's words that he told
his Treasury secretary, Henry Morgenthau, that if he should die the following
day, he wanted Morgenthau to know that he was convinced that Lindbergh
was a Nazi.

Through similar pairings, the Reverend Dr. Anna Shaw's eloquent call
in 1919 for a League of Nations is followed by Henry Cabot Lodge's tren-
chant argument against the League delivered before the Senate later the same
year; Dudley Field Malone faces off against William Jennings Bryan at the
Scopes trial; and Douglas MacArthur's famous speech before the joint session
of Congress in which he bade farewell with the refrain "Old soldiers never
die, they just fade away" is preceded by President Harry Truman's explanation
to the American people of the reasons he fired MacArthur.

Party conventions have provided especially fertile ground for powerful speeches. Included here are Adlai Stevenson's rousing ceremonial welcome at the 1952 Democratic Convention, which paved the way for his nomination as president; Barry Goldwater's defiant acceptance speech in 1964, which paved the way for his defeat in the general election; Ronald Reagan's stirring call for change in his acceptance speech in 1980; Mario Cuomo's passionate defense of liberalism in 1984; and Jesse Jackson's fiery call for action in 1988.

The chronological format of this collection, combined with brief headnotes, provides the reader with the historical context necessary to understand the impact various speeches made at different times. Included here are two powerful speeches calling for an end to segregation—one by W. E. B. Du Bois in 1906, another by Duke Ellington in 1941. Both of these speeches had the qualities necessary to stir an audience—the eloquence, the feeling, the rhythm—but it was not until Martin Luther King's "I Have a Dream" speech in 1963 that the civil rights movement had grown to the point where it could influence the national government and produce the desired result—the long-overdue legislation needed to end legal segregation in the South.

Following the speeches in chronological order also provides poignant moments. As we read John Kennedy's reflective words at an Amherst ceremony in honor of the poet Robert Frost in October 1963, we are chilled by the remembrance that in less than a month his voice would be forever stilled. Similarly, as we read Lyndon Johnson's powerful "Great Society" speech, we cannot help but juxtapose this hopeful moment with the despair of his withdrawal speech only four years later, when the war in Vietnam had cut his beloved Great Society in two.

And beyond politics, this eclectic collection includes humorous and moving speeches in fields ranging from business to labor, from law to sports. So settle down for a fabulous journey through ten decades of American history. Let your imagination carry you beyond the words on the page so that you can hear the music of the speaker's delivery—the pitch of the voice, the inflection, the cadence, the changing rhythm, the alliteration, the pulse, the sense of movement—and most of all, the passion that stirred the heart of an audience and left an indelible mark on history.

Doris Kearns Goodwin
Concord, Massachusetts

ACKNOWLEDGMENTS

FIRST, WE ARE INDEBTED TO ANDREW DUBILL, OUR INDEFATIGABLE CO-editor who contributed enormous amounts of energy and insight to this book. Despite the overwhelming demands of law school, Andrew sacrificed whatever time was needed to help us complete this book on schedule. *In Our Own Words,* quite simply, could not have been done without Andrew, and we are grateful to him beyond words. We are also indebted to Anne Griffin, Amber Mettler, and Alex Vermeychuk, our three research assistants from Princeton University who dedicated their summers to *In Our Own Words.* Undaunted by the stifling heat and humidity of our nation's capital, they prowled the archives of the Library of Congress, pored over spools of microfilm, and paged through countless histories of the twentieth century to gather and transcribe the speeches found in this volume. Throughout it all, they never lost their collective capacity for humor, insight, or judgment. *In Our Own Words* is as much theirs as it is ours.

Deborah Baker, our editor at Kodansha, provided brilliant guidance from start to finish. She has been a joy to work with, and we are grateful to her not just for helping us craft this book, but for understanding the vision of this collection from the very beginning.

Scott Mulhauser and Lona Valmoro dedicated vast amounts of their free time to tracking down obscure speeches, contacts, and permissions. Without their wholehearted support, this book would never have left the conceptual stage.

For the Foreword, we are indebted to Doris Kearns Goodwin, who in the midst of myriad commitments and time constraints graciously crafted a thoughtful and compelling beginning to *In Our Own Words.*

Mel Berger of the William Morris Agency and Miriam Altshuler (Andrew Carroll's agent) inspired faith in our concept from its infancy and provided critical advice throughout every aspect of the writing process. Abbe Lowell and Andrew Genton solidified our deal.

We are indebted also to the following pantheon of intellectuals, scholars, and academics; they include Stephen Ambrose of the University of New Orleans; Dick Baker, the Historian of the United States Senate; Rabbi Menachem Genack of the Orthodox Union; Roger Lannius of NASA; Richard Leone of the Twentieth Century Fund; Don Ritchie, Associate Historian of the Senate; and the staff of the Library of Congress.

In addition, Professors Ann Gordon, Lora Garrison, David L. Lewis, William O'Neill, and David Oshinsky of Rutgers University; Douglas Brinkley of the University of New Orleans; Professor Robert Cox of the University of North Carolina, Chapel Hill; and Professor Carol Rigolot of Princeton University each provided insight with particular historical periods. Patricia Evans and Bryan Stiglemeyer of the United States Supreme Court Library offered us a glimpse into the Court's oral arguments. Fred Courtright provided invaluable permissions advice. Thanks also to the research and archives staffs of the Franklin D. Roosevelt, Harry S. Truman, Dwight D. Eisenhower, John F. Kennedy, Richard M. Nixon, and Ronald Reagan Presidential Libraries, as well as to Regina Thomas; John Sampas from the Estate of Jack Kerouac; Marian Wright Edelman; Kathryn Bina of the Centers for Disease Control; David Meltzer, editor of *Reading Jazz* (Mercury House, San Francisco); Dwight Miller at the Herbert Hoover Library; David Wade in Senator John Kerry's office; Pat Simon; Kevin Bowen at the William Joiner Center for the Study of War and Social Consequences; Jane Smith; Phyllis Schlafly; Bill Henderson; and Jean N. Berry at the Wellesley College Archives.

James Devlin, Joshua Kutlin, and Christopher Seidel each contributed critical assistance with cantankerous computers under difficult deadlines. Ed Gehres lent last-minute hints with permissions. David Tipson and Kevin Joyce reviewed drafts of the manuscripts. Beth Devlin offered continuous assistance with grammar and transcribing. Kathleen, Mary, and Robert Dubill each provided constructive criticism for the manuscript and speech selections.

Frederick D. Atwood, Laurie Covington, Hughlings J. Himwich, John T. Kennedy, and Richard Rouse of Flint Hill School each offered timeless advice on historical rigor and grammatical construction. Journalists Richard Benedetto, Tony Mauro, and Ralph Soda reminded us of events we often overlooked. The Reverend Thomas J. Mullelly of the Aquinas Institute at Princeton University; the Reverend Thomas Hagan of Hands Together; and the Reverend Robert Keeley of the Archdiocese of Chicago not only taught us about important religious figures of the twentieth century, but, more important, provided us spiritual fortitude during the grueling editing stages of this process.

INTRODUCTION

THE CENTER OF MY EARLY LIFE WAS MY MOTHER'S SCHOOL LIBRARY. A lifelong teacher, she tended that collection of books as if it were another child. This might have led to a sibling rivalry. But, as the library grew, I soon realized that I was the principal beneficiary; all damaged or duplicate books became mine, and the walls of my room disappeared behind a covering of publishers' promotions.

As technology progressed, publishers no longer simply sent books, but audio tapes and vinyl records as well. Among the first to arrive was a recording of famous speeches. By today's standards of CD-ROMs and compact discs, these 33 rpm records were of poor quality, the clarity of the speeches faintly obscured by a continuous murmur of pops and hisses. Nevertheless, these scratchy voices reached out from the past and eventually became as familiar to me as neighborhood friends.

The lessons of history learned from these orators varied, and the quality of language and delivery was inconsistent. But this was of no consequence, because an essential lesson emerged overall: Words mattered. Words didn't merely chart or record the unfolding drama of history, they *made* history. The spoken word could incite, console, energize, and instruct. For years I have wanted to convey this power, this spirit of purpose and idealism, in a book of speeches.

In Our Own Words is that book—a collection of over 150 extraordinary orations, eulogies, commencement speeches, sermons, public tributes, testimonies, farewells, courtroom summations, and similar addresses given by Americans in the twentieth century. These are the words that have spurred this nation to war, freed the persecuted, tempered simmering mobs, entertained us with wit and humor, launched cultural and environmental movements, heralded breakthroughs in science and medicine, and reminded us of our ideals in periods of moral and political crisis.

In selecting these speeches we have attempted to capture the triumphs, horrors, discoveries, and travails of the last hundred years. "Extraordinary" in no way implies endorsement of the speakers or their beliefs. The stage of history has showcased not only martyrs and social revolutionaries, but scoundrels, bigots, blowhards, and zealots. As appalling as their words may be—such as Senator Joseph McCarthy's infamous declaration that he held in his hand a list of "card-carrying Communists" or George Wallace's boldly unapologetic defense of "Segregation now! Segregation forever!"—they are reflections of their times. We may recoil at their invective, but we cannot ignore their influence.

Assembled chronologically, the speeches are introduced with as little commentary as possible. Many have been edited—some at the request of the contributors, others because the original speeches were, quite frankly, too prolix for a collection attempting to be both inclusive and historically comprehensive. (All cuts have been designated with ellipses.) The notes preceding—and sometimes following—each speech are intended simply to introduce the speaker and the circumstances that prompted the speech and, when appropriate, relate any repercussions.

Some anecdotes, however, proved too irresistible to omit. General George "Blood and Guts" Patton, for example, had a high-pitched, squeaky voice. Sarah Weddington, the lead attorney in the momentous *Roe v. Wade* decision, was only twenty-five years old when she argued on behalf of Jane Roe before the Supreme Court. Robert Kennedy's tribute to Martin Luther King, considered one of the most heartfelt and poetic eulogies ever delivered, was an impromptu address given to an African American crowd in the heart of an urban neighborhood on April 5, 1969—just hours after King had been slain. Kennedy's aides, fearing for his safety, implored him not to attend the outdoor rally, but he insisted. A potentially explosive moment was defused through the sheer force of Kennedy's impassioned expression of grief and understanding.

Excavating the archives of history produced other gems. We discovered a little-known speech by Mark Twain to a class of young girls expounding on drinking, smoking, lying, and marrying. A budding political activist named Hillary Rodham spoke before her graduating class at Wellesley College in 1969, and, before beginning her scripted remarks, publicly challenged the comments of the Republican senator who spoke before her. (Ms. Rodham, of course, went on to become our nation's First Lady twenty-three years later.) And as America stood on the brink of financial ruin in the early 1930s, Joseph Strauss, the engineer of the Golden Gate Bridge, announced at the bridge's 1933 groundbreaking ceremony that the mighty—and very expensive—structure would serve as a symbol of the resilience of the human spirit.

Throughout these past hundred years we also see technology—most notably radio, film, television, and the Internet—dramatically transform the presentation, preservation, and dissemination of speeches. A collection of oratory from the 1800s would consist almost entirely of appearances before institutional gatherings and events. Even the twentieth century began with public speaking as the central form of political communication. Businesses, labor unions, political parties, and congregations heard their leaders talking to them in formal and, to our impatient ears, lengthy speeches.

When it suddenly became possible to broadcast messages to millions of people nationwide, the style, length, and content of speeches changed to accommodate the dynamics of the new media. Electronic communication, in effect, shortened the national attention span. (A term was even created—the "sound bite"—to describe easily digestible nuggets of rhetoric intended for mass consumption.) Public speeches, as Doris Kearns Goodwin notes in the Foreword, became more colloquial, delivered with substantially fewer rhetorical flourishes. Even on the most solemn occasions, speakers began adopting a more conversational tone.

Speakers, especially those appearing before the television camera's unblinking eye, had to address audiences with different cultural, economic, and political opinions—and prove appealing to them all. No longer could the politician or business leader count on the consensus of a self-selected group of individuals assembled in a convention hall united in purpose. Beyond the last row was a more diverse audience of people watching on their living room sofas or listening on their car radios.

If this new exposure tended to encourage ambiguity and doubletalk, it also made speeches more egalitarian. From some more distant perspective the century might appear to be punctuated solely with the grandiloquence of Roosevelt, Kennedy, or Reagan. But the most lasting impression we hope to leave with this collection is that the power of words is not reserved for the powerful. The use of language to effect change or communicate ideas is limited only by imagination, not birthright. Sixteen-year-old Ryan White, who contracted HIV from a blood transfusion, gave the AIDS epidemic a human face and helped dispel the fear and hysteria surrounding the disease through his courageous public appearances. A former drug addict named Patricia Godley virtually silenced a town hall audience in Washington, D.C., after an emotional, unscripted appeal for all Americans to remember that addicts are human beings "worth fighting for." Broadcast live on ABC's *Nightline,* Godley's message was instantly heard by millions. The sound track of democracy, as it is recorded here, emanates from well beyond the Oval Office or the gilded halls of Congress. Indeed, it is all around us.

So this collection begins with these few observations here but presents no conclusions throughout the chapters themselves. It was not our purpose to write the complete history of this century or encumber these speeches with academic analysis. Rather, it was to have you, the reader, experience firsthand and unfiltered the breathtaking sweep of change and the enormousness of the human experience during these past hundred years. In working on this anthology I have confirmed only what my mother led me to discover a long time ago: There is a power in the spoken word. No image resonates longer or more vividly in the human mind than the picture painted by a well-crafted phrase. It is a power to inspire great good or inflict great harm. Oratory in America during the twentieth century seems to have captured it all.

Senator Robert G. Torricelli
Washington, D.C.

1900–1909

TONIGHT WHEN THE CLOCK STRIKES TWELVE, THE PRESENT century will have come to an end. We look back upon it as a cycle of time within which the achievements in science and in civilization are not less than marvelous. The advance of the human race during the past hundred years has not been equaled by the progress of man within any of the preceding ages. The possibilities of the future for mankind are the subjects of hope and imagination. . . .

On this occasion, which is one of solemnity, I express the earnest wish that the rights of the individual man shall continue to be regarded as sacred, and that the crowning glory of the coming century shall be the lifting up of the burdens of the poor, the annihilation of all misery and wrong, and that the peace and goodwill which the angels proclaimed shall rest on the contending nations as the snowflakes upon the land.

—*Randolph Guggenheimer*
New York Board of Education
December 31, 1899

Don P. Halsey Extols the Virtues of Great Oratory.

"We frequently hear it said," Virginia State Senator Don P. Halsey ruefully observed, "that the age of great orators is past." But Halsey was unwilling to accept this, and, in a speech he gave throughout the late 1890s and early 1900s, he celebrated the enduring art of oratory and its enormous power to influence and inspire humanity.

Oratory is an abiding faculty in mankind, and the supply never greatly exceeds or falls short of the demand. It may just be at its ebb, but it has been so a hundred times before. It has also been at the flood again as often, and so surely as prosperity always follows adversity, so truly will a temporary decadence be followed by a revival in oratory. History shows us that the great orators have appeared, and the great orations have been delivered, in the revolutionary periods. Great orators have always accompanied great epochs, and whenever there have been wrongs to right, whenever there has been truth to spread, whenever there has been the vital spark of independence to kindle into flames of mountain height, then there have been heard the voices of orators, clearing the way and blazing the path for the onward march of right and justice. . . .

As a matter of fact, the men who exercise the most influence today are not the millionaires of whom we hear so much—not the Rockefellers and Goulds and Morgans who dominate the realm of finance, not the mere money grubbers who inhabit the streets called Lombard and Wall. They have a large part in the world's affairs, it is true, but above and beyond them in influence and in power are the statesmen, the preachers, the thinkers, the philosophers, whose eloquence is molding public opinion—that great silent force which is under the world, and which is more powerful to move and uplift it than the lever of Archimedes. These are the men who are shaping the world's future history, and no greater instrumentality is at their command than the queenly art of oratory.

No, my friends, there is no such thing as "decadence of oratory." There are as many great orators living today as have ever existed at any period of the world's history. They may not be known, having never had the opportunity or the occasion to show their powers, but they live, and the world will know it if the occasion arises. The art of oratory is not in decadence. It survives and will survive as long as time shall endure. Humanity does not change, and the influences which have acted upon it from the beginning will continue to act upon it to the end.

This is not the first time that men have claimed oratory to be a thing of the past. As far back as the days of old Rome, Tacitus lamented that the great orators were all gone and that oratory had declined, and yet we have ever seen that, when occasion called it forth, it is followed in as pure and strong a stream as in the days of Cicero himself. Thus it will ever be. As our needs, so shall be our strength. And if ever the time shall come when oppression shall find a place in our land—when the rights of the people shall be trodden down, when patriotism shall need to be awakened to destroy tyrants, or when our social fabric shall become rotten and need renewal—then no one need ever fear that there will not arise great men who, by the power of oratory greater perhaps than the world has ever known before, will arouse the people to a sense of their dangers and lead the van in the upward march of civilization. Thus may it be.

Through all the changes that are to come as "the great world goes spinning down the ringing grooves of change," may the time never come when the voices of orators shall be silenced in the councils of our people, or cease to mingle with the chime of the Sabbath bells when men are gathered together to worship God; but on, on to the time when the shining fabric of our universe shall crumble into unmeaning chaos and take itself where "oblivion broods and memory forgets"; on, on, until the darkness shall come down over all like "the pall of a past world," the stars wander darkling in eternal space, rayless and pathless, and the icy earth like a "lump of death," a "chaos of hard clay," wings "blind and blackening in the moonless air," may the power of oratory survive and wield its mighty influence, consecrated to the cause of liberty and truth, and pointing the way to where the Angel of Progress, leaning over the far horizon of the infinite future, beckons mankind forward and upward and onward forever.

Senator Albert J. Beveridge Defends America's Right to Subjugate "Savage" Peoples and Foreign Governments
&
Senator George F. Hoar Denounces American "Imperialism."

Debate over American "imperialism" in 1902 grew so ferocious in the U.S. Congress that a fistfight broke out on the Senate floor. Senator Tillman (D–SC) slugged his colleague Senator McLaurin (D–SC) above the eye, and McLaurin responded by popping Tillman in the nose. At issue was America's annexation of the Philippines. After the U.S. Navy defeated the Spanish fleet in 1898, President William McKinley ordered Spain to evacuate Cuba and surrender the Philippines, Guam, and Puerto Rico to the United States. Filipino natives rebelled, and American troops were sent in to suppress the insurrection. Senator Albert J. Beveridge (R–IN) traveled to the Philippines in 1899 and returned more determined than ever to promote the annexation of the country. On January 9, 1900, Beveridge stated his case in the Senate.

Mr. President, the times call for candor. The Philippines are ours forever—
"territory belonging to the United States," as the Constitution calls them.
And just beyond the Philippines are China's illimitable markets. We will not
retreat from either. We will not abandon our opportunity in the Orient. We
will not renounce our part in the mission of our race: trustee, under God, of
the civilization of the world. And we will move forward to our work, not
howling our regrets like slaves whipped to their burdens, but with gratitude
for a task worthy of our strength, and thanksgiving to Almighty God that He
has marked us as His chosen people, henceforth to lead in the regeneration
of the world. . . .

Mr. President, self-government and internal development have been the
dominant notes of our first century; administration and the development of
other lands will be the dominant notes of our second century. And administration is as high and holy a function as self-government, just as the care of
a trust estate is as sacred an obligation as the management of our own concerns. Cain was the first to violate the divine law of human society which
makes of us our brother's keeper. And administration of good government is
the first lesson in self-government, that exalted estate toward which all civilization tends.

Administration of good government is not denial of liberty. For what is
liberty? It is not savagery. It is not the exercise of individual will. It is not dictatorship. It involves government, but not necessarily self-government. It
means law. First of all, it is a common rule of action, applying equally to all
within its limits. Liberty means protection of property and life without price,
free speech without intimidation, justice without purchase or delay, government without favor or favorites. What will best give all this to the people of
the Philippines—American administration, developing them gradually toward self-government, or self-government by a people before they know
what self-government means? . . .

Mr. President, this question is deeper than any question of party politics,
deeper than any question of the isolated policy of our country even, deeper
even than any question of constitutional power. It is elemental. It is racial.
God has not been preparing the English-speaking and Teutonic peoples for a
thousand years for nothing but vain and idle self-contemplation and self-
admiration. No! He has made us the master organizers of the world to establish systems where chaos reigns. He has given us the spirit of progress to
overwhelm the forces of reaction throughout the earth. He has made us adept
in government that we may administer government among savage and senile
peoples. Were it not for such a force as this, the world would relapse into bar-
barism and night. And of all our race, He has marked the American people as
His chosen nation to lead finally in the regeneration of the world. This is the

divine mission of America, and it holds for us all the profit, all the glory, all the happiness possible to man. We are trustees of the world's progress, guardians of its righteous peace. The judgment of the Master is upon us: "Ye have been faithful over a few things; I will make you ruler over many things."

What shall history say of us? Shall it say that we renounced that holy trust, left the savage to his base condition, the wilderness to the reign of waste, deserted duty, abandoned glory, forgot our sordid profit even, because we feared our strength and read the charter of our powers with the doubter's eye and the quibbler's mind? Shall it say that, called by history's noblest work, we declined that great commission? Our fathers would not have had it so. No! They founded no paralytic government, incapable of the simplest acts of administration. They planted no sluggard people, passive while the world's work calls them. They established no reactionary nation. They unfurled no retreating flag. . . .

Pray God that spirit never fails. Pray God the time may never come when Mammon and the love of ease shall so debase our blood that we will fear to shed it for the flag and its imperial destiny. Pray God the time may never come when American heroism is but a legend like the story of the Cid, American faith in our mission and our right a dream dissolved, and the glory of our mighty race departed. . . .

Senator George F. Hoar (R–MA) broke with his party to oppose American annexation of the Philippines and other territories. During a May 1902 debate on maintaining American troops in the Philippines, where they were increasingly coming under attack, Hoar gave the following speech in the Senate.

If a strong people try to govern a weak one against its will, the home government will get despotic, too. You cannot maintain despotism in Asia and a republic in America. If you try to deprive even a savage or a barbarian of his just rights you can never do it without becoming a savage or a barbarian yourself.

Gentlemen talk about sentimentalities, about idealism. They like practical statesmanship better. But, Mr. President, this whole debate for the last four years has been a debate between two kinds of sentimentality. There has been practical statesmanship in plenty on both sides. Your side has carried their sentimentalities and ideals out in your practical statesmanship. The other side has tried and begged to be allowed to carry theirs out in practical statesmanship also. On one side have been these sentimentalities. They were the ideals of the fathers of the Revolutionary time, and from their day down till the day of Abraham Lincoln and Charles Sumner was over. The sentimentalities were that all men in political right were created equal; that governments derive their just powers from the consent of the governed and are instituted to secure that equality; that every people—not every scattering neighborhood or settlement without organic life, not every portion of a people who may be temporarily discontented, but the political being that we call a people—has the right to institute a government for itself and to lay its foundation on such principles and organize its powers in such form as to it and not to any other people shall seem most likely to effect its safety and happiness. Now, a good deal of practical statesmanship has followed from these ideals and sentimentalities. They have built forty-five states on firm foundations. They have covered South America with republics. They have kept despotism out of the Western Hemisphere. They have made the United States the freest, strongest, richest of the nations of the world. They have made the word *republic* a name to conjure by the round world over. By virtue the American flag—beautiful as a flower to those who love it, terrible as a meteor to those who hate it— floats everywhere over peaceful seas and is welcomed everywhere in friendly ports as the emblem of peaceful supremacy and sovereignty in the commerce of the world. . . .

You also, my imperialistic friends, have had your ideals and your sentimentalities. One is that the flag shall never be hauled down where it has once floated. Another is that you will not talk or reason with a people with arms in their hands. Another is that sovereignty over an unwilling people may be bought with gold. And another is that sovereignty may be got by force of arms, as the booty of battle or the spoils of victory.

What has been the practical statesmanship which comes from your ideals and your sentimentalities? You have wasted six hundred millions of treasure. You have sacrificed nearly ten thousand American lives—the flower of our youth. You have devastated provinces. You have slain uncounted thousands of the people you desire to benefit. You have established reconcentration camps. Your generals are coming home from their harvest, bringing their sheaves with them, in the shape of thousands of sick and wounded and insane to drag out their miserable lives, wrecked in body and mind. You make the American flag in the eyes of numerous people the emblem of sacrilege in Christian churches, and of the burning of human dwellings, and of the horror of the water torture. Your practical statesmanship, which disdains to take George Washington or Abraham Lincoln or the soldiers of the Revolution or of the Civil War as models, has looked in some cases to Spain for your example. I believe—nay, I know—that in general our officers and soldiers are humane. But in some cases they have carried on your warfare with a mixture of American ingenuity and Castilian cruelty.

Your practical statesmanship has succeeded in converting a people who three years ago were ready to kiss the hem of the garment of the American and to welcome him as a liberator, who thronged after your men when they landed on those islands with benediction and gratitude, into sullen and irreconcilable enemies, possessed of a hatred which centuries cannot eradicate. . . .

Forty-four years later, in 1946, the Philippines achieved independence.

Jane Addams Offers an Impassioned Tribute to George Washington on the Anniversary of His Birthday.

The first American woman to win the Nobel Prize for peace, which she received in 1931, Jane Addams was best known for transforming an abandoned, run-down mansion in one of Chicago's poorest neighborhoods into Hull House, a settlement home for the city's neediest. Addams was only twenty-nine when Hull House opened its doors in 1889, offering medical care, legal aid, educational programs, and other essential services. On February 23, 1903, the Union League Club of Chicago invited Addams to speak in honor of George Washington's birthday. Addams used the opportunity not only to celebrate Washington's extraordinary legacy, but also to encourage her audience to emulate the integrity of his character.

We meet together upon those birthdays of our great men not only to review their lives, but to revive and cherish our own patriotism. This matter is a difficult task. In the first place, we are prone to think that by merely reciting these great deeds we get a reflected glory, and that the future is secure to us because the past has been so fine. In the second place, we are apt to think that we inherit the fine qualities of those great men simply because we have had a common descent and are living in the same territory.

As for the latter, we know full well that the patriotism of common descent is the mere patriotism of the clan—the early patriotism of the tribe. We know that the possession of a like territory is merely an advance upon that, and that both of them are unworthy to be the patriotism of a great cosmopolitan nation, whose patriotism must be large enough to obliterate racial distinction and to forget that there are such things as surveyor's lines. Then when we come to the study of great men it is easy to think only of their great deeds, and not to think enough of their spirit. What is a great man who has made his mark upon history? Every time, if we think far enough, he is a man who has looked through the confusion of the moment and has seen the moral issue involved; he is a man who has refused to have his sense of justice distorted; he has listened to his conscience until conscience becomes a trumpet call to like-minded men, so that they gather about him, and together, with mutual purpose and mutual aid, they make a new period in history.

Let us assume for a moment that if we are going to make this day of advantage to us, we will have to appeal to the present as well as to the past. We will have to rouse our national consciences as well as our national pride, and we will all have to remember that it lies with the young people of this nation whether or not it is going to go on to a finish in any way worthy of its beginning.

If we go back to George Washington, and ask what he would be doing were he bearing our burdens now and facing our problems at this moment, we would, of course, have to study his life bit by bit—his life as a soldier, as a statesman, and as a simple Virginia planter.

First, as a soldier. What is it that we admire about the soldier? It certainly is not that he goes into battle. What we admire about the soldier is that he has the power of losing his own life for the life of a larger cause; that he holds his personal suffering of no account; that he flings down in the rage of battle his all and says, "I will stand or fall with this cause." That, it seems to me, is the glorious thing we most admire, and if we are going to preserve that same spirit of the soldier, we will have to found a similar spirit in the civil life of the people, the same pride in civil warfare, the spirit of courage, and the spirit of self-surrender which lies back of this.

If we look out upon our national perspective, do we not see certainly one great menace which calls for patriotism? We see all around us a spirit of materialism—an undue emphasis put upon material possessions, an inordinate desire to win wealth, an inordinate desire to please those who are the possessors of wealth. Now, let us say, if we feel that this is a menace, that with all our power, with all the spirit of a soldier, we will arouse high-minded youth of this country against this spirit of materialism. We will say today that we will not count the opening of markets the one great field which our nation is concerned in, but that when our flag flies everywhere it shall fly for righteousness as well as for increased commercial prosperity; that we will see to it that no sin of commercial robbery shall be committed where it floats; that we shall see to it that nothing in our commercial history will not bear the most careful scrutiny and investigation; that we will restore a commercial life, however complicated, to such honor and simple honesty as George Washington expressed in his business dealings.

Let us take, for a moment, George Washington as a statesman. What was it he did, during those days when they were framing a Constitution, when they were meeting together night after night, and trying to adjust the rights and privileges of every class in the community? What was it that sustained him during all those days, all those weeks, during all those months and years? It was the belief that they were founding a nation on the axiom that all men are created free and equal. What would George Washington say if he found that, among us, there were causes constantly operating against that equality? If he knew that any child which is thrust prematurely into industry has no chance in life with children who are preserved from that pain and sorrow? If he knew that every insanitary street, and every insanitary house, cripples a man so that he has no health and no vigor with which to carry on his life labor? If he knew that all about us are forces making against skill, making against the best manhood and womanhood? What would he say? He would say that if the spirit of equality means anything, it means like opportunity, and if we once lose like opportunity we lose the only chance we have toward equality throughout the nation.

Let us take George Washington as a citizen. What did he do when he retired from office, because he was afraid holding office any longer might bring a wrong to himself and harm to his beloved nation? We say that he went back to his plantation on the Potomac. What were his thoughts during the all too short days that he lived there? He thought of many possibilities, but, looking out over his country, did he fear that there should rise up a crowd of men who held office not for their country's good, but for their own good? Would he not have foreboded evil if he had known that among us were groups and hordes of professional politicians who, without any blinking or without any pretense that they did otherwise, apportioned the spoils of office, and considered an independent man as a mere intruder, as a mere outsider? If he had seen that the original meaning of office holding and the function of government had become indifferent to us, that we were not using our foresight and our conscience in order to find out this great wrong which was sapping the foundations of self-government? He would tell us that anything which makes for better civic service, which makes for a merit system, which makes for fitness for office, is the only thing which will tell against this wrong, and that this course is the wisest patriotism. What did he write in his last correspondence? He wrote that he felt very unhappy on the subject of slavery, that there was, to his mind, a great menace in the holding of slaves. We know that he neither bought nor sold slaves himself, and that he freed his own slaves in his will. That was a century ago. A man who a century ago could do that, would he, do you think, be indifferent now to the great questions of social maladjustment which we feel all around us? His letters breathe a yearning for a better condition for the slaves as the letters of all great men among us breathe a yearning for the better condition of the unskilled and underpaid. A wise patriotism, which will take hold of these questions by careful, legal enactment, by constant and vigorous enforcement, because of the belief that if the meanest man in the republic is deprived of his rights, then every man in the republic is deprived of his rights, is the only patriotism by which public-spirited men and women, with a thoroughly aroused conscience, can worthily serve this republic. Let us say again that the lessons of great men are lost unless they reinforce upon our minds the highest demands which we make upon ourselves; that they are lost unless they drive our sluggish wills forward in the direction of their highest ideals.

Tammany Hall Politician George Washington Plunkitt Justifies "Honest Graft."

"The politician who steals is worse than a thief. He is a fool," George Washington Plunkitt famously remarked. "With the grand opportunities all around for a man with a political pull there's no excuse for stealin' a cent." Notoriously candid, Plunkitt was one of the most influential ward bosses in New York City's infamous Tammany Hall— a Democratic machine that virtually dominated city politics from the 1850s to the 1930s by doling out patronage jobs and contracts in return for votes, power, and money. Plunkitt flaunted his ability to use the system for his personal gain and saw nothing wrong with what he called, as in the following 1905 address, "honest graft."

Everybody is talkin' these days about Tammany men growin' rich on graft, but nobody thinks of drawin' the distinction between honest graft and dishonest graft. There's all the difference in the world between the two. Yes, many of our men have grown rich in politics. I have myself. I've made a big fortune out of the game, and I'm gettin' richer every day, but I've not gone in for dishonest graft—blackmailin' gamblers, saloonkeepers, disorderly people, et cetera—and neither has any of the men who have made big fortunes in politics.

There is an honest graft, and I'm an example of how it works. I might sum up the whole thing by sayin', "I seen my opportunities and I took 'em."

Just let me explain by examples. My party's in power in the city, and it's goin' to undertake a lot of public improvements. Well, I'm tipped off, say, that they're going to lay out a new park at a certain place. I see my opportunity and I take it. I go to that place and I buy up all the land I can in the neighborhood. Then the board of this or that makes its plan public, and there is a rush to get my land, which nobody cared particular for before. Ain't it perfectly honest to charge a good price and make a profit on my investment and foresight? Of course it is. Well, that's honest graft.

Or supposin' it's a new bridge they're goin' to build. I get tipped off and I buy as much property as I can that has to be taken for approaches. I sell at my own price later on and drop some more money in the bank. Wouldn't you? It's just like lookin' ahead in Wall Street or in the coffee or cotton market. It's honest graft, and I'm lookin' for it every day in the year. I will tell you frankly that I've got a good lot of it, too.

I'll tell you of one case. They were goin' to fix up a big park, no matter

where. I got on to it, and went lookin' about for land in that neighborhood.
I could get nothin' at a bargain but a big piece of swamp, but I took it fast
enough and held on to it. What turned out was just what I counted on. They
couldn't make the park complete without Plunkitt's swamp, and they had to
pay a good price for it. Anything dishonest in that?

Up in the watershed I made some money, too. I bought up several bits of
land there some years ago and made a pretty good guess that they would be
bought up for water purposes later by the city.

Somehow I always guessed about right, and shouldn't I enjoy the profit
of my foresight? It was rather amusin' when the condemnation commissioners came along and found piece after piece of the land in the name of George
Plunkitt of the Fifteenth Assembly District, New York City. They wondered
how I knew just what to buy. The answer is, I seen my opportunity and I took
it. . . .

I've told you how I got rich by honest graft. Now, let me tell you that
most politicians who are accused of robbin' the city get rich the same way.
They didn't steal a dollar from the city treasury. They just seen their opportunities and took them. That is why, when a reform administration comes in
and spends a half-million dollars in tryin' to find the public robberies they
talked about in the campaign, they don't find them.

The books are always all right. The money in the city treasury is all right.
Everything is all right. All they can show is that the Tammany heads of departments looked after their friends, within the law, and gave them what opportunities they could to make honest graft. Now, let me tell you, that's never
goin' to hurt Tammany with the people. Every good man looks after his
friends, and any man who doesn't isn't likely to be popular. If I have a good
thing to hand out in private life, I give it to a friend. Why shouldn't I do the
same in public life?

Another kind of honest graft: Tammany has raised a good many salaries.
There was an awful howl by the reformers, but don't you know that Tammany gains ten votes for every one it lost by salary raisin'? The Wall Street
banker thinks it shameful to raise a department clerk's salary from $1,500 to
$1,800 a year, but every man who draws a salary himself says, "That's all right.
I wish it was me." And he feels very much like votin' the Tammany ticket on
election day, just out of sympathy.

Tammany was beat in 1901 because the people were deceived into be-
lievin' that it worked dishonest graft. They didn't draw a distinction between
dishonest and honest graft, but they saw that some Tammany men grew rich
and supposed they had been robbin' the city treasury or levyin' blackmail on
disorderly houses, or workin' in with the gamblers and lawbreakers. As a matter of policy, if nothing else, why should the Tammany leaders go into such

dirty business, when there is so much honest graft lyin' around when they are in power? Did you ever consider that?

Now, in conclusion, I want to say that I don't own a dishonest dollar. If my worst enemy was given the job of writin' my epitaph when I'm gone, he couldn't do more than write:

"George W. Plunkitt. He Seen His Opportunities, and He Took 'Em."

Plunkitt's speech, far from endangering his position or reputation, seemed only to heighten his influence and appeal. He died in 1924 at the age of eighty-two, an esteemed and very wealthy man.

President Theodore Roosevelt Condemns the "Muckrakers" Who Smear and Slander Honest Men.

One week after President William McKinley was fatally wounded by an assassin on September 6, 1901, Vice President Theodore Roosevelt became, at age forty-two, America's youngest commander in chief. In one of his first actions as president, Roosevelt launched an aggressive anti-corruption campaign, particularly against the nation's most powerful industries and corporate monopolies. Wildly popular with the general public, Roosevelt's "house cleaning" crusade exposed a seemingly endless parade of unscrupulous officials and leaders in both government and the private sector. But there was one unintended result—in the frenzy to root out the bad, many honest men were publicly smeared by rumors and unfounded charges. In an impassioned speech he gave on April 14, 1906, Roosevelt reiterated his desire to combat fraud, but also railed against those who fabricated stories and dug up dirt—"muckrakers," as he called them—merely to sell newspapers or ruin enemies.

In Bunyan's *Pilgrim's Progress,* you may recall the description of the man with the muck rake, the man who could look no way but downward, with the muck rake in his hand; who was offered a celestial crown for his muck rake, but would neither look up nor regard the crown he was offered, but continued to rake to himself the filth of the floor.

In *Pilgrim's Progress,* the man with the muck rake is set forth as the example of him whose vision is fixed on carnal instead of spiritual things. Yet he also typifies the man who in this life consistently refuses to see aught that is lofty, and fixes his eyes with solemn intentness only on that which is vile and debasing. Now it is very necessary that we should not flinch from seeing what is vile and debasing. There is filth on the floor, and it must be scraped up with the muck rake; and there are times and places where this service is the most needed of all the services that can be performed. But the man who never does anything else, who never thinks or speaks or writes save of his feats with the muck rake, speedily becomes not a help to society, not an incitement to good, but one of the most potent forces for evil.

There are in the body politic, economic and social, many and grave evils, and there is urgent necessity for the sternest war upon them. There should be relentless exposure of, and attack upon, every evil man, whether politician or business man, every evil practice, whether in politics, in business, or in social life. I hail as a benefactor every writer or speaker, every man, who on the platform or in a book, magazine, or newspaper, with merciless severity makes such attack, provided always that he in his turn remembers that the attack is of use only if it is absolutely truthful. The liar is no whit better than the thief, and if his mendacity takes the form of slander, he may be worse than most thieves. It puts a premium upon knavery untruthfully to attack an honest man, or even with hysterical exaggeration to assail a bad man with untruth. An epidemic of indiscriminate assault upon character does no good, but very great harm. The soul of every scoundrel is gladdened whenever an honest man is assailed, or when a scoundrel is untruthfully assailed. . . .

Now, it is easy to twist out of shape what I have just said, easy to affect to misunderstand it, and if it is slurred over in repetition not difficult really to misunderstand it. Some persons are sincerely incapable of understanding that to denounce mudslinging does not mean the endorsement of whitewashing; and both the interested individuals who need whitewashing and those others who practice mudslinging like to encourage such confusion of ideas. . . .

At the risk of repetition, let me say again that my plea is not for immunity to, but for the most unsparing exposure of, the politician who betrays his trust, of the big business man who makes or spends his fortune in illegitimate or corrupt ways. There should be a resolute effort to hunt every such man out of the position he has disgraced. Expose the crime and hunt down the criminal, but remember that even in the case of crime, if it is attacked in sensational, lurid, and untruthful fashion, the attack may do more damage to the public mind than the crime itself.

It is because I feel that there should be no rest in the endless war against the forces of evil that I ask the war be conducted with sanity as well as with resolution. The men with the muck rakes are often indispensable to the well-being of society—but only if they know when to stop raking the muck, and to look upward to the celestial crown above them, to the crown of worthy endeavor. There are beautiful things above and round about them, and if they gradually grow to feel that the whole world is nothing but muck, their power of usefulness is gone. . . .

At this moment we are passing through a period of great unrest—social, political, and industrial unrest. It is of the utmost importance for our future that this should prove to be not the unrest of mere rebelliousness against life, of mere dissatisfaction with the inevitable inequality of conditions, but the unrest of a resolute and eager ambition to secure the betterment of the individual and the nation. . . .

It is a prime necessity that if the present unrest is to result in permanent good, the emotion shall be translated into action, and that the action shall be marked by honesty, sanity, and self-restraint. There is mighty little good in a mere spasm of reform. The reform that counts is that which comes through steady, continuous growth. Violent emotionalism leads to exhaustion.

It is important to this people to grapple with the problems connected with the amassing of enormous fortunes and the use of those fortunes, both corporate and individual, in business. We should discriminate in the sharpest way between fortunes well won and fortunes ill won; between those gained as an incident to performing great services to the community as a whole and those gained in evil fashion by keeping just within the limits of mere law honesty. Of course, no amount of charity in spending such fortunes in any way compensates for misconduct in making them. . . .

The men of wealth who today are trying to prevent the regulation and control of their business in the interest of the public by the proper government authorities will not succeed, in my judgment, in checking the progress of the movement. But if they did succeed, they would find that they had sown the wind and would surely reap the whirlwind, for they would ultimately provoke the violent excesses which accompany a reform coming by convulsion instead of by steady and natural growth.

On the other hand, the wild preachers of unrest and discontent, the wild agitators against the entire existing order, the men who act crookedly, whether because of sinister design or from mere puzzle-headedness, the men who preach destruction without proposing any substitute for what they intend to destroy, or who propose a substitute which would be far worse than the existing evils—all these men are the most dangerous opponents of real reform. If they get their way, they will lead the people into a deeper pit than any into which they could fall under the present system. If they fail to get their way, they will still do incalculable harm by provoking the kind of reaction which in its revolt against the senseless evil of their teaching would enthrone more securely than ever the evils which their misguided followers believe they are attacking.

More important than aught else is the development of the broadest sympathy of man for man. The welfare of the wage worker, the welfare of the tiller of the soil—upon these depend the welfare of the entire country. Their good is not to be sought in pulling down others, but their good must be the prime object of all our statesmanship.

Materially we must strive to secure a broader economic opportunity for all men, so that each shall have a better chance to show the stuff of which he is made. Spiritually and ethically we must strive to bring about clean living and right thinking. We appreciate that the things of the body are important, but we appreciate also that the things of the soul are immeasurably more important.

The foundation stone of national life is, and ever must be, the high individual character of the average citizen.

The Reverend Dr. Donald Sage Mackay Addresses the Question "Does God Care?" After an Earthquake Destroys San Francisco.

"San Francisco is gone!" exclaimed the writer Jack London after an earthquake leveled much of his native city on April 18, 1906. "Nothing remains of it but memories and a fringe of dwelling houses on the outskirts." Fires raged for days and one-third of San Francisco was ultimately reduced to ash and rubble. Approximately 800 people were killed—although some estimates put the number of deaths in the thousands—and more than 200,000 citizens were left homeless. On the Sunday after the quake, the Reverend Dr. Donald Sage Mackay of the Collegiate Church in New York City, like many of his fellow clergy, struggled to explain such overwhelming suffering and disaster in spiritual and religious terms.

"Does God care?" is doubtless the question which many people are asking in these days of national calamity. It was different when two weeks ago the lava of Vesuvius engulfed hundreds of our fellow beings in a distant land, but today, when flaming fingers have written ruin and death over one of the fairest cities of our own land, the religious question becomes insistent. In the words of Eliphaz to Job, "It toucheth thee and thou art troubled." And from many pulpits today trite and wholesome lessons will be drawn defending the ways of Providence and commending to the hearts of the faithful a proper spirit of humility. And yet, as Job replied to his comforters of old, "The thunders of the Almighty, who can understand?" His ways are past finding out.

It is not the function of the Christian pulpit to justify, far less defend, the dealings of the Almighty. The calamity of San Francisco has a profound religious significance, but that significance is not to be discovered by human ingenuity scrutinizing the methods of divine judgment. In itself, in all its appalling horrors, the catastrophe, which in a few hours wiped out the pride and glory of a modern city, staggers the mind. It is an impressive picture of the awful resources of natural law working out in periodic course their appointed destiny. That we cannot explain, but we can give to this calamity a profound religious significance by recognizing in it an opportunity, not for vindicating God, but for helping men. God does care for his children, and that love of His is not limited by death. It is for us who believe in that love to mediate its power through the channels of human sympathy and human brotherhood. We make this disaster beautiful in light of our Christian charity.

Ashes make a good fertilizer, and out of the ashes and ruin of San Francisco will grow—not only a statelier city of stone, but, as we believe, a worthier city of good citizenship, stirred to independence and self-control, while also realizing the blessings of helpfulness and comradeship in this hour of its direct distress.

W. E. B. Du Bois Issues a Call to Arms to His Fellow African Americans in the "Battle for Humanity" & Booker T. Washington Warns Against Confrontational Actions That May Do More Harm than Good.

Booker T. Washington's address at the 1895 Atlanta Cotton Exposition offering a course for reconciliation between blacks and whites electrified his audience and won him national acclaim. Washington's central message to blacks was not to dwell on past (or even present) grievances but to focus on economic security through discipline and hard work, no matter how menial. W. E. B. Du Bois, a twenty-seven-year-old African American educator, was impressed with the speech. "Here," Du Bois remarked, "might be the basis of a real settlement between whites and blacks." But Du Bois's admiration for Washington was short lived, and as Du Bois himself gained national prominence as a writer and lecturer, a rivalry between the two black leaders emerged and became increasingly acrimonious. Du Bois was particularly incensed by Washington's suggestion that blacks should exercise "patience, forbearance, and self-control" when faced with racial injustice. As a rebuke to Washington and his followers, Du Bois formed the Niagara Movement—named after the site of their first meeting in 1905 near Niagara Falls in Canada (New York State hotels would not offer rooms to blacks). At their August 1906 meeting, held in Harpers Ferry, Virginia, in honor of John Brown, Du Bois gave the following speech articulating the movement's goals and philosophy.*

---

* On October 16, 1859—less than two years before the beginning of the Civil War—a white abolitionist named John Brown led a group of eighteen men (five black, thirteen white) on a raid at Harpers Ferry to steal munitions from the town's armory and rally the slaves. Pursued by a young lieutenant named Robert E. Lee, ten of Brown's followers, including two of his sons, were killed and the rest were captured and sentenced to death. Brown was hanged on December 2, 1859.

The men of the Niagara Movement coming from the toil of the year's hard work and, pausing a moment from the earning of their daily bread, turn toward the nation and again ask in the name of ten million the privilege of a hearing. In the past year the work of the Negro-hater has flourished in the land. Step-by-step the defenders of the rights of American citizens have retreated. The work of stealing the black man's ballot has progressed, and the fifty and more representatives of stolen votes still sit in the nation's capital. Discrimination in travel and public accommodation has so spread that some of our weaker brethren are actually afraid to thunder against color discrimination as such and are simply whispering for ordinary decencies.

Against this the Niagara Movement eternally protests. We will not be satisfied to take one jot or tittle less than our full manhood rights. We claim for ourselves every single right that belongs to a freeborn American—political, civil, and social—and until we get these rights we will never cease to protest and assail the ears of America. The battle we wage is not for ourselves alone but for all true Americans. It is a fight for ideals, lest this, our common fatherland, false to its founding, become in truth the land of the thief and the home of the slave, a byword and a hissing among the nations for its sounding pretensions and pitiful accomplishment.

Never before in the modern age has a great and civilized folk threatened to adopt so cowardly a creed in the treatment of its fellow citizens born and bred on its soil. Stripped of verbiage and subterfuge and in its naked nastiness, the new American creed says: Fear to let black men even try to rise lest they become the equals of the white. And this is the land that professes to follow Jesus Christ. The blasphemy of such a course is only matched by its cowardice.

In detail, our demands are clear and unequivocal. First, we would vote. With the right to vote goes everything: freedom, manhood, the honor of your wives, the chastity of your daughters, the right to work, and the chance to rise, and let no man listen to those who deny this. We want full manhood suffrage, and we want it now, henceforth, and forever.

Second, we want discrimination in public accommodation to cease. Separation in railway and streetcars, based simply on race and color, is un-American, undemocratic, and silly. We protest against all such discrimination.

Third, we claim the right of free men to walk, talk, and be with them that wish to be with us. No man has a right to choose another man's friends, and to attempt to do so is an impudent interference with the most fundamental human privilege.

Fourth, we want the laws enforced against rich as well as poor; against capitalist as well as laborer; against white as well as black. We are not more lawless than the white race. We are more often arrested, convicted, and mobbed. We want justice even for criminals and outlaws. We want the Constitution of the country enforced. We want Congress to take charge of Congressional elections. We want the Fourteenth Amendment carried out to the letter and every state disenfranchised in Congress which attempts to disenfranchise its rightful voters. We want the Fifteenth Amendment enforced and no state allowed to base its franchise simply on color. . . .

Fifth, we want our children educated. The school system in the country districts of the South is a disgrace, and in few towns and cities are the Negro schools what they ought to be. We want the national government to step in and wipe out illiteracy in the South. Either the United States will destroy ignorance or ignorance will destroy the United States.

And when we call for education we mean real education. We believe in work—we ourselves are workers—but work is not necessarily education. Education is the development of power and ideal. We want our children trained as intelligent human beings should be, and we will fight for all time against any proposal to educate black boys and girls simply as servants and underlings, or simply for the use of other people. They have a right to know, to think, to aspire.

These are some of the chief things which we want. How shall we get them? By voting where we may vote; by persistent, unceasing agitation; by hammering at the truth; by sacrifice and work.

We do not believe in violence, neither in the despised violence of the raid nor the lauded violence of the soldier, nor the barbarous violence of the mob. But we do believe in John Brown, in that incarnate spirit of justice, that hatred of a lie, that willingness to sacrifice money, reputation, and life itself on the altar of right. And here on the scene of John Brown's martyrdom we reconsecrate ourselves, our honor, our property to the final emancipation of the race which John Brown died to make free.

Our enemies, triumphant for the present, are fighting the stars in their courses. Justice and humanity must prevail. We live to tell these dark brothers of ours—scattered in counsel, wavering, and weak—that no bribe of money or notoriety, no promise of wealth or fame, is worth the surrender of a people's manhood or the loss of a man's self-respect. We refuse to surrender the leadership of this race to cowards and trucklers. We are men; we will be treated as men. On this rock we have planted our banners. We will never give up, though the trump of doom find us still fighting.

And we shall win. The past promised it, the present foretells it. Thank God for John Brown! Thank God for Garrison and Douglass, Sumner and Phillips, Nat Turner and Robert Gould Shaw, and all the hallowed dead who died for freedom! Thank God for all those today, few though their voices be, who have not forgotten the divine brotherhood of all men, white and black, rich and poor, fortunate and unfortunate.

We appeal to the young men and women of this nation, to those whose nostrils are not yet befouled by greed and snobbery and racial narrowness: Stand up for the right, prove yourselves worthy of your heritage and, whether born North or South, dare to treat men as men. Cannot the nation that has absorbed ten million foreigners into its political life without catastrophe absorb ten million Negro Americans into that same political life at less cost than their unjust and illegal exclusion will involve?

Courage, brothers! The battle for humanity is not lost or losing. All across the skies sit signs of promise. The slave is rising in his might, the yellow millions are tasting liberty, the black Africans are writhing toward the light, and everywhere the laborer, with ballot in his hand, is voting open the gates of opportunity and peace. The morning breaks over blood-stained hills. We must not falter, we may not shrink. Above are the everlasting stars.

In contrast to Du Bois, Booker T. Washington adopted a more conciliatory tone in his speeches. Even after a major riot broke out in Atlanta in September 1906, resulting in the deaths of twelve blacks, Washington severely admonished those who encouraged Southern blacks to form "self-defense" groups. Washington blamed Northern blacks for inciting further violence and, on October 11, 1906, delivered the following remarks to an audience in New York City.

In the season of disturbances and excitement, if others yield to the temptation of losing control of their judgment and give way to passion and prejudice, let us as a race teach the world that we have learned the great lesson of calmness and self-control; that we are determined to be governed by reason rather than by feeling. Our victories in the past have come to us through our ability to be calm and patient, often while enduring great wrong.

Again, I am most anxious—and I know that in this I speak the sentiment of every conservative member of our race—that our race everywhere bears the reputation of a law-abiding and law-respecting people. If others would break the law and trample it underfoot, let us keep and respect it, and teach to our children to follow our example. In this connection I repeat what I have uttered on a recent occasion: That every iota of influence that we possess should be used to get rid of the criminal and loafing element of our people and to make decent, law-abiding citizens.

To the members of my race who reside in the northern states, let me utter the caution that in your enthusiastic desire to be of service to your brethren in the South you do not make their path more thorny and difficult by rash and intemperate utterances. Before giving advice to the Negro in the South, the Negro in the North should be very sure that what he advises is that which he himself would be willing to take into the heart of the South and put into practice. Be careful not to assist in lighting a fire which you will have no ability to put out.

Some may think that the problems with which we are grappling will be better solved by inducing millions of our people to leave the South for residence in the North, but I warn you that instead of this being a solution it will but add to the complications of the problem.

While condemning the giving of prominence to the work of the mob in the South, we should not fail to give due credit to those of the white race who stood manfully and courageously on the side of law and order during the recent trying ordeals through which this section of our country has been passing. During the racial disturbances the country very seldom hears of the brave and heroic acts of a certain element of southern white people whose deeds are seldom heralded through the press.

The indiscriminate condemnation of all white people on the part of any member of our race is a suicidal and dangerous policy. We must learn to discriminate. We have strong friends, both in the South and in the North, and we should emphasize and magnify the efforts of our friends more than those of them who wish us evil.

I have said we must differentiate between white people in the South. We cannot afford to class all as our enemies, for there are many who are our friends. The country must also learn to differentiate among black people. It is a mistake to place all in the same class when referring to labor, morality, or general conduct. There is a vicious class that disgraces us; there is also a worthy class which should always receive commendation. Further, we must frankly face the fact that the great body of our people are to dwell in the South, and any policy that does not seek to harmonize the two races and cement them is unwise and dangerous.

Creation—construction in the material, civic, educational, moral, and religious world—is what makes races great. Any child can cry and fret, but it requires a full-grown man to create, to construct. Let me implore you to teach the members of our race everywhere that they must become, in an increasing degree, creators of their own careers.

Mark Twain Speaks to Misses Tewksbury's School for Girls on Smoking, Drinking, and Lying.

"I have achieved my seventy years in the usual way," explained the humorist Samuel L. Clemens—better known as Mark Twain—in a 1905 speech, "by sticking strictly to a scheme of life which would kill anybody else." Twain wasn't kidding. A cigar smoker

since childhood, he ate what he pleased, eschewed medicines, and considered exercise "loathsome." At seventy-three, Twain offered a more succinct, though no less spirited, inventory of life lessons to an audience of young ladies graduating from Misses Tewksbury's School in Baltimore.

I don't know what to tell you girls to do. Mr. Martin has told you everything you ought to do, and now I must give you some don'ts. There is nothing for me to do but to tell you young ladies what not to do. There are three things that you should never do on any occasion.

First, girls, don't smoke—that is, don't smoke to excess. I am seventy-three and one half years old, and have been smoking seventy-three of them. But I never smoke to excess. That is, I smoke in moderation—only one cigar at a time.

Second, don't drink—that is, don't drink to excess.

Third, don't marry—I mean, to excess.

Now, if you young ladies will refrain from all these things you will have all the virtues that anyone will honor and respect.

Another thing I want to say, and that is that honesty is the best policy. That is an old proverb, but you don't want ever to forget it in your journey through life.

I remember when I had just written *Innocents Abroad* when I and my partner wanted to start a newspaper syndicate. We needed three dollars and did not know where to get it. While we were in a quandary I espied a valuable dog on the street. I picked up the canine and sold him to a man for three dollars. Afterward the owner of the dog came along and I got three dollars from him for telling him where the dog was. So I went back and gave the three dollars to the man whom I sold it to, and I have lived honestly ever since.

Ida B. Wells-Barnett Calls Attention to the Epidemic of Lynchings and "Mob Murder" in America.

The daughter of Mississippi slaves, Ida B. Wells-Barnett was a fiercely outspoken activist, journalist, and teacher who inveighed against racial discrimination and championed women's rights throughout the late 1800s and early 1900s. Wells-Barnett began a national crusade against lynching in 1892 when one of her closest friends was lynched by a mob during a race riot. In the following 1909 address to the National Association for the Advancement of Colored People, Wells-Barnett assails the mentality that condones lynchings and other forms of "mob" justice.

The lynching record for a quarter of a century merits the thoughtful study of the American people. It presents three salient facts: First, lynching is a color-line murder. Second, crimes against women is the excuse, not the cause. Third, it is a national crime and requires a national remedy.

Proof that lynching follows the color line is to be found in the statistics which have been kept for the past twenty-five years. During the few years preceding this period and while frontier law existed, the executions showed a majority of white victims. Later, however, as law courts and authorized judiciary extended into the far West, lynch law rapidly abated, and its white victims became few and far between. . . .

During the last ten years, from 1899 to 1908 inclusive, the number lynched was 959. Of this number, 102 were white, while the colored victims numbered 857. No other nation, civilized or savage, burns its criminals; only under that Stars and Stripes is the human holocaust possible. Twenty-eight human beings burned at the stake, one of them a woman and two of them children, is the awful indictment against American civilization—the gruesome tribute which the nation pays to the color line.

Why is mob murder permitted by a Christian nation? What is the cause of this awful slaughter? This question is answered almost daily: always the same shameless falsehood that "Negroes are lynched to protect womanhood." Standing before a Chautauqua assemblage, John Temple Graves, at once champion of lynching and apologist for lynchers, said, "The mob stands today as the most potential bulwark between the women of the South and such a carnival of crime as would infuriate the world and precipitate the annihilation of the Negro race." This is the never-varying answer of lynchers and their apologists. All know that it is untrue. The cowardly lyncher revels in murder, then seeks to shield himself from public execration by claiming devotion to woman. But truth is mighty and the lynching record discloses the hypocrisy of the lyncher as well as his crime.

The Springfield, Illinois, mob rioted for two days, the militia of the entire state was called out, two men were lynched, hundreds of people driven from their homes, all because a white woman said a Negro assaulted her. A mad mob went to the jail, tried to lynch the victim of her charge, and, not being able to find him, proceeded to pillage and burn the town and to lynch two innocent men. Later, after the police had found that the woman's charge was false, she published a retraction, the indictment was dismissed, and the intended victim discharged. But the lynched victims were dead, hundreds were homeless, and Illinois was disgraced.

As a final and complete refutation of the charge that lynching is occasioned by crimes against women, a partial record of lynchings is cited; 285

persons were lynched for causes as follows: unknown cause, 92; no cause, 10; race prejudice, 49; miscegenation, 7; informing, 12; making threats, 11; keeping saloon, 3; practicing fraud, 5; practicing voodooism, 2; bad reputation, 8; unpopularity, 3; mistaken identity, 5; using improper language, 3; violation of contract, 1; writing insulting letter, 2; eloping, 2; poisoning horse, 1; poisoning well, 2; by white capes, 9; vigilantes, 14; Indians, 1; moonshining, 1; refusing evidence, 2; political causes, 5; disputing, 1; disobeying quarantine regulations, 2; slapping a child, 1; turning state's evidence, 3; protecting a Negro, 1; to prevent giving evidence, 1; knowledge of larceny, 1; writing letter to white woman, 1; asking white woman to marry, 1; jilting girl, 1; having smallpox, 1; concealing criminal, 2; threatening political exposure, 1; self-defense, 6; cruelty, 1; insulting language to woman, 5; quarreling with white man, 2; colonizing Negroes, 1; throwing stones, 1; quarreling, 1; gambling, 1.

Is there a remedy, or will the nation confess that it cannot protect its protectors at home as well as abroad? Various remedies have been suggested to abolish the lynching infamy, but year after year, the butchery of men, women, and children continues in spite of plea and protest. Education is suggested as a preventive, but it is as grave a crime to murder an ignorant man as it is a scholar. True, few educated men have been lynched, but the hue and cry once started stops at no bounds, as was clearly shown by the lynchings in Atlanta, and in Springfield, Illinois.

Agitation, though helpful, will not alone stop the crime. Year after year statistics are published, meetings are held, resolutions are adopted. And yet lynchings go on. . . . The only certain remedy is an appeal to law. Lawbreakers must be made to know that human life is sacred and that every citizen of this country is first a citizen of the United States and secondly a citizen of the state in which he belongs. This nation must assert itself and protect its federal citizenship at home as well as abroad. The strong men of the government must reach across state lines whenever unbridled lawlessness defies state laws, and must give to the individual under the Stars and Stripes the same measure of protection it gives to him when he travels in foreign lands. Federal protection of American citizenship is the remedy for lynching. . . .

In a multitude of counsel there is wisdom. Upon the grave question presented by the slaughter of innocent men, women, and children there should be an honest, courageous conference of patriotic, law-abiding citizens anxious to punish crime promptly, impartially, and by due process of law, also to make life, liberty, and property secure against mob rule.

Time was when lynching appeared to be sectional, but now it is national—a blight upon our nation, mocking our laws and disgracing our Christianity. "With malice toward none but with charity for all," let us undertake the work of making the "law of the land" effective and supreme upon every foot of American soil—a shield to the innocent; and to the guilty, punishment swift and sure.

No federal antilynching law was ever enacted.

Chief Plenty Coup Confers with His Tribal Council on Achieving Peace Between the Great Tribes of the United States.

Sixty-three years old, Chief Plenty Coup of the Crow Nation had witnessed for decades the forced removal of Native Americans from their homes, the undermining of treaties by U.S. officials, and the steady encroachment of white pioneers and settlers on the lands of Native Americans. But when the Crow Nation held a council to prepare for a meeting with the chiefs of the other Indian nations, Chief Plenty Coup's sentiment was not one of anger but resignation. The end for his people had all but come, he recognized, and his remaining hope was to leave behind a legacy of peace between the Crows and the other nations.

The ground on which we stand is sacred ground. It is the dust and blood of our ancestors. On these plains the Great White Father at Washington sent his soldiers armed with long knives and rifles to slay the Indian. Many of them sleep on yonder hill where Pahaska—White Chief of the Long Hair—so bravely fought and fell. A few more passing suns will see us here no more, and our dust and bones will mingle with these same prairies. I see as in a vision the dying speak of our council fires, the ashes cold and white. I see no longer the curling smoke rising from our lodge poles. I hear no longer the songs of the women as they prepare the meal. The antelope have gone; the buffalo wallows are empty. Only the wail of the coyote is heard. The white man's medicine is stronger than ours; his iron horse rushes over the buffalo trail. He talks to us though his "whispering spirit." We are like birds with a broken wing. My heart is cold within me. My eyes are growing dim. I am old.

Before our red brothers pass on to the happy hunting ground, let us bury the tomahawk. Let us break our arrows. Let us wash off our war paint in the river. And I will instruct our medicine men to tell the women to prepare a great council lodge. I will send our hunters into the hills and pines for deer. I will send my runners to the lodges of the Blackfeet, where in that far north flowers border the snow on the hills. I will send them across the fiery desert to the lodges of the Apaches in the south. I will send them east to the lodges of the Sioux, warriors who have met us in many a hard battle. I will send them to the west, where among the mountains dwell the Cayuse and the Umatillas. I will have the outliers build smoke signals on all the high hills, calling the chiefs of all the tribes together, that we may meet here as brothers and friends in one great last council, that we may eat our bread and meat together, and smoke the council pipe, and say farewell as brothers, never to meet again.

Chief Plenty Coup's invitation was accepted by more than twenty other distinguished chiefs, and in September 1909 the "Last Great Indian Council" was held in the valley of the Little Horn, Montana. Chief Plenty Coup remarked at the assembly's conclusion, it was "the greatest event of my life."

The Reverend Reverdy Ransom on "White Supremacy" and an Upcoming Boxing Match Between Jack Johnson and Jim Jeffries.

When Jack Johnson, the nation's premier African American heavyweight boxer, publicly challenged world heavyweight champion Jim Jeffries (who was white) to a fight, Jeffries dismissed the challenge out of hand: "When there are no white men left to fight, I will quit the business. I am determined not to take a chance of losing the championship to a Negro." Jeffries ultimately retired undefeated. But after Johnson had "slaughtered" (in the words of sportswriters) reigning champion Tommy Burns, a promoter offered a $100,000 prize to the winner of a Johnson–Jeffries match. Both men accepted. Animosity between the races escalated to dangerous levels before the encounter and even emanated from the nation's pulpits. When a white minister mocked Johnson in a sermon delivered two weeks before Christmas, the Reverend Reverdy C. Ransom, from the predominantly black Bethel AME Church in New York, responded with the following.

The great civilizations of the ages have cast in classic form some phase of physical prowess. In Greece, it was Isthmian games; in Rome, the gladiatorial fights; in Spain, the matador of the bullfight; in America, it is the prizefighter who defends his person with his fists.

A week ago last Sunday, the Reverend John Hamilton Timbrell of Cedar Cliff, New Jersey, delivered himself of a sermon on the theme: "Can Jeffries Come Back?" He based it on the story of Sampson resting in the lap of Delilah. He says that Jeffries, the modern Sampson, has come from a life of self-indulgence to meet "the big black gorilla."

We have no concern about all this business save to meet the challenge of the Reverend Mr. Timbrell. To begin with, he is an unchristian-like Christian minister. He seeks to fill his auditors with contempt of horror of Jack Johnson, to whom he refers throughout as "the big black gorilla."

The burden of Mr. Trimbell's theme is "Can Jeffries Come Back?" We confess that we have small sympathy with the supremacy of brute forces in this connection, but it has been made an issue that Jeffries must regain white supremacy by defeating Johnson in the roped arena.

Truly our white brother has set for himself an unending task. If Jeffries with his fists must seek to regain white supremacy, then if some Negro poet, artist, sculptor, or musician seeks to realize his conception, the white race throughout the world will be called upon to regain its supremacy. If in statesmanship, oratory, science, philosophy, business, some of the darker children of mankind forge to the front, what is to become of white supremacy? With our Japanese, with China, India, and Africa brushing the sleep of more than three thousand years from their eyes, what is to become of white supremacy when these awake?

I do not believe that Jack Johnson thinks of black supremacy in relation to his contest with Jeffries. It is simply a case of one man meeting another. The best man wins.

The darker races of mankind, and the black race in particular, will keep the white race busy for the next few hundred years throughout the world in defending the interests of white supremacy. The black singer is coming with his song, the poet with his dreams, the sculptor with his conception of some form of beauty and of awe, the orator with his burning phrase, and the scholar with his truth—in every domain of thought.

The greatest marathon race of the ages is now about to begin between the white race and the darker races of mankind. What Jack Johnson seeks to do to Jeffries in the roped arena will be more and more the ambition of Negroes in every domain of human endeavor.

Johnson and Jeffries finally stood toe-to-toe on July 4, 1910, in Reno, Nevada. Defying convention, the two boxers did not shake hands. The fight lasted fifteen rounds and Johnson, nicknamed the "Negroes' Deliverer," prevailed. As word of the outcome spread swiftly across the nation, riots erupted in every southern state, as well as in New York, Massachusetts, Ohio, Missouri, Oklahoma, and Colorado.

1910–1919

LIFE IS GROWTH, LIFE IS PROGRESS, AND PROGRESS DEPENDS ON new ideas. Without the advent of new ideas, we should still be riding in stagecoaches and reading by the light of tallow candles.

Great ideals are the glory of man alone. No other creature can have them. Only man can get a vision and an inspiration that will lift him above the level of himself and send him forth against all opposition or any discouragement to do and to dare and to accomplish wonderful and great things for the world and for humanity.

To no other of God's creatures is given this power but man alone, and the man that has set before him no great and uplifting ideal and never received a vision of the glory of service has never known the joy of real achievement. There can be no conquest to the man who dwells in the narrow and small environment of a groveling life, and there can be no vision to the man the horizon of whose vision is limited by the bounds of self.

But the great things of the world, the great accomplishments of the world, have been achieved by men who had high ideals and who have received great visions. The path is not easy, the climbing is rugged and hard, but the glory of the vision at the end is worthwhile.

—Lecture notes by Matthew Henson,
African American polar explorer
and aide to Commander Robert Peary,
c. 1910

Anarchist Emma Goldman Derides Patriotism
as a "Menace to Liberty."

After gaining national renown as a dynamic public speaker, the Russian-born radical Emma Goldman attracted crowds of thousands to hear her trumpet the social and personal rewards of anarchism and "free love." Goldman had come to the United States in 1886 and, after toiling in the looms and mills of New York, identified herself with the anarchist cause—the belief in the absolute freedom of the individual and the abolishment of government. She was imprisoned three times for her outspoken stances on labor issues, birth control, and pacificism. (She was deported to the Soviet Union in 1919 and ultimately settled in England.) Goldman's most vehement denunciations, as in the following 1910 speech to a New York audience, focused on patriotism as one of society's most malevolent forces.

What is patriotism? Is it love of one's birthplace, the place of childhood's recollections and hopes, dreams, and aspirations? Is it the place where, in childlike naïveté, we would watch the floating clouds and wonder why we, too, could not run so swiftly? In short, is it love for the spot, every inch representing dear and precious recollections of a happy, joyous, and playful childhood?

If that were patriotism, few American men of today would be called upon to be patriotic, since the place of play has been turned into factory, mill, and mine, while deepening sounds of machinery have replaced the music of the birds. No longer can we hear the tales of great deeds, for the stories our mothers tell today are but those of sorrow, tears, and grief.

What, then, is patriotism? "Patriotism, sir, is the last resort of scoundrels," said Dr. Johnson. Leo Tolstoy, the greatest anti-patriot of our time, defines patriotism as the principle that will justify the training of wholesale murderers.

Indeed, conceit, arrogance, and egotism are the essentials of patriotism. Let me illustrate. Patriotism assumes that our globe is divided into little spots, each one surrounded by an iron gate. Those who have had the fortune of being born on some particular spot consider themselves nobler, better, grander, more intelligent than those living beings inhabiting any other spot. It is, therefore, the duty of everyone living on that chosen spot to fight, kill, and die in the attempt to impose his superiority upon all the others.

The inhabitants of the other spots reason in like manner, of course, with the result that from early infancy the mind of the child is provided with bloodcurdling stories about the Germans, the French, the Italians, Russians, et cetera.

Thinking men and women the world over are beginning to realize that patriotism is too narrow and limited a conception to meet the necessities of our time. The centralization of power has brought into being an international feeling of solidarity among the oppressed nations of the world; a solidarity which represents a greater harmony of interests between the working man of America and his brothers abroad than between the American miner and his exploiting compatriot; a solidarity which fears not foreign invasion, because it is bringing all the workers to the point when they will say to their masters, "Go and do your own killing. We have done it long enough for you."

The proletariat of Europe has realized the great force of that solidarity and has, as a result, inaugurated a war against patriotism and its bloody spectre, militarism. Thousands of men fill the prisons of France, Germany, Russia, and the Scandinavian countries because they dared to defy the ancient superstition.

America will have to follow suit. The spirit of militarism has already permeated all walks of life. Indeed, I am convinced that militarism is a greater danger here than anywhere else, because of the many bribes capitalism holds out to those whom it wishes to destroy.

The beginning has already been made in the schools. Children are trained in military tactics, the glory of military achievements extolled in the curriculum, and the youthful mind perverted to suit the government. Thus innocent boys are morally shanghaied into patriotism, and the military Moloch strides conquering through the nation.

When we have undermined the patriotic lie, we shall have cleared the path for the great structure where all shall be united into a universal brotherhood—a truly free society.

Union Activist Rose Schneiderman on the Deaths of 146 Workers in the Triangle Shirtwaist Fire.

Five hundred employees—most of them immigrant women—of the Triangle Shirtwaist factory in New York City were ending their shift on Saturday, March 25, 1911, when a fire swept through the top three floors of the ten-story building. Exit doors had been locked, there were no sprinklers, and the one accessible fire escape collapsed from the weight of panicked workers fleeing from the blaze. When fire trucks finally arrived, their ladders were unable to reach those clinging to the building's ledge, and many workers fell to their deaths. In all, 146 died—3 men and 143 women and girls. When the owners of the factory were found not guilty of manslaughter, the public was outraged and demanded work safety reforms, many of which were enacted. But labor activist Rose Schneiderman, who had helped organize strikes against the Triangle Shirtwaist Company even before the fire, felt it was too little, too late. At a memorial gathering for the victims in the Metropolitan Opera House, Schneiderman vented her indignation at society's apathy toward the working classes.

I would be a traitor to these poor burned bodies if I came here to talk good fellowship. We have tried you good people of the public and we have found you wanting. This is not the first time girls have been burned alive in the city. Every week I must learn of the untimely death of one of my sister workers. Every year thousands of us are maimed. The life of men and women is so cheap and property is so sacred. There are so many of us for one job it matters little if 143 are burned to death.

We have tried you, citizens; we are trying you now, and you have a couple of dollars for the sorrowing mothers and daughters and sisters by way of a charity gift. But every time the workers come out in the only way they know to protest against conditions which are unbearable, the strong hand of the law is allowed to press down heavily upon us.

Public officials have only words of warning to us—warning that we must be intensely orderly and must be intensely peaceable, and they have the workhouse just back of all their warnings. The strong hand of the law beats us back when we rise into the conditions that make life bearable.

I can't talk fellowship to you who are gathered here. Too much blood has been spilled. I know from my experience it is up to the working people to save themselves. The only way they can save themselves is by a strong working-class movement.

Mrs. D. H. Bishop Offers a Harrowing Eyewitness Account of the Titanic's Last Hours.

Eleven stories high and four city blocks long, the Titanic left England for New York on April 11, 1912, with more than 2,000 passengers and crew. By the early hours of April 15, 1,500 of them would be dead. In the frigid waters east of Nova Scotia, an iceberg tore a gash in the starboard side of Titanic's hull, sending the world's largest ship plunging to the bottom of the Atlantic in two and a half hours. When the Senate conducted hearings on the disaster, Mrs. D. H. Bishop, a survivor, related the horror of the ship's last moments.

We did not begin to understand the situation till we were perhaps a mile or more away from the *Titanic.* Then we could see the rows of lights along the decks begin to slant gradually upward from the bow. Very slowly the lines of light began to point downward at a greater and greater angle. The sinking was so slow that you could not perceive the lights of the deck changing their position. The slant seemed to be greater about every quarter of an hour. That was the only difference.

In a couple of hours, though, she began to go down more rapidly. Then the fearful sight began. The people in the ship were just beginning to realize how great their danger was. When the forward part of the ship dropped suddenly at a faster rate, so that the upward slope became marked, there was a sudden rush of passengers on all the decks towards the stern. It was like a wave. We could see the great black mass of people in the steerage sweeping to the rear part of the boat and breaking through to the upper decks. At the distance of about a mile we could distinguish everything through the night, which was perfectly clear. We could make out the increasing excitement on board the boat as the people, rushing to and fro, caused the deck lights to disappear and reappear as they passed in front of them.

This panic went on, it seemed, for an hour. Then suddenly the ship seemed to shoot up out of the water and stand there perpendicularly. It seemed to us that it stood upright in the water for four full minutes.

Then it began to slide gently downwards. Its speed increased as it went down head first, so that the stern shot down with a rush.

The lights continued to burn till it sank. We could see the people packed densely in the stern till it was gone.

As the ship sank, we could hear the screaming a mile away. Gradually it became fainter and fainter and died away. Some of the lifeboats that had room for more might have gone to their rescue, but it would have meant that those who were in the water would have swarmed aboard and sunk her.

Henry Ford Describes the Bonus He Has Provided His Workers and Its Intended Effects on Their Private Lives.

Henry Ford's 1908 Model-Ts were not the first automobiles sold in the United States, but they were the first cars affordable to average Americans. Ford, who had once worked as the chief engineer at Thomas Edison's Illuminating Company in Detroit, revolutionized the use of mass production lines. In 1914, Ford offered an unprecedented profit-sharing plan to his workers, doubled their pay to five dollars a day, and cut their work week by eight hours. Although Ford, the son of an Irish immigrant, was sympathetic to the burdens placed on working men, he readily acknowledged his motivations were not inspired solely by "charity" but by a desire to reduce employee turnover, to prompt his men to work harder, and to exert moral control over their private lives. Speaking before the Federal Commission on Industrial Relations on January 22, 1915, Ford elaborated on what he offered his workers—and what he expected of them in return.

Every man working for the Ford Motor Company is first entitled to his just wages as such—depending upon efficiency and responsibility—which wages are about 15 percent above the usual market wage for the service in question. And then every one who is eligible is entitled to a certain profit. . . .

Prior to the inauguration of the Ford Motor Company's profit-sharing plan, the company was entirely satisfied with the individual and collective output of its men. There was no thought of betterment in this direction, no measure of economic benefit made in anticipation, no desire for publicity or other gain to the company incorporated into the plan or considered with reference to it. The object was simply to better the financial and moral status of the men.

No man is influenced to change his mode of living, his habits, or character in order to qualify under the profit-sharing plan if he does not willingly so elect. Whereas at start 60 percent of the men were receiving a share of the profits, six months later 75 percent of the men were enrolled as participants, and at the end of the first year 87 percent of the entire force were participating, representing practically all of the men past twenty-two years of age with very few exceptions.

The increased efficiency of the men under the plan has been from 15 to 20 percent with reference to work produced, which is further emphasized when you consider that the improvement was made in an eight-hour day versus the comparison in a nine-hour day. Daily absentees from work have decreased from a total equivalent to 10 percent of the working force under old conditions to three-tenths of 1 percent. . . .

Fear and worry in the struggle for livelihood to properly provide for home and dependents with the dread of what might happen if the job is lost have practically been eliminated. No man is discharged from the service of the company until he has been proven utterly unfit from every standpoint. If he fails to make good in one department, the foreman of that department sends him to the clearing house, and he is given repeated trials, if necessary, until he makes good or it is proven that he does not want to succeed. A recent ruling of the company requires the approval of one of four men before the man can be finally dismissed. Of the four, two are, respectively, the president and vice president of the company.

Bank accounts show an increase during the first six months of 130 percent; life insurance carried, 86 percent; value of homes owned outright, 87 percent; value of lots owned outright, 86 percent. This remarkable showing refers only to such employees as are on the profit-sharing basis.

Careful medical survey reveals a substantial improvement in physical attributes. Upwards of two hundred men have been influenced and helped to obtained citizenship in the United States. A carefully prepared map of the city shows that eight thousand families have changed their place of residence since the plan was started. And a study of the districts into which they have moved and from which they came shows that the migration has been from poor and squalid to healthy, sanitary quarters, with environment conducive to health, happiness, and comfort.

Results on character and steadiness of men may perhaps be best measured and more thoroughly understood by agencies outside the company. Police justices say whereas Ford employees, recognized by their badges, were almost daily seen in the prisoner's dock up to a year ago, since January 1914 they have been noticeably absent and are rarely among the unfortunates brought to justice. From one of the largest Polish Catholic parishes in the city, the father writes: "The work of the Ford Motor Company has been of tremendous benefit to my people. Heavy drinking is characteristic of the Poles I know. Your work, however, has resulted in sobriety now being the rule rather than the exception in my parish. . . ."

The company also had the courage to seize an opportunity for breaking away from old-time habits and customs that were possibly applicable to other periods. The institution of a new order treating men like men in man fashion has brought out much of human salvage and proven that barriers between employers and employees thought to exist, and that often do exist, can be largely removed.

A large proportion of our employees were foreign born, many of them recent arrivals not used to American habits and surroundings. Very few, if any, resented our guiding them into better conditions, into habits of thrift, saving, sobriety, and improved moral and social conditions. No coercion is laid upon any employee, but if he is not living a sober life, or is neglecting his duties as a father or husband, and he persists in such course, he cannot be an associate in our business. . . .

We do not undertake to say what corporations should do in general, but if employees of labor—we mean the men themselves at the head of these enterprises—have a genuine, sincere, and active interest in the improvement of the conditions of labor and a heartfelt personal interest in the welfare of their employees, no conditions that are irksome or distasteful will be laid upon the men.

Theoretically, some persons may argue that we have no right to inquire how a man lives at home, so long as he does his work at the factory, but we are talking of conditions, not of theories. Our experience leads us to conclude, beyond doubt, that the interest taken in employees as to their individual welfare is the most desirable from every standpoint, not only that of the employee and his family, but of the business itself.

President Woodrow Wilson Requests a
Declaration of War Against Germany.

"He kept us out of war" was President Woodrow Wilson's slogan for his 1916 re-election campaign. Even after the 1915 German submarine attack on the British ocean-liner Lusitania, which killed an estimated 1,200 people, including 128 Americans, Wilson did not want the United States entangled in the fighting that erupted in August 1914 between the Central Powers—Germany, Austria-Hungary, Bulgaria, and Turkey—and the Allied Powers, which included France, Belgium, Russia, and the British Empire. Wilson, along with most Americans, wanted to limit U.S. involvement to "impartial mediation" and broker peace. "There is such a thing," President Wilson told one audience, "as a man being too proud to fight. There is such a thing as a nation being so right that it does not need to convince others by force." But when German U-boats sank several American ships on March 18, 1917, an agonized President Wilson knew what the consequences would have to be. On April 2, he went before Congress and requested a formal declaration of war.

Gentlemen of the Congress: I have called the Congress into extraordinary session because there are serious, very serious choices of policy to be made, and made immediately, which it was neither right nor situationally permissible that I should assume the responsibility of making. . . .

American ships have been sunk, American lives taken in ways which it has stirred us very deeply to learn of, but the ships and people of other neutral and friendly nations have been sunk and overwhelmed in the waters in the same way. There has been no discrimination. The challenge is to all mankind. Each nation must decide for itself how it will meet it. The choice we make for ourselves must be made with a moderation of counsel and a temperateness of judgment befitting our character and our motives as a nation. We must put excited feeling away. Our motive will not be revenge or the victorious assertion of the physical might of the nation, but only the vindication of right, of human right, of which we are only a single champion. . . .

Armed neutrality is ineffectual enough at best. In such circumstances and in the face of such pretensions it is worse than ineffectual; it is likely only to produce what it was meant to prevent. It is practically certain to draw us into the war without either the rights or the effectiveness of belligerents. There is one choice we cannot make, we are incapable of making: We will not choose the path of submission and suffer the most sacred rights of our nation and our people to be ignored or violated. The wrongs against which we now array ourselves are no common wrongs; they cut to the very roots of human life.

With a profound sense of the solemn and even tragical character of the step I am taking and of the grave responsibilities which it involves, but in un-hesitating obedience to what I deem my constitutional duty, I advise that Congress declare the recent course of the Imperial German government to be in fact nothing less than war against the government and people of the United States; that it formally accept the status of belligerent which has thus been thrust upon it; and that it take immediate steps not only to put the country in a more thorough state of defense, but also to exert all its power and employ all its resources to bring the government of the German Empire to terms and end war. . . .

We have no quarrel with the German people. We have no feeling towards them but one of sympathy and friendship. It was not upon their impulse that their government acted in entering this war. It was not with their previous knowledge or approval. It was a war determined upon as wars used to be de-termined upon in the old, unhappy days when peoples were nowhere con-sulted by their rulers and wars were provoked and waged in the interest of dynasties or of little groups of ambitious men who were accustomed to use their fellow men as pawns and tools. . . .

We are accepting this challenge of hostile purpose because we know that in such a government, following such methods, we can never have a friend; and that in the presence of its organized power, always lying in wait to ac-complish we know not what purpose, there can be no assured security for the democratic governments of the world. We are now about to accept the gage of battle with this natural foe to liberty and shall, if necessary, spend the whole force of the nation to check and nullify its pretensions and its power. We are glad, now that we see the facts with no veil of false pretense about them, to fight thus for the ultimate peace of the world and for the liberation of its peoples, the German peoples included, for the rights of nations, great and small, and the privilege of men everywhere to choose their way of life and of obedience. The world must be made safe for democracy. Its peace must be planted upon the tested foundations of political liberty. We have no selfish ends to serve. We desire no conquest, no dominion. We seek no indemnities for ourselves, no material compensation for the sacrifices we shall freely make. We are but one of the champions of the rights of mankind. We shall be satisfied when those rights have been made as secure as the faith and the free-dom of nations can make them. . . .

It is a distressing and oppressive duty, gentlemen of the Congress, which I have performed in thus addressing you. There are, it may be, many months of fiery trial and sacrifice ahead of us. It is a fearful thing to lead this great peaceful people into war, into the most terrible and disastrous of all wars, civ-ilization itself seeming to be in the balance. But the right is more precious than the peace, and we shall fight for the things which we have always carried nearest our hearts—for democracy, for the right of those who submit to authority to have a voice in their own governments, for the rights and liberties of small nations, for a universal domination of right by such a concert of free peoples as shall bring peace and safety to all nations and make the world itself at last free. To such a task we can dedicate our lives and our fortunes, everything that we are and everything that we have, with the pride of those who know that the day has come when America is privileged to spend her blood and her might for the principles that gave her birth and happiness and the peace which she has treasured. God helping her, she can do no other.

Wilson's speech was greeted with an explosion of applause. "My message today was a message of death for our young men," Wilson was overheard saying at the White House afterward. "How strange it seems to applaud that." Two days later, the Senate voted 90 to 6 and the House of Representatives voted 373 to 50 to pass a resolution recognizing the existence of a state of war with Germany.

Carrie Chapman Catt Urges the U.S. Congress to Make One "Last, Hard Fight" for Suffrage.

Although Jeannette Rankin of Montana was elected to the U.S. House of Representatives in 1916 and fifteen states had granted women the right to vote by 1918, suffragists could not convince Congress to extend voting rights to women on the national level. One of the movement's most persuasive speakers was a former journalist named Carrie Chapman Catt, who became president of the National American Woman Suffrage Association (NAWSA) from 1900 to 1904 and then again from 1915 to 1947. Speaking before NAWSA in the winter of 1917, Catt gave the following open address to Congress.

Woman suffrage is inevitable. Suffragists knew it before November 4, 1917; opponents afterward. Three distinct causes made it inevitable.

First, the history of our country. Ours is a nation born of revolution, of rebellion against a system of government so securely entrenched in the customs and traditions of human society that in 1776 it seemed impregnable. From the beginning of things, nations had been ruled by kings and for kings, while the people served and paid the cost. The American Revolutionists boldly proclaimed the heresies: "Taxation without representation is tyranny." "Governments derive their just powers from the consent of the governed." The colonists won, and the nation which was established as a result of their victory has held unfailingly that these two fundamental principles of democratic government are not only the spiritual source of our national existence but have been our chief historic pride and at all times the sheet anchor of our liberties.

Eighty years after the Revolution, Abraham Lincoln welded those two maxims into a new one: "Ours is a government of the people, by the people, and for the people." Fifty years more passed and the president of the United States, Woodrow Wilson, in a mighty crisis of the nation, proclaimed to the world: "We are fighting for the things which we have always carried nearest to our hearts: for democracy, for the right of those who submit to authority to have a voice in their own government."

All the way between these immortal aphorisms political leaders have declared unabated faith in their truth. Not one American has arisen to question their logic in the 141 years of our national existence. However stupidly our country may have evaded the logical application at times, it has never swerved from its devotion to the theory of democracy as expressed by those two axioms. . . .

With such a history behind it, how can our nation escape the logic it has never failed to follow, when its last unenfranchised class calls for the vote? Behold our Uncle Sam floating the banner with one hand, "Taxation without representation is tyranny," and with the other seizing the billions of dollars paid in taxes by women to whom he refuses "representation." Behold him again, welcoming the boys of twenty-one and the newly made immigrant citizen to "a voice in their own government" while he denies that fundamental right of democracy to thousands of women public school teachers from whom many of these men learn all they know of citizenship and patriotism, to women college presidents, to women who preach in our pulpits, interpret law in our courts, preside over our hospitals, write books and magazines, and serve in every uplifting moral and social enterprise. Is there a single man who can justify such inequality of treatment, such outrageous discrimination? Not one. . . .

Second, the suffrage for women already established in the United States makes women suffrage for the nation inevitable. When Elihu Root, as president of the American Society of International Law, at the eleventh annual meeting in Washington, April 26, 1917, said, "The world cannot be half democratic and half autocratic. It must be all democratic or all Prussian. There can be no compromise," he voiced a general truth. Precisely the same intuition has already taught the blindest and most hostile foe of woman suffrage that our nation cannot long continue a condition under which government in half its territory rests upon the consent of half of the people and in the other half upon the consent of all the people; a condition which grants representation to the taxed in half of its territory and denies it in the other half; a condition which permits women in some states to share in the election of the president, senators, and representatives and denies them that privilege in others. It is too obvious to require demonstration that woman suffrage, now covering half our territory, will eventually be ordained in all the nation. No one will deny it. The only question left is when and how will it be completely established.

Third, the leadership of the United States in world democracy compels the enfranchisement of its own women. The maxims of the Declaration were once called "fundamental principles of government." They are now called "American principles" or even "Americanisms." They have become the slogans of every movement toward political liberty the world around, of every effort to widen the suffrage for men or women in any land. Not a people, race, or class striving for freedom is there anywhere in the world that has not made our axioms the chief weapon of the struggle. More, all men and women the world around, with farsighted vision into the verities of things, know that the world tragedy of our day is not now being waged over the assassination of an archduke, nor commercial competition, nor national ambitions, nor the freedom of the seas. It is a death grapple between the forces which deny and those which uphold the truths of the Declaration of Independence. . . .

Do you realize that in no other country in the world with democratic tendencies is suffrage so completely denied as in a considerable number of our own states? There are thirteen black states where no suffrage for women exists, and fourteen others where suffrage for women is more limited than in many foreign countries.

Do you realize that when you ask women to take their cause to state referendum you compel them to do this: that you drive women of education, refinement, achievement, to beg men who cannot read for their political freedom?

Do you realize that such anomalies as a college president asking her janitor to give her a vote are overstraining the patience and driving women to desperation?

Do you realize that women in increasing numbers indignantly resent the long delay in their enfranchisement?

Your party platforms have pledged women suffrage. Then why not be honest, frank friends of our cause, adopt it in reality as your own, make it a party program, and "fight with us"? As a party measure—a measure of all parties—why not put the amendment through Congress and the legislatures? We shall all be better friends, we shall have a happier nation, we women will be free to support loyally the party of our choice, and we shall be far prouder of our history.

"There is one thing mightier than kings and armies"—aye, than Congresses and political parties—"the power of an idea when its time has come to move." The time for woman suffrage has come. The woman's hour has struck. If parties prefer to postpone action longer and thus do battle with this idea, they challenge the inevitable. The idea will not perish; the party which opposes it may. Every delay, every trick, every political dishonesty from now on will antagonize the women of the land more and more, and when the party or parties which have so delayed woman suffrage finally let it come, their sincerity will be doubted and their appeal to the new voters will be met with suspicion. This is the psychology of the situation. Can you afford the risk? Think it over.

We know you will meet opposition. There are a few "women haters" left, a few "old males of the tribe," as Vance Thompson calls them, whose duty they believe it to be to keep women in the places they have carefully picked out for them. Treitschke, made world famous by war literature, said some years ago, "Germany, which knows all about Germany and France, knows far better what is good for Alsace-Lorraine than that miserable people can possibly know." A few American Treitschkes we have who know better than women what is good for them. There are women, too, with "slave souls" and "clinging vines" for backbones. There are female dolls and male dandies. But the world does not wait for such as these, nor does liberty pause to heed the plaint of men and women with a grouch. She does not wait for those who have a special interest to serve, nor a selfish reason for depriving other people of freedom. Holding her torch aloft, liberty is pointing the way onward and upward and saying to America, "Come."

To you and the supporters of our cause in Senate and House, and the number is large, the suffragists of the nation express their grateful thanks. This address is not meant for you. We are more truly appreciative of all you have done than any words can express. We ask you to make a last, hard fight for the amendment during the present session. Since last we asked a vote on this amendment, your position has been fortified by the addition to suffrage territory of Great Britain, Canada, and New York.

Some of you have been too indifferent to give more than casual attention to this question. It is worthy of your immediate consideration. A question big enough to engage the attention of our allies in wartime is too big a question for you to neglect.

Some of you have grown old in party service. Are you willing that those who take your places by and by shall blame you for having failed to keep pace with the world and thus having lost for them a party advantage? Is there any real gain for you, for your party, for your nation by delay? Do you want to drive the progressive men and women out of your party?

Some of you hold to the doctrine of states' rights as applying to woman suffrage. Adherence to that theory will keep the United States far behind all other democratic nations upon this question. A theory which prevents a nation from keeping up with the trend of world progress cannot be justified.

Gentlemen, we hereby petition you, our only designated representatives, to redress our grievances by the immediate passage of the Federal Suffrage Amendment and to use your influence to secure its ratification in your own state, in order that the women of our nation may be endowed with political freedom before the next presidential election, and that our nation may resume its world leadership in democracy.

Woman suffrage is coming—you know it. Will you, Honorable Senators and Members of the House of Representatives, help or hinder it?

Later that winter, on January 10, 1918, the House of Representatives passed the suffrage amendment, but the Senate defeated it. The Nineteenth Amendment to the Constitution, guaranteeing women the right to vote, would not be ratified until August 26, 1920.

President Woodrow Wilson Enumerates the "Fourteen Points" That Will Ensure World Peace and "Justice to All Peoples and Nationalities."

To a nation familiar with the horror of war (many Americans alive in 1917 were old enough to have seen firsthand the atrocities of the Civil War), the fighting in Europe was like nothing America—or even the rest of the world—had ever seen. Poison gas, flamethrowers, machine guns, and other "innovations" had brought a horrifying, technological ferocity to warfare. As early as the winter of 1917, President Wilson was drafting his famous "Fourteen Points" for peace. On January 18, 1918, President Wilson gave the following address to Congress and the world.

Gentlemen of the Congress: Once more, as repeatedly before, the spokesmen of the Central Empires have indicated their desire to discuss the objects of war and the possible basis of peace. . . .

We entered this war because violations of right had occurred which touched us to the quick and made the life of our own people impossible unless they were corrected and the world secured once and for all against their recurrence. What we demand in this war, therefore, is nothing peculiar to ourselves. It is that the world must be made fit and safe to live in; and particularly that it be made safe for every peace-loving nation which, like our own, wishes to live its own life, determine its own institutions, be assured of justice and fair dealings by the other peoples of the world, as against force and selfish aggression. All of the peoples of the world are in effect partners in this interest, and for our own part we see very clearly that unless justice be done to others it will not be done to us.

The program of the world's peace, therefore, is our program, and that program, the only possible program, as we see it, is this:

One. Open covenants of peace must be arrived at, after which there will surely be no private international action or rulings of any kind, but diplomacy shall proceed always frankly and in the public view.

Two. Absolute freedom of navigation upon the seas, outside territorial waters, alike in peace and in war, except as the seas may be closed in whole or in part by international action for the enforcement of international covenants.

Three. The removal, so far as possible, of all economic barriers and the establishment of an equality of trade conditions among all the nations consenting to the peace and associating themselves for its maintenance.

Four. Adequate guarantees given and taken that national armaments will reduce to the lowest point consistent with domestic safety.

Five. Free, open-minded, and absolutely impartial adjustment of all colonial claims, based on a strict observance of the principle that in determining all such questions of sovereignty the interests of the population concerned must have equal weight with the equitable claims of the government whose title is to be determined.

Six. The evacuation of all Russian territory and such a settlement of all questions affecting Russia as will secure the best and freest cooperation of the other nations of the world in obtaining for her an unhampered and unembarrassed opportunity for the independent determination of her own political development and national policy, and assure her of a sincere welcome into the society of free nations under institutions of her own choosing. And, more than a welcome, assistance also of every kind that she may need and may herself desire. The treatment accorded Russia by her sister nations in the months to come will be the acid test of their goodwill, of their comprehension of her needs as distinguished from their own interests, and of their intelligent and unselfish sympathy.

Seven. Belgium, the whole world will agree, must be evacuated and restored, without any attempt to limit the sovereignty which she enjoys in common with all other free nations. No other single act will serve as this will serve to restore confidence among the nations in the laws which they have themselves set and determined for the government of their relations with one another. Without this healing act the whole structure and validity of international law is forever impaired.

Eight. All French territory should be freed and the invaded portions restored, and the wrong done to France by Prussia in 1871 in the matter of

Alsace-Lorraine, which has unsettled the peace of the world for nearly fifty years, should be righted, in order that peace may once more be made secure in the interest of all.

Nine. A readjustment of the frontiers of Italy should be effected along clearly recognizable lines of nationality.

Ten. The peoples of Austria-Hungary, whose place among the nations we wish to see safeguarded and assured, should be accorded the freest opportunity of autonomous development.

Eleven. Romania, Serbia, and Montenegro should be evacuated; occupied territories restored; Serbia accorded free and secure access to the sea; and the relations of the several Balkan states to one another determined by friendly counsel along historically established lines of allegiance and nationality; and international guarantees of the political and economic independence and territorial integrity of the several Balkan states should be entered into.

Twelve. The Turkish portions of the present Ottoman Empire should be assured a secure sovereignty, but the other nationalities which are now under Turkish rule should be assured an undoubted security of life and an absolutely unmolested opportunity of autonomous development, and the Dardanelles should be permanently opened as a free passage to the ships and commerce of all nations under international guarantees.

Thirteen. An independent Polish state should be erected which should include the territories inhabited by indisputably Polish populations, which should be assured a free and secure access to the sea, and whose political and economic independence and territorial integrity should be guaranteed by international covenant.

Fourteen. A general association of nations must be formed under specific covenants for the purpose of affording mutual guarantees of political independence and territorial integrity to great and small states alike.

In regard to these essential rectifications of wrong and assertions of right, we feel ourselves to be intimate partners of all the governments and peoples associated together against the imperialists. We cannot be separated in interest or divided in purpose. We stand together until the end. . . .

An evident principle runs through the whole program I have outlined. It is the principle of justice to all peoples and nationalities, and their right to live on equal terms of liberty and safety with one another, whether they be strong or weak. Unless this principle be made its foundation, no part of the structure of international justice can stand. The people of the United States could act upon no other principle, and to the vindication of this principle they are ready to devote their lives, their honor, and everything that they possess. The moral climax of this, the culminating and final war for human liberty, has come, and they are ready to put their own strength, their own highest purpose, their own integrity and devotion to the test.

Ambassador James W. Gerard Encourages German Americans to Be Loyal to the United States—or Else.

German Americans represented one of the nation's largest immigrant groups, and until America's direct involvement in the war, many had publicly expressed support for their native land. Once fighting between Americans and Germans began, however, the majority appeared to rally in support of the United States—or, if they felt otherwise, kept their sentiments to themselves. James W. Gerard, the American ambassador to Germany, gave the following speech in April 1918 observing that German Americans had embraced their new nation's cause unconditionally. Gerard's speech was intended to demoralize the German government and, of course, serve as a not-so-subtle warning to any German Americans who entertained thoughts of treason.

I know that it is hard for Americans to realize the magnitude of the war in which we are involved. We have problems in this war no other nations have. Fortunately, the great majority of American citizens of German descent have, in this great crisis of our history, shown themselves splendidly loyal to our flag. Everyone had a right to sympathize with any warring nation. But now that we are in the war there are only two sides, and the time has come when every citizen must declare himself American—or traitor!

We must disappoint the Germans who have always believed that the German Americans here would risk their property, their children's future, and their own neck and take up arms for the Kaiser. The foreign minister of Germany once said to me, "Your country does not dare do anything against Germany, because we have in your country 500,000 German reservists who will rise in arms against your government if you dare to make a move against Germany." Well, I told him that that might be so, but that we had 500,001 lampposts in this country, and that that was where the reservists would be hanging the day after they tried to rise. And if there are any German Americans here who are so ungrateful for all the benefits they have received that they are still for the Kaiser, there is only one thing to do with them. And that is to hog-tie them, give them back the wooden shoes and the rags they landed in, and ship them back to the Fatherland.

I have traveled this year over all the United States—through the Alleghenies, the White Mountains, and the Catskills, the Rockies, and the Bitterroot Mountains, and the Cascades, the Coast Range, and the Sierras. And in all these mountains, there is no animal that bites and kicks and squeals and scratches, that would bite and squeal and scratch equal to a fat German American, if you commenced to tie him up and told him that he was on his way back to the Kaiser.

Socialist Leader Eugene V. Debs Defends Himself in Court Against Charges of "Disloyalty" and "Sedition."

In June 1918, socialist leader Eugene V. Debs was arrested for violating the Espionage and Sedition Acts, legislation that forbade "uttering words intended to cause insubordination and disloyalty within the American forces, to incite resistance to the war, and to promote the cause of Germany." (Debs had given a speech in Canton, Ohio, on June 16 excoriating the "tyrants" and "exploiters" he believed were bankrolling America's participation in the war.) On September 1, 1918, as his trial neared its conclusion, Debs addressed the jury directly to explain why he—and many other Americans—were opposed to America's war efforts.

May it please the court, and gentlemen of the jury:

For the first time in my life I appear before a jury in a court of law to answer an indictment for crime. I am not a lawyer. I know little about court procedure, about the rules of evidence or legal practice. I know only that you gentlemen are to hear the evidence brought against me, that the court is to instruct you in the law, and that you are then to determine your verdict whether I shall be branded with criminal guilt and be consigned, perhaps to the end of my life, in a felon's cell.

Gentlemen, I do not fear to face you in this hour of accusation, nor do I shrink from the consequences of my utterances or my acts. Standing before you, charged as I am with crime, I can yet look the court in the face, I can look you in the face, I can look the world in the face, for in my conscience, in my soul, there is festering no accusation of guilt.

Permit me to say in the first place that I am entirely satisfied with the court's rulings. I have no fault to find with the assistant district attorney or with the counsel for the prosecution. I wish to admit the truth of all that has been testified to in this proceeding. I have no disposition to deny anything that is true. I would not, if I could, escape the results of an adverse verdict. I would not retract a word that I have uttered that I believe to be true to save myself from going to the penitentiary for the rest of my days.

Gentlemen, you have heard the report of my speech at Canton on June 16, and I submit that there is not a word in that speech to warrant the charges set out in the indictment. I admit having delivered the speech. I admit the accuracy of the speech in all of its main features as reported in this proceeding.

In what I had to say there my purpose was to have the people understand something about the social system in which we live and to prepare them to change this system by perfectly peaceable and orderly means into what I, as a socialist, conceive to be real democracy.

From what you heard in the address of the counsel for the prosecution, you might naturally infer that I am an advocate of force and violence. It is not true. I have never advocated violence in any form. I have always believed in education, in intelligence, in enlightenment; and I have always made my appeal to the reason and to the conscience of the people. I admit being opposed to the present social system. I am doing what little I can, and have been for many years, to bring about a change that shall do away with the rule of the great body of the people by a relatively small class and establish in this country an industrial and social democracy.

When great changes occur in history, when great principles are involved, as a rule the majority are wrong. The minority are usually right. In every age there have been a few heroic souls who have been in advance of their time, who have been misunderstood, maligned, persecuted—sometimes put to death. Long after their martyrdom, monuments were erected to them and garlands woven for their graves.

This has been the tragic history of the race. In the ancient world, Socrates sought to teach some new truths to the people, and they made him drink the fatal hemlock. This has been true all along the track of the ages. The men and women who have been in advance, who have had new ideas, new ideals, who have had the courage to attack the established order of things, have all had to pay the same penalty.

A century and a half ago when the American colonists were still foreign subjects, when there were a few men who had faith in the common people and their destiny and believed that they could rule themselves without a king, in that day to question the divine right of the king to rule was treason. If you will read Bancroft or any other American historian, you will find that a great majority of the colonists were loyal to the king and actually believed that he had a divine right to rule over them. . . . But there were a few men in that day who said, "We don't need a king. We can govern ourselves." And they began an agitation that has immortalized them in history. Washington, Adams, Paine—these were the rebels of their day. At first they were opposed by the people and denounced by the press. But they had the moral courage to stand erect and defy all the storm's detraction. And that is why they are in history, and that is why the great respectable majority of their day sleep in forgotten graves.

At a later time there began another mighty agitation in this country. It was against an institution that was deemed a very respectable one in this time—

the institution of chattel slavery. . . . All of the organized forces of society, all of the powers of government upheld and defended chattel slavery in that day. And again a few advanced thinkers appeared. One of the first was Elijah Lovejoy. Elijah Lovejoy was murdered in cold blood in Alton, Illinois, in 1837 simply because he was opposed to chattel slavery—just as I am opposed to wage slavery. When you go down the Mississippi River and look up at Alton, you see a magnificent white shaft erected there in memory of the man who was true to himself and his convictions of right and duty even unto death.

It was my good fortune to personally know Wendell Phillips. I heard the story of his cruel and cowardly persecution from his own eloquent lips just a little while before they were silenced in death.

William Lloyd Garrison, Geritt Smith, Thaddeus Stevens—these leaders of the abolition movement who were regarded as monsters of depravity were true to their faith and stood their ground. They are all in history. You are now teaching your children to revere their memories, while all of their detractors are in oblivion.

Chattel slavery has disappeared. We are not yet free. We are engaged today in another mighty agitation. It is the rise of the toiling masses who are gradually becoming conscious of their interests, their power, and their mission as a class; who are organizing industrially and politically, who are slowly but surely developing the economic and political power that is to set them free. They are still in a minority, but they have learned how to wait, and to bide their time.

From the beginning of the war to this day, I have never, by word or act, been guilty of the charges that are embraced in this indictment. If I have criticized, if I have condemned, it is because I have believed myself justified in doing so under the laws of the land. I have precedents for my attitude. This country has been engaged in a number of wars, and every one of them has been condemned by some of the most eminent men in the country. The war of the Revolution was opposed. The Tory press denounced its leaders as criminals and outlaws.

The War of 1812 was opposed and condemned, the Mexican War was bitterly condemned by Abraham Lincoln, Charles Sumner, Daniel Webster, and Henry Clay. They were not indicted. They were not tried for crime. They are honored today by all of their countrymen. The war of the Rebellion was opposed and condemned. In the year 1864 the Democratic Party met in convention at Chicago and passed a resolution condemning the war as a failure. What would you say if the Socialist Party were to meet in convention today and condemn the present war as a failure? You would charge us with being disloyalists and traitors. Were the Democrats of 1864 disloyalists and traitors because they condemned the war as a failure?

I believe in the Constitution of the United States. Isn't it strange that we socialists stand almost alone today in defending the Constitution of the United States? The Revolutionary fathers who had been oppressed under king rule understood that free speech, a free press, and the right of free assemblage by the people were fundamental principles in democratic government. The very first amendment to the Constitution reads: "Congress shall make no law respecting an establishment of religion, or prohibiting the free exercise thereof; or abridging the freedom of speech, or of the press; or the right of the people peaceably to assemble, and to petition the government for a redress of grievances."

That is perfectly plain English. It can be understood by a child. I believe the Revolutionary fathers meant just what is here stated—that Congress shall make no law abridging the freedom of speech, or of the press, or of the right of the people to peaceably assemble and to petition the government for a redress of their grievances.

That is the right I exercised at Canton on the sixteenth day of last June, and for the exercise of that right, I now have to answer this indictment. I believe in the right of free speech, in war as in peace. I would not, under any circumstances, suppress free speech. It is far more dangerous to attempt to gag the people than to allow them to speak freely what is in their hearts.

I have told you that I am no lawyer, but it seems to me that I know enough to know that if Congress enacts any law that conflicts with this provision in the Constitution, that law is void. If the Espionage Law finally stands, then the Constitution of the United States is dead. If that law is not the negation of every fundamental principle established by the Constitution, then certainly I am unable to read or to understand the English language.

Now, in the course of this proceeding you gentlemen have perhaps drawn the inference that I am pro-German in the sense that I have sympathy with the imperial government of Germany. My mother and father were born in Alsace. They loved France with a passion that was holy. They understood the meaning of Prussianism and they hated it with all their hearts. I did not need to be taught to hate Prussian militarism. I knew from them what a hateful, oppressive, and brutalizing thing it was and is. I cannot imagine how anyone can suspect for one moment that I could have the slightest sympathy with such a monstrous thing. I have been speaking and writing against it practically all my life. I know that the Kaiser incarnates all there is of brute force and murder.

With every drop of blood in my veins I despise Kaiserism and all that Kaiserism expresses and implies. My sympathy is with the struggling, suffering people everywhere. It matters not under what flag they were born, or where they live. I sympathize with them all, and I would, if I could, establish a social system that would embrace them all. . . .

Gentlemen, I am the smallest part of this trial. I have lived long enough to realize my own personal insignificance in relation to a great issue that involves the welfare of the whole people. What you may choose to do to me will be of small consequence after all. I am not on trial here. There is an infinitely greater issue that is being tried today in this court, though you may not be conscious of it. American institutions are on trial here before a court of American citizens. The future will render the final verdict.

And now, your honor, permit me to return my thanks for your patient consideration. And to you, gentlemen of the jury, for the kindness with which you have listened to me.

I am prepared for your verdict.

The verdict was "Guilty," and Debs was condemned to ten years in prison. Ultimately, however, he only served two years of the sentence. President Warren G. Harding pardoned him in 1921.

The Reverend Dr. Anna Howard Shaw Beseeches Americans to Accept President Wilson's Proposal for a "League of Nations" & Senator Henry Cabot Lodge Rejects the League and Its "Mongrel Banner."

More than 10 million soldiers were dead by the time the armistice was declared on the eleventh hour of the eleventh day on the eleventh month in 1918, and an estimated 20 million were wounded. (Over 113,000 Americans in all were killed in action or died from war-related injuries and illnesses.) A triumphant President Wilson personally made the trip to Paris to help negotiate the terms for peace and, he hoped, create a "League of Nations" that would enforce the rules of the treaty and serve to prevent future wars. Wilson found an impassioned ally in the Reverend Dr. Anna Howard Shaw, a Methodist minister who gained prominence for her role in the battle to secure voting rights for women. Shaw was a dynamic public speaker, having delivered hundreds of speeches a year as president of the National American Woman Suffrage Association. During the war, Shaw served as the chair of the Council of National Defense's Women's Committee to coordinate women's activities in support of the war effort. In May 1919 Shaw gave the following speech at a series of conventions to rally Americans—and women, in particular—behind Wilson's League of Nations.

What are we women to do in this matter of a League of Nations? What part are we to play in it? . . .

Women never had such an opportunity in the world's affairs before as we had during the war just closed. At the beginning of the war, very little attention was paid to the women. But gradually, as the manpower began to leave for the front and as the greater need for munitions and other necessary equipment of war demanded larger bodies of people to the service of the government, more and larger demands were made upon women until it came to such a pass that it is declared by every nation which has been at war that the war could never have been won if it had not been for the work of the women.

And so through this cooperative service of the men and women we have been able to reach this peace which is now so very near and which we trust the Senate of the United States will not retard, as no other nation save Germany has any desire to do so.

During the war women were called upon to serve and the response was universal. . . .

Men told us that, if we made a conquered peace, if we subdued militarism and the militarist spirit which Germany was inciting not only in its own country, but in the countries of the world, it would be conquered forever. "This is the war to end war." It was this thought which brought women together. "This is a war to end war," and women must play their part in helping to end war forever.

We know that men are ready to die in war, but there are a great many things harder than to die. Everybody must die sometime, and it does not make so much difference perhaps as to the number of days we live as it does to the manner in which we live the days we do live. There are some things that are worth a great deal more than life, and one thing which was worth more than life to the men who went out and laid down their lives for their countries was not to leave a dishonored nation, a nation unworthy of the civilization of our time, a nation which had no heart to feel and no understanding to realize the conditions of intimate association between nation and nation and the obligation which one nation has to care for and sympathize with another.

Having grasped this idea of democracy, this idea of the oneness of the human family, we declared that we would give everything that we had and sacrifice everything that we had in the interests of ending war forever. So our women toiled and sacrificed and saved and toiled again, until the war ended.

Now, whether we agree with every part of that peace treaty or not, no matter whether we agree with everything there is in the League of Nations or not, the question remains that now with the Germans, our opponents, defeated on the field of battle, is that the way to end war forever—merely to defeat them on the field of battle? Is there not something to be done afterwards? Everyone knows that no war is ended on the battlefield. The last word in war is spoken in the halls where the people meet together to decide what shall be the result of the war, what shall be the penalties of war, and how peace shall be made.

If President Wilson were to stand before us today and tell us even a part of what he knows that we do not know, we would be the most astonished people in all the world. The Peace Commission with all the facts before them knows, and out of their knowledge, out of what they understand of the relation of nations to each other, they have given us this League of Nations as the best solution they could produce to bring about a just and lasting peace. That is what we women have been working for from the beginning of the war. In a conversation with President Wilson just before he went to Paris, he said, "The most difficult task I have had since the war began, in dealing with foreign nations, has been to convince them that we do not want any material advantage out of this war. They cannot understand it. Never before did any great nation go into war such as this, with our men and our treasure, and then ask nothing in return. I could hardly make them believe that we were perfectly willing to come out with empty hands. And yet," he said, "they are beginning to understand that, because our men over there on the battlefield have shown them their disinterestedness. And they are able to feel that if we can send men to die in this disinterested way, those of us who are at home have perhaps the same spirit. And so they are beginning to trust a little more than they did in the beginning." . . .

We have come to the place now where we can fly in a day from this country to any other country on the earth almost, and we have become so closely interallied that national interests merge the one with the other in such a manner that we cannot go alone. We must look facts in the face: All humanity is one. The world is one. And no nation can suffer unless all nations suffer. No nation can prosper without all nations prospering. We have got to take facts as they are, and we have got to find out the best thing we can have. The best thing that has been given us and the only thing we have before us is this League of Nations. We have only this one. We must take this one or no one can tell what will come. We have no midway point. We have no purgatory. We have to choose either Heaven or Hell. We must take it or we must reject it. . . .

President Lowell, of Harvard, had clearly explained every single idea there is in the League and every purpose of it—simply, that we may be able to have some sort of an organized body by which we may have international cooperation in keeping peace, international cooperation in providing a certain uniformity of law in the protection of the laboring people of the world, international cooperation to prevent the spread of disease and other evils. There is little for me to say on that last proposition. When influenza was sweeping over the country, didn't we wish that we had some kind of an international health bureau by which we could have kept that disease out? And that is only the beginning of many diseases which will sweep the world as a result of the war, of the impoverished condition of Europe, and the unhealthful conditions of living forced upon the soldiers in the trenches.

And from those evils comes back to us the lesson we must learn: that the "sins of the fathers are visited upon the children unto the third and fourth generations." When I read that peace pact and I thought how hard it is, how difficult it is, there appeared before me just as if it were written in words of light: "The sins of the fathers shall be visited upon the children unto the third and fourth generation." So Germany's children will bear the burden to the third and fourth generation of the crimes against them, and the children of the world will bear the burdens of the obligations which they are compelled to assume because of the sins of the people of the world.

We women, the mothers of the race, have given everything, have suffered everything, have sacrificed everything, and we come to you now and say, "The time has come when we will no longer sit quietly by and bear and rear sons to die at the will of a few men. We will not endure it. We demand either that you shall do something to prevent war or that we shall be permitted to try to do something ourselves." Could there be any cowardice, could there be any injustice, could there be any wrong greater than to refuse to hear the voice of a woman expressing the will of women at the peace table of the world and then for men not to provide a way by which the women of the future shall not be robbed of their sons as the women of the past have been?

To you men we look for support. We look for the support of your senators, and from this day until the day when the League of Nations is accepted and ratified by the Senate of the U.S., it should be the duty of every man and every woman to see to it that the senators from their state know the will of the people shall be done; even though not perfect, that there shall be a beginning from which we shall construct something more perfect by and by; that the will of the people is that this League shall be accepted; and that if, in the Senate of the U.S., there are men so blinded by partisan desire for present advantage, so blinded by personal pique and narrowness of vision, that they cannot see the large problems which involve the nations of the world, then the people of the states must see to it that other men sit in the seats of the highest.

Despite the support of Shaw and many other renowned Americans for the League, President Wilson faced opposition throughout the country to creating an international institution that, critics argued, might not always have the best interests of the United States at heart. Wilson's most powerful antagonist was Henry Cabot Lodge (R–MA), the majority leader of the Senate and the chairman of the Foreign Relations Committee. Lodge made his case before the Senate on August 12, 1919.

I am anxious as any human being can be to have the United States render every possible service to the civilization and the peace of mankind, but I am certain we can do it best by not putting ourselves in leading strings or subjecting our policies and our sovereignty to other nations. The independence of the United States is not only more precious to ourselves but to the world than any single possession.

Look at the United States today. We have made mistakes in the past. We have had shortcomings. We shall make mistakes in the future and fall short of our own best hopes. But nonetheless, is there any country today on the face of the earth which can compare with this in ordered liberty, in peace, and in the largest freedom? I feel that I can say this without being accused of undue boastfulness, for it is the simple fact, and in making this treaty and taking on these obligations all that we do is in a spirit of unselfishness and in a desire for the good of mankind. But it is well to remember that we are dealing with nations every one of which has a direct individual interest to serve, and there is grave danger in an unshared idealism.

Contrast the United States with any country on the face of the earth today and ask yourself whether the situation of the United States is not the best to be found. I will go as far as anyone in world service, but the first step to world service is the maintenance of the United States. You may call me selfish, if you will, conservative or reactionary, or use any other harsh adjective you see fit to apply, but an American I was born, an American I have remained all my life. I can never be anything else but an American, and I must think of the United States first. And when I think of the United States first in an arrangement like this I am thinking of what is best for the world, for if the United States fails, the best hopes of mankind fail with it. I have never had but one allegiance. I cannot divide it now. I have loved but one flag, and I cannot share that devotion and give affection to the mongrel banner invented for a league.

Internationalism, illustrated by the Bolshevik and by the men to whom all countries are alike provided they can make money out of them, is to me repulsive. National I must remain, and in that way I, like all other Americans, can render the amplest service to the world. The United States is the world's best hope, but if you fetter her in the interests and quarrels of other nations, if you tangle her in the intrigues of Europe, you will destroy her power for good and endanger her very existence. Leave her to march freely through the centuries to come as in the years that have gone. Strong, generous, and confident, she has nobly served mankind. Beware how you trifle with your marvelous inheritance, this great land of ordered liberty, for if we stumble and fall, freedom and civilization everywhere will go down in ruin.

We are told that we shall "break the heart of the world" if we do not take this League just as it stands. I fear that the hearts of the vast majority of mankind would beat on strongly and steadily and without any quickening if the League were to perish altogether. If it should be effectively and beneficently changed, the people who would lie awake in sorrow for a single night could be easily gathered in one not very large room, but those who would draw a long breath of relief would reach to millions. . . .

Ideals have been thrust upon us as an argument for the League until the healthy mind which rejects cant revolts from them. Are ideals confined to this deformed experiment upon a noble purpose, tainted as it is with bargains and tied to a peace treaty which might have been disposed of long ago to the great benefit of the world if it had not been compelled to carry this rider on its back? . . .

No doubt many excellent and patriotic people see a coming fulfillment of noble ideals in the words "League for Peace." We all respect and share these aspirations and desires, but some of us see no hope, but rather defeat, for them in this murky covenant. For we, too, have our ideals, even if we differ from those who have tried to establish a monopoly of idealism. Our first ideal is our country, and we see her in the future, as in the past, giving service to all her people and to the world. Our ideal of the future is that she should continue to render that service of her own free will. She has great problems of her own to solve, very grim and perilous problems, and a right solution, if we can attain to it, would largely benefit mankind. We would have our country strong to resist a peril from the West, as she has flung back the German menace from the East. We would not have our politics distracted and embittered by the distensions of other lands. We would not have our country's vigor exhausted, or her moral force abated, by everlasting meddling and muddling in every quarrel great and small which afflicts the world. Our ideal is to make her ever stronger and better and finer, because in that way alone, as we believe, can she be of the greatest service to the world's peace and to the welfare of mankind.

Faced with a growing chorus of critics who denounced America's entry into the League of Nations more vehemently than Lodge, Wilson tirelessly traveled the country making the case for the League. On September 25, 1919, an exhausted Wilson was in Colorado when he complained of a blistering headache. His physician canceled the rest of Wilson's trip, and on October 2 Wilson collapsed, the victim of a massive stroke. He survived, but his ability to move, speak, and think was impaired, and, without its most ardent defender, support for the League was all but dead by the end of November. Wilson was crushed by the defeat, but he received some vindication when he was awarded the Nobel Prize for peace in 1919.

New York Governor Alfred E. Smith Assails the "Contemptible" Publishing Tycoon William Randolph Hearst.

The date was October 29, 1919, and the stage at New York's Carnegie Hall was set for an unprecedented confrontation: Alfred E. Smith, the governor of New York, had issued a challenge to debate William Randolph Hearst, the media magnate who owned tabloid newspapers from coast to coast and was the inspiration for Orson Welles's 1941 masterpiece Citizen Kane. Governor Smith was enraged by Hearst and his New York American newspaper for waging a smear campaign against him that bordered, in Smith's opinion, on the libelous. Most egregiously to Smith, the American relentlessly and unfairly blamed him for the city's milk shortage in the summer of 1919, which nearly led to a health crisis for the city's children. When Hearst failed to appear at the debate, Smith launched into a lengthy tirade against Hearst and his sensationalistic tabloids.

I cannot think of a more contemptible man. My power of imagination fails to bring into my mind's eye a more despicable man than the man that exploits the poor. Any man that leads you to believe that your lot in life is not all right, any man that conjures up for you a fancied grievance against your government or against the man at the head of it, to help himself, is breeding the seeds of anarchy and a dissatisfaction more disastrous to the welfare of the community than any other teaching I can think of, because at least the wildest anarchist, the most extreme socialist, the wildest radical that you can think of, may at least be sincere in his own heart. He may think that it is right when he preaches it. But the man that preaches to the poor of this or of any other community discontent and dissatisfaction to help himself and to make good his side of the argument, and to destroy, as he said himself he would, the governor of the state, is a man as low and as mean as I can picture. . . .

Follow back the history of this man's newspapers since he came to this part of the country, and you will have to read out of his newspapers this remarkable fact: that in this great democracy, in this land of the free and in this home of the brave, there has never been a man elected to office yet that has not been tainted in some way. If the Hearst newspapers were the textbooks for the children of our schools, they would have to spell out of its every line that no man can be trusted in this country after he is put into public office; that no man thinks enough about it; no man has enough of regard for it; no man has enough of real Christian charity to do the thing right; no man that ever held great public office had enough of respect and regard for his mother and his wife and his children and his friends to be right in office. About that there can be no question, because no public man in this state, from Grover Cleveland right down to today, has ever escaped this fellow. We all know that. The children on the street know it.

Nobody that ever went to the governor's office went there with a graver sense of the responsibility of that office than I did. What could there possibly be about me that I should be assailed in this reckless manner by this man? I have more reason probably than any man I will meet tonight to have a strong love and a strong devotion for this country, for this state, and for this city. Look at what I have received at its hands: I left school and went to work before I was fifteen years of age. I worked hard, night and day. I worked honestly and conscientiously at every job that I was ever put at until I went to the governor's chair in Albany. What can it be? It has got to be jealousy. It has got to be envy. It has got to be hatred. Or it has to be something that nobody understands, that makes me come down here, into the City of New York, before this audience, and urge them to organize in this city to stay the danger that comes from these papers, to the end that the health, and welfare, and the comfort of this people, of the people of this state, may be promoted, and we may get rid of this pestilence that walks in the darkness.

Hearst did not respond to Smith's accusations, and, somewhat inconceivably, Hearst's New York American *endorsed Smith for governor in 1920.*

1920–1929

JAZZ IS NOT NECESSARILY THE GATEWAY TO HELL. IT MAY BE THE portal to life eternal. For jazz is a protest against machine methods, against the monotony of life. Professional reformers and evangelists and the timid folk to whom everything new is of the devil can see nothing ahead but destruction for those who prefer syncopated time to the long meter doxology as though the tempo of the long meter doxology were the tune of heaven or had been inspired by God.

Jazz is an attempt at individual expression. No two people jazz-dance alike. Others may smile and even sneer at the way the young factory girl and her boyfriend fling themselves into the anarchy of individual jazz experience. But it is *their* dance, and they are finding freedom, liberty, release in it. They need it to get away from the awful humdrum and monotony which are starving their souls.

—*The Reverend Charles Stelzle,*
sermon given in New York City,
c. 1925

Evangelical Preacher Billy Sunday Excoriates
Alcohol as "God's Worst Enemy"
&
Will Rogers Skewers Both the "Wets"
and the "Drys" in the Prohibition Debate.

At midnight on January 16, 1920, the Eighteenth Amendment, prohibiting the "manufacture, sale, or transportation of intoxicating liquors," went into effect. The Anti-Saloon League of New York announced triumphantly: "Now for an era of clean thinking and clean living!" The League and other temperance societies throughout the nation found their greatest allies among religious leaders and church groups who believed that alcohol was the devil's brew. Few endorsed this crusade as enthusiastically, however, as the evangelical preacher William Ashley "Billy" Sunday. A major-league baseball player for eight years, Sunday embraced Christianity and discovered soon after that he had a natural talent for preaching. Sunday eventually became the most recognized preacher of the early twentieth century, traveling across America from one tent revival meeting to the next, mesmerizing crowds with his energetic sermons. The following is one of Sunday's many exhortations on the evils of drinking.

In these days when the question of saloon or no saloon is at the fore in almost every community, one hears a good deal about what is called "personal liberty." These are fine, large, mouth-filling words, and they certainly do sound first rate. But when you get right down and analyze them in light of common old horse sense, you will discover that in their application to the present controversy they mean just about this: "Personal liberty" is for the man who, if he has the inclination and the price, can stand up at the bar and fill his hide so full of red liquor that he is transformed for the time being into an irresponsible, dangerous, evil-smelling brute.

But "personal liberty" is not for his patient, long-suffering wife, who has to endure with what fortitude she can, his blows and curses. Nor is it for his children, who, if they escape his insane rage, are yet robbed of every known joy and privilege of childhood, and too often grow up neglected, uncared for, and vicious as the result of their surroundings and the example before them.

"Personal liberty" is not for the sober, industrious citizen who from the proceeds of honest toil and orderly living has to pay, willingly or not, the tax bills which pile up as a direct result of drunkenness, disorder, and poverty—the items of which are written in the records of every police court and poorhouse in the land. Nor is "personal liberty" for the good woman who goes abroad in the town only at the risk of being shot down by some drink-crazed creature. This rant about "personal liberty" as an argument has no leg to stand upon. . . .

The saloon comes as near to being a rat hole for a wage earner to dump his wages in as anything you can find. The only interest it pays is red eyes and foul breath and the loss of health. You go in with money and you come out with empty pockets. You go in with character and you come out ruined. You go in with a good position and you lose it. You lost your position in the bank, or in the cab of the locomotive. And it pays nothing back but disease and damnation and gives an extra dividend in delirium tremens and a free pass to Hell. And then it will let your wife be buried in the potter's field and your children go to the asylum, and yet you walk out and say the saloon is a good institution when it is the dirtiest thing on earth. It hasn't one leg to stand on and has nothing to commend it to a decent man, not one thing. . . .

The saloon is a coward. It is a thief. It is not an ordinary court offender that steals your money, but it robs you of manhood and leaves you in rags, and takes away your friends, and it robs your family. It impoverishes your children, and it brings insanity and suicide. It will take the shirt off your back, and it will steal the coffin from a dead child and yank the last crust of bread out of the hand of the starving child. It will take the last bucket of coal out of your cellar and the last cent out of your pocket, and will send you home bleary-eyed and staggering to your wife and children. It will steal the milk from the breast of the mother and leave her with nothing with which to feed her infant. It will take the virtue from your daughter. It is the dirtiest, most low-down business that ever crawled out of the pit of Hell. It is a sneak and a thief and a coward.

It is an infidel. It has no faith in God, has no religion. It would close every church in the land. It would bring its beer signs on the abandoned altars. It would close every public school. It respects the thief and it esteems the blasphemer. It fills the prisons and the penitentiaries. It despises heaven, hates love, scorns virtue. It tempts the passions. Its music is the song of the siren. Its sermons are a collection of lewd, vile stories. It wraps a mantle about the mopes of this world and that to come. Its tables are full of the vilest literature. It is the moral clearing house for rot and damnation and poverty and insanity, and it wrecks homes and blights lives today.

The saloon is a liar. It promises good cheer and sends sorrow. It promises health and causes disease. It promises prosperity and sends poverty. It promises happiness and sends misery. Yes, it sends the husband home with a lie on his lips to his wife; and the boy home with a lie on his lips to his mother; and it causes the employee to lie to his employer. It degrades. It is God's worst enemy and the devil's best friend. It spares neither youth nor old age. It is waiting with a dirty blanket for the baby to crawl into the world. It lies in wait for the unborn.

It cocks the highwayman's pistol. It puts the rope in the hands of the mob. It is the anarchist of the world, and its dirty red flag is dyed with the blood of women and children. It sent the bullet through the body of Lincoln; it nerved the arm that sent the bullets through Garfield and William McKinley. Yes, it is a murderer. Every plot that was ever hatched against the government and law was born and bred and crawled out of the grog shop to damn this country.

I tell you that the curse of God Almighty is on the saloon. Legislatures are legislating against it. Decent society is barring it out. The fraternal brotherhoods are knocking it out. The Masons and Odd Fellows and the Knights of Pythias and the AOUW are closing their doors to whisky sellers. They don't want you wriggling your carcass in their lodges. Yes sir, I tell you, the curse of God is on it. It is on the downgrade. It is headed for Hell, and by the grace of God I am going to give it a push, with a whoop, for all I know how. . . .

Will Rogers, on the other hand, couldn't see what all the fuss was about. Through his radio program, syndicated columns, stage shows, and movies, Rogers was the most beloved humorist and entertainer of his time. Rather than argue any one political position or issue, Rogers preferred to point out the silliness of whatever national debate was raging at the time and focus on the hypocrisy and hubris of those in power, making him a folk hero to many Americans. In one radio broadcast Rogers offered his thoughts on Prohibition—not, of course, by coming down firmly one way or the other, but by poking fun at both sides.

I have received more letters in the last few weeks to talk on Prohibition than on any other subject. I haven't said a word about it. I was really ashamed. So many was talking and arguing over it that I wanted to be original and just let it alone. Can you name me one subject in the entire world that there has been as much time and energy wasted on? . . .

I have often said that I wish the wets would become so soused they would be speechless and couldn't say anything, and that the drys would become so perfect that the Lord would come down and take them away from here—and that would leave the country to the rest of us who are tired of listening to both of them. So I got to wondering if it wasn't possible for a fellow to talk on it without being a nut on the other side. I think if I could do that I would be speaking in behalf of practically millions of people.

Now it is not so terribly serious, this Prohibition. It is not a life-or-death problem with us. If it was repealed tomorrow, the lives and habits and morals of the whole country, they wouldn't be ruined; the country would drag along just the same. Taxes and parking spaces would hit us in the face just the same. Henry Ford wouldn't leave the country if it was repealed—you couldn't run him out of here.

Then, on the other hand, if it is never repealed, we will still drag along. The country won't go to the dogs. We lived with the Eighteenth Amendment and we have lived without it, and we are still here under both systems. So you see there is perhaps problems greater. . . . America is getting so big—you know, it really is, this country is getting so big—that no matter what it is, it don't bother us anymore. We just struggle along in spite of ourselves. It takes more than a drink to really interest us anymore. It is not undermining the moral fiber of a great nation. That's a lot of hooey. . . .

Some folks on both sides have just kidded themselves it is our greatest problem. The real wet is going to drink, I don't care what your laws are, and a real dry is going to lecture to him while he is drinking, no matter what your laws about it are. You can't change human nature. But while those two are fighting it out, there will be five hundred passing by tending to their own business, living their own lives, and doing exactly what they think is best for them. . . .

We are trying to settle something here that has been going on since way back in Bible times. Those old prophets couldn't even settle it, and you can't tell me that [Prohibitionist and Republican Senator George Higgins] Moses of New Hampshire and his gang of senators know any more than Moses of Palestine and his troop did. Right in the first book of Genesis, you don't read but just a few pages until Noah was lit up like a pygmy golf course. Here is just how it started—wait a minute, I got it right here on paper—I will read it to you. Right in the start of Genesis, the ninth chapter and twentieth verse, it says, "And Noah became a husbandman and planted a vineyard." The minute he became a husband he started in raising the ingredients that goes with married life. So you can trace all drink to marriage, see. What we got to prohibit is *marriage*. In the very next verse, the twenty-first verse, it says, "And he drank of the wine and was drunk." Now that was Noah himself, our forefather. Practically all of us can trace our ancestry back to him. . . .

Now you see Noah drank and he didn't drink water, and he was a man that knew more about water than practically any man of his time. He was the water commissioner of his day. Old Noah was an expert on water, but the Lord is very far-seeing, and everything He does is for the best. Through Noah partaking of too much wine and going on his little spree, that is just why the Lord picked on him to pick out these animals to take into the Ark—he was the only man that had even *seen* all of them. So if Noah hadn't drunk, today we would be without circuses and menageries. Of course, other men since Noah's time have claimed that they have seen animals that Noah didn't put into the Ark—but they were drinking from a different vineyard. . . .

Noah lived—you know this wine had such ill effects on Noah that he only lived to be 950 years old. That is just nineteen years short of Methuselah, who held the longevity record of his and all times. So Prohibition is not a new problem by any means. There is no need for this generation to feel conceited enough to think that they can settle it. It is like stopping war. We are always going to do something that no other generation has ever been able to do. If you could take politics out of Prohibition, it would be more beneficial to this country than if you took the alcohol out of our drinks. . . .

America ain't as bad off as it might seem. The young are not drinking themselves to death and the old are not worrying themselves to death over the condition of whether the young are drinking or not. Chain stores are worrying this country a lot more than chain saloons are. Turkey is the only other Prohibition country in the world, us and Turkey. There's a fine gang to be linked up with, ain't it? If we enjoyed some of the other privileges, things wouldn't be so bad. We enjoy them, but they are not legal.

Now listen here, folks—honest, this is what I want to get over to you tonight. Let's not all get excited about it and break friendships with our neighbors and fall out with our brother over this Prohibition. Nothing is going to be done about it during our lifetime. There ain't anybody hearing me tonight who will live to see the time when anything is done about it, so don't let's all worry and get all het up about it, get all hot and bothered. Don't let's take it so serious. The drys and wets both combined can't hurt this country. Talking about Prohibition is like whittling used to be: It passes away the time but don't settle anything.

Now go to bed and forget about it, and let's hope that some day our country will be as dry as the speeches made by both the wets and the drys. . . .

Prohibition was repealed on December 5, 1933.

Attorney Edward Prindeville Demands Imprisonment for Eight Chicago White Sox Players Who Intentionally Lost the 1919 World Series.

Reported first in the Chicago Herald and Examiner, *a young fan tugged at the sleeve of "Shoeless" Joe Jackson and pleaded, "Say it ain't so, Joe. Say it ain't so." But Joe confessed that it was: He and seven other Chicago White Sox players conspired to lose the 1919 World Series to the Cincinnati Reds to make $20,000. (The players themselves were cheated by the bookie who arranged the deal, leaving them a total of $10,000 to split among the eight of them.) Outraged that the players could desecrate the sport of baseball—the "national pastime"—the assistant state's attorney, Edward Prindeville, demanded harsh penalties for the eight men in his address to the jury on July 29, 1920.*

What more convincing proof do you want than the statements made by the ballplayers? Joe Jackson, Eddie Cicotte, and Claude Williams sold out the American public for a paltry $20,000. They collected the money, but they could not keep quiet. Their consciences would not let them rest. When the scandal broke, they sought out the state's attorney's office and made their confessions voluntarily. . . .

This is an unusual case as it deals with a class of men who are involved in the great national game which all red-blooded men follow. This game, gentlemen, has been the subject of a crime. The public, the club owners, even the small boys on the sandlots have been swindled. That is why these defendants are charged with conspiracy.

This conspiracy started when Eddie Cicotte told [Bill] Burns in New York that if the White Sox won the pennant there was something on and he would let him in on it. All the way through you will find that Cicotte's statements are corroborated by Burns and vice versa.

Cicotte was advised of his rights, yet he told his story. He told of the $10,000 he got under his pillow. He told of meeting his pals and talking over the conspiracy details. He told of watching while his companions filed one by one from the meeting place so as not to raise suspicions of the honest players. Then what did this idol of the diamond do? He went home and took the $10,000 from under his pillow. Of course he was uneasy!

Then the gamblers met again on the morning before the World Series began. The gamblers accepted the players' terms. It was agreed that Cicotte should lose the first game. Of course he lost. With $10,000 in his pocket, how could you expect him to keep his balance and win. The weight would bear him down! . . .

I say, gentlemen, that the evidence shows that a swindle and a con game has been worked on the American people. The crime in this case warrants the most severe punishment of the law. This country is for sending criminals to the penitentiary whether they are idols of the baseball diamond or gangsters guilty of robbery with a gun. Unless the jury, by convicting the ballplayers in this trial, does its part to stamp out gambling that is corrupting baseball, I predict restrictive legislation for baseball such as has been enacted for boxing and horseracing.

The state is asking in this case for a verdict of guilty with five years in the penitentiary and a fine of $2,000 for each defendant!

The defense's argument that the players were pawns in a larger scam apparently proved successful. The players were ultimately acquitted on all counts, but they did not go without punishment: The eight men were banned from professional baseball for life.

Helen Keller Emphatically Endorses
Communism and the Russian Revolution.

When Vladimir Lenin's Bolsheviks assumed power in Russia in the fall of 1917, they had numerous supporters in the United States. One of them was a young deaf and blind woman named Helen Keller. Born on June 27, 1880, into a staunchly conservative family in Alabama, Keller was stricken at the age of eighteen months with an illness that left her unable to see, hear, or speak. Keller eventually learned to talk, and, despite her parents' political views, she became an ardent socialist who spoke out against racial discrimination, war (she emphatically opposed America's entry into World War I), and capitalism. On December 31, 1920, Keller gave a passionate, almost exclamatory speech to a New York City audience celebrating the Russian Revolution before a crowd of socialists who were about to begin a "grand march" in support of their cause.

The hour has struck for the grand march! Onward, comrades, all together! Fall in line! Let us join the world's procession marching toward a glad tomorrow. Strong of hope and brave in heart the West shall meet the East! March with us, brothers every one! March with us to all things new! Climb with us the hills of God to a wider, holier life. Onward, comrades, all together, onward to meet the dawn!

Leave behind your doubts and fears! What need have we for "ifs" and "buts"? Away with parties, schools, and leagues! Get together, keep in step, shoulder to shoulder, hearts throbbing as one! Face the future, outdaring all you have dared! March on, O comrades, strong and free, out of darkness, out of silence, out of hate and custom's deadening sway! Onward, comrades, all together, onward to the wind-blown dawn!

With us shall go the new day, shining behind the dark. With us shall go power, knowledge, justice, truth. The time is full! A new world awaits us. Its fruits, its joys, its opportunities are ours for the taking! Fear not the hardships of the road—the storm, the parching heat or winter's cold, hunger or thirst or ambushed foe! There are bright lights ahead of us, leave the shadows behind! In the East a new star is risen! With pain and anguish the old order has given birth to the new, and behold in the East a man-child is born! Onward, comrades, all together! Onward to the campfires of Russia! Onward to the coming dawn!

Through the night of our despair rings the keen call of the new day. All the powers of darkness could not still the shout of joy in faraway Moscow! Meteor-like through the heavens flashed the golden words of light, "Soviet Republic of Russia." Words sunlike banishing hate, bidding the teeming world of men to wake and live! Onward, comrades, all together, onward to the bright, redeeming dawn!

With peace and brotherhood make sweet the bitter way of men! Today and all the days to come, repeat the words of Him who said, "Thou shall not kill." Send on psalming winds the angel chorus, "Peace on Earth, good will to men." Onward march, and keep on marching until His will on earth is done! Onward, comrades, all together, onward to the life-giving fountain of dawn!

All along the road beside us throng the peoples sad and broken, weeping women, children hungry, homeless like little birds cast out of their nest. Onward march, comrades, strong to lift and save! Our brothers watch us from barred windows! With their hearts aflame, untamed, glorying in martyrdom they hail us passing quickly, "Halt not, O comrades, yonder glimmers the star of our hope, the red-centered dawn in the East! Halt not, lest you perish ere you reach the land of promise." Onward, comrades, all together, onward to the sun-red dawn!

We march though trackless wilds of hate and death, across Earth's battle-fields. O comrades, pause one panting moment and shed a tear for the youth of the world, killed in its strength and beauty—our brothers, our comrades tenderly loved, the valiant young men of all lands eagerly seeking life's great enterprises, love, adventure, and the fair country of bright dreams. Under our feet they lie, mingling their clean young flesh with the soil, the rain, and the heat! Over our murdered dead we march to the new day. Onward, comrades, all together, onward to the spirit's unquenchable dawn!

Margaret Sanger Promotes Birth Control as an "Ethical Necessity for Humanity."

Founder of the American Birth Control League (later renamed Planned Parenthood Federation), Margaret Sanger established America's first birth control clinic in Brooklyn on October 16, 1916. The police raided the clinic soon after and arrested Sanger for violating New York's Comstock Law, which forbade the dissemination of birth control information. Sanger was imprisoned for thirty days but after her release continued discussing and distributing family-planning materials to women who requested them. Her perseverance, it is speculated, was motivated by the loss of her mother, an Irish Catholic woman who gave birth to eleven children before dying at age fifty. In the following address, which she gave throughout the early 1920s, Sanger articulates her opposition to the church and its teachings.

Religious propaganda against birth control is crammed with contradiction and fallacy. It refutes itself. Yet it brings the opposing views into vivid contrast. In stating these differences we should make clear that advocates of birth control are not seeking to attack the Catholic Church. We quarrel with that

Church, however, when it seeks to assume authority over non-Catholics and to dub their behavior immoral because they do not conform to the dictatorship of Rome. The question of bearing and rearing children we hold is the concern of the mother and the potential mother. If she delegates the responsibility, the ethical education, to an external authority, that is her affair. We object, however, to the state or the Church which appoints itself as arbiter and dictator in this sphere and attempts to force unwilling women into compulsory maternity. . . .

The sex instinct in the human race is too strong to be bound by the dictates of any church. The Church's failure, its century after century of failure, is now evident on every side. For having convinced men and women that only in its baldly propagative phase is sexual expression legitimate, the teachings of the Church have driven sex underground into secret channels, strengthened the conspiracy of silence, concentrated men's thoughts upon the "lusts of the body," have sown, cultivated, and reaped a crop of bodily and mental diseases, and developed a society congenitally and almost hopelessly unbalanced. How is any progress to be made, how is any human expression or education possible when women and men are taught to combat and resist their natural impulses and to despise their bodily functions? . . .

More than ever in history, women need to realize that nothing can ever come to us from another. Everything we attain we must owe to ourselves. Our own spirit must vitalize it. Our own heart must feel it. For we are not passive machines. We are not to be lectured, guided, and molded this way or that. We are alive and intelligent, we women, no less than men, and we must awaken to the essential realization that we are living beings, endowed with will, choice, comprehension, and that every step in life must be our own initiative.

Moral and sexual balance in civilization will only be established by the assertion and expression of power on the part of women. This power will not be found in any futile seeking for economic independence or in the aping of men in industrial or business pursuits, nor by joining the so-called "single standard." Woman's power can only be expressed and make itself felt when she refuses the task of bringing unwanted children into the world to be exploited in industry and slaughtered in wars. When we refuse to produce battalions of babies to be exploited, when we declare to the nation, "Show us that the best possible chance in life is given to every child now brought into the world before you cry for more! At present our children are a glut on the market. You hold infant life cheap. Help us to make the world a fit place for our children. When you have done this, we will bear you children. Then we shall be true women." The new morality will express this power and responsibility on the part of women. . . .

Birth control is an ethical necessity for humanity today because it places in our hands a new instrument of self-expression and self-realization. It gives us control over one of the primordial forces of nature, to which in the past the majority of mankind have been enslaved, and by which it has been cheapened and debased. It arouses us to the possibility of newer and greater freedom. It develops the power, the responsibility, and intelligence to use this freedom in living a liberated and abundant life. It permits us to enjoy this liberty without danger of infringing upon the similar liberty of our fellow men, or of injuring and curtailing the freedom of the next generation. It shows us that we need not seek in the amassing of worldly wealth, nor in the illusion of some extraterrestrial heaven or earthly utopia of a remote future, the road to human development. The kingdom of heaven is in a very definite sense within us. Not by leaving our body and our fundamental humanity behind us, not by aiming to be anything but what we are, shall we become ennobled or immortal. By knowing ourselves, by expressing ourselves, by realizing ourselves more completely than has ever before been possible, not only shall we attain the kingdom ourselves but we shall hand on the torch of life undimmed to our children and the children of our children.

President Warren G. Harding Marvels at the "Majesty" of Yellowstone National Park.

The social critic and journalist H. L. Mencken once described President Warren G. Harding's speeches, which were notoriously long-winded and dull, as the rhetorical equivalent of a "hippopotamus struggling to free itself from a slough of molasses." But while on a cross-country sojourn to visit Alaska (which was not yet a state), Harding passed through Montana's Yellowstone National Park in late June 1923 and gave an uncharacteristically heartfelt and thoughtful speech on the park's beauty and its profound effect on his spirit.

It is a very great pleasure to be greeted so cordially by so many of you on this Sabbath evening. We have been spending two wonderful days in your vicinity. And we spent this Sabbath day, I believe, quite as close to God Almighty as though we worshipped in temples erected by man, for we spent the day amidst the grandeur, the majesty, and the inspirations of the great Yellowstone National Park. . . .

The Yellowstone Park is a wonderful place. It is a great possession for you of Montana and the other states which have territory therein. It is a great possession for those who live nearby. It is a great possession for the United

States of America. I have been marveling at our experiences of the last two days. During that time we have seen literally a fine cross section of the citizenship of our land. I believe that during my brief sojourn in the park I have greeted personally travelers from every state in the American Union, and, in addition to that, I have had the privilege of greeting citizens of England, of Canada, and of Cuba. Manifestly all the country is beginning to turn its face toward the Yellowstone National Park, and I am glad of it, for there is nothing more helpful, nothing more uplifting, nothing that gives one a greater realization of the wonders of creation than a visit to that great national institution.

I have gathered some interesting impressions from my sojourn in the park, and I wonder if similar impressions have come to you who live nearby. For instance, because of the protection of wildlife in the park, there has been created amongst the wild creatures there an air and feeling of confidence which causes them to experience a sense of security. We saw it everywhere; and as I watched the wildlife of the park today unconcerned and unmindful of the human beings about them, manifesting their confidence in the security of the situation, I thought how helpful it would be to humankind if we could have a like confidence in one another in all the relations of life.

There was another incident that appealed strongly to me. As we were nearing the end of our trip this afternoon, and were coming down one of the long grades, our car suddenly approached a mother grouse and a group of little grouse chicks. The excellent driver of the car brought it to too sudden a halt, but he did it out of regard for that young wildlife which was not capable of knowing the danger or protecting itself. The driver did not want to destroy one of those little grouse chicks, not much bigger than a hickory nut—I do not know whether or not you are familiar with hickory nuts in this section—and I liked him for what he did. He exhibited one of the finest impulses that animate the heart of man—namely, to spare innocent, defenseless life. The old mother grouse seemed not to know or care, because she did not realize the danger, but our driver did. I should like to see that example more frequently followed in our relationships with one another. Those who know, those who are strong, those who are in a position to command ought always to be ready to protect the weak, the helpless, and those who do not know. I am sure that if we will more faithfully carry out that principle, we shall be even a better people than we are. . . .

In addition to being able to visit the park, it is good to have the privilege of coming to this wonderful section of our country. You of Montana live in a vast and wonderful state. I hope you will never allow it to become too common to you. Not so very long ago I heard the pastor of a Washington church

deliver a sermon in which he admonished his congregation never to allow
the uncommon things to become common. If I could convey his thought to
you, I would urge you never to allow the grandeur of the mountains and the
majesty of this great western country to become so common to you that you
will lose the ability to appraise the value of their inspiration and worth. You
live in a wonderland, indeed, and we who have come from sections further
east have been marveling and indulging in the most extravagant comment of
admiration and approval.

I speak the plain truth when I say to you that I am rejoiced that I have
come to know better your state and the people of your state. It is a fine thing,
my countrymen, to know each other better. I love to preach the gospel of
understanding. I want you to understand your government, and I think your
government ought to understand you. If we can only have understanding in
the world and, with that understanding, the practice of the Golden Rule, we
shall not only be a peaceful people among ourselves, but we shall always remain at peace with the nations of the earth.

Black Leader Marcus Garvey Finds Common Ground
with the Ku Klux Klan.

*After its six-year murderous reign of terror was suppressed by the federal government
in 1872, the Ku Klux Klan was resurrected in 1915 and counted 4.5 million "white
male, native-born Gentiles" as its members by 1924. In one of the most unlikely developments in race relations during the early part of the century, the Klan found an ally
in Marcus Garvey, the Jamaican-born leader of what was perhaps the largest secular
black movement in America. Ostentatiously dressed in ostrich-plumed hats and military regalia (though he was not and never had been part of an army), Garvey
launched the Universal Negro Improvement Association and its most visible campaign,
a "back to Africa" crusade to create an all-black kingdom of expatriate African Americans in Africa. The Klan was predictably delighted with Garvey's efforts to encourage
African Americans to leave the United States, and in June 1922 the Imperial Wizard
of the Ku Klux Klan hosted Garvey in Atlanta to discuss their common goals. Esteemed black leaders such as W. E. B. Du Bois, cofounder of the NAACP, excoriated
Garvey for meeting with an organization infamous for its brutal and systematic lynchings of black people, but Garvey was unapologetic. Speaking from New York's Liberty
Hall on July 9, 1922, Garvey railed against his critics and defiantly explained his actions.*

In keeping with my duties as leader of a large movement, as one of the advocates of Negro rights and Negro liberty, as an officer of the largest Negro

organization in the world, I became interested in the activities of an organization known as the Ku Klux Klan, not because I wanted to be a member of the Klan, but because I wanted to know the truth about the Klan's attitude toward the race I represent.

For that reason a conference was arranged between the acting Imperial Wizard of the Ku Klux Klan and myself, which took place in Atlanta, Georgia, on the twenty-fifth of June. . . .

You may believe it or not. I made several statements to him, in which he said this: that the Klan is not organized for the absolute purpose of interfering with Negroes, for the purpose of suppressing Negroes, but the Klan is organized for the purpose of protecting the interests of the white race in America. Now anything that does not spell the interests of the white race in America does not come within the scope of the Ku Klux Klan.

I found out, therefore, that the Ku Klux Klan was purely a racial organization standing up in the interests of white folks exclusive of the interests of others. You cannot blame any group of men, whether they are Chinese, Japanese, Anglo-Saxons, or Frenchmen, for standing up for their interests or for organizing in their interest. I am not apologizing for the Klan or endeavoring to excuse the existence of the Klan, but I want a proper understanding about the Ku Klux Klan so that there can be no friction between the Negroes in America and the Ku Klux Klan, because it is not going to help.

The Ku Klux Klan is not an ordinary social club organized around the corner. The Ku Klux Klan is the invisible government of the United States of America. The Ku Klux Klan expresses to a great extent the feeling of every real white American. The attitude of the Ku Klux Klan is that America shall be a white man's country at all hazards, at all costs. The attitude of the Universal Negro Improvement Association is in a way similar to the Ku Klux Klan. Whilst the Ku Klux Klan desires to make America absolutely a white man's country, the Universal Negro Improvement Association wants to make Africa absolutely a black man's country. . . .

We are not going to have any fight as an organization with the Ku Klux Klan because it is not going to help. The Ku Klux Klan, as I said a while ago, is the invisible government of the United States of America. What do I mean by that? The Klan represents the spiritual feeling and even the physical attitude of every white man in the country. There are hundreds of other organizations that feel as the Ku Klux Klan feels. There are millions of individuals in America who feel as the Ku Klux Klan feels. But those individuals, those organizations, are not honest enough to make the confession that the Ku Klux Klan makes. I prefer and I have a higher regard for the man who intends to take my life who will warn me and say, "Garvey, I am going to take your life," so as to give me time to prepare my soul for my God, rather than the man who will pretend to be my friend, and as I turn my back he ushers me into eternity without even giving me a chance to say the Lord's Prayer. . . .

I asked the acting Imperial Wizard of the Ku Klux Klan whether he was interpreting the spirit of just a few people who make up his organization or not, and he said, "No, we are interpreting the spirit of every true white American, but we are honest enough to say certain things that others do not care to say." Now in a nutshell you have the situation. What is the use of staying outside not understanding the attitude and lambasting those people who are in power? Sentiment cannot put down the Ku Klux Klan. Newspaper writings cannot put down the Ku Klux Klan. The Ku Klux Klan is expressing the feeling of over 95 million people. No law can put down the prejudice of a race. You may legislate between now and eternity. If I hate you, no law in the world can make me love you. If I am prejudiced against you for reasons, no law, no constitution in the world can make me change my attitude toward you. . . .

And then we discussed the social side. I said [to the Imperial Wizard], "What is your attitude on white men raping black women?" And he said, "We are as much against that as any self-respecting Negro can be, and we are organized to see that the purity of the race—and especially the purity of the white race—is upheld, and because of that we would not desire to impose upon you that which we do not intend to accept from you."

I asked him, "What would be your attitude if a white man was to go into a colored neighborhood and endeavor to take advantage of the womanhood of our race?" And he said that his attitude would be against that white man. "Let me tell you this," he said further, "that I would be in sympathy with any Negro organization that would uphold the integrity of the Negro race even as the white organization are endeavoring to uphold the integrity of the white race."

The Universal Negro Improvement Association is carrying out that doctrine splendidly. When I arrived at Baton Rouge, in Louisiana, I was visited by the president and some officers of the nearby division. They brought to me this report: Three nights ago seven white men came into a colored neighborhood. We found them at midnight sleeping in homes where they had no business, and they flogged them and drove them out of the neighborhood, and the next day they brought them before the judge, and the judge, who was a Ku Kluxer, let go all the colored men and said, "Do some more of that."

So you realize that the Universal Negro Improvement Association is carrying out just what the Ku Klux Klan is carrying out: the purity of the white race down South. And we are going to carry out the purity of the black race not only down South, but all through the world.

Maud Ballington Booth Expresses Her Belief
That No Prisoner Is "Beyond Hope."

After a visit to the notorious Sing Sing prison in May 1896, the English-born social activist Maud Ballington Booth decided to focus her energies for almost the next fifty years on ministering to convicts. By September 1896 she had opened in the Bronx what is believed to be the nation's first halfway house for released prisoners, Hope Hall No. 1. (Other Hope Halls were later established across the country.) Booth was strict but caring. "I will help you over the rough places," she told incoming ex-cons, "but I will not carry you." Throughout the 1920s she was frequently invited to speak about her work, and, as in the following address, her theme was the rehabilitation of the "given-up" man.

When we look out over the lives of those whose souls have been soiled, whose talents and very manhood have been prostituted to evil, whose hopes and chances in life are blighted, we are prone to be hopeless concerning their future. If the shadow of prison walls is around them, and the stigma of detected crime has blackened their name and character, the world says of them, "That man is done for. He has thrown away his chances. He will never make anything of life after this." If he be one who has lived long in crime, who has been especially reckless, hardened, and desperate in character, one for whom no one has a good word and who has been but a denizen of the underworld, then the world will indeed say that the case is hopeless, that efforts would be wasted in trying to touch the hardened heart of seeking to kindle the star of hope in the dark night that has closed in around the "given-up" man's miserable wreck of a life. Fortunately, the world's harsh judgment is often hasty and based more on what is seen of the difficulties of a situation than upon the possibilities that underlie the surface.

There is an old saying that is often glibly passed from lip to lip and uttered even by good people who would feel deeply incensed if charged with falsehood, and yet it is cruelly, wickedly false: "Once a thief, always a thief. Once a convict, always a convict." When first I undertook to study the questions that involve the present and future welfare of our country's prisoners, this fallacy was quoted to me by those who said that I was entering a field where only bitter disappointment and failure awaited me, and that those who had upon them the taint of crime were beyond hope. Then it was that my heart gloried in the fact that those of us who go as messengers of the great King of love and mercy can view the poor, sin-stained, self-wrecked lives of men from His standpoint, and not from that of the world. Beneath the very evident failure and wrong, we may look deep down in the poor, hopeless heart for the bud of promise that, all unknown to themselves, may yet be awaiting the touch of a higher, stronger power than any that has yet reached them. I believed when I first went to a prison, and I believe a hundredfold more intensely now, that in every human heart there is something to reach, and that there is an influence above that will step in where human love and work and effort could not avail to bring about much-needed awakening and unfold a revelation of future possibility. Yes, thank God, there is a sunshine that can force its way through prison bars and work wondrous and unexpected miracles, and a genuine change of heart where such results seemed the most utterly unlikely and impossible.

Defense Attorney Clarence Darrow
Implores the Court to Spare the Lives of Two Young Murderers.

There was no question as to their guilt. Nathan Leopold and Richard Loeb, two young men from Chicago, confessed that they had killed a boy named Bobby Franks in May 1924 simply to see if they could get away with it. Defending Leopold and Loeb from execution by hanging was Clarence S. Darrow, considered even by his opponents as the nation's most eloquent and persuasive criminal lawyer. In his closing statement, Darrow argued directly to Judge John R. Caverly—and indirectly, no doubt, to a nation held spellbound by the unfolding drama—that putting Leopold and Loeb to death would, far from deterring crime, lead to a more inhumane and uncivilized society.

I do not need to ask mercy from this court for these clients, nor for anybody else, nor for myself, though I have yet found a person who did not need it. But I do not ask mercy for these boys. Your Honor may be as strict in the enforcement of the law as you please and you cannot hang these boys. You can only hang them because back of the law, and back of justice, and back of the common instincts of man, and back of the human feeling for the young, is the hoarse voice of the mob which says, "Kill." I need ask nothing. What is the law of Illinois? If one is found guilty of murder in the first degree by a jury, or if he pleads guilty before a court, the court or jury may do one of three things: He may hang, he may imprison for life, or he may imprison for a term of not less than fourteen years. Now, why is that the law?

Does it follow from the statute that a court is bound to ascertain the impossible, and must necessarily measure the degrees of guilt? Not at all. He may not be able to do it. A court may act from any reason or from no reason. A jury may fix any one of these penalties as they separate. Why was this law passed? Undoubtedly in recognition of the growing feeling in all for a term of not less than fourteen years. Now, why is that the law?

Without any reason whatever, without any facts whatever, Your Honor must make the choice, and you have the same right to make one choice as another. It is Your Honor's province. You may do it, and I need ask nothing in order to have you do it. There is the statute. But there is more than that in this case.

We have sought to tell this court why he should not hang these boys. We have sought to tell this court, and to make this court believe, that they were diseased of mind, and that they were of tender age. . . .

Why did they kill little Bobby Franks? Not for money, not for spite, not for hate. They killed him as they might kill a spider or a fly—for the experience. They killed him because they were made that way. Because somewhere in the infinite process that go to the making up of the boy or the man something slipped, and those unfortunate lads sit here hated, despised, outcasts, with the community shouting for their blood. . . .

Many may say now that they want to hang these boys. But I know that giving the people blood is something like giving them their dinner: When they get it they go to sleep. They may for the time being have an emotion, but they will bitterly regret it. And I undertake to say that if these two boys are sentenced to death, and are hanged on that day, there will be a pall settle over the people of this land that will be dark and deep, and at least cover every human and intelligent person with its gloom. I wonder if it will do good. I marveled when I heard Mr. Savage [one of the prosecutors] talk. Mr. Savage tells this court that if these boys are hanged, there will be no more murder. Mr. Savage is an optimist. He says that if the defendants are hanged there will be no more boys like these. I could give him a sketch of punishment, punishment beginning with the brute which killed something because something hurt it, the punishment of the savage. If a person is injured in the tribe, they must injure somebody in the other tribe. It makes no difference who it is, but somebody. If one is killed, his friends or family must kill in return.

You can trace it all down through the history of man. You can trace the burning, the boilings, the drawings and quarterings, the hangings of people in England at the crossroads, carving them up and hanging them, as examples for all to see. We can come down to the last century when nearly two hundred crimes were punishable by death, and by death in every form. Not only hanging—that was too humane—but burning, boiling, cutting into pieces, torturing in all conceivable forms.

I know that every step in the progress of humanity has been met and opposed by prosecutors, and many times by courts. I know that when poaching and petty larceny was punishable by death in England, juries refused to convict. They were too humane to obey the law, and judges refused to sentence. I know that when the delusion of witchcraft was spreading over Europe, claiming its victims by the millions, many a judge so shaped his cases that no crime of witchcraft could be punished in his court. I know that these trials were stopped in America because juries would no longer convict.

Gradually the laws have been changed and modified, and men look back with horror at the hangings and the killings of the past. What did they find in England? That as they got rid of these barbarous statutes, crimes decreased instead of increased. As the criminal law was modified and humanized, there was less crime instead of more. I will undertake to say, Your Honor, that you can scarcely find a single book written by a student—and I will include all the works on criminology of the past—that has not made the statement over and over again that as the penal code was made less terrible, crimes grew less frequent.

If these two boys die on the scaffold—which I can never bring myself to imagine—if they do die on the scaffold, the details of this will be spread over the world. Every newspaper in the United States will carry a full account. Every newspaper of Chicago will be filled with the gruesome details. It will enter every home and every family. Will it make men better or make men worse? I would like to put that to the intelligence of man, at least such intelligence as they have. I would like to appeal to the feelings. Would it make the human heart softer, or would it make hearts harder?

What influence would it have upon the millions of men who will read it? What influence would it have upon the millions of women who will read it, more sensitive, more impressionable, more imaginative than men? Would it help them if Your Honor should do what the state begs you to do? What influence would it have upon the infinite number of children who will devour its details as Dicky Loeb has enjoyed reading detective stories? Would it make them better or would it make them worse? The question needs no answer. You can answer it from the human heart. What influence, let me ask you, will it have for the unborn babes still sleeping in their mother's womb? Do I need to argue to Your Honor that cruelty only breeds cruelty, that hatred only causes hatred, that if there is any way to kill evil and hatred and all that goes with it, it is not through evil and hatred and cruelty? It is through charity, and love, and understanding.

I am not pleading so much for these boys as I am for the infinite number of others to follow, those who perhaps cannot be as well defended as these have been, those who may go down in the storm, and the tempest, without aid. It is of them I am thinking, and for them I am begging of this court not to turn backward toward the barbarous and cruel past.

Darrow's words proved persuasive, and the two men were sentenced to life in prison. Loeb would ultimately be killed by another prisoner, and Leopold was granted parole after thirty-three years behind bars and moved to Puerto Rico.

William Jennings Bryan Scoffs at Darwin's Theory of Evolution
&
Defense Attorney Dudley Field Malone Argues That Both
"Theology and Science" Should Be Taught in Public Schools.

Less than a year after the Leopold and Loeb sentencing, Clarence Darrow would participate in another of the most famous cases in American history, State of Tennessee v. John T. Scopes. Scopes was a twenty-four-year-old high school science instructor in Dayton, Tennessee, arrested for violating the Butler Act, a statute prohibiting the teaching of Charles Darwin's theory of evolution (or any theory that challenged the biblical account of creation). Assisting the prosecution was the three-time Democratic candidate for president, William Jennings Bryan, a fundamentalist Christian who had lobbied for the Butler Act. Although Darrow's dramatic cross-examination of Bryan, who took the stand as an expert on the Bible, would be immortalized in Jerome Lawrence and Robert Lee's 1950s play Inherit the Wind, *the most pivotal legal showdown came between Bryan and Darrow's assistant Dudley Field Malone on July 16, 1925. (Ironically, Malone had also been an assistant to Bryan when Bryan served as President Woodrow Wilson's secretary of state.) At issue was whether testimony from expert witnesses defending scientific theories of evolution would be allowed. Bryan, who considered such testimony irrelevant to the case, spoke first.*

The statute defines exactly what the people of Tennessee desired and intended and did declare unlawful, and it needs no interpretation. The caption speaks of the evolutionary theory and the statute specifically states that teachers are forbidden to teach in the schools supported by taxation in this state, any theory of creation of man that denies the divine record of man's creation as found in the Bible. . . .

And yet while Mr. Scopes knew what the law was and knew what evolution was, and knew that it violated the law, he proceeded to violate the law.

That is the evidence before the court, and we do not need any expert to tell us what that law means. An expert cannot be permitted to come in here and try to defeat the enforcement of a law by testifying that it's a bad law and it isn't—I mean a bad doctrine—no matter how these people phrase the doctrine, no matter how they eulogize it. This is not the place to try to prove that the law ought never to have been passed. The place to prove that, or teach that, was to the legislature. . . .

Your Honor, I want to show you that we have evidence enough here. We do not need any experts to come in here and tell us about this thing. Here we have Mr. Hunter. Mr. Hunter is the author of this *Biology*, and this is the man who wrote the book Mr. Scopes was teaching. . . . On page 194, we have a diagram, and this diagram purports to give someone's family tree—not only his ancestors but his collateral relatives. We are told just how many animal species there are: 518,900. And in this diagram, beginning with the protozoa, we have the animals classified. We have circles differing in size according to the number of species in them and we have the guess that they give. . . .

And then we run down to the insects, 360,000 insects. Two-thirds of all the species of the animal world are insects. And sometimes in the summertime we feel that we become intimately acquainted with them. A large percentage of the species are mollusks and fishes. Now, we are getting up near our kinfolks, 13,000 fishes. . . . And then we have the reptiles, 3,500. And then we have 13,000 birds. Strange that this should be exactly the same as the number of fishes, round numbers. And then we have mammals, 3,500. And there is a little circle and man is in the circle. Find him, find man.

There is that book! There is the book that we're teaching your children that man was a mammal and so indistinguishable among the mammals that they leave him there with 3,499 other mammals—including elephants. Talk about putting Daniel in the lion's den. How dared those scientists put man in a little ring like that with lions and tigers and everything that is bad! Not only the evolution is possible, but the scientists possibly think of shutting man up in a little circle like that with all these animals, that have an odor that extends beyond the circumference of this circle, my friends.

He tells the children to copy this, copy this diagram. In the notebook, children are to copy this diagram and take it home in their notebooks. To show their parents that you cannot find man. That is the great game to put in the public schools: to find man among animals, if you can.

Tell me that the parents of this day have not any right to declare that children are not to be taught this doctrine? Shall not be taken down from the high plane upon which God put man? Shall be detached from the throne of God and be compelled to link their ancestors with the jungle, tell that to these children? Why, my friend, if they believe it, they go back to scoff at the religion of their parents! And the parents have a right to say that no teacher paid by their money shall rob their children of faith in God and send them back to their homes, skeptical, infidels, or agnostics, or atheists. . . .

And today there is not a scientist in all the world who can trace one single species to any other, and yet they call us ignoramuses and bigots because we do not throw away our Bible and accept it as proved that out of two or three million species not a one is traceable to another. And they say that evolution is a fact when they cannot prove that one species came from another, and if there is such a thing, all species must have come—commencing, as they say—commencing in that one lonely cell down there in the bottom of the ocean that just evolved and evolved until it got to be a man. And they cannot find a single species that came from another, and yet they demand that we allow them to teach this stuff to our children, that they may come home with their imaginary family tree and scoff at their mother's and father's Bible.

Your Honor, we first pointed out that we do not need any experts in science. Here is one plain fact, and the statute defines itself, and it tells the kind of evolution it does not want taught, and the evidence says that this is the kind of evolution that was taught, and no number of scientists could come in here, my friends, and override that statute or take from the jury its right to decide this question, so that all the experts they could bring would mean nothing. . . .

We could have a thousand or a million witnesses, but this case as to whether evolution is true or not is not going to be tried here, within this city. If it is carried to the state's courts, it will not be tried there, and if it is taken to the great court at Washington, it will not be tried there. No, my friends, no court or the law and no jury great or small is going to destroy the issue between the believer and the unbeliever. The Bible is the Word of God. The Bible is the only expression of man's hope of salvation—the Bible, the record of the Son of God, the Savior of the world, born of the Virgin Mary, crucified, and risen again. That Bible is not going to be driven out of this court by experts who come hundreds of miles to testify that they can reconcile evolution, with its ancestors in the jungle, with man made by God in His image, and put here for purposes as a part of the divine plan. No, we are not going to settle that question here.

And I think we ought to confine rules to the law and to the evidence that can be admitted in accordance with the law. Your court is an office of this state, and we who represent the state as counsel are officers of the state, and we cannot humiliate the great state of Tennessee by admitting for a moment that people can come from anywhere and protest against the enforcement of this state's laws on the ground that it does not conform with their ideas, or because it banishes from our schools a thing that they believe in and think ought to be taught in spite of the protest of those who employ the teacher and pay him his salary.

The facts are simple, the case is plain, and if those gentlemen want to enter upon a larger field of educational work on the subject of evolution, let us get through with this case and then convene a mock court for it that will deserve the title of mock court if its purpose is to banish from the hearts of the people the Word of God as revealed.

Malone, who knew expert testimony on the theory of evolution would be pivotal to Scopes's case, began a spirited defense of science and its place in the trial.

Mr. Bryan quoted Mr. Darwin. That theory was evolved and explained by Mr. Darwin seventy-five years ago. Have we learned anything in seventy-five years? Here we have learned the truth of anthropology and we have learned more of archaeology. Not very long since the archaeological museum in London established that a city existed showing a high degree of civilization in Egypt 14,000 years old, showing that on the banks of the Nile River there was a civilization much older than ours. Are we to hold mankind to a literal understanding of the claim that the world is 6,000 years old, because of the limited vision of men who believed the world was flat, and that the earth was the center of the universe, and that man is the center of the earth? It is a dignified position for man to be the center of the universe, that the earth is the center of the universe, and that the heavens revolve about us. And the theory of ignorance and superstition for which they stood are identical, a psychology and ignorance which made it possible for theologians to take old and learned Galileo, who proposed to prove the theory of Copernicus—that the earth was round and did not stand still—and to bring old Galileo to trial for what purpose? For the purpose of proving a literal construction of the Bible against truth, which is revealed. Haven't we learned anything in seventy-five years?

Are we to have our children know nothing about science except what the church says they shall know? I have never seen harm in learning and understanding, in humility and open-mindedness, and I have never seen clearer the need of that learning than when I see the attitude of the prosecution, who attack and refuse to accept the information and intelligence which expert witnesses will give them. . . .

Moreover, let us take the law: "Be it enacted by the state of Tennessee that it shall be unlawful for any teacher in any universities, normals, or any other schools in the state which are supported in whole or in part by public funds of the state, to teach any theory that denies the story of divine creation of man as taught in the Bible, and to teach him that man is descended from a lower order of animals." If that word had been "or" instead of "and," then the prosecution would only have to prove half of its case. But it must prove, according to our contention, that Scopes not only taught a theory that man had descended from a lower order of animal life, but at the same time, instead of that theory, he must teach the theory which denies the story of divine creation set forth in the Bible. . . .

These gentlemen say, "The Bible contains the truth. If the world of science can produce any truth or facts not in the Bible as we understand it, then destroy science, but keep our Bible." And we say, "Keep your Bible." Keep it as your consolation, keep it as your guide, but keep it where it belongs: in the world of your own conscience, in the world of your individual judgment, in the world of the Protestant conscience that I heard so much about when I was a boy. Keep your Bible in the world of theology where it belongs and do not try to tell an intelligent world and the intelligence of this country that these books written by men who knew none of the accepted fundamental facts of science can be put into a course of science, because what are they doing here? The law says what? It says that no theory of creation can be taught in a course of science, except one which conforms with the theory of divine creation as set forth in the Bible. In other words, it says that only the Bible shall be taken as an authority on the subject of evolution in a course on biology. . . .

The least that this generation can do, Your Honor, is to give the next generation all the facts, all the available data, all the theories, all the information that learning, that study, that observation has produced. Give it to the children in the hope of heaven that they will make a better world of this than we have been able to make it. We have just had a war with twenty million dead. Civilization is not so proud of the work of the adults. Civilization need not be so proud of what the grown-ups have done. For God's sake let the children have their minds kept open. Close no doors to their knowledge. Shut no door from them. Make the distinction between theology and science. Let them have both. Let them both be taught. Let them both live. Let them be reverent.

But we come here to say that the defendant is not guilty of violating this law. We have a defendant whom we contend could not violate this law. We have a defendant whom we can prove by witnesses whom we have brought here and are proud to have been brought here, to prove, we say, that there is no conflict between the Bible and whatever he taught. . . .

We have come in here ready for a battle. We have come in here for this duel. I don't know anything about dueling, Your Honor. It is against the law of God. It is against the church. It is against the law of Tennessee. But does the opposition mean by duel that our defendant shall be strapped to a board and that they alone shall carry the sword? Is our only weapon—the witnesses who shall testify to the accuracy of our theory—is our weapon to be taken from us, so that the duel will be entirely one-sided? That isn't my idea of a duel. Moreover it isn't going to be a duel.

There is never a duel with the truth. The truth always wins, and we are not afraid of it. The truth is no coward. The truth does not need the law. The truth does not need the forces of government. The truth does not need Mr. Bryan. The truth is imperishable, eternal, and immortal and needs no human agency to support it. We are ready to tell the truth as we understand it, and we do not fear all the truth that they can present as facts. We are ready. We feel we stand with progress. We feel we stand with science. We feel we stand with intelligence. We feel we stand with fundamental freedom in America. We are not afraid. Where is the fear? We meet it. Where is the fear? We defy it. We ask Your Honor to admit the evidence as a matter of correct law, as a matter of sound procedure, and as a matter of justice to the defense in this case.

Ultimately, the judge sided with Bryan and refused to allow testimony supportive of Darwin's theories. The defense team knew that, on purely legal grounds, Scopes would most likely be found guilty of defying the "monkey law," as it came to be known. After a mere eight minutes of jury deliberation, he was. (The state supreme court later reversed the decision, but on a technicality.) The "monkey law" was repealed in 1967.

Nicola Sacco, Before His Execution, Restates His Innocence.

Despite conflicting evidence and eyewitness accounts that the two men were not at the scene of the crime, Nicola Sacco and Bartolomeo Vanzetti were convicted of murder in 1920 and sentenced to die in the electric chair. What doomed Sacco and Vanzetti, it is commonly believed, is the fact that they were immigrants and radicals. Webster Thayer, the presiding judge, referred to the two men as "anarchist bastards," and the prosecuting attorney repeatedly questioned them on their political convictions, though these beliefs had nothing to do with the crime, a payroll robbery. Before their execution, which ultimately was carried out on August 23, 1927, Sacco addressed the court.

I am not an orator. It is not very familiar with me the English language, and, as I know, as my friend has told me, my comrade Vanzetti will speak more long, so I thought to give him the chance.

I never know, never heard, even read in history anything so cruel as this court. After seven years prosecuting they still consider us guilty. And these gentle people here are arrayed with us in this court today.

I know the sentence will be between two class, the oppressed class and the rich class, and there will be always collision between one and the other. We fraternize the people with the books, with the literature. You persecute the people, tyrannize over them, and kill them. We try the education of people always. You try to put a path between us and some other nationality that hates each other. That is why I am here today on this bench, for having been the oppressed class. Well, you are the oppressor.

You know it, Judge Thayer: You know all my life, you know why I have been here, and after seven years that you have been persecuting me and my poor wife, and you still today abuse us to death. I would like to tell you my life, but what is the use? You know all about what I say before, and my friend—that is, my comrade—will be talking, because he is more familiar with the language, and I will give him a chance. My comrade, the man kind, the kind man to all the children, you sentence him two times, in the Bridge-water case and the Dedham case, connected with me, and you know he is in-nocent. You forget all the population that has been with us for seven years, to sympathize and give us all their energy and all their kindness. You do not care for them. Among that peoples and the comrades and the working class there is a big legion of intellectual people which have been with us for seven years, but to not commit the iniquitous sentence, but still the court goes ahead. And I think I thank you all, you peoples, my comrades who have been with me for seven years, with the Sacco–Vanzetti case, and I will give my friend a chance.

I forget one thing which my comrade remember me. As I said before, Judge Thayer know all my life, and he know that I am never be guilty, never—not yesterday, nor today, nor forever.

Al "Scarface" Capone Bids Farewell to Chicago and Laments Being Unappreciated for Showing Citizens a "Good Time."

After being shot five times outside his Chicago apartment—and miraculously surviv-ing—mob boss Jimmy Torrio decided enough was enough and turned his empire over to his twenty-eight-year-old lieutenant, Al "Scarface" Capone. A go-getter from the start (he had formed his first gang at age fourteen), Capone was soon reaping profits of tens of million of dollars a year, most of it from bootlegging, and symbolized an era that became known as the "Lawless Decade" and the "Roaring Twenties." But, as gang-related murders became more ruthless and widespread, public sentiment began to turn against the mob and authorities hounded gangsters with more frequency. Sensing the backlash, a peeved Capone announced at a December 5, 1927, press conference that he was "retiring" and heading to Florida.

I'm leaving for St. Petersburg, Florida, tomorrow. Let the worthy citizens of Chicago get their liquor the best they can. I'm sick of the job. It's a thankless one and full of grief. I don't know when I'll get back, if ever. But it won't be after the holidays, anyway. . . .

I've been spending the best years of my life as a public benefactor. I've given people the light pleasures, shown them a good time. And all I get is abuse, the existence of a hunted man. I'm called a killer.

Well, tell the folks I'm going away now. I guess murder will stop. There won't be any more booze. You won't be able to find a crap game, even, let alone a roulette wheel or a faro game. I guess Mike Hughes won't need his 3,000 extra cops, after all.

Public service is my motto. Ninety-nine percent of the people in

Chicago drink and gamble. I've tried to serve them decent liquor and square games. But I'm not appreciated. It's no use. . . .

I've got some property in St. Petersburg I want to sell. It's warm there but not too warm.

Say, the coppers won't have to lay all the gang murders on me now. Maybe they'll find a new hero for the headlines. It would be a shame, wouldn't it, if while I was away they would forget about me and find a new gangland chief?

I wish all my friends and enemies a Merry Christmas and Happy New Year. That's all they'll get from me this year. I hope I don't spoil anybody's Christmas by not sticking around. . . .

My wife and mother hear so much about what a terrible criminal I am. It's getting too much for them, and I'm getting sick of it myself.

The other day a man came in here and said that he had to have $3,000. If I'd give it to him, he said, he would make me a beneficiary in a $15,000 insurance policy he'd take out and then kill himself. I had to have him pushed out.

Today I got a letter from a woman in England. Even over there I'm known as a gorilla. She offered to pay my passage to London if I'd kill some neighbors she'd been having a quarrel with.

The papers have made me out a millionaire, and hardly an hour goes by that somebody doesn't want me to invest in some scheme or stake somebody in business.

That's what I've got to put up with just because I give the public what the public wants. I never had to send out high-pressure salesmen. Boy, I could never meet the demand! . . .

Capone nevertheless continued his criminal ways, including ordering one of the most infamous murders in gangland history—the St. Valentine's Day massacre. On February 14, 1929, five of Capone's men (three in civilian clothes and two dressed as police officers) walked into a garage where rival gang members were working and machine-gunned them to death. Police could not link Capone directly to the killings, but he was indicted two years later on twenty-two counts of tax evasion. He served more than seven years in prison.

Republican Presidential Candidate Herbert Hoover Predicts the "Abolition of Poverty" in the United States.

The free-spirited, free-spending "Roaring Twenties" all but promised to continue rolling into the 1930s, if not forever. "Given a chance to go forward with the policies of the last eight years," declared Republican presidential candidate Herbert Hoover, "and we shall soon with the help of God be in sight of the day when poverty will be banished from this nation." Hoover, orphaned at age ten and a self-made millionaire, served as the secretary of commerce under presidents Warren G. Harding and Calvin Coolidge for eight years—eight enormously prosperous years for the nation. The awesome debts incurred from World War I were under control, wages doubled for many workers in as little as a decade, and the stock market soared. During the 1928 presidential campaign, Hoover insisted that the ecomony would only continue to flourish if America held fast to its sense of "rugged individualism" and free-enterprise system. Hoover's most famous speech on the matter was given in New York City on October 22, 1928.

This campaign now draws to a close. The platforms of the two parties, defining principles and offering solutions of various national problems, have been presented and are being earnestly considered by our people. . . .

During the war we necessarily turned to the government to solve every difficult economic problem. The government having absorbed every energy of our people for war, there was no other solution. For the preservation of the state the federal government became a centralized despotism which undertook unprecedented responsibilities, assumed autocratic powers, and took over the business of citizens. To a large degree we regimented our whole people temporarily into a socialistic state. However justified in time of war, if continued in peacetime it would destroy not only our American system but with it our progress and freedom as well.

When the war closed, the most vital of all issues both in our own country and throughout the world was whether governments should continue their wartime ownership and operation of many instrumentalities of productions and distribution. We were challenged with a peacetime choice between the American system of rugged individualism and a European philosophy of diametrically opposed doctrines, doctrines of paternalism and state socialism. The acceptance of ideas would have meant the destruction of self-government through centralization of government. It would have meant the undermining of the individual initiative and enterprise through which our people have grown to unparalleled greatness.

The Republican Party from the beginning resolutely turned its face away from these ideas and these war practices. A Republican Congress cooperated with the Democratic administration to demobilize many of our war activities. At that time the two parties were in accord upon that point. When the Republican Party came into full power it went at once resolutely back to our fundamental conception of the state and the rights and responsibilities of the individual. Thereby it restored confidence and hope in the American people, it freed and stimulated enterprise, it restored the government to its position as an umpire instead of a player in the economic game. For these reasons the American people have gone forward in progress while the rest of the world has halted, and some countries have even gone backward. If anyone will study the causes of retarded recuperation in Europe, he will find much of it due to the stifling of private initiative on one hand, and overloading of the government with business on the other. . . .

I feel deeply on this subject because during the war I had some practical experience with governmental operation and control. I have witnessed not only at home but abroad the many failures of government in business. I have seen its tyrannies, its injustices, its destruction of self-government, its undermining of the very instincts which carry our people forward to progress. I have witnessed the lack of advance, the lowered standards of living, the depressed spirits of people working under such a system. My objection is based not upon theory or upon a failure to recognize wrong or abuse, but I know the adoption of such methods would strike at the very roots of American life and would destroy the very basis of American progress.

Our people have the right to know whether we can continue to solve our great problems without abandonment of our American system. I know we can. We have demonstrated that our system is responsive enough to meet any new and intricate development in our economic and business life. We have demonstrated that we can meet any economic problem and still maintain our democracy as master in our own house, and that we can at the same time preserve equality of opportunity and individual freedom. . . .

And what have been the results of our American system? Our country has become the land of opportunity in those born without inheritance, not merely because of the wealth of its resources equal to ours. Her people are equally industrious, but she has not had the blessings of one hundred and fifty years of our form of government and of our social system.

By adherence to the principles of decentralized self-government, ordered liberty, equal opportunity, and freedom to the individual, our American experiment in human welfare has yielded a degree of well-being unparalleled in all the world. It has come nearer to the abolition of poverty, to the abolition of fear of want, than humanity has ever reached before. . . .

Under administration by the Republican Party in the last seven and one-half years our country as a whole has made unparalleled progress and then has been in generous part reflected to this great city. Prosperity is no idle expression. It is a job for every worker. It is the safety and the safeguard of every business and every home. A continuation of the policies of the Republican Party is fundamentally necessary to the further building up of this prosperity.

I have dwelt at some length on the principles of relationship between the government and business. I make no apologies for dealing with this subject. The first necessity of any nation is the smooth functioning of the vast business machinery for employment, feeding, clothing, housing, and providing luxuries and comforts to a people. Unless these basic elements are properly organized and function there can be no progress in business, in education, literature, music, or art. There can be no advance in the fundamental ideas of a people. A people cannot make progress in poverty.

I have endeavored to present to you that the greatness of America has grown out of a political and social system and a method of control of economic forces distinctly its own—our American system—which has carried this great experiment in all history. We are nearer today to the ideal of the abolition of poverty and fear from the lives of men and women than ever before in any land. And I again repeat that the departure from our American system by injecting principles destructive to it which our opponents propose will jeopardize the very liberty and freedom of our people, will destroy the equality of opportunity, not alone to ourselves, but to our children. . . .

Hoover easily won the 1928 election over Democrat Alfred E. Smith, the first Catholic nominated by a major party. "I have no fears for the future of our country," President Hoover exclaimed at his inauguration. "It is bright with hope." But later that year the American economy imploded. On Tuesday, October 29, 1929, the stock market crashed. Wildly overinflated, the Dow Jones had seen the last day of the Great Bull Market on September 3. Brokers began calling their clients demanding payment of their loans, which most couldn't pay without selling off more stocks, which prompted the market to tumble even further. Pandemonium ensued, and within weeks of "Black Tuesday" more than 1 million Americans had lost a staggering $30 billion. Behind the scenes President Hoover knew the situation was ominous, but he also recognized that signs of panic from the White House would prove catastrophic. "Any lack of confidence in the economic future and the basic strength of business in the United States," Hoover stated on November 15, 1929, "is simply foolish." But what President Hoover—and, no doubt, the rest of the country—had hoped was the end of the financial crisis in fact represented merely a prelude. The Great Depression had just begun.

1930–1939

NEVER BEFORE IN MODERN HISTORY HAVE THE ESSENTIAL differences between the two major American parties stood out in such striking contrast as they do today. Republican leaders not only have failed in material things, they have failed in national vision, because in disaster they have held out no hope, they have pointed out no path for the people below to climb back to places of security and of safety in our American life.

Throughout the nation, men and women, forgotten in the political philosophy of the government of the last years, look to us here for guidance and for more equitable opportunity to share in the distribution of national wealth.

On the farms, in the large metropolitan areas, in the smaller cities, and in the villages, millions of our citizens cherish the hope that their old standards of living and of thought have not gone forever. Those millions cannot and shall not hope in vain.

I pledge you, I pledge myself, to a New Deal for the American people. Let us all assembled constitute ourselves prophets of a new order of competence and of courage. This is more than a political campaign; it is a call to arms. Give me your help, not to win votes alone, but to win in this crusade to restore America to its own people.

—Democratic presidential candidate Franklin D. Roosevelt,
accepting the nomination of his party in Chicago,
July 2, 1932

Oscar Ameringer Describes Intolerable Suffering Throughout the United States as a Result of the Great Depression.

Almost a year after the stock market's collapse, President Hoover and his administration were increasingly frustrated by their inability to bolster public morale. Simeon D. Fess, chairman of the Republican National Committee, remarked in October 1930, "Persons high in Republican circles are beginning to believe that there is some concerted effort on foot to utilize the stock market as a method of discrediting the administration. Every time an administration official gives out an optimistic statement about business conditions, the market immediately drops." But the nation's troubles were moving well beyond Wall Street. By 1932, thousands of banks had failed, utterly wiping out their depositors' life savings, and more than 13 million Americans—a full 25 percent of the labor market—had lost their jobs. Congress began hearings on the degree to which Americans were suffering, and, as one observer named Oscar Ameringer relates in the following testimony, there seemed to be no end in sight to the crisis.

During the last three months I have visited, as I have said, some twenty states of this wonderfully rich and beautiful country. Here are some of the things I heard and saw: In the state of Washington I was told that the forest fires raging in that region all summer and fall were caused by unemployed timber workers and bankrupt farmers in an endeavor to earn a few honest dollars as firefighters. The last thing I saw on the night I left Seattle was numbers of women searching for scraps of food in the refuse piles of the principal market of that city. A number of Montana citizens told me of thousands of bushels of wheat left in the fields uncut on account of its low price that hardly paid for the harvesting. In Oregon I saw thousands of bushels of apples rotting in the orchards. Only absolute flawless apples were still salable, at from 40 to 50 cents a box containing 200 apples. At the same time, there are millions of children who, on account of the poverty of their parents, will not eat one apple this winter.

While I was in Oregon the *Portland Oregonian* bemoaned the fact that thousands of ewes were killed by the sheep raisers because they did not bring enough in the market to pay the freight on them. And while Oregon sheep raisers fed mutton to the buzzards, I saw men picking for meat scraps in the garbage cans in the cities of New York and Chicago. I talked to one man in a restaurant in Chicago. He told me of his experience in raising sheep. He said that he had killed 3,000 sheep this fall and thrown them down the canyon, because it cost $1.10 to ship a sheep, and then he would get less than $1.00 for it. He said he could not afford to feed the sheep, and he would not let them starve, so he just cut their throats and threw them down the canyon.

The roads of the West and Southwest teem with hungry hitchhikers. The campfires of the homeless are seen along every railroad track. I saw men, women, and children walking over the hard roads. Most of them were tenant farmers who had lost their all in the late slump in wheat and cotton. Between Clarksville and Russellville, Arkansas, I picked up a family. The woman was hugging a dead chicken under a ragged coat. When I asked her where she had procured the fowl, first she told me she had found it dead in the road, and then added in grim humor, "They promised me a chicken in the pot, and now I got mine."

In Oklahoma, Texas, Arkansas, and Louisiana, I saw untold bales of cotton rotting in the fields because the cotton pickers could not keep body and soul together on 35 cents paid for picking 100 pounds. The farmers cooperatives who loaned the money to the planters to make the crops allowed the planters $5 a bale. That means 1,500 pounds of seed cotton for the picking of it, which was in the neighborhood of 35 cents a pound. A good picker can pick about 200 pounds of cotton a day, so that the 70 cents would not provide enough pork and beans to keep the picker in the field, so that there is fine staple cotton rotting down there by hundreds and thousands of tons.

As a result of this appalling overproduction on the one side and the staggering underconsumption on the other side, 70 percent of the farmers of Oklahoma were unable to pay the interests on their mortgages. Last week, one of the largest and oldest mortgage companies in that state went into the hands of the receiver. In that and other states we have now the interesting spectacle of farmers losing their farms by foreclosure and mortgage companies losing their recouped holdings by tax sales.

The farmers are being pauperized by the poverty of industrial populations, and the industrial populations are being pauperized by the poverty of the farmers. Neither has the money to buy the product of the other, hence we have overproduction and underconsumption at the same time and in the same country.

Justice Oliver Wendell Holmes, on His Ninetieth Birthday, Offers Profound Advice on Life and Death.

Appointed at the age of sixty-two by President Theodore Roosevelt to the U.S. Supreme Court, Oliver Wendell Holmes, son of the famed American poet of the same name, spent thirty distinguished years on the court before retiring in 1932. On March 7, 1931, a gathering of eminent politicians and leaders from the arts and sciences honored Holmes on his ninetieth birthday. At the conclusion of the tribute, which was broadcast over the radio, Holmes unexpectedly went to the microphone and spoke extemporaneously on his philosophy of life.

In this symposium my part is only to sit in silence. To express one's feelings as the end draws nigh is too intimate a task.

But I may mention one thought that comes to me as a listener-in. The riders in a race do not stop short when they reach the goal. There is a little finishing canter before coming to a standstill. There is time to hear the kind voices of friends and to say to oneself, "The work is done." But just as one says that, the answer comes: "The race is over, but the work never is done while the power to work remains. The canter that brings you to a standstill need not be only coming to rest. It cannot be while you still live. For to live is to function. That is all there is to living."

And so I end with a line from a Latin poet who uttered the message more than fifteen hundred years ago, "Death plucks my ear and says: Live—I am coming."

Notre Dame President the Reverend Father Charles L. O'Donnell Eulogizes the Legendary Football Coach Knute Rockne.

"Go out there and win one for the Gipper," Notre Dame football coach Knute Rockne famously told his players before a crucial game. Immortalized by the 1940 film Knute Rockne, All American, *starring a young Ronald Reagan as the dying football player George Gipp, Rockne's "Gipper" speech, historians now believe, is apocryphal. But there is no doubt that Rockne was (and remains) an American legend, rallying the "Fighting Irish" to five undefeated seasons and three national championships. After Rockne was killed in a plane crash on March 31, 1931, Notre Dame's president, the Reverend Father Charles L. O'Donnell, offered a heartfelt tribute on April 4 heard by millions on the CBS radio network.*

In an age that has stamped itself as the era of the "go-getter"—a horrible, ruthless thing—he was a go-giver. He made use of all the proper machinery and the legitimate methods of modern activity to be not essentially modern at all; to be quite elementary, human, Christian, giving himself, spending himself like water, not for himself, for others.

In this Holy Week a tragic event has occurred which accounts for our presence here today. Knute Rockne is dead. And who was he?

Ask the President of the United States, who dispatched a personal message of tribute to his memory and comfort to his bereaved family. Ask the King of Norway, who sends a special delegation as his personal representative to this solemn service. Ask the several state legislatures now sitting that have passed resolutions of sympathy and condolence. Ask the thousands of newspapermen, whose labor of love in his memory has stirred a reading public of

125 million Americans. Ask men and women from every walk of life. Ask the children, the boys of America. Ask any and all of these, who was this man whose death has struck the nation with dismay and has everywhere bowed heads in grief?

Was he perhaps a martyr who died for some great cause? A patriot who laid down his life for his country? A statesman, a soldier, an admiral of the fleet? Some heaven-born artist, an inventor, a captain of industry or finance? No, he was Knute Rockne, director of athletics and football coach of Notre Dame. He was a man of the people, a husband and father, a citizen of South Bend, Indiana. Yet had he been any one of these personages that have been mentioned, the tribute of admiration and affection which he has received could not be more universal or more sincere.

What was the secret of his irresistible appeal to all sorts and conditions of men? When we say simply, "He was a great American," we shall go far toward satisfying man, for all of us recognize and love the attributes of the true American character. When we say that he was an inspirer of young men in the direction of high ideals that were conspicuously exemplified in his own life, we have covered much that unquestionably was true of him.

When we link his name with the intrinsic chivalry and romance of a great college game, which he perhaps more than any other one man has made fine and cleaner in itself and larger in its popular appeal, here too we touch upon a vital point. But no one of those things, nor all of them together, can quite sum up this man whose tragic death at the early age of forty-three has left the country aghast. Certainly the circumstances of his death do not furnish the answer.

I do not know the answer. I would not dare the irreverence of guessing. But I find myself in this hour of piteous loss and pained bewilderment re-calling the words of Christ: "Thou shalt love the Lord thy God with thy whole heart." This is the first and greatest commandment. And the second is like unto this: "Thou shalt love thy neighbor as thyself." I think, supremely, he loved his neighbor, his fellow man, with genuine, deep love. In his case most illustriously is verified the Christian paradox: He has cast away to keep, he has lost his life to find it. This is not death, but immortality.

We who are here are but a handful of his friends, come to pay our last tribute of devotion to his mortal remains; to give some token of affection so that his dear ones, his loving wife and children, his venerable mother and his sisters, may in their sorrow be a little comforted by our sympathy and the knowledge that we too loved him.

Of necessity we are few in numbers in this hallowed place, though thousands are without the doors. But we represent millions of men and women like ourselves who are here in spirit, in the very spirit of these solemn services, and listening all over America to these holy rites.

It is fitting he should be brought here to his beloved Notre Dame, and that his body should rest a little while in this church where the light of faith broke upon his happy soul, where the waters of baptism were poured on his brow, where he made his first confession, received his first Holy Communion, and was confirmed by the same consecrated hand that today is raised in blessing above his coffin.

He might have gone to any university in the land and been gladly received and forever cherished there. But he chose Our Lady's school, Notre Dame. He honored her in his life as a student, he honored her in the monogram he earned and wore, he honored her in the principles he inculcated and the ideals he set up in the lives of the young men under his care. He was her own true son.

To Our Lady we turn in this hour of anguish and of broken hopes and hearts laid waste. She is the Mother of God, and Mother of God's men, we give him into Thy keeping. Mary, Gate of Heaven, we come to thee. Open to receive him. Mary, Morning Star, shine upon his sea. Mary of Notre Dame, take him into thy house of gold. Our life, our sweetness, and our hope, we lay him in thy bosom.

Eternal rest grant unto him, O Lord, and let perpetual light shine upon him. May his soul and the souls of all the faithful departed, through the mercy of God, rest in peace. Amen.

Walter W. Waters, Leader of the "Bonus Expeditionary Forces," Rallies Americans Against President Herbert Hoover.

In 1924, when America was enjoying economic prosperity, Congress granted a bonus (which would not be due until 1945) in the form of paid-up, twenty-year insurance policies to the nation's veterans. In May 1932, during the worst of the Great Depression, an estimated 20,000 jobless veterans marched to Washington demanding full and immediate payment of the bonus. The House of Representatives passed a bill granting the veterans their money, but the Senate struck it down. Discouraged, some of the veterans returned home. But the majority, led by a former World War I sergeant named Walter W. Waters, defiantly camped out in vacant government buildings and areas of southeast Washington. On July 28, government agents and local police instructed the "Bonus Expeditionary Force," as they called themselves, to clear out. But during the evacuation a riot ensued, resulting in two deaths and many injuries, and an exasperated President Hoover ordered in the army to resolve the matter once and for all. Four troops of cavalry and four infantry companies, with tanks, tear gas, and machine guns—all under the command of General Douglas MacArthur, whose junior officers included George S. Patton and a reluctant Dwight D. Eisenhower—charged into the BEF's shantytown, torched their shacks, fired tear gas into the crowds, and drove the entire BEF into Virginia and Maryland. There were more than two hundred casualties, including two children who died as a result of the gassings. (Among the veterans who died was Joseph T. Angelino, who had won the Distinguished Service Cross for saving the life of none other than George S. Patton.) Enraged by the loss of life and the very idea of the U.S. government attacking its own, BEF leader Walter W. Waters lashed out at President Hoover and his administration.

Immediate organization of an effective body of national scope that will honestly represent the mass of the American people in taking the United States government away from the moneyed powers by legal means, and returning it to the common people, whose government it should be, is a crying need of the country today. I am therefore calling upon every American citizen of voting age, whether man or woman, to join hands now with the Bonus Expeditionary Force to clean out the high places in government and to keep them clean.

The Bonus Expeditionary Force, because it is already a functioning body proved under fire, offers as a nucleus of such an organization to lead the fight at the polls for justice to the veterans, the working people, employed and unemployed, and all others whose rights and interests are forgotten by their misnamed representatives in Washington, in the eagerness of those misrepresentatives to serve the special interests.

We of this organization, law-abiding American citizens and veterans, all have been gradually working toward such a body for weeks. But the tragic affair of yesterday, precipitated by a national administration whose security was threatened because of the dogged lawful resistance of a force of loyal Americans that refused to be dislodged by any of its stratagems and trickery, calls for immediate enlistment of all citizens who have the welfare of true American government at heart.

The people have been betrayed by the servant of Wall Street who sits in the White House. He and his henchmen will continue to betray the people unless the people rise in their own defense and, with the weapon given them by law—the ballot—turn out all whose interests are not the interests of the masses.

The Bonus Expeditionary Force came to Washington to collect a debt that they conscientiously believe is due them. But the movement they began has far outgrown the so-called "bonus." They stand now as the spokesmen for all the people whose welfare is ignored by the plunder band of the White House and Capitol Hill. That their leadership in this is feared is attested by the fact that the administration, in a preconceived plan to drive them from the nation's capital after trickery had failed, set troops upon them to drive them out with bombs and bayonets and set fire to their lowly billets and their few personal belongings.

But the BEF will carry on, no longer as merely a "bonus army" but as torch bearers for the inarticulate masses the country over. Every state will be organized, every community in the country will have its unit in what we hope and expect will be the greatest organization for the promotion of the welfare of the common people that history has ever known.

This organization will brook no revolutionary doctrine. Its principles and procedure will be strictly American for, despite our contempt for those who are mismanaging our country, we are entirely loyal to its institutions and its ideals.

Every American voter is urged to join with us and to spread our doctrine of just treatment for all the people in every town and hamlet of the country. The khaki shirt will be the symbol of our organization, and every supporter, friend, and member is asked to wear such shirts that our strength may be known by all who see.

Although Waters's anger resonated with the American people, the BEF and its supporters ultimately dissipated. But the assault on the unarmed BEF was not without consequences. Coming in the middle of an election year, it all but guaranteed President Hoover's loss to the charismatic governor from the state of New York, Franklin Delano Roosevelt.

Newly Elected President Franklin D. Roosevelt Gives Inspiration and Courage to a Nation Overwhelmed by Poverty and Anxiety.

While President Herbert Hoover seemed, by many Americans, to be dull and aloof, candidate Roosevelt emanated charm and charisma. While President Hoover lacked the ability to uplift a nation mired in economic and social depression, candidate Roosevelt manifested a more passionate desire to renew their circumstances and their spirits. "The country needs and, unless I mistake its temper, the country demands, bold, persistent experimentation," Roosevelt would thunder at campaign stops. "The millions who are in want will not stand by silently forever while the things to satisfy their needs are within easy reach." On November 4, 1932, the American people elected Roosevelt in a popular landslide. Well aware of the daunting task before him, and addressing a nation tired of false promises but yearning for inspiration, President Roosevelt gave the following speech at his inauguration.

This is a day of national consecration, and I am certain that my fellow Americans expect that on my induction into the presidency I will address them with a candor and a decision which the present situation of our nation impels. This is preeminently the time to speak the truth, the whole truth, frankly and boldly. Nor need we shrink from honestly facing conditions in our country today. This great nation will endure as it has endured, will revive, and will prosper. So, first of all, let me assert my firm belief that the only thing we have to fear is fear itself—nameless, unreasoning, unjustified terror which paralyzes needed efforts to convert retreat into advance. In every dark hour of our national life a leadership of frankness and vigor has met with that understanding and support of the people themselves which is essential to victory. I am convinced that you will again give that support to leadership in these critical days.

In such a spirit on my part and on yours we face our common difficulties. They concern, thank God, only material things. Values have shrunken to fantastic levels. Taxes have risen. Our ability to pay has fallen. Government of all kinds is faced by serious curtailment of income. The means of exchange are frozen in the currents of trade. The withered leaves of industrial enterprise lie on every side. Farmers find no markets for their produce. The savings of many years in thousands of families are gone. More important, a host of unemployed citizens face the grim problem of existence, and an equally great number toil with little return. Only a foolish optimist can deny the dark realities of the moment.

Yet our distress comes from no failure of substance. We are stricken by no plague of locusts. Compared with the perils which our forefathers conquered because they believed and were not afraid, we have still much to be thankful for. Nature still offers her bounty, and human efforts have multiplied it. Plenty is at our doorstep, but a generous use of it languishes in the very sight of the supply.

Primarily this is because the rulers of the exchange of mankind's goods have failed, through their own stubbornness and their own incompetence, have admitted their failure, and abdicated. Practices of the unscrupulous money changers stand indicted in the court of public opinion, rejected by the hearts and minds of men. True, they have tried, but their efforts have been cast in the pattern of an outworn tradition. Faced by failure of credit, they have proposed only the lending of more money. Stripped of the lure of profit by which to induce our people to follow their false leadership, they have resorted to exhortations, pleading tearfully for restored confidence. They know only the rules of a generation of self-seekers. They have no vision, and when there is no vision the people perish.

The money changers have fled from their high seats in the temple of our civilization. We may now restore that temple to the ancient truths. The measure of the restoration lies in the extent to which we apply social values more noble than mere monetary profit.

Happiness lies not in the mere possession of money. It lies in the joy of achievement, in the thrill of creative effort. The joy and moral stimulation of work no longer must be forgotten in the mad chase of evanescent profits. These dark days will be worth all they cost us if they teach us that our true destiny is not to be ministered unto but to minister to ourselves and to our fellow men.

Recognition of the falsity of material wealth as the standard of success goes hand in hand with the abandonment of the false belief that public office and high political position are to be valued only by the standards of pride of place and personal profit. And there must be an end to a conduct in banking and in business which too often has given to a sacred trust the likeness of callous and selfish wrongdoing. Small wonder that confidence languishes, for it thrives only on honesty, on honor, on the sacredness of obligations, on faithful protection, on unselfish performance. Without them it cannot live.

Restoration calls, however, not for changes in ethics alone. This nation asks for action, and action now. Our greatest primary task is to put people to work. This is no unsolvable problem if we face it wisely and courageously. It can be accomplished in part by direct recruiting by the government itself, treating the task as we would treat the emergency of a war, but at the same time, through this employment, accomplishing greatly needed projects to stimulate and reorganize the use of our natural resources.

Hand in hand with this we must frankly recognize the overbalance of population in our industrial centers and, by engaging on a national scale in a redistribution, endeavor to provide a better use of the land for those best fitted for the land. The task can be helped by definite efforts to raise the values of agricultural products and with this the power to purchase the output of our cities. It can be helped by preventing realistically the tragedy of the growing loss through foreclosure of our small homes and our farms. It can be helped by insistence that the federal, state, and local governments act forthwith on the demand that their cost be drastically reduced. It can be helped by the unifying of relief activities which today are often scattered, uneconomical, and unequal. It can be helped by national planning for and supervision of all forms of transportation and of communications and other utilities which have a definitely public character. There are many ways in which it can be helped, but it can never be helped merely by talking about it. We must act and act quickly.

Finally, in our progress toward a resumption of work we require two safeguards against a return of the evils of the old order. There must be a strict supervision of all banking and credits and investments. There must be an end to speculation with other people's money. And there must be provision for an adequate but sound currency.

There are the lines of attack. I shall presently urge upon a new Congress in special session detailed measures for their fulfillment, and I shall seek the immediate assistance of the several states. . . .

I am prepared under my constitutional duty to recommend the measures that a stricken nation in the midst of a stricken world may require. These measures, or such other measures as the Congress may build out of its experience and wisdom, I shall seek, within my constitutional authority, to bring to speedy adoption. But in the event that the Congress shall fail to take one of these two courses and in the event that the national emergency is still critical, I shall not evade the clear course of duty that will then confront me. I shall ask the Congress for the one remaining instrument to meet the crisis: broad executive power to wage a war against the emergency, as great as the power that would be given to me if we were in fact invaded by a foreign foe. For the trust reposed in me I will return the courage and the devotion that befit the time. I can do no less.

We face the arduous days that lie before us in the warm courage of the national unity, with the clear consciousness of seeking old and precious moral values, with the clean satisfaction that comes from the stern performance of duty by old and young alike. We aim at the assurance of a rounded and permanent national life. We do not distrust the future of essential democracy. The people of the United States have not failed. In their need they have registered a mandate that they want direct, vigorous action. They have asked for discipline and direction under leadership. They have made me the present instrument of their wishes. In the spirit of the gift I take it.

In this dedication of a nation we humbly ask the blessing of God. May He protect each and every one of us. May He guide me in the days to come.

Joseph Strauss, Engineer of the Golden Gate Bridge, Celebrates the Bridge as a Symbol of "New Hopes and New Aspirations."

Like New York's Empire State Building, which was completed in 1931, the construction of the Golden Gate Bridge in San Francisco was more than an unprecedented feat of engineering—it was a symbol of resolve in anxious times. The chief engineer, Joseph

Baermann Strauss, was faced with seemingly impossible obstacles to overcome logisti-
cally and architecturally: violent winds and currents, channel depths of more than 300
feet, and the constant threat of earthquakes. Undeterred, Strauss created a structure that
blended beauty with strength and remains to this day one of the world's largest and
most stunning bridges. The Golden Gate was opened to the public on May 27, 1937.
But in February 1933, when the groundbreaking began, Strauss gave the following
speech in San Francisco, expressing all that the bridge would represent to the city and
the world.

In all ages men have paused in awe and celebrated with festival and with song each manifestation of the creative urge that links him to his maker, the phenomenon of birth. Tonight we pause once again to celebrate that phenomenon in the birth of a bridge. Firmly do we plant its feet at that vast subaqueous plateau of rock that has buttressed the western outpost of the world for untold centuries. Swiftly do we fashion its towering, tapering sinews of steel. Lift them up, up, through the clouds into the pure sunlight of the true California! Over their tall, naked shoulders we thread the far-flung drapery of slender cables. Pendant from these, piece by piece, we fasten a necklace around the throat of San Francisco Bay. Gaily do we caparison it with brilliants of gleaming lights and festoon it with long, white ribbons of roadway and sidewalks. A finishing touch here and there, and California presents to the world her contribution to its gallery of immortals, her answer to the call of her people and her rebuke to the irreconcilable iconoclasts and the gospel of inertia.

But that is not all. In these giant arms of steel, clasping hands above the tumbling waters of the Golden Gate, San Francisco returns to her bosom her own flesh and blood, torn from her by the gods of fire and water in that shadowy long ago. She recaptures the lost Pleiad of a brilliant constellation. She restores the geographical unity of a homogenous people and weaves still closer the ties of community kinship. She welds the first link that binds the separated fragments of a scattered dynasty into a new world metropolis. She reunites the severed arteries of communication so that the quickened lifeblood of commerce and travel may pulsate through them to the uttermost recesses of a vast empire. At the threshold of that empire, she builds a vestibule to the redwood highway, chancel aisle of a great cathedral whose pillars are the colonnaded sequoias, row on row, like which there are none other. And so, concurrent and concomitant at this one spot in all the world, are joined the greatest of God's living creatures, and the greatest of man's feeble attempts at dominion, born of his ceaseless struggle to conquer this strange kingdom in which his restless spirit is marooned. . . .

Life is motion, and absence of motion is death! The new San Francisco, whose hub is the center of the Golden Gate, has chosen life! And the Golden Gate Bridge is the crest upon the apex of that new San Francisco that tells the world of a new city, reborn to lead the thundering legions upon whose banners are blazoned the story of the world's progress.

In one leap this new San Francisco has emerged from bridge obscurity to bridge supremacy. For the Golden Gate Bridge is the climax of the superlatives in an age of superlatives. It is a thing apart, even in a land where the unusual is the usual, a thing apart in a competitive world in which men strive feverishly for supremacy in endless contests, in a frenzied world where deeds of daring and of skill are a commonplace and the spectacular and sensational are our daily portion. But remote from that frenzied sphere of ceaseless striving, there is another realm, a saner realm where men still labor for purposeful accomplishment, labor patiently and devotedly, careless of applause, immune from the lure of the front page; a realm in which the breaking of records is not just a passing thrill, but a service that achieves greatest happiness for humanity; a realm in which, day by day, mankind acquires an increasing command over nature and paves the difficult path to continuing progress for the human race. In that realm the Golden Gate Bridge takes its proper place, and in that realm it records a definite advance in the technique and artistry of bridge design. To that extent, and to the extent of the vast benefits it will convey to the Commonwealth of California, it has enriched the world. . . .

Mute though it is, the bridge sounds your call to freedom, a call that to you is the voice of opportunity, of new leisure, new prosperity, new hopes, new ideals, new aspirations, new outlooks, a finer and a better life.

To me, it speaks in other terms, in terms of a dream come true, a vision fulfilled, a task performed; speaks as one who knows its very mood, who saw its image within, before it met the light of day without; speaks as a glorious painting speaks, when entranced we stand before the canvas and live the vivid scenes depicted there—as an immortal elegy speaks in its rhythmic logic—as a lovely song speaks when its soft, sweet noises steal their way to the soul of humanity, to stifle its sobs, to still its longing, to uplift and to inspire, to make us one with the Creator from whence it came.

And to the world, it speaks in still other terms, in terms of the master bridge, last born and greatest of a noble line, scion of a royal house—strong, clean, fearless, humble, true, efficient, unselfish, loyal—exemplar of those simple virtues which, applied to the conduct of human affairs, would be a panacea for all our ills and build for us a happier and a better world.

So shall it speak in after years when we, out of fitful flame of life extinguished, shall fail to hear. Standing at the gateway of the Pacific, at the crossroads of the redwood empire, a new Statue of Liberty, with its fingers

gripping the boundary lines of British Columbia and Mexico, its face up-
turned to the sun, rich in promise and vibrant with eternal youth, the swift
wings of the wind that caresses it shall beat to the farthest corners of the
Earth its inspiring message to posterity forever.

Mary McLeod Bethune Commemorates the Sacrifices and Achievements of African American Women Over the Past 100 Years.

*Overcoming formidable odds—she was the fifteenth of seventeen children born to im-
poverished former slaves—Mary McLeod Bethune elevated herself to unprecedented
heights for a black woman in American society. In 1904 she started a boarding school
for African American girls that eventually became Bethune–Cookman College. In 1935
she was appointed by President Franklin D. Roosevelt as director of the Office of Minority Affairs of the National Youth Administration, the highest government position
ever held by an African American woman. Throughout Roosevelt's presidency she
served as an informal adviser and friend to First Lady Eleanor Roosevelt. In June 1933
Bethune spoke before the Chicago Women's Federation on a theme she knew intimately, "the progress of Negro women."*

To Frederick Douglass is credited the plea that "the Negro be not judged by
the heights to which he is risen, but by the depths from which he has
climbed." Judged on that basis, the Negro woman embodies one of the modern miracles of the New World.

One hundred years ago she was the most pathetic figure on the American continent. She was not a person, in the opinion of many, but a thing—a
thing whose personality had no claim to the respect of mankind. She was a
household drudge, a means for getting distasteful work done. She was an an-
imated agricultural implement to augment the service of mules and plows in
cultivating and harvesting the cotton crop. Then she was an automatic incu-
bator, a producer of human livestock, beneath whose heart and lungs more
potential laborers could be bred and nurtured and brought to the light of day.

Today she stands side by side with the finest manhood the race has been
able to produce. Whatever the achievements of the Negro man in letters,
business, art, pulpit, civic progress, and moral reform, he cannot but share
them with his sister of darker hue. Whatever glory belongs to the race for a
development unprecedented in history for the given length of time, a full
share belongs to the womanhood of the race.

By the very force of circumstances, the part she has played in the progress
has been of necessity to a certain extent subtle and indirect. She has not always been permitted a place in the front ranks where she could show her face

and make her voice heard with effect. But she has been quick to seize every opportunity which presented itself to come more and more into the open and strive directly for the uplift of the race and nation. In that direction, her achievements have been amazing. . . .

When the ballot was made available to the womanhood of America, the sister of darker hue was not slow to seize the advantage. In sections where the Negro could gain access to the voting booth, the intelligent, forward-looking element of the race's women have taken hold of political issues with an en- thusiasm and mental acumen that might well set worthy examples for other groups. Oftentimes she has led the struggle toward moral improvement and political record, and has compelled her reluctant brother to follow her deter- mined lead.

In time of war as in time of peace, the Negro woman has ever been ready to serve for the people's and the nation's good. During the recent World War she pleaded to go in the uniform of the Red Cross nurse and was denied the opportunity only on the basis of racial distinction. . . .

Negro women have thrown themselves wholeheartedly into the organi- zation of groups to direct the social uplift of their fellowmen, one of the greatest achievements of the race. . . .

In no field of modern social relationship has the hand of service and the influence of the Negro woman been felt more distinctly than in the Negro orthodox church. It may be safely said that the chief sustaining force in sup- port of the pulpit and the various stages of missionary enterprise has been the feminine element of the membership. The development of the Negro church since the Civil War has been another of the modern miracles. Throughout its growth the untiring effort, the unflagging enthusiasm, the sacrificial contri- bution of time, effort, and cash earnings of the black woman have been the most significant factors, without which the modern Negro church would have no history worth the writing.

Both before and since emancipation, by some rare gift, she has been able to hold on to the fibers of family unity and keep the home one unimpaired whole. In recent years it has become increasingly the case where in many in- stances, the mother is the sole dependence of the home and, single-handed, fights the wolf from the door, while the father submits unwillingly to en- forced idleness and unavoidable unemployment. Yet in myriads of instances she controls home discipline with a tight rein and exerts a unifying influence that is the miracle of the century.

The true worth of a race must be measured by the character of its wom- anhood. As the years have gone on the Negro woman has touched the most vital fields in the civilization of today. Wherever she had contributed she has left the mark of a strong character. The educational institutions she has established and directed have met the needs of her young people. Her cultural development has concentrated itself into artistic presentation accepted and acclaimed by meritorious critics. She is successful as a poet and a novelist. She is shrewd in business and capable in politics. She recognizes the importance of uplifting her people through social, civic, and religious activities. Starting at the time when as a "mammy" she nursed the infants of the other race and taught him her meager store of truth, she has been a contributing factor of note to interracial relations. Finally, through the past century she has made and kept her home intact, humble though it may have been in many instances. She has made and is making history.

Populist Senator Huey P. Long Advances His "Share Our Wealth" Plan to Make "Every Man a King."

In 1934 the United States was threatening to plunge even deeper into economic chaos, and President Roosevelt's New Deal was not providing the swift relief Americans were fervently expecting. Few other political leaders capitalized on the nation's fear with more zeal than Huey P. Long, the U.S. senator and former governor of Louisiana. Known as the "Kingfish" by his admirers and the "Dictator of Louisiana" by his detractors, Long excoriated the rich and championed the downtrodden through his fiery— many would say demagogic—rhetoric and "share the wealth" social policies. (Long upped taxes on the wealthy to pay for new schools, roads, medical care, textbooks, and tax breaks for his state's poorest citizens.) His most memorable speech and first national radio broadcast, "Every Man a King," aired February 23, 1934.

I contend, my friends, that we have no difficult problem to solve in America, and that is the view of nearly everyone with whom I have discussed the matter here in Washington and elsewhere throughout the United States: that we have no very difficult problem to solve.

It is not the difficulty of the problem which we have. It is the fact that the rich people of this country—and by rich people I mean the super-rich—will not allow us to solve the problems, or rather the one little problem that is afflicting this country, because in order to cure all of our woes it is necessary to scale down the big fortunes, that we may scatter the wealth to be shared by all the people.

We have a marvelous love for this government of ours. In fact, it is almost a religion, and it is well that it should be, because we have a splendid set of laws. We have everything here that we need, except that we have neglected the fundamentals upon which the American government was principally predicated.

How many of you remember the first thing that the Declaration of Independence said? It said, "We hold these truths to be self-evident, that there are certain inalienable rights for the people, and among them are life, liberty, and the pursuit of happiness." And it said further, "We hold the view that all men are created equal."

Now, what did they mean by that? Did they mean, my friends, to say that all men are created equal and that that meant that any one man was born to inherit $10 billion and that another child was to be born to inherit nothing? Did that mean, my friends, that someone would come into this world without having had an opportunity, of course, to have hit one lick of work, should be born with more than it and all of its children and children's children could ever dispose of, but that another one would have to be born into a life of starvation?

That was not the meaning of the Declaration of Independence when it said that all men are created or "that we hold that all men are created equal." Nor was it the meaning of the Declaration of Independence when it said that they held that there were certain rights that were inalienable—the right of life, liberty, and the pursuit of happiness.

Is that right of life, my friends, when the young children of this country are being reared into a sphere which is more owned by twelve men than it is by 120 million people? Is that, my friends, giving them a fair shake of the dice or anything like the inalienable right of life, liberty, and the pursuit of happiness—or anything resembling the fact that all people are created equal—when we have today in America thousands and hundreds of thousands and millions of children on the verge of starvation in a land that is overflowing with too much to eat and too much to wear? . . .

[W]e have in America today, my friends, a condition by which about ten men dominate the means of activity in at least 85 percent of the activities that you own. They either own directly everything or they have got some kind of mortgage on it, with a very small percentage to be excepted. They own the banks, they own the steel mills, they own the railroads, they own the bonds, they own the mortgages, they own the stores, and they have chained the country from one end to the other until there is not any kind of business that a small, independent man could go into today and make a living, and there is not any kind of business that an independent man can go into and make any money to buy an automobile with. And they have finally and gradually and steadily eliminated everybody from the fields in which there is a living to be made, and still they have got little enough sense to think they ought to be able to get more business out of it anyway.

If you reduce a man to the point where he is starving to death and bleeding and dying, how do you expect that man to get hold of any money to spend with you? It is not possible. Then, ladies and gentlemen, how do you expect people to live, when the wherewith cannot be had by the people? . . .

Now, we have organized a society, and we call it "Share Our Wealth," a society with the motto "Every Man a King." Every man a king, so there would be no such thing as a man or woman who did not have the necessities of life, who would not be dependent upon the whims and caprices and ipse dixit of the financial barons for a living. What do we propose by this society? We propose to limit the wealth of big men in the country. There is an average of $15,000 in wealth to every family in America. That is right here today.

We do not propose to divide it up equally. We do not propose a division of wealth, but we propose to limit poverty that we will allow to be inflicted upon any man's family. We will not say we are going to try to guarantee any equality, or $15,000 to a family. No, but we do say that one-third of the average is low enough for any one family to hold, that there should be a guarantee of a family wealth of around $5,000—enough for a home, an automobile, a radio, and the ordinary conveniences, and the opportunity to educate their children; a fair share of the income of this land thereafter to that family so there will be no such thing as merely the select to have those things, and so there will be no such thing as a family living in poverty and distress. . . .

Another thing we propose is old-age pension of $30 a month for everyone that is sixty years old. Now, we do not give this pension to a man making $1,000 a year, and we do not give it to him if he has $10,000 in property, but outside of that we do.

We will limit hours of work. There is not any necessity of having overproduction. I think all you have got to do, ladies and gentlemen, is just limit the hours of work to such as extent as people will work only so long as it is necessary to produce enough for all of the people to have what they need. Why, ladies and gentlemen, let us say that all of these labor-saving devices reduce hours down to where you do not have to work but four hours a day. That is enough for these people, and then praise be the name of the Lord if it gets that good. Let it be good and not a curse, and then we will have five hours a day and five days a week, or even less than that. And we might give a man a whole month off during the year, or give him two months. And we might do what other countries have seen fit to do, and what I did in Louisiana, by having schools by which adults could go back and learn the things that have been discovered since they went to school. . . .

We will not have any trouble taking care of the agricultural situation. All you have to do is balance your production with your consumption. You simply have to abandon a particular crop that you have too much of, and all you have to do is store the surplus for the next year, and the government will take it over. . . .

Those are the things we propose to do. "Every Man a King." Every man to eat when there is something to eat. All to wear something when there is something to wear. That makes us all sovereign.

You cannot solve these things through these various and sundry alphabetical codes. You can have the NRA and PWA and CWA and the UUG and GIN, and any other kind of dad-gummed lettered code. You can wait until doomsday and see twenty-five more alphabets, but that is not going to solve this proposition. Why hide? Why quibble? You know what the trouble is. The man that says he does not know what the trouble is just hiding his face to keep from seeing the sunlight. . . .

Now, my friends, we have got to hit the root with the ax. Centralized power in the hands of a few is the trouble. Get together in your community tonight or tomorrow and organize one of our Share Our Wealth societies. If you do not understand it, write me and let me send you the platform. Let me give you the proof of it. . . .

I thank you, my friends, for your kind attention, and I hope you will enroll with us, take care of your own work in the work of this government, and share or help in the Share Our Wealth societies.

Within a month of Long's address, 800,000 Americans joined Share Our Wealth societies, and by September 1935 there were an estimated 7 million members. Originally a supporter of President Roosevelt, Long became one of his harshest critics and planned to oust Roosevelt in the 1936 election. But Long's flourishing political career—and his life—ended on September 8, 1935, when he was gunned down in the Louisiana State-house by Carl Austin Weiss, the son-in-law of a political enemy. Weiss was immediately killed by Long's bodyguards, who shot him sixty-one times.

Radio Broadcaster Herb Morrison Reports Live as the Hindenburg Explodes and Crashes to the Ground.

It remains to this day one of the most horrifying eyewitness accounts ever broadcast on radio. Herb Morrison from WLS radio of Chicago was covering the landing of the Hindenburg, the largest aircraft of its time, at an airfield in Lakehurst, New Jersey. Spanning 800 feet in length, the Hindenburg was designed to carry approximately 50 passengers across the Atlantic in unrivaled luxury. As the Hindenburg began its descent, the rear end of the aircraft suddenly exploded—the result, many believe, of sabotage—and immediately consumed the hydrogen-filled aircraft and everyone on board in flames. (A few leaped to the ground and miraculously survived.) Morrison's breath-

less narration of the Hindenburg's *fate, beginning with its peaceful arrival, was heard live the evening of May 6, 1937.*

Oh, here it comes, ladies and gentlemen. We're out now, outside of the hangar, and what a great sight it is. A thrilling one, it's a marvelous sight, coming down out of the sky, pointed directly toward us and toward the mooring mast. The propellers fighting into the air and throwing it back into a galelike whirlpool. No one in this great floating palace can travel through the air at such a speed without these powerful motors behind it. The sun is striking the windows of the observation deck on the eastward side and sparkling like jewels on a background of black velvet.

Now the field that we thought anxious when we first arrived has turned into a moving mass of cooperative action. The landing crews have rushed to their posts and spots, and orders are being passed along, and last-minute preparations are being completed for the moment we have waited for so long.

Orders are being shouted at the crew, the passengers are looking down, getting a glimpse of the mooring mast. These giant flagships standing here, the American Airlines flagships waiting to direct them to all points in the United States, when they get the ship moored. There are a number of important persons on board.

It's practically standing still now. It's roped out of the nose of the ship and it's been taken a hold of down on the field by a number of men. It's starting to rain again. The back motors of the ship are just holding enough to keep it from—

It burst into flames! It burst into flames and it's falling, it's crashing! Get out of the way! Get out of the way! It's crashing, it's crashing—terrible. Oh my, get out of the way, please! It's burning, bursting into flames, and it's falling into the mooring mast and—oh, this is terrible—this is one of the worst catastrophes in the world. Ball of flame four or five hundred feet into the sky. And it's a terrific crash, ladies and gentlemen. There's smoke and there's flames now and the frame is crashing to the ground—not quite to the mooring mast. Oh the humanity! I can't talk. I can't talk, ladies and gentlemen. Oh, it's just laying there a mess, the smoking wreckage and everybody can hardly breathe and talk—and—I'm sorry, honest I can hardly breathe, I'm going to step inside while I can. It's terrible. Listen folks, I'm going to have to stop for a minute because this is the worst thing I have ever witnessed. . . .

Ladies and gentlemen, I'm back again. I've sort of recovered from that terrific explosion and the terrific crash that occurred just as it was being pulled down to the mooring mast, it's still smoking and flaming and crackling down there and I don't know how many of the ground crew were under when it fell. There's not a possible chance for anyone to be saved. The relatives of the people who are waiting here ready to welcome their loved ones that came off this great ship—oh, I'm broken up—they're carrying them in to give them first aid, and to be sure, some of them have fainted, and the people are rushing down to the burning ship. They've all gone down to see if they can extinguish any of the blaze whatsoever. But the terrible amount of hydrogen gas in it just caught. The tail surface broke into flames first, then there was a terrific explosion and then the burning of the nose and the crashing nose into the ground, and everybody carrying back at breakneck speed to get out from underneath it, because it was over the people at the time it burst into flames. Now whether it fell on the people who were witnessing it, we do not know. But as it exploded, they rushed back and now it's smoking—a terrific black smoke floating up in the sky—the flames are still leaping maybe 30, 40 feet from the ground the entire 811-feet length of it. They're frantically calling for ambulances and—the wires are humming with activity.

Will you pardon me just a moment. I'm not going to stop talking, I'm just going to swallow several times until I can keep on. I should imagine that the nose is not more than 500 feet or maybe 700 feet from the mooring mast. They had dropped two ropes and whether or not some spark or something set it on fire, we don't know, or whether something—on the inside of the ship causing that spark and causing it to explode in the tail surface. But everything crashed to the ground and there's not a possible chance of anybody being saved. . . .

Union Leader John L. Lewis Excoriates Big Business for Its "Brutality and Oppression" Against Organized Labor.

Between 1936 and 1937 union membership nearly doubled in America, from just under 4 million members to over 7 million. One of the men responsible for the surge was John L. Lewis, president of the first major industrial union in the United States, the United Mine Workers. Lewis himself came from a long line of Welsh miners. After being expelled from the American Federation of Labor for clashing with the AFL's leadership, Lewis formed the Congress of Industrial Organizations in 1936, which soon became one of nation's most confrontational labor organizations at a time when tensions between unions and employers were extremely volatile. In May 1937 police shot and killed ten strikers outside a Chicago steel plant, and in Detroit, Henry Ford's company guards brutally beat leaders of the United Automobile Workers. During a September 3, 1937, speech, Lewis railed against the corporate barons he believed were responsible for the bloody clashes.

The United States Chamber of Commerce, the National Association of Manufacturers, and similar groups representing industry and financial interests are rendering a disservice to the American people in their attempts to frustrate the organization of labor and in their refusal to accept collective bargaining as one of our economic institutions. These groups are encouraging a systematic organization under the sham pretext of local interests. They equip these vigilantes with tin hats, wooden clubs, gas masks, and lethal weapons and train them in the arts of brutality and oppression.

No tin hat brigade of goose-stepping vigilantes or bibble-babbling mob of blackguarding and corporation-paid scoundrels will prevent the onward march of labor, or divert its purpose to play its natural and rational part in the development of the economic, political, and social life of our nation.

Unionization, as opposed to communism, presupposes the relation of employment. It is based upon the wage system, and it recognizes fully and unreservedly the institution of private property and the right to investment profits. It is upon the fuller development of collective bargaining, the wider expansion of the labor movement, the increased influence of labor in our national councils, that the perpetuity of our democratic institutions must largely depend. The organized workers of America, free in their industrial life, conscious partners of production, secure in their homes, and enjoying a decent standard of living, will prove the finest bulwark against the intrusion of alien doctrines of government.

Do those who hatched this foolish cry of communism in the CIO fear the increased influence of labor in our democracy? Do they fear its influence will be cast on the side of shorter hours, a better system of distributed employment, better homes for the underprivileged, Social Security for the aged, a fairer distribution of our national income? Certainly the workers that are being organized want a voice in the determination of these objectives of social justice. Certainly labor wants a fairer share of the national income. Assuredly labor wants a larger participation in increased productive efficiency. Obviously the population is entitled to participate in the fruits of the genius of our men of achievement in the field of material sciences.

Labor has suffered just as our farm population has suffered from a viciously unequal distribution of the national income. In the exploitation of both classes of workers has been the source of panic and depression, and upon the economic welfare of both rests the best assurance of a sound and permanent prosperity.

Under the banner of the Committee for Industrial Organization, American labor is on the march. Its objectives today are those it had in the beginning: to strive for the unionization of our unorganized millions of workers and for the acceptance of collective bargaining as a recognized American institution. It seeks peace with the industrial world. It seeks cooperation and mutuality of effort with the agricultural population. It would avoid strikes. It would have its rights determined under the law by the peaceful negotiations and contract relationships that are supposed to characterize American commercial life.

Until an aroused public opinion demands that employers accept that rule, labor has no recourse but to surrender its rights or struggle for their realization with its own economic power. Labor, like Israel, has many sorrows. Its women weep for their fallen, and they lament for the future of the children of the race. It ill behooves one who has supped at labor's table and who has been sheltered in labor's house to curse with equal fervor and fine impartiality both labor and its adversaries when they become locked in deadly embrace.

I repeat that labor seeks peace and guarantees its own loyalty, but the voice of labor, insistent upon its rights, should not be annoying to the ears of justice nor offensive to the conscience of the American people.

Orson Welles Tries to Assure Terrified Listeners That They Are Not Being Attacked by Martians.

"Ladies and gentlemen," the radio announcer intoned with a note of urgency, "we interrupt our program of dance music to bring you a special bulletin from the Intercontinental Radio News." To an American public still reeling from deep economic insecurity, labor strikes and riots, and the ominous expansion of fascism overseas, the incoming reports were the last thing they wanted to hear: Hostile aliens from Mars had invaded Earth and were killing all humans in their path. Masterminded by a twenty-three-year-old Orson Welles and a small group of actors working out of a New York studio, the remarkably realistic news flashes provoked hysteria across the nation. Telephone lines were overwhelmed. Roads became impassable with traffic. Churches were filled with whole families praying to God for protection or, if it were too late for that, absolution. At the end of the October 30, 1938, broadcast, a calm and composed Welles made the following statement.

This is Orson Welles, ladies and gentlemen, out of character to assure you that the *War of the Worlds* has no further significance than as the holiday offering it was intended to be: the Mercury Theatre's own radio version of dressing up in a sheet and jumping out of a bush and saying, "Boo!" Starting now, we couldn't soap all your windows and steal all your garden gates by tomorrow night, so we did the next best thing. We annihilated the world before your

very ears, and utterly destroyed the Columbia Broadcasting System. You will
be relieved, I hope, to learn that we didn't mean it, and that both institutions
are still open for business. So good-bye everybody, and remember, please, for
the next day or so the terrible lesson you learned tonight: That grinning,
glowing, globular invader of your living room is an inhabitant of the pump-
kin patch, and if your doorbell rings and nobody's there, that was no Mar-
tian—it's Halloween.

*But hundreds of thousands of listeners, either too caught up in the frenzy of the mo-
ment or already hiding under their beds, remained convinced of the attack. Panic continued into the next morning, and the story of Welles's terrifying dramatization
remained front-page news for days.*

Baseball Great Lou Gehrig, Suffering from a Fatal Disease, Thanks His Fans and Considers Himself the "Luckiest Man on the Face of the Earth."

*Diagnosed with a fatal, paralyzing disease, baseball great Lou Gehrig spoke before
more than 60,000 New York Yankees fans to express his love for baseball, his team-
mates, and everyone who supported him over the years. Nicknamed the "Iron Horse,"
Gehrig had batted a career average of .340 and played a record 2,130 consecutive
major-league games. (Gehrig's record remained for almost sixty years, when, in September 1995, it was broken by the Baltimore Orioles' Cal Ripken Jr.) In a voice trembling with emotion, Gehrig addressed a packed Yankee Stadium on July 4, 1939, two
years before he would succumb to the disease that now bears his name.*

Fans, for the past two weeks you have been reading about a bad break I got.
Yet today I consider myself the luckiest man on the face of the earth. I have
been in ballparks for seventeen years and have never received anything but
kindness and encouragement from you fans.

　　Look at these grand men. Which of you wouldn't consider it the high-
light of his career just to associate with them for one day?

　　Sure, I'm lucky. Who wouldn't consider it an honor to have known Jacob
Ruppert; also the builder of baseball's greatest empire, Ed Barow; to have
spent six years with that wonderful little fellow Miller Huggins; then to have
spent the next nine years with that outstanding leader, that smart student of
psychology—the best manager in baseball today—Joe McCarthy!

　　Sure, I'm lucky. When the New York Giants, a team you would give your right arm to beat, and vice versa, sends you a gift, that's something. When everybody down to the groundskeepers and those boys in white coats remember you with trophies, that's something.

When you have a wonderful mother-in-law who takes sides with you in squabbles against her own daughter, that's something. When you have a father and mother who work all their lives so that you can have an education and build your body, it's a blessing. When you have a wife who has been a tower of strength and shown more courage than you dreamed existed, that's the finest I know.

So I close in saying that I might have had a tough break, but I have an awful lot to live for!

1940–1949

WE SHOULD BE CLEAR ON THIS POINT: WHAT IS CONVULSING the world today is not merely another old-fashioned war. It is a counterrevolution against our ideas and ideals, against our sense of justice and our human values.

Three systems today compete for world domination. Communism, fascism, and democracy are struggling for social-economic-political world control. As the conflict sharpens, it becomes clear that the other two, fascism and communism, are merging into one. They have one common enemy: democracy. They have one common goal: the destruction of democracy.

This is why the war is not an ordinary war. It is not a conflict for markets or territories. It is a desperate struggle for the possession of the souls of men.

—Secretary of the Interior Harold L. Ickes,
addressing a crowd in New York's Central Park
on "I Am an American Day,"
May 18, 1941

CBS Newsman Edward R. Murrow Describes Nazi Air Attacks on the City of London.

"You burned the city of London in our houses," remarked the poet and statesman Archibald Macleish of Edward R. Murrow, "and we felt the flames." Of Murrow's estimated 5,000 radio broadcasts, few were as dramatic or influential as the news bulletins of the German blitz on London beginning in the summer of 1940. The fires of World War II had been raging since September 1939, when Britain and France officially declared war on Germany after Nazi troops invaded Poland without provocation. Murrow traveled to Europe in 1937 to head up CBS's foreign bureau, and when Hitler's forces stormed through Austria in March 1938, Murrow immediately chartered a plane to Vienna to describe the invasion. Transmitted back to an American public unwilling to become embroiled in another world war, Murrow's live reports—such as the following broadcast on September 13, 1940—gave listeners in the United States an eyewitness account of what it was like to be in the eye of the Nazi storm.

This is London at 3:30 in the morning. This has been what might be called a "routine night": air-raid alarm at about nine o'clock and intermittent bombing ever since. I had the impression that more high explosives and few incendiaries have been used tonight. Only two small fires can be seen on the horizon. Again the Germans have been sending their bombers in singly or in pairs. The anti-aircraft barrage has been fierce, but sometimes there have been periods of twenty minutes when London has been silent. Then the big red buses would start up and move on till the guns started working again. That silence is almost hard to bear. One becomes accustomed to rattling windows and the distant sound of bombs, and then there comes a silence that can be felt. You know the sound will return. You wait, and then it starts again. That waiting is bad. It gives you a chance to imagine things. I have been walking tonight. There is a full moon, and the dirty-gray buildings appear white. The stars, the empty windows, are hidden. It's a beautiful and lonesome city where men and women and children are trying to snatch a few hours' sleep underground.

In the fashionable residential districts I could read the "To Let" signs on the front of big houses in the light of the bright moon. Those houses have big basements underneath—good shelters—but they're not being used. Many people think that they should be.

The scale of this air war is so great that the reporting of it is not easy. Often we spend hours traveling about this sprawling city, viewing damage, talking with people, and occasionally listening to the bombs come down, and then more hours wondering what you'd like to hear about these people who are citizens of no mean city. We've told you about the bombs, the fires, the smashed houses, and the courage of the people. We've read you the communiqués and tried to give you an honest estimate of the wounds inflicted upon this, the best bombing target in the world. But the business of living and working in this city is very personal. The little incidents, the things the mind retains, are in themselves unimportant, but they somehow weld together to form the hard core of memories that will remain when the last "all clear" has sounded.

That's why I want to talk for just three or four minutes about the things we haven't talked about before. For many of these impressions it is necessary to reach back through only one long week. There was a rainbow bending over the battered and smoking East End of London just when the "all clear" sounded one afternoon. One night I stood in front of a smashed grocery store and heard a dripping inside. It was the only sound in all London. Two cans of peaches had been drilled clean through by flying glass, and the juice was dripping down onto the floor.

Talking from a studio with bodies lying about on the floor, sleeping on mattresses, still produces a strange feeling, but we'll probably get used to that. Today I went to buy a hat. My favorite shop had gone, blown to bits. The windows of my shoe store were blown out. I decided to have a haircut. The windows of the barbershop were gone, but the Italian barber was still doing business. "Someday," he said, "we smile again, but the food it doesn't taste so good since being bombed." I went on to another shop to buy flashlight batteries. I bought three. The clerk said, "You needn't buy so many. We'll have enough for the whole winter." But I said, "What if you aren't here?" There were buildings down in that street, and he replied, "Of course we'll be here. We've been in business here for a hundred and fifty years."

President Franklin D. Roosevelt Tries to Convince a Skeptical Nation Why It Must Defend the World Against Nazism.

One by one the nations of Europe were being hammered into defeat by Hitler's war machine. Austria, Czechoslovakia, Poland, Denmark, Norway, the Netherlands, Belgium, Luxembourg, and France had all surrendered to the German army by June 1940, and Hitler showed no signs of relenting. Prime Minister Neville Chamberlain, who until 1939 had espoused appeasing Hitler, was replaced by Winston Churchill in May 1940. Churchill implored the United States to assist Britain before it too fell to the Nazis, but the American public remained essentially unmoved. Wendell Wilkie, Franklin D. Roosevelt's Republican opponent in the 1940 presidential campaign, warned Americans that their sons would be sent overseas if the president remained in office. Roosevelt's response, directed to anxious parents, was unwavering: "I have said this before, but I shall say it again and again and again. Your boys are not going to be sent into any foreign wars." Roosevelt was also restricted by the Johnson Act of 1934, which prohibited loans to governments that were in default—such as Britain, now verging on bankruptcy. Roosevelt soundly defeated Wilkie in the November election, and in December he had a flash of inspiration: Instead of sending funds to Britain, the United States would "lend" weapons and supplies, which Britain would then either return or repay in kind after the war. Hoping to win over a skeptical Congress and public, Roosevelt argued on January 6, 1941, for the necessity of the Lend-Lease Act (which was ultimately passed) and the enormity of the threat facing Europe—and the world.

I address you, the members of this new Congress, at a moment unprecedented in the history of the union. I use the word *unprecedented* because at no previous time has American security been as seriously threatened from without as it is today. . . .

I suppose that every realist knows that the democratic way of life is at this moment being directly assailed in every part of the world—assailed either by arms or by secret spreading of poisonous propaganda by those who seek to destroy unity and promote discord in nations that are still at peace. During sixteen months this assault has blotted out the whole pattern of democratic life in an appalling number of independent nations, great and small. And the assailants are still on the march, threatening other nations, great and small.

Therefore, as your president, performing my constitutional duty to "give to the Congress information of the state of the union," I find it unhappily necessary to report that the future and the safety of our country and of our democracy are overwhelmingly involved in events far beyond our borders.

Armed defense of democratic existence is now being gallantly waged in four continents. If that defense fails, all the population and all the resources of Europe and Asia, Africa, and Australia will be dominated by the conquerors. And let us remember that the total of those populations and their resources greatly exceeds the sum total of the population and resources of the whole of the Western Hemisphere—yes, many times over. . . .

No realistic American can expect from a dictator's peace international generosity, or return of true independence, or world disarmament, or freedom of expression, or freedom of religion—or even good business. Such a peace would bring no security for us or for our neighbors. . . .

Our national policy is this:

First, by an impressive expression of the public will and without regard to partisanship, we are committed to all-inclusive national defense.

Second, by an impressive expression of the public will and without regard to partisanship, we are committed to full support of all those resolute
people everywhere who are resisting aggression and are thereby keeping war
away from our hemisphere. By this support we express our determination
that the democratic cause shall prevail, and we strengthen the defense and the
security of our own nation.

Third, by an impressive expression of the public will and without regard
to partisanship, we are committed to the proposition that principles of morality and considerations for our own security will never permit us to ac-
quiesce in a peace dictated by aggressors and sponsored by appeasers. We
know that enduring peace cannot be bought at the cost of other people's
freedom.

In the recent national election there was no substantial difference between the two great parties in respect to that national policy. No issue was
fought out on this line before the American electorate. And today it is abun-
dantly evident that American citizens everywhere are demanding and supporting speedy and complete action in recognition of obvious danger.

Therefore, the immediate need is a swift and driving increase in our ar-
mament production. . . . Our most useful and immediate role is to act as an
arsenal for them as well as for ourselves. They do not need man power, but
they do need billions of dollars worth of the weapons of defense. . . . Let us
say to the democracies: "We Americans are vitally concerned in your defense
of freedom. We are putting forth our energies, our resources, and our organizing powers to give you the strength to regain and maintain a free world.
We shall send you, in ever-increasing numbers, ships, planes, tanks, guns. That
is our purpose and our pledge." . . .

As men do not live by bread alone, they do not fight by armaments alone.
Those who man our defenses and those behind them who build our defense
must have the stamina and the courage which come from an unshakable belief in the manner of life which they are defending. The mighty action that
we are calling for cannot be based on a disregard of all the things worth fighting for.

The nation takes great satisfaction and much strength from the things
which have been done to make its people conscious of their individual stake
in the preservation of democratic life in America. Those things have tough-
ened the fiber of our people, have renewed their faith and strengthened their
devotion to the institutions we make ready to protect.

Certainly this is no time for any of us to stop thinking about the social
and economic problems which are the root cause of the social revolution
which is today a supreme factor in the world. For there is nothing mysterious about the foundations of a healthy and strong democracy.

The basic things expected by our people of their political and economic systems are simple. They are: quality and opportunity for youth and for others, jobs for those who can work, security for those who need it, the ending of special privilege for the few, the preservation of civil liberties for all, the enjoyment of the fruits of scientific progress in a wider and constantly rising standard of living.

These are the simple, the basic things that must never be lost sight of in the turmoil and unbelievable complexity of our modern world. The inner and abiding strength of our economic and political systems is dependent upon the degree to which they fulfill these expectations. . . .

I have called for personal sacrifice, and I am assured of the willingness of almost all Americans to respond to that call. . . .

In the future days which we seek to make secure, we look forward to a world founded upon four essential human freedoms.

The first is freedom of speech and expression—everywhere in the world.

The second is freedom of every person to worship God in his own way—everywhere in the world.

The third is freedom from want—which, translated into world terms, means economic understandings which will secure to every nation a healthy peacetime life for its inhabitants—everywhere in the world.

The fourth is freedom from fear—which, translated into world terms, means a worldwide reduction of armaments to such a point and in such a thorough manner that no nation will be in a position to commit an act of physical aggression against any neighbor—anywhere in the world.

That is no vision of a distant millennium. It is a definite basis for a kind of world attainable in our own time and generation. That kind of world is the very antithesis of the so-called "new order" of tyranny which the dictators seek to create with the crash of a bomb. To that new order we oppose the greater conception—the moral order. A good society is able to face schemes or world domination and foreign revolutions alike without fear.

Since the beginning of our American history we have been engaged in change, in a perpetual, peaceful revolution which goes on steadily, quietly, adjusting itself to changing conditions without the concentration camp or the quicklime in the ditch. The world order which we seek is the cooperation of free countries working together in a friendly, civilized society.

This nation has placed its destiny in the hands, heads, and hearts of millions of free men and women, and its faith in freedom under the guidance of God. Freedom means the supremacy of human rights everywhere. Our support goes to those who struggle to gain those rights and keep them. Our strength is in our unity of purpose.

To that high concept there can be no end save victory.

Legendary Composer Duke Ellington Exalts the Artistic, Intellectual, and Spiritual Contributions Made by African Americans.

Considered one of the greatest composers of the twentieth century, Edward Kennedy "Duke" Ellington listened with the rest of America as the nation's leaders inveighed against the horrors of fascism and totalitarianism overseas. But Ellington, like many African Americans, perceived a dissonance between what the United States espoused and what it practiced. Racial discrimination and segregation were still firmly entrenched, socially and legally, throughout the country. As the possibility of U.S. involvement in World War II loomed ever closer, Ellington, in a February 12, 1941, talk before Los Angeles churchgoers, offered his thoughts on the contributions blacks had made—and, undoubtedly, would continue to make—both culturally and militarily.

First of all, I should like to extend my sincere appreciation to the Reverend Karl Downs for the opportunity to appear on this very fine program and express myself in a manner not often at my disposal. Music is my business, my profession, my life, but even though it means so much to me, I often feel that I'd like to say something, have my say, on some of the burning issues confronting us, in another language: in words of mouth.

There is a good deal of talk in the world today. Some view that as a bad sign. One of the Persian poets, lamenting the great activity of men's tongues, cautioned them to be silent with the reminder that, "In much of your talking, thinking is half-murdered." This is true no doubt. Yet in this day when so many men are silent because they are afraid to speak—indeed, have been forbidden to speak—I view the volubility of the unrestricted with great satisfaction. Here in America, the silence of Europe—silent, that is, except for the harsh echoes of the dictators' voices—has made us conscious of our privileges of free speech, and like the dumb suddenly given tongue, or the tongue-tied eased of restraint, we babble and bay to beat the band. Singly, as individuals, we don't say much of consequence perhaps, but put together, heard in chorus, the blustering half-truths, the lame and halting logic, the painfully sincere convictions of Joe and Mary Doaks compose a powerful symphony which, like the small boy's brave whistle in the dark, serves notice on the hobgoblins that we are not asleep, not prey to the unchallenged attack. And so it is with the idea in mind of adding my bit to the meaningful chorus that I address you briefly this evening.

I have been asked to take as the subject of my remarks the title of a very significant poem, "We, Too, Sing America," written by the distinguished poet and author Langston Hughes.

In the poem, Mr. Hughes argues the case for democratic recognition of the Negro on the basis of the Negro's contribution to America, a contribution of labor, valor, and culture. One hears that argument repeated frequently in the race press, from the pulpit and rostrum. America is reminded of the feats of Crispus Attucks, Peter Salem, black armies in the Revolution, the War of 1812, the Civil War, the Spanish-American War, the World War. Further, forgetful America is reminded that we sing without false notes, as borne out by the fact that there are no records of black traitors in the archives of American history. This is all well and good, but I believe it to be only half the story.

We play more than a minority role in singing "America." Although numerically but 10 percent of the mammoth chorus that today, with an eye overseas, sings "America" with fervor and thanksgiving, I say our 10 percent is the very heart of the chorus: the sopranos, so to speak, carrying the melody; the rhythm section of the band; the violins, pointing the way.

I contend that the Negro is the creative voice of America, *is* creative America, and it was a happy day in America when the first unhappy slave was landed on its shores. There, in our tortured induction into this "land of liberty," we built its most graceful civilization. Its wealth, its flowering fields, its handsome homes, its pretty traditions, its guarded leisure, and its music were all our creations.

We stirred in our shackles, and our unrest awakened justice in the hearts of a courageous few, and we re-created in America the desire for true democracy, freedom for all, the brotherhood of man, principles on which the country had been founded.

We were freed and as before, we fought America's wars, provided her labor, gave her music, kept alive her flickering conscience, prodded her on toward the yet unachieved goal, democracy, until we became more than a part of America! We—this kicking, yelling, touchy, sensitive, scrupulously demanding minority—are the personification of the ideal begun by the Pilgrims almost 350 years ago.

It is our voice that sang "America" when America grew too lazy, satisfied, and confident to sing, before the dark threats and fire-lined clouds of destruction frightened it into a thin, panicky quaver.

We are more than a few isolated instances of courage, valor, achievement. We're the injection, the shot in the arm, that has kept America and its gotten principles alive in the fat and corrupt years intervening between our divine conception and our near-tragic present.

Famed Pilot Charles Lindbergh Argues That the United States Would Meet with "Defeat and Failure" Against the German Army.

By far the most visible and vocal fraternity of isolationists in the United States, the Committee to Defend America First represented a who's who of power and prestige, including automobile magnate Henry Ford, Ambassador Joseph P. Kennedy, radio demagogue Father Charles E. Coughlin, and most notably Charles A. Lindbergh. It had been fourteen years since his historic nonstop solo flight across the Atlantic, but Lindbergh remained one of the most admired men in America. While isolationism was by no means a euphemism for anti-Semitism, Lindbergh himself lauded Hitler as a "great man" and maligned Jews in his speeches. "The three most important groups who have been pressing this country toward war," Lindbergh once famously declared, "are the British, the Jewish, and the Roosevelt administration." (Lindbergh would later adamantly deny that he was an anti-Semite or Nazi apologist.) On April 23, 1941, Lindbergh continued his campaign against American intervention in a speech in New York City.

There are many viewpoints from which the issues of this war can be argued. Some are primarily idealistic. Some are primarily practical. One should, I believe, strive for a balance of both. But, since the subjects that can be covered in a single address are limited, tonight I shall discuss the war from a viewpoint which is primarily practical. It is not that I believe ideals are unimportant, even among the realities of war, but if a nation is to survive in a hostile world its ideals must be backed by the hard logic of military practicability. If the outcome of war depended on ideals alone, this would be a different world than it is today.

I know I will be severely criticized by the interventionists in America when I say we should not enter a war unless we have a reasonable chance of winning. That, they will claim, is far too materialistic a viewpoint. They will advance again the same arguments that were used to persuade France to declare war against Germany in 1939. But I do not believe that our American ideals and our way of life will gain through an unsuccessful war. And I know that the United States is not prepared to wage war in Europe successfully at this time. We are no better prepared today than France was when the interventionists in Europe persuaded her to attack the Siegfried Line.

I have said before, and I will say again, that I believe it will be a tragedy to the entire world if the British Empire collapses. That is one of the main reasons why I opposed this war before it was declared, and why I have constantly advocated a negotiated peace. I did not feel that England and France had a reasonable chance of winning. France has now been defeated, and despite the propaganda and confusion of recent months it is now obvious that

England is losing the war. I believe this is realized even by the British government. But they have one last desperate plan remaining: They hope that they may be able to persuade us to send another American Expeditionary Force to Europe and to share with England militarily, as well as financially, the fiasco of this war.

I do not blame England for this hope, or for asking for our assistance. But we now know that she declared war under circumstances which led to the defeat of every nation that sided with her from Poland to Greece. We know that in the desperation of war, England promised to all these nations armed assistance that she could not send. We know that she misinformed them, as she has misinformed us, concerning her state of preparation, her military strength, and the progress of the war.

In the time of war, truth is always replaced by propaganda. I do not believe we should be too quick to criticize the actions of a belligerent nation. There is always the question whether we ourselves would do better under similar circumstances. But we in this country have a right to think of the welfare of America first, just as the people in England thought first of their own country when they encouraged the smaller nations of Europe to fight against hopeless odds. When England asks us to enter this war, she is considering her own future and that of her empire. In making our reply, I believe we should consider the future of the United States and that of the Western Hemisphere.

It is not only our right, but it is our obligation as American citizens to look at this war objectively, and to weigh our chances for success if we should enter it. I have attempted to do this, especially from the standpoint of aviation, and I have been forced to the conclusion that we cannot win this war for England, regardless of how much assistance we extend.

I ask you to look at the map of Europe today and see if you can suggest any way in which we could win this war if we entered it. Suppose we had a large army in America, trained and equipped. Where would we send it to fight? The campaigns of the war show only too clearly how difficult it is to force a landing or to maintain an army on a hostile coast. Suppose we took our navy from the Pacific and used it to convoy British shipping. That would not win the war for England. It would, at best, permit her to exist under the constant bombing of the German air fleet. Suppose we had an air force that we could send to Europe. Where could it operate? Some of our squadrons might be based in the British Isles, but it is physically impossible to base enough aircraft in the British Isles alone to equal in strength the aircraft that can be based on the continent of Europe.

I have asked these questions on the supposition that we had in existence an army and an air force large enough and well enough equipped to send to Europe; and that we would dare to remove our navy from the Pacific. Even on this basis, I do not see how we could invade the continent of Europe successfully as long as all of that continent and most of Asia is under Axis domination. But the fact is that none of these suppositions are correct. We have only a one-ocean navy. Our army is still untrained and inadequately equipped for a foreign war. Our air force is deplorably lacking in modern fighting planes, because most of them have already been sent to Europe.

When these facts are cited, the interventionists shout that we are defeatists, that we are undermining the principles of democracy, and that we are giving comfort to Germany by talking about our military weakness. But everything I mention here has been published in our newspapers and in the reports of congressional hearings in Washington. Our military position is well known to the governments of Europe and Asia. Why, then, should it not be brought to the attention of our own people?

I say it is the interventionist in America, as it was in England and in France, who gives comfort to the enemy. I say it is they who are undermining the principles of democracy when they demand that we take a course to which more than 80 percent of our citizens are opposed. I charge them with being the real defeatists, for their policy has led to the defeat of every country since this war began. There is no better way to give comfort to an enemy than to divide the people of a nation over the issue of foreign war. There is no shorter road to defeat than by entering a war with inadequate preparation. Every nation that has adopted the interventionist policy of depending on someone else for its own defense has met with nothing but defeat and failure.

When history is written, the responsibility for the downfall of the democracies of Europe will rest squarely upon the shoulders of the interventionists who led their nations into war uninformed and unprepared. With their shouts of defeatism and their disdain of reality, they have already sent countless thousands of young men to death in Europe. From the campaign of Poland to that of Greece, their prophecies have been false and their policies have failed. Yet these are the people who are calling us defeatists in America today. And they have led this country, too, to the verge of war.

There are many such interventionists in America, but there are more people among us of a different type. That is why you and I are assembled here tonight. There is a policy open to this nation that will lead to success, a policy that will leave us free to follow our own way of life and to develop our own civilization. It is not a new and untried idea. It was advocated by Washington. It was incorporated in the Monroe Doctrine. Under its guidance, the United States became the greatest nation in the world. It is based upon the belief that the security of a nation lies in the strength and character of its own people. It recommends the maintenance of armed forces sufficient to defend this hemisphere from attack by any combination of foreign powers. It demands faith in an independent American destiny. This is a policy of the America First Committee today. It is a policy that led this nation to success during the most trying years of our history, and it is a policy that will lead us to success again. . . .

The time has come when those of us who believe in an independent American destiny must band together and organize for strength. We have been led toward war by a minority of our people. This minority has power. It has influence. It has a loud voice. But it does not represent the American people. During the last several years I have traveled over this country from one end to the other. I have talked to many hundreds of men and women, and I have had letters from tens of thousands more who feel the same way as you and I. These people—the majority of hardworking American citizens—are with us. They are the true strength of our country. And they are beginning to realize, as you and I, that there are times when we must sacrifice our normal interests in life in order to insure the safety and the welfare of our nation.

Such a time has come. Such a crisis is here. That is why the America First Committee has been formed—to give voice to the people who have no newspaper or newsreel or radio station at their command, to the people who must do the paying and the fighting and the dying if this country enters the war.

Whether or not we do enter the war rests upon the shoulders of you in this audience, upon us here on this platform, upon meetings of this kind that are being held by Americans in every section of the United States today. It depends upon the action we take and the courage we show at this time. If you believe in an independent destiny for America, if you believe that this country should not enter the war in Europe, we ask you to join the America First Committee in its stand. We ask you to share our faith in the ability of this nation to defend itself, to develop its own civilization, and to contribute to the progress of mankind in a more constructive and intelligent way than has yet been found by the warring nations of Europe. We need your support, and we need it now. The time to act is here.

Writing in his journal on December 8, 1941—the day after the Japanese attacked Pearl Harbor—Lindbergh noted, "I can see nothing to do under these circumstances except to fight. If I had been in Congress, I certainly would have voted for a declaration of war." Lindbergh volunteered to serve his country "any way [he] could," but President Roosevelt and his Cabinet—still furious over Lindbergh's isolationist speeches, as well as his verbal attacks on the administration—refused his offer. "I ardently hope that this confirmed fascist," Secretary of the Interior Harold Ickes wrote to the president, "will not be given the opportunity to wear the uniform of the United States. He should be buried in merciful oblivion." Humiliated, Lindbergh went to work for Henry Ford, who used his auto factories and assembly lines to build bombers and other weapons of war for the government.

Journalist Dorothy Thompson Imagines the Horror of a World Controlled by Adolf Hitler.

"The eyes alone are notable," wrote the American journalist Dorothy Thompson upon meeting Adolf Hitler for the first time. "Dark gray and hyperthyroid—they have the peculiar shine which often distinguishes geniuses, alcoholics, and hysterics." Thompson, who wired her reports from Berlin back to the United States for the Saturday Evening Post, *witnessed firsthand Hitler's murderous rise in the 1930s to become chancellor of the Reich. Watching Hitler's stormtroopers parade down the street shouting "Jude Verriecke! [Kill the Jews]" and "Heil Hitler," Thompson lamented, "I saw, in my mind's eye, the machine guns that would soon be in their hands, the planes that would fly over their heads, the tanks that would rumble and roll with their tread." Years later her vision became bloody reality, and after leaving Germany, Thompson spoke with urgency to audiences throughout North America of Hitler's ruthlessness and insatiable thirst for domination. On May 2, 1941, she addressed a convention in Toronto, Canada, and encouraged the audience to visualize a world overrun by Hitler's forces.*

Every nation on this globe and every individual on this globe will presently learn what a few have always known: that there are times in history where the business of one is the business of all, when life or death is a matter of choice, and when no one alive can avoid making that choice. These times occur seldom in history, these times of inevitable decisions. But this is one of those times.

Before this epoch is over, every living human being will have chosen. Every living human being will have lined up with Hitler or against him. Every living human being will either have opposed this onslaught or supported it. For if he tries to make no choice, that in itself will be a choice. If he takes no side, he is on Hitler's side. If he does not act, that is an act—for Hitler.

The *Japan Times Advertiser,* which is a controlled organ of the Japanese Foreign Office, has set them forth. They have appeared along with the suggestion that [Hitler ally and foreign minister of Japan, Yosuke Matsuoka] come to America and induce President Roosevelt to join Japan in an attempt to mediate the war. The proposed terms affect Canada no less than any other part of the British Empire and affect us as intimately as though we were already an active belligerent. They reveal with complete clarity what is in the minds of the Axis powers. They reveal what they consider to be the New Order of a Thousand Years.

Let us take a look at them. Let us see what is the price for peace.

The British Empire and Commonwealth will be utterly destroyed. . . . All western and all eastern bases of the British Empire—Gibraltar, Malta, Aden, the Red Sea, Singapore, Hong Kong—are to be demilitarized in a world bristling with Axis weapons. The Dutch East Indies and French Indochina are to be liberated from oppressive rule and put under Japanese economic control.

The seat of authority of the British Empire is to remain, for the time being, on the British Isles. But these islands will be able to exercise no authority over themselves or over any part of the world. For across from them will be the mightiest, consolidated, regimented, and enslaved block of human beings ever gathered together under one despot in the history of the human race.

Nazi Germany is to organize the entire continent as one corporate state, with its capital in Berlin. This means that nationality in Europe, except for minor matters of local administration, is to be abolished. The whole of western Europe is to be organized as a huge vertical trust in which the executives, directors, and majority stockholders will be the German Nazi Party. . . .

Over a year ago I received the information that this was Hitler's plan for Britain. He intends to remove from those islands as he has removed from Poland all those persons who, whether by virtue of superior intelligence, or popular leadership, or executive ability, or ardent patriotism, are capable of keeping alive in masses of people the memory of a great past and the hope of a future. He intends to reduce the population of those isles—first to reduce the leadership, then to reduce the actual numbers and send them to Canada. What happened to the Jews, and then happened to the Czechs and the Poles, is proposed for the English: the greatest diaspora in the human history. . . .

In this world people get what they passionately desire, and woe unto them if they desire the wrong thing. If we desire isolation, we shall have it— the isolation of a prison camp in a hostile community. We shall be penned up on this continent while hostile nations east of us, and west of us, and north of us, and south of us do their level best—their vicious scheming, organized, subsidized, ruthless best—to destroy us from inside, to set Canadians against the people of the States, to set labor against capital and capital against labor, the masses against the intelligentsia and the intelligentsia against the masses, the Irish against the English, the Catholics against the Protestants, the Negroes against the whites, the whites against the Negroes, and everybody against the Jews, in order that the war which we sought to avoid elsewhere may occur here in an internecine fight, the running amok and berserk of an imprisoned colony.

This is their plan. This has always been their plan, to stir nationality against nationality, race against race, class against class, creed against creed, that their mutual destruction of each other may work out for the glory of Hitler and the grandeur of Japan. They count on our freedom—our individual freedom, our individual interests, our individual pursuit of pleasure and happiness—as the means of our destruction of ourselves.

And good men, honest men, unwitting men work together with the frustrated, the fanatic, the sick, the bitter, the cowardly, the corrupt, the greedy, the selfish for the end that this civilization may perish from this earth. And democracy and freedom face the bitterest of all tests. It is not the test of arms. It is truly the test of whether they are worthy to survive.

President Franklin D. Roosevelt Requests from Congress a Declaration of War Against Japan.

"Tora! Tora! Tora!" Japanese Commander Mitsuo Fuchida hollered to his fellow pilots, signaling that they had caught the U.S. Navy by total surprise. At 7:49 A.M. on December 7, 1941, the attack on Pearl Harbor had begun. Bombs rained down on the unsuspecting base, ultimately destroying 188 planes and 18 warships and killing an estimated 2,400 Americans. Admiral Husband Kimmel, commander of the Pacific fleet, watched the first wave of the ambush in disbelief from his front lawn. (Moments later an errant bullet shattered a window and bounced harmlessly off Kimmel's chest.) As word of the unprovoked assault spread throughout the country, twenty years of American isolationism evaporated in an instant. In Washington the president and his advisers huddled around Roosevelt's private secretary, Grace Tully, as she swiftly typed out the incoming reports relayed over the telephone from naval operations chief Admiral Harold Stark. "The Boss maintained greater outward calm than anybody else," Tully later recalled of Roosevelt, "but there was rage in his very calmness. With each new message he shook his head grimly and tightened the expression of his mouth." Hours later Roosevelt met privately with Tully and carefully dictated the first draft of the speech he would deliver the next day. On December 8, Roosevelt appeared before Congress and officially requested a declaration of war against Japan.

Yesterday, December 7, 1941, a date which will live in infamy, the United States of America was suddenly and deliberately attacked by naval and air forces of the Empire of Japan.

The United States was at peace with that nation and, at the solicitation

of Japan, was still in conversation with its government and its emperor looking toward the maintenance of peace in the Pacific.

Indeed, one hour after Japanese air squadrons had commenced bombing
Oahu, the Japanese ambassador to the United States and his colleague delivered to the secretary of state a formal reply to a recent American message.
While this reply stated that it seemed useless to continue the existing diplomatic negotiations, it contained no threat or hint of war or armed attack.

It will be recorded that the distance of Hawaii from Japan makes it obvious that the attack was deliberately planned many days or even weeks ago.
During the intervening time, the Japanese government has deliberately
sought to deceive the United States by false statements and expressions of
hope for continued peace. The attack yesterday on the Hawaiian Islands
has caused severe damage to American naval and military forces. Very
many American lives have been lost. In addition, American ships have
been reported torpedoed on the high seas between San Francisco and Honolulu.

Yesterday the Japanese government also launched an attack against
Malaya. Last night Japanese forces attacked Hong Kong. Last night Japanese
forces attacked Guam. Last night Japanese forces attacked the Philippine Islands. Last night the Japanese attacked Wake Island. This morning the Japanese attacked Midway Island. Japan has, therefore, undertaken a surprise
offensive extending throughout the Pacific area. The facts of yesterday speak
for themselves. The people of the United States have already formed their
opinions and well understand the implications to the very life and safety of
our nation.

As commander in chief of the army and navy, I have directed that all
measures be taken for our defense. Always will we remember the character of
the onslaught against us.

No matter how long it may take us to overcome this premeditated invasion, the American people in their righteous might will win through to absolute victory. I believe I interpret the will of the Congress and of the people
when I assert that we will not only defend ourselves to the uttermost but will
make very certain that this form of treachery shall never endanger us again.

Hostilities exist. There is no blinking at the fact that our people, our territory, and our interests are in grave danger.

With confidence in our armed forces, with the unbounding determination of our people, we will gain the inevitable triumph. So help us God.

I ask that the Congress declare that since the unprovoked and dastardly
attack by Japan on Sunday, December 7, a state of war has existed between
the United States and the Japanese Empire.

Congress immediately and overwhelmingly passed the resolution. (Only one member, Representative Jeannette Rankin of Montana, voted against it.) Germany and Italy, presuming the United States to be weakened and demoralized by the bombardment of Pearl Harbor, officially announced a state of war with the United States on the morning of December 11. Again Roosevelt sent a message to Congress to declare war on the two countries, and again Congress did so. Believing he had already stated his case, Roosevelt did not formally address the American public or Congress, but in a statement days after the initial attacks, he proclaimed, "In the past few years—and, most violently, in the past few days—we have learned a terrible lesson. We must begin the great task that is before us by abandoning once and for all the illusion that we can ever again isolate ourselves from the rest of humanity." He added defiantly, "We are going to win the war, and we are going to win the peace that follows."

Nobel Laureate Pearl Buck Contends That to Defeat Fascism Abroad, Americans Must Fight for Equality at Home.

When the United States officially announced its entry in World War II, sudden and sweeping changes were required in virtually all aspects of American life. Millions of soldiers had to be drafted. Food had to be rationed. An unprecedented number of planes, aircraft carriers, tanks, bombs, guns, and other weapons of war had to be built in an impossibly short amount of time. (The government ordered over $100 billion in war contracts in the first six months of 1942 alone, and the tax system consequently needed to be overhauled almost entirely.) For a country just awakening from an economic nightmare, the task ahead was both daunting and galvanizing. Many of the nation's most prominent social, religious, and political leaders encouraged citizens to unite solidly behind the war effort, while others used the war to accentuate what they saw as American hypocrisy. They contended that the United States was willing to fight and spend lavishly for freedom overseas but not for those at home mired in poverty or victimized by racial discrimination. Pearl Buck, the first American woman to win the Nobel Prize for literature and an adamant proponent of civil rights, believed the two positions were not mutually exclusive. In a June 5, 1942, commencement speech at Howard University, Buck, who spent most of her life in China, said that the defeat of fascism overseas would be a victory for human rights throughout the world, and she encouraged the graduating students to recognize their role in defeating oppression both overseas and within the United States.

I believe this is the first time in my life that I have ever made a commencement address. The invitations I have had I have refused until now because it has always seemed to me presumptuous to offer advice or even to forecast for those who have not yet entered in the sort of life that lies ahead of college. Life is so individual a thing in ordinary times, so much depends on the person who is to live it, that all I have ever felt I could say was easily said in a sentence: The only way to find out anything about life is to live it as heartily as you can. So what was the use of making a speech about what could be said in one sentence? But I accepted the invitation this particular year to this particular university for a very special reason: These are not ordinary times, and this is no ordinary graduating class. . . .

I am asking today only one question: How can every citizen in this country fulfill his responsibility as a citizen of our democracy? I repeat, it is as a democracy that we will win this war. If we cease to be a democracy, we will not win this war, and there will not be any peace if we don't win this war. Therefore, it is not enough merely to join the army and the navy and the air force if they will have us, and to do nothing if they won't. It is not enough to pour our savings into war bonds. It is not enough to put our lives into factories and war work so far as we are allowed. We will not win this war unless we win it as a nation where human beings are equal and human rights are respected. The peace will be no peace unless it is based upon the principles of human equality.

In profound belief in democracy, thus in deepest love of our country, let us now realize that when we work for democracy and our own nation we are in the most important sense working for victory in war and in peace.

Therefore, today I believe that discrimination in our country must go, because until it does, we will not have won the war. We cannot fight for freedom unless we fight for freedom for all. We are not better than fascists if we fight for freedom of one group and not another, for the benefit of one race and not another, for the aggrandizement of a part and not the betterment of the whole. And we must be better than fascists. We cannot allow in our nation the evil root of something which Hitler has developed into a system of slavery the like of which the world has never seen, where the individual is nothing but a piece of property seized and used and tossed aside by a robber government. Japan's militarists, too, have for generations conceived the individual to be nothing but a tool, and the history of Japan during the last four generations has been the history of the struggle between the individual and the possessor state. And the beginning of that struggle anywhere is always in the degradation of a class, the condemnation for some trivial cause of a group of individuals.

It is ironic that in Germany the death grip of the state today upon the individual arose not out of too much unity but too little. Germany has never really achieved a sense of nationhood. A loose handful of states, her people have longed for unity. But in the desire to be integrated into a nation, they have handed themselves over to a handful of persons who have wrecked them not only as a nation but as individuals.

We, too, are not a unified people. We have sprung from many sources and many places, and we too have a deep-seated longing for unity. Perhaps that is why we exalt more than most democracies in the power of our government. In a common government we find a sort of unity which otherwise we lack. Perhaps that is why we look to government instead of to our wise men, as the Chinese and Indians do. But this desire to be unified must not lead us in the directions of the Nazis, where first a race was despised and then where every individual who differed from the unifying force was eliminated. The danger of race prejudice always is that it tends to lump people together and ignore the individual. Any nation which tolerates prejudice against one group in its people carries inside itself the potentialities of developing fascism, as a persistent sore is always a potential cancer. It has to be watched, and the body is never safe until the sore is cut out.

The equality of opportunity, therefore, which you have not been given in your country has now become more than an individual handicap, more than a group misfortune. It has become a national danger of the sharpest sort, a rock upon which our whole nation may founder. It is now necessary that all of us who believe with all our hearts in democracy work together to bring about human equality in the world of which our nation is only a part. . . .

We are in the midst of a struggle in the hour of change, when by action for freedom we can still shape the world toward freedom. We ought so to act that all we do is designed to break down that which denies equality and forbids freedom.

Therefore you are to be congratulated. You have come to your majority at a time in history when more than ever before all effort for freedom can count. You are trained, intelligent, and ready to work. You are citizens in a country which still allows free speech and individual effort. But most important of all—and here is your greatest advantage—you [as African Americans] belong to a group which more than any in the world knows what race prejudice is, and how even political freedom cannot do away with it, and you know that it must be done away with if democracy is to prevail. The white citizens of this country in their general ignorance cannot realize as clearly as you do how our nation is threatened by our inner division and what it means to the world if we do not achieve democracy. But you can realize it. You know what it does in your own lives, in your own minds and wills and characters. . . .

You are in a superior position in America: It is not you who bare the stigma of not practicing democracy. You have now the advantage over the white man. You can be free from hypocrisy. Do not for one moment, therefore, accept the status which race prejudice puts upon you. Consider what you can do best and do it, determined never to yield to undemocratic behavior and prejudice which denies all that America means. You belong here in America. You have a purpose to fulfill in this country, and I am grateful today that the people of our country are of more races than one. It gives us matchless opportunity of working out upon our own soil the world problems of equality and of cooperation between different peoples. Do not yield to discouragement or to hopelessness and do not expect an easy life or seek a sheltered one. The times are demanding that every one of you thinks not of yourself or of your own race or group life, but of the life of the nation as a whole. All that we have done for democracy and for history will have been lost if we do not achieve a democracy now. . . .

You are not simply a group of people in one country. You are part of the great war of the peoples for freedom. They are not only colored peoples against white. There are many white people on your side and white people in many parts of the world who are subject, too, to tyrants. You must understand the meaning of the war, and you must wage it on its true scale. By linking your particular battle for your own place in your own country to the whole war for freedom and human equality in the world, you will enlarge your forces and strengthen your cause, and help to win the war for democracy.

And you must remember that if we are really to achieve human equality in the world the war must not degenerate into a war of the races or a war of East against West. Such a struggle against prejudices will win nothing. Your enemies are not of one nation. Your enemies are all those who do not believe in human equality, who judge a man by his skin and not by what he is as an individual. Your allies are those who believe in and practice human equality and who judge an individual solely by what he is and what he does. As simply as that you may know your enemies and your allies. You must not yield to race prejudice. It is wrong for you to hate the white man because he is white, as it is for him to hate you because you are not white. Keep yourselves free from jealousy and revenge that you may do your work in the world in this time. . . .

As far as you are able really to believe in your own equality, so far will you be able to bring human equality about in our country and in the world. You will not grow bigger than your own feelings. You will not accomplish more than you are. This fight for equality begins in your own soul, and then it must spread as wide as the world. The battle against race prejudice is no longer a family quarrel in our own house. The great storm that now sweeps humanity has swept us all with it, and our own fight against discrimination has become part of the tremendous struggle for human freedom upon this globe.

General Dwight D. Eisenhower Drafts a
Message of Apology for His Failure at D-Day
&
General Eisenhower Issues His "Order of the Day"
to the Men Who Will Storm the Beaches of Normandy.

Even his troops could see the anxiety on his face before the fateful invasion. As a grim Dwight D. Eisenhower reviewed his men, one soldier called out to the supreme commander of Allied forces, "Quit worrying, General, we'll take care of this thing for you." But Eisenhower had reason to worry. Operation Overlord, as it was known, would almost certainly determine the outcome of World War II. In the two years since the beginning of the war, Allied forces had made extraordinary gains, but the key to defeating the Nazis hinged on breaching the infamous Atlantic Wall and liberating German-occupied France. The invasion of Normandy was planned for June 1944, and the enormousness and complexity of the assault were unprecedented in the history of warfare. "In one night and day," explained the historian Stephen Ambrose, "175,000 fighting men and their equipment, including 50,000 vehicles of all types, were transported across 60 to 100 miles of open water and landed on a hostile shore against intense opposition. They were either carried by or supported by 5,333 ships and craft of all types and almost 11,000 airplanes." One of Eisenhower's greatest concerns was how the troops would react once they hit the beaches. If they froze, the operation would be a catastrophe. At 3:30 A.M. the morning of June 5, Eisenhower woke after only a few hours of sleep. He received an update that the rainstorm over Normandy, which was the deciding factor in ordering or delaying the invasion, would break by dawn. Eisenhower silently paced for a few moments, faced his subordinates, and stated, "Okay, let's go." Hours later, and preparing for the worst, Eisenhower wrote out the following message to the American people and their allies around the world.

Our landings in the Cherbourg–Havre area have failed to gain a satisfactory foothold and I have withdrawn the troops.

My decision to attack at this time and place was based upon the best information available. The troops, the air, and the navy did all that bravery and devotion to duty could do. If any blame or fault attaches to the attempt it is mine alone.

Eisenhower tucked the statement in his wallet and soon forgot about it. (He later threw it in the trash, but an aide, recognizing its historic value, salvaged it.) The statement Eisenhower ultimately issued to his troops, however, could not—and did not—contain even a hint of anxiety. On June 6, Eisenhower released the order of the day, which was read aloud to Allied forces before they stormed the beaches of Normandy.

Soldiers, sailors and airmen of the Allied Expeditionary Force: You are about to embark upon a great crusade, toward which we have striven these many months. The eyes of the world are upon you. The hopes and prayers of liberty-loving people everywhere march with you.

In company with our brave Allies and brothers in arms on other fronts, you will bring about the destruction of the German war machine, the elimination of Nazi tyranny over the oppressed peoples of Europe, and security for ourselves in a free world.

Your task will not be an easy one. Your enemy is well trained, well equipped and battle-hardened. He will fight savagely.

But this is the year 1944. Much has happened since the Nazi triumphs of 1940–41. The United Nations have inflicted upon the Germans great defeats in open battle, man to man. Our air offensive has seriously reduced their strength in the air and their capacity to wage war on the ground.

Our home fronts have given us an overwhelming superiority in weapons and munitions of war, and placed at our disposal great reserves of trained fighting men.

The tide has turned. The free men of the world are marching together to victory. I have full confidence in your courage, devotion to duty and skill in battle. We will accept nothing less than full victory. Good luck.

Let us all beseech the blessing of Almighty God, upon this great and noble undertaking.

Whatever apprehension the Allied commanders may have had about the courage and bravery of their men was immediately put to rest once the assault commenced. American, British, and Canadian troops rushed headlong into a steel blizzard of enemy fire and ultimately penetrated the heavily fortified Atlantic Wall. The operation, though not without excruciating losses, was a phenomenal success. Paris would be liberated a mere eleven weeks later.

General George S. Patton Tells His Troops That War Is the "Most Magnificent Competition in Which a Human Being Can Indulge."

An admitted megalomaniac with an explosive temper, George S. "Blood and Guts" Patton, commander of the Third Army in Europe, was one of the most feared and despised generals in the American military. Intolerant of the slightest display of weakness, Patton famously slapped an ailing soldier and even pulled his gun on the young man after calling him a "goddamned whimpering coward." When the Saturday Evening

Post and other media sources reported the incident, it almost permanently derailed Patton's military career. But he survived, and despite the rancor directed toward him personally, Patton was also recognized as a brilliant general who could inspire his men like no other leader. Frustrated that he would not be part of the D-Day invasion—"It is hell to be on the sidelines and see all the glory eluding me," he wrote to his wife on June 6, 1944, "but I guess there will be enough for all"—Patton traveled to England to rally American troops with the following profanity-laced call to arms. (And unlike the actor George C. Scott, who gave a more sanitized version of the speech in the 1970 classic Patton, *the real Patton did not have a husky baritone but, rather surprisingly, a voice that was described as a "high-pitched, womanish squeak.")*

Men, this stuff that some sources sling around about America wanting out of this war, not wanting to fight, is a crock of bullshit. Americans love to fight, traditionally. All real Americans love the sting and clash of battle. You are here today for three reasons. First, because you are here to defend your homes and your loved ones. Second, you are here for your own self-respect, because you would not want to be anywhere else. Third, you are here because you are real men, and all real men like to fight. When you here—every one of you—were kids, you all admired the champion marble player, the fastest runner, the big-league ballplayers, and the all-American football players. Americans love a winner. Americans will not tolerate a loser. Americans despise cowards. Americans play to win all the time. I wouldn't give a hoot in hell for a man who lost and laughed. That's why Americans have never lost nor will ever lose a war, for the very thought of losing is hateful to an American.

You are not all going to die. Only 2 percent of you right here today would die in a major battle. Death must not be feared. Death, in time, comes to all men. Yes, every man is scared in his first battle. If he says he's not, he's a liar! Some men are cowards but they fight just the same as the brave men, or they get the hell slammed out of them watching men fight who are just as scared as they are. The real hero is the man who fights even though he is scared. Some men get over their fright in a minute under fire. For some, it takes an hour. For some, it takes days. But a real man will never let his fear of death overpower his honor, his sense of duty to his country, and his innate manhood. Battle is the most magnificent competition in which a human being can indulge. It brings out all that is best and it removes all that is base. Americans pride themselves on being he-men, and they are he-men. Remember that the enemy is just as frightened as you are, and probably more so. They are not supermen.

All through your army careers, you men have bitched about what you call "chickenshit drilling." That, like everything else in this army, has a definite purpose. That purpose is alertness. Alertness must be bred into every soldier. I don't give a fuck for a man who is not always on his toes. You men are veterans or you wouldn't be here. You are ready for what's to come. A man must be alert at all times if he expects to stay alive. If you're not alert, some time a German son of an asshole bitch is going to sneak up behind you and beat you to death with a sockful of shit! There are four hundred neatly marked graves somewhere in Sicily, all because one man went to sleep on the job. But they are German graves, because we caught the bastard asleep before they did.

An army is a team. It lives, sleeps, eats, and fights as a team. This individual heroic stuff is pure horseshit. The bilious bastards who write that kind of stuff for the *Saturday Evening Post* don't know any more about real fighting under fire than they know about fucking! We have the finest food, the finest equipment, the best spirit, and the best men in the world. Why, by God, I actually pity those poor sons of bitches we are going up against. By God, I do.

My men don't surrender. I don't want to hear of any soldier under my command being captured unless he has been hit. Even if you are hit, you can still fight back. That's not just bullshit either. The kind of a man that I want in my command is just like the lieutenant in Libya who, with a Luger against his chest, jerked off his helmet, swept the gun aside with one hand, and busted the hell out of the Kraut with his helmet. Then he jumped on the gun and went out and killed another German before they knew what the hell was coming off. And all of that time, this man had a bullet through a lung. There was a real man!

All the real heroes are not storybook combat fighters, either. Every single man in this army plays a vital role. Don't ever let up. Don't ever think that your job is unimportant. Every man has a job to do and he must do it. Every man is a vital link in the great chain. What if every truck driver suddenly decided that he didn't like the whine of those shells overhead, turned yellow, and jumped headlong into a ditch? The cowardly bastard could say, "Hell, they won't miss me, just one guy in thousands." But, what if every man thought that way? Where in the hell would we be now? What would our country, our loved ones, our homes, even the world, be like? No, goddamnit, Americans don't think like that. Every man does his job. Every man serves the whole. Every department, every unit, is important to the vast scheme of this war. The ordnance men are needed to supply the guns and machinery of war to keep us rolling. The quartermaster is needed to bring up food and clothes for us because where we are going there isn't a hell of a lot to steal. Every last man on KP has a job to do, even the one who heats our water to keep us from getting the "G.I. shits."

Each man must not only think of himself, but also of his buddy fighting beside him. We don't want yellow cowards in this army. They should be killed off like rats. If not, they will go home after this war and breed more cowards. The brave men will breed more brave men. One of the bravest men that I ever saw was a fellow on top of a telegraph pole in the midst of a furious fire-fight in Tunisia. I stopped and asked what the hell he was doing up there at a time like that. He answered, "Fixing the wire, Sir." I asked, "Isn't that a little unhealthy right about now?" He answered, "Yes, Sir, but the goddamned wire has to be fixed." I asked, "Don't those planes strafing the road bother you?" And he answered, "No, Sir, but you sure as hell do!" Now, there was a real man, a real soldier. There was a man who devoted all he had to his duty, no matter how seemingly insignificant his duty might appear at the time, no matter how great the odds. And you should have seen those trucks on the road to Tunisia. Those drivers were magnificent. All day and all night they rolled over those son-of-a-bitching roads, never stopping, never faltering from their course, with shells bursting all around them all of the time. We got through on good old American guts. Many of those men drove for over forty consecutive hours. Those men weren't combat men, but they were all soldiers with a job to do. They did it, and in one hell of a way they did it. They were part of a team. Without team effort, without them, the fight would have been lost. All of the links in the chain pulled together, and the chain became unbreakable.

Don't forget, you men don't know that I'm here. No mention of that fact is to be made in any letters. The world is not supposed to know what the hell happened to me. I am not supposed to be commanding this army. I'm not even supposed to be here in England. Let the first bastards to find out be the goddamned Germans. Someday I want to see them raise up on their piss-soaked hind legs and howl, "Jesus Christ, it's the goddamned Third Army again and that son-of-a-fucking-bitch Patton again!"

We want to get the hell over there. The quicker we clean up this god-damned mess, the quicker we can take a little jaunt against the purple-pissing Japs and clean out their nest, too—before the goddamned Marines get all of the credit. Sure, we want to get home. We want this war over with. The quickest way to get it over with is to go get the bastards who started it. The quicker they are whipped, the quicker we can go home. The shortest way home is through Berlin and Tokyo. And when we get to Berlin, I am person-ally going to shoot that paper-hanging son of a bitch Hitler, just like I'd shoot a snake!

When a man is lying in a shell hole, if he just stays there all the day, a Ger-man will get to him eventually. The hell with that idea. The hell with taking it. My men don't dig foxholes. I don't want them to. Foxholes only slow up an offensive. Keep moving. And don't give the enemy time to dig one either. We'll win this war, but we'll win it only by fighting and by showing the Ger-mans that we've got more guts than they have, or ever will have. We're not going to just shoot the sons of bitches, we're going to rip out their living goddamned guts and use them to grease the treads of our tanks. We're going to murder those lousy Hun cocksuckers by the bushel-fucking-basket. War is a bloody, killing business. You've got to spill their blood, or they will spill yours. Rip them up the belly. Shoot them in the guts. When shells are hitting all around you and you wipe the dirt off your face and realize that instead of dirt it's the blood and guts of what once was your best friend beside you, you'll know what to do!

I don't want to get any messages saying, "I am holding my position." We are not holding a goddamned thing. Let the Germans do that. We are advancing constantly and we are not interested in holding on to anything except the enemy's balls. We are going to twist his balls and kick the living shit out of him all the time. Our basic plan of operation is to advance and to keep on advancing regardless of whether we have to go over, under, or through the enemy. We are going to go through him like crap through a goose—like shit through a tin horn!

From time to time there will be some complaints that we are pushing our people too hard. I don't give a goddamn about such complaints. I believe in the old and sound rule that an ounce of sweat will save a gallon of blood. The harder we push, the more Germans we will kill. The more Germans we kill, the fewer of our men will be killed. Pushing means fewer casualties. I want you all to remember that.

There is one great thing that you men will all be able to say after this war is over and you are home once again. You may be thankful that twenty years from now when you are sitting by the fireplace with your grandson on your knee and he asks you what you did in the great World War II, you won't have to cough, shift him to the other knee, and say, "Well, your granddaddy shoveled shit in Louisiana." No, sir, you can look him straight in the eye and say, "Son, your granddaddy rode with the great Third Army and a son-of-a-goddamned-bitch named Georgie Patton!"

Eisenhower's victory at D-Day and the liberation of Paris in August 1944 infused the Allies with new optimism. But as they approached Germany's western border that winter, they confronted a fierce German counterattack in the dead of winter in the Ardennes. Eisenhower called in neighboring troops for reinforcement, including Patton's Third Army. But even Patton was intimidated by the challenge of routing the Nazi offensive in the freezing conditions, and he appealed directly to the Almighty for assistance. Patton offered his prayer on December 23, 1944, in the Pescatore Chapel in Luxembourg, which purportedly began, "Sir, this is Patton talking. The past fourteen days have been straight hell—rain, snow, more rain, more snow—and I am beginning to wonder what's going on in Your headquarters. Whose side are You on anyway? . . . I am sick of the unnecessary butchery of American youth, and in exchange for four days of fighting weather, I will deliver You enough Krauts to keep Your bookkeepers months behind in their work. Amen." *The weather cleared. Days later, and after encountering Patton's Third Army, the German forces were soundly annihilated.*

President Harry S. Truman Addresses a Nation Grief-Stricken by the Death of Franklin D. Roosevelt.

A few minutes past 5:00 P.M. on April 12, 1945, Vice President Harry S. Truman walked into the private office of Speaker of the House Sam Rayburn, to have a drink. An urgent message was waiting for Truman from President Roosevelt's press secretary, Steve Early. Truman called Early and was told to come to the White House as "quickly and quietly" as possible. The vice president left in such a rush that he made the trip from the Capitol without his Secret Service detail. Moments later he was met by First Lady Eleanor Roosevelt, who put her arm on Truman's shoulder and said, "Harry, the president is dead." Truman, visibly stunned, asked Mrs. Roosevelt, "Is there anything I can do for you?" She responded, "Is there anything we can do for you, for you are the one in trouble now." The first lady was serious. Truman, a senator from Missouri, had served as vice president for only eighty-two days, replacing Henry Wallace in the 1944 election. Within a few hours he would be the new commander in chief of a nation in the throes of a world war. Looking "absolutely dazed," as one observer noted, Truman took the oath of office and immediately issued the following press release: "The world may be sure that we will prosecute the war on both fronts, east and west, with all the vigor we possess, to a successful conclusion." Four days later, President Truman addressed a nation mourning the loss of an enormously popular four-term president.

It is with a heavy heart that I stand before you, my friends and colleagues, in the Congress of the United States.

Only yesterday we laid to rest the mortal remains of our beloved president, Franklin Delano Roosevelt. At times like this, words are inadequate. The most eloquent tribute would be a reverent silence. Yet in this decisive hour, when world events are moving so rapidly, our silence might be misunderstood and might give comfort to our enemies.

In His infinite wisdom, Almighty God has seen fit to take from us a great man who loved, and was beloved by, all humanity. No man could possibly fill the tremendous void left by the passing of that noble soul. No words can ease the aching hearts of untold millions of every race, creed, and color. The world knows it has lost a heroic champion of justice and freedom.

Tragic fate has thrust upon us grave responsibilities. We *must* carry on. Our departed leader never looked backward. He looked forward and moved forward. That is what he would want us to do. That is what America *will* do. So much blood has already been shed for the ideals which we cherish, and for which Franklin Delano Roosevelt lived and died, that we dare not permit even a momentary pause in the hard fight for victory.

Today, the entire world is looking to America for enlightened leadership to peace and progress. Such a leadership requires vision, courage, and tolerance. It can be provided only by a united nation deeply devoted to the highest ideals. With great humility I call upon all Americans to help me keep our nation united in defense of those ideals with all my strength and all my heart. That is my duty, and I shall not shirk it.

So that there can be no possible misunderstanding, both Germany and Japan can be certain beyond any shadow of a doubt that America will continue the fight for freedom until no vestige of resistance remains. We are deeply conscious of the fact that much hard fighting is still ahead of us. Having to pay such a heavy price to make complete victory certain, America will never become a party to any plan for partial victory. To settle for merely another temporary respite would surely jeopardize the future security of all the world. Our demand has been—and it remains—unconditional surrender. We will not traffic with the breakers of the peace on the terms of the peace.

The responsibility for the making of the peace—and it is a very grave responsibility—must rest with the defenders of the peace. We are not unconscious of the dictates of humanity. We do not wish to see unnecessary or unjustified suffering. But the laws of God and of man have been violated, and the guilty must not go unpunished. Nothing shall shake our determination to punish the war criminals even though we must pursue them to the ends of the earth.

Lasting peace can never be secured if we permit our dangerous opponents to plot future wars with impunity at any mountain retreat, however distant. In this shrinking world, it is futile to seek safety beyond geographical barriers. Real security will be found only in law and in justice. Here in America, we have labored long and hard to achieve a social order worthy of our great heritage. In our time, tremendous progress has been made toward a really democratic way of life. Let me assure the forward-looking people of America that there will be no relaxation in our efforts to improve the lot of the common people.

In the difficult days ahead, unquestionably we shall face problems of staggering proportions. However, with the faith of our fathers in our hearts, we do not fear the future. On the battlefields, we have frequently faced overwhelming odds—and won! At home, Americans will not be less resolute. We shall never cease our struggle to preserve and maintain our American way of life.

At this moment, America, along with her brave Allies, is paying again a heavy price for the defense of our freedom. With characteristic energy, we are assisting in the liberation of entire nations. Gradually, the shackles of slavery are being broken by the forces of freedom. All of us are praying for a speedy victory. Every day peace is delayed costs a terrible toll. . . .

America must assist suffering humanity back along the path of peaceful progress. This will require time and tolerance. We shall need also an abiding faith in the people, the kind of faith and courage which Franklin Delano Roosevelt always had!

Today, America has become one of the most powerful forces for good on earth. We must keep it so. We have achieved a world leadership which does not depend solely upon our military and naval might. We have learned to fight with other nations in common defense of our freedom. We must now learn to live with other nations for our mutual good. We must learn to trade with other nations so that there may be—for our mutual advantage—increased production, increased employment, and better standards of living throughout the world. May we Americans all live up to our glorious heritage. In that way, America may well lead the world to peace and prosperity.

At this moment, I have in my heart a prayer. As I have assumed my heavy duties, I humbly pray Almighty God, in the words of King Solomon: "Give therefore thy servant an understanding heart to judge thy people, that I may discern between good and bad, for who is able to judge this thy so great a people?"

I ask only to be a good and faithful servant of my Lord and my people.

Although momentarily buoyed by the news of President Roosevelt's death, Adolf Hitler knew by late April that the end had finally arrived. Soviet troops had reached Germany's capital from the east, and Allied forces were approaching from the west. The Nazi war machine, once seemingly invincible, was now little more than a thinning army of elderly men and young boys. At approximately 3:00 P.M. on April 30, 1945, Hitler and his new wife, Eva Braun, retired to the führer's private quarters in his Berlin bunker and ingested cyanide. Hitler simultaneously shot himself with a pistol. Germany's unconditional surrender followed one week later.

President Truman Announces That an Atomic Bomb—
the Largest Bomb Ever Used in the History of
Warfare—Has Been Dropped on Japan
&
General Douglas MacArthur Offers Words of Peace
After Japan Signs the Official Declaration of Surrender.

The formal ceremony of Germany's surrender took place in Eisenhower's headquarters in Reims, France, on May 7. (Germany surrendered to the Russians in Berlin the next day.) But there was still the matter of the war with Japan. After some of the bloodiest fighting of the war, including hand-to-hand combat, U.S. forces finally took control of the islands of Iwo Jima and Okinawa, providing them with crucial positioning for a full-scale attack on Japan itself. President Truman scheduled an assault for November, but after learning of the fierce resistance of Japanese soldiers and civilians alike, he feared an invasion would result in even more vicious and protracted combat as well as heavy American casualties. There was another option, he soon discovered, and it was a military secret so confidential that even as vice president Truman was not informed of it: the atomic bomb. Less than two weeks after Roosevelt's death, Truman was told of the existence of, in the words of Secretary of War Henry L. Stimson, "the most terrible weapon ever known in human history." Determined to end the war without the loss of another American soldier, Truman gave the order for the bomb to be used, and on August 6, 1945, he justified his actions in a radio address to the American public.

Sixteen hours ago an American airplane dropped one bomb on Hiroshima, an important Japanese army base. That bomb had more power than twenty thousand tons of TNT. It had more than two thousand times the blast power of the British "grand slam," which is the largest bomb ever yet used in the history of warfare.

The Japanese began the war from the air at Pearl Harbor. They have been repaid manyfold. And the end is not yet. With this bomb we have now added a new and revolutionary increase in destruction to supplement the growing power of our armed forces. In their present form these bombs are now in production, and even more powerful forms are in development.

It is an atomic bomb. It is a harnessing of the basic power of the universe. The force from which the sun draws its power has been loosed against those who brought war to the Far East.

Before 1939, it was the accepted belief of scientists that it was theoretically possible to release atomic energy, but no one knew any practical method of doing it. By 1942, however, we knew that the Germans were working feverishly to find a way to add atomic energy to the other engines of war with which they hoped to enslave the world, but they failed. We may be grateful to

Providence that the Germans got the V-1's and V-2's late and in limited quantities and even more grateful that they did not get the atomic bomb at all.

The battle of the laboratories held fateful risks for us as well as the battles of the air, land, and sea, and we have now won the battle of the laboratories as we have won the other battles. . . .

But the greatest marvel is not the size of the enterprise, its secrecy, nor its cost, but the achievement of scientific brains in putting together infinitely complex pieces of knowledge held by many men in different fields of science into a workable plan. And hardly less marvelous has been the capacity of industry to design, and of labor to operate, the machines and methods to do things never done before so that the brainchild of many minds came forth in physical shape and performed as it was supposed to do. Both science and industry worked under the direction of the United States Army, which achieved a unique success in managing so diverse a problem in the advancement of knowledge in an amazingly short time. It is doubtful if such another combination could be got together in the world. What has been done is the greatest achievement of organized science in history. It was done under high pressure and without failure.

We are now prepared to obliterate more rapidly and completely every productive enterprise the Japanese have above ground in any city. We shall destroy their docks, their factories, and their communications. Let there be no mistake: We shall completely destroy Japan's power to make war.

It was to spare the Japanese people from utter destruction that the ultimatum of July 26 was issued at Potsdam. Their leaders promptly rejected that ultimatum. If they do not now accept our terms, they may expect a rain of ruin from the air the like of which has never been seen on this earth. Behind this air attack will follow sea and land forces in such numbers and power as they have not yet seen and with the fighting skill of which they are already well aware. . . .

The fact that we can release atomic energy ushers in a new era in man's understanding of nature's forces. Atomic energy may in the future supplement the power that now comes from coal, oil, and falling water, but at present it cannot be produced on a basis to compete with them commercially. Before that comes, there must be a long period of intensive research.

It has never been the habit of the scientists of this country or the policy of this government to withhold from the world scientific knowledge. Normally, therefore, everything about the work with atomic energy would be made public. But under present circumstances it is not intended to divulge the technical processes of production or all the military applications, pending further examination of possible methods of protecting us and the rest of the world from the danger of sudden destruction.

I shall recommend that the Congress of the United States consider promptly the establishment of an appropriate commission to control the production and use of atomic power within the United States. I shall give further consideration and make further recommendations to the Congress as to how atomic power can become a powerful and forceful influence towards the maintenance of world peace.

The bomb, nicknamed "Little Boy," detonated at 8:16 A.M. on August 6, killing an estimated 100,000 people, many of whom were vaporized almost instantly. (Another 100,000 would die from cancer and other radiation-related illnesses in the decades to come.) Three days later, with still no word of surrender from Japan, another atomic bomb was dropped on the city of Nagasaki. Five days after that, the emperor himself resolved, over the protests of many of his senior military officers, that Japan must surrender. The official surrender ceremony was held in Tokyo Bay on Sunday, September 2, 1945, aboard the USS Missouri, *the newest warship in the American fleet. General Douglas MacArthur, who had masterminded much of the victory in the Pacific, offered the following words of peace.*

Today the guns are silent. A great tragedy has ended. A great victory has been won. The skies no longer rain death. The seas bear only commerce. Men everywhere walk upright in the sunlight. The entire world lies quietly at peace. The holy mission has been completed. And in reporting this to you, the people, I speak for the thousands of silent lips forever stilled among the jungles and the beaches and in the deep waters of the Pacific which marked the way. I speak for the unnamed brave millions homeward bound to take up the challenge of that future which they did so much to salvage from the brink of disaster.

As I look back on the long, tortuous trail from those grim days of Bataan and Corregidor, when an entire world lived in fear, when democracy was on the defensive everywhere, when modern civilization trembled in the balance, I thank a merciful God that he has given us the faith, the courage, and the power from which to mold victory. We have known the bitterness of defeat and the exultation of triumph, and from both we have learned there can be no turning back. We must go forward to preserve in peace what we won in war.

A new era is upon us. Even the lesson of victory itself brings with it profound concern both for our future security and the survival of civilization. The destructiveness of the war potential, through progressive advances in scientific discovery, has in fact now reached a point which revises the traditional concept of war.

Men since the beginning of time have sought peace. Various methods through the ages have been attempted to devise an international process to prevent or settle disputes between nations. From the very start, workable methods were found insofar as individual citizens were concerned, but the mechanics of an instrumentality of larger international scope have never been successful. Military alliances, balances of power, leagues of nations—all in turn failed, leaving the only path to be by way of the crucible of war. The utter destructiveness of war now blots out this alternative. We have had our last chance. If we will not devise some greater and more equitable system, Armageddon will be at our door. The problem basically is theological and involves a spiritual recrudescence and improvement of human character that will synchronize with our almost matchless advances in science, art, literature, and all material and cultural developments of the past 2,000 years. It must be of the spirit if we are to save the flesh.

We stand in Tokyo today reminiscent of our countryman Commodore Perry ninety-two years ago. His purpose was to bring to Japan an era of enlightenment and progress by lifting the veil of isolation to the friendship, trade, and commerce of the world. But alas, the knowledge thereby gained of Western science was forged into an instrument of oppression and human enslavement. Freedom of expression, freedom of action, even freedom of thought were denied through suppression of liberal education, through appeal to superstition, and through the application of force. We are committed by the Potsdam Declaration of Principles to see that the Japanese people are liberated from this condition of slavery. It is my purpose to implement this commitment just as rapidly as the armed forces are demobilized and other essential steps are taken to neutralize the war potential. The energy of the Japanese race, if properly directed, will enable expansion vertically rather than horizontally. If the talents of the race are turned into constructive channels, the country can lift itself from its present deplorable state into a position of dignity.

To the Pacific basin has come the vista of a new emancipated world. Today, freedom is on the offensive, democracy is on the march. Today, in Asia as well as in Europe, unshackled peoples are tasting the full sweetness of liberty, the relief from fear. In the Philippines, America has evolved a model for this new free world of Asia. In the Philippines, America has demonstrated that peoples of the East and peoples of the West may walk side by side in mutual respect and with mutual benefit. The history of our sovereignty there has now the full confidence of the East.

And so, my fellow countrymen, today I report to you that your sons and daughters have served you well and faithfully with the calm, deliberate, determined fighting spirit of the American soldier and sailor based upon a tradition of historical truth, as against the fanaticism of an enemy supported only by mythological fiction. Their spiritual strength and power has brought us through to victory. They are homeward bound. Take care of them.

Even the Japanese delegation was profoundly moved by MacArthur's statement. Toshikazu Kazu of the foreign ministry later told the emperor that MacArthur was a "man of light" with a "magnificent soul," and General Torashiro Kawabe reported that he had just encountered "a truly cultured nation." Unbeknownst to everyone at the official ceremony, however, a self-appointed squadron of Japanese fighter pilots, infuriated by their country's capitulation, were preparing to dive-bomb the Missouri. They refrained at the last minute only because of the arrival of Prince Takamatsu, the emperor's younger brother.

J. Robert Oppenheimer, Creator of the Atomic Bomb, Beseeches His Colleagues Not to Forget Morality in Their Pursuit of Science.

With tens of millions of soldiers and civilians dead throughout the world, World War II had officially come to an end. But the legacy of the war would haunt future generations, and no threat was more ominous than the proliferation of nuclear arms. The scientists and engineers who created the first atomic bombs were aware of the enormous moral questions these weapons raised, and two of the men most responsible for their development—J. Robert Oppenheimer and Albert Einstein—were especially concerned about the military implications of nuclear power. In the desert laboratory of Los Alamos, New Mexico, it was Oppenheimer who led the team that built the bombs dropped on Japan. Racked with guilt, he resigned his position and later fought the creation of the even more powerful hydrogen bomb. (Oppenheimer's antagonists were so enraged by his protests that they accused him of being an agent for the Soviet Union. After a 1954 hearing, Oppenheimer was cleared of being a spy but nevertheless deemed a "security risk.") On November 2, 1945, Oppenheimer addressed the Association of Los Alamos Scientists on the responsibilities of scientists to expand the boundaries of knowledge but, in doing so, to recognize as well that they are human beings whose discoveries can have grave results.

The reason that we did this job is because it was an organic necessity. If you are a scientist you cannot stop such a thing. If you are a scientist you believe that it is good to find out how the world works, that it is good to find out what the realities are, that it is good to turn over to mankind at large the greatest possible power to control the world and to deal with it according to its lights and its values.

There has been a lot of talk about the evil of secrecy, of concealment, of control, of security. Some of that talk has been on a rather low plane, limited really to saying that it is difficult or inconvenient to work in a world where you are not free to do what you want. I think that the talk has been justified, and that the almost unanimous resistance of scientists to the imposition of control and secrecy is a justified position, but I think that the reason may lie a little deeper. I think that it comes from the fact that secrecy strikes at the very root of what science is, and what it is for. It is not possible to be a scientist unless you believe that it is good to learn. It is not good to be a scientist, and it is not possible, unless you think that it is of the highest value to share your knowledge, to share it with anyone who is interested. It is not possible to be a scientist unless you believe that the knowledge of the world, and the power which this gives, is a thing which is of intrinsic value to humanity, and that you are using it to help in the spread of knowledge, and are willing to take the consequences. And, therefore, I think that this resistance which we feel and see all around us to anything which is an attempt to treat science of the future as though it were rather a dangerous thing, a thing that must be watched and managed, is resisted not because of its inconvenience—I think that we are in a position where we must be willing to take on any inconveniences—but resisted because it is based on a philosophy incompatible with that by which we live, and learned to live in the past.

There are many people who try to wriggle out of this. They say the real importance of atomic energy does not lie in the weapons that have been made. The real importance lies in all the great benefits which atomic energy, which the various radiations, will bring to mankind. There may be some truth in this. I am sure that there is truth in it, because there has never in the past been a new field opening up where the real fruits of it have not been invisible at the beginning. I have a very high confidence that the fruits—the so-called peacetime applications—of atomic energy will have in them all we think and more. There are others who try to escape the immediacy of this situation by saying that, after all, war has always been very terrible; after all, weapons have always gotten worse and worse; that this is just another weapon and it doesn't create a great change; that they are not so bad; bombings have been bad in this war and this is not a change in that—it just adds a little to the effectiveness of bombing; that some sort of protection will be found. I think that these efforts to diffuse and weaken the nature of the crisis make it only more dangerous. I think it is for us to accept it as a very grave crisis, to realize that these atomic weapons which we have started to make are very terrible, that they involve a change, that they are not just a slight modification—to accept this, and to accept it with the necessity for those transformations in the world that will make it possible to integrate these developments into human life. . . .

I think that we have no hope at all if we yield in our belief in the value of science, in the good that it can be to the world to know about reality, about nature, to attain a gradually greater and greater control of nature, to learn, to teach, to understand. I think that if we lose our faith in this, we stop being scientists. We sell out our heritage. We lose what we have most of value for this time of crisis.

But there is another thing: We are not only scientists. We are men, too. We cannot forget our dependence on our fellow men. I mean not only our material dependence, without which no science would be possible, and without which we could not work; I mean also our deep moral dependence, in that the value of science must lie in the world of men, that all our roots lie there. These are the strongest bonds in the world, stronger than those even that bind us to one another. These are the deepest bonds that bind us to our fellow men.

***

Robert H. Jackson Demands a Verdict of Guilty for the Nazi Leaders on Trial at Nuremberg
&
Holocaust Survivor Hadassah Rosensaft Describes the Day She Was Liberated from a Nazi Extermination Camp
&
Zionist Leader Abba Hillel Silver Implores the United Nations to Authorize the Creation of a Homeland for Jews in Palestine.

The end of World War II also confronted humanity with the most savage act of state-organized genocide ever seen: the Holocaust. Almost every aspect of German society, from government officials and bureaucrats to doctors and engineers, conspired either directly or tacitly to exterminate an entire community—Europe's Jews—from the face of the earth. Adolf Hitler's "Final Solution," as it was called, almost succeeded. Six million Jews, almost one-third of world Jewry, perished in concentration camps. (Homosexuals, Gypsies, Catholics, children and adults with mental illness, and others considered by the Nazis to be socially or medically "undesirable" were also targeted, though not as relentlessly as Jews.) After the war, British Prime Minister Winston Churchill wanted the Nazi leaders gathered together and shot. President Truman demanded instead that they be tried and punished. Beginning in November 1945 in Nuremberg, Germany—the city where many of the same Nazi leaders had staged anti-Semitic rallies—the International Military Tribunal's eight judges (two each from America, France, Britain, and the Soviet Union) heard eyewitness accounts from survivors, pored through incriminating documents, and watched films chronicling conditions in the most infamous of the Nazi camps. Leading the prosecution was former

U.S. Attorney General Robert H. Jackson, who passionately railed against the Nazi leaders and their unconscionable crimes against humanity.

In eight months we have introduced evidence which embraces as vast and varied a panorama of events as have ever been compressed within the framework of a litigation. It is impossible in summation to do more than outline with bold strokes the vitals of this trial's mad and melancholy record, which will live as the historical text of the twentieth century's shame and depravity.

It is common to think of our own time as standing at the apex of civilization. The reality is that in the long perspective of history the present century will not hold an admirable position, unless its second half is to redeem its first. These twoscore years in the twentieth century will be reported in the book of years as one of the most bloody in all annals. Two world wars have left a legacy of dead which number more than all the armies engaged in any way that make ancient or medieval history. No half century ever witnessed slaughter on such a scale, such cruelties and inhumanities. The terror of Torquemada pales before the Nazi inquisition. If we cannot eliminate the causes and prevent the repetition of these barbaric events, it is not an irresponsible prophecy to say that this twentieth century may yet succeed in bringing the doom of civilization.

Of one thing we may be sure: The future will never have to ask with misgiving what the Nazis could have said in their favor. The fact is that the testimony of the defendants has removed any doubt of guilt which, because of the extraordinary nature and magnitude of these crimes, may have existed before they spoke. They have helped write their own judgment of condemnation.

We are not trying them for the possession of obnoxious ideas. It is their right, if they choose, to renounce the Hebraic heritage in the civilization of which Germany was once a part. Nor is it our affair that they repudiated the Hellenic influence as well. The intellectual bankruptcy and moral perversion of the Nazi regime might have been no concern of international law had it not been utilized to goosestep the *Herrenvolk* across international frontiers. It is not their thoughts, it is their overt actions which we charge to be crimes.

The time has come for final judgment, and if the case I present seems hard and uncompromising, it is because the evidence makes it so. A glance over the dock will show that, despite quarrels among themselves, each defendant has played a part which fitted in with every other, and that all advanced the common plan.

The large and varied role of Göring was half militarist and half gangster. He stuck his pudgy finger in every pie. In order to entrench that power, he contrived to have the Reichstag burned, established the Gestapo, and created the concentration camps. He was equally adept at massacring opponents and at framing scandals to get rid of stubborn generals. He built up the Luftwaffe and hurled it at his defenseless neighbors. He was among the foremost in harrying Jews out of the land. By mobilizing the total economic resources of Germany, he made possible the waging of the war which he had taken a large part in planning. He was, next to Hitler, the man who tied the activities of all the defendants together in a common effort.

The zealot Hess, before succumbing to wanderlust, was the engineer tending the party machinery. Keitel, the weak and willing tool, delivered the armed forces, the instrument of aggression, over to the party and directed them in executing its felonious designs. Kaltenbrunner, the grand inquisitor, took up the bloody mantle of Heydrich to stifle opposition and terrorize compliance. It was Rosenberg, the intellectual high priest of the "master race," who provided the doctrine of hatred which gave the impetus for the annihilation of Jewry, and who put his infidel theories into practice against the eastern occupied territories. The fanatical Frank proceeded to export his lawlessness to Poland, which he governed with the lash of Caesar, and whose population he reduced to sorrowing remnants. Frick, as the ruthless organizer, helped the party to seize power, supervised the police agencies to ensure that it stayed in power, and chained the economy of Bohemia and Moravia to the German war machine.

Streicher, the venomous vulgarian, manufactured and distributed obscene racial libels which incited the populace to accept and assist the progressively more savage operations of "race purification." As minister of economics, Funk accelerated the pace of rearmament, and as Reichsbank president he banked for the SS the gold teeth fillings of concentration camp victims—probably the most ghoulish collateral in banking history. It was Schacht, the facade of starched respectability, who in the early days provided window dressing and whose wizardry later made it possible for Hitler to finance the colossal rearmament program, and to do it secretly.

Dönitz, Hitler's legatee of defeat, promoted the success of the Nazi aggressions by instructing his pack of submarine killers to conduct warfare at sea with the illegal ferocity of the jungle. Raeder, the political admiral, stealthily built up the German navy in defiance of the Versailles Treaty, and then put it to use in a series of aggressions which he had taken a leading part in planning. Von Schirach, poisoner of a generation, initiated the German youth in Nazi doctrine, trained them in legions for services in the SS and Wehrmacht, and delivered them up to the party as fanatic, unquestioning executors of its will.

Sauckel, the greatest and cruelest slaver since the pharaohs of Egypt, produced desperately needed manpower by driving foreign people into the land of bondage on a scale unknown even in the ancient days of tyranny in the kingdom of the Nile. Jodl, betrayer of the traditions of his profession, led the Wehrmacht in violating its own codes of military honor in order to carry out the barbarous aims of Nazi politics. Von Papen, pious agent of an infidel regime, held the stirrups while Hitler vaulted into the saddle.

Seyss-Inquart, spearhead of the Austrian fifth column, took over the government of his own country only to make a present of it to Hitler, and then, moving north, brought terror and oppression to the Netherlands. Von Neurath, the old-school diplomat who cast the pearls of his experience before the Nazis, guided Nazi diplomacy in the early years, soothed the fears of prospective victims, and, as Reich Protector of Bohemia and Moravia, strengthened the German position for the coming attack on Poland. Speer joined in planning and executing the program to dragoon prisoners of war and foreign workers into German war industries, which waxed in output while the laborers waned in starvation. Fritzsche, radio propaganda chief, by manipulation of the truth goaded German public opinion into frenzied support of the regime and anesthetized the independent judgment of the population so that they did without question their masters' bidding. And Bormann, who has not accepted our invitation to this reunion, sat at the throttle of the vast and powerful engine of the party, guiding it in the ruthless execution of Nazi politics, from the scourging of the Christian Church to the lynching of captive Allied airmen.

These men destroyed free government in Germany and now plead to be excused from responsibility because they became slaves. They are in the position of the fictional boy who murdered his father and mother and then pleaded for leniency because he was an orphan.

What these men have overlooked is that Adolf Hitler's acts are their acts. It was these men among millions of others, and it was these men leading millions of others, who built up Adolf Hitler and vested in his psychopathic personality not only innumerable lesser decisions but the supreme issue of war or peace. They intoxicated him with power and adulation. They fed his hate and aroused his fears. They put a loaded gun in his eager hands. It was left to Hitler to pull the trigger, and when he did they all at that time approved. His guilt stands admitted, by some defendants reluctantly, and some vindictively. But his guilt is the guilt of the whole dock, and of every man in it. . . .

No one lives who, at least until the very last moments of the war, outranked Göring in position, power, and influence. No soldier stood above Keitel and Jodl, and no sailor above Raeder and Dönitz. Who can be responsible for the diplomacy of duplicity if not the foreign ministers Von Neurath and Ribbentrop and the diplomatic handyman Von Papen? Who should be answerable for the oppressive administration of occupied countries if gauleiters, protectors, governors, and commissars such as Frank, Seyss-Inquart, Frick, Von Schirach, Von Neurath, and Rosenberg are not? Where shall we look for those who mobilized the economy for total war if we overlook Schacht and Speer and Funk? Who was the master of the great slaving enterprise if it was not Sauckel? Where shall we find the hand that ran the concentration camps if it was not the hand of Kaltenbrunner? And who whipped up the hate and fears of the public and manipulated the party organizations to incite these crimes if not Hess, Von Schirach, Fritzsche, Bormann, and the unspeakable Julius Streicher?

The defendants have been unanimous, when pressed, in shifting the blame on other men, sometimes on one and sometimes on another. . . . The chief villain on whom blame is placed—some of the defendants vie with each other in producing appropriate epithets—is Hitler. He is the man at whom nearly every defendant has pointed an accusing finger.

I shall not dissent from this consensus. It may well be said that Hitler's final crime was against the land he had ruled. He was a mad messiah who started the war without cause and prolonged it without reason. I admit that Hitler was the chief villain. But for the defendants to put all blame on him is neither manly nor true. Other legs must run his errands; other hands must execute his plans. On whom did Hitler rely on for such things more than upon these men in the dock?

The fact is that the Nazi habit of economizing in the use of truth pulls the foundations out from under their own defenses. Lying has always been a highly approved Nazi technique. Hitler, in *Mein Kampf,* advocated mendacity as a policy. Nor is the lie direct the only means of falsehood. They all speak with a Nazi doubletalk with which to deceive the unwary. In the Nazi dictionary of sardonic euphemisms "final solution" of the Jewish problem was a phrase which meant extermination; "special treatment" of prisoners of war meant killing; "protective custody" meant concentration camps. Rosenberg was stated by his counsel to have always had in mind a "chivalrous solution" to the Jewish problem. When it was necessary to remove Schuschnigg after the Anschluss, Ribbentrop would have had us believe that the Austrian chancellor was resting at a "villa." It was left to cross-examination to reveal that the "villa" was Buchenwald concentration camp. The record is full of other examples of dissimulations and evasions.

This was the philosophy of the National Socialists. It is against such a background that these defendants now ask this tribunal to say that they are not guilty of planning, executing, or conspiring to commit this long list of crimes and wrongs. They stand before the record of this trial as bloodstained Gloucester stood by the body of his slain king. He begged of the widow, as they beg of you, "Say I slew them not." And the queen replied, "Then say they were not slain. But dead they are." If you were to say of these men that they are not guilty, it would be as true to say that there has been no war, there are no slain, there has been no crime.

On October 1, 1946, the Nuremberg judges handed down their verdicts: "death by hanging" for Göring (who committed suicide before his execution), Hess, Keitel, Kaltenbrunner, Rosenberg, Frank, Frick, Sauckel, Jodl, and Seyss-Inquart; "imprisonment" for Funk (life), Dönitz (ten years), Raeder (life), Von Shirach (twenty years), Von Neurath (fifteen years), and Speer (twenty years); and "acquittal" for Schacht, Von Papen, and Fritzsche. Thirty-five years after the Nuremberg trials, the International Liberators Conference convened in Washington, D.C., bringing together Holocaust survivors, veterans, medical personnel, and others who were either confined in or helped liberate the Nazi camps. Dr. Hadassah Rosensaft, who became an American citizen, was imprisoned at Bergen-Belsen and related her memories of the day she was rescued.

My name is Hadassah Bimko Rosensaft. I am a Jew, born in Sosnowiec, Poland. My parents, my first husband, and my six-year-old son were gassed by the Germans in the extermination camp of Auschwitz-Birkenau. My entire family perished during the Holocaust, gassed by the Germans in Treblinka and Auschwitz. I was in Auschwitz-Birkenau more than a year, and thereafter I was in the concentration camp of Bergen-Belsen, where I was liberated by the British army on April, 15, 1945. . . .

I will never forget that day. It was Sunday, a very hot day. It was quiet. Nobody was to be seen outside the barracks. The camp seemed to have become abandoned almost like a cemetery. I was sitting with the children with whom I lived in the same barrack.

Suddenly we felt the tremors of the earth—something was moving—and then we heard the sound of rolling tanks. We were convinced that the Germans were about to blow up the camp. But then—it was three o'clock in the afternoon—we heard a loud voice say in German: "Hello, hello, you are free! We are British soldiers, and we came to liberate you!"

We ran out of the barracks and saw in the middle of the road a British army car with a loudspeaker on top going through the camp and repeating the same message over and over again. Within minutes, hundreds of women stopped the car, screaming, laughing, and crying with us. (The soldier was the late Captain Derek Sington.) It seemed a dream which soon turned into reality. How tragic it was that the great majority did not even realize that we were free, because they were unconscious or too sick to understand what was happening.

The British tanks rolled on in pursuit of the German army, and for one day the camp remained in the charge of a group of Hungarian SS guards who in this one day killed 72 Jews and 11 non-Jews. The British came back to us on April 17, this time to stay. They found 58,000 inmates, both men and women, 90 percent of whom were Jews. The vast majority were living skeletons. Most of them were too ill and too weak even to walk. Within the following eight weeks, 13,944 more died. In addition, there were more than 10,000 unburied corpses lying around the camp. The late Brigadier General H. L. Glyn Hughes, as the chief medical officer of the British Army of the Rhine, came to see the camp. I was asked to take him around. What he saw was a sea of crying, screaming bones. At the sight of the huts with their dead and near-dead, General Glyn Hughes, a medical officer hardened to human suffering, cried unashamedly. He decided on the spot to try to save as many sick as possible in spite of the conflicting needs of the military casualties for whom he was responsible.

Not far from the concentration camp were German army barracks, strong brick buildings with all necessary amenities. General Glyn Hughes decided to transform these barracks into a hospital for some 17,000 patients—the more desperately ill among the survivors. I was asked to help and was appointed administrator of the hospital for the survivors. I was honored and privileged to work with him and the other British medical personnel. My first task was to issue a call to the doctors and nurses among the survivors to come forward. Twenty-eight doctors and 590 female and 30 male nurses reported immediately. Not all the nurses were qualified, and most of them were extremely weak, but they all worked with great devotion. General Glyn Hughes said about them, and I quote, "I would like to pay a special tribute to those who, although inmates for a long period, had survived and retained their moral standards and sense of responsibility. By their unselfish devotion to others, they must themselves have saved countless lives. After the liberation, they continued their excellent work and were invaluable to the helpers who came in."

We started to work immediately. It took several weeks to evacuate the concentration camp. Once this process was completed, and all the survivors had been relocated in the former German military barracks, the British on May 21 burned down the barracks of the concentration camp in order to contain the spread of the epidemics. The burning down of the old camp also marked the beginning of regular medical attention for the sick of Belsen, instead of the emergency measures of the past month.

As far as our own feelings are concerned, it is hard for me to put them into words. At first, we paid our respects to the tens of thousands of our dead brothers and sisters for whom the help came too late and who were buried in mass grave after mass grave.

For the greatest part of the liberated Jews of Bergen-Belsen, there was no ecstasy, no joy at our liberation. We had lost our families, our homes. We had no place to go to, nobody to hug. Nobody was waiting for us anywhere. We had been liberated from death and the fear of death, but not from the fear of life.

The Holocaust also gave new urgency to Zionism, the movement to create a Jewish homeland in Palestine, where Jews and Arabs had been coexisting since 1922 under British rule. In 1947 the British government resolved to remove itself from the growing hostilities in Palestine and referred the debate to the United Nations. Dr. Abba Hillel Silver, an eastern European Jew by birth, served as the president of the Zionist Organization of America and was called upon to argue the Zionist case before the UN General Assembly and its Committee of Inquiry. In an impassioned speech on May 8, 1947, Dr. Silver implored the Assembly to visit Palestine and understand firsthand how imperative it was for Jews to be given the opportunity to establish a new homeland— something they had not had since the destruction of the Second Temple in 70 A.D.

I believe that the Committee of Inquiry should most certainly visit Palestine. Written documents are important, but infinitely more instructive are the living documents, the visible testimony of creative effort and achievement. In Palestine they will see what the Jewish people, inspired by the hope of reconstituting their national home after the long, weary centuries of their homelessness, and relying upon the honor and the pledged word of the world community, have achieved in a few short years against great odds and seemingly insurmountable physical handicaps. The task was enormous: untrained hands, inadequate means, overwhelming difficulties. The land was stripped and poor, neglected through the centuries. And the period of building took place between two disastrous world wars when European Jewry was shattered and impoverished. Nevertheless, the record of pioneering achievement of the Jewish people in Palestine has received the acclaim of the entire world. And what was built there with social vision and high human idealism has proved a blessing, we believe, not only to the Jews of Palestine, but to the Arabs and other non-Jewish communities as well.

That the return of the Jews to Palestine would prove a blessing not only to themselves but also to their Arab neighbors was envisaged by the Emir Feisal, who was a great leader of the Arab peoples at the Peace Conference following the First World War. On March 3, 1919, he wrote:

"We Arabs . . . look with deepest sympathy on the Zionist movement. Our deputation here in Paris is fully acquainted with the proposals submitted yesterday by the Zionist Organization to the Peace Conference, and we regard them as moderate and proper. We will do our best, insofar as we are concerned, to help them through. We will wish the Jews a most hearty welcome home. . . . I look forward, and my people with me look forward, to a future in which we will help you and you will help us, so that the countries in which we are mutually interested may once again take their places in the community of civilized peoples of the world."

Your Committee of Inquiry will conclude, we are confident, that if allowed to develop uninterruptedly, the standards of life which are being developed in Palestine, the concepts of social justice, and the modern scientific methods will serve as a great stimulus to the rebirth and progress of the entire Near East with which Palestine and the destinies of the Jewish national home are naturally bound up.

Your Committee of Inquiry should also consider the potentialities of the country which, if properly developed, can, according to the expert testimony of those most qualified to speak on the subject, sustain a population much greater than the present one. Many more projects, which will result in great economic and social improvement not alone in Palestine but in all the neighboring countries, are awaiting development pending a satisfactory political solution.

Your Committee of Inquiry should, while in Palestine, also look into the real—the fundamental—causes of the tragic unrest and violence which today mar the life of the holy land to which our Jewish pioneers came not with weapons, but with tools. They will inquire, I am sure, why a peace-loving community whose sole interest was in building a peaceful home and future for themselves and their children is being driven to a pitch of resentment and tension and lamentably driving some of its members to actions which we all deplore. They will ask themselves, I am sure, why shiploads of helpless Jewish refugees, men and women and children, who have been through all the hells of Nazi Europe, are being driven away from the shores of the Jewish national home by a mandatory government which assumed as its prime obligations the facilitation of Jewish immigration into that country. They will also investigate, I hope, how the mandatory government is carrying out another of its obligations, which is to encourage close settlement of the Jews on the land. In actual practice it is today severely restricting free Jewish settlement to an area less than 6 percent of that tiny country and is enforcing today in the Jewish national home discriminatory racial laws which the mandate, as well as the charter of the United Nations, severely condemns. . . .

We hope most earnestly that the Committee of Inquiry will also visit the displaced person camps in Europe and see with their own eyes the appalling human tragedy which mankind is permitting to continue unabated two years—it is exactly two years today since V-E Day—after the close of a war in which the Jewish people were the greatest sufferers. While committees of investigation and study are reporting on their sad plight, and while intergovernmental discussions and negotiations are going on, these war-ravaged men and women are languishing in their misery, still waiting for salvation. They ask for the bread of escape and hope. They are given the stone of inquiries and investigations. Their morale is slumping terribly. A spiritual deterioration, I am afraid, is setting in among them. It is only the hope that tomorrow—perhaps tomorrow—redemption may come that keeps their spirits from breaking utterly.

Most of them are desperately eager to go to the Jewish national home. I hope that the conscience of mankind, speaking through you and through your Committee of Inquiry, will make it possible for these weary men and women to find peace at last and healing in the land of their fondest hopes, and that their liberation will not be delayed until the report of the committee is finally made and the action of the assembly is finally taken but that, pending ultimate decisions and implementations, these unfortunate people will be permitted forthwith to migrate in substantial numbers to Palestine. . . .

I hope, Mr. Chairman, that I have not abused your patience and the patience of the representatives of the United Nations here assembled. Permit me to conclude with this observation: The Jewish people place great hope upon the outcome of the deliberations of this great body. They have faith in its collective sense of justice and fairness and in the high ideals which inspire it. We are an ancient people, and though we have often, on the long, hard road which we have traveled, been disillusioned, we have never been disheartened. We have never lost faith in the sovereignty and the ultimate triumph of great moral principles. In these last tragic years when the whole household of Israel became one great hostelry of pain, we could not have built what we did build had we not preserved our unshakable trust in the victory of truth. It is in that strong faith and hope that we wish to cooperate with you in this task which you have undertaken.

The Jewish people belong in this society of nations. Surely the Jewish people are no less deserving than other people whose national freedom and independence have been established and whose representatives are now seated here. The Jewish people were your allies in the war and joined their sacrifices to yours to achieve a common victory. The representatives of the Jewish people of Palestine should sit in your midst—the representatives of the people and of the land which gave to mankind spiritual and ethical values, inspiring human personalities, and sacred texts which are your treasured possessions. We hope that people, now again rebuilding its national life in its ancient homeland, will be welcomed before long by you to this noble fellowship of the United Nations.

In May 1948, Britain terminated its mandate to rule Palestine, and Jews announced that the land was now the republic of Israel. In Washington, President Truman's national security advisers strenuously discouraged the president from officially recognizing Israel, fearing it would alienate Arab nations and their vast resources of oil. But Truman, acting out of humanitarian and political impulses, formally recognized Israel on May 14.

Secretary of State George Marshall Announces a Plan to Save War-Ravaged Europe from Descending Into "Chaos."

In the spring of 1947, Winston Churchill grieved over the condition of postwar Europe, which he described as "a rubble-heap, a charnel house, a breeding ground of pestilence and hate." Major cities remained in shambles, both physically and economically. Food shortages were rampant. Diseases such as tuberculosis ravaged the population. President Truman warned of the inherent dangers of the situation: "The seeds of totalitarian regimes are nurtured by misery and want. They spread and grow in the evil soil of poverty and strife." After an extensive tour of Europe, the U.S. assistant secretary of state for economic affairs, Will Clayton, was emotionally overwhelmed by the suffering he saw firsthand and drafted an urgent memo to Assistant Secretary of State Dean Acheson detailing the immediate need for relief. With the blessing of President Truman, Acheson and his boss, the newly appointed Secretary of State George Marshall, initiated an enormously far-reaching and expensive plan to aid Europe. Acheson presented the first public outlines of the effort in a speech on May 8, 1947, but it went almost entirely unnoticed. It was not until Secretary of State Marshall himself announced the plan at Harvard's commencement on June 5 that it gained attention.

I need not tell you gentlemen that the world situation is very serious. That must be apparent to all intelligent people. I think one difficulty is that the problem is one of such enormous complexity that the very mass of facts presented to the public by press and radio make it exceedingly difficult for the man in the street to reach a clear appraisement of the situation. Furthermore, the people of this country are distant from the troubled areas of the earth, and it is hard for them to comprehend the plight and consequent reactions of the long-suffering peoples, and the effect of those reactions on their governments in connection with our efforts to promote peace in the world.

In considering the requirements for the rehabilitation of Europe, the physical loss of life, the visible destruction of cities, factories, mines, and railroads was correctly estimated, but it has become obvious during recent months that this visible destruction was probably less serious than the dislocation of the entire fabric of the European economy. For the past ten years conditions have been highly abnormal. The feverish preparation for war and the more feverish maintenance of the war effort engulfed all aspects of national economies. Machinery has fallen into disrepair or is entirely obsolete. Under the arbitrary and destructive Nazi rule, virtually every possible enterprise was geared into the German war machine. Long-standing commercial ties, private institutions, banks, insurance companies, and shipping companies disappeared through loss of capital, absorption through nationalization, or by simple destruction. In many countries, confidence in the local currency has been severely shaken. The breakdown of the business structure of Europe during the war was complete. Recovery has been seriously retarded by the fact that two years after the close of hostilities a peace settlement with Germany and Austria has not been agreed upon. But even given a more prompt solution of these difficult problems, the rehabilitation of the economic structure of Europe quite evidently will require a much longer time and greater effort than had been foreseen.

There is a phase of this matter which is both interesting and serious. The farmer has always produced the foodstuffs to exchange with the city dweller for the other necessities of life. This division of labor is the basis of modern civilization. At the present time, it is threatened with breakdown. The town and city industries are not producing adequate goods to exchange with the food-producing farmer. Raw materials and fuel are in short supply. Machinery is lacking or worn out. The farmer or the peasant cannot find the goods for sale which he desires to purchase. So the sale of his farm produce for money which he cannot use seems to him an unprofitable transaction. He therefore has withdrawn many fields from crop cultivation and is using them for grazing. He feeds more grain to stock and finds for himself and his family an ample supply of food, however short he may be on clothing and the other ordinary gadgets of civilization. Meanwhile, people in the cities are short of food and fuel. So the governments are forced to use their foreign money and credits to procure these necessities abroad. This process exhausts funds which are urgently needed for reconstruction.

The truth of the matter is that Europe's requirements for the next three or four years of foreign food and other essential products—principally from America—are so much greater than her present ability to pay that she must have substantial additional help or face economic, social, and political deterioration of a very grave character.

The remedy lies in breaking the vicious circle and restoring the confidence of the European people in the economic future of their own countries and of Europe as a whole. The manufacturer and the farmer throughout wide areas must be able and willing to exchange their products for currencies the continuing value of which is not open to question.

Aside from the demoralizing effect on the world at large and the possibilities of disturbances arising as a result of the desperation of the people concerned, the consequences to the economy of the United States should be apparent to all. It is logical that the United States should do whatever it is able to do to assist in the return of normal economic health in the world, without which there can be no political stability and no assured peace. Our policy is directed not against any country or doctrine but against hunger, poverty, desperation, and chaos. Its purpose should be the revival of a working economy in the world so as to permit the emergence of political and social conditions in which free institutions can exist. Such assistance, I am convinced, must not be on a piecemeal basis as various crises develop. Any assistance that this government may render in the future should provide a cure rather than a mere palliative. Any government that is willing to assist in the task of recovery will find full cooperation, I am sure, on the part of the United States government. Any government which maneuvers to block the recovery of other countries cannot expect help from us. Furthermore, governments, political parties, or groups which seek to perpetuate human misery in order to profit therefrom politically or otherwise will encounter the opposition of the United States.

It is already evident that, before the United States government can proceed much further in its efforts to alleviate the situation and help start the European world on its way to recovery, there must be some arrangement among the countries of Europe as to the requirements of the situation and the part those countries themselves will take in order to give proper effect to whatever action might be undertaken by this government. It would be neither fitting nor efficacious for this government to undertake to draw up unilaterally a program designed to place Europe on its feet economically. This is the business of Europeans. The initiative, I think, must come from Europe. The role of this country should consist of friendly aid in the drafting of a European program and of later support of such a program so far as it may be practical for us to do so. The program should be a joint one, agreed to by a number if not all European nations.

An essential part of any successful action on the part of the United States is an understanding on the part of the people of America of the character of the problem and the remedies to be applied. Political passion and prejudice should have no part. With foresight and a willingness on the part of our people to face up to the vast responsibility which history has clearly placed upon our country, the difficulties I have outlined can and will be overcome.

Although formally titled the European Recovery Program, it became known as the Marshall Plan and was considered by many Americans and the vast majority of Europeans to be the greatest act of humanitarian aid ever implemented. The Soviet Union (which Marshall had invited to assist with the plan's creation) viewed it as "economic imperialism," however, and refused to participate, further deepening the tensions between the world's two superpowers. Marshall received the Nobel Prize for peace in 1953 for his efforts.

World-Renowned Performer Paul Robeson Adamantly Defends His Love for the Soviet Union and Its Government & Major-League Baseball Player Jackie Robinson Appears Before the House Un-American Activities Committee to Comment on Robeson's Remarks.

Scholar, athlete, and internationally renowned performer Paul Robeson was arguably the most famous African American of the 1930s and 1940s. A Phi Beta Kappa graduate and football star of Rutgers University in 1919, Robeson went on to Columbia University Law School in New York, where he began acting in community theaters. He soon found himself on Broadway and, with no formal training, became a celebrated actor and bass singer. Robeson's meteoric career suddenly began to plunge, however, when he expressed pro-communist sentiments. The first of eight children born into a lower-class family, Robeson sympathized with the plight of working people everywhere, and he believed the Soviet Union had created a social and political system superior to America's. Criticism of Robeson turned to sheer hatred and harassment when, at the Paris Peace Conference of 1949, he purportedly stated that, should the United States and the Soviet Union ever go to war, it was "inconceivable that American Negroes would fight with those who have oppressed them for generations against the Soviet Union, which, in a generation, has raised them to a position of equality." (Robeson later said the statement was taken out of context.) After being reported in the United States, the remarks sparked a national boycott against Robeson, and violence erupted at two of his concerts. Not all of Robeson's fans turned on him, however, and many organized a welcome-home rally for him in New York City on June 19, 1949. Robeson used the opportunity to discuss his travels abroad and express once again his love for the Soviet Union.

My last weeks abroad were spent in these countries to the east, Czechoslovakia, Poland, and finally the Soviet Union. Here thousands of people—men, women, children—cried to me to thank progressive America for sending one of its representatives, begged me so to take back their love, their heartfelt understanding of the suffering of their Negro brothers and sisters, that I wept time and time again. Whole nations of people gave me a welcome I can never forget—a welcome not for me, Paul Robeson, but in your name, the name of the Negro people of America, of the colonies, in the name of the progressive America of Wallace and the Progressive Party, and in the name of the twelve Communist leaders. Outstanding people in the government treated me with the greatest respect and dignity because I represented you, but there were no calls from the American embassies.

Here in these countries are the people. Their spokesmen are in the forefront of our struggle for liberation—on the floor of the United Nations, in the highest councils of world diplomacy. Here in the Soviet Union, in Czechoslovakia, in battered but gallant Warsaw with its brave saga of the ghetto are the nations leading the battle for peace and freedom. They were busy building, reconstructing, and the very mention of war caused one to look at you as if you were insane.

I was in Stalingrad. I saw a letter from President Roosevelt—no equivocation here. It said that in Stalingrad came the turning point in the battle for civilization. I stood in the little rectangle where the heroic people of Stalingrad fought with their backs to the mighty Volga and saved us—saved you and me—from Hitler's wrath. We loved them then. What has happened to us? For they are the same, only braver. 'Midst their ruins, they sing and laugh and dance. Their factories are restored 50 percent above prewar. I sang at their tractor factory and saw a tractor—not a tank—coming off the line every fifteen minutes. It was a factory built by Soviet hands, Soviet brains, Soviet know-how.

They want peace and an abundant life. Freedom is already theirs. The children cried, "Take back our love to the Negro children and the working-class children." And they clasped and embraced me literally and symbolically for you. I love them.

Here is a whole one-sixth of the earth's surface, including millions of brown, yellow, and black people who would be Negroes in America and subject to the same awful race prejudice that haunts us. In this Soviet Union, the very term *backward country* is an insult, for in one generation former colonial peoples have been raised to unbelievable industrial and social levels. It is indeed a vast new concept of democracy. And these achievements make completely absurd the solemn pronouncements that it will take several generations, maybe hundreds of years, before we Negro people in the West Indies, Africa, and America can have any real control over our own destiny.

Here is a white nation which is now doing honor to our poet Pushkin, one of the greatest poets in history, the Soviet people's and our proud world possession. Could I find a monument to Pushkin in a public square of Birmingham or Atlanta or Memphis, as one stands in the center of Moscow? No. One perhaps to Goethe, but not to the dark-skinned Pushkin.

Yes, I love this Soviet people more than any other nation, because of their suffering and sacrifices for us, the Negro people, the progressive people, the people of the future in this world.

At the Paris Peace Conference, I said it was unthinkable that the Negro people of America or elsewhere in the world could be drawn into war with the Soviet Union. I repeat it with a hundredfold emphasis. They will not.

And don't ask a few intellectuals who are jealous of their comfort. Ask the sugar workers whom I saw starving in Louisiana, the workers in the cotton lands and the tobacco belts in the South. Ask the sugar workers in Jamaica. Ask the Africans in Malan's South Africa. Ask them if they will struggle for peace and friendship with the Soviet people, with the peoples of China and the new democracies, or if they will help their imperialist oppressors to return them to an even worse slavery. The answer lies there in the millions of my struggling people, not only the 14 million in America, but the 40 million in the Caribbean and Latin America and the 150 million in Africa. No wonder all the excitement! For one day this mighty mass will strike for freedom, and a new strength like that of gallant China will add its decisive weight to insuring a world where all men can be free and equal.

I am born and bred in the America of ours. I want to love it. I love a part of it. But it's up to the rest of America when I shall love it with the same intensity that I love the Negro people from whom I spring, in the way that I love progressives in the Caribbean, the black and Indian peoples of South and Central America, the peoples of China and Southeast Asia—yes, suffering people the world over—and in the way that I deeply and intensely love the Soviet Union. That burden of proof rests upon America.

Now these peoples of the Soviet Union, of the new eastern democracies, of progressive western Europe, and the representatives of the Chinese people whom I met in Prague and Moscow, were in great part communists. They were the first to die for our freedom and for the freedom of all mankind. So I'm not afraid of communists. No, far from that. I will defend them as they defended us, the Negro people. And I stand firm and immovable by the side of that great leader who has given his whole life to the struggle of the American working class. . . . Their struggle is our struggle.

But to fulfill our responsibilities as Americans, we must unite, especially we Negro people. We must know our strength. We are the decisive force. That's why they terrorize us. That's why they fear us. And if we unite in all our might, this world can fast be changed. Let us create that unity now. And this important, historic role of the Negro people our white allies here must fully comprehend. This means increasing understanding of the Negro, his tremendous struggle, his great contributions, his potential for leadership at all levels in the common task of liberation. It means courage to stand by our side whatever the consequences, as we the Negro people fulfill our historic duty in freedom's struggle.

If we unite, we'll get our law against lynching, our right to vote and to labor. Let us march on Washington, representing 14 million strong. Let us push aside the sycophants who tell us to be quiet.

The so-called western democracies—including our own, which so fiercely exploits us and daily denies us our simple constitutional guarantees— can find no answer before the bar of world justice for their treatment of the Negro people. Democracy indeed! We must have the courage to shout at the top of our voices about our injustices and we must lay the blame where it belongs and where it has belonged for over three hundred years of slavery and misery: right here on our own doorstep, not in any far away place. This is the very time when we can win our struggle.

And we cannot win it by being lured into any kind of war with our closest friends and allies throughout the world. For any kind of decent life, we need, we want, and we demand our constitutional rights right here in America. We do not want to die in vain any more on foreign battlefields for Wall Street and the greedy supporters of domestic fascism. If we must die, let it be in Mississippi or Georgia! Let it be wherever we are lynched and deprived of our rights as human beings!

Let this be a final answer to the warmongers. Let them know that we will not help to enslave our brothers and sisters and eventually ourselves. Rather, we will help to insure peace in our time, the freedom and liberation of the Negro and other struggling peoples, and the building of a world where we can all walk in full equality and full human dignity.

Theater houses and concert halls soon closed their doors to Robeson, libraries banned his books, and radio stations refused to play his records, which counted in the hundreds. Robeson's comments also entangled another of America's great African American heroes, Jackie Robinson, in the controversy. Major-league baseball was segregated until Robinson broke the color barrier and joined the Brooklyn Dodgers in 1947. Although hate mail and taunts from fans were a common occurrence, many Americans admired Robinson for his talent and his courage. After Robeson's pro-communist remarks in Paris, Robinson was asked to appear before the House Un-American Activities Committee to attest to the loyalty of all black Americans. Although he was privately disgusted by the nature of the request, Robinson believed he could respond in a way that would both defuse mounting racial tensions over the issue and satisfy the committee, as well as his own conscience. On July 18, 1949, Robinson made the following statement.

I've been asked to express my views on Paul Robeson's statement in Paris to the effect that American Negroes would refuse to fight in any war against

Russia because we love Russia so much. I haven't any comment to make except that the statement, if Mr. Robeson actually made it, sounds very silly to me. But he has a right to his personal views, and if he wants to sound silly when he expresses them in public, that's his business and not mine. He's still a famous ex-athlete and a great singer and actor.

I understand that there are some few Negroes who are members of the Communist Party, and in event of war with Russia, they would probably act just as any other Communists would. So would members of other minority and majority groups. There are some colored pacifists, and they'd act just like pacifists of any color. And most Negroes—and Italians and Irish and Jews and Swedes and Slavs and other Americans—would act just as all these groups did in the last war: They'd do their best to help their country stay out of war. If unsuccessful, they'd do their best to help their country win the war—against Russia or any other enemy that threatened us.

This isn't said as any defense of the Negro's loyalty, because any loyalty that needs defense can't amount to much in the long run. And no one has ever questioned my race's loyalty except a few people who don't amount to very much.

What I'm trying to get across is that the American public is off on the wrong foot when it begins to think of radicalism in terms of any special minority group. It is thinking of this sort that gets people scared because one Negro speaking to a communist group in Paris threatens an organized boycott by fifteen million members of his race.

I can't speak for any fifteen million people more than any other one person can, but I know that I've got too much invested for my wife and child and myself in the future of this country, and I and other Americans of many races and faiths have too much invested in our country's welfare for any of us to throw it away because of a siren song sung in bass.

I am a religious man. Therefore I cherish America, where I am free to worship as I please, a privilege which some countries do not give. And I suspect that 999 out of almost any thousand colored Americans you meet will tell you the same thing.

At a news conference in New York on July 20, Paul Robeson was asked to respond to Jackie Robinson's comments. "I am not going to permit the issue to boil down to a personal feud between myself and Jackie," Robeson replied. "To do that would be to do exactly what the other group wants us to do." Robeson then added, "The committee's efforts to make the loyalty of the Negro people an issue is an insult. How do they dare question our loyalty? I challenge the loyalty of the Un-American Activities Committee." It was a challenge that many Americans, both black and white, would become particularly concerned with in the decade to come.

1950–1959

WE ARE CURRENTLY WEALTHY, FAT, COMFORTABLE, AND COM-
placent. We have currently a built-in allergy to unpleasant or
disturbing information. Our mass media reflect this. But unless we get
off our fat surpluses and recognize that television in the main is being
used to distract, delude, amuse, and insulate us, then television and
those who finance it, those who look at it, and those who work at it
may see a totally different picture too late.

I do not advocate that we turn television into a twenty-seven-
inch wailing wall, where longhairs constantly moan about the state of
our culture and our defense. But I would like to see it reflect occasionally the hard, unyielding realities of the world in which we live. . . .

This instrument can teach, it can illuminate—yes, it can even inspire. But it can do so only to the extent that humans are determined
to use it to those ends. Otherwise it is merely wires and lights in a box.
There is a great and perhaps decisive battle to be fought against ignorance, intolerance, and indifference. This weapon of television could be
useful.

Stonewall Jackson, who knew something about the use of
weapons, is reported to have said, "When war comes, you must draw
the sword and throw away the scabbard." The trouble with television
is that it is rusting in the scabbard during a battle for survival.

—*Broadcaster Edward R. Murrow,*
speaking before the Radio and Television News Directors Association in
Chicago,
October 15, 1958

Senator Joseph McCarthy Launches a "Final, All–Out Battle" Against Communist Sympathizers in the United States
&
Senator Margaret Chase Smith Warns Against Those Who Use "Fear, Ignorance, Bigotry, and Smear [Tactics]" for Political Gain.

In August 1948 a magazine editor named Whittaker Chambers accused Alger Hiss, a former high-level U.S. State Department official, of spying for the Soviet Union. (Hiss emphatically denied the charges and, after being vilified by a young congressman named Richard M. Nixon, became a hero to the left.) In September 1949 the Soviets tested their first atomic bomb, bringing a sudden end to America's four-year nuclear monopoly. And in October 1949 the world's most populated country, China, declared itself a communist nation. Event after event fueled the fires of anti-communism in America until, by the beginning of the 1950s, it had become a blaze of fear and suspicion. Few politicians capitalized on this anxiety more effectively than a little-known Republican senator from Wisconsin named Joseph McCarthy. McCarthy's most infamous statement came during an address to a women's group in Wheeling, West Virginia, where he announced that he had in his possession a list of 205—later he would claim the number was only 57—names of communist subversives in the U.S. government (he never released the list). The speech, which was given on February 9, 1950, was ostensibly to honor the memory of Abraham Lincoln. But this was merely a pretext for a series of accusations that would launch one of the darkest periods in twentieth-century American politics.

Today we are engaged in a final, all-out battle between communistic atheism and Christianity. The modern champions of communism have selected this as the time. And, ladies and gentlemen, the chips are down. They are truly down.

Lest there be any doubt that the time has been chosen, let us go directly to the leader of communism today, Joseph Stalin. Here is what he said, not back in 1928, not before the war, not during the war, but two years after the last war was ended: "To think that the communist revolution can be carried out peacefully, within the framework of a Christian democracy, means one has either gone out of one's mind and lost all normal understanding, or has grossly and openly repudiated the communist revolution."

Ladies and gentlemen, can there be anyone here tonight who is so blind as to say that the war is not on? Can there be anyone who fails to realize that the communist world has said, "The time is now," that this is the time for the showdown between the democratic Christian world and the communist atheistic world?

Unless we face this fact, we shall pay the price that must be paid by those who wait too long.

Six years ago, at the time of the first conference to map out the peace—Dumbarton Oaks—there was within the Soviet orbit 180 million people. Lined up on the anti-totalitarian side there were in the world at that time roughly 1.625 billion people. Today, only six years later, there are 800 million people under the absolute domination of Soviet Russia, an increase of over 400 percent. On our side, the figure has shrunk to around 500 million. In other words, in less than six years the odds have changed from 9 to 1 in our favor to 8 to 5 against us. This indicates the swiftness of the tempo of communist victories and American defeats in the Cold War. As one of our outstanding historical figures once said, "When a great democracy is destroyed, it will not be because of enemies from without, but rather because of enemies from within."

The truth of this statement is becoming terrifyingly clear as we see this country each day losing on every front.

At war's end we were physically the strongest nation on earth and, at least potentially, the most powerful intellectually and morally. Ours could have been the honor of being a beacon in the desert of destruction, a shining living proof that civilization was not yet ready to destroy itself. Unfortunately, we have failed miserably and tragically to rise to that opportunity.

The reason why we find ourselves in a position of impotency is not because our only powerful potential enemy has sent men to invade our shores, but rather because of the traitorous actions of those who have been treated so well by this nation. It has not been the less fortunate or members of minority groups who have been selling this nation out, but rather those who have had all the benefits that the wealthiest nation on earth has had to offer—the finest homes, the finest college education, and the finest jobs in government we can give.

This is glaringly true in the State Department. There the bright young men who are born with silver spoons in their mouths are the ones who have been worst. . . . In my opinion the State Department, which is one of the most important government departments, is thoroughly infested with communists.

I have here in my hand a list of 205—a list of names that were made known to the secretary of state as being members of the Communist Party and who nevertheless are still working and shaping policy in the State Department.

One thing to remember in discussing the communists in our government is that we are not dealing with spies who get thirty pieces of silver to steal the blueprints of a new weapon. We are dealing with a far more sinister type of activity because it permits the enemy to guide and shape our policy. . . .

This brings us to the case of one Alger Hiss, who is important not as an individual anymore, but rather because he is so representative of a group in the State Department. It is unnecessary to go over the sordid events showing how he sold out the nation which had given him so much. Those are rather fresh in all of our minds.

However, it should be remembered that the facts in regard to his connection with this international communist spy ring were made known to the then Under Secretary of State Berle three days after Hitler and Stalin signed the Russo-German alliance pact. At that time one Whittaker Chambers, who was also part of the spy ring, apparently decided that with Russia on Hitler's side, he could no longer betray our nation to Russia. He gave Under Secretary of State Berle—and this is all a matter of record—practically all, if not more, of the facts upon which Hiss's conviction was based. . . .

As you hear this story of high treason, I know that you are saying to yourself, "Well, why doesn't the Congress do something about it?" Actually, ladies and gentlemen, one of the important reasons for the graft, the corruption, the dishonesty, the disloyalty, the treason in high government positions—one of the most important reasons why this continues is a lack of moral uprising on the part of the 140 million American people. In the light of history, however, this is not hard to explain.

It is the result of an emotional hangover and a temporary moral lapse which follows every war. It is the apathy to evil which people who have been subjected to the tremendous evils of war feel. As the people of the world see mass murder, the destruction of defenseless and innocent people, and all of the crime and lack of morals which go with war, they become numb and apathetic. It has always been thus after war.

However, the morals of our people have not been destroyed. They still exist. This cloak of numbness and apathy has only needed a spark to rekindle them. Happily, this spark has finally been supplied.

As you know, very recently the secretary of state proclaimed his loyalty to a man guilty of what has always been considered as the most abominable of all crimes—of being a traitor to the people who gave him a position of great trust. The secretary of state, in attempting to justify his continued devotion to the man who sold out the Christian world to the atheistic world, referred to Christ's Sermon on the Mount as a justification and reason therefore, and the reaction of the American people to this would have made the heart of Abraham Lincoln happy. When this pompous diplomat in striped pants, with a phony British accent, proclaimed to the American people that Christ on the Mount endorsed communism, high treason, and betrayal of a sacred trust, the blasphemy was so great that it awakened the dormant indignation of the American people.

He has lighted the spark which is resulting in a moral uprising and will end only when the whole sorry mess of twisted, warped thinkers are swept from the national scene so that we may have a new birth of national honesty and decency in government.

The allegations shocked the country and elevated McCarthy to a position of enormous power and prestige. Few dared to challenge him lest they too be labeled communist sympathizers. But one representative—America's only female senator, in fact—Margaret Chase Smith, stood before her colleagues on June 1, 1950, and requested a "declaration of conscience" affirming the principles on which the Constitution was founded and castigating those who sullied them through "irresponsible sensationalism."

Mr. President, I would like to speak briefly and simply about a serious national condition. It is a national feeling of fear and frustration that could result in national suicide and the end of everything that we Americans hold dear. It is a condition that comes from the lack of effective leadership either in the legislative branch or the executive branch of our government. . . .

Mr. President, I speak as a Republican. I speak as a woman. I speak as a United States senator. I speak as an American.

The United States Senate has long enjoyed worldwide respect as the greatest deliberative body in the world. But recently that deliberative character has too often been debased to the level of a forum of hate and character assassination sheltered by the shield of congressional immunity.

It is ironical that we senators can in debate in the Senate, directly or indirectly, by any form of words, impute to any American who is not a senator any conduct or motive unworthy or unbecoming an American—and without that non-senator American having any legal redress against us—yet if we say the same thing in the Senate about our colleagues, we can be stopped on the grounds of being out of order. . . .

I think that it is high time for the United States Senate and its members to do some real soul searching and to weigh our consciences as to the manner in which we are performing our duty to the people of America and the manner in which we are using or abusing our individual powers and privileges. I think that it is high time that we remembered that we have sworn to uphold and defend the Constitution. I think that it is high time that we remembered that the Constitution, as amended, speaks not only of the freedom of speech but also of trial by jury instead of trial by accusation. Whether it be a criminal prosecution in court or a character prosecution in the Senate, there is little practical distinction when the life of a person has been ruined.

Those of us who shout the loudest about Americanism in making character assassinations are all too frequently those who, by our own words and acts, ignore some of the basic principles of Americanism: the right to criticize, the right to hold unpopular beliefs, the right to protest, the right of independent thought. The exercise of these rights should not cost one single American citizen his reputation or his right to a livelihood, nor should he be in danger of losing his reputation or livelihood merely because he happens to know someone who holds unpopular beliefs. Who of us does not? Otherwise none of us could call our souls our own. Otherwise thought control would have set in.

The American people are sick and tired of being afraid to speak their minds lest they be politically smeared as communists or fascists by their opponents. Freedom of speech is not what it used to be in America. It has been so abused by some that it is not exercised by others.

The American people are sick and tired of seeing innocent people smeared and guilty people whitewashed. But there have been enough proved cases—such as the Amerasia case, the Hiss case, the Coplon case, the Gold case—to cause nationwide distrust and strong suspicion that there may be something to the unproved, sensational accusations.

As a Republican, I say to my colleagues on this side of the aisle that the Republican Party faces a challenge today that is not unlike the challenge which it faced back in Lincoln's day. The Republican Party so successfully met that challenge that it emerged from the Civil War as the champion of a united nation, in addition to being a party which unrelentingly fought loose spending and loose programs.

Today our country is being psychologically divided by the confusion and the suspicions that are bred in the United States Senate to spread like cancerous tentacles of "know nothing, suspect everything" attitudes. Today we have a Democratic administration that has developed a mania for loose spending and loose programs. History is repeating itself, and the Republican Party again has the opportunity to emerge as the champion of unity and prudence.

The record of the present Democratic administration has provided us with sufficient campaign issues without the necessity of resorting to political smears. America is rapidly losing its position as leader of the world simply because the Democratic administration has pitifully failed to provide effective leadership. . . .

The nation sorely needs a Republican victory. But I do not want to see the Republican Party ride to political victory on the Four Horsemen of Calumny—Fear, Ignorance, Bigotry, and Smear. I doubt if the Republican Party could do so, simply because I do not believe the American people will uphold any political party that puts political exploitation above the national interest. Surely we Republicans are not that desperate for victory. I do not want to see the Republican Party win that way. While it might be a fleeting victory for the Republican Party, it would be a more lasting defeat for the American people. Surely it would ultimately be suicide for the Republican Party and the two-party system that has protected our American liberties from the dictatorship of a one-party system.

As members of the minority party, we do not have the primary authority to formulate the policy of our government. But we do have the responsibility of rendering constructive criticism, of clarifying issues, of allaying fears by acting as responsible citizens. As a woman, I wonder how the mothers, wives, sisters, and daughters feel about the way in which members of their families have been politically mangled in Senate debate—and I use the word *debate* advisedly. As a United States senator, I am not proud of the way in which the Senate has been made a publicity platform for irresponsible sensationalism. I am not proud of the reckless abandon in which unproved charges have been hurled from this side of the aisle. I am not proud of the obviously staged, undignified countercharges which have been attempted in retaliation from the other side of the aisle. . . .

As an American, I am shocked at the way Republicans and Democrats alike are playing directly into the communist design of "confuse, divide, and conquer." As an American, I do not want a Democratic administration whitewash or cover-up any more than I want a Republican smear or witch hunt.

As an American, I condemn a Republican fascist just as much as I condemn a Democrat communist. I condemn a Democrat fascist just as much as I condemn a Republican communist. They are equally dangerous to you and me and to our country. As an American, I want to see our nation recapture the strength and unity it once had when we fought the enemy instead of ourselves.

As the nation's anxieties over Communism heightened, particularly after the 1950 invasion of South Korea by North Korea's communist troops and the 1951 trial and eventual execution of Julius and Ethel Rosenberg, whom the American left defended (like Alger Hiss), McCarthy's popularity and influence surged. In 1953 he was made chairman of the Permanent Subcommittee on Investigations, which bullied Americans, both famous and unknown, into answering a series of hostile questions, including: "Are you now or have you ever been a member of the Communist Party?" Many who testified before the committee saw their careers destroyed (some even committed suicide as a result), and those who refused to appear were blacklisted and imprisoned. McCarthy finally met his match in Joseph Welch, chief counsel for the U.S. Army, who excoriated the senator as a man with "no sense of decency." A television broadcast by the esteemed newsman Edward R. Murrow on McCarthy and his tactics proved damning as well. McCarthy's reputation plunged in the months to come, and the Senate censured him in December 1954. Decades after McCarthy's death from alcohol-related illnesses in

1957, the collapse of the Soviet Union would exonerate those, like McCarthy, who accused Alger Hiss and Julius Rosenberg of being spies. Soviet intelligence files, now open to scholars, confirmed their guilt as communist agents. But even those who aided McCarthy later recognized there was no excuse for his scorched-earth policy. "I was all for kicking communists out of Hollywood," confessed a famous actor who had informed on his fellow artists in the 1950s for the FBI, "but some members of [McCarthy's committee], ignoring standards of truth and fair play, ganged up on innocent people." The actor, commenting in 1990, was Ronald Reagan.

Nobel Laureate William Faulkner Expresses His Heartfelt Belief That "Man Will Not Merely Endure: He Will Prevail."

When William Faulkner first received word that he had won the Nobel Prize for literature, the most prestigious literary award in the world, he gratefully accepted the prize but regretted he would not be able to attend the official ceremony in Stockholm, Sweden. "I doubt if I know anything worth talking two minutes about," the fifty-three-year-old author of The Sound and the Fury and As I Lay Dying explained to the Nobel committee. More likely, though, as a man who was uncomfortable speaking in public, Faulkner was anxious about addressing such a large and distinguished audience. He ultimately did go to Stockholm and, in an effort to settle his nerves, drank heavily the night before. On December 10, 1950, Faulkner, haggard and hungover, delivered what has been hailed as one of the finest Nobel acceptance speeches ever given.

I feel that this award was not made to me as a man, but to my work—a life's work in the agony and sweat of the human spirit, not for glory and least of all for profit, but to create out of the materials of the human spirit something which did not exist before. So this award is only mine in trust. It will not be difficult to find a dedication for the money part of it commensurate with the purpose and significance of its origin. But I would like to do the same with the acclaim, too, by using this moment as a pinnacle from which I might be listened to by the young men and women already dedicated to the same anguish and travail, among whom is already that one who will some day stand where I am standing.

Our tragedy today is a general and universal physical fear so long sustained by now that we can even bear it. There are no longer problems of the spirit. There is only the question: When will I be blown up? Because of this, the young man or woman writing today has forgotten the problems of the human heart in conflict with itself which alone can make good writing because only that is worth writing about, worth the agony and the sweat.

He must learn them again. He must teach himself that the basest of all things is to be afraid, and teaching himself that, forget it forever, leaving no room in his workshop for anything but the old verities and truths of the heart, the universal truths lacking which any story is ephemeral and doomed—love and honor and pity and pride and compassion and sacrifice. Until he does so, he labors under a curse. He writes not of love but of lust, of defeats in which nobody loses anything of value, of victories without hope and, worst of all, without pity or compassion. His griefs grieve on no universal bones, leaving no scars. He writes not of the heart but of the glands.

Until he learns these things, he will write as though he stood among and watched the end of man. I decline to accept the end of man. It is easy enough to say that man is immortal simply because he will endure, that when the last ding-dong of doom has clanged and faded from the last worthless rock hanging tideless in the last red and dying evening, that even then there will still be one more sound: that of his puny, inexhaustible voice still talking. I refuse to accept this. I believe that man will not merely endure: He will prevail. He is immortal, not because he alone among creatures has an inexhaustible voice, but because he has a soul, a spirit capable of compassion and sacrifice and endurance. The poet's and writer's duty is to write about these things. It is his privilege to help man endure by lifting his heart, by reminding him of the courage and honor and hope and pride and compassion and pity and sacrifice which have been the glory of his past. The poet's voice need not merely be the record of man. It can be one of the props, the pillars to help him endure and prevail.

President Harry S. Truman Defends Sending Troops to Korea and Firing General Douglas MacArthur
&
General MacArthur Explains His Actions in the Korean War and Refutes Charges of Being a "Warmonger."

When the Japanese colony of Korea was divided in 1945 by the United States and the Soviet Union along the 38th Parallel, the Soviet-backed People's Democratic Republic assumed control of the North, while the U.S.-supported Republic of Korea took over the South. In 1949 Soviet and American forces withdrew from Korea, presuming the region to have stabilized, but on June 25, 1950, 90,000 North Korean troops stormed across the 38th Parallel in a surprise invasion of the South. President Truman viewed the attack as proof of a larger communist plot to dominate the world and immediately—and without Congress's consent—ordered American troops to Korea under the leadership of General Douglas MacArthur, who had served as supreme commander of

Allied forces in the southwest Pacific during World War II. Despite brilliant and daring assaults by MacArthur (particularly at Inchon) that regained all of the territory the South had lost, MacArthur insisted on pushing the North Korean army past the 38th Parallel and, if need be, going to war with China. (MacArthur requested that atomic bombs be dropped on North Korean and Chinese forces and territories.) When MacArthur's recklessness, insubordination, and disparaging comments about President Truman became more than Truman could endure—not to mention potentially perilous to American soldiers and international security—Truman fired him. On April 11, 1951, the president addressed a country both weary of war and enraged by his dismissal of the revered general to explain, point by point, his actions.

I want to talk to you tonight about what we are doing in Korea and about our policy in the Far East. In the simplest terms what we are doing in Korea is this: We are trying to prevent a third world war.

I think most people in this country recognized that fact last June. And they warmly supported the decision of the government to help the Republic of Korea against the communist aggressors. Now, many persons, even some who applauded our decision to defend Korea, have forgotten the basic reasons for our action. It is right for us to be in Korea now. It was right last June. It is right today. I want to remind you why this is true.

The communists in the Kremlin are engaged in a monstrous conspiracy to stamp out freedom all over the world. If they were to succeed, the United States would be numbered among their principal victims. It must be clear to everyone that the United States cannot and will not sit idly by and await foreign conquest. The only question is: When is the best time to meet the threat and how?

The best time to meet the threat is in the beginning. It is easier to put out a fire in the beginning when it is small than after it has become a roaring blaze. And the best way to meet the threat of aggression is for the peace-loving nations to act together. If they don't act together, they are likely to be picked off, one by one. If they had followed the right policies in the 1930s—if the free countries had acted together to crush the aggression of the dictators, and if they had acted in the beginning, when the aggression was small—there probably would have been no World War II.

If history has taught us anything, it is that aggression anywhere in the world is a threat to the peace everywhere in the world. When that aggression is supported by the cruel and selfish rulers of a powerful nation who are bent on conquest, it becomes a clear and present danger to the security and independence of every free nation. This is a lesson that most people in this country have learned thoroughly. This is the basic reason why we have joined in creating the United Nations. And, since the end of World War II, we have been putting that lesson into practice. We're working with other free nations to check the aggressive designs of the Soviet Union before they can result in a third world war. . . .

The aggression against Korea is the boldest and most dangerous move the communists have yet made. The attack on Korea was part of a greater plan for conquering all of Asia. I would like to read to you from a secret intelligence report which came to us after the attack. I have that report right here. It is a report of a speech a communist army officer in North Korea gave to a group of spies and saboteurs last May, one month before South Korea was invaded. The report shows in great detail how this invasion was a part of a carefully prepared plot. Here is part of what the communist officer, who had been trained in Moscow, told his men: "Our forces," he said, "are scheduled to attack South Korean forces about the middle of June. . . . The coming attack on South Korea marks the first step toward the liberation of Asia." Notice that he used the word *liberation*. This is communist double-talk meaning conquest.

I have another secret intelligence report here. This one tells what another communist officer in the Far East told his men several months before the invasion of Korea. And here's what he said: "In order to successfully undertake the long-awaited world revolution, we must first unify Asia. . . . Java, Indochina, Malaya, India, Tibet, Thailand, Philippines, and Japan are our ultimate targets. . . . The United States is the only obstacle on our road for the liberation of all countries in Southeast Asia. In other words we must unify the people of Asia and crush the United States." Again, *liberation* in the commie language means conquest.

That's what the communist leaders are telling their people, and that is what they've been trying to do. They want to control all Asia from the Kremlin. This plan of conquest is in flat contradiction to what we believe. We believe that Korea belongs to the Koreans. We believe that India belongs to the Indians. We believe that all nations of Asia should be free to work out their affairs in their own way. This is the basis of peace in the Far East, and it is the basis of peace of everywhere else.

The whole communist imperialism is backing the attack on peace in the Far East. It was the Soviet Union that trained and equipped the North Koreans for aggression. The Chinese communists massed forty-four well-trained and well-equipped divisions on the Korean frontier. These were the troops they threw into battle when the North Korean communists were beaten.

The question we have had to face is whether the communist plan of conquest can be stopped without a general war. Our government and other countries associated with us in the United Nations believe that the best chance of stopping it without a general war is to meet the attack in Korea and defeat it there. That is what we have been doing. It is a difficult and bitter task, but so far is has been successful. So far, we have prevented World War III. So far, by fighting a limited war in Korea, we have prevented aggression from succeeding and bringing on a general war. And the ability of the whole free world to resist communist aggression has been greatly improved.

We have taught the enemy a lesson. He has found out that aggression is not cheap or easy. Moreover, men all over the world who want to remain free have been given new courage and new hope. They know now that the champions of freedom can stand up and fight, and that they *will* stand up and fight. Our resolute stand in Korea is helping the forces of freedom now fighting in Indochina and other countries in that part of the world. It has already slowed down the timetable of conquest.

In Korea itself, there are signs that the enemy is building up his ground forces for a new mass offensive. We also know that there have been large increases in the enemy's available air forces. If a new attack comes, I feel confident it will be turned back. The United Nations fighting forces are tough and able and well equipped. They are fighting for a just cause. They are proving to all the world that the principle of collective security will work. We are proud of all these forces for the magnificent job they have done against heavy odds. We pray that their efforts may succeed, for upon their success may hinge the peace of the world.

The communist side must now choose its course of action. The communist rulers may press the attack against us. They may take further action which will spread the conflict. They have that choice and with it the awful responsibility for what may follow. The communists also have the choice of a peaceful settlement which could lead to general relaxation of the tensions in the Far East. The decision is theirs, because the forces of the United Nations will strive to limit the conflict if possible.

We do not want to see the conflict in Korea extended. We are trying to prevent a world war, not to start one. And the best way to do that is to make it plain that we and the other free countries will continue to resist the attack. But you may ask why can't we take other steps to punish the aggressor. Why don't we bomb Manchuria and China itself? Why don't we assist the Chinese nationalist troops to land on the mainland of China?

If we were to do these things, we would be running a very grave risk of starting a general war. If that were to happen, we would have brought about the exact situation we are trying to prevent. If we were to do these things, we would become entangled in a vast conflict on the continent of Asia, and our task would become immeasurably more difficult all over the world. What would suit the ambitions of the Kremlin better than for our military forces to be committed to a full-scale war with Red China? It may well be that, in spite of our best efforts, the communists may spread the war. But it would be wrong—tragically wrong—for us to take the initiative in extending the war.

The dangers are great. Make no mistake about it. Behind the North Koreans and Chinese communists in the front lines stand additional millions of Chinese soldiers. And behind the Chinese stand the tanks, the planes, the submarines, the soldiers, and the scheming rulers of the Soviet Union. . . .

I have thought long and hard about this question of extending the war in Asia. I have discussed it many times with the ablest military advisers in the country. I believe with all my heart that the course we are following is the best course. I believe that we must try to limit the war to Korea for these vital reasons: to make sure that the precious lives of our fighting men are not wasted; to see that the security of our country and the free world is not needlessly jeopardized; and to prevent a third world war.

A number of events have made it evident that General MacArthur did not agree with that policy. I have therefore considered it essential to relieve General MacArthur so that there would be no doubt or confusion as to the real purpose and aim of our policy. It was with the deepest personal regret that I found myself compelled to take this action. General MacArthur is one of our greatest military commanders. But the cause of world peace is more important than any individual.

The change in commands in the Far East means no change whatever in the policy of the United States. We will carry on the fight in Korea with vigor and determination in an effort to bring the war to a speedy and successful conclusion. The new commander, Lieutenant General Matthew Ridgway, has already demonstrated that he has the good qualities of military leadership needed for the task.

We are ready, at any time, to negotiate for a restoration of peace in the area. But we will not engage in appeasement. We are only interested in real peace. Real peace can be achieved through a settlement based on the following factors: One, the fighting must stop. Two, concrete steps must be taken to insure that the fighting will not break out again. Three, there must be an end of the aggression. A settlement founded upon these elements would open the way for the unification of Korea and the withdrawal of all foreign forces.

In the meantime, I want to be clear about our military objective. We are fighting to resist an outrageous aggression in Korea. We are trying to keep the Korean conflict from spreading to other areas. But at the same time we must conduct our military activities so as to insure the security of our forces. This is essential if they are to continue the fight until the enemy abandons its ruthless attempts to destroy the Republic of Korea. That is our military objective—to repel attack and to restore peace.

In the hard fighting in Korea, we are proving that collective action among nations is not only a high principle but a workable means of resisting aggression. Defeat of aggression in Korea may be the turning point in the world's search for a practical way of achieving peace and security.

The struggle of the United Nations in Korea is a struggle for peace. The free nations have united their strength in an effort to prevent a third world war. That war can come if the communist rulers want it to come. But this nation and its allies will not be responsible for its coming. We do not want to widen the conflict. We will use every effort to prevent that disaster. And in so doing, we know that we are following the great principles of peace, freedom, and justice.

A cheering crowd of 500,000 met Douglas MacArthur upon his return to the United States, and millions turned out for a ticker-tape parade in New York City. Eight days after Truman's speech, MacArthur stood before a joint session of Congress to bid farewell to a long and distinguished military career.

Mr. President, Mr. Speaker, and the distinguished members of Congress: I stand on this rostrum with a sense of deep humility and great pride—humility in the wake of those great American architects of our history who have stood here before me, pride in the reflection that this home of legislative debate represents human liberty in the purest form yet devised. Here are centered the hopes and aspirations and faith of the entire human race.

I do not stand here as advocate for any partisan cause, for the issues are fundamental and reach quite beyond the realm of partisan consideration. They must be resolved on the highest plane of national interest if our course is to prove sound and our future protected. I trust, therefore, that you will do me the justice of receiving that which I have to say solely expressing the considered viewpoint of a fellow American. I address you with neither rancor nor bitterness in the fading twilight of life but with one purpose in mind—to serve my country. . . .

The communist threat is a global one. Its successful advance in one sector threatens the destruction of every other sector. You cannot appease or otherwise surrender to communism in Asia without simultaneously undermining our efforts to halt its advance in Europe. Beyond pointing out these general truisms, I shall confine my discussion to the general areas of Asia. . . .

While I was not consulted prior to the President's decision to intervene in support of the Republic of Korea, that decision, from a military standpoint, proved a sound one. As I say, it proved a sound one, as we hurled back the invader and decimated his forces. Our victory was complete, and our objectives within reach, when Red China intervened with numerically superior ground forces.

This created a new war and an entirely new situation, a situation not contemplated when our forces were committed against the North Korean invaders, a situation which called for new decisions in the diplomatic sphere to permit the realistic readjustment of military strategy. Such decisions have not been forthcoming. While no man in his right mind would advocate sending our ground forces into continental China and such was never given a thought, the new situation did urgently demand a drastic revision of strategic planning if our political aim was to defeat this new enemy as we had defeated the old.

Apart from the military need as I saw it to neutralize the sanctuary protection given the enemy north of the Yalu, I felt that military necessity in the conduct of the war made mandatory: first, the intensification of our economic blockade against China; second, the imposition of a naval blockade against the China coast; third, removal of restrictions on air reconnaissance of China's coast areas and of Manchuria; fourth, removal of restrictions on the forces of the Republic of China on Formosa with logistical support to contribute to their effective operations against the common enemy.

For entertaining these views—all professionally designed to support our forces committed to Korea and bring hostilities to an end with the least possible delay and at a saving of countless American and Allied lives—I have been severely criticized in lay circles, principally abroad, despite my understanding that from a military standpoint the above views have been fully shared in the past by practically every military leader concerned with the Korean campaign, including our own joint chiefs of staff.

I called for reinforcements but was informed that reinforcements were not available. I made clear that if not permitted to destroy the build-up bases north of the Yalu; if not permitted to utilize the friendly Chinese force of some 600,000 men on Formosa; if not permitted to blockade the China coast to prevent the Chinese reds from getting succor from without; and if there were to be no hope of major reinforcements, the position of the command from the military standpoint forbade victory.

We could hold in Korea by constant maneuver and at an approximate area where our supply line advantages were in balance with the supply line disadvantages of the enemy, but we could hope at best for only an indecisive campaign, with its terrible and constant attrition upon our forces if the enemy utilized his full military potential. I have consistently called for the new political decisions essential to a solution. Efforts have been made to distort my position. It has been said, in effect, that I am a warmonger. Nothing could be further from the truth. I know war as few other men now living know it, and nothing to me is more revolting. I have long advocated its complete abolition, as its very destructiveness on both friend and foe has rendered useless as a means of settling international disputes. . . . But once war is forced upon us, there is no other alternative than to apply every available means to bring it to a swift end. War's very object is victory, not prolonged indecision. In war, indeed, there can be no substitute for victory.

There are some who for varying reasons would appease Red China. They are blind to history's clear lesson. For history teaches us with unmistakable emphasis that appeasement but begets new and bloodier war. It points to no single instance where the end has justified that means—where appeasement has lead to more than a sham peace. Like blackmail, it lays the basis for new and successively greater demands, until, as in blackmail, violence becomes the only other alternative. Why, my soldiers asked of me, surrender military advantages to any enemy in the field? I could not answer. Some may say to avoid spread of the conflict into an all-out war with China; others, to avoid Soviet intervention. Neither explanation seems valid. For China is already engaging with the maximum power it can commit, and the Soviet [Union] will not necessarily mesh its actions with our moves. Like a cobra, any new enemy will likely strike whenever it feels that the relativity in military or other potential is in its favor on a worldwide basis.

The tragedy of Korea is further heightened by the fact that as military action is confined to its territorial limits, it condemns that nation, which it is our purpose to save, to suffer the devastating impact of full naval and air bombardment, while the enemy's sanctuaries are fully protected from such attack and devastation. Of the nations of the world, Korea alone, up to now, is the sole one which has risked its all against communism. The magnificence of the courage and fortitude of the Korean people defies description. They have chosen to risk death rather than slavery. Their last words to me were, "Don't scuttle the Pacific. . . ."

I am closing my fifty-two years of military service. When I joined the Army even before the turn of the century, it was the fulfillment of all my boyish hopes and dreams. The world has turned over many times since I took the oath on the plain at West Point, and the hopes and dreams have long since vanished. But I still remember the refrain of one of the most popular barrack ballads of that day, which proclaimed most proudly that "Old soldiers never die, they just fade away."

And like the old soldier of that ballad, I now close my military career and just fade away—an old soldier who tried to do his duty as God gave him the light to see that duty. Good-bye.

Over thirty million Americans either watched or listened to MacArthur's address, and President Truman was overheard calling it "nothing but a bunch of damn bullshit." After the Senate Foreign Relations and Armed Services committees launched an inquiry into the firing of MacArthur, Truman's action appeared more justified, and MacArthur, as he himself prophesied, "faded away." The war in Korea, however, raged on. A cease-fire would not be brokered until July 1953, and the border between the North and the South remained essentially where it had been on the day of the invasion. Well over two and a half million people, including more than fifty-four thousand American servicemen, were killed in the war.

Democratic Governor Adlai Stevenson Reminds Members of His Party of All That They Have Accomplished in the Past Twenty Years
&
Vice Presidential Candidate Richard M. Nixon Confronts Allegations That He Used Campaign Funds for His Personal Gain.

Even Democratic candidate Adlai Stevenson knew he didn't have a prayer against the Republican Dwight D. Eisenhower in the 1952 presidential campaign. "Who did I think I was," he later joked, "running against George Washington?" Not only was Stevenson competing with the man who brought victory to the Allies in World War II, the Democratic Party itself was on the defensive. President Truman's approval ratings were at an abysmal 23 percent, the war in Korea was dragging on (the cease-fire would not come until 1953), and Senator Joseph McCarthy's anti-communist witch-hunts had many Americans believing that virtually every other member of Truman's administration was a personal friend of Joseph Stalin. Stevenson himself did not want to run, but on July 16 at the Chicago convention he gave the following speech—a ceremonial welcome—that proved so rousing, the delegates drafted him as the party's nominee.

As governor of the host state to the 1952 Democratic convention, I have the honor of welcoming you to Illinois. And in the name of our nine millions of people, I extend to you the heartiest of greetings. Chicago and Illinois are proud that once again the party conventions by which we restate our principles and choose our candidates for the greatest temporal office on earth are held here in Chicago, at the crossroads of the continent.

Here, on the prairies of Illinois and the Middle West, we can see a long way in all directions. We look to east, to west, to north, and south. Our commerce, our ideas, come and go in all directions. Here there are no barriers, no defenses, to ideas and aspirations. We want none. We want no shackles on the mind or the spirit, no rigid patterns of thought, no iron conformity. We want only the faith and conviction that triumph in a free and fair contest. . . .

You are very welcome here. Indeed, we think you were very wise to come here for your deliberations in this fateful year of grace. For it was in

Chicago that the modern Democratic story began. It was here, just twenty years ago, in the depths of shattering national misery at the end of a dizzy decade of Republican rule that you commenced the greatest economic and social progress in our history with the nomination of Franklin Roosevelt; twenty years during which we fought total depression to victory and have never been more prosperous; twenty years during which we fought total war to victory, both east and west, and launched the United Nations, history's most ambitious experiment in international security; twenty years that close this very month in grim contest with the communist conspiracy on every continent.

But our Republican friends say it was all a miserable failure. For almost a week pompous phrases marched over this landscape in search of an idea, and the only idea they found was that the two great decades of progress in peace, victory in war, and bold leadership in this anxious hour were the misbegotten spawn of socialism, bungling, corruption, mismanagement, waste, and worse. They captured, tied, and dragged that ragged idea in here and furiously beat it to death. After listening to this everlasting procession of epithets about our misdeeds, I was even surprised the next morning when the mail was delivered on time! I guess our Republican friends were out of patience, out of sorts, and, need I add, out of office. But we Democrats were not the only victims here. First they slaughtered each other, and then they went after us. And the same vocabulary was good for both exercises, which was a great convenience. Perhaps the proximity of the stockyards accounts for the carnage.

The constructive spirit of the great Democratic decades must not die here on its twentieth anniversary in destructive indignity and disorder. And I hope and pray, as you all do, that we can conduct our deliberations with a businesslike precision and a dignity befitting our responsibility, and the solemnity of the hour of history in which we meet.

For it is a very solemn hour indeed, freighted with the hopes and fears of millions of mankind who see in us, the Democratic Party, sober understanding of the breadth and depth of the revolutionary currents in the world. Here and abroad they see in us awareness that there is no turning back, that, as Justice Holmes said, "We must sail sometimes with the wind, sometimes against it, but we must sail and not drift or lie at anchor." They see in us the Democratic Party that has steered this country through a storm of spears for twenty years, an understanding of a world in the torment of transition from an age that has died to an age struggling to be born. They see in us relentless determination to stand fast against the barbarian at the gate, to cultivate allies with a decent respect for the opinion of others, to patiently explore every misty path to peace and security which is the only certainty of lower taxes and a better life.

This is not the time for superficial solutions and endless elocution, for frantic boast and foolish word. For words are not deeds and there are no cheap and painless solutions to war, hunger, ignorance, fear, and to the new imperialism of Soviet Russia. Intemperate criticism is not a policy for the nation. Denunciation is not a program for our salvation. Words calculated to catch everyone may catch no one. And I hope we can profit from Republican mistakes not just for our partisan benefit, but for the benefit of all of us, Republicans and Democrats alike.

Where we have erred, let there be no denial. Where we have wronged the public trust, let there be no excuses. Self-criticism is the secret weapon of democracy, and candor and confession are good for the political soul. But we will never appease, nor will we apologize for our leadership in the great events of this critical century from Woodrow Wilson to Harry Truman! We glory rather in these imperishable pages of our country's chronicle. But a great record of past achievement is not good enough. There can be no complacency, perhaps for years to come. We dare not just look back to great yesterdays. We must look forward to great tomorrows.

What counts now is not just what we are against, but what we are for. Who leads us is less important than *what* leads us—what convictions, what courage, what faith—win or lose. A man doesn't save a century, or a civilization, but a militant party wedded to a principle can. So I hope our preoccupation here is not just with personalities but with objectives. And I hope the spirit of this convention is confident reaffirmation that the United States is strong, resolved, resourceful, and rich; that we know the duty and the destiny of this heaven-rescued land; that we can and we will pursue a strong, consistent, and honorable policy abroad, and meanwhile preserve the free institutions of life and of commerce at home. What America needs and the world wants is not bombast, abuse, and double-talk, but a sober message of firm faith and confidence. St. Francis said, "Where there is patience and humility there is neither anger nor worry." That might well be our text.

And let us remember that we are not meeting here alone. All the world is watching and listening to what we say, what we do, and how we behave. So let us give them a demonstration of democracy in action at its best—our manners good, our proceedings orderly, fairly, not by the processes of synthetic excitement or mass hysteria but, as these solemn times demand, by earnest thought and prayerful deliberation. Thus can the people's party reassure the people and vindicate and strengthen the forces of democracy throughout the world.

After reluctantly accepting the nomination, Stevenson articulated with passion and candor the challenges that he and the party faced and, most important, his desire for the

race to be won honorably and honestly. "Better we lose the election," Stevenson ex-
claimed, "than mislead the people." Which, in the minds of many American voters and
reporters, is precisely what "Ike" Eisenhower and his running mate, Richard M.
Nixon, were guilty of doing. Even General Omar Bradley, Ike's World War II col-
league, was appalled by his campaign tactics, condemning Ike for "hypocritically calling
into question policies he himself had helped formulate or approved or carried out." But
it was Nixon who earned the enmity of millions for his belligerent attacks on the in-
tegrity of his opponents and their supporters, whom Nixon even referred to as traitors
to their country. But Nixon would find himself embroiled in scandal when front-page
headlines announced on September 18, 1952, a "secret fund" that supposedly paid for
lavish personal items unrelated to the campaign. Although the charges would later
prove to be false, Ike was pressured to get rid of Nixon as quickly as possible. Before
making a final decision, he allowed Nixon to defend himself, which Nixon did on Sep-
tember 23 on national television.

I come before you tonight as a candidate for the vice presidency and as a man whose honesty and integrity have been questioned.

The usual political thing to do when charges are made against you is to either ignore them or to deny them without giving details. I believe we've had enough of that in the United States, particularly with the present administration in Washington, D.C. To me the office of the vice presidency of the United States is a great office, and I feel that the people have got to have confidence in the integrity of the men who run for that office and who might obtain it. I have a theory, too, that the best and only answer to a smear or to an honest misunderstanding of the facts is to tell the truth. And that's why I'm here tonight. I want to tell you my side of the case.

I am sure that you have read the charge and you've heard that I, Senator Nixon, took $18,000 from a group of my supporters. Now, was that wrong? And let me say that it was wrong—I'm saying, incidentally, that it was *wrong* and not just illegal. Because it isn't a question of whether it was legal or illegal—that isn't enough. The question is, was it morally wrong?

I say that it was morally wrong if any of that $18,000 went to Senator Nixon for my personal use. I say that it was morally wrong if it was secretly given and secretly handled. And I say that it was morally wrong if any of the contributors got special favors for the contributions that they made.

And now, to answer those questions, let me say this: Not one cent of the $18,000 or any other money of that type ever went to me for my personal use. Every penny of it was used to pay for political expenses that I did not think should be charged to the taxpayers of the United States.

It was not a secret fund. As a matter of fact, when I was on *Meet the Press*—some of you may have seen it last Sunday—[reporter] Peter Edson came up to me after the program and he said, "Dick, what about this fund we hear about?" And I said, "Well, there's no secret about it. Go out and see Dana Smith, who is the administrator of the fund." And I gave him his address, and I said that you will find that the purpose of the fund simply was to defray political expenses that I did not feel should be charged to the government.

And third, let me point out—and I want to make this particularly clear— that no contributor to this fund, no contributor to any of my campaigns, has ever received any consideration that he would not have received as an ordinary constituent.

But then some of you will say and rightly, "Well, what did you use the fund for, Senator? Why did you have to have it?" Let me tell you in just a word how a Senate office operates. First of all, a Senator gets $15,000 a year in salary. He gets enough money to pay for one trip a year, a round trip that is, for himself and his family between his home and Washington, D.C. And then he gets an allowance to handle the people that work in his office, to handle his mail. And the allowance for my state of California is enough to hire thirteen people. But there are other expenses which are not covered by the government. And I think I can best discuss those expenses by asking you some questions.

Do you think that when I or any other senator makes a political speech, has it printed, should charge the printing of that speech and the mailing of that speech to the taxpayers? Do you think, for example, when I or any other senator makes a trip to his home state to make a purely political speech, that the cost of that trip should be charged to the taxpayers? Do you think when a senator makes political broadcasts or political television broadcasts, radio or television, that the expense of those broadcasts should be charged to the taxpayers?

Well, I know what your answer is. It is the same answer that audiences give me whenever I discuss this particular problem. The answer is, "No." The taxpayers shouldn't be required to finance items which are not official business but which are primarily political business. . . .

And so I felt that the best way to handle these necessary political expenses of getting my message to the American people and the speeches I made—the speeches that I had printed, for the most part, concerned this one message: of exposing this administration, the communism in it, the corruption in it—the only way that I could do that was to accept the aid which people in my home state of California who contributed to my campaign and who continued to make these contributions after I was elected were glad to make.

And let me say I am proud of the fact that not one of them has ever asked me for a special favor. I'm proud of the fact that not one of them has ever asked me to vote on a bill other than as my own conscience would dictate. And I am proud of the fact that the taxpayers by subterfuge or otherwise have never paid one dime for expenses which I thought were political and shouldn't be charged to the taxpayers. . . .

I realize that there are still some who may say, and rightly so—and let me say that I recognize that some will continue to smear regardless of what the truth may be—but that there has been understandably some honest misunderstanding on this matter. And there's some that will say, "Well, maybe you were able, Senator, to fake this thing. How can we believe what you say? After all, is there a possibility that maybe you got some sums in cash? Is there a possibility that you may have feathered your own nest?" And so now what I am going to do—and incidentally this is unprecedented in the history of American politics—I am going at this time to give this television and radio audience a complete financial history: everything I've earned, everything I've spent, everything I owe. And I want you to know the facts. I'll have to start early.

I was born in 1913. Our family was one of modest circumstances, and most of my early life was spent in a store out in East Whittier. It was a grocery store, one of those family enterprises. The only reason we were able to make it go was because my mother and dad had five boys and we all worked in the store.

I worked my way through college and to a great extent through law school. And then, in 1940, probably the best thing that ever happened to me happened: I married Pat, who is sitting over here. We had a rather difficult time after we were married, like so many of the young couples who may be listening to us. I practiced law. She continued to teach school. Then in 1942 I went into the service.

Let me say that my service record was not a particularly unusual one. I went to the South Pacific. I guess I'm entitled to a couple of battle stars. I got a couple of letters of commendation, but I was just there when the bombs were falling and then I returned. I returned to the United States, and in 1946 I ran for Congress.

When we came out of the war, Pat and I—Pat during the war worked as a stenographer, and in a bank, and as an economist for a government agency—and when we came out the total of our saving from both my law practice, her teaching, and all the time that I was in the war—the total for that entire period—was just a little less than $10,000. Every cent of that, incidentally, was in government bonds.

Well, that's where we started when I got into politics. Now, what I've earned since I went into politics? Well, here it is. I jotted it down. Let me read the notes. First of all, I've had my salary as a congressman and as a senator.

Second, I have received a total in this past six years of $1,600 from estates which were in my law firm the time that I severed my connection with it.

And, incidentally, as I said before, I have not engaged in any legal practice and have not accepted any fees from business that came to the firm after I went into politics. I have made an average of approximately $1,500 a year from nonpolitical speaking engagements and lectures. And then, fortunately, we've inherited a little money. Pat sold her interest in her father's estate for $3,000, and I inherited $1,500 from my grandfather.

We live rather modestly. For four years we lived in an apartment in Park Fairfax, in Alexandria, Virginia. The rent was $80 a month. And we saved for the time that we could buy a house.

Now, that was what we took in. What did we do with this money? What do we have today to show for it? This will surprise you, because it is so little, I suppose, as standards generally go, of people in public life. First of all, we've got a house in Washington which cost $41,000 and on which we owe $20,000. We have a house in Whittier, California, which cost $13,000 and on which we owe $3,000. My folks are living there at the present time.

I have just $4,000 in life insurance, plus my G.I. policy, which I've never been able to convert and which will run out in two years. I have no insurance whatever on Pat. I have no life insurance on our youngsters, Patricia and Julie. I own a 1950 Oldsmobile car. We have our furniture. We have no stocks and bonds of any type. We have no interest of any kind, direct or indirect, in any business.

Now, that's what we have. What do we owe? Well, in addition to the mortgage, the $20,000 mortgage on the house in Washington, the $10,000 one on the house in Whittier, I owe $4,500 to the Riggs Bank in Washington, D.C., with interest 4½ percent. I owe $3,500 to my parents, and the interest on that loan—which I pay regularly, because it's the part of the savings they made through the years they were working so hard—I pay regularly 4 percent interest. And then I have a $500 loan which I have on my life insurance.

Well, that's about it. That's what we have and that's what we owe. It isn't very much, but Pat and I have the satisfaction that every dime that we've got is honestly ours. I should say this: that Pat doesn't have a mink coat, but she does have a respectable Republican cloth coat. And I always tell her that she'd look good in anything.

One other thing I probably should tell you, because if we don't they'll probably be saying this about me too: We did get something, a gift, after the election. A man down in Texas heard Pat on the radio mention the fact that our two youngsters would like to have a dog. And, believe it or not, the day before we left on this campaign trip we got a message from Union Station in Baltimore saying they had a package for us. We went down to get it. You know what it was? It was a little cocker spaniel dog in a crate that he'd sent all the way from Texas. Black and white spotted. And our little girl—Tricia, the six-year-old—named it Checkers. And you know, the kids, like all kids, love the dog, and I just want to say this right now that regardless of what they say about it, we're gonna keep it.

It isn't easy to come before a nationwide audience and air your life as I've done. But I want to say some things before I conclude that I think most of you will agree on. Mr. Mitchell, the chairman of the Democratic National Committee, made the statement that if a man couldn't afford to be in the United States Senate, he shouldn't run for the Senate. And I just want to make my position clear. I don't agree with Mr. Mitchell when he says that only a rich man should serve his government in the United States Senate or in Congress. I don't believe that represents the thinking of the Democratic Party, and I know it doesn't represent the thinking of the Republican Party. I believe that it's fine that a man like Governor Stevenson, who inherited a fortune from his father, can run for president. But I also feel that it's essential in this country of ours that a man of modest means can also run for president. . . .

And now, finally, I know that you wonder whether or not I am going to stay on the Republican ticket or resign. Let me say this: I don't believe that I ought to quit, because I'm not a quitter. And, incidentally, Pat's not a quitter. After all, her name was Patricia Ryan and she was born on St. Patrick's Day, and you know the Irish never quit.

But the decision, my friends, is not mine. I would do nothing that would harm the possibilities of Dwight Eisenhower to become president of the United States. And for that reason I am submitting to the Republican National Committee tonight through this television broadcast the decision which it is theirs to make. Let them decide whether my position on the ticket will help or hurt. And I am going to ask you to help them decide. Wire and write the Republican National Committee whether you think I should stay or whether I should get off. And whatever the decision is, I will abide by it.

But just let me say this last word. Regardless of what happens I'm going to continue this fight. I'm going to campaign up and down America until we drive the crooks and the communists and those that defend them out of Washington. And remember, folks, Eisenhower is a great man. Believe me, he's a great man. And a vote for Eisenhower is a vote for what's good for America.

Calls and telegrams overwhelmingly in favor of Nixon flooded the Republican National Committee. "Let there be no doubt about it," Ike boasted, "America has taken Dick Nixon to its heart. He is vindicated as a man of courage and honor." Nixon's "Checkers" speech, as it came to be known, gave the campaign a boost, and the election six weeks later was a landslide: 442 electoral votes for Eisenhower, 89 for Stevenson.

John W. Davis Contends That "Separate but Equal" Is a Matter for the Legislature, Not the Courts, to Decide
&
NAACP Attorney Thurgood Marshall Argues That "Separate but Equal" Schools and Other Institutions Are Unconstitutional

It all began when an eight-year-old girl named Linda Brown was denied entrance to the all-white school in her neighborhood solely because she was black. Her father, Oliver, sued the board of education, and the case eventually made its way to the U.S. Supreme Court. Representing the Brown family was the great-grandson of a slave, NAACP lawyer Thurgood Marshall, who hoped the Court's decision not only would end segregation in schools, but would tear down Plessy v. Ferguson, the 1896 ruling that declared "separate but equal" facilities constitutional. Marshall argued before the Court on December 9, 1952, that the very act of separating black and white students instilled in blacks a sense of inferiority and inequality. "Witnesses testified," Marshall contended, "that segregation deterred the development of the personalities of these children. Two witnesses testified that it deprives them of equal status in the school community, that it destroys their self-respect." Representing the defense was John W. Davis, an eighty-year-old lawyer and Democrat who had run against Calvin Coolidge in the 1924 presidential election. Brown v. Board of Education of Topeka, Kansas would be Davis's last case of an estimated 140 appearances before the Court, and he took issue with Marshall's claim that segregation psychologically harmed children. More fundamentally, though, Davis argued that desegregation was a matter for the legislatures, not the courts, to decide.

It is true that in the Constitution of the United States there is no equal protection clause [sic]. It is true that the Fourteenth Amendment was addressed primarily to the states. . . .

At the time the amendment was submitted, there were thirty-seven states in the Union. Thirty of them had ratified the amendment at the time it was proclaimed in 1868. Of those thirty ratifying states, twenty-three either then had, or immediately installed, separate schools for white and colored children under their public school systems. Were they violating the amendment which they had solemnly accepted? Were they conceiving of it in any other sense than that it did not touch their power over their public schools?

How do they stand today? Seventeen states in the Union today provide for separate schools for white and colored children, and four others make it permissive with their school boards. Those four are Wyoming, Kansas of which we heard yesterday, New Mexico, and Arizona, so that you have twenty-one states today which conceive it their power and right to maintain separate schools if it suits their policy.

When we turn to the judicial branch, it has spoken on this question perhaps with more repetition and in more cases than any other single separate constitutional question that now occurs to me. . . .

What does this Court say? I repeat, I shall not undertake to interpret for Your Honors the scope and weight of your own opinions. In *Plessy v. Ferguson, Cumming v. Richmond County Board of Regents, Gaines v. Canada, Sweatt v. Painter,* and *McLaurin v. Oklahoma,* and there may be others for all I know, certainly this Court has spoken in the most clear and unmistakable terms to the effect that this segregation is not unlawful. I am speaking for those with whom I am associated. We find nothing in the latest cases that modified that doctrine of "separate but equal" in the least. *Sweatt v. Painter* and similar cases were decided solely on the basis of inequality, as we think and as we believe the Court intended.

It is a little late, said the court below—after this question has been presumed to be settled for ninety years—it is a little late to arrive that the question is still at large. . . .

[C]ounsel for the plaintiffs, or appellants, [say] "We have the uncontradicted testimony of expert witnesses that segregation is hurtful, and in their opinion hurtful to the children of both races, both colored and white." . . . These learned witnesses do not have the whole field to themselves. They do not speak without contradiction from other sources. . . . Let me read a sentence or two from Dr. [W. E. B.] Du Bois. I may be wrong about this, but I should think that he has been perhaps the most constant and vocal opponent of Negro oppression of any of his race in the country. Says he:

It is difficult to think of anything more important for the development of a people than proper training for their children; and yet I have repeatedly seen wise and loving colored parents take infinite pains to force their little children into schools where the white children, white teachers, and white parents despised and resented the dark child, make mock of it, neglected and bullied it, and literally rendered its life a living hell. Such parents want their children to fight this thing out—but, dear God, at what a cost.

He goes on: "We shall get a finer, better balance of spirit, an infinitely more capable and rounded personality, by putting children in schools where they are wanted and where they are happy and inspired, than in thrusting them into hells where they are ridiculed and hated."

If this question is a judicial question, if it is to be decided on the varying opinions of scholars, students, writers, authorities, and what you will, certainly it cannot be said that the testimony will be all one way. Certainly it cannot be said that a legislature conducting its public schools in accordance with the wishes of its people—it cannot be said that they are acting merely by caprice or by racial prejudice. . . .

Once more, Your Honors, I might say: What underlies this whole question? What is the great national and federal policy on this matter? Is it not a fact that the very strength and fiber of our federal system is local self-government in those matters for which local action is competent? Is it not, of all the activities of government, the one which most nearly approaches the hearts and minds of people, the question of the education of their young? Is it not the height of wisdom that the manner in which that shall be conducted should be left to those most immediately affected by it, and that the wishes of the parents, both white and colored, should be ascertained before their children are forced into what may be an unwelcome contact?

I respectfully submit to the Court, there is no reason assigned here why this Court or any other should reverse the findings of ninety years.

Marshall's final summation to the court contended that "separate but equal" was, in fact, a judicial matter.

May it please the Court:

So far as the appellants are concerned in this case, at this point it seems to me that the significant factor running through all these arguments up to this point is that for some reason, which is still unexplained, Negroes are taken out of the mainstream of American life in these states. There is nothing involved in this case other than race and color, and I do not need to go to the background of the statutes or anything else. I just read the statutes, and they say, "white and colored."

While we are talking about the feeling of the people in South Carolina, I think we must once again emphasize that under our form of government, these individual rights of minority people are not to be left to even the most mature judgment of the majority of the people, and that the only testing ground as to whether or not individual rights are concerned is in this Court.

If I might digress just for a moment, on this question of the will of the people of South Carolina, if [African American diplomat and winner of the Nobel Prize for peace] Ralph Bunche were assigned to South Carolina, his children would have to go to a Jim Crow school. No matter how great anyone becomes, if he happens to have been born Negro, regardless of his color, he is relegated to that school. . . .

I think, considering the legislatures, that we have to bear in mind that I know of no Negro legislator in any of these states, and I do not know whether they consider the Negro's side or not. It is just a fact. But I assume that there are people who will say that ["separate but equal"] was and is necessary, and my answer to that is, even if the concession is made that it was necessary in 1895, it is not necessary now because people have grown up and understand each other. They are fighting together and living together.

For example, today they are working together in other places. As a result of the ruling of this Court, they are going together on the higher level. Just how far it goes—I think when we predict what might happen, I know in the South where I spent most of my time, you will see white and colored kids going down the road together to school. They separate and go to different schools, and they come out and they play together. I do not see why there would necessarily be any trouble if they went together. . . .

I think, sir, that the ultimate authority for the asserted right by an individual in a minority group is in a body set aside to interpret our Constitution, which is our Court. . . .

[T]he rights of the minorities, as has been our whole form of government, have been protected by our Constitution, and the ultimate authority for determining that is this Court. I think that is the real difference. As to whether or not I, as an individual, am being deprived of my right is not legislative but judicial.

Although the hearing took only forty-eight hours, it would be a year and a half before the ruling was announced. And when it came, on May 17, 1954, it would be unanimous in favor of Brown. The Court ordered states to move with "all deliberate speed" (Marshall had argued for a specific date) and Southern institutions, not surprisingly, resisted complying. The White House offered integrationists virtually no support, and President Eisenhower, who had appointed Chief Justice Earl Warren to the Court, was later heard calling his appointment "the biggest damn fool mistake" he had ever made. (Eisenhower only reluctantly sent in federal troops to escort nine black teenagers to the Central High School in Little Rock, Arkansas.) Thurgood Marshall would later become the nation's first black Supreme Court justice, appointed to Warren's Court in 1967 by President Lyndon Johnson.

Former First Lady Eleanor Roosevelt Addresses the Question: "Hasn't the United Nations Failed?"

In recognition of the former first lady's lifelong commitment to peace and human rights, President Harry S. Truman appointed Eleanor Roosevelt as the U.S. representative to the nascent United Nations organization in 1945. Created to serve as a stabilizing force in a postwar world, the United Nations, almost from its inception, was perceived instead as an arena of animosity where countries endlessly bickered over grievances both large and petty. The dream of world peace seemed particularly elusive with the explosion of the Korean War, and doubts were raised in the United States and abroad as to whether any organization could promote international equilibrium. Mrs. Roosevelt had lobbied for the establishment of the United Nations and, with its image tarnished, toured the country touting its purpose in the world. In the spring of 1953, Mrs. Roosevelt offered the following defense of the United Nations and its mission before the Illinois Congress of Parents and Teachers.

You have heard, as many of us have heard, the current saying, "What good has come from the United Nations? Hasn't the United Nations failed? It was set up to bring us peace, and we don't have peace." But that is really a most unfortunate misconception. The object that the sovereign states hoped for when they wrote the charter in San Francisco was that we could use this machinery as united nations to achieve a peaceful world. But it's only machinery, and machinery doesn't work by itself. It's the people that make it work.

We have also heard it said that the United Nations is just a debating society, that it never accomplishes anything. Yet we have found over the years that it requires a good deal of talk for people to learn to understand one another. Even in the Congress of the United States we don't always find an immediate meeting of minds. Well, you take sixty sovereign nations, all representing peoples with different customs and habits, frequently different religions, frequently different legal systems. How can you expect them immediately—within six or seven years, that is—to arrive at a meeting of minds? True, the breach has widened between us and the Soviets, but that breach might have broadened into a war if there hadn't been a place where we had to meet and where we were able to talk.

And if the United Nations is a debating society, do you feel that you have learned all you should about what conditions are all over the world—for instance, in India? I am sure that many of you have no conception of what it is to live in a country where there is always a famine somewhere. I know it wasn't until I went to India and saw the famine districts that I realized what it would be like if some part of my own country was always living under famine conditions. I know of no way in which we can learn these things as quickly as we are learning them from the information that comes to us through channels provided by the United Nations.

I get a lot of letters from people who say, "How can you expect the United Nations to succeed when you do not recognize God in the United Nations?" We have in the U.N. building a little room known as a prayer room to serve all devout people. From those who live according to their own religious standards I have learned a tremendous amount. I have learned to respect them, for I sometimes think that the same spirit pervades the good people in all religions. If you want others to respect your beliefs, you must in return give respect for theirs.

These are some of the things that you learn as you find yourself in close association with people from different parts of the world. It is because they are things that we all need to learn that I believe parents and teachers today have such a tremendous responsibility. They have to prepare our children for living as leaders in a world that will follow their leadership, if the world can respect it. And that will require of our children a greater knowledge of the rest of the world than any of us have ever had before. They are going to be leaders in a world where not only are there different religions and habits and customs but different races—and two-thirds of that world is made up of peoples of different colors. . . .

When all is said and done, then, what we need is to know more about the United Nations and its action groups—the specialized agencies—if only because this is machinery that we people of the different nations must use. For if we do not know about it and if we do not back it up, it isn't going to be used as well as it might be. Furthermore, I feel very strongly that with more knowledge, many of the fears we have had about the United Nations will be dispelled.

Remember, this cooperation is so new, so new in every field, that it's very hard for any of us to work together even on what we think are simple things. So we shouldn't be discouraged when we do not achieve peace all at once. Peace is not going to drop on us from heaven. It is going to have to be worked for, with the hearts and minds and wills of human beings. I believe it can be achieved, but we are going to have to work much harder. We must strengthen it, at the same time learning about the rest of the world.

This is why parents and teachers today must have courage enough to stand up against waves of public opinion. At present we are going through a period of what I call unreasonable fears, fears that cause great suspicion among us. Many people are afraid to say what they think because it might by chance be something that somebody else might think subversive. Yet our nation has been built on differences of opinion, stated openly. Throughout our history we have had quite a number of people who stood for almost revolutionary ideas. But we have weathered the years, and we have come to be the leading nation of the world. And now it is a question of how well we prepare the next generation to take the burden from their elders. These young people have to know much more than we knew. We had to know about our own country; they have to know about the world. They have to feel and understand things that we didn't have to feel and understand at all. . . .

We have to have unity. We have to believe in each other. We cannot be suspicious of everybody. Surely there are people among us who perhaps do not believe in the things that we think essential, but I think the vast majority of us are well rooted in the beliefs of freedom.

I think we can stand up against any infiltration or propaganda, but first we must have a feeling of confidence. We must really care about bringing to the people of the world a leadership that is good, a leadership that is strong. I do not mean strong just in a military and economic way but in a spiritual and moral way. If we do have that feeling and can impart it to our young people, I believe we can do this job, the biggest job any nation has ever had. We are at the crossroads. It is up to us whether we move forward—slowly, to be sure, but step by step—to a better world or whether we fail.

What is going to happen? I do not know. If we succeed, it will be because you and I, as individuals, believe in ourselves and in the need to work with our neighbors throughout the world. I think we will hand on to our children a struggle, but a struggle that will give our nation the capacity to lead the world toward peace and righteousness and freedom.

Environmentalist Rachel Carson Muses on the "Exceeding Beauty of the Earth" and Its Effect on the Human Spirit.

A year before publishing the book that would launch the modern environmental movement, the marine biologist Rachel Carson deliberated over two possible titles for her work, The War Against Nature *and* At War with Nature. *But Carson ultimately settled on the more poetic* Silent Spring, *referring to the eerie hush of natural areas, once populous with birds and wildlife, now barren after years of pesticide use. Carson's lucid prose and lyrical style attracted millions of Americans to her message, which celebrated the interconnectedness of humans, animals, and the natural world and exposed how man-made chemicals were endangering them all. Carson's book became an immediate best-seller and prompted legislation that eventually banned DDT and other harmful insecticides. On April 21, 1954, soon after the release of her first major book,* The Sea Around Us, *but still eight years before* Silent Spring's *publication, Carson poignantly expressed to an audience in Columbus, Ohio, how vital a love for nature is to the well-being of both individuals and a nation.*

The pleasures, the values of contact with the natural world are not reserved for the scientists. They are available to anyone who will place himself under the influence of a lonely mountain top, or the sea, or the stillness of a forest, or who will stop to think about so small a thing as the mystery of a growing seed.

I am not afraid of being thought a sentimentalist when I stand here tonight and tell you that I believe natural beauty has a necessary place in the spiritual development of any individual or any society. I believe that whenever we destroy beauty, or whenever we substitute something man-made and artificial for a natural feature of the earth, we have retarded some part of man's spiritual growth.

I believe this affinity of the human spirit for the earth and its beauties is deeply and logically rooted. As human beings, we are part of the whole stream of life. We have been human beings for perhaps a million years. But life itself passes on something of itself to other life—that mysterious entity that moves and is aware of itself and its surroundings, and so is distinguished from rocks or senseless clay [from which] life arose many hundreds of millions of years ago. Since then it has developed, struggled, adapted itself to its surroundings, evolved an infinite number of forms. But its living protoplasm is built of the same elements as air, water, and rock. To these the mysterious spark of life was added. Our origins are of the earth. And so there is in us a deeply seated response to the natural universe, which is part of our humanity.

Now, why do I introduce such a subject tonight—a serious subject for a night when we are supposed to be having fun? First, because you have asked me to tell you something of myself, and I can't do that without telling you some of the things I believe in so intensely.

Also, I mention it because it is not often I have a chance to talk to a thousand women. I believe it is important for women to realize that the world of today threatens to destroy much of that beauty that has immense power to bring us a healing release from tension. Women have a greater intuitive understanding of such things. They want for their children not only physical health but mental and spiritual health as well. I bring these things to your attention tonight because I think your awareness of them will help, whether you are practicing journalists, or teachers, or librarians, or housewives and mothers.

What are these threats of which I speak? What is this destruction of beauty—this substitution of man-made ugliness—this trend toward a perilously artificial world? Unfortunately, that is a subject that could require a whole conference extending over many days. So in the few minutes that I have to devote to it, I can only suggest the trend.

We see it in small ways in our own communities, and in larger ways in the community of the state of the nation. We see the destruction of beauty and the suppression of human individuality in hundreds of suburban real estate developments where the first act is to cut down all the trees and the next is to build an infinitude of little houses, each like its neighbor.

We see it in distressing form in the nation's capital, where I live. There in the heart of the city, we have a small but beautiful woodland area, Rock Creek Park. It is a place where one can go, away from the noise of traffic and of man-made confusions, for a little interval of refreshing and restoring quiet, where one can hear the soft water sounds of a stream on its way to river and sea, where the wind flows through the trees and a veery sings in the green twilight. Now they propose to run a six-lane arterial highway through the heart of that narrow woodland valley, destroying forever its true and immeasurable value to the city and the nation.

Those who place so great a value on a highway apparently do not think the thoughts of an editorial writer for the *New York Times* who said, "But a little lonesome space, where nature has her own way, where it is quiet enough at night to hear the patter of small paws on leaves and the murmuring of birds, can still be afforded. The gift of tranquility, wherever found, is beyond price."

We see the destructive trend on a national scale in proposals to invade the national parks with commercial schemes such as the building of power dams. The parks were placed in trust for all the people, to preserve for them just such recreational and spiritual values as I have mentioned. Is it the right of this, our generation in its selfish materialism, to destroy these things because we are blinded by the dollar sign? Beauty and all the values that derive from beauty are not measured and evaluated in terms of the dollar.

Years ago I discovered in the writings of the British naturalist Richard Jefferies a few lines that so impressed themselves upon my mind that I have never forgotten them. May I quote them for you now? "The exceeding beauty of the earth, in her splendor of life, yields a new thought with every petal. The hours when the mind is absorbed by beauty are the only hours when we really live. All else is illusion, or mere endurance." Those lines are, in a way, a statement of the creed I have lived by, for as perhaps you have seen tonight, a preoccupation with the wonder and beauty of the earth has strongly influenced the course of my life.

Since *The Sea Around Us* was published, I have had the privilege of receiving many letters from people who, like myself, have been steadied and reassured by contemplating the long history of the earth and sea, and the deeper meanings of the world of nature. These letters have come from all sorts of people. There have been hairdressers and fishermen and musicians; there have been classical scholars and scientists. So many of them have said, in one phrasing or another, "We have been troubled about the world and had almost lost faith in man. It helps to think about the long history of the earth, and of how life came to be. And when we think in terms of millions of years, we are not so impatient that our own problems be solved tomorrow."

In contemplating "the exceeding beauty of the earth" these people have found calmness and courage. For there is symbolic as well as actual beauty in the migration of birds, in the ebb and flow of the tides, in the folded bud ready for the spring. There is something infinitely healing in these repeated refrains of nature—the assurance that dawn comes after night, and spring after winter.

Mankind has gone very far into an artificial world of his own creation. He has sought to insulate himself, with steel and concrete, from the realities of earth and water. Perhaps he is intoxicated with his own power, as he goes farther and farther into experiments for the destruction of himself and his world. For this unhappy trend there is no single remedy, no panacea. But I believe that the more clearly we can focus our attention on the wonders and realities of the universe about us, the less taste we shall have for destruction.

Architect Frank Lloyd Wright Encourages His Students to Create Buildings That Are "Beneficial to Humankind."

"No house should ever be built on any hill or on anything. It should be of the hill," insisted one of the twentieth century's most influential American architects, Frank Lloyd Wright. Described as "organic architecture," Wright's philosophy espoused a harmony between a building and its surrounding landscape. Every structure, Wright believed, should have a spirit that emanates from within that inspires and uplifts individuals through its beauty. Wright elaborated on the spiritual nature of both humanity and architecture in a presentation to his apprentices on April 15, 1956, encouraging them to become not merely great architects, but exemplary human beings—"the greatest thing [a person] can be."

When we speak of humanity we mean a quality, and it is interior. It is a quality of light that proceeds from the light of the world, the light of the universe, light as it is. And according to that light, you grow as a son of—well, I think they call it God, but I never knew exactly why. That's a good name for it, maybe. But I don't think it's outside of yourselves, a mystery that someday you're going to inherit. I think that all you'll see of it you've got right now.

And the thing for you to do is to look, listen, and conform to that. It's the only conformity I would suggest to you. It's different for each of you. It's different for us all. It wouldn't be the same for me. It wouldn't be the same for Olgivanna. It wouldn't be the same for Tom. It wouldn't be the same for David. It wouldn't be the same for anybody, except that it is one, it is the light, and as you are respectful, cognizant, obedient, in a way you grow. You grow stronger in spirit.

Stronger in spirit is the only strength that this country, or any country, or any man needs. There is enough physical strength, God knows, on earth. And the machine has augmented our physical strength. And today by way of scientific invention we can do a hundred to one anything man ever did, but how about *him?* Meantime what's happened to him? What's he got? What has he gained? Is *he* any stronger? Is he any more competent to beautify his life—and no man can beautify his life without beautifying the life of others. If you think that you can get away with it by something that you do for yourself, you've got to guess again, because it won't work.

Instinctively and naturally if you beautify your own life, you beautify the life of everybody around you—just as that flower there in itself is having a happy time, realizing a principle, no doubt. But we share it, we get from it, it belongs to us as we see it. To the extent that we take it in, we are that thing. And so it is when you do this thing for yourselves, and become your self's expression, make yourself an expression of this light within we call the spirit, just so long are you beneficial to humankind. If they can say, "Well, he's a great human being," no greater compliment can be paid you.

In architecture we want a humane architecture. We don't want buildings that simply say things by rhyme or without reason, nor by rhyme and reason even, without a soul. We want the thing to be extremely humane, of the spirit. From man to man according to man's higher nature, and that higher nature is never exterior. That higher nature is ever inside. And when we say that the reality of the building consists of the space within to be lived in, don't you see that philosophically we have abandoned all exterior thought, idea—that anything outside it matters. It all must come from within. That is what gives charm and grace and beauty and integrity to the buildings that we build. And the more you can strengthen that in your own natures, the more of a break you give it, the more respect you pay to it, the more powerful you will be in making things beautiful. The principle will always be there and always working according to what you are yourselves, what you've got, how far you've come.

Homer Hickam Relates How Sputnik Inspired Him to Become a Rocket Engineer for NASA.

Not much larger than a basketball, Sputnik I, *the world's first artificial satellite, sent a shudder of fear through the American psyche after it was launched into orbit by the Soviet Union on October 4, 1957.* Sputnik I *also emitted a signal that could be heard on radios and televisions—a signal that sounded both mysterious and mocking—continually reminding Americans that the Soviet-made satellite was simultaneously over their heads and in their living rooms. One American, however, seemed absolutely unbothered by the development. "This launching of the satellite," President Dwight D. Eisenhower remarked dismissively of the Soviets, "proves that they can hurl an object a considerable distance." (Eisenhower's casual tone belied genuine concern. The former general knew the military advantages of such a satellite, particularly if it were armed with a nuclear device.) For countless younger Americans, the launch of* Sputnik I*— and later,* Sputnik II*—inspired them to dream of one day participating in an American space program. Homer Hickam Jr., a fourteen-year-old student in a small mining town in West Virginia, was so smitten with such an idea that he began experimenting with homemade rockets in his backyard. Hickam, who would later write about his life in the national bestseller* Rocket Boys, *related to a New York audience in March 1999 the impact* Sputnik I *and* Sputnik II *had on his life as a young boy.*

On November 3, the Russians struck again, launching *Sputnik II.* This one had a dog in it—Laika was her name—and by her picture in the paper, she looked a little like Poteet. I went out into the yard and called Poteet over and picked her up. She wasn't a big dog, but she felt pretty heavy. Mom saw me and came outside. "What are you doing to that dog?"

"I just wondered how big a rocket it would take to put her into orbit."

"If she don't stop peeing on my rosebushes, she's going into orbit—won't need any rocket," Mom said.

Poteet whined and ducked her head in my armpit. She might not have known every word, but she knew very well what Mom was saying. As soon as Mom went back inside, I put Poteet down and she went over and sat by one of the rosebushes. I didn't watch to see what she did after that.

My dad got two magazines in the mail every week, *Newsweek* and *Life.* When they came, he read them from cover to cover, and I got them next. In a November issue of *Life,* I found, to my great interest, drawings of the internal mechanisms of a variety of different kinds of rockets. I studied them carefully, and then I remembered reading how Wernher von Braun had built rockets when he was a youngster. An inspiration came to me. At the supper table that night, I put down my fork and announced that I was going to build a rocket. Dad, musing into his glass of corn bread and milk, said nothing. He was probably working through some ventilation problem, and I doubt if he even heard me. [My brother] Jim snickered. He probably thought it was a sister thing to do. Mom stared at me for a long while and then said, "Well, don't blow yourself up."

I gathered Roy Lee, O'Dell, and Sherman in my room. My mom's pet squirrel, Chipper, was hanging upside down on the curtains, watching us. Chipper had the run of the house and loved to join a gathering. "We're going to build a rocket," I said as the little rodent launched himself at my shoulder. He landed and snuggled up against my ear. I petted him absently.

The other boys looked at one another and shrugged. "Where will we launch it?" was all that Roy Lee wanted to know. Chipper wiggled his nose in Roy Lee's direction and then hopped off my shoulder to the bed and then to the floor. The sneak attack was Chipper's favorite game.

"The fence by the rosebushes," I said. My house was narrowly fitted between two mountains and a creek, but there was a small clearing behind Mom's rose garden.

"We'll need a countdown," Sherman stated flatly.

"Well of course we have to have a countdown," O'Dell argued, even though no one was arguing with him. "But what will we make our rocket out of? I can get stuff if you tell me what we need." O'Dell's father, Red, was the town garbageman. On weekends, O'Dell and his brothers helped out on the truck and saw just about every kind of stuff there was in Coalwood one time or another.

Sherman was always a practical boy with an orderly mind. "Do we know how to build a rocket?" he wondered.

I showed them the *Life* magazine. "All you have to do is put fuel in a tube and a hole at the bottom of it."

"What kind of fuel?"

I had already given the matter some thought. "I've got twelve cherry bombs left over from the Fourth of July," I said. "I've been saving them for New Year's. We'll use the powder out of them."

Satisfied, Sherman nodded. "Okay, that ought to do it. We'll start the countdown at ten."

"How high will it fly?" O'Dell wondered.

"High," I guessed.

We all sat around in a little circle and looked at one another. I didn't have to spell it out. It was an important moment and we knew it. We boys in Coalwood were joining the space race. "All right, let's do it," Roy Lee said just as Chipper landed on his D.A. Roy Lee leapt to his feet and flailed ineffectually at his attacker. Chipper giggled and then jumped for the curtain.

"Chipper! Bad squirrel!" I yelled, but he just closed his beady eyes and vibrated in undisguised delight.

Roy Lee rolled up the *Life* magazine, but before he could raise his arm, Chipper was gone in a flash, halfway down the stairs toward the safety of Mom in the kitchen. "I can't wait for squirrel season," Roy Lee muttered.

I appointed myself chief rocket designer. O'Dell provided me with a small discarded plastic flashlight to use as the body of the rocket. I emptied its batteries and then punched a hole in its base with a nail. I cracked open my cherry bombs and poured the powder from them into the flashlight and then wrapped it all up in electrical tape. I took one of the cherry bomb fuses left over and stuck it in the hole and glued the entire apparatus inside the fuselage of a de-winged plastic model airplane—I recall it was an F-100 Super Sabre. Since Sherman couldn't run very fast—and also because it was his idea—he was placed in charge of the countdown, a position that allowed him to stand back. Roy Lee was to bring the matches. O'Dell was to strike the match and hand it to me. I would light the fuse and make a run for it. Everybody had something to do.

When night came, we balanced our rocket, looking wicked and sleek, on top of my mother's rose garden fence. The fence was a source of pride and satisfaction to her. It had taken six months of her reminding Dad before he finally sent Mr. McDuff down from the mine to build it. The night was cold and clear—all the better, we thought, for us to track our rocket as it streaked across the dark, starry sky. We waited until some coal cars rumbled past, and then I lit the fuse and ran back to the grass at the edge of the rosebushes. O'Dell smacked his hand over his mouth to smother his excited giggle.

Sparkles of fire dribbled out of the fuse. Sherman was counting backward from ten. We waited expectantly, and then Sherman reached zero and yelled, "*Blast off!*" just as the cherry bomb powder detonated.

There was an eyewitness, a miner waiting for a ride at the gas station across the street. For the edification of the fence gossipers, he would later describe what he had seen. There was, he reported, a huge flash in the Hickams' yard and a sound like God himself had clapped His hands. Then an arc of fire lifted up and up into the darkness, turning and cartwheeling and spewing bright sparks. The way the man told it, our rocket was a beautiful and glorious sight, and I guess he was right as far as it went. The only problem was, it wasn't our rocket that streaked into that dark, cold, clear, and starry night.

It was my mother's rose garden fence.

Soon after, Hickam and his friends would have better results. One rocket even soared six miles into the sky. Against enormous odds, the group of amateur "rocket boys"

*would go on to win the gold and silver medals at the National Science Fair. Hickam
later realized a loftier goal; twenty years after learning about* Sputnik I *and* Sputnik
II, *Homer Hickam Jr. was working on Space Shuttle missions and training astronauts
as an engineer with the National Aeronautics and Space Administration.*

Jack Kerouac, in a Rare Public Appearance, Describes What the "Beat Generation" Is—and Is Not.

*"Always considered writing my duty on earth," remarked Jack Kerouac in the intro-
duction to his 1960 book* Lonesome Traveler. *"Also the preachment of universal
kindness, which hysterical critics have failed to notice beneath the frenetic activity of my
true-story novels about the 'beat' generation.—Am actually not 'beat' but strange solitary crazy Catholic mystic." But despite his protestations, it would ultimately be the
"Beat" label that would forever stick to Kerouac, author of over a dozen books, including his 1957 classic* On the Road. *A notoriously shy public speaker, Kerouac gave
almost no formal speeches or talks, with the exception of numerous poetry readings. He
did, however, deliver an address on "Beat and Its Beginnings" in late 1958 at Hunter
College in New York City. Although there are no known recordings or transcripts of
that speech, the following statement was written by Kerouac based on his notes and recollections from the event.*

Much of the misunderstanding about hipsters and the Beat Generation
in general today derives from the fact that there are two distinct styles of hip-
sterism: the cool today is your bearded laconic sage, or schlerm, before a
hardly touched beer in a beatnik dive, whose speech is low and unfriendly,
whose girls say nothing and wear black: the "hot" today is the crazy talkative
shining eyed (often innocent and openhearted) nut who runs from bar to bar,
pad to pad looking for everybody, shouting, restless, lushy, trying to "make it"
with the subterranean beatniks who ignore him. Most Beat Generation
artists belong to the hot school, naturally since that hard gemlike flame needs
a little heat. In many cases the mixture is 50–50. It was a hot hipster like myself who finally cooled it in Buddhist meditation, though when I go in a jazz
joint I still feel like yelling, "Blow baby blow!" to the musicians though
nowadays I'd get 86d for this. In 1948 the "hot hipsters" were racing around
in cars like in *On the Road* looking for wild bawling jazz like Willis Jackson
or Lucky Thompson (the early) or Chubby Jackson's big band while the
"cool hipsters" cooled it in dead silence before formal and excellent musical
groups like Lennie Tristano or Miles Davis. It's still just about the same, ex-

cept that it has begun to grow into a national generation and the name "Beat" has stuck (though all hipsters hate the word).

The word "beat" originally meant poor, down and out, deadbeat, on the bum, sad, sleeping in subways. Now that the word is belonging officially it is being made to stretch to include people who do not sleep in subways but have a certain new gesture, or attitude, which I can only describe as a new *more*. "Beat Generation" has simply become the slogan or label for a revolution in manners in America. Marlon Brando was not really the first to portray it on the screen. Dane Clark with his pinched Dostoyevskyan face and Brooklyn accent, and of course, Garfield, were first. The private eyes were Beat, if you will recall. Bogart. Lorre was Beat. In *M,* Peter Lorre started a whole revival, I mean the slouchy street walk.

I wrote *On the Road* in three weeks in the beautiful month of April 1951 while living in the Chelsea district of lower West Side Manhattan, on a 100-foot roll and put the Beat Generation in words there, saying at the point where I am taking part in a wild kind of collegiate party with a bunch of kids in an abandoned miner's shack: "These kids are great but where are Dean Moriarty and Carlo Marx? Oh well I guess they wouldn't belong in this gang, they're too *dark*, too strange, too subterranean and I am slowly beginning to join a new kind of *beat* generation." The manuscript of *Road* was turned down on the grounds that it would displease the sales manager of my publisher at that time, though the editor, a very intelligent man, said, "Jack this is just like Dostoyevsky, but what can I do at this time?" It was too early. . . .

But when the publishers finally took a dare and published *On the Road* in 1957 it burst open, it mushroomed, everybody began yelling about a Beat Generation. I was being interviewed everywhere I went for "what I meant" by such a thing. People began to call themselves beatniks, beats, jazzniks, bopniks, bugniks, and finally I was called the "avatar" of all this.

Yet it was as a Catholic, it was not at the insistence of any of these "niks" and certainly not with their approval either, that I went one afternoon to the church of my childhood (one of them), Ste. Jeanne d'Arc in Lowell, Massachusetts, and suddenly with tears in my eyes had a vision of what I must have really meant with "Beat" anyhow when I heard the holy silence in the church (I was the only one in there, it was five p.m., dogs were barking outside, children yelling, the fall leaves, the candles were flickering alone just for me), the vision of the word Beat as being to mean beatific. There's the priest preaching on Sunday morning, all of a sudden through a side door of the church comes a group of Beat Generation characters in strapped raincoats like the I.R.A. coming in silently to "dig" the religion—I knew it then.

But this was 1954, so then what horror I felt in 1957 and later 1958 naturally to suddenly see "Beat" being taken up by everybody, press and TV and Hollywood borscht circuit to include the "juvenile delinquency" shot and the horrors of a mad teeming billyclub New York and L.A. and they began to call *that* Beat, *that* beatific—bunch of fools marching against the San Francisco Giants protesting baseball, as if (now) in my name and I, my childhood ambition to be a big league baseball star hitter like Ted Williams so that when Bobby Thomson hit that home run in 1951 I trembled with joy and couldn't get over it for days and wrote poems about how it is possible for the human spirit to win after all! Or, when a murder, a routine murder took place in North Beach, they labeled it a Beat Generation slaying. . . .

But yet, but yet, woe, woe unto those who think that the Beat Generation means crime, delinquency, immorality, amorality; woe unto those who attack it on the grounds that they simply don't understand history and the yearnings of human souls; woe unto those who don't realize that America must, will, is, changing now, for the better I say. Woe unto those who believe in the atom bomb, who believe in hating mothers and fathers, who deny that most important of the Ten Commandments, woe unto those (though) who don't believe in the unbelievable sweetness of sex love, woe unto those who are the standard bearers of death, woe unto those who believe in conflict and horror and violence and fill our books and screens and living rooms with all that crap, woe in fact to those who make evil movies about the Beat Generation where innocent housewives are raped by beatniks! Woe unto those who are the real dreary sinners that even God finds room to forgive. Woe unto those who spit on the Beat Generation, the wind'll blow it back.

———————

Poet Carl Sandburg, Before a Joint Session of Congress, Honors Abraham Lincoln on the 150th Anniversary of His Birth.

On February 12, 1959, an elderly poet addressed a joint session of the U.S. Congress, an honor no poet (and only one other private citizen) had ever been granted before. But the occasion was a momentous one—the 150th anniversary of Abraham Lincoln's birth, and the poet was one of America's most revered—Carl Sandburg. His four-volume work, Abraham Lincoln: The War Years, *earned Sandburg the Pulitzer Prize in 1940 and national acclaim. The eighty-one-year-old Sandburg was invited to speak before Congress not only as an expert on Lincoln, but as a poet who celebrated the integrity, compassion, strength, and humor of the common American—characteristics Sandburg believed Lincoln himself embodied.*

Not often in the story of mankind does a man arrive on earth who is both steel and velvet, who is as hard as rock and soft as drifting fog, who holds in his heart and mind the paradox of terrible storm and peace unspeakable and perfect. Here and there across centuries come reports of men alleged to have these contrasts. And the incomparable Abraham Lincoln, born 150 years ago this day, is an approach if not a perfect realization of this character.

In the time of the April lilacs in the year 1865, on his death, the casket with his body was carried north and west a thousand miles, and the American people wept as never before. Bells sobbed, cities wore crepe, people stood in tears and with hats off as the railroad burial car paused in the leading cities of seven states, ending its journey at Springfield, Illinois, the home town.

During the four years he was president, he at times, especially in the first three months, took to himself the powers of a dictator. He commanded the most powerful armies till then assembled in modern warfare. He enforced conscription of soldiers for the first time in American history. Under imperative necessity he abolished the right of habeas corpus. He directed politically and spiritually the wild, massive, turbulent forces let loose in civil war.

He argued and pleaded for compensated emancipation of the slaves. The slaves were property, they were on the tax books along with horses and cattle, the valuation of each slave next to his name on the tax assessor's books. Failing to get action on compensated emancipation, as a chief executive having war powers, he issued the paper by which he declared the slaves to be free under "military necessity." In the end nearly $4 million worth of property was taken away from those who were legal owners of it, property confiscated, wiped out as by fire and turned to ashes, at his instigation and executive direction. Chattel property recognized and lawful for 300 years was expropriated, seized without payment.

In the month the war began he told his secretary, John Hay, "My policy is to have no policy." Three years later in a letter to a Kentucky friend made public, he confessed plainly, "I have been controlled by events." His words at Gettysburg were sacred, yet strange with a color of the familiar: "We cannot consecrate—we cannot hallow—this ground. The brave men, living and dead, who struggled here, have consecrated it, far beyond our poor power to add or detract."

He could have said "the brave Union men." Did he have a purpose in omitting the word *Union?* Was he keeping himself and his utterance clear of the passion that would not be good to look at when the time came for peace and reconciliation? Did he mean to leave an implication that there were brave Union men, and brave Confederate men, living and dead, who had struggled there? We do not know of a certainty. Was he thinking of the Kentucky father whose two sons died in battle, one in Union blue, the other in Confederate gray, the father inscribing on the stone over their double grave, "God knows which was right"? We do not know. . . .

While the war winds howled, he insisted that the Mississippi was one river meant to belong to one country, that railroad connection from coast to coast must be pushed through and the Union Pacific Railroad made a reality. While the luck of war wavered and broke and came again, as generals failed and campaigns were lost, he held enough forces of the North together to raise new armies and supply them, until generals were found who made war as victorious war has always been made—with terror, frightfulness, destruction, and on both sides, North and South, valor and sacrifice past words of man to tell.

In the mixed shame and blame of the immense wrongs of two crashing civilizations, often with nothing to say, he said nothing, slept not at all, and on occasions he was seen to weep in a way that made weeping appropriate, decent, majestic. . . .

The people of many other countries take Lincoln now for their own. He belongs to them. He stands for decency, honest dealing, plain talk, and funny stories. "Look where he came from. Don't he know all us strugglers, and wasn't he a kind of tough struggler all his life right up to the finish?" Something like that you can hear in any nearby neighborhood and across the seas.

Millions there are who take him as a personal treasure. He had something they would like to see spread everywhere over the world. Democracy? We can't find words to say exactly what it is, but he had it. In his blood and bones he carried it. In the breath of his speeches and writings it is there. Popular government? Republican institution? Government where the people have the say-so, one way or another telling their elected leaders what they want? He had the idea. It's there in the lights and shadows of his personality, a mystery that can be lived but never fully spoken in words.

Our good friend the poet and playwright Mark Van Doren tells us, "To me, Lincoln seems, in some ways, the most interesting man who ever lived. He was gentle, but his gentleness was combined with a terrific toughness, an iron strength."

How did Lincoln say he would like to be remembered? His beloved friend, Representative Owen Lovejoy of Illinois, had died in May of 1864 and friends wrote to Lincoln and he replied that the pressure of duties kept him from joining them in efforts for a marble monument to Lovejoy, the last sentence of his letter saying, "Let him have the marble monument along with the well-assured and more enduring one in the hearts of those who love liberty, unselfishly, for all men."

So perhaps we may say that the well-assured and most enduring memorial to Lincoln is invisibly there, today, tomorrow, and for a long time yet to come in the hearts of lovers of liberty, men and women who understand that wherever there is freedom there have been those who fought, toiled, and sacrificed for it.

Green Bay Packers Coach Vince Lombardi Orders His Players to "Make Any Sacrifice to Win."

"Pro football," exclaimed Vince Lombardi, "is a violent, dangerous sport. To play it other than violently would be imbecile." Head coach of the Green Bay Packers, Lombardi led his team to five championships, including Super Bowls I and II, in the 1960s. Although raised to be a priest, Lombardi found his true love in football, working as an assistant coach at the high school, college, and eventually professional levels throughout the 1940s and 1950s. Finally, in 1959, Lombardi was named the head coach of an NFL team, the Packers, and the evening before their first game on September 27 against the Chicago Bears, the notoriously bombastic coach launched into the following tirade on his intolerance for losing.

Gentlemen, we're going to have a football team. We are going to win some games. Do you know why? Because you are going to have confidence in me and my system. By being alert you are going to make fewer mistakes than your opponents. By working harder you are going to outexecute, outblock, outtackle every team that comes your way.

I've never been a losing coach, and I don't intend to start here. There is nobody big enough to think he's got the team made or can do what he wants. Trains and planes are coming in and going in and coming out of Green Bay every day, and he'll be on one of them. I won't. I'm going to find thirty-six men who have the pride to make any sacrifice to win. There are such men. If they're not here, I'll get them. If you are not one, if you don't want to play, you might as well leave right now. . . .

I've been up here all year and I've learned a lot. I know how the townspeople are and what they think of you men and I know that in a small town you need definite rules and regulations. And anybody who breaks the rules will be taken care of in my own way. . . . You may not be a tackle. You may not be a guard. You may not be a back. But you *will* be a professional.

The Packers beat the Bears.

1960–1969

As I HAVE WALKED AMONG THE DESPERATE, REJECTED, AND angry young men I have told them that Molotov cocktails and rifles would not solve their problems. I have tried to offer them my deepest compassion while maintaining my conviction that social change comes most meaningfully through nonviolent action. But they asked—and rightly so—what about Vietnam? They asked if our own nation wasn't using massive doses of violence to solve its problems, to bring about the changes it wanted. Their questions hit home, and I knew that I could never again raise my voice against the violence of the oppressed in the ghettos without having first spoken clearly to the greatest purveyor of violence in the world today—my own government. For the sake of those boys, for the sake of this government, for the sake of the hundreds of thousands trembling under our violence, I cannot be silent.

—*Dr. Martin Luther King Jr.,*
speaking at the Riverside Church, New York City,
April 4, 1967

Dwight D. Eisenhower Ends His Presidency with a Heartfelt Message of Peace and a Warning About the Growing "Military Establishment" in America
&
President John F. Kennedy Summons the Nation and the World to Join Together in the Fight Against "Tyranny, Poverty, Disease, and War."

Before President Dwight D. Eisenhower left office to be succeeded by the forty-three-year-old dynamic senator from Massachusetts, John F. Kennedy, he had one last message to the American public: Beware the country's growing military-industrial complex. Coming from the celebrated general, the theme was an astonishing one to many. But it was not entirely without precedent. In one of the most dramatic speeches of his presidency, Eisenhower proclaimed in April 1953, "Every gun that is made, every warship launched, every rocket fired signifies, in that final sense, a theft from those who hunger and are not fed, those who are cold and are not clothed. The world in arms is not spending its money alone. It is spending the sweat of its laborers, the genius of its scientists, the hopes of its children." It was a sentiment Eisenhower continued in his farewell address on January 17, 1961.

My fellow Americans, three days from now, after half a century in the service of our country, I shall lay down the responsibilities of office as, in traditional and solemn ceremony, the authority of the presidency is vested in my successor. This evening I come to you with a message of leave taking and farewell, and to share a few final thoughts with you, my countrymen. . . .

We now stand ten years past the midpoint of a century that has witnessed four major wars among great nations. Three of these involved our own country. Despite these holocausts, America is today the strongest, the most influential, and most productive nation in the world. Understandably proud of this preeminence, we yet realize that America's leadership and prestige depend not merely upon our unmatched material progress, riches, and military strength, but on how we use our power in the interests of world peace and human betterment. . . .

Crises there will continue to be. In meeting them, whether foreign or domestic, great or small, there is a recurring temptation to feel that some spectacular and costly action could become the miraculous solution to all current difficulties. A huge increase in newer elements of our defense, development of unrealistic programs to cure every ill in agriculture, a dramatic expansion in basic and applied research—these and many other possibilities, each possibly promising in itself, may be suggested as the only way to the road we wish to travel.

But each proposal must be weighed in the light of a broader consideration: the need to maintain balance in and among national programs—balance between the private and the public economy, balance between cost and hoped for advantage, balance between the clearly necessary and the comfortably desirable, balance between our essential requirements as a nation and the duties imposed by the nation upon the individual, balance between actions of the moment and the national welfare of the future. Good judgment seeks balance and progress. Lack of it eventually finds imbalance and frustration. . . .

A vital element in keeping the peace is our military establishment. Our arms must be mighty, ready for instant action, so that no potential aggressor may be tempted to risk his own destruction. Our military organization today bears little relation to that known by any of my predecessors in peacetime, or indeed by the fighting men of World War II or Korea. Until the latest of our world conflicts, the United States had no armaments industry. American makers of plowshares could, with time and as required, make swords as well. But now we can no longer risk emergency improvisation of national defense. We have been compelled to create a permanent armaments industry of vast proportions. Added to this, three-and-a-half million men and women are directly engaged in the defense establishment. We annually spend on military security more than the net income of all United States corporations.

This conjunction of an immense military establishment and a large arms industry is new in the American experience. The total influence—economic, political, even spiritual—is felt in every city, every statehouse, every office of the federal government. We recognize the imperative need for this development. Yet we must not fail to comprehend its grave implications. Our toil, resources, and livelihood are all involved. So is the very structure of our society.

In the councils of government, we must guard against the acquisition of unwarranted influence, whether sought or unsought, by the military–industrial complex. The potential for the disastrous rise of misplaced power exists and will persist.

We must never let the weight of this combination endanger our liberties or democratic processes. We should take nothing for granted. Only an alert and knowledgeable citizenry can compel the proper meshing of the huge industrial and military machinery of defense with our peaceful methods and goals, so that security and liberty may prosper together. . . .

Down the long lane of the history yet to be written, America knows that this world of ours, ever growing smaller, must avoid becoming a community of dreadful fear and hate and be instead a proud confederation of mutual trust and respect. Such a confederation must be one of equals. The weakest must come to the conference table with the same confidence as do we, protected as we are by our moral, economic, and military strength. That table, though scarred by many past frustrations, cannot be abandoned for the certain agony of the battlefield.

Disarmament, with mutual honor and confidence, is a continuing imperative. Together we must learn how to compose differences not with arms, but with intellect and decent purpose. Because this need is so sharp and apparent, I confess that I lay down my official responsibilities in this field with a definite sense of disappointment. As one who has witnessed the horror and lingering sadness of war—as one knows that another war could utterly destroy this civilization which has been so slowly and painfully built over thousands of years—I wish I could say tonight that a lasting peace is in sight. Happily, I can say that war has been avoided. Steady progress toward our ultimate goal has been made. But so much remains to be done. As a private citizen, I shall never cease to do what little I can to help the world advance along that road.

So, in this my last good night to you as your president, I thank you for the many opportunities you have given me for public service in war and peace. I trust that in that service you find some things worthy. As for the rest of it, I know you will find ways to improve performance in the future. You and I, my fellow citizens, need to be strong in our faith that all nations, under God, will reach the goal of peace with justice. May we be ever unswerving in devotion to principle, confident but humble with power, diligent in pursuit of the nation's great goals.

To all the peoples of the world, I once more give expression to America's prayerful and continuing aspiration: We pray that peoples of all faiths, all races, all nations, may have their great human needs satisfied; that those now denied opportunity shall come to enjoy it to the full; that all who yearn for freedom may experience its spiritual blessings; that those who have freedom will understand also its heavy responsibilities; that all who are insensitive to the needs of others will learn charity; that the scourges of poverty, disease, and ignorance will be made to disappear from the earth; and that, in the goodness of time, all peoples will come to live together in a peace guaranteed by the binding force of mutual respect and love.

Three days later, President John F. Kennedy, who had defeated Richard M. Nixon by only 120,000 votes (out of almost 70 million cast), took the oath of office on the steps of the Capitol. In the bitter cold, Kennedy sent a message to the American people—and to the nations of the world—that his administration was fiercely committed to preventing the international spread of communism. Kennedy also issued one of the most memorable challenges to the American people ever heard in a presidential inauguration.

We observe today not a victory of party but a celebration of freedom, symbolizing an end as well as a beginning, signifying renewal as well as change. For I have sworn before you and Almighty God the same solemn oath our forebears prescribed nearly a century and three-quarters ago.

The world is very different now, for man holds in his mortal hands the power to abolish all forms of human poverty and all forms of human life. And yet the same revolutionary beliefs for which our forebears fought are still at issue around the globe—the belief that the rights of man come not from the generosity of the state but from the hand of God.

We dare not forget today that we are the heirs of that first Revolution. Let the word go forth from this time and place, to friend and foe alike, that the torch has been passed to a new generation of Americans born in this century, tempered by war, disciplined by a hard and bitter peace, proud of our ancient heritage, and unwilling to witness or permit the slow undoing of those human rights to which this nation has always been committed, and to which we are committed today at home and around the world. Let every nation know, whether it wishes us well or ill, that we shall pay any price, bear any burden, meet any hardship, support any friend, oppose any foe to assure the survival and the success of liberty. This much we pledge—and more.

To those old allies whose cultural and spiritual origins we share, we pledge the loyalty of faithful friends. United there is little we cannot do in a host of cooperative ventures. Divided there is little we can do, for we dare not meet a powerful challenge at odds and split asunder.

To those new states whom we welcome to the ranks of the free, we pledge our word that one form of colonial control shall not have passed away merely to be replaced by a far more iron tyranny. We shall not always expect to find them supporting our view, but we shall always hope to find them strongly supporting their own freedom—and to remember that, in the past, those who foolishly sought power by riding the back of the tiger ended up inside.

To those people in the huts and villages of half the globe struggling to break the bonds of mass misery, we pledge our best efforts to help them help themselves, for whatever period is required—not because the communists may be doing it, not because we seek their votes, but because it is right. If a free society cannot help the many who are poor, it cannot save the few who are rich.

To our sister republics south of our border, we offer a special pledge: to convert our good words into good deeds in a new alliance for progress to assist free men and free governments in casting off the chains of poverty. But this peaceful revolution of hope cannot become the prey of hostile powers. Let all our neighbors know that we shall join with them to oppose aggression or subversion anywhere in the Americas. And let every other power know that this hemisphere intends to remain the master of its own house.

To that world assembly of sovereign states, the United Nations, our last best hope in an age where the instruments of war have far outpaced the instruments of peace, we renew our pledge of support to prevent it from becoming merely a forum for invective, to strengthen its shield of the new and the weak, and to enlarge the area in which its writ may run.

Finally, to those nations who would make themselves our adversary, we offer not a pledge but a request: that both sides begin anew the quest for peace before the dark powers of destruction unleashed by science engulf all humanity in planned or accidental self-destruction. We dare not tempt them with weakness. For only when our arms are sufficient beyond doubt can we be certain beyond doubt that they will never be employed. But neither can two great and powerful groups of nations take comfort from our present course: both sides overburdened by the cost of modern weapons, both rightly alarmed by the steady spread of the deadly atom, yet both racing to alter that uncertain balance of terror that stays the hand of mankind's final war.

So let us begin anew, remembering on both sides that civility is not a sign of weakness and sincerity is always subject to proof. Let us never negotiate out of fear, but let us never fear to negotiate. Let both sides explore what problems unite us instead of belaboring those problems which divide us. Let both sides, for the first time, formulate serious and precise proposals for the inspection and control of arms, and bring the absolute power to destroy other nations under the absolute control of all nations. Let both sides seek to invoke the wonders of science instead of its terrors. Together let us explore the stars, conquer the deserts, eradicate disease, tap the ocean depths, and encourage the arts and commerce. Let both sides unite to heed in all corners of the earth the command of Isaiah to "undo the heavy burdens . . . (and) let the oppressed go free." And if a beachhead of cooperation may push back the jungle of suspicion, let both sides join in creating a new endeavor, not a new balance of power, but a new world of law, where the strong are just and the weak secure and the peace preserved.

All this will not be finished in the first one hundred days. Nor will it be finished in the first one thousand days, nor in the life of this administration, nor even perhaps in our lifetime on this planet. But let us begin. In your hands, my fellow citizens, more than mine, will rest the final success or failure of our course. Since this country was founded, each generation of Americans has been summoned to give testimony to its national loyalty. The graves of young Americans who answered the call to service surround the globe. Now the trumpet summons us again—not as a call to bear arms, though arms we need; not as a call to battle, though embattled we are—but a call to bear the burden of a long twilight struggle, year in and year out, "rejoicing in hope, patient in tribulation," a struggle against the common enemies of man: tyranny, poverty, disease, and war itself. Can we forge against these enemies a grand and global alliance, North and South, East and West, that can assure a more fruitful life for all mankind? Will you join in that historic effort?

In the long history of the world, only a few generations have been granted the role of defending freedom in its hour of maximum danger. I do not shrink from this responsibility—I welcome it. I do not believe that any of us would exchange places with any other people or any other generation. The energy, the faith, the devotion which we bring to this endeavor will light our country and all who serve it, and the glow from that fire can truly light the world.

And so, my fellow Americans, ask not what your country can do for you—ask what you can do for your country. My fellow citizens of the world, ask not what America will do for you, but what together we can do for the freedom of man.

Finally, whether you are citizens of America or citizens of the world, ask of us here the same high standards of strength and sacrifice which we ask of you. With a good conscience our only sure reward, with history the final judge of our deeds, let us go forth to lead the land we love, asking His blessing and His help, but knowing that here on earth God's work must truly be our own.

President John F. Kennedy Informs Americans of the Installation of Nuclear Missiles in Cuba—a "Reckless and Provocative Threat to World Peace."

On October 14, 1962, an American U-2 spy plane conclusively photographed the installation of nuclear missiles in Cuba, only ninety miles from the United States. The threat could not have been more menacing. National security analysts estimated that nuclear missiles launched from Cuba could reach the United States within two to three minutes and kill eighty million Americans. On October 22, President Kennedy went before the country to explain in no uncertain terms the gravity of the situation and the unconditional demands the Soviet leadership must abide by in order to resolve the crisis. Until the time of his televised address, the American public had no idea of the unfolding drama. Kennedy's spokesman, Pierre Salinger, released a statement at noon that the president would talk to the nation on a matter "of the greatest urgency" later that evening. As Kennedy spoke, the military's "Defense Condition" (DefCon) was lowered to 3; DefCon 5 representing peace, DefCon 1 full-scale nuclear war.

This government, as promised, has maintained the closest surveillance of the Soviet military buildup on the island of Cuba. Within the past week, unmistakable evidence has established the fact that a series of offensive missile sites are now in preparation on that imprisoned island. The purpose of these bases can be none other than to provide a nuclear strike capability against the Western Hemisphere.

Upon receiving the first preliminary hard information of this nature last Tuesday morning at 9 A.M., I directed that our suveillance be stepped up. And having now confirmed and completed our evaluation of the evidence and our decision on a course of action, this government feels obliged to report this new crisis to you in fullest detail.

The characteristics of these new missile sites indicate two distinct types of installations. Several of them include medium-range ballistic missiles capable of carrying a nuclear warhead for a distance of more than 1,000 nautical miles. Each of these missiles, in short, is capable of striking Washington, D.C., the Panama Canal, Cape Canaveral, Mexico City, or any other city in the southeastern part of the United States, in Central America, or in the Caribbean area.

Additional sites not yet completed appear to be designed for intermediate-range ballistic missiles capable of traveling more than twice as far and thus capable of striking most of the major cities in the Western Hemisphere, ranging as far north as Hudson Bay, Canada, and as far south as Lima, Peru. In addition, jet bombers capable of carrying nuclear weapons are now being uncrated and assembled in Cuba, while the necessary air bases are being prepared.

This urgent transformation of Cuba into an important strategic base—by the presence of these large, long-range, and clearly offensive weapons of sudden mass destruction—constitutes an explicit threat to the peace and security of all the Americas, in flagrant and deliberate defiance of the Rio Pact of 1947, the traditions of this nation and hemisphere, the joint resolution of the 87th Congress, the charter of the United Nations, and my own public warnings to the Soviets on September 4 and 13. This action also contradicts the repeated assurances of Soviet spokesmen, both publicly and privately delivered, that the arms buildup in Cuba would retain its original defensive character, and that the Soviet Union had no need or desire to station strategic missiles on the territory of any other nation. . . .

But this secret, swift, and extraordinary buildup of communist missiles—in an area well known to have a special and historical relationship to the United States and the nations of the Western Hemisphere, in violation of Soviet assurances, and in defiance of American and hemispheric policy—this sudden, clandestine decision to station strategic weapons for the first time outside of Soviet soil is a deliberately provocative and unjustified change in the status quo which cannot be accepted by this country if our courage and our commitments are ever to be trusted again by either friend or foe.

The 1930s taught us a clear lesson: Aggressive conduct, if allowed to go unchecked and unchallenged, ultimately leads to war. This nation is opposed to war. We are also true to our word. Our unswerving objective, therefore, must be to prevent the use of these missiles against this or any other country, and to secure their withdrawal or elimination from the Western Hemisphere.

Our policy has been one of patience and restraint, as befits a peaceful and powerful nation, which leads a worldwide alliance. We have been determined not to be diverted from our central concerns by mere irritants and fanatics. But now further action is required, and it is under way. And these actions may only be the beginning. We will not prematurely or unnecessarily risk the costs of worldwide nuclear war in which even the fruits of victory would be ashes in our mouth, but neither will we shrink from that risk at any time it must be faced.

Acting therefore in the defense of our own security and of the entire Western Hemisphere, and under the authority entrusted to me by the Constitution as endorsed by the resolution of the Congress, I have directed that the following initial steps be taken immediately.

First, to halt this offensive buildup, a strict quarantine on all offensive military equipment under shipment to Cuba is being initiated. All ships of any kind bound for Cuba from whatever nation or port will, if found to contain cargoes of offensive weapons, be turned back. This quarantine will be extended, if needed, to other types of cargo and carriers. We are not at this time, however, denying the necessities of life as the Soviets attempted to do in their Berlin blockade of 1948.

Second, I have directed the continued and increased close surveillance of Cuba and its military buildup. . . .

Third, it shall be the policy of this nation to regard any nuclear missile launched from Cuba against any nation in the Western Hemisphere as an attack by the Soviet Union on the United States, requiring a full retaliatory response upon the Soviet Union.

Fourth, as a necessary military precaution, I have reinforced our base at Guantanamo, evacuated today the dependents of our personnel there, and ordered additional military units to be on a standby alert basis.

Fifth, we are calling tonight for an immediate meeting of the organ of consultation under the Organization of American States to consider this threat to hemispheric security and to invoke articles 6 and 8 of the Rio Treaty in support of all necessary action. . . .

Sixth, under the charter of the United Nations, we are asking tonight that an emergency meeting of the Security Council be convoked without delay to take action against this latest Soviet threat to world peace. Our resolution will call for the prompt dismantling and withdrawal of all offensive weapons in Cuba under the supervision of U.N. observers before the quarantine can be lifted.

Seventh and finally, I call upon Chairman Khrushchev to halt and eliminate this clandestine, reckless, and provocative threat to world peace and stable relations between our two nations. I call upon him further to abandon this course of world domination and to join in an historic effort to end the perilous arms race and to transform the history of man. . . .

We have in the past made strenuous efforts to limit the spread of nuclear weapons. We have proposed the elimination of all arms and military bases in a fair and effective disarmament treaty. We are prepared to discuss new proposals for the removal of tensions on both sides, including the possibility of a genuinely independent Cuba free to determine its own destiny. We have no wish to war with the Soviet Union, for we are a peaceful people who desire to live in peace with all other peoples. But it is difficult to settle or even discuss these problems in an atmosphere of intimidation. That is why this latest Soviet threat—or any other threat which is made independently or in response to our actions this week—must and will be met with determination. . . .

My fellow citizens, let no one doubt that this is a difficult and dangerous effort on which we have set out. No one can see precisely what course it will take or what costs or casualties will be incurred. Many months of sacrifice and self-discipline lie ahead, months in which both our patience and our will will be tested, months in which many threats and denunciations will keep us aware of our dangers. But the greatest danger of all would be to do nothing.

The path we have chosen for the present is full of hazards, as all paths are, but it is the one most consistent with our character and courage as a nation and our commitments around the world. The cost of freedom is always high, and Americans have always paid it. And one path we shall never choose, and that is the path of surrender or submission.

Our goal is not the victory of might, but the vindication of right—not peace at the expense of freedom, but both peace and freedom, here in this hemisphere, and, we hope, around the world. God willing, that goal will be achieved.

The world held its breath as Soviet vessels, presumably carrying more missiles, steadily approached the American warships. Had either side fired on the other, it almost certainly would have started World War III. The Soviet ships ultimately turned back, but the conflict was not over—the matter of the existing missiles still had to be settled. On

October 26 Kennedy received a long, emotional letter from Soviet leader Nikita Khrushchev on the horrors of nuclear war and offering to remove the missiles if the United States would end the quarantine and agree not to invade Cuba. (The United States had backed such a maneuver at the Bay of Pigs in April 1961, and it was a humiliating failure.) But before Kennedy could answer, a second letter from Khrushchev was received the next morning. Its tone was stern and insisted on more concessions, including the removal of American missiles in Turkey, a demand many of Kennedy's security advisors found unacceptable. Robert Kennedy, serving as the U.S. Attorney General, advised his brother simply to ignore the second letter and respond to the first. Kennedy accepted the terms of Khrushchev's first letter, and in a secret verbal message forwarded to the Soviet Ambassador, agreed that he would remove America's missiles in Turkey. Never before had the world come closer to utter annihilation than during the Cuban Missile Crisis—nor has it since.

Alabama Governor George Wallace Promises His State: "Segregation Now! Segregation Tomorrow! Segregation Forever!"

Campaigning as a moderate in the 1958 gubernatorial race in Alabama, George Wallace was defeated for being too timid in his support for segregation. Vowing he would never, in his words, be "out-niggered again," Wallace adopted a staunchly segregationist platform and handily won the 1962 race. During the inaugural ceremony on January 14, 1963, Wallace reaffirmed his support of segregation in a speech that his supporters perceived as an eloquent articulation of states' rights and that integrationists—both black and white—viewed as indefensibly racist and demagogic.

This is the day of my inauguration as governor of the state of Alabama. And on this day I feel a deep obligation to renew my pledges, my covenants with you, the people of this great state.

Gen. Robert E. Lee said that *duty* is the sublimest word in the English language, and I have come increasingly to realize what he meant. I shall do my duty to you, God helping, to every man, to every woman, yes, and to every child in this state. I shall fulfill my duty toward honesty and economy in our state government so that no man shall have a part of his livelihood cheated and no child shall have a bit of his future stolen away. . . .

Today I have stood where once Jefferson Davis stood, and took an oath to my people. It is very appropriate then that from this cradle of the Confederacy, this very heart of the great Anglo-Saxon Southland, that today we sound the drum for freedom as have our generations of forebears before us done, time and again down through history. Let us rise to the call of freedom-loving blood that is in us and send our answer to the tyranny that clanks the name of the greatest people that have ever trod this earth. I draw the line in the dust and toss the gauntlet before the feet of tyranny, and I say segregation now! Segregation tomorrow! Segregation forever! . . .

Hear me, Southerners! You sons and daughters who have moved north and west throughout this nation, we call on you from your native soil to join with us in national support and vote. And we know wherever you are, away from the hearths of the Southland, that you will respond, for though you may live in the farthest reaches of this vast country, your heart has never left Dixieland.

And you native sons and daughters of old New England's rockribbed patriotism, and you sturdy natives of the great Midwest, and you descendants of the Far West, flaming spirit of pioneer freedom, we invite you to come and be with us, for you are of the Southern mind and the Southern spirit and the Southern philosophy. You are Southerners too and brothers with us in our fight. . . .

We are faced with an idea that if a centralized government assumes enough authority, enough power over its people, that it can provide a utopian life; that if given the power to dictate, to forbid, to require, to demand, to distribute, to edit, and to judge what is best and enforce that will of judgment upon its citizens from unimpeachable authority, then it will produce only "good," and it shall be our father and our god. It is an idea of government that encourages our fears and destroys our faith, for where there is faith, there is no fear, and where there is fear, there is no faith. In encouraging our fears of economic insecurity, it demands we place that economic management and control with government. In encouraging our fear of educational development it demands we place that education and the minds of our children under management and control of government. And even in feeding our fears of physical infirmities and declining years, it offers and demands to father us through it all and even into the grave. . . .

Not so long ago men stood in marvel and awe at the cities, the buildings, the schools, the autobahns that the government of Hitler's Germany had built, just as centuries before they stood in wonder at Rome's building. It could not stand, for the system that built it had rotted the souls of the builders and in turn rotted the foundation of what God meant that men should be. Today that same system on an international scale is sweeping the world. It is the "changing world" of which we are told, it is called "new" and "liberal." It is as old as the oldest dictator. It is degenerate and decadent. As the national racism of Hitler's Germany persecuted a national minority to the whim of a national majority, so the international racism of the liberals seek to persecute the international white minority to the whim of the international colored majority, so that we are footballed about according to the favor of the Afro-Asian bloc. But the Belgian survivors of the Congo cannot present their case to a war crimes commission, nor the Portuguese of Angola, nor the survivors of Castro, nor the citizens of Oxford, Mississippi.

It is this theory of international power politics that led a group of men on the Supreme Court for the first time in American history to issue an edict based not on legal precedent, but upon a volume, the editor of which has said our Constitution is outdated and must be changed and the writers of which some had admittedly belonged to as many as half a hundred communist front organizations. It is this theory that led this same group of women to briefly bare the ungodly core of that philosophy in forbidding little school children to say a prayer.

And we find evidence of that ungodliness even in the removal of the words "In God We Trust" from some of our dollars, which was placed there as like evidence by our Founding Fathers as the faith upon which this system of government was built.

It is the spirit of power thirst that caused a president in Washington to take up Caesar's pen and with one stroke of it, make a law. A law which the law-making body of Congress refused to pass: a law that tells us that we can or cannot buy or sell our very homes, except by his conditions, and except at his discretion. It is the spirit of power thirst that led that same president to launch a full offensive of 25,000 troops against a university—of all places—in his country and against his own people, when this nation maintains only 6,000 troops in the beleaguered city of Berlin.

We have witnessed such acts of "might makes right" over the world as men yielded to the temptation to play God, but we have never before witnessed it in America. We reject such acts as free men. We do not defy, for there is nothing to defy, since as free men we do not recognize any government right to give freedom or deny freedom. No government erected by man has that right. As Thomas Jefferson has said, "The God who gave us life gave us liberty at the same time. No king holds the right of liberty in his hands." Nor does any ruler in American government. . . .

This nation was never meant to be a unit of one, but a united of the many. That is the exact reason our freedom-loving forefathers established the states, so as to divide the rights and powers among the many states, insuring that no central power could gain master government control.

In united effort we were meant to live under this government, whether Baptist, Methodist, Presbyterian, Church of Christ, or whatever one's denomination or religious belief, each respecting the others' right to a separate denomination; each, by working to develop his own, enriching the total of all our lives through united effort. And so it was meant in our political lives, whether Republican, Democrat, Prohibition, or whatever political party, each striving from his separate political station, respecting the rights of others to be separate and work from within their political framework, and each separate political station making its contribution to our lives.

And so it was meant in our racial lives. Each race within its own framework has the freedom to teach, to instruct, to develop, to ask for and receive deserved help from others of separate racial stations. This is the great freedom of our American Founding Fathers. But if we amalgamate into one unit as advocated by the communist philosophers, then the enrichment of our lives, the freedom of our development, is gone forever. We become therefore a mongrel unit of one under a single all-powerful government, and we stand for everything and for nothing. The true brotherhood of America, of respecting the separateness of others and uniting in effort, has been so twisted and distorted from its original concept that there is small wonder that communism is winning the world.

We invite the Negro citizens of Alabama to work with us from his separate racial station—as we will work with him—to develop, to grow in individual freedom and enrichment. We want jobs and a good future for both our races. We want to help the physically and mentally sick of both races, the tubercular and the infirm. This is the basic heritage of my religion, of which I make full practice, for we are all the handiwork of God. . . .

My pledge to you to "stand up for Alabama" is a stronger pledge today than it was the first day I made that pledge. I shall stand up for Alabama as governor of our state. You stand with me, and we together can give courageous leadership to millions of people throughout this nation who look to the South for their hope in this fight to win and preserve our freedoms and liberties. So help me God.

And my prayer is that the Father who reigns above us will bless all the people of this great sovereign state and nation, both white and black.

Later that year, on June 11, Wallace physically placed himself in "the school house door" to block two African American students from attending the University of Alabama. President Kennedy federalized the Alabama National Guard, and the two students, James Hood and Vivian Malone, were allowed to enter. Wallace would go on to serve four terms as governor and run four times for president. In 1972 he was crippled by a would-be assassin, Arthur Bremer, who shot Wallace five times at a campaign rally. Before he died at the age of seventy-nine in September 1998, Wallace expressed deep remorse for his past and made peace with many of those he had antagonized—including James Hood.

Standing in Front of the Berlin Wall, President John F. Kennedy Reminds the World of the "Failures of Communism."

Situated deep within Soviet-dominated East Germany, the city of Berlin became a battleground of political ideology and military bluster between the United States and the Soviet Union after World War II. East Berlin was controlled by the communists, and in 1948 Soviet leader Joseph Stalin cut off all power and food supplies to the western, pro-democracy sector of the city and blockaded the area with tanks in hopes West Berlin would submit to Soviet authority. Undeterred, the United States and its allies commenced a nonstop, eleven-month airlift to provide citizens with coal, food, and other necessities to survive. Although Stalin capitulated, his successor, Nikita Khrushchev, would prove more belligerent. Meeting face to face on June 4, 1961, with President Kennedy (who later fumed that Khrushchev treated him like "a little boy"), the Soviet leader issued an ultimatum—West Berlin or war. "If that is true," Kennedy replied, "then, Mr. Chairman, there will be war." After weeks of increasing tension between the two superpowers, Khrushchev devised a third alternative: beginning in the middle of August, a twenty-eight-mile barrier made of barbed wire—later replaced by electrified fences and concrete barriers guarded by soldiers with orders to shoot to kill— was swiftly erected between East and West Berlin. Hundreds of thousands of East Berliners had been fleeing to the West in hopes of escaping communist oppression, and Khrushchev wanted to stem the flow. Kennedy grudgingly accepted the barrier. "Better a wall," he privately said, "than a war." But when Kennedy traveled to Germany in June of 1963 and looked over the wall to see the conditions of those trapped in East Berlin, he was profoundly shocked. "He looks like a man who just glimpsed hell," journalist Hugh Sidey observed. Back in his motorcade, Kennedy immediately began redrafting the remarks he had planned to deliver, crafting a speech that would resonate with more power and intensity than any other he had given—or would ever give—on foreign soil.

I am proud to come to this city as the guest of your distinguished mayor, who has symbolized throughout the world the fighting spirit of West Berlin. And I am proud to visit the federal republic with your distinguished chancellor who for so many years has committed Germany to democracy and freedom and progress, and to come here in the company of my fellow American, General Clay, who has been in this city during its great moments of crisis and will come again if ever needed.

Two thousand years ago the proudest boast was *"Civis Romanus sum."* Today, in the world of freedom, the proudest boast is *"Ich bin ein Berliner."* There are many people in the world who really don't understand, or say they don't, what is the great issue between the free world and the communist world. Let them come to Berlin. There are some who say that communism is the wave of the future. Let them come to Berlin. And there are some who say in Europe and elsewhere we can work with the communists. Let them come to Berlin. And there are even a few who say that it is true that communism is an evil system, but it permits us to make economic progress. *Lass' sic nach Berlin Kommen.* Let them come to Berlin.

Freedom has many difficulties and democracy is not perfect, but we have never had to put a wall up to keep our people in, to prevent them from leaving us. I want to say, on behalf of my countrymen who live many miles away on the other side of the Atlantic, who are far distant from you, that they take the greatest pride that they have been able to share with you, even from a distance, the story of the last eighteen years. I know of no town, no city, that has been besieged for eighteen years that still lives with the vitality and the force and the hope and the determination of the city of West Berlin. While the wall is the most obvious and vivid demonstration of the failures of the communist system for all the world to see, we take no satisfaction in it, for it is, as your mayor has said, an offense not only against history but an offense against humanity, separating families, dividing husbands and wives and brothers and sisters, and dividing a people who wish to be joined together.

What is true of this city is true of Germany: Real, lasting peace in Europe can never be assured as long as one German out of four is denied the elementary right of free men, and that is to make a free choice. In eighteen years of peace and good faith, this generation of Germans has earned the right to be free, including the right to unite their families and their nation in lasting peace, with goodwill to all people. You live in a defended island of freedom, but your life is part of the main. So let me ask you, as I close, to lift your eyes beyond the dangers of today, to the hopes of tomorrow, beyond the freedom merely of this city of Berlin, or your country of Germany, to the advance of freedom everywhere, beyond the wall to the day of peace with justice, beyond yourselves and ourselves to all mankind.

Freedom is indivisible, and when one man is enslaved, all are not free. When all are free, then we can look forward to that day when this city will be joined as one and this country and this great continent of Europe in a peaceful and hopeful globe. When that day finally comes, as it will, the people of West Berlin can take sober satisfaction in the fact that they were in the front lines for almost two decades.

All free men, wherever they may live, are citizens of Berlin, and therefore, as a free man, I take pride in the words *"Ich bin ein Berliner."*

Thirty-five years later, after Mikhail Gorbachev's perestroika *policies swept through the Soviet Union and Eastern Europe, the Berlin Wall came down and East and West Berlin (and later East and West Germany) were reunited.*

Dr. Martin Luther King Jr. Electrifies a Nation with His
Call for an End to Segregation and Racial Discrimination
&
Dr. King Eulogizes Four Little Black Girls
Murdered by the Ku Klux Klan
&
Malcolm X Scoffs at Dr. King's Pacifism, Declaring:
"There's No Such Thing as a Nonviolent Revolution."

Fears of a racial war in America were not unfounded in the summer of 1963. Armed federal marshals had to be called in to protect black students registering at universities in Mississippi and Alabama. Thirty-seven-year-old NAACP activist Medgar Evers was shot dead outside his house and in full view of his family by a racist assassin. Police chief "Bull" Connor unleashed high-pressured firehoses and ferocious dogs on peaceful civil rights demonstrators in Birmingham, Alabama, as televised images of the brutality horrified millions of viewers—black and white. When civil rights leaders A. Philip Randolph and Dr. Martin Luther King Jr. proposed a March on Washington, President Kennedy expressed concern that the event would only further enflame tensions and jeopardize the passage of a civil rights bill pending in Congress. King later remarked, "I have never engaged in any direct-action movement which did not seem ill timed." On August 28, 1963, an estimated quarter of a million people— 200,000 black, 50,000 white—gathered together around the Lincoln Memorial to hear entertainers such as Harry Belafonte, Sidney Poitier, Joan Baez, and Bob Dylan appeal for justice and harmony. (President Kennedy had secretly positioned thousands of troops in the surrounding areas and had aides stand by the controls of the microphone ready to pull the plug in case the rhetoric became too incendiary.) As evening approached, it was time for the keynote speaker—King—to address the hushed audience at the memorial, as well as the tens of millions of Americans watching the event live on television. King's deep Baptist baritone mesmerized the crowd, and as they responded to his energy and eloquence King disregarded his prepared text and extemporaneously delivered one of the most soul-stirring orations of the twentieth century.

I am happy to join with you today in what will go down in history as the greatest demonstration for freedom in the history of our nation.

Five score years ago, a great American in whose symbolic shadow we stand today signed the Emancipation Proclamation. This momentous decree came as a great beacon light of hope to millions of Negro slaves who had been seared in the flames of withering injustice. It came as a joyous daybreak to end the long night of their captivity.

But one hundred years later, the Negro still is not free. One hundred years later, the life of the Negro is still sadly crippled by the manacles of segregation and the chains of discrimination. One hundred years later, the Negro lives on a lonely island of poverty in the midst of a vast ocean of material prosperity. One hundred years later, the Negro is still languishing in the corners of American society and finds himself an exile in his own land.

So we have come here today to dramatize a shameful condition. In a sense we have come to our nation's capital to cash a check. When the architects of our republic wrote the magnificent words of the Constitution and the Declaration of Independence, they were signing a promissory note to which every American was to fall heir. This note was a promise that all men—yes, black men as well as white men—would be guaranteed the inalienable rights of life, liberty, and the pursuit of happiness.

It is obvious today that America has defaulted on this promissory note insofar as her citizens of color are concerned. Instead of honoring this sacred obligation, America has given the Negro people a bad check, a check which has come back marked "insufficient funds." But we refuse to believe that the bank of justice is bankrupt. We refuse to believe that there are insufficient funds in the great vaults of opportunity of this nation. So we have come to cash this check, a check that will give us upon demand the riches of freedom and the security of justice.

We have also come to this hallowed spot to remind America of the fierce urgency of now. This is no time to engage in the luxury of cooling off or to take the tranquilizing drug of gradualism. Now is the time to make real the promises of democracy. Now it the time to rise from the dark and desolate valley of segregation to the sunlit path of racial justice. Now is the time to lift our nation from the quicksands of racial injustice to the solid rock of brotherhood. Now is the time to make justice a reality for all of God's children. It would be fatal for the nation to overlook the urgency of the moment. This sweltering summer of the Negro's legitimate discontent will not pass until there is an invigorating autumn of freedom and equality.

Nineteen sixty-three is not an end, but a beginning. And those who hope that the Negro needed to blow off steam and will now be content will have a rude awakening if the nation returns to business as usual. There will be neither rest nor tranquility in America until the Negro is granted his citizenship rights. The whirlwinds of revolt will continue to shake the foundations of our nation until the bright day of justice emerges.

But there is something that I must say to my people who stand on the warm threshold which leads into the palace of justice. In the process of gaining our rightful place we must not be guilty of wrongful deeds. Let us not seek to satisfy our thirst for freedom by drinking from the cup of bitterness and hatred. We must forever conduct our struggle on the high plane of dignity and discipline. We must not allow our creative protest to degenerate into physical violence. Again and again we must rise to the majestic heights of meeting physical force with soul force.

The marvelous new militancy which has engulfed the Negro community must not lead us to a distrust of all white people, for many of our white brothers, as evidenced by their presence here today, have come to realize that their destiny is tied up with our destiny. They have come to realize that their freedom is inextricably bound to our freedom. We cannot walk alone.

And as we walk, we must make the pledge that we shall always march ahead. We cannot turn back. There are those who are asking the devotees of civil rights, "When will you be satisfied?" We can never be satisfied as long as the Negro is the victim of the unspeakable horrors of police brutality. We can never be satisfied as long as our bodies, heavy with the fatigue of travel, cannot gain lodging in the motels of the highways and the hotels of the cities. We cannot be satisfied as long as a Negro in Mississippi cannot vote, and a Negro in New York believes he has nothing for which to vote. No, no, we are not satisfied, and we will not be satisfied until justice rolls down like waters and righteousness like a mighty stream.

I am not unmindful that some of you have come here out of great trials and tribulation. Some of you come fresh from narrow jail cells. Some of you have come from areas where your quest for freedom left you battered by the storms of persecution and staggered by the winds of police brutality. You have been the veterans of creative suffering. Continue to work with the faith that unearned suffering is redemptive. Go back to Mississippi. Go back to Alabama. Go back to South Carolina. Go back to Georgia. Go back to Louisiana. Go back to the slums and ghettos of our northern cities, knowing that somehow this situation can and will be changed. Let us not wallow in the valley of despair.

I say to you today my friends, even though we face the difficulties of today and tomorrow, I still have a dream. It is a dream deeply rooted in the American dream. I have a dream that one day this nation will rise up and live out the true meaning of its creed: "We hold these truths to be self-evident, that all men are created equal."

I have a dream that one day on the red hills of Georgia the sons of former slaves and the sons of former slaveowners will be able to sit down together at the table of brotherhood.

I have a dream that one day, even the state of Mississippi, a state sweltering with the heat of injustice, a state sweltering with the heat of oppression, will be transformed into an oasis of freedom and justice.

I have a dream that my four little children will one day live in a nation where they will not be judged by the color of their skin but by the content of their character. I have a dream today.

I have a dream that one day, down in Alabama, with its vicious racists, with its governor having his lips dripping with the words of interposition and nullification, that one day right down in Alabama, little black boys and black girls will be able to join hands with little white boys and white girls as sisters and brothers. I have a dream today.

I have a dream that one day every valley shall be exalted, every hill and mountain shall be made low, the rough places will be made plain and the crooked places will be made straight and the glory of the Lord shall be revealed and all flesh shall see it together.

This is our hope. This is the faith that I go back to the South with. With this faith we will be able to hew out of the mountain of despair a stone of hope. With this faith we will be able to transform the jangling discords of our nation into a beautiful symphony of brotherhood. With this faith we will be able to work together, to pray together, to struggle together, to go to jail together, to stand up for freedom together, knowing that we will be free one day. This will be the day, this will be the day when all of God's children will be able to sing with new meaning, "My country 'tis of thee,/ sweet land of liberty,/ of thee I sing./ Land where my fathers died,/ land of the Pilgrims' pride,/ from every mountainside,/ let freedom ring!" And if America is to be a great nation, this must become true.

So let freedom ring from the prodigious hilltops of New Hampshire. Let freedom ring from the mighty mountains of New York. Let freedom ring from the heightening Alleghenies of Pennsylvania. Let freedom ring from the snowcapped Rockies of Colorado. Let freedom ring from the curvaceous slopes of California. But not only that, let freedom ring from Stone Mountain of Georgia. Let freedom ring from Lookout Mountain of Tennessee. Let freedom ring from every hill and molehill of Mississippi. From every mountainside, let freedom ring.

And when this happens, when we allow freedom to ring, when we let it ring from every village and every hamlet, from every state and every city, we will be able to speed up that day when all of God's children—black men and white men, Jews and Gentiles, Protestants and Catholics—will be able to join hands and sing in the words of the old Negro spiritual, "Free at last, free at last. Thank God Almighty, we are free at last."

The surge of euphoria and expectations of racial unity generated by King's riveting speech were imperiled eighteen days later by an act of sheer evil: on September 15, four little black girls attending Sunday school at the Sixteenth Street Baptist Church in Birmingham were killed by a bomb set off by members of the Ku Klux Klan. Even the civil rights movement's staunchest advocates of peaceful resistance questioned whether they could remain nonviolent in the wake of such barbarity. In the following

eulogy for the slain children, King exhorted his followers to hold fast to their sense of
urgency, but not to succumb to the impulses of hate.

This afternoon we gather in the quiet of this sanctuary to pay our last
tribute of respect to these beautiful children of God. They entered the stage
of history just a few years ago, and in the brief years that they were privileged
to act on this mortal stage, they played their parts exceedingly well. Now the
curtain falls; they move through the exit; the drama of their earthly life comes
to a close. They are now committed back to that eternity from which they
came. These children—unoffending, innocent, and beautiful—were the victims of one of the most vicious, heinous crimes ever perpetrated against humanity.

Yet they died nobly. They are the martyred heroines of a holy crusade for
freedom and human dignity. So they have something to say to us in their
death. They have something to say to every minister of the Gospel who has
remained silent behind the safe security of stained-glass windows. They have
something to say to every politician who has fed his constituents the stale
bread of hatred and the spoiled meat of racism. They have something to say
to a federal government that has compromised with the undemocratic practices of southern Dixiecrats and the blatant hypocrisy of right-wing northern Republicans. They have something to say to every Negro who passively
accepts the evil system of segregation and stands on the sidelines in the midst
of a mighty struggle for justice. They say to each of us, black and white alike,
that we must substitute courage for caution. They say to us that we must be
concerned not merely about who murdered them, but about the system, the
way of life and the philosophy which produced the murderers. Their death
says to us that we must work passionately and unrelentingly to make the
American dream a reality.

So they did not die in vain. God still has a way of wringing good out of
evil. History has proven over and over again that unmerited suffering is redemptive. The innocent blood of these little girls may well serve as the redemptive force that will bring new light to this dark city. The holy Scripture
says, "A little child shall lead them." The death of these little children may lead
our whole Southland from the low road of man's inhumanity to man to the
high road of peace and brotherhood. These tragic deaths may lead our nation
to substitute an aristocracy of character for an aristocracy of color. The spilt
blood of these innocent girls may cause the whole citizenry of Birmingham
to transform the negative extremes of a dark past into the positive extremes
of a bright future. Indeed, this tragic event may cause the white South to
come to terms with its conscience.

So in spite of the darkness of the hour we must not despair. We must not become bitter, nor must we harbor the desire to retaliate with violence. We must not lose faith in our white brothers. Somehow we must believe that the most misguided among them can learn to respect the dignity and worth of all human personality.

May I now say a word to you, the members of the bereaved families. It is almost impossible to say anything that can console you at this difficult hour and remove the deep clouds of disappointment which are floating in your mental skies. But I hope you can find a little consolation from the universality of this experience. Death comes to every individual. There is an amazing democracy about death. It is not aristocracy for some of the people, but a democracy for all of the people. Kings die and beggars die; rich men die and poor men die; old people die and young people die; death comes to the innocent and it comes to the guilty. Death is the irreducible common denominator of all men.

I hope you can find some consolation from Christianity's affirmation that death is not the end. Death is not a period that ends the great sentence of life, but a comma that punctuates it to more lofty significance. Death is not a blind alley that leads the human race into a state of nothingness, but an open door which leads man into life eternal. Let this daring faith, this great invincible surmise, be your sustaining power during these trying days.

At times life is hard, as hard as crucible steel. It has its bleak and painful moments. Like the ever-flowing waters of a river, life has its moments of drought and its moments of flood. Like the ever-changing cycle of the seasons, life has the soothing warmth of the summers and the piercing chill of its winters. But through it all, God walks with us. Never forget that God is able to lift you from fatigue of despair to the buoyancy of hope, and transform dark and desolate valleys into sunlit paths of inner peace.

Your children did not live long, but they lived well. The quantity of their lives was disturbingly small, but the quality of their lives was magnificently big. Where they died and what they were doing when death came will remain a marvelous tribute to each of you and an eternal epitaph to each of them. They died not in a den or dive nor were they hearing and telling filthy jokes at the time of their death. They died within the sacred walls of the church after discussing a principle as eternal as love.

Shakespeare had Horatio utter some beautiful words over the dead body of Hamlet. I paraphrase these words today as I stand over the last remains of these lovely girls. Good-night, sweet princesses. May the flight of angels take thee to thy eternal rest.

Millions of blacks throughout the country could not, however, share Dr. King's aspirations for racial equality realized only through peaceful means. And no black leader proved more threatening to King's nonviolent philosophy than Malcolm X. He was born Malcolm Little. When he was a child, his family home was burned to the ground by a white vigilante group, and years later his father, a Baptist clergyman, was found dismembered on their town's trolley tracks—murdered, Malcolm suspected, by whites. Malcolm was a sharp-minded, promising student, but his desire to remain in school and eventually become a lawyer was crushed by a teacher who cautioned, "You've got to be realistic about being a nigger." Incarcerated as a young man for burglary, Malcolm dropped his "slave name" and replaced it with an X, representing the unknown surname of his African ancestors. He also converted to the Muslim faith and, after being released from prison, so impressed Nation of Islam leader Elijah Muhammad that Muhammad made him a minister. (Malcolm X would later break with the Nation of Islam, leading to his assassination by three of its members on February 21, 1965.) On November 10, 1963—several months after Dr. King's March on Washington, which Malcolm X dismissed as a "farce"—Malcolm X spoke before a Detroit audience and scoffed at the notion of a "peaceful, turn-the-other-cheek" revolution.

We want to have just an off-the-cuff chat between you and me, us. We want to talk right down to earth in a language that everybody here can easily understand. . . .

I would like to make a few comments concerning the difference between the black revolution and the Negro revolution. Are they both the same? And if they're not, what is the difference? What is the difference between a black revolution and a Negro revolution? First, what is a revolution? Sometimes I'm inclined to believe that many of our people are using this word *revolution* loosely, without taking careful consideration of what this word actually means and what its historic characteristics are. When you study the historic nature of revolutions, the motive of a revolution, the objective of a revolution, the result of a revolution, and the methods used in a revolution, you may change words. You may devise another program, you may change your goal and you may change your mind.

Look at the American Revolution in 1776. That revolution was for what? For land. Why did they want land? Independence. How was it carried out? Bloodshed. Number one, it was based on land, the basis of independence. And the only way they could get it was bloodshed. The French Revolution— what was it based on? The landless against the landlord. What was it for? Land. How did they get it? Bloodshed—was no love lost, was no compromise, was no negotiation. I'm telling you, you don't know what a revolution is. Because when you find out what it is, you'll get back in the alley, you'll get out of the way. The Russian Revolution—what was it based on? Land; the landless against the landlord. How did they bring it about? Bloodshed. You haven't got a revolution that doesn't involve bloodshed. And you're afraid to bleed. I said, you're afraid to bleed. . . .

I cite these various revolutions, brothers and sisters, to show you that you don't have a peaceful revolution. You don't have a turn-the-other-cheek revolution. There's no such thing as a nonviolent revolution. The only kind of revolution that is nonviolent is the Negro revolution. The only revolution in which the goal is loving your enemy is the Negro revolution. It's the only revolution in which the goal is a desegregated lunch counter, a desegregated theater, a desegregated park, and a desegregated public toilet. You can sit down next to white folks—on the toilet. That's no revolution. Revolution is based on land. Land is the basis of all independence. Land is the basis of freedom, justice, and equality.

The white man knows what a revolution is. He knows that the black revolution is worldwide in scope and in nature. The black revolution is sweeping Asia, is sweeping Africa, is rearing its head in Latin America. How do you think he'll react to you when you learn what a real revolution is? You don't know what a revolution is. If you did, you wouldn't use that word.

Revolution is bloody, revolution is hostile, revolution knows no compromise, revolution overturns and destroys everything that gets in its way. And you, sitting around here like a knot on the wall, saying, "I'm going to love these folks no matter how much they hate me." No, you need a revolution. Whoever heard of a revolution where they lock arms, as Reverend Cleage was pointing out beautifully, singing, "We shall overcome"? You don't do that in a revolution. You don't do any singing, you're too busy swinging. It's based on land. A revolutionary wants land so he can set up his own nation, an independent nation. These Negroes aren't asking for any nation—they're trying to crawl back on the plantation.

When you want a nation, that's called nationalism. When the white man became involved in a revolution in this country against England, what was it for? He wanted this land so he could set up another white nation. That's white nationalism. The American Revolution was white nationalism. The French Revolution was white nationalism. The Russian Revolution, too. Yes, it was white nationalism. You don't think so? Why do you think Khrushchev and Mao can't get their heads together? White nationalism. All the revolutions that are going on in Asia and Africa are based on what? Black nationalism. A revolutionary is a black nationalist. He wants a nation. I was reading some beautiful words by Reverend Cleage, pointing out why he couldn't get together with someone else in the city because all of them were afraid of being identified with black nationalism. If you're afraid of black nationalism, you're afraid of revolution. And if you love revolution, you love black nationalism. . . .

President John F. Kennedy Pays Tribute to the Poet Robert Frost and All of America's Writers and Artists.

The world was not on the brink of nuclear annihilation, and there was no domestic or international crisis immediately calling upon President Kennedy's oratorical finesse to reassure or inspire the nation. The only obligation facing the president on October 26, 1963, was to participate in a small ceremony at Amherst College in honor of the poet Robert Frost. The event nevertheless allowed Kennedy, who could recite whole passages of poetry by heart, an opportunity to offer one of the most thoughtful tributes ever spoken by a politician on the place and purpose of artistic expression in society.

This day devoted to the memory of Robert Frost offers an opportunity for reflection which is prized by politicians as well as by others, and even by poets, for Robert Frost was one of the granite figures of our time in America. He was supremely two things: an artist and an American. A nation reveals itself not only by the men it produces but also by the men it honors, the men it remembers.

In America, our heroes have customarily run to men of large accomplishments. But today this college and country honors a man whose contribution was not to our size but to our spirit, not to our political beliefs but to our insight, not to our self-esteem, but to our self-comprehension. In honoring Robert Frost, we therefore can pay honor to the deepest sources of our national strength. That strength takes many forms, and the most obvious forms are not always the most significant. The men who create power make an indispensable contribution to the nation's greatness, but the men who question power make a contribution just as indispensable, especially when that questioning is disinterested, for they determine whether we use power or power uses us.

Our national strength matters, but the spirit which informs and controls our strength matters just as much. This was the special significance of Robert Frost. He brought an unsparing instinct for reality to bear on the platitudes and pieties of society. His sense of the human tragedy fortified him against self-deception and easy consolation. "I have been," he wrote, "one acquainted with the night." And because he knew the midnight as well as the high noon, because he understood the ordeal as well as the triumph of the human spirit, he gave his age strength with which to overcome despair. At bottom, he held a deep faith in the spirit of man, and it is hardly an accident that Robert Frost coupled poetry and power, for he saw poetry as the means of saving power from itself. When power leads men towards arrogance, poetry reminds him of his limitations. When power narrows the areas of man's concern, poetry reminds him of the richness and diversity of his existence. When power corrupts, poetry cleanses. For art establishes the basic human truth which must serve as the touchstone of our judgment.

The artist, however faithful to his personal vision of reality, becomes the last champion of the individual mind and sensibility against an intrusive society and an officious state. The great artist is thus a solitary figure. He has, as Frost said, a lover's quarrel with the world. In pursuing his perceptions of reality, he must often sail against the currents of his time. This is not a popular role. If Robert Frost was much honored in his lifetime, it was because a good many preferred to ignore his darker truths. Yet in retrospect, we see how the artist's fidelity has strengthened the fiber of our national life.

If sometimes our great artists have been the most critical of our society, it is because their sensitivity and their concern for justice, which must motivate any true artist, makes him aware that our nation falls short of its highest potential. I see little of more importance to the future of our country and our civilization than full recognition of the place of the artist.

If art is to nourish the roots of our culture, society must set the artist free to follow his vision wherever it takes him. We must never forget that art is not a form of propaganda; it is a form of truth. And as Mr. MacLeish once remarked of poets, there is nothing worse for our trade than to be in style. In free society art is not a weapon and it does not belong to the spheres of polemic and ideology. Artists are not engineers of the soul. It may be different elsewhere, but democratic society—in it—the highest duty of the writer, the composer, the artist is to remain true to himself and to let the chips fall where they may. In serving his vision of the truth, the artist best serves his nation. And the nation which disdains the mission of art invites the fate of Robert Frost's hired man, the fate of having "nothing to look backward to with pride, and nothing to look forward to with hope."

I look forward to a great future for America, a future in which our country will match its military strength with our moral restraint, its wealth with our wisdom, its power with our purpose. I look forward to an America which will not be afraid of grace and beauty, which will protect the beauty of our natural environment, which will preserve the great old American houses and squares and parks of our national past, and which will build handsome and balanced cities for our future.

I look forward to an America which will reward achievement in the arts as we reward achievement in business or statecraft. I look forward to an America which will steadily raise the standards of artistic accomplishment and which will steadily enlarge cultural opportunities for all of our citizens. And I look forward to an America which commands respect throughout the world not only for its strength but for its civilization as well. And I look forward to a world which will be safe not only for democracy and diversity but also for personal distinction.

Robert Frost was often skeptical about projects for human improvement, yet I do not think he would disdain this hope. As he wrote during the uncertain days of the Second War:

> Take human nature altogether since time began . . .
> And it must be a little more in favor of man,
> Say a fraction of one percent at the very least . . .
> Our hold on this planet wouldn't have so increased.

Because of Mr. Frost's life and work, because of the life and work of this college, our hold on this planet has increased.

Cardinal Richard Cushing Offers a Final Prayer for President John F. Kennedy, Slain by an Assassin's Bullet.

At 2:38 P.M. on November 22, 1963, a visibly shaken Walter Cronkite interrupted the afternoon television broadcast to issue a report almost surreal in its abruptness: "From Dallas, Texas, the flash apparently official. President Kennedy died at 1:00 P.M. Central Standard Time, two o'clock Eastern Standard Time, some 38 minutes ago." Kennedy, the very embodiment of life and vitality, was only forty-five years old at the time. And in a moment, he was gone forever. Shell-shocked, the nation watched a parade of indelible images over the next several days: Vice President Johnson being sworn in next to Jacqueline Kennedy—still wearing her blood-splattered dress—aboard Air Force One on the day of the killing; Lee Harvey Oswald, the assassin, led by police officers through a garage basement in chains when Jack Ruby suddenly stepped in his path and shot him dead; the funeral cortege moving slowly across Memorial Bridge and into Arlington National Cemetery; and, most heartbreaking of all, the picture of the president's three-year-old son saluting his father's coffin as it passed by. On November 24, Cardinal Richard Cushing, who had known John F. Kennedy as a young man, eulogized the slain leader during a nationally televised address from Kennedy's hometown of Boston.

In the name of the Father, and of the Son, and of the Holy Ghost. Amen.

My dearly beloved, friends in Christ, and guests: A shocked and stricken world stands helpless before the fact of death, that death brought to us through a tragically successful assault upon the life of the president of the United States. Our earliest disbelief has slowly given way to unprecedented sorrow as millions all over the earth join us in lamenting a silence that can never again be broken and the absence of a smile that can never again be seen.

For those of us who knew the president as a friend as well as a statesman, words mock our attempts to express the anguish of our hearts. It was my privilege to have been associated with John F. Kennedy from the earliest days of his public life, and even prior to that time, my privilege to have watched him mature with ever-expanding responsibility, to have known some of the warmth of his hearty friendship, to see tested under pain and loss the steely strength of his character. I have been with him in joy and in sorrow, in decision and in crisis, among friends and with strangers, and I know of no one who has combined in more noble perfection the qualities of greatness that marked his cool, calculating intelligence and his big, brave, bountiful heart. Now all of a sudden, he has been taken from us, and I dare say we shall never see his like again.

Many there are who will appropriately pay tribute to the president as a world figure, a tribute due him for his skill in political life and his devotion to public service. Many others will measure the wide interests of his mind, the swiftness of his resolution, the power of his persuasion, the efficiency of his action, and the courage of his conviction. For me, however, it is more fitting and proper to recall him during these days of mourning as husband and father, surrounded by his young and beloved family. Although the demands of his exalted position carried him often on long journeys and filled even his days at home with endless labors, how often he would make time to share with his little son and sweet daughter whatever time would be his own. What a precious treasure it is now and will be forever in the memories of the two fatherless children. Who among us can forget those childish ways which from time to time enhance the elegance of the executive mansion with the touching scenes of a happy family life? Charming Caroline stealing the publicity, jovial John-John on all fours ascending the stairs of an airplane to greet his daddy, and a loving mother like all mothers joyfully watching the two children of her flesh and blood, mindful always of three others in nurseries in the Kingdom of Heaven.

At the side of the president in understanding devotion and affection behold his gracious and beautiful Jacqueline. True always to the obligations of her role as mother, she has given new dimensions to the trying demands of being America's first lady. The pride in her husband which he so eminently justified was plainly reciprocated in his pride of her. The bonds of love that made them one in marriage became like hoops of steel binding them together. From wherever men may look out from eternity to see the workings of our world, Jack Kennedy must beam with new pride in that valiant woman who shared his life, especially to the moment of its early and bitter end. It will never be forgotten by her, for her clothes are now stained with the blood of her assassinated husband.

Those days of sorrow must be difficult for her—more difficult than for any others. A divine Providence has blessed her as few such women in history by allowing her hero husband to have the dying comfort of her arms. When men speak of this sad hour in times to come, they will ever recall how well her frail beauty matched in courage the stalwart warrior who was her husband. We who had so many reasons for holding her person in a most profound respect must now find an even wider claim for the nobility of her spirit.

One cannot think, my dearly beloved, especially one such as myself, of the late president without thinking also of the legacy of public service which was bequeathed to him by his name and his family. For several generations in a variety of tasks, this republic on one level or another has been enriched by the blood that was so wantonly shed on Friday last. Jack Kennedy fulfilled in the highest office available to him the long dedication of his family. It is a consolation for us all to know that his tragic death does not spell the end of this public service but commits to new responsibilities the energies and the abilities of one of the truly great families of America. What comfort can I extend to their heavy hearts today—mother, father, sisters, brothers? What beyond the knowledge that they have given history a youthful Lincoln, who in his time and in his sacrifice had made more sturdy the hopes of this nation and its people.

The late president was even in death a young man, and he was proud of his youth. We can never forget the words with which he began his short term as president of the United States: "Let the word go forth," he said, "from this time and place, to friend and foe alike, that the torch has been passed to a new generation of Americans born in this century, tempered by war, disciplined by a hard and bitter peace, proud of our ancient heritage." No words could describe better the man himself who spoke, one whose youth supplied an almost boundless energy, despite illness and physical handicap, whose record in war touched heroic proportions, whose service in Congress was positive and progressive.

It was against this background that he continued by saying: "Let every nation know . . . that we shall pay any price, bear any burden, meet any hardship, support any friend, oppose any foe to assure the survival and success of liberty. This we pledge—and more." All that the young president promised in these words, he delivered before his assassination. He has written in unforgettable language his own epitaph. Two days ago, he was the leader of the free world, full of youth, vigor, and promise, full of conflict, excitement, pressure, and change. His was a fully human life, one in which he lived, felt dawn, saw sunset glow, loved, and was loved. Now in the inscrutable ways God, he has been summoned to an eternal life beyond all striving, where everywhere is peace.

All of us who knew personally and loved Jack Kennedy—his youth, his drive, his ideals, his heart, generosity, and his hopes—mourn now more for ourselves and each other than for him. We will miss him. He only waits for us in another place. He speaks to us today from there in the words of Paul to Timothy: "As for me, my blood has already flown in sacrifice. I have fought the good fight; I redeemed the pledge; I look forward to the prize that awaits me, the prize I have earned. The Lord whose award never goes amiss will grant it to me—to me, yes, and to all those who have learned to welcome His coming." . . .

May his noble soul rest in peace. May his memory be perpetuated in our hearts as a symbol and love for God, country, and all mankind, the foundation upon which a new world must be built if our civilization is to survive. Eternal peace grant unto him, O Lord, and let perpetual light shine upon him.

In the name of the Father, and the Son, and the Holy Ghost. Amen.

President Lyndon Johnson Orders "Air Action" Against North Vietnam After U.S. Destroyers Are Attacked in the Gulf of Tonkin.

Five days after Kennedy's assassination, President Lyndon Baines Johnson, the former senator from Texas and Kennedy's vice president, stood before Congress to assure the American people that the spirit and policies of Kennedy's administration would continue. President Johnson also stated, in relation to foreign affairs, that "there can be no losers in peace and no victors in war." But Johnson would not heed his own words when he focused his sights on the mounting tensions in southeast Asia between North and South Vietnam. In 1961 and 1962 President Kennedy had sent thousands of U.S. military advisers into South Vietnam to help the Army of the Republic of Vietnam (ARVN) strategize against the Vietcong, who threatened to topple the South Vietnamese government. When Johnson assumed the presidency, he increased the number of troops to 23,000. But what had begun as a relatively minor military operation exploded into full-scale war after the destroyer USS Maddox was purportedly fired on by North Vietnamese PT boats on August 2, 1964, in the Gulf of Tonkin. Two days later another American warship was reported to have come under attack. Although later investigations would cast serious doubts on the accuracy of these reports, Johnson used the incidents to justify air strikes against North Vietnamese targets. On the evening of August 4, Johnson spoke to the nation shortly before midnight on North Vietnam's "aggression" and the U.S. military's "reply."

As president and commander in chief, it is my duty to the American people to report that renewed hostile actions against United States ships on the high seas in the Gulf of Tonkin have today required me to order the military forces of the United States to take action in reply.

The initial attack on the destroyer *Maddox* on August 2 was repeated today by a number of hostile vessels attacking U.S. destroyers with torpedoes. The destroyers and supporting aircraft acted at once on the orders I gave after the initial act of aggression. We believe at least two of the attacking boats were sunk. There were no U.S. losses.

The performance of commanders and crews in this engagement is in the highest tradition of the United States Navy. But repeated acts of violence against the armed forces of the United States must be met not only with alert defense, but with positive reply. That reply is being given as I speak to you tonight. Air action is now in execution against gunboats and certain supporting facilities in North Vietnam which have been used in these hostile operations.

In the larger sense this new act of aggression, aimed directly at our own forces, again brings home to all of us in the United States the importance of the struggle for peace and security in southeast Asia. Aggression by terror against the peaceful villagers of South Vietnam has now been joined by open aggression on the high seas against the United States of America. The determination of all Americans to carry out our full commitment to the people and to the government of South Vietnam will be redoubled by this outrage. Yet our response, for the present, will be limited and fitting. We Americans know, although others appear to forget, the risks of spreading conflict. We still seek no wider war.

I have instructed the secretary of state to make this position totally clear to friends and to adversaries and, indeed, to all. I have instructed Ambassador Stevenson to raise this matter immediately and urgently before the Security Council of the United Nations. Finally, I have today met with the leaders of both parties in the Congress of the United States, and I have informed them that I shall immediately request the Congress to pass a resolution making it clear that our government is united in its determination to take all necessary measures in support of freedom and in defense of peace in southeast Asia. I have been given encouraging assurance by these leaders of both parties that such a resolution will be promptly introduced, freely and expeditiously debated, and passed with overwhelming support. And just a few minutes ago I was able to reach Senator Goldwater and I am glad to say that he has expressed his support of the statement that I am making to you tonight.

It is a solemn responsibility to have to order even limited military action by forces whose overall strength is as vast and as awesome as those of the

United States of America, but it is my considered conviction, shared through-out your government, that firmness in the right is indispensable today for peace, that firmness will always be measured. Its mission is peace.

Congress passed the Gulf of Tonkin Resolution almost unanimously—88 to 2 in the Senate, 416 to 0 in the House—authorizing President Johnson to "take all necessary steps, including the use of armed force" to assist the South Vietnamese. By the end of 1965, more than 185,000 American troops would be in Vietnam. Three years later, there would be almost half a million.

Senator Barry Goldwater Exclaims at the 1964 Republican Convention That "Extremism in the Defense of Liberty Is No Vice."

It was, in the end, a child pulling petals off a flower that doomed Arizona senator Barry Goldwater to one of the worst defeats in a presidential election. In a political ad conceived by President Johnson's campaign, a little girl plucked a daisy as a voiceover ominously counted down from ten to one—and then, in a flash, an atomic bomb exploded. Goldwater's name wasn't even mentioned, but the unmistakable message to voters was that his hotheaded, blindly anti-communist foreign policy might well spark a nuclear war. (Goldwater's campaign slogan, "In your heart, you know he's right" was refashioned by Democrats into "In your heart, you know he might.") Uncompromising and bombastic, Goldwater tossed one rhetorical grenade after another at liberals and moderate Republicans alike, blasting Social Security (which he thought should be privatized), government subsidies, and even the historic Civil Rights Act of 1964. On July 16 of that same year, Goldwater's image as a firebrand was clinched during his rousing acceptance speech at the Republican National Convention in San Francisco.

From this moment, united and determined, we will go forward together, dedicated to the ultimate and undeniable greatness of the whole man. To-gether, we will win. I accept your nomination with a deep sense of humility. I accept the responsibility that goes with it. I seek your continued help and guidance. Our cause is too great for any man to feel worthy of it.

Our task would be too great for any man, did he not have with him the hearts and hands of this great Republican Party. I promise you that every fiber of my being is consecrated to our cause, that nothing shall be lacking from the struggle that can be brought to it by enthusiasm and devotion and hard work. In this world, no person—no party—can guarantee anything. What we can do, and what we shall do, is to deserve victory.

The good Lord raised up this mighty republic to be a home for the brave and to flourish as the land of the free—not to stagnate in the swampland of collectivism, not to cringe before the bullying of communism. The tide has been running against freedom. Our people have followed false prophets. We must and we shall return to proven ways—not because they are old, but because they are true. We must and we shall set the tides running again in the cause of freedom.

This party, with its every action, every word, every breath and every heartbeat has but a single resolve: Freedom. Freedom made orderly for this nation by our constitutional government. Freedom under a government limited by the laws of nature and of nature's God. Freedom balanced so that order, lacking liberty, will not become a slavery of the prison cell; balanced so that liberty, lacking order, will not become the license of the mob and the jungle. We Americans understand freedom. We have earned it, lived for it, and died for it. This nation and its people are freedom's model in a searching world. We can be freedom's missionaries in a doubting world. But first we must renew freedom's vision in our own hearts and in our own homes.

During four futile years, the administration which we shall replace has distorted and lost that vision. It has talked and talked and talked the words of freedom. But it has failed and failed and failed in the works of freedom. . . . It has been during Democratic years that our strength to deter war has stood still and even gone into a planned decline. It has been during Democratic years that we have weakly stumbled into conflict, timidly refusing to draw our own lines against aggression, deceitfully refusing to tell even our own people of our full participation, and tragically letting our finest men die on battlefields unmarked by purpose, pride, or the prospect of victory. Yesterday it was Korea. Today it is Vietnam. We are at war in Vietnam, yet the president who is the commander in chief of our forces refuses to say whether or not the objective is victory. His secretary of defense continues to mislead and misinform the American people.

It has been during Democratic years that a billion persons were cast into communist captivity and their fate cynically sealed. Today, we have an administration which seems eager to deal with communism in every coin known—from gold to wheat, from consulates to confidences, and even human freedom itself.

The Republican cause demands that we brand communism as the principal disturber of peace in the world today—indeed, the only significant disturber of the peace. We must make clear that until its goals of conquest are absolutely renounced, and its relations with all nations tempered, communism and the governments it now controls are enemies of every man on earth who is or wants to be free.

We can keep the peace only if we remain vigilant and strong. Only if we keep our eyes open and keep our guard up can we prevent war. I do not intend to let peace or freedom be torn from our grasp because of lack of strength or lack of will. That I promise you. I believe that we must look beyond the defense of freedom today to its extension tomorrow. I believe that the communism which boasts it will "bury us" will instead give way to the forces of freedom. And I can see, in the distant and yet recognizable future, the outlines of a world worthy of our dedication, our every risk, our every effort, our every sacrifice along the way. Yes, a world that will redeem the suffering of those who will be liberated from tyranny. . . .

I pledge that the America I envision in the years ahead will extend its hand in help, in teaching, and in cultivation, so that all new nations will at least be encouraged to go our way—so that they will not wander down the dark alleys of tyranny, or the dead-end streets of collectivism. We do no man a service by hiding freedom's light under a bushel of mistaken humility.

I seek an America proud of its past, proud of its ways, proud of its dreams, and determined actively to proclaim them. But our example to the world must, like charity, begin at home. In our vision of a good and decent future, free and peaceful, there must be room for the liberation of the energy and the talent of the individual. Otherwise our vision is blind at the outset. We must assure a society here which, while never abandoning the needy or forsaking the helpless, nurtures incentives and opportunities for the creative and the productive. . . .

We do not seek to live anyone's life for him. We seek only to secure his rights, guarantee him opportunity to strive, with government performing only those needed and constitutionally sanctioned tasks which cannot otherwise be performed. We seek a government that attends to its inherent responsibilities of maintaining a stable monetary and fiscal climate, encouraging a free and competitive economy, and enforcing law and order.

Thus do we seek inventiveness, diversity, and creative difference within a stable order. For we Republicans define government's role, where needed, at many levels, preferably the one closest to the people involved. Our towns and our cities, then our counties and states, then our regional compacts—and only then the national government. That is the ladder of liberty built by decentralized power. On it, also, we must have balance between branches of government at every level.

Balance, diversity, creative difference—these are the elements of the Republican equation. Republicans agree on these elements and they heartily agree to disagree on many, many of their applications. This is a party for free men, not for blind followers and not for conformists. In 1858 Lincoln said of the Republican Party that it was composed of "strange, discordant, and even hostile elements." Yet all of the elements agreed on one paramount objective: to arrest the progress of slavery and place it in the course of ultimate extinction.

Today as then, but more urgently and more broadly than then, the task of preserving and enlarging freedom at home, and of safeguarding it from the forces of tyranny abroad, is enough to challenge all our resources and to require all our strength. Any who join us in all sincerity, we welcome. Those who do not care for our cause we do not expect to enter our ranks in any case. And let our Republicanism, so focused and so dedicated, not be made fuzzy and futile by unthinking labels. Extremism in the defense of liberty is no vice. Moderation in the pursuit of justice is no virtue.

The beauty of the very system we Republicans are pledged to restore and revitalize, the beauty of this federal system of ours, is in its reconciliation of diversity with unity. We must not see malice in honest differences of opinion, no matter how great, so long as they are not inconsistent with the pledges we have given to each other in and through the Constitution.

Our Republican cause is not to level out the world or make its people reform in computer-regimented sameness. Our Republican cause is to free our people and light the way for liberty throughout the world. Ours is a very human cause for very humane goals. This party, its good people, and its unquenchable devotion to freedom will not fulfill the high purpose of the campaign which we launch here and now until our cause has won the day, inspired the world, and shown the way to a tomorrow worthy of all our yesterdays.

Although Goldwater's speech antagonized the more moderate "Rockefeller Republicans," whom Goldwater derided as blue-blooded elites, the force and conviction of his ideas endeared him to a new generation of emphatically anti-government Republicans, including Ronald Reagan, Dan Quayle, and Pat Buchanan. The modern conservative movement was born.

Berkeley University Student Mario Savio Criticizes the School Administration's Attempts to Stifle Free Speech.

"You can't trust anyone over thirty" was coined by a graduate student at the University of California at Berkeley named Jack Weinberg, and it became the catchphrase of young activists in the mid-1960s. In the beginning of October 1964, Weinberg sparked the first and most famous campus uprising of the era when, despite a ban on the dissemination of political literature, he distributed civil rights pamphlets in Berkeley's

Sproul Plaza. University administrators called the police, and Weinberg was literally dragged away. But the commotion caught the attention of other students who surrounded the squad car carrying Weinberg and caused a stand-off that lasted thirty-two hours. The crowd swelled to thousands of young people, and one student, Mario Savio, climbed atop a police car and gave an impromptu address on freedom of expression. Two months later, on December 2, Savio would again denounce the university for its unconstitutional actions, as well as the bureaucracy that allowed such policies to continue.

Last summer I went to Mississippi to join the struggle there for civil rights. This fall I am engaged in another phase of the same struggle, this time in Berkeley. The two battlefields may seem quite different to some observers, but this is not the case. The same rights are at stake in both places: the right to participate as citizens in a democratic society and the right to due process of law. Further, it is a struggle against the same enemy. In Mississippi an autocratic and powerful minority rules through organized violence to suppress the vast, virtually powerless majority. In California, the privileged minority manipulates the University bureaucracy to suppress the students' political expression. That "respectable" bureaucracy masks the financial plutocrats; that impersonal bureaucracy is the efficient enemy in a "brave new world."

In our free speech fight at the University of California, we have come up against what may emerge as the greatest problem of our nation: depersonalized, unresponsive bureaucracy. We have encountered the organized status quo in Mississippi, but it is the same in Berkeley. Here we find it impossible usually to meet with anyone but secretaries. Beyond that, we find functionaries who cannot make policy but can only hide behind the rules. We have discovered total lack of response on the part of the policy makers. To grasp a situation which is truly Kafkaesque, it is necessary to understand the bureaucratic mentality. And we have learned quite a bit about it this fall, more outside the classroom than in.

As bureaucrat, an administrator believes that nothing new happens. He occupies an ahistorical point of view. In [early October], to get the attention of this bureaucracy which had issued arbitrary edicts suppressing student political expression and refused to discuss its action, we held a sit-in on the campus. We sat around a police car and kept it immobilized for over thirty-two hours. At last, the administrative bureaucracy agreed to negotiate. But instead, on the following Monday, we discovered that a committee had been appointed in accordance with usual regulations to resolve the dispute. Our attempt to convince any of the administrators that an event had occurred, that something new had happened, failed. They saw this simply as something to be handled by normal university procedures.

The same is true of all bureaucrats. They begin as tools, means to certain legitimate goals, and they end up feeding their own existence. The conception that bureaucrats have is that history has in fact come to an end. . . .

The university is the place where people begin seriously to question the conditions of their existence and raise the issue of whether they can be committed to the society they have been born into. After a long period of apathy during the fifties, students have begun not only to question but, having arrived at answers, to act on those answers. This is part of a growing understanding among many people in America that history has not ended, that a better society is possible, and that it is worth dying for.

This free speech fight points up a fascinating aspect of contemporary campus life. Students are permitted to talk all they want so long as their speech has no consequences. . . . The administration of the Berkeley campus has admitted that external, extralegal groups have pressured the university not to permit students on campus to organize picket lines, not to permit on campus any speech with consequences. And the bureaucracy went along. Speech with consequences, speech in the area of civil rights, speech which some might regard as illegal must stop.

Many students here at the university, many people in society, are wandering aimlessly about. Strangers in their own lives, there is no place for them. They are people who have not learned to compromise, who for example have come to the university to learn to question, to grow, to learn—all the standard things that sound like clichés because no one takes them seriously. And they find at one point or other that for them to become part of society, to become lawyers, ministers, businessmen, people in government, that very often they must compromise those principles which were most dear to them. They must suppress the most creative impulses that they have. This is a prior condition for being part of the system. The university is well structured, well tooled, to turn out people with all the sharp edges worn off—the well-rounded person. The university is well equipped to produce that sort of person, and this means that the best among the people who enter must, for four years, wander aimlessly much of the time questioning why they are on campus at all, doubting whether there is any point in what they are doing, and looking toward a very bleak existence afterward in a game in which all of the rules have been made up, which one cannot really amend.

It is a bleak scene, but it is all a lot of us have to look forward to. Society provides no challenge. American society in the standard conception it has of itself is simply no longer exciting. The most exciting things going on in America today are movements to change America. America is becoming ever more the utopia of sterilized, automated contentment. The "futures" and "careers" for which American students now prepare are for the most part intellectual and moral wastelands. This chrome-plated consumers' paradise would have us grow up to be well-behaved children. But an important minority of men and women coming to the front today have shown that they will die rather than be standardized, replaceable, and irrelevant.

Emboldened by Savio's speech, over a thousand students marched into Sproul Hall and staged a sit-in. Governor Edmund G. Brown (father of future governor, presidential candidate, and Oakland mayor Jerry Brown) brought in the police, who arrested 700 protestors. After a widely supported strike among other students and faculty, the administration capitulated. One of the unintended consequences of the Berkeley demonstrations was the political ammunition it gave to gubernatorial candidate Ronald Reagan, who referred to the students as "those Berkeley bastards." Reagan pointed to the marches, sit-ins, and strikes as proof that, under Governor Brown, California was plunging into anarchy. The message worked—in 1966 Reagan was elected governor.

———

President Lyndon Johnson Envisions Transforming America Into a "Great Society" Free of Poverty, Crime, and Racism
&
President Johnson Makes an Impassioned Plea to Congress to Pass the Voting Rights Act of 1965.

Less than two months after his landslide victory over Barry Goldwater, President Johnson outlined before Congress on January 5, 1965, the most ambitious domestic agenda since Franklin D. Roosevelt's New Deal of the 1930s. The "Great Society," as Johnson boldly envisioned it, would solve poverty, crime, racism, unemployment, and virtually every other seemingly intractable problem that had, in Johnson's belief, impeded Americans from reaching their full potential as individuals. In May 1964 President Johnson announced to the graduating class of the University of Michigan his dramatic blueprint for the Great Society.

I have come today from the turmoil of your capital to the tranquility of your campus to speak about the future of your country.

The purpose of protecting the life of our nation and preserving the liberty of our citizens is to pursue the happiness of our people. Our success in that pursuit is the test of our success as a nation. For a century we labored to settle and to subdue a continent. For half a century we called upon unbounded invention and untiring industry to create an order of plenty for all of our people. The challenge of the next half-century is whether we have the wisdom to use that wealth to enrich and elevate our national life and to advance the quality of our American civilization. Your imagination, your initiative, and your indignation will determine whether we build a society where progress is the servant of our needs or a society where old values and new visions are buried under unbridled growth. For in your time we have the opportunity to move not only toward the rich society and the powerful society, but upward to the Great Society.

The Great Society rests on abundance and liberty for all. It demands an end to poverty and racial injustice, to which we are totally committed in our time. But that is just the beginning. The Great Society is a place where every child can find knowledge to enrich his mind and to enlarge his talents. It is a place where leisure is a welcome chance to build and reflect, not a feared cause of boredom and restlessness. It is a place where the city of man serves not only the needs of the body and the demands of commerce but the desire for beauty and the hunger for community. It is a place where man can renew contact with nature. It is a place which honors creation for its own sake and for what it adds to the understanding of the race. It is a place where men are more concerned with the quality of their goals than the quantity of their goods. But most of all, the Great Society is not a safe harbor, a resting place, a final objective, a finished work. It is a challenge constantly renewed, beckoning us toward a destiny where the meaning of our lives matches the marvelous products of our labor.

So I want to talk to you today about three places where we begin to build the Great Society: in our cities, in our countryside, and in our classrooms. Many of you will live to see the day, perhaps fifty years from now, when there will be 400 million Americans—four-fifths of them in urban areas. In the remainder of this century urban population will double, city land will double, and we will have to build homes, highways, and facilities equal to all those built since this country was first settled. So in the next forty years we must rebuild the entire urban United States.

Aristotle said, "Men come together in cities in order to live, but they remain together in order to live the good life." It is harder and harder to live the good life in American cities today. The catalog of ills is long: There is the decay of the centers and the despoiling of the suburbs. There is not enough housing for our people or transportation for our traffic. Open land is vanishing and old landmarks are violated. Worst of all, expansion is eroding the precious and time honored values of community with neighbors and communion with nature. The loss of these values breeds loneliness and boredom and indifference.

Our society will never be great until our cities are great. Today the frontier of imagination and innovation is inside those cities and not beyond their borders. New experiments are already going on. It will be the task of your generation to make the American city a place where future generations will come not only to live, but to live the good life.

I understand that if I stayed here tonight I would see that Michigan students are really doing their best to live the good life.

This is the place where the Peace Corps was started. It is inspiring to see how all of you, while you are in this country, are trying so hard to live at the level of the people.

A second place where we begin to build the Great Society is in our countryside. We have always prided ourselves on being not only America the strong and America the free, but America the beautiful. Today that beauty is in danger. The water we drink, the food we eat, the very air that we breathe, are threatened with pollution. Our parks are overcrowded, our seashores overburdened. Green fields and dense forests are disappearing. A few years ago we were greatly concerned about the "ugly American." Today we must act to prevent an ugly America. For once the battle is lost, once our natural splendor is destroyed, it can never be recaptured. And once man can no longer walk with beauty or wonder at nature, his spirit will wither and his sustenance be wasted.

A third place to build the Great Society is in the classrooms of America. There your children's lives will be shaped. Our society will not be great until every young mind is set free to scan the farthest reaches of thought and imagination. We are still far from that goal.

Today, 8 million adult Americans, more than the entire population of Michigan, have not finished five years of school. Nearly 20 million have not finished eight years of school. Nearly 54 million—more than one-quarter of all America—have not even finished high school. Each year more than 100,000 high school graduates with proven ability do not enter college because they cannot afford it. And if we cannot educate today's youth, what will we do in 1970 when elementary school enrollment will be 5 million greater than 1960? And high school enrollment will rise by 5 million. College enrollment will increase by more than 3 million.

In many places, classrooms are overcrowded and curricula are outdated. Most of our qualified teachers are underpaid, and many of our paid teachers are unqualified. So we must give every child a place to sit and a teacher to learn from. Poverty must not be a bar to learning, and learning must offer an escape from poverty.

But more classrooms and more teachers are not enough. We must seek an educational system which grows in excellence as it grows in size. This means better training for our teachers. It means preparing youth to enjoy their hours of leisure as well as their hours of labor. It means exploring new techniques of teaching, to find new ways to stimulate the love of learning and the capacity for creation.

These are three of the central issues of the Great Society. While our government has many programs directed at those issues, I do not pretend that we have the full answer to those problems. But I do promise this: We are going to assemble the best thought and the broadest knowledge from all over the world to find those answers for America. I intend to establish working groups to prepare a series of White House conferences and meetings on the cities, on natural beauty, on the quality of education, and on other emerging challenges. And from these meetings and from this inspiration and from these studies we will begin to set our course toward the Great Society.

The solution to these problems does not rest on a massive program in Washington, nor can it rely solely on the strained resources of local authority. They require us to create new concepts of cooperation, a creative federalism, between the national capital and the leaders of local communities.

Woodrow Wilson once wrote: "Every man sent out from his university should be a man of his nation as well as a man of his time." Within your lifetime, powerful forces already loosed will take us toward a way of life beyond the realm of our experience, almost beyond the bounds of our imagination. For better or for worse, your generation has been appointed by history to deal with those problems and to lead America toward a new age. You have the chance never before afforded to any people in any age. You can help build a society where the demands of morality and the needs of the spirit can be realized in the life of the nation.

So, will you join in the battle to give every citizen the full equality which God enjoins and the law requires, whatever his belief, or race, or the color of his skin? Will you join in the battle to give every citizen an escape from the crushing weight of poverty? Will you join in the battle to make it possible for all nations to live in enduring peace as neighbors and not as mortal enemies? Will you join in the battle to build the Great Society, to prove that our material progress is only the foundation on which we will build a richer life of mind and spirit?

There are those timid souls who say this battle cannot be won, that we are condemned to a soulless wealth. I do not agree. We have the power to shape the civilization that we want. But we need your will, your labor, your hearts if we are to build that kind of society. Those who came to this land sought to build more than just a new country. They sought a new world. So I have come here today to your campus to say that you can make their vision our reality. So let us from this moment begin our work so that in the future men will look back and say, "It was then, after a long and weary way, that man turned the exploits of his genius to the full enrichment of his life."

One by one President Johnson's Great Society initiatives were passed by Congress, a political triumph not seen in thirty years. The Civil Rights Act, Medicare, Medicaid, Head Start, Job Corps, the National Foundation on the Arts and Humanities, and many more agencies and legislative acts were all established, fundamentally altering American culture and society. Although Johnson fought for each of his Great Society programs with considerable zeal, he mounted his most impassioned defense on behalf of the Voting Rights Act. Johnson frequently spoke out against racism in America, but his call to end discrimination gained renewed vigor when peaceful marchers in Selma, Alabama, were viciously assaulted in early March of 1965. A white clergyman, the Reverend James Reed, was surrounded by white supremacists and clubbed to death. Johnson was infuriated by the attacks and, in his characteristically blunt style, ordered Attorney General Nicholas Katzenbach "to write the goddamnedest toughest Voting Rights Act you can devise." On the evening of March 15, 1965, Johnson gave a nationally televised speech before a joint session of Congress.

Mr. Speaker, Mr. Vice President, Members of the Congress:

I speak tonight for the dignity of man and the destiny of democracy.

I urge every member of both parties, Americans of all religions and of all colors, from every section of this country, to join me in that cause.

At times history and fate meet at a single time in a single place to shape a turning point in man's unending search for freedom. So it was at Lexington and Concord. So it was a century ago at Appomattox. So it was last week in Selma, Alabama. There, long-suffering men and women peacefully protested the denial of their rights as Americans. Many were brutally assaulted. One good man, a man of God, was killed.

There is no cause for pride in what has happened in Selma. There is no cause for self-satisfaction in the long denial of equal rights of millions of Americans. But there is cause for hope and for faith in our democracy in what is happening here tonight. For the cries of pain and the hymns and protests of oppressed people have summoned into convocation all the majesty of this great government—the government of the greatest nation on earth.

Our mission is at once the oldest and the most basic of this country: to right wrong, to do justice, to serve man.

In our time we have come to live with moments of great crisis. Our lives have been marked with debate about great issues; issues of war and peace, issues of prosperity and depression. But rarely in any time does an issue lay bare the secret heart of America itself. Rarely are we met with a challenge, not to our growth or abundance, our welfare or our security, but rather to the values and the purposes and the meaning of our beloved nation.

The issue of equal rights for American Negroes is such an issue. And should we defeat every enemy, should we double our wealth and conquer the stars, and still be unequal to this issue, then we will have failed as a people and as a nation. For with a country as with a person, "What is a man profited, if he shall gain the whole world, and lose his own soul?"

There is no Negro problem. There is no Southern problem. There is no Northern problem. There is only an American problem. And we are met here tonight as Americans—not as Democrats or Republicans—we are met here as Americans to solve that problem.

This was the first nation in the history of the world to be founded with a purpose. The great phrases of that purpose still sound in every American heart, North and South: "All men are created equal"; "government by consent of the governed"; "give me liberty or give me death." Well, those are not just clever words and those are not just empty theories. In their name Americans have fought and died for two centuries, and tonight around the world they stand there as guardians of our liberty, risking their lives.

Those words are a promise to every citizen that he shall share in the dignity of man. This dignity cannot be found in a man's possessions; it cannot be found in his power, or in his position. It really rests on his right to be treated as a man equal in opportunity to all others. It says that he shall share in freedom, he shall choose his leaders, educate his children, and provide for his family according to his ability and his merits as a human being.

To apply any other test—to deny a man his hopes because of his color or race, his religion or the place of his birth—is not only to do injustice, it is to deny America and to dishonor the dead who gave their lives for American freedom.

Our fathers believed that if this noble view of the rights of man was to flourish, it must be rooted in Democracy. The most basic right of all was the right to choose your own leaders. The history of this country, in large measure, is the history of the expansion of that right to all of our people.

Many of the issues of civil rights are very complex and most difficult. But about this there can and should be no argument: Every American citizen must have an equal right to vote. There is no reason which can excuse the denial of that right. There is no duty which weighs more heavily on us than the duty we have to ensure that right.

Yet the harsh fact is that in many places in this country men and women are kept from voting simply because they are Negroes. Every device of which human ingenuity is capable has been used to deny this right. The Negro citizen may go to register only to be told that the day is wrong, or the hour is late, or the official in charge is absent. And if he persists, and if he manages to present himself to the registrar, he may be disqualified because he did not spell out his middle name or because he abbreviated a word on the application.

And if he manages to fill out an application he is given a test. The registrar is the sole judge of whether he passes this test. He may be asked to recite the entire Constitution, or explain the most complex provisions of state law. And even a college degree cannot be used to prove that he can read and write. For the fact is that the only way to pass these barriers is to show a white skin.

Experience has clearly shown that the existing process of law cannot overcome systematic and ingenious discrimination. No law that we now have on the books—and I have helped to put three of them there—can ensure the right to vote when local officials are determined to deny it.

In such a case our duty must be clear to all of us. The Constitution says that no person shall be kept from voting because of his race or his color. We have all sworn an oath before God to support and to defend that Constitution. We must now act in obedience to that oath.

Wednesday, I will send to Congress a law designed to eliminate illegal barriers to the right to vote.

The broad principles of that bill will be in the hands of the Democratic and Republican leaders tomorrow. After they have reviewed it, it will come here formally as a bill. I am grateful for this opportunity to come here tonight at the invitation of the leadership to reason with my friends, to give them my views, and to visit with my former colleagues.

I have had prepared a more comprehensive analysis of the legislation which I had intended to transmit to the clerk tomorrow but which I will submit to the clerks tonight. But I want to discuss with you now briefly the main proposals of this legislation.

This bill will strike down restrictions to voting in all elections—federal, state, and local—which have been used to deny Negroes the right to vote.

This bill will establish a simple, uniform standard which cannot be used, however ingenious the effort, to flout our Constitution.

It will provide for citizens to be registered by officials of the United States Government if the state officials refuse to register them.

It will eliminate tedious, unnecessary lawsuits which delay the right to vote.

Finally, this legislation will ensure that properly registered individuals are not prohibited from voting.

I will welcome the suggestions from all of the members of Congress—I have no doubt that I will get some—on ways and means to strengthen this law and to make it effective. But experience has plainly shown that this is the only path to carry out the command of the Constitution.

To those who seek to avoid action by their national government in their own communities; who want to and who seek to maintain purely local control over elections, the answer is simple: Open your polling places to all your people. Allow men and women to register and vote whatever the color of their skin. Extend the rights of citizenship to every citizen of this land.

There is no constitutional issue here. The command of the Constitution is plain.

There is no moral issue. It is wrong—deadly wrong—to deny any of your fellow Americans the right to vote in this country.

There is no issue of states' rights or national rights. There is only the struggle for human rights.

I have not the slightest doubt what will be your answer.

The last time a president sent a civil rights bill to the Congress it contained a provision to protect voting rights in federal elections. That civil rights bill was passed after eight long months of debate. And when that bill came to my desk from the Congress for my signature, the heart of the voting provision had been eliminated. This time, on this issue, there must be no delay, no hesitation and no compromise with our purpose.

We cannot, we must not, refuse to protect the right of every American to vote in every election that he may desire to participate in. And we ought not and we cannot and we must not wait another eight months before we get a bill. We have already waited a hundred years and more, and the time for waiting is gone.

So I ask you to join me in working long hours—nights and weekends, if necessary—to pass this bill. And I don't make that request lightly. For from the window where I sit with the problems of our country I recognize that outside this chamber is the outraged conscience of a nation, the grave concern of many nations, and the harsh judgment of history on our acts.

But even if we pass this bill, the battle will not be over. What happened in Selma is part of a far larger movement which reaches into every section and state of America. It is the effort of American Negroes to secure for themselves the full blessings of American life.

Their cause must be our cause too. Because it is not just Negroes, but really it is all of us, who must overcome the crippling legacy of bigotry and injustice.

And we shall overcome.

As a man whose roots go deeply into Southern soil I know how agonizing racial feelings are. I know how difficult it is to reshape the attitudes and the structure of our society. But a century has passed, more than a hundred years, since the Negro was freed. And he is not fully free tonight.

It was more than a hundred years ago that Abraham Lincoln, a great president of another party, signed the Emancipation Proclamation, but emancipation is a proclamation and not a fact.

A century has passed, more than a hundred years, since equality was promised. And yet the Negro is not equal.

A century has passed since the day of promise. And the promise is unkept.

The time of justice has now come. I tell you that I believe sincerely that no force can hold it back. It is right in the eyes of man and God that it should come. And when it does, I think that day will brighten the lives of every American. For Negroes are not the only victims. How many white children have gone uneducated, how many white families have lived in stark poverty, how many white lives have been scarred by fear, because we have wasted our energy and our substance to maintain the barriers of hatred and terror?

So I say to all of you here, and to all in the nation tonight, that those who appeal to you to hold on to the past do so at the cost of denying you your future.

This great, rich, restless country can offer opportunity and education and hope to all: black and white, North and South, sharecropper and city dweller. These are the enemies: poverty, ignorance, disease. They are the enemies and not our fellow man, not our neighbor. And these enemies, too—poverty, disease and ignorance—we shall overcome.

Now let none of us in any sections look with prideful righteousness on the troubles in another section, or on the problems of our neighbors. There is really no part of America where the promise of equality has been fully kept. In Buffalo as well as in Birmingham, in Philadelphia as well as in Selma, Americans are struggling for the fruits of freedom.

This is one nation. What happens in Selma or in Cincinnati is a matter of legitimate concern to every American. But let each of us look within our own hearts and our own communities, and let each of us put our shoulder to the wheel to root out injustice wherever it exists.

As we meet here in this peaceful, historic chamber tonight, men from the South, some of whom were at Iwo Jima, men from the North who have carried Old Glory to far corners of the world and brought it back without a stain on it, men from the East and from the West, are all fighting together without regard to religion, or color, or region, in Vietnam. Men from every region fought for us across the world twenty years ago.

And in these common dangers and these common sacrifices the South made its contribution of honor and gallantry no less than any other region of the great Republic—and in some instances, a great many of them, more.

And I have not the slightest doubt that good men from everywhere in this country, from the Great Lakes to the Gulf of Mexico, from the Golden

Gate to the harbors along the Atlantic, will rally together now in this cause to vindicate the freedom of all Americans. For all of us owe this duty; and I believe that all of us will respond to it. Your President makes that request of every American. . . .

My first job after college was as a teacher in Cotulla, Texas, in a small Mexican-American school. Few of them could speak English, and I couldn't speak much Spanish. My students were poor and they often came to class without breakfast, hungry. They knew even in their youth the pain of prejudice. They never seemed to know why people disliked them. But they knew it was so, because I saw it in their eyes. I often walked home late in the afternoon, after the classes were finished, wishing there was more that I could do. But all I knew was to teach them the little that I knew, hoping that it might help them against the hardships that lay ahead.

Somehow you never forget what poverty and hatred can do when you see its scars on the hopeful face of a young child. I never thought then, in 1928, that I would be standing here in 1965. It never even occurred to me in my fondest dreams that I might have the chance to help the sons and daughters of those students and to help people like them all over this country. But now I do have that chance—and I'll let you in on a secret—I mean to use it. And I hope that you will use it with me.

This is the richest and most powerful country which ever occupied the globe. The might of past empires is little compared to ours. But I do not want to be the president who built empires, or sought grandeur, or extended dominion.

I want to be the president who educated young children to the wonders of their world. I want to be the president who helped to feed the hungry and to prepare them to be taxpayers instead of taxeaters. I want to be the president who helped the poor to find their own way and who protected the right of every citizen to vote in every election. I want to be the president who helped to end hatred among his fellow men and who promoted love among the people of all races and all regions and all parties. I want to be the president who helped to end war among the brothers of this earth.

And so at the request of your beloved Speaker and the Senator from Montana; the majority leader, the Senator from Illinois; the minority leader, Mr. McCulloch, and other Members of both parties, I came here tonight—not as President Roosevelt came down one time in person to veto a bonus bill, not as President Truman came down one time to urge the passage of a railroad bill—but I came down here to ask you to share this task with me and to share it with the people that we both work for. I want this to be the Congress, Republicans and Democrats alike, which did all these things for all these people.

Beyond this great chamber, out yonder in fifty states, are the people that we serve. Who can tell what deep and unspoken hopes are in their hearts tonight as they sit there and listen. We all can guess, from our own lives, how difficult they often find their own pursuit of happiness, how many problems each little family has. They look most of all to themselves for their futures. But I think that they also look to each of us.

Above the pyramid on the great seal of the United States it says—in Latin—"God has favored our undertaking."

God will not favor everything that we do. It is rather our duty to divine His will. But I cannot help believing that He truly understands and that He really favors the undertaking that we begin here tonight.

Congress erupted in cheers. Dr. Martin Luther King, watching in Alabama, reportedly wept. On August 6, 1965, President Johnson signed the Voting Rights Act into law, which, among other things, prohibited states from using literacy tests, poll taxes, and other means to intimidate minorities from voting. Despite the Voting Rights Act and many of Johnson's other extraordinary legislative accomplishments, the mounting number of American casualties in the Vietnam war cast a pall on Johnson's legacy.

FBI Director J. Edgar Hoover Explains Why Only "Clean Cut" Men (and No "Beatniks") Can Serve in the FBI.

With a pit-bull countenance that matched his no-nonsense demeanor, J. Edgar Hoover served eight presidents as the dictatorial and ruthlessly effective director of the Federal Bureau of Investigation. Hoover ordered his men to "act first, talk afterward," browbeat witnesses, and illegally wiretap both suspected criminals and political enemies, including, at the behest of President Franklin D. Roosevelt, hundreds of FDR's Republican opponents in the 1940 campaign. Insistent that each of his agents not only act but look the part of a G-man, Hoover's FBI selected only "all-American" types and enforced a strict dress code. In the following testimony on February 10, 1966, before the House Committee on Appropriations, Hoover described exactly the kind of man he wanted to serve under him.

As regards appearance, Mr. Congressman, I certainly would not want to have any of the beatniks with long sideburns and beards as employees in the Bureau. . . . No member of the Mattachine Society [an early gay rights organization] or anyone who is a sex deviate will ever be appointed to the FBI. If I find one in the FBI, he will be dismissed.

As to appearance, our special agents in a broad sense are really salesmen.

They interview the presidents of large banks, the chairmen of the boards of large corporations, longshoremen, and laborers. They have to sell themselves to them to get their confidence to obtain the information that they need. In addition they go on the witness stand and appear before juries. They must convince a jury of twelve people that they are testifying objectively, impartially, and without emotion. Their personal appearance plays a great part in this.

I am not looking for the "collar ad" type, but I am looking for men who are clean-cut, mature, and who will measure up to the image which I think the American people feel an FBI man should be. In this regard, we cooperate with a weekly TV show. It is called *The FBI*. I have received hundreds of letters from people saying that the inspector portrays what they thought an FBI inspector would portray. Efrem Zimbalist Jr. is the inspector in the show. In other words, there is an image that people have of the FBI. I want our special agents to live up to that image.

President Lyndon Johnson Outlines the "First Steps" to Limiting the War in Vietnam and Makes a Stunning Personal Announcement to the American People.

Campaigning almost solely on an antiwar platform, Minnesota Senator Eugene Mc-Carthy launched a formidable challenge to President Johnson during the New Hampshire presidential primary on March 12, 1968. Six weeks earlier, tens of thousands of communist soldiers ambushed U.S. troops throughout South Vietnam during the Tet Offensive, precipitating three weeks of brutal combat. Although they failed militarily, the communists made a mockery of U.S. leaders who had claimed that American forces were gaining ground. Antiwar activists screamed at Johnson wherever he appeared, "Hey! Hey! L.B.J.! How many kids did you kill today?" His popularity plummeted. (U.S. fatalities in Vietnam soared from 1,400 in 1965 to 10,000 in 1967.) And then came McCarthy's victory, followed four days later by Robert F. Kennedy's announcement that he, too, would seek the presidency. At 9 P.M. on March 31, 1968, President Johnson addressed the nation to announce a temporary halt to the bombings in North Vietnam. The news came as a surprise to the 85 million Americans watching the televised speech, as did the statement Johnson made at the end of the broadcast.

Good evening, my fellow Americans. Tonight I want to speak to you of peace in Vietnam and Southeast Asia. No other question so preoccupies our people. No other dream so absorbs the 250 million human beings who live in that part of the world. No other goal motivates American policy in southeast Asia.

For years, representatives of our government and others have traveled the world seeking to find a basis for peace talks. Since last September, they have carried the offer that I made public at San Antonio. That offer was this: That the United States would stop its bombardment of North Vietnam when that would lead promptly to productive discussions, and that we would assume that North Vietnam would not take military advantage of our restraint.

Hanoi denounced this offer, both privately and publicly. Even while the search for peace was going on, North Vietnam rushed their preparations for a savage assault on the people, the government, and the allies of South Vietnam. Their attack during the Tet holidays failed to achieve its principal objectives. It did not collapse the elected government of South Vietnam or shatter its army, as the communists had hoped. It did not produce a general uprising among the people of the cities, as they had predicted. The communists were unable to maintain control of any of the more than thirty cities that they attacked. And they took very heavy casualties. But they did compel the South Vietnamese and their allies to move certain forces from the countryside into the cities. They caused widespread disruption and suffering. Their attacks, and the battles that followed, made refugees of half a million human beings.

The communists may renew their attack any day. They are, it appears, trying to make 1968 the year of decision in South Vietnam—the year that brings, if not final victory or defeat, at least a turning point in the struggle. This much is clear: If they do mount another round of heavy attacks, they will not succeed in destroying the fighting power of South Vietnam and its allies. But tragically, this is also clear: Many men on both sides of the struggle will be lost. A nation that has already suffered twenty years of warfare will suffer once again. Armies on both sides will take new casualties. And the war will go on.

There is no need for this to be so. There is no need to delay the talks that could bring an end to this long and this bloody war. Tonight, I renew the offer I made last August to stop the bombardment of North Vietnam. We ask that talks begin promptly, that they be serious talks on the substance of peace. We assume that during those talks Hanoi will not take advantage of our restraint. We are prepared to move immediately toward peace through negotiations.

So, tonight, in the hope that this action will lead to early talks, I am taking the first step to de-escalate the conflict. We are reducing—substantially reducing—the present level of hostilities. And we are doing so unilaterally, and at once. Tonight, I have ordered our aircraft and our naval vessels to make no attacks on North Vietnam, except in the area north of the demilitarized zone where the continuing enemy buildup directly threatens allied forward positions and where the movements of their troops and supplies are clearly related to that threat. The area in which we are stopping our attacks includes almost 90 percent of North Vietnam's population, and most of its territory. Thus there will be no attacks around the principal populated areas, or in the food-producing areas of North Vietnam. Even this very limited bombing of the North could come to an early end if our restraint is matched by restraint in Hanoi. But I cannot in good conscience stop all bombing so long as to do so would immediately and directly endanger the lives of our men and our allies. Whether a complete bombing halt becomes possible in the future will be determined by events.

Our purpose in this action is to bring about a reduction in the level of violence that now exists. It is to save the lives of brave men and to save the lives of innocent women and children. It is to permit the contending forces to move closer to a political settlement. . . . But if peace does not come now through negotiations, it will come when Hanoi understands that our common resolve is unshakable, and our common strength is invincible. Tonight, we and the other allied nations are contributing 600,000 fighting men to assist 700,000 South Vietnamese troops in defending their little country.

Our presence there has always rested on this basic belief: The main burden of preserving their freedom must be carried out by them—by the South Vietnamese themselves. We and our allies can only help to provide a shield behind which the people of South Vietnam can survive and can grow and develop. On their efforts—on their determination and resourcefulness—the outcome will ultimately depend.

That small, beleaguered nation has suffered terrible punishment for more than twenty years. I pay tribute once again tonight to the great courage and endurance of its people. South Vietnam supports armed forces tonight of almost 700,000 men, and I call your attention to the fact that this is the equivalent of more than 10 million in our own population. Its people maintain their firm determination to be free of domination by the North.

There has been substantial progress, I think, in building a durable government during these last three years. The South Vietnam of 1965 could not have survived the enemy's Tet Offensive of 1968. The elected government of South Vietnam survived that attack, and is rapidly repairing the devastation that it wrought. . . .

One day, my fellow citizens, there will be peace in Southeast Asia. It will come because the people of Southeast Asia want it—those whose armies are at war tonight, and those who, though threatened, have thus far been spared. Peace will come because Asians were willing to work for it, and to sacrifice for it, and to die by the thousands for it. But let it never be forgotten: Peace will come also because America sent her sons to help secure it.

It has not been easy—far from it. During the past four years, it has been my fate and my responsibility to be commander in chief. I have lived—daily and nightly—with the cost of this war. I know the pain that it has inflicted. I know, perhaps better than anyone, the misgivings that it has aroused. Throughout this entire, long period, I have been sustained by a single principle: that what we are doing now in Vietnam is vital not only to the security of southeast Asia, but it is vital to the security of every American.

Surely we have treaties which we must respect. Surely we have commitments that we are going to keep. Resolutions of the Congress testify to the need to resist aggression in the world and in southeast Asia. But the heart of our involvement in South Vietnam—under three different presidents, three separate administrations—has always been America's own security. And the larger purpose of our involvement has always been to help the nations of southeast Asia become independent and stand alone, self-sustaining, as members of a great world community at peace with themselves and at peace with all others.

With such an Asia, our country and the world will be far more secure than it is tonight. I believe that a peaceful Asia is far nearer to reality because of what America has done in Vietnam. I believe that the men who endure the dangers of battle—fighting there for us tonight—are helping the entire world avoid far greater conflicts, far wider wars, far more destruction than this one.

The peace that will bring them home someday will come. Tonight I have offered the first in what I hope will be a series of mutual moves toward peace. I pray that it will not be rejected by the leaders of North Vietnam. I pray that they will accept it as a means by which the sacrifices of their own people may be ended. And I ask your help and your support, my fellow citizens, for this effort to reach across the battlefield toward an early peace.

Finally, my fellow Americans, let me say this: Of those to whom much is given, much is asked. I cannot say and no man could say that no more will be asked of us. Yet, I believe that now, no less than when the decade began, this generation of Americans is willing to "pay any price, bear any burden, meet any hardship, support any friend, oppose any foe to assure the survival and the success of liberty." Since those words were spoken by John F. Kennedy, the people of America have kept that compact with mankind's noblest cause, and we shall continue to keep it.

Yet I believe that we must always be mindful of this one thing, whatever the trials and the tests ahead: The ultimate strength of our country and our cause will lie not in powerful weapons or infinite resources or boundless wealth, but will lie in the unity of our people. This I believe very deeply.

Throughout my entire public career I have followed the personal philosophy that I am a free man, an American, a public servant, and a member of my party, in that order always and only. For thirty-seven years in the service of our nation, first as a congressman, as a senator, and as vice president, and now as your president, I have put the unity of the people first. I have put it ahead of any divisive partisanship. And in these times as in times before, it is true that a house divided against itself by the spirit of faction, of party, of region, of religion, of race, is a house that cannot stand.

There is division in the American house now. There is divisiveness among us all tonight. And holding the trust that is mine, as president of all the people, I cannot disregard the peril to the progress of the American people and the hope and the prospect of peace for all peoples. So I would ask all Americans, whatever their personal interests or concern, to guard against divisiveness and all its ugly consequences.

Fifty-two months and ten days ago, in a moment of tragedy and trauma, the duties of this office fell upon me. I asked then for your help and God's that we might continue America on its course, binding up our wounds, healing our history, moving forward in new unity to clear the American agenda and to keep the American commitment for all of our people. United we have kept that commitment. United we have enlarged that commitment. Through all time to come, I think America will be a stronger nation, a more just society, and a land of greater opportunity and fulfillment because of what we have all done together in these years of unparalleled achievement. Our reward will come in the life of freedom, peace, and hope that our children will enjoy through ages ahead. What we won when all of our people united just must not now be lost in suspicion, distrust, selfishness, and politics among any of our people.

Believing this as I do, I have concluded that I should not permit the presidency to become involved in the partisan divisions that are developing in this political year. With America's sons in the fields far away, with America's future under challenge right here at home, with our hopes and the world's hopes for peace in the balance every day, I do not believe that I should devote an hour or a day of my time to any personal partisan causes or to any duties other than the awesome duties of this office, the presidency of your country. Accordingly, I shall not seek and I will not accept the nomination of my party for another term as your president. But let men everywhere know, however, that a strong, a confident, and a vigilant America stands ready tonight to seek an honorable peace—and stands ready tonight to defend an honored cause—whatever the price, whatever the burden, whatever the sacrifice that duty may require.

Thank you for listening. Good night and God bless all of you.

Labor Leader Cesar Chavez, Recovering from a Three-Week Fast, Explains to His Followers Why "Sacrifice" Is Integral to Their Struggle.

"I don't subscribe to the belief that nonviolence is cowardice," labor leader Cesar Chavez once remarked. "In some instances nonviolence requires more militancy than violence." Inspired by Gandhi and Dr. Martin Luther King Jr., Chavez founded the United Farm Workers (UFW)—the first union of its kind—which organized migrant workers to protest substandard wages, unfair labor practices, and unhealthy conditions (such as the spraying of pesticides over fields as farmworkers picked produce) through peaceful means. During a boycott of California table grapes, Chavez began a hunger strike in February 1968. After fasting for over three weeks, he assembled with more than 8,000 farmworkers and supporters, including Senator Robert F. Kennedy, in Delano, California's, Memorial Park, to pray and break bread. Chavez had wanted to speak to the crowd but found himself too feeble to do so. The following speech, which Chavez wrote, was read aloud on March 10 by a minister who assisted the UFW in its mission.

I have asked the Reverend James Drake to read this statement to you because my heart is so full and my body too weak to be able to say what I feel.

My warm thanks to all of you for coming today. Many of you have been here before, during the fast. Some have sent beautiful cards and telegrams and made offerings at the Mass. All of these expressions of your love have strengthened me, and I am grateful.

We should all express our thanks to Senator Kennedy for his constant work on behalf of the poor, for his personal encouragement to me, and for taking the time to break bread with us today.

I do not want any of you to be deceived about the fast. The strict fast of water only which I undertook on February 16 ended after the twenty-first day because of the advice of our doctor, James McKnight, and other physicians. Since that time I have been taking liquids in order to prevent serious damage to my kidneys.

We are gathered here today not so much to observe the end of the fast but because we are a family bound together in a common struggle for justice. We are a union family celebrating our unity and the nonviolent nature of our movement. Perhaps in the future we will come together at other times and places to break bread and to renew our courage and to celebrate important victories.

The fast has had different meanings for different people. Some of you may still wonder about its meaning and importance. It was not intended as a pressure against any growers. For that reason we have suspended negotiations and arbitration proceedings and relaxed the militant picketing and boycotting of the strike during this period. I undertook this fast because my heart was filled with grief and pain for the sufferings of farm workers. The fast was first for me and then for all of us in this union. It was a fast for nonviolence and a call to sacrifice.

Our struggle is not easy. Those who oppose our cause are rich and powerful and they have many allies in high places. We are poor. Our allies are few. But we have something the rich do not own. We have our own bodies and spirits and the justice of our cause as our weapons.

When we are really honest with ourselves we must admit that our lives are all that really belong to us. So it is how we use our lives that determines what kind of men we are. It is my deepest belief that only by giving our lives do we find life. I am convinced that the truest act of courage, the strongest act of manliness, is to sacrifice ourselves for others in a totally non-violent struggle for justice. To be a man is to suffer to others. God help us to be men!

Robert F. Kennedy Calms a Mostly Black Crowd of 1,000 After Informing Them That Martin Luther King Jr. Has Just Been Assassinated & Two Months Later, Robert F. Kennedy Is Killed by an Assassin's Bullet and Is Eulogized by His Younger Brother, Senator Ted Kennedy.

On the evening of April 3, 1968, Dr. Martin Luther King Jr. concluded an electrifying speech at a church in Memphis on a foreboding note. "Like anybody, I would like to live a long life," King thundered. "Longevity has its place. But I'm not concerned about that now. I just want to do God's will. And He's allowed me to go up to the mountain. And I've looked over, and I've seen the promised land. I may not get there with you. But I want you to know tonight that we as a people will get to the promised land. And I'm happy tonight. I'm not worried about anything. I'm not fearing any man. Mine eyes have seen the glory of the coming of the Lord." These would be the last words King would ever speak in public. On April 4, as he stepped onto the second floor walkway of the Lorraine Motel, he was shot dead by James Earl Ray. After news of King's assassination tore through the country, riots flared in more than seventy-five cities. Robert F. Kennedy, campaigning for the presidential primary in Indiana, was scheduled to speak at an outdoor rally in a black neighborhood in Indianapolis at 9:00 P.M., just three hours after King had been shot. Kennedy's aides and even the chief of police strenuously encouraged him to cancel the event, fearing for his safety. But Kennedy insisted on going. Speaking from the back of a flatbed truck in the freezing *cold without notes, Kennedy offered the crowd of 1,000 the following impromptu eulogy for Dr. King.*

I have bad news for you, for all of our fellow citizens, and people who love peace all over the world, and that is that Martin Luther King was shot and killed tonight. Martin Luther King dedicated his life to love and to justice for his fellow human beings, and he died because of that effort.

In this difficult day, in this difficult time for the United States, it is perhaps well to ask what kind of a nation we are and what direction we want to move in. For those of you who are black—considering the evidence there evidently is that there were white people who were responsible—you can be filled with bitterness, with hatred, and a desire for revenge. We can move in that direction as a country, in great polarization—black people amongst black, white people amongst white, filled with hatred toward one another. Or we can make an effort, as Martin Luther King did, to understand and to comprehend, and to replace that violence, that stain of bloodshed that has spread across our land, with an effort to understand with compassion and love.

For those of you who are black and are tempted to be filled with hatred and distrust at the injustice of such an act, against all white people, I can only say that I feel in my own heart the same kind of feeling. I had a member of my family killed, but he was killed by a white man. But we have to make an effort in the United States, we have to make an effort to understand, to go beyond these rather difficult times. My favorite poet was Aeschylus. He wrote, "In our sleep, pain which cannot forget falls drop by drop upon the heart until, in our own despair, against our will, comes wisdom through the awful grace of God."

What we need in the United States is not division. What we need in the United States is not hatred. What we need in the United States is not violence or lawlessness, but love and wisdom and compassion toward one another, and a feeling of justice toward those who still suffer within our country, whether they be white or they be black.

So I shall ask you tonight to return home, to say a prayer for the family of Martin Luther King, that's true, but more importantly to say a prayer for our own country, which all of us love—a prayer for understanding and that compassion of which I spoke.

We can do well in this country. We will have difficult times. We've had difficult times in the past. We will have difficult times in the future. It is not the end of violence. It is not the end of lawlessness. It is not the end of disorder. But the vast majority of white people and the vast majority of black people in this country want to live together, want to improve the quality of our life, and want justice for all human beings who abide in our land. Let us dedicate ourselves to what the Greeks wrote so many years ago: to tame the savageness of man and make gentle the life of this world. Let us dedicate ourselves to that, and say a prayer for our country and for our people.

Much to the surprise of Kennedy's aides, who anticipated the worst, the crowd quietly returned to their homes. "We went there for trouble," a gang member confessed, "[but] after he spoke we couldn't get nowhere. I don't understand why. I don't understand." Two months after Dr. King's assassination, Robert Kennedy himself would join the ranks of martyred leaders when he was fatally wounded by a gunman on June 5, 1968, in a Los Angeles hotel after celebrating his victory in the California primary. Quoting extensively from Robert's own words, Senator Ted Kennedy paid tribute to his older brother in St. Patrick's Cathedral in New York City on June 8.

Love is not an easy feeling to put into words. Nor is loyalty, or trust or joy. But he was all of these. He loved life completely and lived it intensely.

A few years back, Robert Kennedy wrote some words about his own father and they expressed the way we in his family feel about him. He said of what his father meant to him, "What it really all adds up to is love—not love as it is described with such facility in popular magazines, but the kind of love that is affection and respect, order, encouragement, and support. Our awareness of this was an incalculable source of strength, and because real love is something unselfish and involves sacrifice and giving, we could not help but profit from it.

"Beneath it all, he has tried to engender a social conscience. There were wrongs which needed attention. There were people who were poor and who needed help. And we have a responsibility to them and to this country. Through no virtues and accomplishments of our own, we have been fortunate enough to be born in the United States under the most comfortable conditions. We, therefore, have a responsibility to others who are less well off."

This is what Robert Kennedy was given. What he leaves us is what he said, what he did, and what he stood for. A speech he made to the young people of South Africa on their Day of Affirmation in 1966 sums it up the best, and I would read it now:

"There is a discrimination in this world and slavery and slaughter and starvation. Governments repress their people, and millions are trapped in poverty while the nation grows rich, and wealth is lavished on armaments everywhere.

"These are differing evils, but they are common works of man. They reflect the imperfection of human justice, the inadequacy of human compassion, our lack of sensibility toward the sufferings of our fellows. But we can perhaps remember—even if only for a time—that those who live with us are our brothers; that they share with us the same short moment of life; that they seek—as we do—nothing but the chance to live out their lives in purpose and happiness, winning what satisfaction and fulfillment they can. Surely this bond of common faith, this bond of common goal, can begin to teach us something. Surely we can learn, at least, to look at those around us as fellow men. And surely we can begin to work a little harder to bind up the wounds among us and to become in our own hearts brothers and countrymen once again.

"Our answer is to rely on youth—not a time of life but a state of mind, a temper of the will, a quality of imagination, a predominance of courage over timidity, of the appetite for adventure over the love of ease. The cruelties and obstacles of this swiftly changing planet will not yield to obsolete dogmas and outworn slogans. They cannot be moved by those who cling to a present that is already dying, who prefer the illusion of security to the excitement and danger that come with even the most peaceful progress. It is a revolutionary world we live in, and this generation at home and around the world has had thrust upon it a greater burden of responsibility than any generation that has ever lived.

"Some believe there is nothing one man or one woman can do against the enormous array of the world's ills. Yet many of the world's great movements, of thought and action, have flowed from the work of a single man. A young monk began the Protestant Reformation, a young general extended an empire from Macedonia to the borders of the earth, and a young woman reclaimed the territory of France. It was a young Italian explorer who discovered the New World, and the thirty-two-year-old Thomas Jefferson who proclaimed that all men are created equal.

"These men moved the world, and so can we all. Few will have the greatness to bend history itself, but each of us can work to change a small portion of events, and in the total of all those acts will be written the history of this generation. It is from numberless diverse acts of courage and belief that human history is shaped. Each time a man stands up for an ideal, or acts to improve the lot of others, or strikes out against injustice, he sends forth a tiny ripple of hope, and crossing each other from a million different centers of energy and daring, those ripples build a current that can sweep down the mightiest walls of oppression and resistance.

"Few are willing to brave the disapproval of their fellows, the censure of their colleagues, the wrath of their society. Moral courage is a rarer commodity than bravery in battle or great intelligence. Yet it is the one essential, vital quality for those who seek to change a world that yields most painfully to change. And I believe that in this generation those with the courage to enter the moral conflict will find themselves with companions in every corner of the globe.

"For the fortunate among us, there is the temptation to follow the easy and familiar paths of personal ambition and financial success so grandly spread before those who enjoy the privilege of education. But that is not the road history has marked out for us. Like it or not, we live in times of danger and uncertainty. But they are also more open to the creative energy of men than any other time in history. All of us will ultimately be judged—and as the years pass we will surely judge ourselves—on the effort we have contributed to building a new world society and the extent to which our ideals and goals have shaped that effort.

"The future does not belong to those who are content with today, apathetic toward common problems and their fellow man alike, timid and fearful in the face of new ideas and bold projects. Rather it will belong to those who can blend vision, reason, and courage in a personal commitment to the ideals and great enterprises of American society.

"Our future may lie beyond our vision, but it is not completely beyond our control. It is the shaping impulse of America that neither fate nor nature nor the irresistible tides of history, but the work of our own hands, matched to reason and principle, that will determine our destiny. There is pride in that, even arrogance, but there is also experience and truth. In any event, it is the only way we can live."

This is the way he lived. My brother need not be idealized, or enlarged in death beyond what he was in life, to be remembered simply as a good and decent man, who saw wrong and tried to right it, saw suffering and tried to heal it, saw war and tried to stop it. Those of us who loved him and who take him to his rest today, pray that what he was to us and what he wished for others will someday come to pass for all the world.

As he said many times, in many parts of this nation, to those he touched and who sought to touch him, "Some men see things as they are and say why. I dream things that never were and say why not."

With Robert F. Kennedy's death, the Democrats lost their best hope for winning the 1968 presidential election. Richard M. Nixon, who declared in his nomination speech that "the time has come for an honest government," defeated Vice President Hubert Humphrey by less than 1 percent of the vote.

Crew Members of the Apollo 8 Spacecraft Offer a Christmas Eve Message of Peace and Hope to a Nation Reeling from Social and Political Turmoil.

In April 1961 the Soviet Union, having already humiliated the United States with the launchings of Sputnik I *and* Sputnik II *in 1957, sent the first man into space, Yuri*

*Gagarin. The announcement of Gagarin's triumphant mission so nettled President
John F. Kennedy that he publicly demanded the United States be the first to put a man
on the moon. "We choose to go to the moon in this decade and do other things,"
Kennedy proclaimed at Rice University on September 12, 1962, "not because they are
easy, but because they are hard, because that goal will serve to organize and measure
the best of our energies and skills, because that challenge is one that we are willing to
accept, one we are unwilling to postpone, and one which we intend to win." In December 1968, with less than a year to meet Kennedy's deadline, three astronauts—
Frank Borman, Jim Lovell, and Bill Anders—left the earth in a Saturn V rocket, the
most powerful thrust device ever created, and successfully completed a lunar orbit. No
other man-made craft had ever accomplished such a feat, and it was a necessary last step
before sending astronauts to the moon itself. On Christmas Eve, Borman transmitted
the following broadcast back to the United States—a message that resonated deeply to
a country reeling from assassinations, riots, and an overall sense that the world was
tumbling into chaos.*

This is *Apollo 8* coming to you live from the moon. We've had to switch to
the TV camera now. We showed you first the view of earth as we've been
watching it for the past sixteen hours. Now we're switching so we can
show you the moon that we've been flying over at sixty miles altitude for
the last sixteen hours. Bill Anders, Jim Lovell, and myself have spent the
day before Christmas up here and doing experiments, taking pictures, and
firing our spacecraft engines to maneuver around. What we'll do now is follow the trail we've been following all day and take you on through a lunar
sunset.

The moon is a different thing to each one of us. I think that each one
carries his own impressions of what he's seen today. I know my own impression is that it's a vast, lonely, forbidding-type expanse of nothing. It looks
rather like clouds and clouds of pumice stone. And it certainly does not appear to be a very inviting place to live or work. . . .

What we've noticed especially that you cannot see in the computers are
the small, bright impact craters that dominate the lunar surface.

The horizon here is very, very stark. The sky is pitch black and the moon
is quite light, and the contrast between the sky and the moon is a vivid
dark line. Coming into view of the camera now are some interesting old
double-ring craters, some interesting features that are quite common in
the mare regions and have been filled by some material, same consistency of
the mare and the same color. Here are three or four of these interesting features.

The mountains coming up now are heavily impacted with numerous
craters whose central peaks you can see in many of the larger ones. Actually,

I think the best way to describe this is really a vastness of black and white—absolutely no color.

The sky up here is also a rather forbidding, foreboding expanse of blackness with no stars visible when flying over the moon in the daylight.

You can see by the numerous craters that this planet has been bombarded through the eons with numerous small asteroids and meteoroids pockmarking the surface, every square inch. One of the amazing features of the surface is the vastness of most of the craters. It seems that most of them have a round type appearance instead of sharp jagged rocks. Only the very newest features have any sharp definition to them, and eventually they get eroded down by the constant bombardment of fallen meteorites.

We're now going over—approaching one of our future landing sites selected in this moon region called the Sea of Tranquility, smooth in order to make it easy for the initial landing attempts, in order to preclude having to dodge mountains.

Now you can see the long shadows of the lunar sunrise.

We are now approaching lunar sunrise and for all the people back on Earth, the crew of *Apollo 8* has a message that we would like to send to you:

In the beginning God created the heaven and the earth.

And the earth was without form and void, and darkness was upon the face of the deep.

And the spirit of God moved upon the face of the waters. And God said: Let there be light.

And God saw the light; that it was good.

And God divided the light from the darkness.

And God called the light day.

And the darkness he called night. And the evening and the morning were the first day.

And God said let there be a firmament in the midst of the waters, and let it divide the waters from the waters.

And God made the firmament, and divided the waters which were under the firmament from the waters which were above the firmament; and it was so.

And God called the firmament heaven. And the evening and the morning were the second day.

And God said, Let the waters under the heaven be gathered together into one place, and let the dry land appear; and it was so.

And God called the dry land Earth; and the gathering together of the waters He called Seas; and God saw that it was good.

And from the crew of *Apollo 8* we close with good night, good luck, a Merry Christmas, and God bless all of you—all of you on the good Earth.

Seven months later, Apollo 11 *astronaut Neil Armstrong descended from the landing vehicle* Eagle *and placed his foot on the powdery surface of the moon. "That's one small step for man," Armstrong observed, a quarter million miles from Earth, "one giant leap for mankind." Armstrong's achievement represented the fulfillment of President Kennedy's vision of putting a man on the moon by the end of the decade (and with only months to spare). Cut down by an assassin's bullet in 1963, Kennedy was not alive to see his dream realized. But soon after the* Apollo 11 *mission, a brief note was left on Kennedy's grave at the Arlington National Cemetery. "Mr. President," the message read simply, "the* Eagle *has landed."*

Congresswoman Shirley Anita St. Hill Chisholm Demands That the United States Spends Its Resources on "People and Peace, Not Profits and War."

The first African American woman elected to Congress, Shirley Anita St. Hill Chisholm worked as a teacher and educational consultant before becoming a representative in 1969. Chisholm had hoped to serve on a committee that addressed the problems of her constituents, who were predominantly black and lived in Brooklyn, New York. Instead, she was appointed to the House Agricultural Subcommittee on Forestry and Rural Villages. After protesting to the House leadership, Chisholm was reassigned to the Veterans Affairs Committee, which was an improvement but far from ideal. Undaunted, Chisholm capitalized on her position to speak out against increased military spending, particularly at a time when social programs were, in her opinion, being unnecessarily slashed. On March 16, 1969, Chisholm offered an impassioned speech on the subject.

Mr. Speaker, on the same day President Nixon announced he had decided the United States will not be safe unless we start to build a defense system against missiles, the Head Start program in the District of Columbia was cut back for the lack of money.

As a teacher, and as a woman, I do not think I will ever understand what kind of values can be involved in spending $9 billion—and more, I am sure— on elaborate, unnecessary, and impractical weapons when several thousand disadvantaged children in the nation's capital get nothing.

When the new administration took office, I was one of the many Americans who hoped it would mean that our country would benefit from the fresh perspectives, the new ideas, the different priorities of a leader who had no part in the mistakes of the past. Mr. Nixon had said things like this: "If our cities are to be livable for the next generation, we can delay no longer in launching new approaches to the problems that beset them and to the tensions that tear them apart." And he said, "When you cut expenditures for education, what you are doing is shortchanging the American future."

But frankly, I have never cared too much what people say. What I am interested in is what they do. We have waited to see what the new administration is going to do. The pattern is now becoming clear. Apparently launching those new programs can be delayed for a while, after all. It seems we have to get some missiles launched first. Recently the new secretary of commerce spelled it out. The secretary, Mr. Stans, told a reporter that the new administration is "pretty well agreed it must take time out from major social objectives" until it can stop inflation.

The new secretary of health, education, and welfare, Robert Finch, came to the Hill to tell the House Education and Labor Committee that he thinks we should spend more on education, particularly in city schools. But, he said, unfortunately we cannot "afford" to, until we have reached some kind of honorable solution to the Vietnam War. I was glad to read that the distinguished Member from Oregon [Mrs. Green] asked Mr. Finch this: "With the crisis we have in education, and the crisis in our cities, can we wait to settle the war? Shouldn't it be the other way around? Unless we can meet the crisis in education, we really can't afford the war."

Secretary of Defense Melvin Laird came to Capitol Hill, too. His mission was to sell the antiballistic missile insanity to the Senate. He was asked what the new administration is doing about the war. To hear him, one would have thought it was 1968, that the former secretary of state was defending the former policies, that nothing had ever happened, a president had never decided not to run because he knew the nation would reject him in despair over this tragic war we have blundered into. Mr. Laird talked to being prepared to spend at least two more years in Vietnam.

Two more years. Two more years of hunger for Americans, of death for our best young men, of children here at home suffering the lifelong handicap of not having a good education when they are young. Two more years of high taxes collected to feed the cancerous growth of a Defense Department budget that now consumes two-thirds of our federal income.

Two more years of too little being done to fight our greatest enemies—poverty, prejudice, and neglect—here in our own country. Two more years of fantastic waste in the Defense Department and of penny pinching on social programs. Our country cannot survive two more years, or four, of these kinds of policies. It must stop this year—now.

Now, I am not a pacifist. I am deeply, unalterably opposed to this war in Vietnam. Apart from all other considerations—and they are many—the main fact is that we cannot squander the lives, the money, the energy that we need desperately here, in our cities, in our schools.

I wonder whether we cannot reverse our whole approach to spending. For years, we have given the military, the defense industry, a blank check. New weapons systems are dreamed up, billions are spent, and many times they are found to be impractical, inefficient, unsatisfactory, even worthless. What do we do then? We spend more money on them. But with social programs, what do we do? Take the Job Corps. Its failure has been mercilessly exposed and criticized. If it had been a military research and development project, they would have been covered up or explained away, and Congress would have been ready to pour more billions after those that had been wasted on it.

The case of Pride, Inc., is interesting. This vigorous, successful black organization here in Washington, conceived and built by young, inner-city men, has been ruthlessly attacked by its enemies in the government, in this Congress. At least six auditors from the General Accounting Office were put to work investigating Pride. They worked seven months and spent more than $100,000. They uncovered a fraud. It was something less than $2,100. Meanwhile, millions of dollars—billions of dollars, in fact—were being spent by the Department of Defense, and how many auditors and investigators were checking into their negotiated contracts? Five.

We Americans have come to feel that it is our mission to make the world free. We believe that we are the good guys everywhere—in Vietnam, in Latin America, wherever we go. We believe that we are the good guys at home, too. When the Kerner Commission told white America what black America had always known, that prejudice and hatred built the nation's slums, maintain them, and profit by them, white America would not believe it. But it is true. Unless we start to fight and defeat the enemies of poverty and racism in our own country and make our talk of equality and opportunity ring true, we are exposed as hypocrites in the eyes of the world when we talk about making other people free.

I am deeply disappointed at the clear evidence that the number-one priority of the new administration is to buy more and more weapons of war, to return to the era of the Cold War, to ignore the war we must fight here—the war that is not optional. There is only one way, I believe, to turn these policies around. The Congress can respond to the mandate that the American people have clearly expressed. They have said, "End this war. Stop the waste. Stop the killing. Do something for your own people first." We must find the money to "launch the new approaches," as Mr. Nixon said. We must force the administration to rethink its distorted, unreal scale of priorities. Our children, our jobless men, our deprived, rejected, and starving fellow citizens must come first.

For this reason, I intend to vote "No" on every money bill that comes to the floor of this House that provides any funds for the Department of Defense—any bill whatsoever—until the time comes when our values and priorities have been turned rightside up again, until the monstrous waste and the shocking profits in the defense budget have been eliminated and our country starts to use its strength, its tremendous resources, for people and peace, not for profits and war.

It was Calvin Coolidge, I believe, who made the comment that "the business of America is business." We are now spending $80 billion a year on defense. That is two-thirds of every tax dollar. At this time, gentlemen, the business of America is war, and it is time for a change.

Wellesley Graduate Hillary Diane Rodham Defends Her Generation's Use of "Constructive Protest" to Create Social Change.

Chosen to be the first student ever to speak at her school's commencement, a twenty-one-year-old Hillary Diane Rodham surprised the audience of parents, classmates, administrators, and faculty by abandoning her opening remarks and rebuking the speaker who preceded her, the distinguished Republican senator from Massachusetts, Edward William Brooke III. While conceding that "productive dissent" was fundamental to a thriving democracy, Brooke castigated "self-proclaimed radicals" who were "merely exploiting issues for the sake of some ulterior purpose" and, through their "primitive breast-beating," were responsible for the outbreak of turbulent student protests throughout the country. Introduced by Wellesley's president, Ruth Adams, Rodham, a political science major and president of the student government, took issue with Brooke's contentions.

I am very glad that Miss Adams made it clear that what I am speaking for today is all of us—the four hundred of us—and I find myself in a familiar position, that of reacting, something that our generation has been doing for quite a while now. We're not in the positions yet of leadership and power, but we do have that indispensable task of criticizing and constructive protest, and I find myself reacting just briefly to some of the things that Senator Brooke said. This has to be brief because I do have a little speech to give.

Part of the problem with empathy with professed goals is that empathy doesn't do us anything. We've had lots of empathy, we've had lots of sympathy, but we feel that for too long our leaders have used politics as the art of the possible. And the challenge now is to practice politics as the art of making what appears to be impossible, possible. . . .

The question about possible and impossible was one that we brought with us to Wellesley four years ago. We arrived not yet knowing what was not possible. Consequently, we expected a lot. Our attitudes are easily understood, having grown up, having come to consciousness in the first five years of this decade—years dominated by men with dreams, men in the civil rights movement, the Peace Corps, the space program—so we arrived at Wellesley and we found, as all of us have found, that there was a gap between expectation and realities. But it wasn't a discouraging gap, and it didn't turn us into cynical, bitter old women at the age of eighteen. It just inspired us to do something about that gap. What we did is often difficult for some people to understand. They ask us quite often, "Why, if you're dissatisfied, do you stay in a place?" Well, if you didn't care a lot about it you wouldn't stay. It's almost as though my mother used to say, "I'll always love you, but there are times when I certainly won't like you." Our love for this place, this particular place, Wellesley College, coupled with our freedom from the burden of an inauthentic reality, allowed us to question basic assumptions underlying our education.

Before the days of the media-orchestrated demonstrations, we had our own gathering in Founder's parking lot. We protested against the rigid academic distribution requirement. We worked for a pass-fail system. We worked for a say in some of the process of academic decision-making. And luckily we were in a place where, when we questioned the meaning of a liberal arts education, there were people with enough imagination to respond to that questioning. So we have made progress. We have achieved some of the things that we initially saw as lacking in that gap between expectation and reality. Our concerns were not, of course, solely academic as all of us know. We worried about—inside Wellesley—questions of admissions, the kind of people that were coming to Wellesley, the kind of people that should be coming to Wellesley, the process for getting them here. We questioned about what responsibility we should have both for our lives as individuals and for our lives as members of a collective group. . . .

Many of the issues that I've mentioned—those of sharing power and responsibility, those of assuming power and responsibility—have been general concerns on campuses throughout the world. But underlying those concerns there is a theme, a theme which is so trite and so old because the words are so familiar. It talks about integrity and trust and respect. Words have a funny way of trapping our minds on the way to our tongues, but there are necessary means even in this multimedia age for attempting to come to grasps with some of the inarticulate—maybe inarticulable—things that we're feeling. We are, all of us, exploring a world that none of us understands and attempting to create within that uncertainty. But there are some things we feel, feelings that our prevailing, acquisitive, and competitive corporate life, including, tragically, the universities, is not the way of life for us. We're searching for more immediate, ecstatic, and penetrating modes of living. And so our questions, our questions about our institutions, about our colleges, about our churches, about our government, continue. The questions about those institutions are familiar to all of us. We have seen them heralded across the newspapers. Senator Brooke has suggested some of them this morning. But along with using these words—integrity, trust, and respect—in regard to institutions and leaders, we're perhaps harshest with them in regard to ourselves.

Every protest, every dissent, whether it's an individual academic paper, or a Founder's parking lot demonstration, is unabashedly an attempt to forge an identity in this particular age. That attempt at forging for many of us over the past four years has meant coming to terms with our humanness. Within the context of a society that we perceive—now, we can talk about reality, and I would like to talk about reality sometime, authentic reality, inauthentic reality, and what we have to accept of what we see—but our perception of it is that it hovers often between the possibility of disaster and the potentiality for imaginatively responding to men's needs. There's a very strange conservative strain that goes through a lot of the New Left, collegiate protests that I find very intriguing because it harkens back to a lot of the old virtues, to the fulfillment of original ideas. And it's also a very unique American experience. It's such a great adventure. If the experiment in human living doesn't work in this country, in this age, it's not going to work anywhere.

But we also know that to be educated, the goal of it must be human liberation, a liberation enabling each of us to fulfill our capacity so as to be free to create within and around ourselves. To be educated to freedom must be evidenced in action, and here again is where we ask ourselves, as we have asked our parents and our teachers, questions about integrity, trust, and respect. Those three words mean different things to all of us. Some of the things they can mean, for instance: integrity—the courage to be whole, to try to mold an entire person in this particular context, living in relation to one another in the full poetry of existence. If the only tool we have, ultimately, to use is our lives, so we use it in the way we can by choosing a way to live that will demonstrate the way we feel and the way we know.

Trust. This is one word that when I asked the class at our rehearsal what it was they wanted me to say for them, everyone came up to me and said, "Talk about trust, talk about the lack of trust both for us and the way we feel about others. Talk about the trust bust." What can you say about it? What can you say about a feeling that permeates a generation and that perhaps is not even understood by those who are distrusted? All they can do is keep trying again and again and again. There's that wonderful line in "East Coker" by Eliot about there's only the trying, again and again and again, to win again what we've lost before.

And then respect. There's that mutuality of respect between people where you don't see people as percentage points, where you don't manipulate people, where you're not interested in social engineering for people. The struggle for an integrated life existing in an atmosphere of communal trust and respect is one with desperately important political and social consequences. And the word *consequences* of course catapults us into the future. One of the most tragic things that happened yesterday, a beautiful day, was that I was talking to a woman who said that she wouldn't want to be me for anything in the world. She wouldn't want to live today and look ahead to what it is she sees because she's afraid. Fear is always with us, but we just don't have time for it—not now.

There are two people that I would like to thank before concluding. That's Ellie Acheson, who is the spearhead for this, and also Nancy Scheibner, who wrote this poem which is the last thing that I would like to read.

My entrance into the world of so-called "social problems"
Must be with quiet laughter, or not at all.
The hollow men of anger and bitterness
The bountiful ladies of righteous degradation
All must be left to a bygone age.
And the purpose of history is to provide a receptacle
For all those myths and oddments
Which oddly we have acquired
And for which we would become unburdened
To create a newer world
To translate the future into the present.

We have no need of false revolutions
In a world where categories tend to tyrannize our minds
And hang our lives up on narrow pegs.
It is well at every given moment to seek the limits in our lives.
And once those limits are understood
To understand that limitations no longer exist.
Earth could be fair. And you and I must be free
Not to save the world in a glorious crusade
Not to kill ourselves with a nameless gnawing pain
But to practice with all the skill of our being
The art of making possible.

After graduating from Wellesley, Rodham attended Yale Law School, where she met a young classmate from Arkansas named Bill Clinton. The two married in 1975, and in January 1993 the Clintons moved from Arkansas to Washington, D.C., when Mrs. Clinton's husband became president of the United States.

Vice President Spiro Agnew Blasts the "Effete Corps of Impudent Snobs" and "Professional Anarchists" Who Oppose the War in Vietnam.

"Hysterical hypochondriacs of history," "nattering nabobs of negativism," and "pusillanimous pussyfooters" were just a handful of Vice President Spiro Agnew's memorably alliterative attacks on the media and political opponents. Inflammatory, blunt, and unrepentant, Agnew was so disliked that President Nixon considered him insurance against assassination: "Who would want President Agnew?" Nixon joked. But Agnew had his enthusiasts, too, who admired his candid verbal assaults on liberals, such as the following October 1969 speech against the leaders of the antiwar movement and their allies in the press.

Sometimes it appears that we are reaching a period when our senses and our minds will no longer respond to moderate stimulation. We seem to be approaching an age of the gross. Persuasion through speeches and books is too often discarded for disruptive demonstrations aimed at bludgeoning the unconvinced into action.

The young—and by this I don't mean by any stretch of the imagination all the young, but I'm talking about those who claim to speak for the young—at the zenith of physical power and sensitivity, overwhelm themselves with drugs and artificial stimulants. Subtlety is lost, and fine distinctions based on acute reasoning are carelessly ignored in a headlong jump to a predetermined conclusion. Life is visceral rather than intellectual, and the most visceral practitioners of life are those who characterize themselves as intellectuals.

Truth to them is "revealed" rather than logically proved, and the principal infatuations of today revolve around the social sciences, those subjects which can accommodate any opinion and about which the most reckless conjecture cannot be discredited.

Education is being redefined at the demand of the uneducated to suit the ideas of the uneducated. The student now goes to college to proclaim rather than to learn. The lessons of the past are ignored and obliterated in a contemporary antagonism known as the generation gap. A spirit of national masochism prevails, encouraged by an effete corps of impudent snobs who characterize themselves as intellectuals.

It is in this setting of dangerous oversimplification that the war in Vietnam achieves its greatest distortion.

The recent Vietnam Moratorium is a reflection of the confusion that exists in America today. Thousands of well-motivated young people, conditioned since childhood to respond to great emotional appeals, saw fit to demonstrate for peace. Most did not stop to consider that the leaders of the moratorium had billed it as a massive public outpouring of sentiment against the foreign policy of the president of the United States. Most did not care to be reminded that the leaders of the moratorium refused to disassociate themselves from the objective enunciated by the enemy in Hanoi.

If the moratorium had any use whatever, it served as an emotional purgative for those who felt the need to cleanse themselves of their lack of ability to offer a constructive solution to the problem.

Unfortunately, we have not seen the end. The hard-core dissidents and the professional anarchists within the so-called "peace movement" will continue to exacerbate the situation. . . .

Great patriots of past generations would find it difficult to believe that Americans would ever doubt the validity of America's resolve to protect free men from totalitarian attack. Yet today we see those among us who prefer to side with an enemy aggressor rather than stand by this free nation. We see others who are shortsighted enough to believe that we need not protect ourselves from attack by governments that depend upon force to control their people, governments which came into being through force alone and continue to exist by force alone.

I do not want to see this nation spend one dollar more on defense than is absolutely necessary, but I would hate to see this nation spend one dollar less on defense than is absolutely necessary. Until the principle of open representative government exists among all nations, the United States must not abandon its moral obligations to protect by any means necessary the freedoms so hard won by past generations—the freedoms so hard won by the 400,000 Americans who made the ultimate sacrifice in the dedicated belief that some things are more precious than life itself.

Four years later, Agnew would be forced to resign as vice president when it was discovered he had accepted payoffs and failed to report almost $30,000 of income in 1967. Agnew, who was replaced by Representative Gerald Ford, was fined and put on three years' probation.

Betty Friedan Explains Why the Feminist Movement Is Imperative Not Only for Women, But for Men As Well.

In the words of Betty Friedan, it was "the problem that has no name"—the unspoken desire of millions of American women, constrained by the dictates of a patriarchal society, to define themselves as something other than housewives and mothers. Friedan had given up a professional life as a journalist to stay home and care for her three children, but despite the nice house and happy family life, she asked herself the question that resonated as well with readers of her 1963 best-seller, The Feminine Mystique: *"Is this all?" Friedan would go on to help establish the National Organization for Women in 1966, the National Women's Political Caucus in 1973, and the organization that would eventually become the National Abortion Rights Action League. Invited to address the First National Conference for Repeal of Abortion Laws in 1969 (four years before* Roe v. Wade *legalized abortion throughout the country), Friedan gave a fiery address that railed against the objectification and subjugation of women and how their plight adversely affected all Americans, both female and male.*

Women, even though they are almost too visible as sex objects in this country, are invisible people. As the Negro was the invisible man, so women are the invisible people in American today. We must now become visible women who have a share in the decisions of the mainstream of government, of politics, of the church, who don't just cook the church supper, but preach the sermon; who don't just look up the ZIP codes and address the envelopes, but make the political decisions; who don't just do the housework of industry, but make some of the executive decisions; women, above all, who say what their own lives and personalities are going to be, and no longer listen to or even permit male experts to define what "feminine" is or isn't.

The essence of the denigration of women is our definition as sex object. To confront our inequality, therefore, we must confront both society's denigration of us in these terms and our own self-denigration as people.

Am I saying that women must be liberated from sex? No. I am saying that sex will only be liberated to be a human dialogue, sex will only cease to be a sniggering, dirty joke and an obsession in this society, when women become active, self-determining people liberated to a creativity beyond motherhood to a full human creativity.

Am I saying that women must be liberated from motherhood? No. I am saying that motherhood will only be a joyous and responsible human act when women are free to make, with full conscious choice and full human responsibility, the decisions to become mothers. Then and only then will they be able to define themselves not just as somebody's mother, not just as servants of children, not just as breeding receptacles, but as people for whom motherhood is a freely chosen part of life, freely celebrated while it lasts, but for whom creativity has many more dimensions, as it has for men.

Then and only then will motherhood cease to be a curse and a chain for men and for children. For despite all the lip service paid to motherhood today, all the roses sent on Mother's Day, all the commercials and the hypothetical ladies magazines' celebration of women in their roles as housewives and mothers, the fact is that all television or nightclub comics have to do is go before a microphone and say the words "my wife," and the whole audience erupts into gales of guilty, vicious, and obscene laughter.

The hostility between the sexes has never been worse. The image of women in avant-garde plays, novels, and movies and behind the family situation comedies on television is that mothers are man-devouring, cannibalistic monsters, or else Lolitas, sex objects—and objects not even of heterosexual impulse, but of sadomasochism. That impulse—the punishment of women—is much more of a factor in the abortion question than anybody ever admits.

Motherhood is a bane almost by definition, or at least partly so, as long as women are forced to be mothers—and only mothers—against their will. Like a cancer cell living its life through another cell, women today are forced to live too much through their children and husbands. They are too dependent on them, and therefore are forced to take too much varied resentment, vindictiveness, inexpressible resentment, and rage out on their husbands and children.

Perhaps it is the least understood fact of American political life, the enormous buried violence of women in this country today. Like all oppressed people, women have been taking their violence out on their own bodies, in all the maladies with which the plague the M.D.'s and the psychoanalysts. Inadvertently, and in subtle and insidious ways, they have been taking their violence out, too, on their children and on their husbands—and sometimes they're not so subtle.

The battered-child syndrome that we are hearing more and more and more about from our hospitals is almost always to be found in the instance of unwanted children, and women are doing the battering as much or more than men. In the case histories of psychologically and physically maimed children, the woman is always the villain, and the reason is our definition of her: not only as passive sex object, but as mother, servant, someone else's mother, someone else's wife.

Am I saying that women have to be liberated from men? That men are the enemy? No. I am saying the men will only be truly liberated to love women and to be fully themselves when women are liberated to have a full say in the decisions of their lives and their society.

Until that happens, men are going to bear the guilty burden of the passive destiny they have forced upon women, the suppressed resentment, the sterility of love when it is not between two fully active, joyous people, but has in it the element of exploitation. And men will not be free to be all they can be as long as they must live up to an image of masculinity that disallows all the tenderness and sensitivity in a man, all that might be considered feminine. Men have enormous capacities in them that they have to repress and fear in order to live up to the obsolete, brutal, bear-killing, Ernest Hemingway, crew-cut, Prussian, napalm-all-the-children-in-Vietnam, bang-bang-you're-dead image of masculinity. Men are not allowed to admit that they sometimes are afraid. They are not allowed to express their own sensitivity, their own need to be passive sometimes and not always active. Men are not allowed to cry. So they are only half-human, as women are only half-human, until we can go this next step forward. All the burdens and responsibilities that men are supposed to shoulder alone makes them, I think, resent women's pedestal, much as that pedestal may be a burden for women.

This is the real sexual revolution, not the cheap headlines in the papers about at what age boys and girls go to bed with each other and whether they do it with or without the benefit of marriage. That's the least of it. The real sexual revolution is the emergence of women from passivity, from the point where they are the easiest victims for all the seductions, the waste, the worshipping of false gods in our affluent society, to full self-determination and full dignity. And it is the emergence of men from the stage where they are inadvertent brutes and masters to sensitive, complete humanity.

This revolution cannot happen without radical changes in the family as we know it today—in our concepts of marriage and love, in our architecture, our cities, our theology, our politics, our art. Not that women are special, not that women are superior, but these expressions of human creativity are bound to be infinitely more various and enriching when women and men are allowed to relate to each other beyond the strict confines of the *Ladies Home Journal*'s definition of the mama-and-papa marriage.

If we are finally allowed to become full people, not only will children be born and brought up with more love and responsibility than today, but we will break out of the confines of that sterile little suburban family to relate to each other in terms of all of the possible dimensions of our personalities—male and female, as comrades, as colleagues, as friends, as lovers. And without so much hate and jealousy and buried resentment and hypocrisies, there will be a whole new sense of love that will make what we call love on Valentine's Day look very pallid. . . .

1970–1979

LADIES AND GENTLEMEN, WE HAVE COME TOGETHER IN THE midst of one of our country's most difficult periods. After two years of turmoil, a president of the United States has resigned his office. His chosen successor, in whom Democrats and Republicans alike had at first placed such hope, has granted a "full, free, and absolute pardon" to the fallen president in advance of any charges filed against him.

This pardon has again opened the wounds of Watergate. It has undermined respect for law and order. It has prejudiced pending trials. It has tormented the families of those already in prison for the administration's political crimes. It is yet another blow to that vast body of law-abiding Americans, whose faith in equal justice under law has been shaken, then repaired, and is now shaken again.

—Twenty-eight-year-old William Jefferson Clinton,
speaking before the Arkansas State Democratic Convention,
September 13, 1974

Herbert L. Carter Describes in Graphic Detail His Eyewitness Account of the Atrocities Committed at My Lai
&
Twenty-eight-Year-Old Veteran and War Hero John Kerry Asks the U. S. Senate "Where Are the Leaders" to End This "Barbaric War" in Vietnam?

The official press release could not have been more straightforward: "The America Division's 11th Brigade infantrymen from Task Force Barker raided a Viet Cong stronghold [in My Lai] six miles northeast of Quang Ngai, killing 128 enemy in a running battle." But the "battle" at My Lai was, in fact, a massacre of hundreds of unarmed villagers, including infants and elderly men and women. The true nature of the killings would not be revealed until a year later when Ron Ridenhour, a helicopter gunner, heard of the atrocities and sent a letter to political and military leaders, prompting congressional hearings in 1970. Herbert L. Carter was one of several men in Charlie Company who refused commanding officer Lt. William Calley's orders to shoot the defenseless villagers. (Calley was the only member of Charlie Company ultimately convicted. He was sentenced to life in prison but was released after just three years.) In the following account, given to the U.S. Army's Criminal Investigation Division before Congress began its full-scale investigation, Carter related in graphic detail what occurred in My Lai on the morning of March 16, 1968.

We were picked up by helicopters at LZ Dottie early in the morning, and we were flown to My Lai. We landed outside the village in a dry rice paddy. There was no resistance from the village. There was no armed enemy in the village. We formed a line outside the village.

The first killing was an old man in a field outside the village who said some greeting in Vietnamese and waved his arms at us. Someone—either [Captain Ernest] Medina or Calley—said to kill him and a big heavyset white fellow killed the man. I do not know the name of the man who shot this Vietnamese. This was the first murder.

Just after the man killed the Vietnamese, a woman came out of the village and someone knocked her down and Medina shot her with his M16 rifle. I was fifty or sixty feet from him and saw this. There was no reason to shoot this girl. Mitchell, Conti, Meadlo, Stanley, and the rest of the squad and the command group must have seen this. It was pure out-and-out murder.

Then our squad entered the village. We were making sure no one escaped from the village. Seventy-five or a hundred yards inside the village we came to where the soldiers had collected fifteen or more Vietnamese men, women, and children in a group. Medina said, "Kill everybody. Leave no one standing." Wood was there with an M60 machine gun and, at Medina's orders, he fired into the people. Sgt. Mitchell was there at this time and fired into the people with his M16 rifle, also. Widmer was there and fired into the group, and after they were down on the ground, Widmer passed among them and finished them off with his M16 rifle. Medina himself did not fire into this group.

Just after this shooting, Medina stopped a seventeen- or eighteen-year-old man with a water buffalo. Medina said for the boy to make a run for it—he tried to get him to run—but the boy wouldn't run, so Medina shot him with his M16 rifle and killed him. The command group was there. I was seventy-five or eighty feet away at the time and saw it plainly. There were some demolition men there, too, and they would be able to testify about this. I don't know any other witnesses to this murder. Medina killed the buffalo, too. . . .

We went on through the village. Meadlo shot a Vietnamese and asked me to help him throw the man in the well. I refused and Meadlo had Carney help him throw the man in the well. I saw this murder with my own eyes and know that there was no reason to shoot the man. I also know from the wounds that the man was dead.

Also in the village the soldiers had rounded up a group of people. Meadlo was guarding them. There were some other soldiers with Meadlo. Calley came up and said that he wanted them all killed. I was right there within a few feet when he said this. There were about twenty-five people in this group. Calley said, "When I walk away, I want them all killed." Meadlo and Widmer fired into this group with his M16 on automatic fire. Cowan was there and fired into the people too, but I don't think he wanted to do it. There were others firing into this group, but I don't remember who. Calley had two Vietnamese with him at this time and he killed them, too, by shooting them with his M16 rifle on automatic fire. I didn't want to get involved and I walked away. There was no reason for this killing. These were mainly women and children and a few old men. They weren't trying to escape or attack or anything. It was murder.

A woman came out of a hut with a baby in her arms and she was crying. She was crying because her little boy had been in front of her hut and between the well and the hut someone had killed the child by shooting it. She came out of the hut with her baby and Widmer shot her with an M16 and she fell. When she fell, she dropped the baby and then Widmer opened up on the baby with his M16 and killed the baby, too.

I also saw another woman come out of a hut and Calley grabbed her by the hair and shot her with a caliber .45 pistol. He held her by the hair for a minute and then let go and she fell to the ground. Some enlisted man standing there said, "Well, she'll be in the big rice paddy in the sky."

While many in the military and the Nixon administration downplayed the My Lai massacre as an aberration, testimony by another young Vietnam veteran, twenty-eight-year-old John Kerry, suggested such atrocities were not uncommon. What made Kerry's appearance before the U.S. Senate Foreign Relations Committee on April 23, 1971, particularly compelling was not just the horrors he related, but the fact that Kerry was a highly decorated Navy officer, having earned a Silver Star, a Bronze Star, and three Purple Hearts for injuries sustained in combat. Kerry's statement was a powerful testimony to the corrosive effect the war was having on American soldiers and the countries of Vietnam and the United States.

I would like to talk on behalf of all those veterans and say that several months ago in Detroit we had an investigation at which over 150 honorably discharged, and many very highly decorated, veterans testified to war crimes committed in southeast Asia. These were not isolated incidents but crimes committed on a day-to-day basis with the full awareness of officers at all levels of command.

It is impossible to describe to you exactly what did happen in Detroit, the emotions in the room and the feelings of the men who were reliving their experiences in Vietnam. They relived the absolute horror of what this country, in a sense, made them do.

They told stories that at times they had personally raped, cut off ears, cut off heads, taped wires from portable telephones to human genitals and turned up the power, cut off limbs, blown up bodies, randomly shot at civilians, razed villages in fashion reminiscent of Genghis Khan, shot cattle and dogs for fun, poisoned food stocks, and generally ravaged the countryside of South Vietnam in addition to the normal ravage of war and the normal and very particular ravaging which is done by the applied bombing power of this country.

We call this investigation the Winter Soldier Investigation. The term *winter soldier* is a play on words of Thomas Paine's in 1776 when he spoke of the sunshine patriots and summertime soldiers who deserted at Valley Forge because the going was rough.

We who have come here to Washington have come here because we feel we have to be winter soldiers now. We could come back to this country, we could be quiet, we could hold our silence, we could not tell what went on in Vietnam, but we feel because of what threatens this country—not the reds, but the crimes which we are committing that threaten it—that we have to speak out. . . .

In our opinion and from our experience, there is nothing in South Vietnam which could happen that realistically threatens the United States of America. And to attempt to justify the loss of one American life in Vietnam,

Cambodia, or Laos by linking such loss to the preservation of freedom, which those misfits supposedly abuse, is to us the height of criminal hypocrisy, and it is that kind of hypocrisy which we feel has torn this country apart.

We found that not only was it a civil war, an effort by a people who had for years been seeking their liberation from any colonial influence whatsoever, but also we found that the Vietnamese whom we had enthusiastically molded after our own image were hard put to take up the fight against the threat we were supposedly saving them from.

We found most people didn't even know the difference between communism and democracy. They only wanted to work in rice paddies without helicopters strafing them and bombs with napalm burning their villages and tearing their country apart. They wanted everything to do with the war, particularly with this foreign presence of the United States of America, to leave them alone in peace, and they practiced the art of survival by siding with whichever military force was present at a particular time, be it Vietcong, North Vietnamese, or American.

We found also that all too often American men were dying in those rice paddies for want of support from their allies. We saw firsthand how monies from American taxes were used for a corrupt dictatorial regime. We saw that many people in this country had a one-sided idea of who was kept free by the flag, and blacks provided the highest percentage of casualties. We saw Vietnam ravaged equally by American bombs and search and destroy missions, as well as by Vietcong terrorism, and yet we listened while this country tried to blame all of the havoc on the Vietcong.

We rationalized destroying villages in order to save them. We saw America lose her sense of morality as she accepted very coolly a My Lai and refused to give up the image of America soldiers who hand out chocolate bars and chewing gum. We learned the meaning of free-fire zones, shooting anything that moves, and we watched while America placed a cheapness on the lives of Orientals.

We watched the United States' falsification of body counts, in fact the glorification of body counts. We listened while month after month we were told the back of the enemy was about to break. We fought using weapons against "Oriental human beings." We fought using weapons against those people which I do not believe this country would dream of using were we fighting in the European theater. We watched while men charged up hills because a general said that hill has to be taken, and after losing one platoon or two platoons they marched away to leave the hill for reoccupation by the North Vietnamese. We watched pride allow the most unimportant battles to be blown into extravaganzas, because we couldn't lose, and we couldn't retreat, and because it didn't matter how many American bodies were lost to prove that point, and so there were Hamburger Hills and Khe Sanhs and Hill 81s and Fire Base 6s, and so many others.

Now we are told that the men who fought there must watch quietly while American lives are lost so that we can exercise the incredible arrogance of Vietnamizing the Vietnamese.

Each day to facilitate the process by which the United States washes her hands of Vietnam someone has to give up his life so that the United States doesn't have to admit something that the entire world already knows, so that we can't say that we have made a mistake. Someone has to die so that President Nixon won't be, and these are his words, "the first president to lose a war." We are asking Americans to think about that because how do you ask a man to be the last man to die in Vietnam? How do you ask a man to be the last man to die for a mistake? . . .

We are here in Washington to say that the problem of this war is not just a question of war and diplomacy. It is part and parcel of everything that we are trying as human beings to communicate to people in this country: the question of racism which is rampant in the military, and so many other questions such as the use of weapons, the hypocrisy in our taking umbrage at the Geneva Conventions and using that as justification for a continuation of this war when we are more guilty than any other body of violations of those Geneva Conventions, in the use of free-fire zones, harassment interdiction fire, search and destroy missions, the bombings, the torture of prisoners—all accepted policy by many units in South Vietnam. That is what we are trying to say. It is part and parcel of everything.

An American Indian friend of mine who lives in the Indian Nation of Alcatraz put it to me very succinctly. He told me how as a boy on an Indian reservation he had watched television and he used to cheer the cowboys when they came in and shot the Indians, and then suddenly one day he stopped in Vietnam and he said, "My God, I am doing to these people the very same thing that was done to my people," and he stopped. And that is what we are trying to say, that we think this thing has to end.

We are here to ask, and we are here to ask vehemently: Where are the leaders of our country? Where is the leadership? We're here to ask where are McNamara, Rostow, Bundy, Gilpatrick, and so many others? Where are they now that we, the men they sent off to war, have returned? These are the commanders who have deserted their troops. And there is no more serious crime in the laws of war. The Army says they never leave their wounded. The Marines say they never even leave their dead. These men have left all the casualties and retreated behind a pious shield of public rectitude. They've left the real stuff of their reputations bleaching behind them in the sun in this country. . . .

We wish that a merciful God could wipe away our own memories of that service as easily as this administration has wiped away their memories of us. But all that they have done and all that they can do by this denial is to make more clear than ever our own determination to undertake one last mission: to search out and destroy the last vestige of this barbaric war, to pacify our own hearts, to conquer the hate and fear that have driven this country these last ten years and more. And so when thirty years from now our brothers go down the street without a leg, without an arm, or a face, and small boys ask why, we will be able to say "Vietnam" and mean not a desert, not a filthy obscene memory, but mean instead where America finally turned and where soldiers like us helped it in the turning.

John Kerry went on to earn a law degree at Boston College in 1976 and, after serving as an assistant district attorney, became the lieutenant governor of Massachusetts in 1982. Two years later Kerry was elected to the U.S. Senate, where he serves to this day.

TV Reporter Dorothy Fuldheim, Who Covered the Kent State Shootings, Responds to Critics of Her "Pro-Student" Sympathies.

Of the four students shot dead at Kent State University by Ohio National Guardsmen on May 4, 1970, only one was actually part of the group of antiwar demonstrators that had clashed with the guardsmen. Two of the students were merely spectators, and the third was caught in the crossfire on her way to class. A poll conducted a week after the shootings found the majority of Americans—58 percent—blamed the students, while only 11 percent condemned the guardsmen. "When dissent turns to violence," President Nixon remarked matter-of-factly, "it invites tragedy." Dorothy Fuldheim, who covered the shootings for WEWS–TV news in Cleveland, became engulfed in controversy after criticizing the guardsmen for opening fire on the unarmed students. After months of hate mail and other personal attacks, Fuldheim responded to those enraged by her pro-student sentiments.

A few weeks before the fatal day when four students were killed on the Kent State University campus, I had thrown [antiwar activist] Jerry Rubin off my show for his bad manners and his obscenity. I was hailed as a Joan of Arc, and everywhere I went I was patted on the back and received hundreds of letters, flowers, wine, telegrams, et cetera. But on that fatal day when I returned from Kent and went on the air and expressed my deep feeling that the killings were unwarranted, that no guardsmen had been wounded, sent to the hospital, or killed, that the killing of the students was therefore inexplicable, and that the whole tragic event was an aberration of the American spirit, I became a villain.

I pointed out that an American who is accused of a crime is given an opportunity to defend himself in court. But these students who had been shot down had not been asked what their philosophy or intentions were. It is true that students did engage in destruction. They burned the ROTC building and they created disturbances in the town. For this it would have been legitimate to arrest them as anyone who disturbs the peace is arrested. But the slaughter occurred not in the town but on the campus.

As an American who believes in fair play, I felt that the students had been the victims of some sort of hysteria on the part of the National Guard. Further, I said I was deeply agitated that such an occurrence could take place on a university campus and that the student movement now had their martyrs.

It seemed to me that my statements were a legitimate appraisal of what had taken place, but not to my viewers. We were deluged with calls, hundreds of them. Some threatened to kill me. All insisted on talking to me personally. It was apparently no longer the message but the messenger who was being attacked. This time not hundreds but thousands of letters came in. Seventy-five percent at least criticized my stand vehemently and even savagely. I was accused of being emotional and that what we needed were a few more of these killings and that the students should be taught a lesson, et cetera. There was even a petition signed by some of the townspeople to get me off the air. Many reluctantly said they would never listen to me again.

In my twenty-four years on television, nothing that I ever said drew such an avalanche of disapproval, and some of it couched in savage and brutal words. I admit to being emotional about this matter, but I am still bewildered at the intensity of the feeling against the students and support of the shooting by the National Guard, who undoubtedly were unnerved by the whole bizarre situation.

Inmate L. D. Barkley Reads Aloud the Prisoners' Demands During a Hostage Crisis in New York State's Attica Prison.

When asked on live television what would happen to him if Governor Nelson Rockefeller did not offer clemency to his captors, Sergeant Edward Cunningham responded simply, "I'm dead." Cunningham was one of nine guards taken hostage in the New York State Correctional Facility at Attica by inmates protesting inhumane living conditions. The crisis began after a riot on September 9, 1971, and continued for almost a week. A young prisoner named Elliott "L. D." Barkley read the inmates' demands aloud on national television.

The rebellion of inmates at Attica is part of the long struggle of people demanding that their basic needs be met. The slaughter of these prisoners over demands for their survival—health care, diet, political freedom, legal assistance—clearly shows the contempt the government has for oppressed people.

Rockefeller's response to their demands has shown us his willingness to commit genocide and kill his own people in order to save the system that keeps him rich. Harassment, beatings, and illegal questioning of inmates continues at Attica, but the prisoners' struggle continues also. From San Quentin to Attica, prisoners are organizing and collectivizing to fight for their needs. Attica has made it clear to us the steps the government will take to keep us in our place. And now we've no other alternative than to fight even harder.

Following is a statement from our brothers at Attica and a list of their demands:

To the People of America

The incident that has erupted here at Attica is not a result of the dastardly bushwhacking of the POW prisoners September 8, 1971, but of the unmitigated oppression wrought by the racist administration network of this prison throughout the year.

We are men! We are not beasts and do not intend to be beaten or driven as such. The entire prison populace has set forth to change forever the ruthless brutalization and disregard for the lives of the prisoners here and throughout the United States. What has happened here is but the sound before the fury of those who are oppressed.

We will not compromise on any terms except those that are agreeable to us. We call upon all the conscientious citizens of America to assist us in putting an end to this situation that threatens the lives of not only us [inmates], but each and every one of us [Americans] as well.

We have set forth demands that will bring closer to reality the demise of these prison institutions that serve no useful purpose to the people of America but to those who would enslave and exploit the people of America.

1. We demand that all inmates be given adequate food, water, and shelter.
2. We will return to our cells only under our own power.
3. We want complete amnesty, meaning freedom from any physical, mental, and legal reprisals.
4. We demand that the New York State Minimum Wage Law be enforced in all State Institutions. Stop slave labor! Inmates at Attica are getting 25 cents an hour for their work.
5. Give us by October 1 a permanent group who will represent our views at the prison to be made up of people acceptable to us from the nearby communities.
6. There must be no intimidation or reprisals for all New York State prisoners who are politically active.

7. Give us true religious freedom.

8 End all censorship of newspaper, magazines, letters, and other publications coming from the publisher.

9. Allow all inmates, at our own expense, to communicate with anyone we please.

10. We demand effective rehabilitation programs for all inmates. No real attempts are made to rehabilitate prisoners. The main emphasis is on punishment, and the majority of prisoners in the U.S. are just kept in their cells.

11. Modernize the inmate educational system which would include a Spanish-language library and a criminal law library.

12. There must be an effective drug treatment program for all inmates who request it. Attica inmates addicted to heroin are given therapy sessions only once a month.

13. All inmates requesting legal assistance must be given that assistance either from outsides lawyers or inmates, depending on their choice.

14. Give us less cell time and more recreation time with better recreational equipment and facilities.

15. Give us a healthy diet, stop feeding us so much pork, and give us some fresh fruit daily.

16. Give us a doctor that will examine and treat all inmates that request treatment. Spanish-speaking doctors must be available for Spanish-speaking inmates.

17. We demand a significant increase in the number of black and Spanish-speaking officers.

18. Give us an institutional delegation comprised of one inmate from each company authorized to speak to the institution administration concerning grievances so that we may participate in the decision-making processes that affect our lives.

19. Investigate the charges of money taken from inmate funds and investigate how the profits from metal and other shops are being used.

20. Cease administrative resentencing of inmates returned for parole violations.

21. No parole violation changes without legal representation.

22. There must be more funds to expand work-relief programs.

23. End approval lists for correspondence and visitors.

24. Remove visitation screens.

25. No one must spend more than thirty days for any one offense.

26. Paroled inmates shall not be charged with parole violations for traffic offenses.

27. We demand that outside dentists and doctors be allowed to treat inmates within the institution.

28. Members of the Observer Committee must be permitted into the institution to see if all the provisions are being carried out.

We want safe transportation to a nonimperialist country. We demand removal of Mancusi, warden of Attica. We demand amnesty also from all authorities outside the prison administration, including the State of New York.

Department of Correctional Services Commissioner Russell Oswald agreed to consider all of the demands except the last three. To the inmates, this was unacceptable. Gathered in Attica's outdoor D Yard, the inmates and hostages, with knives to their throats, watched tensely as helicopters hovered overhead and snipers took position around the area. Oswald implored the inmates one last time to accept the terms of the negotiation, but they refused. Moments after 9:45 A.M. on September 13, the order was given and a hail of bullets rained down on prisoners and hostages alike. Forty men—thirty-one inmates and nine guards, including Edward Cunningham, who predicted his fate, and inmate Barkley—were shot to death. Reports of the killings, which are believed to be the worst in America's penal history, prompted prison reforms nationwide.

Twenty-five-Year-Old Attorney Sarah Weddington Argues Before the U.S. Supreme Court Why Abortions Should Be Legal Throughout America.

Dallas County District Attorney Henry Wade had already earned his place in history when he prosecuted the case of JFK assassin Lee Harvey Oswald's killer, Jack Ruby. But Wade would become a household name after being sued by plaintiffs seeking to prevent his office from ever again prosecuting another abortion case in Texas. The plaintiffs represented a poor, single, twenty-one-year-old woman in Dallas named Norma McCorvey—known in the trial as "Jane Roe"—who wanted an abortion but was prohibited by a Texas law dating back to 1854. The case of Roe v. Wade *ultimately made its way to the Supreme Court and would become one of the Court's most far-reaching and disputed judgments of the twentieth century. A twenty-five-year-old attorney named Sarah Weddington argued before the Court that the Constitution guaranteed a "right to privacy" and that no right could be more private or fundamental to a woman than choosing to continue or end a pregnancy. On December 13, 1971, Weddington articulated the impossible situation women were placed in by present abortion laws (coupled with unfair work policies that allowed pregnant women to be fired) and the imperative of having these laws overturned.*

Mr. Chief Justice, and may it please the Court: . . .
In Texas, the woman is the victim. The state cannot deny the effect that

this law has on the women of Texas. Certainly there are problems regarding even the use of contraception. Abortion now, for a woman, is safer than childbirth. In the absence of abortions—or, legal, medically safe abortions—women often resort to the illegal abortions, which certainly carry risks of death, all the side effects such as severe infections, permanent sterility, all the complications that result. And, in fact, if the woman is unable to get either a legal abortion or an illegal abortion in our state, she can do a self-abortion, which is certainly, perhaps, by far the most dangerous. And that is no crime.

Texas, for example, it appears to us, would not allow any relief at all, even in situations where the mother would suffer perhaps serious physical and mental harm. There is certainly a great question about it. If the pregnancy would result in the birth of a deformed or defective child, she has no relief. Regardless of the circumstances of conception, whether it was because of rape, incest, whether she is extremely immature, she has no relief.

I think it's without question that pregnancy to a woman can completely disrupt her life. Whether she's unmarried, whether she's pursuing an education, whether she's pursuing a career, whether she has family problems—all of the problems of personal and family life for a woman are bound up in the problem of abortion.

For example, in our state there are many schools where a woman is forced to quit if she becomes pregnant. In the City of Austin that is true. A woman, if she becomes pregnant, and if in high school, must drop out of the regular education process. And that's true of some colleges in our state. In the matter of employment, she often is forced to quit at an early point in her pregnancy. She has no provision for maternity leave. She has—she cannot get unemployment compensation under our laws, because the laws hold that she is not eligible for employment, being pregnant, and therefore is eligible for no unemployment compensation. At the same time, she can get no welfare to help her at a time when she has no unemployment compensation and she's not eligible for any help in getting a job to provide for herself.

There is no duty for employers to rehire women if they must drop out to carry a pregnancy to term. And, of course, this is especially hard on the many women in Texas who are heads of their own households and must provide for their already existing children. And, obviously, the responsibility of raising a child is a most serious one, and at times an emotional investment that must be made cannot be denied.

So a pregnancy to a woman is perhaps one of the most determinative aspects of her life. It disrupts her body. It disrupts her education. It disrupts her employment. And it often disrupts her entire family life. And we feel that, because of the impact on the woman, this certainly—in as far as there are any rights which are fundamental—is a matter which is of such fundamental and basic concern to the woman involved that she should be allowed to make the choice as to whether to continue or to terminate her pregnancy.

I think the question is equally serious for the physicians of our state. They are seeking to practice medicine in what they consider the highest methods of practice. We have affidavits in the back of our brief from each of the heads of public—of heads of obstetrics and gynecology departments from each of our public medical schools in Texas. And each of them points out that they were willing and interested to immediately begin to formulate methods of providing care and services for women who are pregnant and do not desire to continue the pregnancy. They were stopped cold in their efforts, even with the declaratory judgment, because of the DA's position that they would continue to prosecute. . . .

[Concerning the constitutionality of the case], in the lower court, as I'm sure you're aware, the court held that the right to determine whether or not to continue a pregnancy rested upon the Ninth Amendment—which, of course, reserves those rights not specifically enumerated to the government to the people. I think it is important to note, in a law review article recently submitted to the Court and distributed among counsel by Professor Cyril Means Jr. entitled "The Phoenix of Abortional Freedom," that at the time the Constitution was adopted there was no common-law prohibition against abortions, that they were available to the women of this country. . . .

[And] insomuch as members of the Court have said that the Ninth Amendment applies to rights reserved to the people, and those which were most important—and certainly this is—that the Ninth Amendment is the appropriate place insofar as the Court has said that life, liberty, and the pursuit of happiness involve the most fundamental things of people; that this matter is one of those most fundamental matters. I think, in as far as the Court has said there is a penumbra that exists to encompass the entire purpose of the Constitution, I think one of the purposes of the Constitution was to guarantee to individuals the right to determine the course of their own lives. . . .

Weddington's arguments proved persuasive, and on January 22, 1973, the Court ruled 7 to 2 in favor of Roe, prompting cheers from pro-choice advocates and furious denunciations from pro-life proponents. John Krol, president of the pro-life National Catholic Conference, denounced the Court for opening the doors to the "greatest slaughter of innocent life in the history of mankind." Twenty-two years after the decision, "Jane Roe" herself, Norma McCorvey, reconsidered her position and joined the pro-life movement.

Actress Jane Fonda Broadcasts Pro-Communist Radio Messages in Hanoi to Demoralize American Servicemen Fighting in Vietnam.

A two-time Academy Award winner, Jane Fonda starred in her most controversial role during the Vietnam War—as herself. A fervently outspoken antiwar activist, Fonda traveled to the capital of communist Vietnam, Hanoi, and recorded a series of pro–North Vietnamese radio messages in the summer of 1972 to demoralize American servicemen and POWs. "Hanoi Jane," as she was nicknamed, particularly infuriated her detractors when she posed in the gunner's seat of an anti-aircraft gun used to shoot down U.S. planes. (Fonda later apologized for the stunt, but still accused POWs of being "war criminals" for their involvement in the conflict.) The following is a verbatim transcript of one of Fonda's broadcasts.

This is Jane Fonda. I have come to North Vietnam to bear witness to the damage being done to the Vietnamese land and to Vietnamese lives.

Just like the Thieu regime in Saigon, which is sending its ARVN soldiers recklessly into dangerous positions for fear that it will be replaced by the U.S. government if it fails to score some strategic military gains, so Nixon is continuing to risk your lives and the lives of the American prisoners of war under the bomb in a last desperate gamble to keep his office come November. How does it feel to be used as pawns? You may be shot down, you may perhaps even be killed, but for what, and for whom?

Eighty percent of the American people, according to a recent poll, have stopped believing in the war and think we should get out, think we should bring all of you home. The people back home are crying for you. We are afraid of what, what must be happening to you as human beings. For it isn't possible to destroy, to receive salary for pushing buttons and pulling levers that are dropping illegal bombs on innocent people, without having that damage your own souls.

Tonight when you are alone, ask yourselves: What are you doing? Accept no ready answers fed to you by rote from basic training on up, but as men, as human beings, can you justify what you are doing? Do you know why you are flying these missions, collecting extra combat pay on Sunday?

The people beneath your planes have done us no harm. They want to live in peace. They want to rebuild their country. They cannot understand what kind of people could fly over their heads and drop bombs on them. Did you know that the antipersonnel bombs that are thrown from some of your planes were outlawed by the Hague Convention of 1907, of which the United States was a signatory? I think that if you knew what these bombs were doing, you would get very angry at the men who invented them. They cannot destroy bridges or factories. They cannot pierce steel or cement. Their only target is unprotected human flesh. The pellet bombs now contain rough-edged plastic pellets, and your bosses, whose minds think in terms of statistics, not human lives, are proud of this new perfection. The plastic pellets don't show up on X-rays and cannot be removed. The hospitals here are filled with babies and women and old people who will live for the rest of their lives in agony with these pellets embedded in them.

Can we fight this kind of war and continue to call ourselves Americans? Are these people so different from our own children, our mothers, or grandmothers? I don't think so, except that perhaps they have a surer sense of why they are living and for what they are willing to die.

I know that if you saw and if you knew the Vietnamese under peaceful conditions, you would hate the men who are sending you on bombing missions. I believe that in this age of remote-controlled push-button war, we must all try very, very hard to remain human beings.

President Richard M. Nixon Announces a Cease-Fire Between the U.S. Military and the North Vietnamese.

"The more divided we are at home, the less likely the enemy is to negotiate," President Nixon solemnly warned on October 15, 1969. "North Vietnam cannot defeat or humiliate the United States. Only Americans can do that." But President Nixon's attempts to unite the public behind the war in Vietnam unraveled with every image of flag-draped coffins containing the bodies of Americans soldiers (well over 58,000 would be killed in all) and with every new war-related atrocity at home or abroad. In 1970 it was the deaths of antiwar activists at Kent State and the exposé of the My Lai massacre. In 1971 it was the release of the "Pentagon Papers," a damning 7,000-page top secret report leaked to the media by former Pentagon analyst Daniel Ellsberg. Commissioned by President Lyndon B. Johnson's secretary of defense, Robert McNamara, and officially entitled "The History of U.S. Decision-Making Process in Vietnam," the document recounted a pattern of incompetence and outright deception by the U.S. military. The war, Nixon knew, had to end. After protracted negotiations in Paris between the North Vietnamese and Secretary of State Henry Kissinger, a peace agreement was reached in January 1973. On January 23, President Nixon announced to the nation that America's involvement in the Vietnam war had finally come to a conclusion.

I have asked for this radio and television time for the purpose of announcing that we today have concluded an agreement to end the war and bring peace with honor in Vietnam and in southeast Asia. The following statement is being issued at this moment in Washington and Hanoi:

At 12:30 Paris time today, January 23, 1973, the Agreement on Ending the War and Restoring Peace in Vietnam was initialed by Dr. Henry Kissinger on behalf of the United States, and Special Adviser Le Duc Tho on behalf of the Democratic Republic of Vietnam.

The agreement will be formally signed by the parties participating in the Paris Conference on Vietnam on January 27, 1973, at the International Conference Center in Paris.

The cease-fire will take effect at 24:00 Greenwich Mean Time, January 27, 1973. The United States and the Democratic Republic of Vietnam express the hope that this agreement will ensure stable peace in Vietnam and contribute to the preservation of lasting peace in Indochina and southeast Asia.

That concludes the formal statement.

Throughout the years of negotiations, we have insisted on peace with honor. In my addresses to the nation from this room of January 25 and May 8, I set forth the goals that we considered essential for peace with honor. In the settlement that has now been agreed to, all the conditions that I laid down then have been met:

A cease-fire, internationally supervised, will begin at 7 P.M. this Saturday, January 27, Washington time. Within sixty days from this Saturday, all Americans held prisoners of war throughout Indochina will be released. There will be the fullest possible accounting for all of those who are missing in action. During the same sixty-day period, all American forces will be withdrawn from South Vietnam. The people of South Vietnam have been guaranteed the right to determine their own future, without outside interference. By joint agreement, the full text of the agreement and the protocols to carry it out will be issued tomorrow.

Throughout these negotiations, we have been in the closest consultation with President Thieu and other representatives of the Republic of Vietnam. This settlement meets the goals and has the full support of President Thieu and the government of the Republic of Vietnam, as well as that of our other allies who are affected.

The United States will continue to recognize the government of the Republic of Vietnam as the sole legitimate government of South Vietnam. We shall continue to aid South Vietnam within the terms of the agreement, and we shall support efforts by the people of South Vietnam to settle their problems peacefully among themselves.

We must recognize that ending the war is only the first step toward building the peace. All parties must now see to it that this is a peace that lasts, and also a peace that heals, and a peace that not only ends the war in southeast Asia but contributes to the prospects of peace in the whole world. This will mean that the terms of the agreement must be scrupulously adhered to. We shall do everything the agreement requires of us, and we shall expect the other parties to do everything it requires of them. We shall also expect other interested nations to help ensure that the agreement is carried out and peace is maintained.

As this long and very difficult war ends, I would like to address a few special words to each of those who have been parties in the conflict. First, to the people and government of South Vietnam: By your courage, by your sacrifice, you have won the precious right to determine your own future, and you have developed the strength to defend that right. We look forward to working with you in the future, friends in peace as we have been allies in war.

To the leaders of North Vietnam: As we have ended the war through negotiation, let us now build a peace of reconciliation. For our part, we are prepared to make a major effort to achieve that goal. But just as reciprocity was needed to end the war, so too will it be needed to build and strengthen the peace.

To the other major powers that have been involved, even indirectly: Now is the time for mutual restraint so that the peace we have achieved can last.

And finally, to all of you who are listening, the American people: Your steadfastness in supporting our insistence on peace with honor has made peace with honor possible. I know that you would not have wanted the peace jeopardized. With our secret negotiations at the sensitive stage they were in during this recent period, for me to have discussed publicly our efforts to secure peace would not only have violated our understanding with North Vietnam, it would have seriously harmed and possibly destroyed the chances for peace. Therefore, I know that you now can understand why, during these past several weeks, I have not made any public statements about those efforts. The important thing was not to talk about peace, but to get peace—and to get the right kind of peace. This we have done.

Now that we have achieved an honorable agreement, let us be proud that America did not settle for a peace that would have betrayed our allies, that would have abandoned our prisoners of war, or that would have ended the war for us but would have continued the war for the fifty million people of Indochina. Let us be proud of the two and a half million young Americans who served in Vietnam, who served with honor and distinction in one of the most selfless enterprises in the history of nations. And let us be proud of those who sacrificed, who gave their lives so that the people of South Vietnam might live in freedom and so that the world might live in peace.

In particular, I would like to say a word to some of the bravest people I have ever met—the wives, the children, the families of our prisoners of war and the missing in action. When others called on us to settle on any terms, you had the courage to stand for the right kind of peace so that those who died and those who suffered would not have died and suffered in vain, and so that where this generation knew war, the next generation would know peace. Nothing means more to me at this moment than the fact that your long vigil is coming to an end.

Just yesterday, a great American who once occupied this office died. In his life, President Johnson endured the vilification of those who sought to portray him as a man of war. But there was nothing he cared about more deeply than achieving a lasting peace in the world.

I remember the last time I talked with him. It was just the day after New Year's. He spoke then of his concern with bringing peace, with making it the right kind of peace, and I was grateful that he once again expressed his support for my efforts to gain such a peace. No one would have welcomed this peace more than he.

And I know he would join me in asking—for those who died and for those who live—let us consecrate this movement by resolving together to make the peace that we have achieved a peace that will last.

Thank you and good evening.

South Vietnamese leader General Nguyen Van Thieu was in fact reluctant to accept the terms of the treaty, fearing that without the United States his military would be vulnerable to another invasion. President Nixon assured Thieu that the United States would "respond with full force should the settlement be violated by the North Vietnamese." But when Thieu's regime was attacked in March 1975, President Nixon could not come to his aid: Nixon had resigned the presidency in disgrace in 1974. President Ford appealed to Congress for emergency assistance, but there was no desire on the part of Congress or the public to become embroiled yet again in the conflict. Two months later, South Vietnam fell to communism.

Pat Simon, the Mother of a Young Soldier Killed in the Vietnam War, Asks That Amnesty Be Granted to All Draft Resisters.

The horrible legacy of the war in Vietnam would continue, long after the fighting had ended, to haunt the families who lost loved ones and the young veterans scarred both emotionally and physically by their combat experiences. The war in Vietnam would also continue to cast a shadow over the lives of those who resisted the draft, particularly those who fled to foreign countries rather than serve in the armed forces. Although there are no precise numbers of how many men actually became expatriates (most estimates put the number between 60,000 and 100,000), 25 percent are believed to have remained abroad and 10 percent were imprisoned for being deserters. On January 6, 1974, the day before a resister named Richard Bucklin was to be tried in court for avoiding the draft, Pat Simon, the mother of a soldier killed in Vietnam, voiced her support for Bucklin's refusal to participate in the war and expressed her desire that all deserters be granted amnesty.

Today is the twenty-fifth anniversary of the birth of my son. Friday was the sixth anniversary of his death in Vietnam.

It feels very good to be here in Denver in support of Richard Bucklin, who will be tried by military court martial tomorrow at nine o'clock. My son would be happy that I'm here. He knew before he went to Vietnam that he was being used in a bad cause and talked of going AWOL. On his Christmas card from Vietnam was pictured a maze and through it ran the words "They who have walked in darkness have seen a great light." His light came too late for him to extricate himself from the trap we had all created. But this awareness came in time for many courageous men to make the conscious choice of life and peace over war and killing and death. As Roger Williams says in *The New Exiles,* there is nothing sad or negative or tragic about this kind of choice. "The tragedy is not in the fleeing but in what is being fled."

What was fled was the fact that most of the population, because it did not have to choose between life and death, was allowing leaders with completely upside-down priorities, and drunk with the power of our position and technology, to wage an undeclared war on a peasant population which was opposing an oppressive regime. Thousands of young men applied for CO [conscientious objector] status and were refused. As one resister said, "You've got to have a showable ideology. You can have it in your head, but if you can't verbalize it you've had it." They fled a Selective Service system that discriminated against the poor and uneducated, and which allowed 20 million draft-age men to legally avoid the war.

Our president [Richard Nixon] has said, "America will not turn her back on those who served, nor make a mockery of their sacrifice by granting amnesty. The two and a half million who served have paid a price. The few hundred who chose to desert America must pay a price." In the first place, men who have left the country or gone underground have paid dearly for those who demand a price. The decisions were for the most part agonizing. The more than half million veterans with less than honorable discharges suffer from permanent loss of civil rights, discrimination in employment, and they receive no veterans benefits.

And the president's statement reflects and encourages that common, narrow definition of service to one's country—service which says that only blind obedience is patriotic when service actually can take many forms. It also involves a traditional definition of masculinity which says that to be a man one must pick up a gun and go to war, that might makes right. When the resisters refused to participate in the war, they were not deserting the country but rather its disastrous policy. Information and insight came to all of us at different times in and out of the military. My son followed his conscience and went into the army. With a little more time to question rather than trust our leaders, his conscience would have probably led him in a different direction. I wish it had.

Dr. Robert Brown of Stanford points out that amnesty is a way of showing that America still respects the right of an informed conscience to act against public opinion. He says we must remember how much we need citizens who will take risks for the sake of the convictions and will jeopardize their futures so that their country does not jeopardize its future. . . .

Perhaps the time is more receptive now. Watergate has shocked and roused the country, where the ten-year war has not. The dishonesty and deceptions recently revealed seem to offend people more than enormous destruction to life and culture, as long as it is not one's own.

Even if it were not an American tradition to grant amnesty, wouldn't the gruesome experience, suggested a conscientious objector in Brookline, Massachusetts, provide a fitting place to begin the tradition in view of the awesome destruction? It would seem that an unprecedented amnesty is called for in view of the unprecedented barbarity dealt by our technological warfare, which has not been war at all but slaughter.

When I first heard that I was to be with you this morning, I was told the topic was to be "Amnesty: A Question of Forgiveness." I had trouble with that, for I feel there is nothing to forgive. To forgive would be to imply wrongdoing by the resisters. Also it would be treating the symptom—the refusal of hundreds of thousands of our youth to participate in the violence—instead of the illness, which is the war itself. If we treat only the symptom we deny ourselves as a nation the possibility, the opportunity, of health and of growing up. So the real question is, Can we face up to what we've done in Vietnam and forgive ourselves? It's the fear that we cannot that prevents the facing up. Or perhaps the lack of understanding that one can and must, first of all, forgive oneself.

A Harvard Ph.D. candidate in an amnesty debate said, "What is required by those who have lost sons in Vietnam is psychological compensation, and that compensation is punishment." I realize that this reflects a widespread attitude, and there are a number of Gold Star parents who feel an obligation to counteract this. We need to convey to the country that there is no compensation for the loss of our sons in an illegal, undeclared war—certainly not in the punishment of those who resisted it. We would like to say to all the exiles here and abroad, and to all those in prison, Forgive us for presenting you with such cruel choices. We can't bring back our sons, but we can restore a part of life to those who can be an influence against violence. To further punish them delays the consciousness, individual and national, that is essential to the resurrection of some of the ideals on which our country was founded, and the consciousness that is essential to the humane use of our country's power.

The other parents and I feel that a universal, unconditional amnesty would be a living memorial to all the young dead soldiers who leave us the task of giving meaning to their deaths.

Amnesty would not come until January 21, 1977, when President Jimmy Carter issued a blanket pardon for all draft resisters.

Representative Barbara Jordan Argues for the Impeachment of President Richard M. Nixon
&
President Nixon Bids an Emotional Farewell to His Staff
&
President Gerald R. Ford Explains His Motivations for Pardoning Richard M. Nixon.

When five black-clad intruders were discovered in the offices of the Democratic National Committee (DNC) close to midnight on June 17, 1972, the "third-rate burglary," as President Nixon's press secretary Ron Ziegler dismissed it, was virtually ignored by the media. Voters didn't seem particularly concerned, either. Nixon crushed democratic candidate George McGovern months later in the 1972 presidential election, winning every state except Massachusetts. Undaunted, two young Washington Post metro reporters, Bob Woodward and Carl Bernstein, investigated suspicious connections between the burglars and the Committee to Re-Elect the President, or "CREEP" as it was more notoriously known. Although President Nixon almost certainly did not order the Watergate break-in (though he had recommended the infiltration of a Washington think tank, the Brookings Institute), he immediately initiated a far-reaching cover-up. Assisted by an unnamed and inside (it is assumed) source known only as "Deep Throat," Woodward and Bernstein meticulously began to disentangle the threads of corruption that led from the Watergate complex, where the DNC was headquartered, to the White House itself. Throughout 1973 and 1974 Woodward and Bernstein reported allegations of money laundering, illegal wiretapping, bribery, abuse of power, and obstruction of justice. Through it all, Nixon denied any personal wrongdoing. Senate hearings brought the scandal to a boil as, one by one, former Nixon staff members testified to a litany of crimes committed by White House aides and the president himself. But nothing electrified the proceedings like the revelation by former Nixon assistant Alexander Butterfield that an Oval Office taping system existed with recordings of the president's conversations. When Nixon claimed "executive privilege" and refused to hand over the tapes, the Supreme Court unanimously ordered Nixon to surrender them. Indeed, once made public, they exposed a president who was fully complicit in the Watergate cover-up and, to the shock of many, was also profane, paranoid, and bigoted. On the evening of July 25, 1974, as tens of millions of television sets flickered in homes across the country—many tuned to the House Judiciary Committee's impeachment proceedings—an African American congresswoman from Texas named Barbara Jordan offered the followed opening statement. The national audience became riveted by Jordan's eloquent yet unflinching assessment of the president and the grave threat his actions posed to the United States and the Constitution.

Mr. Chairman, I join my colleague Mr. Rangel in thanking you for giving the junior members of this committee the glorious opportunity of sharing the pain of this inquiry. Mr. Chairman, you are a strong man, and it has not been easy but we have tried as best we can to give you as much assistance as possible.

Earlier today we heard the beginning of the Preamble to the Constitution of the United States: "We, the people." It is a very eloquent beginning. But when that document was completed, on the seventeenth of September in 1787, I was not included in that "We, the people." I felt somehow for many years that George Washington and Alexander Hamilton just left me out by mistake. But through the process of amendment, interpretation, and court decision I have finally been included in "We, the people."

Today I am an inquisitor. I believe hyperbole would not be fictional and would not overstate the solemnness that I feel right now. My faith in the Constitution is whole, it is complete, it is total. I am not going to sit here and be an idle spectator to the diminution, the subversion, the destruction of the Constitution.

"Who can so properly be the inquisitors for the nation as the representatives of the nation themselves? The subject of its jurisdiction are those offenses which proceed from the misconduct of public men" [*Federalist Papers,* no. 65]. That is what we are talking about. In other words, the jurisdiction comes from the abuse of violation of some public trust. It is wrong, I suggest, it is a misreading of the Constitution for any member here to assert that for a member to vote for an article of impeachment means that that member must be convinced that the president should be removed from office. The Constitution doesn't say that.

The powers relating to impeachment are an essential check in the hands of this body, the legislature, against and upon the encroachment of the executive. In establishing the division between the two branches of the legislature, the House and the Senate, assigning to the one the right to accuse and to the other the right to judge, the Framers of this Constitution were very astute. They did not make the accusers and the judges the same person.

We know the nature of impeachment. We have been talking about it awhile now. "It is chiefly designed for the president and his high ministers" to somehow be called into account. It is designed to "bridle" the executive if he engages in excesses. "It is designed as a method of national inquest into the public men." The Framers confined in the Congress the power if need be, to remove the president in order to strike a delicate balance between a president swollen with power and grown tyrannical, and preservation of the independence of the executive. The nature of impeachment is a narrowly channeled exception to the separation-of-powers maxim; the federal Convention of 1787 said that. It limited impeachment to high crimes and misdemeanors and discounted and opposed the term *maladministration*. "It is to be used only for great misdemeanors," so it was said in the North Carolina ratification convention. And in the Virginia ratification convention: "We do not trust our liberty to a particular branch. We need one branch to check the others." The North Carolina ratification convention: "No one need be afraid that officers who commit oppression will pass with immunity." "Prosecutions of impeachments will seldom fail to agitate the passions of the whole community," said Hamilton in the *Federalist Papers,* no. 65. "And to divide it into parties more or less friendly or inimical to the accused." I do not mean political parties in that sense. The drawing of political lines goes to the motivation behind impeachment, but impeachment must proceed within the confines of the constitutional term "high crimes and misdemeanors."

Of the impeachment process, it was Woodrow Wilson who said that "nothing short of the grossest offenses against the plain law of the land will suffice to give them speed and effectiveness. Indignation so great as to overgrow party interest may secure a conviction, but nothing else can." Common sense would be revolted if we engaged upon this process for insurance, campaign finance reform, housing, environmental protection, energy sufficiency, mass transportation. Pettiness cannot be allowed to stand in the face of such overwhelming problems. So today we are not being petty. We are trying to be big because the task we have before us is a big one.

This morning, in a discussion of the evidence, we were told that the evidence which purports to support the allegations of misuse of the CIA by the president is thin. We are told that that evidence is insufficient. What that recital of the evidence this morning did not include is what the president did know on June 23, 1972. The president did know that it was Republican money, that it was money from the Committee [to Re-Elect the President], which was found in the possession of one of the burglars arrested on June 17.

What the president did know on June 23 was the prior activities of E. Howard Hunt, which included his participation in the break-in of Daniel Ellsberg's psychiatrist, which included Howard Hunt's participation in the

Dita Beard ITT affair, which included Howard Hunt's fabrication of cables designed to discredit the Kennedy administration.

We were further cautioned today that perhaps these proceedings ought to be delayed because certainly there would be new evidence forthcoming from the president. The committee subpoena is outstanding, and if the president wants to supply that material, the committee sits here. The fact is that yesterday, the American people waited with great anxiety for eight hours, not knowing whether their president would obey an order of the Supreme Court of the United States.

At this point I would like to juxtapose a few of the impeachment criteria with some of the president's actions.

Impeachment criteria: James Madison, from the Virginia ratification convention: "If the president be connected in any suspicious manner with any person and there be grounds to believe that he will shelter him, he may be impeached." We have heard time and time again that the evidence reflects payment to the defendants of money. The president had knowledge that these funds were being paid and that these were funds collected for the 1972 presidential campaign. We know that the president met with Mr. Henry Petersen twenty-seven times to discuss matters related to Watergate and immediately thereafter met with the very persons who were implicated in the information Mr. Petersen was receiving and transmitting to the president. The words are "if the president be connected in any suspicious manner with any person and there be grounds to believe that he will shelter that person, he may be impeached."

Justice Story: "Impeachment is intended for occasional and extraordinary cases where a superior power acting for the whole people is put into operation to protect their rights and rescue their liberties from violations." We know about the Huston plan. We know about the break-in of the psychiatrist's office. We know that there was absolute complete direction in August 1971 when the president instructed Ehrlichman to "do whatever is necessary." This instruction led to a surreptitious entry into Dr. Fielding's office. "Protect their rights." "Rescue their liberties from violation." The South Carolina ratification convention impeachment criteria: Those are impeachable "who behave amiss or betray their public trust." Beginning shortly after the Watergate break-in and continuing to the present time, the president has engaged in a series of public statements and actions designed to thwart the lawful investigation by government prosecutors. Moreover, the president has made public announcements and assertions bearing on the Watergate case which the evidence will show he knew to be false. These assertions, false assertions, impeachable, those who misbehave. Those who "behave amiss or betray their public trust."

James Madison, again at the Constitutional Convention: "A president is impeachable if he attempts to subvert the Constitution." The Constitution charges the president with the task of taking care that the laws be faithfully executed, and yet the president has counseled his aides to commit perjury, willfully disregarded the secrecy of grand jury proceedings, concealed surreptitious entry, attempted to compromise a federal judge while publicly displaying his cooperation with the processes of criminal justice. "A president is impeachable if he attempts to subvert the Constitution."

If the impeachment provision in the Constitution of the United States will not reach the offenses charged here, then perhaps that eighteenth-century Constitution should be abandoned to a twentieth-century paper shredder. Has the president committed offenses and planned and directed and acquiesced in a course of conduct which the Constitution will not tolerate? That is the question. We know that. We know the question. We should now forthwith proceed to answer the question. It is reason, and not passion, which must guide our deliberations, guide our debate, and guide our decision.

Impeachment by the House was a certainty, and the trial in the Senate would undoubtedly lead to a conviction. After over two years of lies and evasions, President Nixon recognized the end had arrived. "You soldiers have the best way of dealing with a situation like this," the president told his chief of staff, General Alexander Haig. "You just leave a man alone in a room with a loaded pistol." Just after 9 P.M. on August 8, 1974, President Nixon gave a televised address from the Oval Office to announce his resignation. "I have never been a quitter," Nixon said, "but as President, I must put the interests of America first. America needs a full-time President and a full-time Congress, particularly at this time with problems we face at home and abroad." At 9:30 the next morning, Nixon bade farewell to his staff.

I think the record should show that this is one of those spontaneous things that we always arrange whenever the president comes in to speak, and it will be so reported in the press, and we don't mind, because they have to call it as they see it. But on our part, believe me, it is spontaneous. You are here to say good-bye to us, and we don't have a good word for it in English. The best is *au revoir:* We'll see you again.

I just met with the members of the White House staff, you know, those who serve here in the White House day in and day out, and I asked them to do what I ask all of you to do to the extent that you can and, of course, are requested to do so: to serve our next president as you have served me and previous presidents—because many of you have been here for many years— with devotion and dedication, because this office, great as it is, can only be as great as the men and women who work for and with the president.

This house, for example—I was thinking of it as we walked down this hall, and I was comparing it to some of the great houses of the world that I have been in. This isn't the biggest house. Many, and most, in even smaller countries, are much bigger. This isn't the finest house. Many in Europe, particularly, and in China, Asia, have paintings of great, great value, things that we just don't have here and probably will never have until we are 1,000 years old or older.

But this is the best house. It is the best house, because it has something far more important than numbers of people who serve, far more important than numbers of rooms or how big it is, far more important than numbers of magnificent pieces of art.

This house has a great heart, and that heart comes from those who serve. I was rather sorry they didn't come down. We said good-bye to them upstairs. But they are really great. And I recall after so many times I have made speeches, and some of them pretty tough, yet I always come back, or after a hard day—and my days usually have run rather long—I would always get a lift from them, because I might be a little down but they always smiled.

And so it is with you. I look around here, and I see so many on this staff that, you know, I should have been by your offices and shaken hands, and I would love to have talked to you and found out how to run the world—everybody wants to tell the president what to do, and boy, he needs to be told many times—but I just haven't had the time. But I want you to know that each and every one of you, I know, is indispensable to this government.

I am proud of this Cabinet. I am proud of all the members who have served in our Cabinet. I am proud of our sub-Cabinet. I am proud of our White House staff. As I pointed out last night, sure, we have done some things wrong in this administration, and the top man always takes the responsibility, and I have never ducked it. But I want to say one thing: We can be proud of it—five and a half years. No man or no woman came into this administration and left it with more of this world's goods than when he came in. No man or no woman ever profited at the public expense or the public till. That tells something about you.

Mistakes, yes. But for personal gain, never. You did what you believed in. Sometimes right, sometimes wrong. And I only wish that I were a wealthy man—at the present time, I have got to find a way to pay my taxes—and if I were, I would like to recompense you for the sacrifices that all of you have made to serve in government.

But you are getting something in government—and I want you to tell this to your children, and I hope the nation's children will hear it, too—something in government service that is far more important than money. It is a cause bigger than yourself. It is the cause of making this the greatest nation in the world, the leader of the world, because without our leadership, the world will know nothing but war, possibly starvation or worse, in the years ahead. With our leadership it will know peace, it will know plenty.

We have been generous, and we will be more generous in the future as we are able to. But most important, we must be strong here, strong in our hearts, strong in our souls, strong in our belief, and strong in our willingness to sacrifice, as you have been willing to sacrifice, in a pecuniary way, to serve in government.

There is something else I would like for you to tell your young people. You know, people often come in and say, "What will I tell my kids?" They look at government and say, sort of a rugged life, and they see the mistakes that are made. They get the impression that everybody is here for the purpose of feathering his nest. That is why I made this earlier point—not in this administration, not one single man or woman. And I say to them, there are many fine careers. This country needs good farmers, good businessmen, good plumbers, good carpenters.

I remember my old man. I think that they would have called him sort of a little man, common man. He didn't consider himself that way. You know what he was? He was a streetcar motorman first, and then he was a farmer, and then he had a lemon ranch. It was the poorest lemon ranch in California, I can assure you. He sold it before they found oil on it. And then he was a grocer. But he was a great man, because he did his job, and every job counts up to the hilt, regardless of what happens.

Nobody will ever write a book, probably, about my mother. Well, I guess all of you would say this about your mother—my mother was a saint. And I think of her, two boys dying of tuberculosis, nursing four others in order that she could take care of my older brother for three years in Arizona, and seeing each of them die, and when they died, it was like one of her own.

Yes, she will have no books written about her. But she was a saint.

Now, however, we look to the future. I had a little quote in the speech last night from T.R. [Theodore Roosevelt]. As you know, I kind of like to read books. I am not educated, but I do read books. And the T.R. quote was a pretty good one. Here is another one I found as I was reading, my last night in the White House, and this quote is about a young man. He was a young lawyer in New York. He had married a beautiful girl, and they had a lovely daughter, and then suddenly she died, and this is what he wrote. This was in his diary.

He said, "She was beautiful in face and form and lovelier still in spirit. As a flower she grew and as a fair young flower she died. Her life had been always in the sunshine. There had never come to her a single great sorrow. None ever knew her who did not love and revere her for her bright and sunny temper and her saintly unselfishness. Fair, pure, and joyous as a maiden; loving, tender, and happy as a young wife. When she had just become a mother, when her life seemed to be just begun and when the years seemed so bright before her, then by a strange and terrible fate death came to her. And when my heart's dearest died, the light went from my life forever."

That was T.R. in his twenties. He thought the light had gone from his life forever—but he went on. And he not only became president but, as an ex-president, he served his country, always in the arena, tempestuous, strong, sometimes wrong, sometimes right. But he was a man.

And as I leave, let me say, that is an example I think all of us should remember. We think sometimes when things happen that don't go the right way, we think that when you don't pass the bar exam the first time—I happened to, but I was just lucky. I mean, my writing was so poor the bar examiner said, "We have just got to let the guy through." We think that when someone dear to us dies, we think that when we lose an election, we think that when we suffer a defeat that all is ended. We think, as T.R. said, that the light had left his life forever. Not true.

It is only a beginning, always. The young must know it. The old must know it. It must always sustain us, because the greatness comes not when things go always good for you, but the greatness comes and you are really tested, when you take some knocks, some disappointments, when sadness comes, because only if you have been in the deepest valley can you ever know how magnificent it is to be on the highest mountain.

And so I say to you on this occasion, as we leave, we leave proud of the people who have stood by us and worked for us and served this country. We want you to be proud of what you have done. We want you to continue to serve in government, if that is your wish.

Always give your best, never get discouraged, never be petty. Always remember, others may hate you, but those who hate you don't win unless you hate them, and then you destroy yourself.

And so we leave with high hopes, in good spirit, and with deep humility, and with very much gratefulness in our hearts. I can only say to each and every one of you, we come from many faiths, we pray perhaps to different gods—but really the same God in a sense—but I want to say for each and every one of you, not only will we always remember you, not only will we always be grateful to you, but always you will be in our hearts and you will be in our prayers.

Thank you very much.

By 12:03 P.M., the transfer of power was complete when Gerald Ford, the country's first president never to have been elected by the American people (he had been named vice president after Spiro Agnew was convicted of accepting bribes), became the nation's new commander in chief. Infuriated by Nixon's rampant abuse of power, many in Congress and the nation wanted Nixon to be tried in a court of law. Determined to put Watergate to rest once and for all, President Ford braced himself and announced a decision he knew would be politically calamitous but, in his opinion, was best for the country: pardon Richard M. Nixon. On September 8, 1974, President Ford made his case to the American public.

I have come to a decision which I felt I should tell you and all of my fellow American citizens, as soon as I was certain in my own mind and in my own conscience that it is the right thing to do. . . .

I have promised to uphold the Constitution, to do what is right as God gives me to see the right, and to do the very best that I can for America. I have asked your help and your prayers, not only when I became president but many times since. The Constitution is the supreme law of our land and it governs our actions as citizens. Only the laws of God, which govern our consciences, are superior to it.

As we are a nation under God, so I am sworn to uphold our laws with the help of God. And I have sought such guidance and searched my own conscience with special diligence to determine the right thing for me to do with respect to my predecessor in this place, Richard Nixon, and his loyal wife and family. Theirs is an American tragedy in which we all have played a part. It could go on and on and on, or someone must write the end to it. I have concluded that only I can do that, and if I can, I must.

There are no historic or legal precedents to which I can turn in this matter, none that precisely fit the circumstances of a private citizen who has resigned the presidency of the United States. But it is common knowledge that serious allegations and accusations hang like a sword over our former president's head, threatening his health as he tries to reshape his life, a great part of which was spent in the service of this country and by the mandate of its people.

After years of bitter controversy and divisive national debate, I have been advised and I am compelled to conclude that many months and perhaps more years will have to pass before Richard Nixon could obtain a fair trial by jury in any jurisdiction of the United States under governing decisions of the Supreme Court. I deeply believe in equal justice for all Americans, whatever their station or former station. The law, whether human or divine, is no respecter of persons, but the law is a respecter of reality.

The facts, as I see them, are that a former president of the United States, instead of enjoying equal treatment with any other citizen accused of violating the law, would be cruelly and excessively penalized either in preserving the presumption of his innocence or in obtaining a speedy determination of his guilt in order to repay a legal debt to society. During this long period of delay and potential litigation, ugly passions would again be aroused. And our people would again be polarized in their opinions. And the credibility of our free institutions of government would again be challenged at home and abroad. In the end, the courts might well hold that Richard Nixon had been denied due process, and the verdict of history would even more be inconclusive with respect to those charges arising out of the period of his presidency, of which I am presently aware.

But it is not the ultimate fate of Richard Nixon that most concerns me, though surely it deeply troubles every decent and every compassionate person. My concern is the immediate future of this great country. In this, I dare not depend upon my personal sympathy as a long-time friend of the former president, nor my professional judgment as a lawyer, and I do not. As president, my primary concern must always be the greatest good of all the people of the United States whose servant I am. As a man, my first consideration is to be true to my own convictions and my own conscience.

My conscience tells me clearly and certainly that I cannot prolong the bad dreams that continue to reopen a chapter that is closed. My conscience tells me that only I, as president, have the constitutional power to firmly shut and seal this book. My conscience tells me it is my duty not merely to proclaim domestic tranquillity but to use every means that I have to ensure it.

I do believe that the buck stops here, that I cannot rely upon public opinion polls to tell me what is right. I do believe that right makes might and that if I am wrong, ten angels swearing I was right would make no difference. I do believe, with all my heart and mind and spirit, that I, not as president but as a humble servant of God, will receive justice without mercy if I fail to show mercy. Finally, I feel that Richard Nixon and his loved ones have suffered enough and will continue to suffer no matter what I do, no matter what we as a great and good nation can do together to make his goal of peace come true.

Now, therefore, I, Gerald R. Ford, president of the United States, pursuant to the pardon power conferred upon me by Article II, Section 2, of the Constitution, have granted and by these presents do grant a full, free, and absolute pardon unto Richard Nixon for all offenses against the United States which he, Richard Nixon, has committed or may have committed or taken part in during the period from July [January] 20, 1969, through August 9, 1974.

In witness whereof, I have hereunto set my hand this eighth day of September, in the year of our Lord nineteen hundred and seventy-four, and of the Independence of the United States of America the one hundred and ninety-ninth.

Ford's popularity began to tumble almost immediately. By 1976, with the fall of South Vietnam, escalating inflation, urban blight, an increasing dependence on foreign oil, and an overall souring of the nation's economy and faith in its political leadership, Ford's election prospects were bleak. The Democratic Party's hopes rested on a virtually unknown former governor of Georgia named Jimmy Carter, who famously assured voters, "I'll never lie to you." As presumed, Carter won the election, becoming the first Democrat president in thirteen years.

Astronomer Carl Sagan Discusses the Implications of Finding Life on Other Planets
&
The Message (Recorded by President Jimmy Carter) Enclosed in the Voyager I and Voyager II Spacecrafts.

Through his many best-selling books, his award-winning PBS series Cosmos, *and his national television appearances (Johnny Carson, an amateur astronomer, had him on the* Tonight Show *over thirty times), Dr. Carl Sagan inspired millions of Americans to look skyward and contemplate what other life-forms might exist on other planets. Sagan was especially interested in the possibility that life may have once survived—if only in its most rudimentary form—on Mars. During a special broadcast on August 1, 1976, Jim Hartz of NBC asked Sagan what such a discovery would mean to us here on Earth, and Sagan replied with the following.*

Well, I think its historical significance is immense because we are—or at least our machines are—breaking the shackles that tie us to the Earth. We're putting our toes in the cosmic ocean and seeing that it's kind of warm, benign, and interesting. And I think in the long historical perspective this time will be considered as significant and important as the time between, say, the voyages of Columbus and the voyages of Magellan, that early period when the European sailors spread out from Europe and saw what the globe was about, what the significance of the Earth was, what there was on the planet.

Well, we are profoundly ignorant of what the other planets are about. And that ignorance carries over to our own planet. It's very difficult to understand your own planet until you've looked at a few others so you have something to compare against it.

And that's why I think that there are both enormous excitement and adventure. There's no doubt about that, everyone [responding] to the excitement of seeing the first pictures from Mars, but also there's a practical implication for Earthbound sciences like geology, meteorology, biology, that have till now been stuck on one planet. They have been limited in their perspectives. It's not the fault of the practitioners. It's the fault of the subject matter.

We're getting weather reports from Mars to test theories of weather on

Earth. Our geological perceptions of the Earth are being challenged by what we see on Mars. And if we're lucky enough to find life on Mars—an open question—it certainly would be a revolution to biology, because all the organisms on Earth are the same. I know we kind of look different from begonias, whales, or beetles or microbes, but if you look on the fundamental chemical scale, it turns out that the genetic material of all these organisms is made of precisely the same molecule, DNA. And that DNA works to the same molecules in all those organisms called proteins. Even the code book, which translates nucleic acid information to protein, is identical. The oak tree could read your genetic code. It has the right code book.

So we are all the same on this planet. We have no idea what possibilities exist in biology. We only know one kind. Were we to find another example of life, no matter how primitive—microbes are fine—we would then have an opening of horizons. We would know what's possible in biology. We would also have a good idea about the likelihood [of life] evolving elsewhere. If there are two planets and they both had life independently originating, that's a key clue that life is easy to come. And then I think it would be a short stop to the grand conclusion that we live in a populated galaxy, that there is life through the galaxy. And I think the step to intelligent life would then only be a small one.

On the other hand, if we do not find life on Mars, we will of course be disappointed. But there are a lot of positive aspects to that. We're in a no-lose situation. First of all, it would eliminate the problem of the origin of life. Two planets, kind of like each other, same age, similar conditions—life arises on one and not the other. Why? That will say something about what you have to have for the origin of life.

Also, I think, that case will give us a sense of the preciousness of our little planet. Either way, whether we find life or not, I think the point of the uniqueness of human beings, the uniqueness of all the organisms on the Earth, will be driven home powerfully, because the clear lesson of evolution is that nowhere else can there be life like here. There may be intelligence elsewhere. They may be smarter and have better music and all the rest of it, but there cannot be human beings.

And I think that kind of perspective, deprovincialization, is a major outcome of this space program.

In the spring of 1977 Sagan assisted NASA in compiling a series of audio recordings to be placed aboard the Voyager I *and* Voyager II *spacecrafts. The golden phonograph records enclosed in the two* Voyagers, *which were designed only to explore the Jupiter and Saturn systems, had a shelf-life of a billion years. In his 1994 best-seller,* Pale Blue Dot, *Sagan enumerates the phonograph's contents: "greetings in 59 human languages and one whale language; a 12-minute sound essay including a kiss, a baby's cry, and an EEG record of the meditations of a young woman in love; . . . and 90 minutes of the Earth's greatest hits—Eastern and Western, classical and folk, including a Navajo night chant, . . . Stravinsky, Louis Armstrong, Blind Willie Johnson, and Chuck Berry's 'Johnnie B. Goode.'" Of the fifty-nine human greetings, one was by President Jimmy Carter.*

This *Voyager* spacecraft was constructed by the United States of America. We are a community of 240 million human beings among the more than 4 billion who inhabit the planet Earth. We human beings are still divided into nation-states, but these states are rapidly becoming a single global civilization.

We cast this message into the cosmos. It is likely to survive a billion years into our future, when our civilization is profoundly altered and the surface of the Earth may be vastly changed. Of the 200 billion stars in the Milky Way galaxy, some—perhaps many—may have inhabited planets and space-faring civilizations. If one such civilization intercepts *Voyager* and can understand these recorded contents, here is our message:

This is a present from a small distant world, a token of our sounds, our science, our images, our music, our thoughts, and our feelings. We are attempting to survive our time so that we may live into yours. We hope someday, having solved the problems we face, to join a community of galactic civilizations. This record represents our hope and our determination and our goodwill in a vast and awesome universe.

To this day, both Voyager I *and* Voyager II *continue hurtling through space.*

Native American Activist Leonard Peltier, on Trial for Murder, Denounces the Judge as a "Member of the White Racist American Establishment."

On June 26, 1975, two FBI special agents named Ronald Williams and Jack Coler were shot to death at point-blank range on the Pine Ridge Sioux Reservation in South Dakota. These are the confirmed facts of the crime. What is fiercely debated is whether Leonard Peltier, a member of the American Indian Movement (AIM), and other tribal activists ambushed the agents and killed them without provocation. (The agents were on the reservation to arrest another man accused of theft and assault.) Indicted for murder, Peltier, who strenuously asserted his innocence, escaped to Canada but was apprehended and returned to the United States for trial. His defenders claim the prosecution's case was based on circumstantial evidence and excluded information that indicated Peltier's innocence, while the government argued that, among other things, the bullets that killed the two agents had been fired from a gun belonging to Peltier and that Peltier had been identified as the gunman by an eyewitness. On June 1, 1977, the day of his sentencing, Peltier lashed out at Judge Paul Benson not only for what he believed was his own mistreatment, but for the persecution of all Native Americans by white people.

There is no doubt in my mind or my peoples' minds you are going to sentence me to two consecutive life terms. You are and have always been prejudiced against me and any Native Americans who have stood before you. You have openly favored the government all through this trial, and you are happy to do whatever the FBI would want you to do in this case.

I did not always believe this to be so. When I first saw you in the courtroom in Sioux Falls, your dignified appearance misled me into thinking that you were a fair-minded person who knew something of the law and who would act in accordance with the law, which meant that you would be impartial and not favor one side or the other in this lawsuit. That has not been the case, and I now firmly believe that you will impose consecutive life terms solely because that's what you think will avoid the displeasures of the FBI. Neither my people nor myself know why you would be so concerned about an organization that has brought so much shame to the American people, but you are. Your conduct during this trial leaves no doubt that you will do the bidding of the FBI without any hesitation.

You are about to perform an act which will close one more chapter in the history of the failure of the United States courts and the failure of the people of the United States to do justice in the case of a Native American. After centuries of murder of millions of my brothers and sisters by white racist America, could I have been wise in thinking that you would break that tradition and commit an act of justice? Obviously not. Because I should have realized that what I detected was only a very thin layer of dignity and surely not of fine character. If you think my accusations have been harsh and unfounded, I will explain why I have reached these conclusions and why I think my criticism has not been harsh enough:

[E]ach time my defense team tried to expose FBI misconduct in their investigation of this lawsuit and tried to present evidence of this, you claimed it was irrelevant to this trial. But the prosecution was allowed to present their case with evidence that was in no way relevant to this lawsuit—for example, an automobile blowing up on a freeway in Wichita, Kansas; an attempted murder in Milwaukee, Wisconsin, for which I have not been found innocent or guilty; or a van loaded with legally purchased firearms; and a policeman who claims someone fired at him in Oregon state. The Supreme Court of the United States tried to prevent convictions of this sort by passing into law that only past convictions may be presented as evidence if it is not prejudicial to the lawsuit, and only evidence of said case may be used. This court knows very well I have no prior convictions, nor am I even charged with some of these alleged crimes; therefore, they cannot be used as evidence in order to receive a conviction in this farce called a trial. This is why I strongly believe you will impose two life terms, running consecutively, on me. . . .

You do not have the ability to see that the government must suppress the fact that there is a growing anger amongst Indian people and that Native Americans will resist any further encroachments by the military forces of the capitalistic Americans, which is evidenced by the large number of Pine Ridge residents who took up arms on June 27, 1975, to defend themselves. Therefore, you do not have the ability to carry out your responsibility towards me in an impartial way and will run my two life terms consecutively. . . .

I stand before you as a proud man. I feel no guilt. I have done nothing to feel guilty about. I have no regrets of being a Native American activist. Thousands of people in the United States, Canada, and around the world have and will continue to support me to expose the injustices which have occurred in this courtroom. I do feel pity for your people that they must live under such an ugly system. Under your system, you are taught greed, racism, and corruption—and most serious of all, the destruction of Mother Earth. Under the Native American system, we are taught all people are brothers and sisters, to share the wealth with the poor and needy. But the most important of all is to respect and preserve the Earth, who we consider to be our mother. We feed from her breast. Our mother gives us life from birth and when it's time to leave this world, who again takes us back into her womb. But the main thing we are taught is to preserve her for our children and our grandchildren, because they are the next who will live upon her.

No, I'm not the guilty one here. I'm not the one who should be called a criminal. White racist America is the criminal for the destruction of our lands and my people. To hide your guilt from the decent human beings in America and around the world, you will sentence me to two consecutive life terms without any hesitation. . . .

[T]here are less than 400 federal judges for a population of over 200 million Americans. Therefore, you have a very powerful and important responsibility which should be carried out impartially. But you have never been impartial where I was concerned. You have the responsibility of protecting the constitutional rights and laws, but where I was concerned, you neglected to even consider mine or Native Americans' constitutional rights. But, the most important of all, you neglected our human rights.

If you were impartial, you would have had an open mind on all the factual disputes in this case. But you were unwilling to allow even the slightest possibility that a law enforcement officer would lie on the stand. Then how could you possibly be impartial enough to let my lawyers prove how important it is to the FBI to convict a Native American activist in this case? You do not have the ability to see that such a conviction is an important part of the efforts to discredit those who are trying to alert their brothers and sisters to the new threat from the white man, and the attempt to destroy what little Indian land remains in the process of extracting our uranium, oil, and other minerals. Again, to cover up your part in this, you will call me a heartless, cold-blooded murderer who deserves two life sentences consecutively. . . .

I cannot expect a judge who has openly tolerated the conditions I have been jailed under to make an impartial decision on whether I should be sentenced to concurrent or consecutive life terms. You have been made aware of the following conditions which I had to endure at the Grand Forks County Jail, since the time of the verdict: First, I was denied access to a phone to call my attorneys concerning my appeal; second, I was locked in solitary confinement without shower facilities, soap, towels, sheets, or pillow; third, the food was inedible, what little there was of it; fourth, my family—brothers, sisters, mother, and father—who traveled long distances from the reservation, were denied visitation.

No human being should be subjected to such treatment, and while you parade around pretending to be decent, impartial, and law abiding, you knowingly allowed your fascist chief deputy marshal to play stormtrooper. Again, the only conclusion that comes to mind is that you know and always knew that you would sentence me to two consecutive life terms.

Finally, I honestly believe that you made up your mind long ago that I was guilty and that you were going to sentence me to the maximum sentence permitted under the law. But this does not surprise me, because you are a high-ranking member of the white racist American establishment which has consistently said, "In God We Trust," while they went about the business of murdering my people and attempting to destroy our culture.

Leonard Peltier was, as he predicted, condemned to two life terms in prison, where he remains to this day.

Nobel Laureate Isaac Bashevis Singer Reflects on the Role of Stories and Literature to "Uplift the Spirit."

"Yiddish," Isaac Bashevis Singer rhapsodized in his acceptance speech for the 1978 Nobel Prize for literature, "was the tongue of martyrs and saints, of dreamers and kabbalists— rich in humor and in memories. In a figurative way, Yiddish is the wise and humble language of us all, the idiom of frightened and hopeful humanity." Born in Leoncin,

Poland, in 1904, Singer immigrated to the United States in 1935 out of fear that the
Nazis would invade Poland, which they did in 1939. Singer gave his introductory re-
marks at the Nobel ceremony in the language he so adored, and then gave the follow-
ing speech in English celebrating the ability of all writers and poets, regardless of their
language, to embolden humanity and fortify society's moral and spiritual foundations.

The storyteller and poet of our time, as in any other time, must be an entertainer of the spirit in the full sense of the word, not just a preacher of social
or political ideals. There is no paradise for bored readers and no excuse for tedious literature that does not intrigue the reader, uplift his spirit, give him the
joy and the escape that true art always grants. Nevertheless, it is also true that
the serious writer of our time must be deeply concerned about the problems
of his generation. He cannot but see that the power of religion, especially belief in revelation, is weaker today than it was in any other epoch in human
history. More and more children grow up without faith in God, without belief in reward and punishment, in the immortality of the soul, and even in the
validity of ethics. The genuine writer cannot ignore the fact that the family is
losing its spiritual foundation. All the dismal prophecies of [German philoso-
pher and historian] Oswald Spengler have become realities since the Second
World War. No technological achievements can mitigate the disappointment
of modern man, his loneliness, his feeling of inferiority, and his fear of war,
revolution, and terror. Not only has our generation lost faith in Providence,
but also in man in himself, in his institutions, and often in those who are
nearest to him.

In their despair a number of those who no longer have confidence in the
leadership of our society look up to the writer, the master of words. They
hope against hope that the man of talent and sensitivity can perhaps rescue
civilization. Maybe there is a spark of the prophet in the artist after all.

As the son of a people who received the worst blows that human mad-
ness can inflict, I have many times resigned myself to never finding a true way
out. But a new hope always emerges, telling me that it is not yet too late for
all of us to take stock and make a decision. I was brought up to believe in free
will. Although I came to doubt all revelation, I can never accept the idea that
the universe is a physical or chemical accident, a result of blind evolution.
Even though I learned to recognize the lies, the clichés, and the idolatries of
the human mind, I still cling to some truths which I think all of us might accept someday. There must be a way for man to attain all possible pleasures, all
the powers and knowledge that nature can grant him, and still serve God—a
God who speaks in deeds, not in words, and whose vocabulary is the universe.

I am not ashamed to admit that I belong to those who fantasize that lit-

erature is capable of bringing new horizons and new perspectives—philosophical, religious, aesthetical, and even social. In the history of old Jewish literature there was never any basic difference between the poet and the
prophet. Our ancient poetry often became law and a way of life.

Some of my cronies in the cafeteria near the *Jewish Daily Forward* in New
York call me a pessimist and a decadent, but there is always a background of
faith behind resignation. I found comfort in such pessimists and decadents as
Baudelaire, Verlaine, Edgar Allan Poe, and Strindberg. My interest in psychic
research made me find solace in such mystics as your Swedenborg and in our
own Rabbi Nachman Bratzlaver, as well as in a great poet of my time, my
friend Aaron Zeitlin, who died a few years ago and left a spiritual inheritance
of high quality, most of it in Yiddish.

The pessimism of the creative person is not decadence but a mighty passion for the redemption of man. While the poet entertains, he continues to
search for eternal truths, for the essence of being. In his own fashion he tries
to solve the riddle of time and change, to find an answer to suffering, to reveal love in the very abyss of cruelty and injustice. Strange as these words may
sound, I often play with the idea that when all the social theories collapse and
wars and revolutions leave humanity in utter gloom, the poet—whom Plato
banned from his Republic—may rise up and save us all.

Conservative Leader Phyllis Schlafly Denounces the Women's Movement as Incompatible with a "Successful Family Life and Motherhood."

Propelled by Betty Friedan's 1963 national best-seller, The Feminine Mystique, *modern feminism began achieving significant gains in the 1970s. In 1972 Congress overwhelmingly passed the Equal Rights Amendment, which was first proposed in 1923 and stated simply, "Equality of rights under the law shall not be denied or abridged by the United States or any state on account of sex." (The states, however, failed to ratify the amendment, and political support for the ERA cause ultimately waned.) In 1973 the Supreme Court legalized abortion in all fifty states. Throughout the decade women saw increases in their salaries, as well as advances in academic and professional opportunities. But even though the women's liberation movement, as it came to be known, grew in numbers and strength, it by no means represented the views of all women in America. The movement's most prominent opponent, in fact, was a con-servative activist named Phyllis Schlafly, who encouraged women to find fulfillment in motherhood and family life. Schlafly frequently spoke out against feminism and the ERA, and on March 27, 1979, she promoted the "positive woman's movement" to an audience of Southern Baptists meeting in Orlando, Florida.*

Good morning friends. The subject assigned today is, indeed, an important one: the women's movement and family life. It is important that we first of all define the term. I would not agree that there is just *the* women's movement. In order to make sure we know what we are talking about, I will first of all describe what I think could be more appropriately called the women's liberation movement. It could be defined as the movement of women who have, in a general way, been working for the Equal Rights Amendment.

This movement was born in the mid-1960s with the publication of Betty Friedan's book *The Feminine Mystique*. This movement accomplished the task of getting the Equal Rights Amendment through Congress in 1972. It reached its peak in November 1977 in Houston at the National Conference of the Commission on International Women's Year. Since that date, it's no longer a nebulous thing. It is a very precise movement that can be definitely defined with particular people and particular goals.

Participating in that Houston Conference were all the leaders of the women's liberation movement. These included the head of the National Organization for Women (NOW), the head of the Women's Political Caucus, the head of ERAmerica (the lobbying group for the ERA), the head of the Gay Task Force, the person who put the ERA through the Senate, the person who put ERA though the House, Gloria Steinem, and Bella Abzug was the chairman. These were all presidential appointees, and they gathered in Houston. They had $5 million of federal funds and they passed twenty-five resolutions, which represent the goals of the women's liberation movement.

The four "hot button" issues, the term used by *Newsweek* magazine—their most important goals—were ratification of the Equal Rights Amendment, government-funded abortion, lesbian privileges to be recognized with the same dignity as husbands and wives and with the right to teach in schools, and massive, universal, federal child care, which *Time* magazine estimated would cost us an additional $25 billion a year. There were other resolutions, too, but the four "hot button" issues were admitted by everybody—the media plus both sides—as being the main ones.

These are the goals and those are the personalities of the women's liberation movement in our country today. It is my belief, based on working with this movement for quite a number of years, that the movement is having an adverse effect on family life, that it is a major cause of divorce today, and that it is highly detrimental to our country and to our families. . . .

For a woman to function effectively in the family, it is necessary for her to believe in the worth of her position, to have a certain amount of self-esteem, to believe that her task as wife and mother is worthy, is honorable, is useful, and is fulfilling. The fundamental attitude by the women's liberation movement takes all that away from women. I have listened to thousands of their speeches, and basically those speeches inculcate in woman a negative attitude toward life, toward the family, toward their country, and most of all toward themselves. It was best summed up in an advertisement developed by the principal women's liberation organization, the National Organization for Women. It was run as a spot announcement on many television stations and as ads in many magazines and newspapers. This advertisement shows a darling, curly-headed child. The caption under the picture is: "This normal, healthy child was born with a handicap. It was born female."

Think about that. That is the startling assumption of the woman's liberation movement: That somebody—it isn't clear who, God or the establishment or a conspiracy of male chauvinist pigs—has dealt women a foul blow by making them female; that it is up to society to remedy these centuries of oppression, of bondage, even of slavery. Women are told that they are not even persons in our society. They are told that they are second-class citizens. I have given speeches where women have been picketing up and down outside, wearing placards saying, "I am a second-class citizen." I feel so sorry for women who are deliberately inculcating this inferiority complex. Women are not second-class citizens in our society. Whatever women may have been hundreds of years ago, in other lands, or in other countries, that is not the condition of women in our country today.

The thesis of the speeches that women's liberation movement speakers are giving runs basically like this: "Sister, when you wake up in the morning, the cards are stacked against you. You won't get a job, and if you get one, it won't be a good one. You'll never be paid what you're really worth. You won't be promoted as you deserve to be. You simply will never get a fair break in our society. And if you get married, your husband will treat you like a servant, like a chattel"—that's one of their favorite words—"and life is nothing but a bunch of dirty diapers and dirty dishes."

It's no wonder that women have problems when they listen to that line. The women's liberation movement literature is the greatest put-down of women that anything could possibly be. It's difficult to pick yourself up off the floor after you have listened to those tirades about how women are kept in bondage and enslaved, and how the home is a cage or a prison from which women must be liberated. This line creates a natural hostility between men and women. No longer are men people with whom we work in harmony. Men are the enemy who must make it up to us for these centuries of injustice.

Whatever lowly status women may endure in other lands, that is not the situation of American women. It is also true that nobody in this world who wakes up in the morning with a chip on your shoulder, whether it is man or woman, is going to have a happy or fulfilling life, or get ahead in this world.

This is not to say that there aren't any problems. The world is full of problems. I don't know anybody who doesn't have problems. Women face all kinds of problems: husbands out of a job, handicapped children, senile parents, or not enough money. The world is full of problems. But you don't solve your problems by waking up in the morning with a chip on your shoulder, believing and telling yourself hour after hour that you've been oppressed, and that it is up to somebody to remedy years of injustice.

After having flattened women by spreading this negative attitude, the women's liberation movement then comes along and offers its solution. The solution can be best described as the "new narcissism." You remember the story of Narcissus: the Greek youth who fell in love with his own image in the reflecting pool and finally died of unrequited desire.

The women's liberation movement teaches women this fundamental approach to life: "Seek your own self-fulfillment over every other value." It's a free country for those who choose to establish their scale of values that way. Some women make that choice, and they are free to do so if that is what they want. But I simply have to tell women that *that* attitude, that choice of goals, is not compatible with a happy marriage. It is *not* compatible with a successful family life and it is *not* compatible with motherhood.

In order to live in harmony in family life, with a man who's been brought up in another environment, you have to make social compromises, and most of us think that marriage is worth the price.

Motherhood must be a self-sacrificing role, a role of dedication and service. The mother must be able to subordinate her self-fulfillment and her desire for a career to the well-being of her children so that she can answer her child's call any hour of the day or night. This is what marriage and motherhood are all about, and it is not compatible with the dogmas of the women's liberation movement.

The women's liberation movement preaches that the greatest oppression of women is that women get pregnant and men don't get pregnant, and so women must be relieved of this oppression! The second greatest oppression of women, according to the liberation movement, is that society expects mothers to look after their babies, that society reduces women to this menial, tedious, tiresome, confining, repetitious chore of looking after babies.

Well, I suppose it's all in your point of view. Many of us believe that the ability to participate in the creation of human life is the great gift that God gave to women. The task of taking care of babies, despite its tedious drudgery, is better than most of the jobs of the world. Women should find out how exhausting most of the rest of the jobs of the world are. Besides, a mother has something to show for her efforts after twenty years: You've got a living, breathing human being, a good citizen, a wonderful human being you've given to this world.

But the women's movement is causing wives with relatively good families to walk out. Women's lib is a dogma that is especially contagious among women in their forties and fifties after their children are in school. Wives who "catch" the disease of women's liberation are walking out on marriage—not because of the traditional problems in marriage such as alcohol, or money, or adultery, but just to seek their own self-fulfillment.

I speak almost every week on college campuses and I see these abandoned teenagers. Young women come up to me and say, "My mother has left. What can you say to my mother, who has brought up four children and now thinks her whole life is wasted?" The women who "catch" women's liberation are walking out. It makes no difference whether they're northern and eastern liberal homes or southern and western conservative homes. Once they get this message, they go out into emptiness, abandoning their families.

This women's liberation dogma is also very contagious among young college women. They have bought a large part of it. The biggest thing that hits you on the college campuses today is that the educated young women of our nation are rejecting marriage and motherhood. Most important, they're rejecting motherhood. They're saying that if they have a baby, they don't want it to interfere with their careers. I have young men coming to me now saying that they want to marry a young woman, but she tells them very frankly, "If we have a baby, I'm not going to let that baby interfere with my career. I see nothing the matter with putting the baby in some child-care facility at the age of three or four weeks." Remember, this is not a matter of need. These are not hungry people. These are a class of women who expect to have degrees but they don't want that baby to interfere with their careers. Of course, my answer to those young men is, "Forget her." A woman who is unwilling to take care of her own baby is a pathetic sight, and there's nothing in marriage for a man to have a relationship like that. This is what the women's liberation movement is doing to the young women of our nation. . . .

There *is* another women's movement. You don't hear much about it, but I believe it is more powerful. It is the Positive Woman's Movement: the woman who knows who she is. The Positive Woman is not searching for her identity. She knows God made her, she knows why she's here, and she has her scale of values in order. This movement was born in 1972 when some of us realized we had to protect ourselves against the takeaway of the legal rights of the homemaker that was embodied in the Equal Rights Amendment. This movement showed itself at the marvelous Pro-Family Rally in Houston in 1977 where 15,000 people came at their own expense—not like the other one where people came at the taxpayers' expense. Our movement of Positive Women came of age on March 22, 1979 in Washington, D.C., when we celebrated, at a marvelous dinner in Washington, the expiration of the seven years that was set as the time period for ratification of the Equal Rights Amendment. . . .

Our Positive Women are not seeking their own self-fulfillment as the highest value, as the women's liberation movement tries to teach women. Our Positive Women are dedicated to service, to faith and trust in God, to the family, and to this great country that we have been fortunate enough to live in. We are not seeking to get our bit at the price of taking benefits away from others, as the woman's liberation movement is doing. We have taken on these great odds, believing, as we are told in II Chronicles, "Be not afraid, nor dismayed by reason of the great multitude, for the battle is not yours but God's."

We have fought the greatest political forces that anybody has ever fought in our country in this century. We have won, with God's help, because we are Positive Women. We don't wake up in the morning mad at anybody. We have women who are talented, articulate, capable. We have lady legislators and successful career women. We have some who are solely successful career women, others who are wives and mothers but who are also successful in an auxiliary career. The great thing about woman's role is that she can have different careers at different times in her life. But our Positive Women have their scale of values in order: no matter what they may seek for their own self-fulfillment, they know that the family is more important.

Our women are, I believe, the greatest positive force in our country today. We believe that we can do great things. Now that we move into the more positive phase of our activity, we will work for the restoration of the family unit, which is coming apart at the seams in many areas. We want to show women how, in this great country, women can do whatever they want and have all kinds of exciting lives. But for a woman to be a successful wife and mother, during that period of her life, marriage and motherhood must come first over selfish values.

In conclusion, I share with you the comment attributed to a French writer who traveled our country in another century and wrote many commentaries which are still studied in our schools. When he came to the conclusion of his travels, Alexis de Tocqueville wrote, "I sought for the greatness and genius of America in her commodious harbors and ample rivers, but it was not there. I sought for the greatness of America in her fertile lands and boundless prairies, but it was not there. It was not until I went into the churches of America and found her pulpits aflame with righteousness that I understood the secret of her genius and her power. America is great because America is good, and if America ever ceases to be good, she will cease to be great." The Positive Women of America are pledging themselves to do our part to make sure that America continues to be good.

President Jimmy Carter Addresses the "Crisis of Confidence" Affecting the "Heart and Soul and Spirit" of the Nation.

By the summer of 1979, President Jimmy Carter's popularity ratings were in a nose-dive. Heading into the mid-twenties in July (Nixon's were in the thirties during the worst of Watergate), Carter suffered from both horrible luck and poor political judgment. With every foreign policy triumph, such as the historic Camp David Accords Carter brokered establishing peace between Egypt and Israel, there came an intractable crisis, such as the Soviet invasion of Afghanistan. Domestically, the economy was reeling: Unemployment was in the double digits in many areas of the country, inflation hit a staggering 10 percent, interest rates were over 20 percent, and oil and gas, which Americans had always taken for granted, were scarce. (The United States imported more than 30 percent of its oil in 1973. By 1977 it was up to 50 percent, and two years after Carter's inauguration, the Organization of Petroleum Exporting Countries [OPEC] jacked up oil prices more than 100 percent.) Carter's "Washington outsider" status appealed to Watergate-weary voters in 1976, but in the face of what seemed to be one disaster after another, many wondered if Carter had the political aptitude needed to effect dramatic change. Even Carter's vaunted idealism and moral piety—once admired in the aftermath of White House corruption—now appeared arrogant and stubborn. Carter recognized he had to confront the nation's anxieties head on, and on July 15, 1979, he spoke to a radio and television audience of sixty million Americans.

I want to talk to you right now about a fundamental threat to American democracy. I do not mean our political and civil liberties. They will endure. And I do not refer to the outward strength of America, a nation that is at peace tonight everywhere in the world, with unmatched economic power and military might. The threat is nearly invisible in ordinary ways. It is a crisis of confidence. It is a crisis that strikes at the very heart and soul and spirit of our national will. We can see this crisis in the growing doubt about the meaning of our own lives and in the loss of a unity of purpose for our nation. The erosion of our confidence in the future is threatening to destroy the social and the political fabric of America.

The confidence that we have always had as a people is not simply some romantic dream or a proverb in a dusty book that we read just on the Fourth of July. It is the idea which founded our nation and has guided our development as a people. Confidence in the future has supported everything else—public institutions and private enterprise, our own families, and the very Constitution of the United States. Confidence has defined our course and has served as a link between generations. We've always believed in something called progress. We've always had a faith that the days of our children would be better than our own.

Our people are losing that faith not only in government itself but in the ability as citizens to serve as the ultimate rulers and shapers of our democracy. As a people we know our past and we are proud of it. Our progress has been part of the living history of America, even the world. We always believed that we were part of a great movement of humanity itself called democracy, involved in the search for freedom, and that belief has always strengthened us in our purpose. But just as we are losing our confidence in the future, we are also beginning to close the door on our past.

In a nation that was proud of hard work, strong families, close-knit communities, and our faith in God, too many of us now tend to worship self-indulgence and consumption. Human identity is no longer defined by what one does, but by what one owns. But we've discovered that owning things and consuming things does not satisfy our longing for meaning. We've learned that piling up material goods cannot fill the emptiness of lives which have no confidence or purpose.

The symptoms of this crisis of the American spirit are all around us. For the first time in the history of our country a majority of our people believe that the next five years will be worse than the past five years. Two-thirds of our people do not even vote. The productivity of American workers is actually dropping, and the willingness of Americans to save for the future has fallen below that of all other people in the Western world. As you know, there is a growing disrespect for government and for churches and for schools, the news media, and other institutions. This is not a message of happiness or reassurance, but it is the truth and it is a warning.

These changes did not happen overnight. They've come upon us gradually over the last generation, years that were filled with shocks and tragedy. We were sure that ours was a nation of the ballot, not the bullet, until the murders of John Kennedy and Robert Kennedy and Martin Luther King Jr. We were taught that our armies were always invincible and our causes were always just, only to suffer the agony of Vietnam. We respected the presidency as a place of honor until the shock of Watergate. We remember when the phrase "sound as a dollar" was an expression of absolute dependability, until ten years of inflation began to shrink our dollar and our savings. We believed that our nation's resources were limitless until 1973, when we had to face a growing dependence on foreign oil.

Often you see paralysis and stagnation and drift. You don't like it, and neither do I. What can we do? First of all, we must face the truth, and then we can change our course. We simply must have faith in each other, faith in our ability to govern ourselves, and faith in the future of this nation. Restoring that faith and that confidence to America is now the most important task we face. It is a true challenge of this generation of Americans. . . .

We know the strength of America. We are strong. We can regain our unity. We can regain our confidence. We are the heirs of generations who survived threats much more powerful and awesome than those that challenge us now. Our fathers and mothers were strong men and women who shaped a new society during the Great Depression, who fought world wars, and who carved out a new charter of peace for the world.

We ourselves are the same Americans who just ten years ago put a man on the moon. We are the generation that dedicated our society to the pursuit of human rights and equality. And we are the generation that will win the war on the energy problem and in that process rebuild the unity and confidence of America.

We are at a turning point in our history. There are two paths to choose. One is a path I've warned about tonight, the path that leads to fragmentation and self-interest. Down that road lies a mistaken idea of freedom, the right to grasp for ourselves some advantage over others. That path would be one of constant conflict between narrow interests ending in chaos and immobility. It is a certain route to failure. . . .

Little by little we can and we must rebuild our confidence. We can spend until we empty our treasuries, and we may summon all the wonders of science. But we can succeed only if we tap our greatest resources: America's people, America's values, and America's confidence. I have seen the strength of America in the inexhaustible resources of our people. In the days to come, let us renew that strength in the struggle for an energy-secure nation.

In closing, let me say this: I will do my best, but I will not do it alone. Let your voice be heard. Whenever you have a chance, say something good about our country. With God's help and for the sake of our nation, it is time for us to join hands in America. Let us commit ourselves together to a rebirth of the American spirit. Working together with our common faith, we cannot fail.

Later ridiculed by opponents as the "malaise" speech—though the word was never used—Carter's address to the nation actually buoyed his approval rating by 11 percent. But the success would prove short-lived. When the newly deposed Shah of Iran was allowed to seek asylum in the United States after a revolution led by the Ayatollah Khomeini, Iranian fundamentalists stormed the U.S. embassy in Teheran and took fifty-two Americans hostage. The Ayatollah publicly mocked the American president for not having "the guts to use military force." Even more catastrophically, the military did attempt a rescue, but it failed horribly when two of the aircraft collided, killing eight U.S. servicemen. It was a devastating blow to an already demoralized nation.

1980–1989

WE HEAR MUCH FROM MOSCOW ABOUT A NEW POLICY OF RE-
form and openness. Some political prisoners have been released. Certain foreign news broadcasts are no longer being jammed.
Some economic enterprises have been permitted to operate with
greater freedom from state control. Are these the beginnings of profound changes in the Soviet state? Or are they token gestures, intended
to raise false hopes in the West, or to strengthen the Soviet system
without changing it? We welcome change and openness, for we believe that freedom and security go together, that the advance of human
liberty can only strengthen the cause of world peace.

There is one sign the Soviets can make that would be unmistakable, that would advance dramatically the cause of freedom and peace.
General Secretary Gorbachev, if you seek peace, if you seek prosperity
for the Soviet Union and eastern Europe, if you seek liberalization,
come here to this gate! Mr. Gorbachev, open this gate! Mr. Gorbachev,
tear down this wall!

—President Ronald Reagan,
standing before the Berlin Wall, June 12, 1987
(the Wall came down on November 9, 1989)

Presidential Candidate Ronald Reagan Vows a "National Crusade to Make America Great Again."

As President Jimmy Carter predicted in his July 15, 1979, speech, America would indeed regain its confidence. But the country's renewed sense of strength and security would be inspired not by Carter but by his political opponent in the 1980 presidential race, the telegenic former governor of California, Ronald Wilson Reagan. Even his detractors conceded that Reagan, a former Democrat who cast his first vote in 1932 for FDR, radiated charm and an almost contagious sense of optimism—qualities that Jimmy Carter, despite his famous grin, regrettably lacked. Throughout the 1980 campaign Democrats struggled to convince voters that underneath Reagan's genial demeanor was a trigger-happy nuclear cowboy unsympathetic to the plight of the less fortunate. But Reagan, the onetime movie star, stuck to his script and remained upbeat, promising to cut taxes, reduce government, and rebuild the military. On July 17, 1980, Reagan elaborated on these themes at the Republican National Convention, offering one of the most masterful performances of his political career.

Mr. Chairman, Mr. Vice President–to–be, this convention, my fellow citizens of this great nation:

With a deep awareness of the responsibility conferred by your trust, I accept your nomination for the presidency of the United States. I do so with deep gratitude, and I think also I might interject on behalf of all of us, our thanks to Detroit and the people of Michigan and to this city for the warm hospitality they have shown. And I thank you for your wholehearted response to my recommendation in regard to George Bush as a candidate for the vice president. . . .

The major issue in this campaign is the direct political, personal, and moral responsibility of Democratic Party leadership—in the White House and in the Congress—for this unprecedented calamity which has befallen us. They tell us they've done the most that humanly could be done. They say that the United States has had its day in the sun, that our nation has passed its zenith. They expect you to tell your children that the American people no longer have the will to cope with their problems, that the future will be one of sacrifice and few opportunities.

My fellow citizens, I utterly reject that view. The American people, the most generous on earth, who created the highest standard of living, are not going to accept the notion that we can only make a better world for others by moving backwards ourselves. And those who believe we *can* have no business leading this nation.

I will not stand by and watch this great country destroy itself under mediocre leadership that drifts from one crisis to the next, eroding our national will and purpose. We have come together here because the American people deserve better from those to whom they entrust our nation's highest offices, and we stand united in our resolve to do something about it.

We need a rebirth of the American tradition of leadership at every level of government and in private life as well. The United States of America is unique in world history because it has a genius for leaders—many leaders on many levels. But back in 1976, Mr. Carter said, "Trust me." And a lot of people did. And now, many of those people are out of work. Many have seen their savings eaten away by inflation. Many others on fixed incomes, especially the elderly, have watched helplessly as the cruel tax of inflation wasted away their purchasing power. And, today, a great many who trusted Mr. Carter wonder if we can survive the Carter policies of national defense.

"Trust me" government asks that we concentrate our hopes and dreams on one man, that we trust him to do what's best for us. But my view of government places trust not in one person or one party, but in those values that transcend persons and parties. The trust is where it belongs—in the people. The responsibility to live up to that trust is where it belongs—in their elected leaders. That kind of relationship between the people and their elected leaders is a special kind of compact. . . .

The first task of national leadership is to set realistic and honest priorities in our policies and our budget, and I pledge that my administration will do that. When I talk of tax cuts, I am reminded that every major tax cut in this century has strengthened the economy, generated renewed productivity, and ended up yielding new revenues for the government by creating new investment, new jobs, and more commerce among our people.

The present administration has been forced by the Republicans to play follow-the-leader with regard to a tax cut. But in this election year we must take with the proverbial "grain of salt" any tax cut proposed by those who have already given us the greatest tax increase in our nation's history.

When those in leadership give us tax increases and tell us we must also do with less, have they thought about those who've always had less, especially the minorities? This is like telling them that just as they step on the first rung of the ladder of opportunity, the ladder is being pulled out from under them. That may be the Democratic leadership's message to the minorities, but it won't be ours. Our message will be: We have to move ahead, but we're not going to leave anyone behind.

Thanks to the economic policies of the Democratic Party, millions of Americans find themselves out of work. Millions more have never even had a fair chance to learn new skills, hold a decent job, or secure for themselves and their families a share in the prosperity of this nation.

It is time to put America back to work, to make our cities and towns resound with the confident voices of men and women of all races, nationalities and faiths bringing home to their families a paycheck they can cash for honest money. For those without skills, we'll find a way to help them get new skills. For those without job opportunities, we'll stimulate new opportunities, particularly in the inner cities where they live. For those who've abandoned hope, we'll restore hope and we'll welcome them into a great national crusade to make America great again.

When we move from domestic affairs and cast our eyes abroad, we see an equally sorry chapter in the record of the present Administration: a Soviet combat brigade trains in Cuba, just ninety miles from our shores; a Soviet army of invasion occupies Afghanistan, further threatening our vital interests in the Middle East; America's defense strength is at its lowest ebb in a generation, while the Soviet Union is vastly outspending us in both strategic and conventional arms; our European allies, looking nervously at the growing menace from the east, turn to us for leadership and fail to find it; and incredibly, more than fifty of our fellow Americans have been held captive for over eight months by a dictatorial foreign power that holds us up to ridicule before the world. Adversaries large and small test our will and seek to confound our resolve, but we are given weakness when we need strength, vacillation when the times demand firmness. . . .

The administration which has brought us to this state is seeking your endorsement for four more years of weakness, indecision, mediocrity, and incompetence. No American should vote until he or she has asked: Is the United States stronger and more respected now than it was three-and-a-half years ago? Is the world safer, a safer place in which to live?

It is the responsibility of the president of the United States, in working for peace, to insure that the safety of our people cannot successfully be threatened by a hostile foreign power. As president, fulfilling that responsibility will be my number-one priority. We're not a warlike people. Quite the opposite. We always seek to live in peace. We resort to force infrequently and with great reluctance, and only after we've determined that it is absolutely necessary. We are awed—and rightly so—by the forces of destruction at loose in the world in this nuclear era. But neither can we be naive or foolish. Four times in my lifetime America has gone to war, bleeding the lives of its young men into the sands of island beachheads, the fields of Europe, and the jungles and rice paddies of Asia. We know only too well that war comes not when the forces of freedom are strong—it is when they are weak that tyrants are tempted. We simply cannot learn these lessons the hard way again without risking our destruction.

Of all the objectives we seek, first and foremost is the establishment of lasting world peace. We must always stand ready to negotiate in good faith, ready to pursue any reasonable avenue that holds forth the promise of lessening tensions and furthering the prospects of peace. But let our friends and those who may wish us ill take note: The United States has an obligation to its citizens and to the people of the world never to let those who would destroy freedom dictate the future course of life on this planet. I would regard my election as proof that we have renewed our resolve to preserve world peace and freedom, that this nation will once again be strong enough to do that. . . .

Tonight, let us dedicate ourselves to renewing the American compact. I ask you not simply to "trust me," but to trust your values—our values—and to hold me responsible for living up to them. I ask you to trust that American spirit which knows no ethnic, religious, social, political, regional, or economic boundaries; the spirit that burned with zeal in the hearts of millions of immigrants from every corner of the earth who came here in search of freedom.

Some say that spirit no longer exists. But I've seen it—I've felt it—all across the land, in the big cities, the small towns, and in rural America. It's still there, ready to blaze into life if you and I are willing to do what has to be done. We have to do the practical things, the down-to-earth things, such as creating policies that will stimulate our economy, increase productivity, and put America back to work.

The time is now to resolve that the basis of a firm and principled foreign policy is one that takes the world as it is and seeks to change it by leadership and example, not by harangue, harassment, or wishful thinking. The time is now to say that we shall seek new friendships and expand others and improve others, but we shall not do so by breaking our word or casting aside old friends and allies. And the time is now to redeem promises once made to the American people by another candidate, in another time, and another place. He said, "For three long years I have been going up and down this country preaching that government—federal, state, and local—costs too much. I shall not stop that preaching. As an immediate program of action, we must abolish useless offices. We must eliminate unnecessary functions of government. We must consolidate subdivisions of government and, like the private citizen, give up luxuries which we can no longer afford." And then he said: "I propose to you, my friends, and through you, that government of all kinds, big and little, be made solvent and that the example be set by the president of the United States and his Cabinet." That was Franklin Delano Roosevelt's words as he accepted the Democratic nomination for president in 1932.

The time is now, my fellow Americans, to recapture our destiny, to take it into our own hands. And to do this it will take many of us working together. I ask you tonight, all over this land, to volunteer your help in this cause so that we can carry our message throughout the land. Yes, isn't now the time that we, the people, carried out these unkept promises? Let us pledge to each other and to all America on this July day forty-eight years later, we intend to do *just that*.

I have thought of something that is not part of my speech and I'm worried over whether I should do it. Can we doubt that only a divine Providence placed this land, this island of freedom, here as a refuge for all those people in the world who yearn to breathe free? Jews and Christians enduring persecution behind the Iron Curtain; the boat people of Southeast Asia, Cuba, and of Haiti; the victims of drought and famine in Africa; the freedom fighters of Afghanistan; and our own countrymen held in savage captivity.

I'll confess that I've been a little afraid to suggest what I'm going to suggest. I'm more afraid not to. Can we begin our crusade joined together in a moment of silent prayer?

God bless America.

In the minds of many voters, Reagan offered a compelling argument for change. The Democrats' convention in New York City a month later gave Carter a small bump in the polls, and the delegates were invigorated by Senator Kennedy's speech and its stirring conclusion: "For all those whose cares have been our concern, the work goes on, the cause endures, the hope still lives, and the dream shall never die." But the economy remained in shambles, the American hostages in Iran still languished in captivity, and John Anderson, the Illinois congressman running as a candidate on the Independent ticket, further diluted Carter's support. The election was a landslide. Reagan won 44 states—449 electoral votes to Carter's 49. Republicans also swept the Senate. The Reagan Revolution had begun.

Dr. Rayna Green, Cherokee, Offers a "Modest Proposal" for a "Museum of the Plains White Person."

Proving that even academics can have a sense of humor, Cherokee scholar and writer Rayna Green modestly proposed at a 1981 national meeting of American Indian women educators and political activists the need for a "Museum of the Plains White Person." Green, who is the Director of the American Indian Program at the Smithsonian's National Museum of American History, expressed anxiety that white people and their culture were "dying out." Green then outlined what she and other concerned Native Americans planned to do about it.

I am deeply honored to speak before you here in my own homeland of the Cherokee Nation. As you know, all over the country and for the past hundred years, Indian nations have created and maintained a vast number of excellent museums, tribally-specific museums as well as great national cultural institutions which explore and preserve the long and triumphant history of the First Peoples of North America. However, as many of us, now elders in the Native museums and tribal governments, have reflected on our achievements, many of us feel that something is missing. Late one night, in a serious scholarly and philosophical discussion right here in Tahlequah, Oklahoma, I and Louis LaRose, the distinguished ex-chairman of the Winnebago Nation, developed the following proposal and fund-raising plan for an exciting, essential and educational new museum.

We call it the Museum of the Plains White Person. It represents something that Indian people have needed and wanted for a long time. Like many of you, we have been worried about the culture and history of White People. Taking note of their increasingly diminished numbers, we are deeply concerned that White Culture appears to be dying out. We are afraid that, centuries from now, Indian children of the future will have little that remains to tell them about White Culture at its pinnacle, in its heyday. The once elegant and distinguished language of White People has deteriorated so severely that almost none of those remaining speak it well; furthermore, they seem to share no mutually intelligible language. Their religion is in a virtual state of collapse. And their traditional art forms have been devastated, of course. Virtually no one engages in the old performance arts of White People; there are few alive who remember their traditional dances and songs, much less the entirety of their great ceremonies and rituals.

We have been asking ourselves, what will the last surviving White People do when they have no one left to ask what their language was like, what their religions, customs and clothes were like when they were at their peak? In that respect, we've created a new museum in which we can test out some of the notions about white people that we've learned from observing their long-held and simplistic, though somewhat adorable notions about us. And, we've created a museum meant primarily for Indians, though it will assuredly be appreciated by the few remaining white persons who are able to visit it. Native foundations have rushed to put money into this great project. Indian people everywhere have really responded to our call. I cannot tell you how many shawl dances, blanket raffles and bingoes have been given to pay for this museum, and moreover, how our pinions of the world market economy—Native casinos—have responded to the call for support.

We have begun a massive campaign of collection of white artifacts, and I want to engage each of you in this campaign, because we are desperately in need of acquiring these artifacts before they deteriorate and disappear. White

People don't, of course, know how to take care of their artifacts, and we know that many of you have been buying examples of their quaint and decorative material culture in order to save them.

Let me tell you something of the plans for our museum. First, we will be building the museum over an abandoned ceremonial ballcourt, called a "football field," somewhere in what the Omaha Nation called "Nebraska." Our Indian archaeologists made, as you know, the great discovery of an ancient white ceremonial cult called the Cornhuskers, right there, and this ballcourt was the site of their annual rites for that once-great religion. Its major gallery, of course, will be a hall of ancestral remains, and that is the major emphasis of our first collecting effort. We have organized collecting expeditions throughout the country, and, as we speak, Indian backhoes are excavating the sadly abandoned white cemetaries of the United States. We have, through our powers of eminent domain, acquired at least eighty percent of the white cemetaries in this country.

We have begun our national campaign to acquire the bones of famous white people, since they themselves insisted for centuries that that we can all learn so much from studying and displaying such remains. And, accepting their notions of reverence for the exhibition of the dead and goods from graves, White People will be honored to have the remains of their grandmothers and grandfathers on display. We have just acquired what I think is quite an important and moving find, the bones of John Wayne, the White Culture Hero, and we plan to acquire the remains of many other famous white persons. You might guess who we have our sights on. What a great significance this can have for our scholars, as they attempt to interpret the important aspects of white culture from this most American of mythological characters. Although thus far we little understand and are even repelled by the reasons why white people so revere the display of their ancestors, we accept such display as a hallmark of white civilization. We want Indian children, and of course Native scholars, to be able to study them, to pore over the different skull shapes and speculate as to their ancestral heritage and personality disorders as reflected in the remains.

Let me tell you about some of our other collections and exhibition plans that I think are quite exciting. There will be a White Foodways Gallery where we examine the great and holy foods of the quintessential white culture— mayonnaise, white bread, iceberg lettuce, peanut butter, lime Jell-O and little marshmallows. We will reconstruct one of their temples to food, a so-called "McDonald's," in its entirety. We are currently doing a study of some of the ceremonial foodways of the Cornhuskers, and we are particularly interested in the great Weenie Burning rites that occurred in the summer, a religious behavior perhaps related to their reverence for the Little Marshmallows. And, of course, we are doing research on white hunting and foraging techniques, which appeared to be called "making reservations."

We will have several exhibits about their strange but wonderful customs. We have found a few remaining White People who know fragments of their quaint dances and songs, and we will offer living history programs of their dances, the waltz, the fox trot, the Texas Two-Step, the disco, frug, bop and polka. Additionally, we have discovered people who actually remember and can interpret the meaningless vocables—bop-shu-bop, do-wop, do-wop, and ooooh, ooooh, ooooh baby—of many of their ceremonial and courting songs. We are creating an entire photographic exhibition on a form of ritual performance revered by white people, a kind of symbolic warfare they called "talk shows."

We are busily acquiring examples of their most important elaborate ceremonial and shamanistic costumes and instruments of power—a typical chieftain's three-piece suit and briefcase, a medicine man's stethoscope and a Barbie shaman's spike heels and bikini underpants. And we are assembling, in large numbers, examples of an artifact called "handkerchiefs," used by White People to preserve the effluence from their nostrils, only one example of their desire, according to some of our elders' observations, to save everything. And finally, we will be assembling a stellar and major collection of items of costume associated with their centuries-old significant, though puzzling, form of ritual behavior called "playing Indian," taken from their subcults called the Boy Scouts, the Improved Order of Red Men, the Tammany Society, the Washington Redskins, and an obscure but significant group of the twentieth century called the "New Age."

Well, I don't want to burden your patience further with this scholarly exegesis, but I think you'll agree that the Museum of the Plains White Person is one of the most exciting contributions Native people can make to world cultural history. As an Indian scholar, I'm pleased to be involved in addressing our responsibilities to the documentation, preservation and celebration of a once-great but clearly endangered species. When one notes that our great buffalo are now more numerous in North America than White People, it becomes a sad, perhaps ironic commentary on the need for the Museum. I am particularly honored, as today I accept the ancient White title, "Queen for a Day," conferred upon me, to ask Indian women to join in this great enterprise. Since we have, at last, reassumed the roles of leadership for the country that once we held so long ago, it is especially satisfying to ask you to stand with me and sing our national anthem, "This Land Is My Land." Thank you.

UN Ambassador Jeanne Kirkpatrick Excoriates the Soviet Union for Shooting Down a Passenger Plane, Killing Everyone On Board.

"They are the focus of evil in the modern world," President Reagan bluntly exclaimed of the Soviet Union before an audience of evangelical Christians in March 1983. Reagan went on to condemn the Soviet government as an "evil empire" hell-bent on the "eventual domination of all peoples of the earth." Reagan's tirade dramatically increased tensions between the two nations, and many accused the president of recklessly inciting hostilities. But criticisms were muted—if only temporarily—months later when Soviet jets shot down a Korean Air Lines passenger plane that had flown off course over Soviet airspace. On September 6, 1983, Jeanne Kirkpatrick, America's first female ambassador to the United Nations, issued a blistering condemnation of the Soviets for the "murder" of the estimated 270 people aboard.

Most of the world outside the Soviet Union has heard by now of the Korean [Air Lines] flight 007 carrying 269 persons between New York and Seoul which strayed off course into Soviet airspace, was tracked by Soviet radar, was targeted by a Soviet SU-15, whose pilot coolly, and after careful consideration, fired two air-launched missiles which destroyed the Korean airliner and apparently its 269 passengers and crew. . . .

In the days following the destruction of KAL 007, Soviet leaders and the Soviet press have said repeatedly they do not understand what all the fuss is about. They began by accusing the United States of creating a hullabaloo about nothing, and more recently they have accused us of a provocation, implying, though never quite saying, that we provoked them into shooting down an airliner that strayed into their space, provoked them into violating the internationally agreed upon standards and practices of behavior. They have spoken as though a plane's straying off course is a crime punishable by death. They have suggested that "like any self-respecting state" they are doing no more than looking after their sovereignty, which they shall permit no one to violate. They have claimed, still without acknowledging that they shot down the Korean airliner, that "our anti-aircraft defense has fulfilled its duty for the defense of the security of our motherland." They have suggested that they may have mistaken the Korean airliner for an American reconnaissance plane, but still do not admit that they attacked and destroyed it.

But none of these lies, half-lies, and excuses can withstand examination. Straying off course is not recognized as a capital crime by civilized nations. No nation has the sovereign right to shoot down any person or vehicle that may stray across its border in peacetime. . . .

There are internationally agreed upon standards for intercepting unwelcome aircraft. Those internationally agreed upon standards call for serious efforts at identification, verification, warning, and—if the case is serious—for intercepting the intruder and forcing it to land or to leave one's airspace. Sovereignty neither requires nor permits shooting down airliners in peacetime.

Recently the Soviets have implied that the KAL 007 may have been mistaken for a U.S. aerial reconnaissance flight, but that is no more persuasive. The Korean Air Lines Boeing 747 was on a routine scheduled flight. At the time it was shot down the U.S. reconnaissance plane referred to by the Soviets had been on the ground for more than one hour, more than 1,500 miles away. Moreover, the United States does not fly reconnaissance missions in Soviet airspace. . . .

It is depressing to consider seriously our global prospects if those prospects must be built on relations devoid of truth, devoid of trust. It is depressing to consider a world in which a major nation, equipped with the most powerful modern weapons, believes it has a sovereign right to fire on a commercial airliner lost over its territory.

These Soviet actions and claims illuminate the Soviet conception of appropriate relations among nations in peacetime. They illuminate the world in which we live and work and make policy. Of course, some sophisticated observers believe that the destruction of Flight 007 was neither the work of an isolated Strangelove unconcerned about human life—nor of that Strangelove and his ground controller—but was instead a deliberate stroke designed to intimidate: a brutal, decisive act meant to instill fear and hesitation in all who observed its ruthless violence, much as the destruction of an Afghan village or the imprisonment of the Helsinki monitors are intended to secure compliance through terror. Whichever the case—whether the destruction of KAL 007 and its passengers reflect only utter indifference to human life or whether that destruction was designed to intimidate—we are dealing here not with pilot error, but with decisions and priorities characteristic of a system. Not only did Soviet officials shoot down a stray commercial airliner and lie about it, they have callously refused offers of international participation in search-and-rescue efforts, in spite of clearly stated international standards and recommended practices of the International Civil Aviation Organization. . . .

We are reminded once again that the Soviet Union is a state based on the dual principles of callousness and mendacity dedicated to the rule of force. Here is how Lenin described the dictatorship of the proletariat in 1920. He said, "The scientific concept of dictatorship means nothing more than unrestricted power, absolutely unimpeded by law or regulations and resting directly on force." It is this principle of force, this mentality of force, that lies at the root of the Korean Air Line tragedy. This is the reality revealed to the world by the tragedy. It is a reality we must all ponder as we consider threats to peace and human rights that face us today.

The United States deeply believes that immediate steps should be taken here in the United Nations to decrease the likelihood of any repetition of the tragedy of KAL 007. We ask our colleagues to join with us in the coming days in the effort to wrest from this tragedy new clarity about the character of our world and new, constructive efforts to render us all more secure, in the air and on the ground.

Eleven-Year-Old "Ambassador of Peace" Samantha Smith Shares Her Vision of the Future.

"Dear Mr. Andropov," a ten-year-old American girl named Samantha Smith wrote to Soviet leader Yuri Andropov, "I would like to know why you want to conquer the world or at least our country. God made the world for us to live in together in peace and not to fight." Samantha's letter, which also expressed her fears of a nuclear war between the two superpowers, actually made its way to Andropov, who not only responded but invited Samantha and her parents to come to the Soviet Union as his personal guests. An articulate, personable girl, Samantha became an overnight celebrity and, after her 1983 visit to the Soviet Union, traveled the world as a symbolic ambassador of peace. Later that year, on December 26, Samantha shared her vision of the future with an audience in Japan.

I have to begin with an apology. My father helped me with my speech, and look [holds up speech]—I discovered that he doesn't know a single word of Japanese!

Luckily, I have learned some of your language. Since I got here, I've been trying to learn as much as possible. So let me begin by saying *Nihon no minasan Konnichiwa* [Hello everybody in Japan].

I think maybe you should know something about me and the way I live back home. I was born in northern Maine, and we lived at the edge of the wilderness for most of my life. We even had bears and bobcats and moose visiting our backyard. Now I live in a town called Manchester, Maine. It is a small, country town. The number of people in town is about 2,000. I probably saw more people than that at the airport here. Like most kids eleven years old, I'm in the sixth grade and the subjects I study are English, reading, math, science, and social studies. Until last April, I had never traveled outside the eastern United States. I had never even heard of sushi!

Then, because I had written a letter to Yuri Andropov, I found myself in

Moscow, in Leningrad, and at a beautiful camp on the Black Sea near Yalta. I was on airplanes that took me over many foreign countries. After my trip to Russia—which actually should be called the Soviet Union—I came back to the same school and the same teachers and the same kids in Manchester, Maine. I didn't think I had changed at all, but, boy, had they changed!

Well, they were all asking questions like they had never asked before: What was the Soviet Union like? What were the kids like over there? How was the food? I discovered that my trip had made us all aware of parts of the world and people of the world that none of us had ever paid much attention to before.

And now I'll admit that I discovered I had changed, too. I don't feel so nervous in front of new people anymore. And I don't worry so much about understanding how people act in other lands. If I could bring the people of Maine here, you'd see that they're peaceful and easy to get along with. And I discovered that I grew up a lot this year.

But today, we're not here to look back on the summer or to look backward at all. We're here to look ahead. I spent the last several weeks picturing myself in the year 2001, and thought of all the things that I would like the world to be eighteen years from today.

First of all, I don't want to have these freckles anymore, and I want this tooth straightened, and I hope I'll like the idea of being almost thirty. Maybe it's because I've traveled a lot and maybe it's because I've met so many wonderful people who look a little different from the way I look—maybe their skin, or their eyes, or their language is not like mine—but I can picture them becoming my best friends. . . . Maybe it's because of these things that I think the year 2001 and the years that follow are going to be just great.

When I close my eyes and think about the future, this is what I see. I see a computer, and stored in that computer is information on exactly how much food there is in the world. It tells where there are large crops. It tells where the wheat supply is good for that year, and also about the crops of corn and rice and potatoes, and it won't forget the beef and poultry and fish.

This computer will also show where the people are who don't have enough food. By the year 2001, the computer can also tell us where the ships and the airplanes are that can take the food from where it is directly to the people who need it.

In my computer of the year 2001, it also says where the wood for houses and the steel and concrete for buildings can be found, and it shows where the work are for building the new houses and roads and hospitals and schools and factories.

And when I close my eyes, guess what? I know how to work that computer and match up all of the things that will be needed for the people who will need them. And soon we will know how to move one to the other regardless of what country they're in or what borders have to be crossed.

My computer of 2001 will transfer good food, good shelter, and good clothing to the people who need them, and all of it will come from places and countries where these things are plentiful so that it won't hurt what my teacher explains is "the balance of trade."

In my 2001, there's an abundance of everything, and lots of ways to harvest it and transport it to people in need.

By the way, my computer is made up of microchips and wires and electric gizmos from probably 158 different countries. It's a very friendly international computer, and I hope you'll join me in 2001, to help push all the buttons.

Next, I would like to share with you a wish not for 2001, but for this year 1984, the new year.

What I wish for is something I'll call the International Granddaughter Exchange. I guess if I were a boy, I'd call it the International Grandson Exchange. But, I'm not a boy, so I'll stick with granddaughter. The International Granddaughter Exchange would have the highest political leaders in nations all over the world sending their granddaughters or nieces—(or, okay, grandsons or nephews)—to live with families of opposite nations. Soviet leaders' granddaughters would spend two weeks in America. American leaders' granddaughters would spend two weeks in the Soviet Union. And, wherever possible, granddaughters of other opposing countries would exchange visits, and we would have better understanding all over the world.

And now I will say my wish in Japanese: *Sekaiju ni heiwa ga kimasu yo ni* [I wish for world peace and understanding].

Last summer, I had the amazing chance to visit the beautiful and awesome Soviet Union. I loved making friends with those girls and boys, and I think they enjoyed meeting an American kid. Lets keep doing it! Lets find a way to get some of those girls and boys to visit Japan, and America, and China, and Peru. And let's find a way for you to visit Soviet kids and American kids, kids who can't speak a word of Japanese—even kids who drive in American cars.

If we start with an International Granddaughter Exchange and keep expanding it and expanding it, then the year 2001 can be the year when all of us can look around and see only friends, no opposite nations, no enemies, and no bombs.

My grandparents are not important political leaders. In fact, one grandfather of mine was a doctor and one is a retired minister. But I've had the privilege of being an international granddaughter, and let me tell you that it is one terrific experience.

We have started our exciting trip to the year 2001. I've told you two of my favorite visions: the far-off vision of a computer to help deliver the world's abundance to the world's needy, and a closer vision, the International Granddaughter Exchange.

My father, who is back in Maine, didn't help me with the end of my speech, so he'll probably be surprised when I say, Why don't you all come back home with me and meet my friends there!

Thank you for your attention. *Dōmo arigato gozai mashita* [Thank you very much]!

Tragically, Samantha Smith and her father, Arthur, were killed in a plane crash in 1985. Samantha was only thirteen years old.

New York Governor Mario Cuomo Challenges President Reagan's Portrayal of America as a "Shining City on a Hill."

"Four years ago we raised a banner of bold colors," President Reagan declared in a 1984 re-election speech. "We proclaimed a dream of an America that would be a 'shining city on a hill.' . . . Well, now it's all coming together." Reagan's words struck a chord with the public. Compared to the Carter years, employment was up, inflation was down, and prices had stabilized. It was, as Reagan's cheerful commercials heralded, "morning again in America." And once again, the Democrats seemed to be little more than a minor obstacle in the path of the Reagan juggernaut. The party's candidate for president, Walter Mondale, was a man of integrity and compassion, but as Jimmy Carter's vice president he represented to voters all of the failures of the Carter administration and virtually none of its successes. Disheartened by the prospects of yet another humiliating defeat, Democrats experienced a momentary surge of rejuvenation by a single event. For many who heard it live on radio or television or were in the San Francisco convention hall on July 17, 1984, when it occurred, it is remembered simply as "the speech." In a voice that resonated with power, clarity, and urgency, New York Governor Mario Cuomo implored the nation to look beneath the shiny gloss of Reagan's campaign rhetoric and see the suffering and despair in America ignored by the president and his administration.

On behalf of the great Empire State and the whole family of New York, let me thank you for the great privilege of being able to address this convention. Please allow me to skip the stories and the poetry and the temptation to deal in nice but vague rhetoric. Let me instead use this valuable opportunity to deal immediately with the questions that should determine this election and that we all know are vital to the American people.

Ten days ago, President Reagan admitted that although some people in this country seemed to be doing well nowadays, other were unhappy, even worried, about themselves, their families, and their futures. The President said that he didn't understand that fear. He said, "Why, this country is a shining city on a hill." And the President is right. In many ways we are "a shining city on a hill." But the hard truth is that not everyone is sharing in this city's splendor and glory.

A shining city is perhaps all the president sees from the portico of the White House and the veranda of his ranch, where everyone seems to be doing well. But there's another city. There's another part of the "shining city": the part where some people can't pay their mortgages and most young people can't afford one, where students can't afford the education they need and middle-class parents watch the dream they hold for their children evaporate. In this part of the city there are more poor than ever, more families in trouble. More and more people who need help but can't find it. Even worse, there are elderly people who tremble in the basements of the houses there. And there are people who sleep in the city's streets, in the gutter, where the glitter doesn't show. There are ghettoes where thousands of young people, without a job or an education, give their lives away to drug dealers every day. There is despair, Mr. President, in the faces that you don't see, in the places that you don't visit in your shining city. In fact, Mr. President, this nation is more a "Tale of Two Cities," than it is just a "Shining City on a Hill."

Maybe, Mr. President, if you visited some more places; maybe if you went to Appalachia where some people still live in sheds; maybe if you went to Lackawanna where thousands of unemployed steel workers wonder why we subsidize foreign steel while we surrender their dignity to unemployment and to welfare checks; maybe, Mr. President, if you stopped in at a shelter in Chicago and spoke to the homeless there; maybe, Mr. President, if you asked a woman who had been denied the help she needed to feed her children because you said you needed the money for a tax break for a millionaire or for a missile we couldn't afford to use—maybe then you'd understand.

Maybe, Mr. President. But I'm afraid not, because the truth is, ladies and gentlemen, that this is how we were warned it would be. President Reagan told us from the beginning that he believed in a kind of social Darwinism, survival of the fittest. "Government can't do everything," we were told, "so it should settle for taking care of the strong and hope that economic ambition and charity will do the rest. Make the rich richer and what falls from their tables will be enough for the middle class and those who are trying desperately to make it into the middle class." . . .

The president has asked us to judge him on whether or not he's fulfilled the promises he made four years ago. I believe as Democrats that we ought to accept that challenge. And just, for a moment, let us consider what he has said and what he has done.

Inflation is down since 1980. But not because of the supply-side miracle promised to us by the president. Inflation was reduced the old-fashioned way, with a recession, the worst since 1932. Now how did he—we could have brought inflation down that way—do it? Fifty-five thousand bankruptcies, two years of massive unemployment, 200,000 farmers and ranchers forced off the land, more homeless than at any time since the Great Depression in 1932, more hungry in this world of enormous affluence, the United States of America, more hungry, more poor—and most of them women. And he created one other thing: a nearly $200 billion deficit threatening our future.

Now, we must make the American people understand this deficit, because they don't. The president's deficit is a direct and dramatic repudiation of his promise in 1980 to balance our budget by 1983. How large is it? That deficit is the largest in the history of the universe. President Carter's last budget had a deficit less than one-third of this deficit. It is a deficit that, according to the president's own fiscal advisor, may grow as much as $300 billion a year, for "as far as the eye can see." And, ladies and gentlemen, it is a debt so large that almost one-half of our revenue from the income tax goes just to pay the interest on it each year. It is a mortgage on our children's futures that can only be paid in pain and that could bring this nation to its knees. . . .

And what about foreign policy? They said that they would make us and the whole world safer. They say they have, by creating the largest defense budget in history, one that even they now admit is excessive; by escalating to a frenzy the nuclear arms race; by incendiary rhetoric; by refusing to discuss peace with our enemies; by the loss of 279 young Americans in Lebanon in pursuit of a plan and a policy that no one can find or describe. We give monies to Latin American governments that murder nuns and then lie about it. We have been less than zealous in support of our only real friend, it seems to me, in the Middle East, the one democracy there, our flesh and blood ally, the state of Israel. Our foreign policy drifts with no real direction other than a hysterical commitment to an arms race that leads nowhere, if we're lucky. And if we're not, it could lead us to bankruptcy or war.

Of course we must have a strong defense! Of course Democrats are for a strong defense. Of course Democrats believe that there are times when we must stand and fight, and we have. Thousands of us have paid for freedom with our lives. But always when this country has been at its best, our purposes were clear.

Now they're not. Now our allies are as confused as our enemies. Now we have no real commitment to our friends or our ideals, not to human rights, not to the refuseniks, not to Sakharov, not to Bishop Tutu and the others struggling for freedom in South Africa. We have in the last few years spent more time than we can afford. We have pounded our chest and made bold speeches. But we lost 279 young Americans in Lebanon and we live behind sandbags in Washington.

How can anyone say that we are stronger, safer, or better? . . . Where would four years more take us? How much larger will the deficit be? How much deeper the cuts in programs for the struggling middle class and the poor to limit that deficit? How high will the interest rates be? How much more acid rain killing our forests and fouling our lakes?

And, ladies and gentlemen, please think of this. The nation must think of this: What kind of Supreme Court will we have? We must ask ourselves what kind of Court and country will be fashioned by the man who believes in having government mandate people's religion and morality? The man who believes that trees pollute the environment, the man that believes the laws against discrimination against people go too far, the man who threatens Social Security and Medicaid and help for the disabled.

How high will we pile the missiles? How much deeper will be the gulf be between us and our enemies? And, ladies and gentlemen, will four years more make meaner the spirit of our people? This election will measure the record of the past four years. But more than that, it will answer the question of what kind of people we want to be.

We Democrats still have a dream. We still believe in this nation's future, and this is our answer to the question. This is our credo: We believe in only the government we need, but we insist on all the government we need. We believe in a government that is characterized by fairness and reasonableness, a reasonableness that goes beyond labels, that doesn't distort or promise to do things we know it can't do.

We believe in a government strong enough to use the words *love* and *compassion* and smart enough to convert our noblest aspirations into practical realities.

We believe in encouraging the talented, but we believe that while survival of the fittest may be a good working description of the process of evolution, a government of humans should elevate itself to a higher order. Our government should be able to rise to the level where it should be able to fill the gaps left by chance or a wisdom we don't understand.

We would rather have laws written by the patron of this great city, the man called the "world's most sincere Democrat," St. Francis of Assisi, than laws written by Darwin.

We believe, as Democrats, that a society as blessed as ours, the most affluent democracy in the world's history, one that can spend trillions on instruments of destruction, ought to be able to help the middle class in its struggle, ought to be able to find work for all who can do it, room at the table, shelter for the homeless, care for the elderly and infirm, and hope for the destitute.

And we proclaim as loudly as we can the utter insanity of nuclear proliferation and the need for a nuclear freeze, if only to affirm the simple truth that peace is better than war because life is better than death.

We believe in firm but fair law and order. We believe proudly in the union movement. We believe in privacy for people, openness by government. We believe in civil rights, and we believe in human rights.

We believe in a single fundamental idea that describes better than most textbooks and any speech that I could write what a proper government should be: the idea of family, mutuality, the sharing of benefits and burdens for the good of all, feeling one another's pain, sharing one another's blessings, reasonably, honestly, fairly, without respect to race or sex or geography or political affiliation.

We believe we must be the family of America, recognizing that at the heart of the matter we are bound one to another, that the problems of a retired school teacher in Duluth are *our* problems. That the future of the child in Buffalo is *our* future. That the struggle of a disabled man in Boston to survive and to live decently is *our* struggle. That the hunger of a woman in Little Rock, *our* hunger. That the failure anywhere to provide what reasonably we might to avoid pain is *our* failure.

For fifty years we Democrats created a better future for our children using traditional democratic principles as a fixed beacon, giving us direction and purpose but constantly innovating, adapting to new realities. Roosevelt's alphabet programs, Truman's NATO and the G.I. Bill of Rights, Kennedy's intelligent tax incentives and the Alliance For Progress, Johnson's civil rights, Carter's human rights and the nearly miraculous Camp David Peace Accord. Democrats did it, and Democrats can do it again.

We can build a future that deals with our deficit. Remember this: that fifty years of progress never cost us what the last four years of stagnation have. And we can deal with that deficit intelligently, by shared sacrifice, with all parts of the nation's family contributing, building partnerships with the private sector, providing a sound defense without depriving ourselves of what we need to feed our children and care for our people. We can have a future that provides for all the young of the present by marrying common sense and compassion. We know we can, because we did it for nearly fifty years before 1980.

And we can do it again, if we do not forget, forget that this entire nation has profited by these progressive principles. That they helped lift up generations to the middle class and higher. That they gave us a chance to work, to go to college, to raise a family, to own a house, to be secure in our old age, and before that to reach heights that our own parents would not have dared dream of.

That struggle to live with dignity is the real story of the shining city. And it's a story, ladies and gentlemen, I didn't read in a book or learn in a classroom. I saw it and lived it, like many of you. I watched a small man with thick calluses on both hands work fifteen and sixteen hours a day. I saw him once literally bleed from the bottoms of his feet, a man who came here uneducated, alone, unable to speak the language, who taught me all I needed to know about faith and hard work by the simple eloquence of his example. I learned about our kind of democracy from my father. And I learned about our obligation to each other from him and from my mother. And they asked to be protected in those moments when they would not be able to protect themselves. This nation and its government did that for them.

And that they were able to build a family and live in dignity and see one of their children go from behind their little grocery store in south Jamaica on the other side of the tracks where he was born, to occupy the highest seat in the greatest state in the greatest nation in the only world we know, is an ineffably beautiful tribute to the democratic process.

And, ladies and gentlemen, on January 20, 1985, it will happen again. Only on a much, much grander scale. We will have a new president of the United States [Walter Mondale], a Democrat born not to the blood of kings but to the blood of pioneers and immigrants. We will have America's first woman vice president [Geraldine Ferraro], the child of immigrants, and she will open with one magnificent stroke a whole new frontier for the United States. It will happen, if we make it happen—if you and I make it happen.

I ask you, ladies and gentlemen, brothers and sisters, for the good of all of us, for the love of this great nation, for the family of America, for the love of God: Please make this nation remember how futures are built. Thank you, and God bless you.

Walter Mondale's convention speech would also prove memorable when he disastrously stated, "Let's tell the truth. Mr. Reagan will raise taxes and so will I. He won't tell you. I just did." Mondale's prediction would be correct—Reagan did raise taxes after his re-election—but Mondale's candid announcement nevertheless didn't endear him to voters. At the age of 73, the oldest man ever to serve as president, Ronald Reagan earned a staggering 525 electoral votes to Mondale's 13. Reagan lost only the District of Columbia and Minnesota, Mondale's home state.

Susan Baker of the PMRC Recommends Putting Warning Labels on Records with "Sexually Explicit and Violent" Rock Lyrics
&
Musician Frank Zappa Dismisses the PMRC's Proposal as an "Ill-Conceived Piece of Nonsense."

To the members of the Parents Music Resource Center, co-founded by the wives of U.S. Senators, the request seemed reasonable enough: The music industry should place warning labels on all albums if the lyrics "portray explicit sex and violence and glorify the use of drugs and alcohol." But to musicians and industry executives, the PMRC's recommendations smacked of censorship. Senate hearings on the issue were held in September 1985, and Susan Baker, wife of former Senator Howard Baker (R-TN), testified first on behalf of PMRC.

It is no secret that today's rock music is a very important part of adolescents' and teenagers' lives. It always has been, and we don't question their right to have their own music. We think that is important. They use it to identify and give expression to their feelings, their problems, their joys, sorrows, loves, and values. It wakes them up in the morning and it is in the background as they get dressed for school. It is played on the bus. It is listened to in the cafeteria during lunch. It is played as they do their homework. They even watch it on MTV now. It is danced to at parties, and puts them to sleep at night.

Because anything that we are exposed to that much has some influence on us, we believe that the music industry has a special responsibility as the message of songs goes from the suggestive to the blatantly explicit.

As Ellen Goodman stated in a recent column, "Rock Ratings": "The outrageous edge of rock and roll has shifted its focus from Elvis's pelvis to the saw protruding from Blackie Lawless's codpiece on a WASP album. Rock lyrics have turned from 'I can't get no satisfaction' to 'I am going to force you at gunpoint to eat me alive.'" The material we are concerned with cannot be compared with "Louie Louie," Cole Porter, Billie Holiday, et cetera. Cole Porter's "The birds do it, the bees do it," can hardly be compared with WASP, "I F-U-C-K like a beast." There is a new element of vulgarity and violence toward women that is unprecedented.

While a few outrageous recordings have always existed in the past, the proliferation of songs glorifying rape, sadomasochism, incest, the occult, and suicide by a growing number of bands illustrates this escalating trend that is alarming. Some have suggested that the records in question are only a minute element in this music. However, these records are not few, and have sold millions of copies, like Prince's "Darling Nikki," about masturbation, sold over ten million copies. Judas Priest, the one about forced oral sex at gunpoint, has sold over two million copies. Quiet Riot, *Metal Health,* has songs about explicit sex, over five million copies. Mötley Crüe, *Shout at the Devil,* which contains violence and brutality to women, over two million copies.

Some say there is no cause for concern. We believe there is. Teen pregnancies and teenage suicide rates are at epidemic proportions today. The Noedecker Report states that in the United States of America we have the highest teen pregnancy rate of any developed country: 96 out of 1,000 teenage girls become pregnant. Rape is up 7 percent in the latest statistics, and the suicide rates of youth between sixteen and twenty-four have gone up 300 percent in the last three decades while the adult level has remained the same.

There certainly are many causes for these ills in our society, but it is our contention that the pervasive messages aimed at children which promote and glorify suicide, rape, sadomasochism, and so on, have to be numbered among the contributing factors. Some rock artists actually seem to encourage teen suicide. Ozzie Osbourne sings "Suicide Solution." Blue Oyster Cult sings "Don't Fear the Reaper." AC/DC sings "Shoot to Thrill." Just last week in Centerpoint, a small Texas town, a young man took his life while listening to the music of AC/DC. He was not the first.

Now that more and more elementary school children are becoming consumers of rock music, we think it is imperative to discuss this question: What can be done to help parents who want to protect their children from these messages if they want to?

Today, parents have no way of knowing the content of music products that their children are buying. While some album covers are sexually explicit or depict violence, many others give no clue as to the content. One of the top ten today is Morris Day and the Time, "Jungle Love." If you go buy the album *Ice Cream Castles* to get "Jungle Love," you also get, "If the Kid Can't Make You Come, Nobody Can," a sexually explicit song. The pleasant cover picture of the members of the band gives no hint that it contains material that is not appropriate for young consumers.

Our children are faced with so many choices today. What is available to them through the media is historically unique. The Robert Johnson study on teen environment states that young people themselves often feel that they have: one, too many choices to make; two, too few structured means for arriving at decisions; and three, too little help to get there.

We believe something can be done. . . .

Tipper Gore, wife of then Senator Albert Gore (D-TN), then made a statement that the PMRC was merely encouraging the music industry to affix the warning labels vol-

untarily and was not "advocating any federal intervention or legislation whatsoever."
Frank Zappa, the legendary musician who testified after Mrs. Gore, suspected other-
wise and lambasted the PMRC and its founders.

The first thing I would like to do, because I know there is some foreign press involved here and they might not understand what the issue is about is the First Amendment to the Constitution, and it is short and I would like to read it so they will understand. It says: "Congress shall make no law respecting an establishment of religion or prohibiting the free exercise thereof, or abridging the freedom of speech or of the press, or the right of the people peaceably to assemble and to petition the government for a redress of grievances." That is for reference.

These are my personal observations and opinions. I speak on behalf of no group or professional organization.

The PMRC proposal is an ill-conceived piece of nonsense which fails to deliver any real benefits to children, infringes the civil liberties of people who are not children, and promises to keep the courts busy for years dealing with the interpretational and enforcemental problems inherent in the proposal's design.

It is my understanding that in law First Amendment issues are decided with a preference for the least restrictive alternative. In this context, the PMRC demands are the equivalent of treating dandruff by decapitation.

No one has forced Mrs. Baker or Mrs. Gore to bring Prince or Sheena Easton into their homes. Thanks to the Constitution, they are free to buy other forms of music for their children. Apparently they insist on purchasing the works of contemporary recording artists in order to support a personal illusion of aerobic sophistication. Ladies, please be advised: The $8.98 purchase price does not entitle to you to a kiss on the foot from the composer or performer in exchange for a spin on the family Victrola.

Taken as a whole, the complete list of PMRC demands reads like an instruction manual for some sinister kind of toilet training program to housebreak all composers and performers because of the lyrics of a few. Ladies, how dare you? . . .

Is the basic issue morality? Is it mental health? Is it an issue at all? The PMRC has created a lot of confusion with improper comparisons between song lyrics, videos, record packaging, radio broadcasting, and live performances. These are all different mediums and the people who work in them have the right to conduct their business without trade-restraining legislation, whipped up like an instant pudding by "the wives of Big Brother." . . .

Children in the vulnerable age bracket have a natural love for music. If as a parent you believe they should be exposed to something more uplifting than "Sugar Walls," support music appreciation programs in schools. Why have you not considered your child's need for consumer information? Music appreciation costs very little compared to sports expenditures. Your children have a right to know that something besides pop music exists. It is unfortunate that the PMRC would rather dispense governmentally sanitized heavy metal music than something more uplifting. Is this an indication of the PMRC's personal taste or just another manifestation of the low priority this administration has placed on education for the arts in America? . . .

The establishment of a rating system, voluntary or otherwise, opens the door to an endless parade of moral quality control programs based on things certain Christians do not like. What if the next bunch of Washington wives demands a large yellow *J* written on all material written or performed by Jews, in order to save helpless children from exposure to concealed Zionist doctrine?

Record ratings are frequently compared to film ratings. Apart from the quantitative difference, there is another that is more important: People who act in films are hired to pretend. No matter how the film is rated, it will not hurt them personally. Since many musicians write and perform their own material and stand by it as their art, whether you like it or not, an imposed rating will stigmatize them as individuals. How long before composers and performers are told to wear a festive little PMRC armband with their scarlet letter on it?

Bad facts make bad law, and people who write bad laws are in my opinion more dangerous than songwriters who celebrate sexuality. Freedom of speech, freedom of religious thought, and the right to due process for composers, performers, and retailers are imperiled if the PMRC and the major labels consummate this nasty bargain. . . .

No legislation to impose warning labels was passed, and the music industry voluntarily began labeling its records, tapes, and CDs.

Holocaust Survivor Elie Wiesel Criticizes President Reagan at the White House for Planning to Visit a German Cemetery Where Nazi Officers Are Buried.

Soon after President Reagan accepted Chancellor Helmet Kohl's invitation to visit a historic cemetery in Bitburg, West Germany, Reagan's staff made a horrible discovery: Almost fifty members of Adolf Hitler's savage Waffen SS were buried at the cemetery. Reluctant to insult Chancellor Kohl by backing out, Reagan considered proceeding with the visit, infuriating Jews throughout America, including Holocaust survivor and acclaimed novelist Elie Wiesel. (Wiesel would go on to win the Nobel Prize for peace in December 1986.) Wiesel was scheduled to be honored at the White House with a medal of achievement before Reagan left for West Germany, and he decided to use the opportunity to voice his criticism of the planned Bitburg visit. Jewish leaders, despite their anger at Reagan, tried to dissuade Wiesel from publicly confronting the enormously popular president, but their admonitions proved futile. On April 19, 1985, Wiesel stood just a few feet from Reagan and gave the following heartfelt address.

Mr. President, . . . I am grateful to you for the medal. But this medal is not mine alone. It belongs to all those who remember what SS killers have done to their victims.

It was given to me by the American people for my writings, teaching, and for my testimony. When I write, I feel my invisible teachers standing over my shoulders, reading my words and judging their veracity. And while I feel responsible for the living, I feel equally responsible to the dead. Their memory dwells in my memory.

Forty years ago, a young man awoke, and he found himself an orphan in an orphaned world. What have I learned in the last forty years? Small things. I learned the perils of language and those of silence. I learned that in extreme situations when human lives and dignity are at stake, neutrality is a sin. It helps the killers, not the victims. I learned the meaning of solitude, Mr. President. We were alone, desperately alone.

Today is April 19, and on April 19, 1943, the Warsaw Ghetto rose in arms against the onslaught of the Nazis. They were so few and so young and so helpless. And nobody came to their help. And they had to fight what was then the mightiest legion in Europe. Every underground received help except the Jewish underground. And yet they managed to fight and resist and push back those Nazis and their accomplices for six weeks. And yet the leaders of the free world, Mr. President, knew everything and did so little, or nothing, or at least nothing specifically to save Jewish children from death. You spoke of Jewish children, Mr. President. One million Jewish children perished. If I spent my entire life reciting their names, I would die before finishing the task.

Mr. President, I have seen children, I have seen them being thrown in the flames alive. Words, they die on my lips. So I have learned, I have learned, I have learned the fragility of the human condition.

And I am reminded of a great moral essayist. The gentle and forceful Abe Rosenthal, having visited Auschwitz, once wrote an extraordinary reportage about the persecution of Jews, and he called it "Forgive Them Not, Father, For They Knew What They Did."

I have learned that the Holocaust was a unique and uniquely Jewish event, albeit with universal implications. Not all victims were Jews. But all

Jews were victims. I have learned the danger of indifference, the crime of indifference—for the opposite of love, I have learned, is not hate but indifference. Jews were killed by the enemy but betrayed by their so-called allies who
found political reasons to justify their indifference or passivity.

But I have also learned that suffering confers no privileges. It all depends
what one does with it. And this is why survivors of whom you spoke, Mr.
President, have tried to teach their contemporaries how to build on ruins,
how to invent hope in a world that offers none, how to proclaim faith to a
generation that has seen it shamed and mutilated. And I believe, we believe,
that memory is the answer, perhaps the only answer.

A few days ago, on the anniversary of the liberation of Buchenwald, all of
us Americans watched with dismay and anger as the Soviet Union and East
Germany distorted both past and present history.

Mr. President, I was there. I was there when American liberators arrived,
and they gave us back our lives. And what I felt for them then nourishes me
to the end of my days and will do so. If you only knew what we tried to do
with them then. We who were so weak that we couldn't carry our own lives,
we tried to carry them in triumph.

Mr. President, we are grateful to the American army for liberating us. We
are grateful to this country, the greatest democracy in the world, the freest nation in the world, the moral nation, the authority in the world. And we are
grateful, especially, to this country for having offered us haven and refuge, and
grateful to its leadership for being so friendly to Israel.

And, Mr. President, do you know that the ambassador of Israel, who sits
next to you, who is my friend, and has been for so many years, is himself a
survivor? And if you knew all the causes we fought together for the last thirty
years, you should be prouder of him. And we are proud of him.

And we are grateful, of course, to Israel. We are eternally grateful to Israel
for existing. We needed Israel in 1948 as we need it now. And we are grateful
to Congress for its continuous philosophy of humanism and compassion for
the underprivileged.

And as for yourself, Mr. President, we are so grateful to you for being a
friend of the Jewish people, for trying to help the oppressed Jews in the Soviet Union, and to do whatever we can to save Shcharansky and Abe Stolar
and Iosif Begun and Sakharov and all the dissidents who need freedom. And
of course, we thank you for your support of the Jewish state of Israel.

But, Mr. President, I wouldn't be the person I am, and you wouldn't respect me for what I am, if I were not to tell you also of the sadness that is in
my heart for what happened during the last week. And I am sure that you,
too, are sad for the same reasons.

What can I do? I belong to a traumatized generation. And to us, as to you, symbols are important. And furthermore, following our ancient tradition—and we are speaking about Jewish heritage—our tradition commands us "to speak truth to power." So may I speak to you, Mr. President, with respect and admiration, of the events that happened?

We have met four or five times. And each time I came away enriched, for I know of your commitment to humanity. And therefore I am convinced, as you have told us earlier when we spoke, that you were not aware of the presence of SS graves in the Bitburg cemetery. Of course you didn't know, but now we all are aware. May I, Mr. President, if it's possible at all, implore you to do something else, to find a way, to find another way, another site? That place, Mr. President, is not your place. Your place is with the victims of the SS.

Oh, we know there are political and strategic reasons, but this issue, as all issues related to that awesome event, transcends politics and diplomacy. The issue here is not politics, but good and evil. And we must never confuse them. Mr. President, there was a degree of suffering and loneliness in the concentration camps that defies imagination. Cut off from the world with no refuge anywhere, sons watched hopelessly their fathers being beaten to death. Mothers watched their children die of hunger. And then there was Mengele and his selections. Terror, fear, isolation, torture, gas chambers, flames, flames rising to the heavens.

But, Mr. President, I know and I understand, we all do, that you seek reconciliation. And so do I, so do we. And I too wish to attain true reconciliation with the German people. I do not believe in collective guilt, nor in collective responsibility. Only the killers were guilty. Their sons and daughters are not.

And I believe, Mr. President, that we can and we must work together with them and with all people. And we must work to bring peace and understanding to a tormented world that, as you know, is still awaiting redemption.

I thank you, Mr. President.

Despite Wiesel's protest, President Reagan visited Bitburg.

President Ronald Reagan Honors the Memory of the Seven Astronauts Killed in the Space Shuttle Challenger Explosion.

Officially, it was "Shuttle Mission 51-L," but every American knew it as "the flight with the teacher" because one of the crew members was a thirty-seven-year-old teacher named Christa McAuliffe. The first civilian to venture into space, McAuliffe had been chosen out of 11,000 volunteers to join six astronauts on the space shuttle Challenger. *Promising "the ultimate field trip," NASA heavily promoted the launch, and tens of millions of Americans—many of them schoolchildren—tuned in to witness the historic event live on January 28, 1986. At 11:39 A.M., cheers erupted at Cape Canaveral and at McAuliffe's school back in Concord, New Hampshire, as the* Challenger *soared skyward into a picture-perfect, cloudless sky. And then suddenly, inconceivably, the shuttle disappeared into a massive fireball as the two booster rockets sailed on, leaving behind a billowy pitchfork of smoke. Shock immediately turned to grief as the realization sank in: The shuttle had exploded, killing everyone on board. President Reagan was scheduled to give the State of the Union address before Congress that evening, but instead focused solely on the seven crew members who lost their lives—the first American astronauts ever to die in flight.*

Ladies and gentlemen, I'd planned to speak to you tonight to report on the state of the Union, but the events of earlier today have led me to change those plans. Today is a day for mourning and remembering. Nancy and I are pained to the core by the tragedy of the shuttle *Challenger.* We know we share this pain with all of the people of our country. This is truly a national loss.

Nineteen years ago, almost to the day, we lost three astronauts in a terrible accident on the ground. But we've never lost an astronaut in flight. We've never had a tragedy like this. And perhaps we've forgotten the courage it took for the crew of the shuttle. But they, the *Challenger* Seven, were aware of the dangers, overcame them, and did their jobs brilliantly. We mourn seven heroes: Michael Smith, Dick Scobee, Judith Resnik, Ronald McNair, Ellison Onizuka, Gregory Jarvis, and Christa McAuliffe. We mourn their loss as a nation together.

To the families of the seven: We cannot bear, as you do, the full impact of this tragedy. But we feel the loss, and we're thinking about you so very much. Your loved ones were daring and brave, and they had that special grace, that special spirit that says, "Give me a challenge, and I'll meet it with joy." They had a hunger to explore the universe and discover its truths. They wished to serve, and they did. They served all of us. We've grown used to wonders in this century. It's hard to dazzle us, but for twenty-five years the United States space program has been doing just that. We've grown used to the idea of space, and perhaps we forget that we've only just begun. We're still pioneers. They, the members of the *Challenger* crew, were pioneers.

And I want to say something to the schoolchildren of America who were watching the live coverage of the shuttle's takeoff. I know it is hard to understand, but sometimes painful things like this happen. It's all part of the process of exploration and discovery. It's all part of taking a chance and expanding man's horizons. The future doesn't belong to the fainthearted; it belongs to the brave. The *Challenger* crew was pulling us into the future, and we'll continue to follow them.

I've always had great faith in and respect for our space program, and what happened today does nothing to diminish it. We don't hide our space program. We don't keep secrets and cover things up. We do it all up front and in public. That's the way freedom is, and we wouldn't change it for a minute. We'll continue our quest in space. There will be more shuttle flights and more shuttle crews and, yes, more volunteers, more civilians, more teachers in space. Nothing ends here. Our hopes and our journeys continue. I want to add that I wish I could talk to every man and woman who works for NASA or who worked on this mission and tell them, "Your dedication and professionalism have moved and impressed us for decades, and we know of your anguish. We share it."

There's a coincidence today. On this day 390 years ago, the great explorer Sir Francis Drake died aboard ship off the coast of Panama. In his lifetime the great frontiers were the oceans, and an historian later said, "He lived by the sea, died on it, and was buried in it." Well today we can say of the *Challenger* crew, Their dedication was, like Drake's, complete.

The crew of the space shuttle *Challenger* honored us by the manner in which they lived their lives. We will never forget them, nor the last time we saw them, this morning, as they prepared for their journey and waved good-bye and "slipped the surly bonds of earth" to "touch the face of God."

Corporate Raider Ivan Boesky Encourages Graduating Business Students to "Seek Wealth" in a "Virtuous and Honest Way."

They were the kings and queens of real estate, Wall Street, and corporate America—Donald Trump, Leona Helmsley, Michael Milken, Ivan Boesky—and there seemed to be no limit to their financial power. They were the names that symbolized the "Decade of Greed," an era of virtually unprecedented economic growth and ostentatious spending. Inflation and interest rates were down, employment was up, and the stock market was soaring, producing untold millionaires and even many billionaires. On May 18, 1986, Boesky spoke before the graduating class of the Berkeley Business School and reminded them of the great advantages—and obligations—of acquiring enormous wealth.

I am pleased to stand here before you and tell you I am working class. My father was a Russian immigrant Jew, and I am here to tell you, dear students, you will be running this nation's enterprises. I urge you to do so in a manner that will enhance the mantle *businessman* with dignity and honor. Since it is your charge to administer, do so as aggressively and as promptly as possible. Do not be patient. Be restless. Do not be orderly because that's the way it's done. Be anxious to be heard. Demonstrate the virtues of those who, in many cases, founded the businesses that will be employing you. Dare to stretch, imagine, create, and then market your skills. Be entrepreneurial in spirit. Earn positions of leadership and earn your right to remain in those positions.

I urge you, as a part of your mission, to seek wealth. It's all right. Does anyone disagree with that? No! But do it in a virtuous and honest way, the purer the process gathering in that way, it is one of the surest ways to having a voice in the system. Having wealth, if you aim high, can allow you to be what you want to become in this great land. You could be more of a person who would make a difference. As you accumulate wealth and power, you must remain God fearing and responsible to the system that has given you this opportunity. Be respectful of the history of your people and your nation. Give back to the system with humility, and don't take yourself too seriously.

You know, I think of my own circumstance, and my father was one of six children whose brother took a Russian army officer's overshoe one winter day. For that act the family was going to be persecuted and killed and therefore [my father] came to America and began the process of working and supporting his family, and a mere few years later, here I am. So it wasn't my fault; my history had a lot to do with it. Don't be too certain as you progress that it's your fault either. Be thankful for all those who laid down their paths and their futures for you.

Beware of a society that sorely needs retraining to keep up with modern technology and thereby is currently losing so many citizens to hopeless ghettoes. Let your American dream reflect itself in a way that will make it more possibile for all Americans to be able to dream. Let your wealth redound to needy institutions that are organized to stamp out bigotry, to increase jobs, reconcile Christian and Jew, white, black, Jew, and Arab—institutions that will unify people and keep us a free society. As businessmen and women, we must be missionaries with financial clout. To enter business to create goods and services, the successful are given money as a reward. The businessmen of today have the responsibility of nobility of old to look after our cultural institutions, the arts and sciences, politics. Do not be narrow in your sense of who you are as a custodian of the nation's affairs. This land is your land, and you have all the common obligation to be uncommon and enlightened in your stewardship. With the privilege of wealth and power comes enormous obligation. As I look out at this audience and this class, I see a significant diversity of background, a splendid array of colors and cultures. You are the noble trustees of the future of this country, and I do salute you. . . .

Soon after this speech, Boesky was accused of insider trading on Wall Street and, by December 1986, had negotiated a plea bargain that included penalties amounting to $100 million and a three-year prison sentence. (Leona Helmsley would later be convicted and imprisoned for tax evasion. Michael Milken would be fined $600 million and sentenced to ten years in prison, in what would prove to be the largest securities fraud case in U.S. history. And Wall Street itself would see its single worst drop in history on October 19, 1987, losing 508 points in one day.)

An Unrepentent Oliver North Defends His Role in the Iran–Contra Scandal and Blames Congress for Its "Fickle, Vacillating" Foreign Policy.

Spoken from the Oval Office on November 13, 1986, President Reagan's denial of "wildly speculative and false stories about [trading] arms for hostages" could not have been more forceful: "We did not—repeat, did not—trade weapons or anything else for hostages." Indeed, the insinuation that Reagan, who had vilified Iranian leaders as the most "squalid criminals since the advent of [Adolf Hitler's] Third Reich," would allow the United States to break its own policy against negotiating with terrorists and risk the nation's credibility throughout the world seemed ludicrous. But, in fact, the allegations were true. The United States had indeed illegally sold military weapons to Iran in hopes it would facilitate the release of seven American hostages. (Only three were eventually freed.) What proved even more astonishing was the discovery that profits from the arms sales were being used—in direct defiance of Congress's Boland Amendments—to support the Nicaraguan Contras. Again Reagan denied it, and again it was later confirmed to be true. But despite the immensity of the crimes, which were arguably more serious than Watergate, Reagan survived the ordeal virtually unscathed, earning him the nickname "the Teflon president." The administration placed most of the blame for the scandal on CIA Director William Casey, who died of a stroke as the controversy was intensifying. But the person most responsible for the day-to-day operations of Iran–Contra was a boyishly handsome, all-American Marine lieutenant colonel named Oliver "Ollie" North. Straight out of Central Casting, the forty-three-year-old North looked every bit the loyal and patriotic soldier when he appeared in full military regalia before the joint congressional hearings in July 1987. North not only defended his covert dealings, he audaciously faulted Congress for making his actions necessary.

I believe that this is a strange process that you are putting me and others through. Apparently, the president has chosen not to assert his prerogatives, and you have been permitted to make the rules. You called before you the officials of the executive branch. You put them under oath for what must be collectively thousands of hours of testimony. You dissect that testimony to find inconsistencies and declare some to be truthful and others to be liars. You make the rulings as to what is proper and what is not proper. You put the testimony which you think is helpful to your goals up before the people and leave others out. It's sort of like a baseball game in which you are both the player and the umpire. It's a game in which you call the balls and strikes and where you determine who is out and who is safe. And in the end you determine the score and declare yourselves the winner.

From where I sit, it is not the fairest process. One thing is, I think, for certain: that you will not investigate yourselves in this matter. There is not much chance that you will conclude at the end of these hearings that the Boland Amendments and the frequent policy changes therefore were unwise or that your restrictions should not have been imposed on the executive branch. You are not likely to conclude that the administration acted properly by trying to sustain the freedom fighters in Nicaragua when they were abandoned, and you are not likely to conclude by commending the president of the United States who tried valiantly to recover our citizens and achieve an opening that is strategically vital—Iran.

I would not be frank with you if I did not admit that the last several months have been difficult for me and my family. It has been difficult to be on the front pages of every newspaper in the land day after day, be photographed thousands of times by bands of photographers who chase us around since November just because my name arose at the hearings. It is difficult to be caught in the middle of a constitutional struggle between the executive and legislative branches over who will formulate and direct the foreign policy of this nation. It is difficult to be vilified by people in and out of this body, some who have proclaimed that I am guilty of criminal conduct even before they have heard me. Others have said that I would not tell the truth when I came hear to testify, and one member asked a person testifying before this body whether he would believe me under oath. I asked when I got here, If you don't believe me, why call me at all? It has been difficult to see questions raised about my character and morality, my honesty, because only partial evidence was provided. And, as I indicated yesterday, I think it was insensitive of this committee to place before the cameras my home address at a time when my family and I are under twenty-four-hour armed guard by over a dozen government agents of the Naval Investigative Service because of fear that terrorists will seek revenge for my official acts and carry out their announced intentions to kill me.

It is also difficult to comprehend that my work at the NSC [National Security Council]—all of which was approved and carried out in the best interests of our country—has led to two massive parallel investigations staffed by over 200 people. It is mind-boggling to me that one of those investigations is criminal and that some here have attempted to criminalize policy differences between coequal branches of government and the executive's conduct of foreign affairs.

I believe it is inevitable that the Congress will in the end blame the executive branch, but I suggest to you that it is the Congress which must accept at least some of the blame in the Nicaraguan freedom fighters matter. Plain and simple, the Congress is to blame because of the fickle, vacillating, unpredictable, on-again, off-again policy toward the Nicaraguan Democratic Resistance—the so-called Contras. I do not believe that the support of the Nicaraguan freedom fighters can be treated as the passage of a budget. I suppose that if the budget doesn't get passed on time again this year, it will be inevitably another extension of another month or two. But the Contras, the Nicaraguan freedom fighters, are people—living, breathing young men and women who have had to suffer a desperate struggle for liberty with sporadic and confusing support from the United States of America.

Armies need food and consistent help. They need a flow of money, of arms, clothing, and medical supplies. The Congress of the United States left soldiers in the field unsupported and vulnerable to their communist enemies. When the executive branch did everything possible within the law to prevent them from being wiped out by Moscow's surrogates in Havana and Managua, you then had this investigation to blame the problem on the executive branch. It does not make sense to me.

In my opinion, these hearings have caused serious damage to our national interest. Our adversaries laugh at us and our friends recoil in horror. I suppose it would be one thing if the intelligence committees wanted to hear all this in private and thereafter pass laws which in the view of Congress make for better policies or better functioning government. But to hold them publicly for the whole world to see strikes me as very harmful. Not only does it embarrass our friends and allies with whom we have worked, many of whom have helped us in various programs, but must also make them very wary of helping us again. . . .

I don't mind telling you that I'm angry that what some have attempted to do to me and my family. I believe that these committee hearings will show that you have struck some blows. But I am going to walk from here with my head high and my shoulders straight because I am proud of what we accomplished. I am proud of the efforts that we made, and I am proud of the fight that we fought. I am proud of serving the administration of a great president. I am not ashamed of anything in my professional or personal conduct.

As we go through this process, I ask that you continue to please keep an open mind. Please be open-minded and able to admit that perhaps your preliminary conclusions about me were wrong. And please also do not mistake my attitude for lack of respect. I am in awe of this great institution just as I am in awe of the presidency. Both are equal branches of government with separate areas of responsibility under the Constitution that I have taken an oath to support and defend—and I have done so, as many of you have. And although I do not agree with what you are doing, or the way that it is being done, I do understand your interest in obtaining the facts, and I have taken an oath to tell the truth and helping you to do so. In closing, Mr. Chairman— and I thank you for this opportunity—I would just simply like to thank the tens of thousands of Americans who have communicated their support, encouragement, and prayers for me and my family in this difficult time.

Thank you, sir.

Although North was later convicted by Independent Counsel Lawrence E. Walsh for his participation in the Iran-Contra affair, a federal appeals court reversed the decision, ruling that North's congressional testimony—given under immunity—was unfairly used against him.

The Reverend Jesse Jackson Rallies All Americans— Particularly the Most Disadvantaged—to "Keep Hope Alive!"

Like Mario Cuomo in 1984, the Reverend Jesse Jackson served as the conscience of the 1988 Democratic convention in Atlanta, delivering a speech so charged and dynamic it established him as a charismatic national leader with a broad base of support. During the primaries, Jackson, a civil rights activist who had worked closely with Dr. Martin Luther King Jr., stunned the Democratic Party by mounting a serious challenge to the party's frontrunner, Massachusetts governor Michael Dukakis. On "Super Tuesday," a day in early March when twenty-one caucuses and primaries took place nationwide, Jackson either won or came in second in sixteen of them. Four months later, Jackson still had his eye on the White House (and jokingly assured voters he would still call it that if he were elected), but Dukakis was clearly the frontrunner. On July 17, 1984, in a speech ablaze with passion, Jackson resisted rehashing his quarrels with Dukakis and instead exhorted all Americans to seek out "common ground" with one another.

Tonight, I salute Governor Michael Dukakis. He has run a well-managed and a dignified campaign. No matter how tired or how tried, he always resisted the temptation to stoop to demagoguery.

I've watched a good mind fast at work, with steel nerves, guiding his campaign out of the crowded field without appeal to the worst in us. I've watched his perspective grow as his environment has expanded. I've seen his toughness and tenacity close up. I know his commitment to public service.

Mike Dukakis's parents were a doctor and a teacher; my parents, a maid, a beautician, and a janitor. There's a great gap between Brookline, Massachusetts, and Haney Street, the Fieldcrest Village housing projects in Greenville, South Carolina. He studied law; I studied theology. There are differences of religion, region, and race; differences in experiences and perspectives. But the genius of America is that out of the many, we become one. Providence has enabled our paths to intersect. His foreparents came to America on immigrant ships; my foreparents came to America on slave ships. But whatever the original ships, we're in the same boat tonight.

Our ships could pass in the night if we have a false sense of independence, or they could collide and crash. We would lose our passengers. But we can seek a higher reality and a greater good apart. We can drift on the broken pieces of Reaganomics, satisfy our baser instincts, and exploit the fears of our people. At our highest, we can call upon noble instincts and navigate this vessel to safety. The greater good is the common good. As Jesus said, "Not my will, but thine be done." It was his way of saying there's a higher good beyond personal comfort or position.

The good of our nation is at stake—its commitment to working men and women, to the poor and vulnerable, to the many in the world. With so many guided missiles, and so much misguided leadership, the stakes are exceedingly high. Our choice: full participation in a democratic government, or more abandonment and neglect. And so this night, we choose not a false sense of independence, not our capacity to survive and endure.

Tonight we choose interdependency in our capacity to act and unite for the greater good. The common good is finding commitment to new priorities, to expansion and inclusion, a commitment to expanded participation in the Democratic Party at every level, a commitment to a shared national campaign strategy and involvement at every level, a commitment to new priorities that ensure that hope will be kept alive. . . .

Wherever you are tonight, I challenge you to hope and to dream. Don't submerge your dreams. Dream above all else, even on drugs, dream of the day you're drug free. Even in the gutter, dream of the day that you'll be up on your feet again. You must never stop dreaming. Face reality, yes. But don't stop with the way things are; dream of things as they ought to be. Dream. Face pain, but love, hope, faith, and dreams will help you rise above the pain.

Use hope and imagination as weapons of survival and progress, but you keep on dreaming, young America. Dream of peace. Peace is rational and reasonable. War is irrational in this age and unwinnable.

Dream of doctors who are concerned more about public health than private wealth. Dream of lawyers more concerned about justice than a judgeship. Dream of preachers who are concerned more about prophecy than profiteering. Dream on the high road of sound values.

And in America, as we go forth to September, October, and November, and then beyond, America must never surrender to a high moral challenge.

Do not surrender to drugs. The best drug policy is no first use. Don't surrender with needles and cynicism. Let's have no first use on the one hand, or clinics on the other. Never surrender, young America.

Go forward. America must never surrender to malnutrition. We can feed the hungry and clothe the naked. We must never surrender. We must go forward. We must never surrender to illiteracy. Invest in our children. Never surrender; and go forward.

We must never surrender to inequality. Women cannot compromise ERA or comparable worth. Women are making sixty cents on the dollar to what a man makes. Women cannot buy meat cheaper. Women cannot buy bread cheaper. Women cannot buy milk cheaper. Women deserve to get paid for the work that you do. It's right and it's fair.

Don't surrender, my friends. Those who have AIDS tonight, you deserve our compassion. Even with AIDS you must not surrender.

In your wheelchairs, I see you sitting here tonight in those wheelchairs. I've stayed with you. I've reached out to you across our nation. Don't you give up. I know it's tough sometimes. People look down on you. It took you a little more effort to get here tonight. And no one should look down on you, but sometimes mean people do. The only justification we have for looking down on someone is that we're going to stop and pick them up. But even in your wheelchairs, don't you give up. We cannot forget fifty years ago when our backs were against the wall, Roosevelt was in a wheelchair. I would rather have Roosevelt in a wheelchair than Reagan and Bush on a horse. Don't you surrender and don't you give up.

Don't surrender and don't give up! Why can I challenge you this way? "Jesse Jackson, you don't understand my situation. You be on television. You don't understand. I see you with the big people. You don't understand my situation." I understand. You see me on TV, but you don't know the me that makes me, me. They wonder, "Why does Jesse run?" because they see me running for the White House. They don't see the house I'm running from.

I have a story. I wasn't always on television. Writers were not always outside my door. When I was born late one afternoon, October eighth, in Greenville, South Carolina, no writers asked my mother her name. Nobody chose to write down our address. My mama was not supposed to make it, and I was not supposed to make it. You see, I was born of a teenage mother, who was born of a teenage mother.

I understand. I know abandonment, and people being mean to you, and saying you're nothing and nobody and can never be anything. I understand. Jesse Jackson is my third name. I'm adopted. When I had no name, my grandmother gave me her name. My name was Jesse Burns until I was twelve. So I wouldn't have a blank space, she gave me a name to hold me over. I understand when nobody knows your name. I understand when you have no name. I understand.

I wasn't born in the hospital. Mama didn't have insurance. I was born in the bed at home. I really do understand. Born in a three-room house, bathroom in the backyard, slop jar by the bed, no hot and cold running water. I understand. Wallpaper used for decoration? No, for a windbreaker. I understand. I'm a working person's person. That's why I understand you whether you're black or white.

I understand work. I was not born with a silver spoon in my mouth. I had a shovel programmed for my hand. My mother, a working woman. So many of the days she went to work early, with runs in her stockings. She knew better, but she wore runs in her stockings so that my brother and I could have matching socks and not be laughed at at school.

I understand. At three o'clock on Thanksgiving Day, we couldn't eat turkey because Mama was preparing somebody else's turkey at three o'clock. We had to play football to entertain ourselves. And then around six o'clock she would get off the Alta Vista bus and she would bring us the leftovers and eat our turkey—leftovers, the carcass, the cranberries—around eight o'clock at night. I really do understand.

Every one of these funny labels they put on you, those of you who are watching this broadcast tonight in the projects, on the corners, I understand. Call you outcast, low down, you can't make it, you're nothing, you're from nobody, subclass, underclass. When you see Jesse Jackson, when my name goes in nomination, your name goes in nomination.

I was born in the slum, but the slum was not born in me. And it wasn't born in you, and you can make it. Wherever you are tonight, you can make it. Hold your head high, stick your chest out. You can make it. It gets dark sometimes, but the morning comes. Don't you surrender. Suffering breeds character, character breeds faith. In the end, faith will not disappoint.

You must not surrender. You may or may not get there, but just know that you're qualified. And you hold on, and hold out. We must never surrender. America will get better and better. Keep hope alive. Keep hope alive. Keep hope alive. On tomorrow night and beyond, keep hope alive!

I love you very much. I love you very much.

Ryan White Relates the Prejudices and Hatred He Has Endured Since Being Diagnosed with AIDS.

In June 1981 the Centers for Disease Control (CDC) in Atlanta issued a press release that two "previously healthy" young men in Los Angeles had died as a result of a mysterious sickness. The release went virtually unnoticed. One year and several hundred deaths later, the fatal illness was given a name—Acquired Immune Deficiency Syndrome, better known as AIDS—and it soon became an epidemic of staggering proportions. Although the disease is transmitted almost solely through sexual activity or shared needles, thousands of hemophiliacs were infected before 1985 due to blood transfusions tainted with the human immunodeficiency virus (HIV), the virus that causes AIDS. (All blood donated and received in the United States is now thoroughly screened.) One of them was a twelve-year-old boy named Ryan White, who would eventually succumb to the disease at the age of eighteen. Before his death, White demonstrated exemplary character and courage when he went public with his story, braving unimaginable discrimination at a time when people with AIDS were often reviled for their condition. On March 3, 1988, White testified before the Presidential Commission on AIDS to offer the public an idea of what it was like to suffer from the disease not only physically, but socially as well.

Thank you, commissioners. My name is Ryan White. I am sixteen years old. I have hemophilia, and I have AIDS. When I was three days old, the doctors told my parents I was a severe hemophiliac, meaning my blood does not clot. Lucky for me, there was a product just approved by the Food and Drug Administration. It was called Factor VIII, which contains the clotting agent found in blood.

While I was growing up, I had many bleeds—or hemorrhages—in my joints which make it very painful. Twice a week I would receive injections or IV's of Factor VIII which clotted the blood and then broke it down. A bleed occurs from a broken blood vessel or vein. The blood then had nowhere to go, so it would swell up in a joint. You could compare it to trying to pour a quart of milk into a pint-sized container of milk.

The first five to six years of my life were spent in and out of the hospital. All in all I led a pretty normal life.

Most recently my battle has been against AIDS and the discrimination surrounding it. On December 17, 1984, I had surgery to remove two inches of my left lung due to pneumonia. After two hours of surgery, the doctors told my mother I had AIDS. I contracted AIDS through my Factor VIII which is made from blood. When I came out of surgery, I was on a respirator and had a tube in my left lung. I spent Christmas and the next thirty days in the hospital. A lot of my time was spent searching, thinking, and planning my life.

M?? I came face to face with death at thirteen years old. I was diagnosed with AIDS, a killer. Doctors told me I'm not contagious. Given six months to live and being the fighter that I am, I set high goals for myself. It was my decision to live a normal life, go to school, be with my friends, and enjoy day-to-day activities. It was not going to be easy. *understatement*

The school I was going to said they had no guidelines for a person with AIDS. The school board, my teachers, and my principal voted to keep me out of the classroom even after the guidelines were set by the ISTH [International Society of Thrombosis and Hemostasis, a nonprofit organization that focuses on blood disorders], for fear of someone getting AIDS from me by casual contact. Rumors of sneezing, kissing, tears, sweat, and saliva spreading AIDS caused people to panic. *another metaphor*

We began a series of court battles for nine months, while I was attending classes by telephone. Eventually, I won the right to attend school, but the prejudice was still there. Listening to medical facts was not enough. People wanted 100 percent guarantees. There are no 100 percent guarantees in life, but concessions were made by Mom and me to help ease the fear. We decided to meet everyone halfway—separate rest rooms, no gym, separate drinking fountains, disposable eating utensils—even though we knew AIDS was not spread through casual contact. Nevertheless, parents of twenty students started their own school. They were still not convinced.

Because of the lack of education on AIDS, discrimination, fear, panic, and lies surrounded me: one, I became the target of Ryan White jokes; two, lies about me biting people; three, spitting on vegetables and cookies; four, urinating on bathroom walls; five, some restaurants threw away my dishes; six, my school locker was vandalized inside and folders were marked "fag" and other obscenities. I was labeled a troublemaker, my mom an unfit mother, and I was not welcome anywhere. People would get up and leave so they would not have to sit anywhere near me. Even at church, people would not shake my hand. . . .

It was difficult at times to handle, but I tried to ignore the injustice, because I knew the people were wrong. My family and I held no hatred for those people, because we realized they were victims of their own ignorance. We had great faith that, with patience, understanding, and education, my family and I could be helpful in changing their minds and attitudes around.

Financial hardships were rough on us, even though Mom had a good job at GM. The more I was sick, the more work she had to miss. Bills became impossible to pay. My sister, Andrea, was a championship roller skater who had to sacrifice, too. There was no money for her lessons and travel. AIDS can destroy a family if you let it, but luckily for my sister and me, Mom taught us to keep going, don't give up, be proud of who you are, and never feel sorry for yourself. M

After two-and-a-half years of declining health, two attacks of pneumocystis, shingles, a rare form of whooping cough, and liver problems, I faced fighting chills, fevers, coughing, tiredness, and vomiting. I was very ill and being tutored at home. The desire to move into a bigger house, to avoid living AIDS daily, and a dream to be accepted by a community and school became possible and a reality with a movie about my life, *The Ryan White Story*.

My life is better now. At the end of the school year, my family and I decided to move to Cicero, Indiana. We did a lot of hoping and praying that the community would welcome us, and they did. For the first time in three years, we feel we have a home, a supportive school, and lots of friends. The communities of Cicero, Atlanta, Arcadia, and Noblesville, Indiana, are now what we call home. I'm feeling great.

I am a normal, happy teenager again. I have a learner's permit [to drive]. I attend sports functions and dances. My studies are important to me. I made the honor role just recently, with two A's and two B's. I'm just one of the kids, and all because the students at Hamilton Heights High School listened to the facts, educated their parents and themselves, and believed in me. I believe in myself as I look forward to graduating from Hamilton Heights High School in 1991. Hamilton Heights High School is proof that AIDS education in schools works.

———————

Patricia Godley, a Former Drug Addict, Stands Before a Town Hall Meeting on Drug Abuse and Implores: "Make Me Know I'm Worth Fighting For."

A noxious recipe of baking soda, water, and cocaine, "crack" was a cheap and fiercely addictive street drug that tore through America's cities in the mid-1980s with a vengeance. Families were ripped apart by parents too addicted to work or care for their children. Muggings, gang warfare, drive-by shootings, and other violent crimes exploded throughout the country. Gun sales—legal and illegal—soared. The overall murder rate increased from 7.9 deaths per 100,000 people in 1985 to 9.8 deaths in 1991. On April 30, 1989, ABC's Nightline *broadcast a town hall meeting in Washington, D.C., focusing on America's drug epidemic. Near the end of the volatile show, a thirty-seven-year-old mother named Patricia Godley stood up and, without notes or preparation, described her own agonizing battles with abuse and pleaded with policy makers and judges to treat drug addicts as human beings and not just criminals. (Godley was particularly incensed that William Bennett, who was then serving as President Bush's "drug czar," left the town hall meeting before it was over.)*

I'm—I'm a mother, you understand. I heard a lot of things in here said. My son passed two weeks ago when he got killed, but that's okay. That's not even—that's not even the issue, that he's dead. The issue is that I have another one. And if other people have sons, you understand what I'm saying. I heard the man say on the television—this is addressed to you, sir—that parents need to get more involved. Okay, I'm a recovering addict. I'm a recovering convict. I've never been a parent, you understand? Society says that I have to be responsible. I'm trying to be responsible. I'm trying to be a productive member of society. I came from nothing because I thought nothing of myself. Today I see myself as someone, something.

I lost my child, but I have not had a drink or a drug behind his death, because that's not going to bring him back to me. What I do know is that I have another child that I know that needs me desperately. You all take us to jail, you all think I'm going steer straight. Bullshit! Pardon my expression. We learn how to survive in the penal system. That's no problem. All we have to do is overlook somebody telling us when to get up and when to go to bed. But all your friends are there with you. How can it be rough?

You sent my son to Oak Hill to teach him a lesson. Judge, that city was a menace to society. No one took the time once to work with him, to evaluate him, to see what the penal system could do to help him be more productive. My son was handicapped. He could not read or write. And it was not his fault. I'm bad, not him. I brought him into this world, suffering. I did not know any better at the time, but that does not fix the wrong that I did. I can't give it back, I can't take it back. But I'm trying today. What can you do to help me to be something I've never been, a parent? I'm trying to assist my child. Can you do that?

I want that sister that said something about her brother to understand that there is a program, although they do close doors on programs every day. They're making the time shorter and shorter. It don't get you in seven days, it's not going to get you to take a look at yourself, to see what you need on the inside. It's not the outside, it's the inside that needs help, you understand, that makes me feel like I'm worth fighting for my life. Seven days in the detox, that ain't gonna give me that. That's not going to make me look at me, to feel like I'm worth fighting for my life.

Because that's what I'm fighting for today, you understand that? I'm not fighting for your seat. I don't want your damn job. I'm working hard. I pay my bills, goddamn it, I ain't on welfare. You understand what I'm saying? I'm a working taxpayer today. I'm off parole. I walked it down, because I wanted to. You can open up all the jails in the world that you choose to, but if you don't get to the core of the human being that you are incarcerating, nothing is ever going to change, nothing. Make me know that I'm worth fighting for, instead of closing the door in my damn face. It took a judge, one judge, A. Franklin Burgess Jr., to see something in me that I didn't see in myself. When you shooting drugs you can't see nothing. You don't care about nothing. How could I care about me?

You got a lot of addicts out there that are suffering. I am recovering today, but you have a lot of them out there, man, that are suffering still, that don't see no hope, that don't see no way out. Do you know that the jail is a relief? They glad when you lock them up! They get three meals, a hot and a cot. They get more than they get out on the street. They need some help. We're learning that their life is worth something more than a piece of rock in a pipe or a piece of junk in a hype, you understand? I got a fourteen-year-old baby that I want to live to see. I swear to God, I do.

But I'm powerless over that part. I'm powerless over that part. You all also told me one thing to remember, that I'll run nothing, that I can't make my child do nothing, and you understand that. I can't put enough locks on my goddamn door to keep him in. If I'm going to work, if I'm going to take care, where do you go when you got people—you got young boys twenty-one years old out there with apartments of their own, seventeen, pay their own rent. Ain't no mother in there. They tell them, "Well, look, if you see my son, please send him home." Ain't nobody in there but kids. Kids dictating to kids.

Some of you all need to come down off them high horses you're up on and deal with it. Because you're watched on TV, you got a lot of clout. Mr. Koppel, you got a lot of clout. You understand? Granted, I ain't mad 'cause you had it. I have no animosity in my heart, because you had the potential to excel. I don't have that. I want the chance to excel. Make me feel like I can do it. That's what our children are asking for. The punk rock, the rapping, all that, that's not what I'm talking about. I'm talking about trying to give a child, the child, while they're young, man. You can take them off them porch out there and teach them that they have the potential to excel because somebody cares. Not just mouth service. The mouth'll say anything, but, hey, you don't lie. Thank you.

1990–1999

FEW HUMAN BEINGS ARE BLESSED TO ANTICIPATE OR EXPERIENCE the beginning of a new century and millennium. How will we say thanks for the life, earth, nations, and children God has entrusted to our care? What legacies, principles, values, and deeds will we stand for and send to the future through our children to their children and to a spiritually confused, balkanized, and violent world desperately hungering for moral leadership and community?

How will progress be measured over the next thousand years if we survive them? Will we be remembered in this last part of the twentieth century by how many material things we can manufacture, advertise, sell, and consume, or by our rediscovery of more lasting, nonmaterial measures of success? By how rapidly technology and corporate mergermania can render human beings and human work obsolete, or by our search for a better balance between corporate profits and corporate caring for children, families, and communities? Will we be remembered by the glitz, style, and banality of too much of our culture in the world's electronic global village, or by the substance of our efforts to rekindle an ethic of caring, community, and justice in a world driven too much by money, technology, and weaponry?

The answers lie in the values we stand for and in the actions we take today. What an opportunity for good or evil we personally and collectively hold in our hands as parents, citizens, religious, community, and political leaders, and—for those Americans among us—as titular world leader in this post–Cold War and postindustrial era on the cusp of the third millennium.

—*Marian Wright Edelman,*
president of the Children's Defense Fund,
addressing the State of the World Forum in San Francisco,
October 3, 1996

Student Dissident Shen Tong Offers a Firsthand Account of the Violent Crackdown in Tiananmen Square, China.

It was a stand-off that captured the attention of the world. A single Chinese protestor, unarmed, placed himself directly in front of a row of tanks rumbling toward Tiananmen Square. When the lead tank moved to the left, the young man moved to the left. When the tank went right, so did the young man. For sixty excruciating seconds the show-down continued, a symbol of the larger confrontation between a new generation of Chinese citizens yearning for democracy and an old communist regime intent on crushing them. Although the lone protestor survived his face-off (horrified onlookers eventually raced onto the street and pulled him away), the Chinese government prevailed over the demonstrators. On June 4, 1989, the military opened fire on the peaceful crowd, killing many of them. Although the Chinese students had been emboldened by Soviet leader Mikhail Gorbachev's recent pro-democracy reforms, the spirit of the movement was also inspired by the teachings of Dr. Martin Luther King Jr. One of the leaders of the demonstration was a student named Shen Tong, who escaped from China one week after the crackdown and now lives in the United States. On January 13, 1990, Tong was a featured speaker at a student conference honoring Dr. King's legacy in Atlanta, where he related the barbarity he witnessed in Beijing and described both the difficulty and the necessity of remaining nonviolent through the worst of it.

It is such a great honor to be speaking with you here today. I cannot begin to find the words which express how moved I am to be here surrounded by an atmosphere of Dr. King and his nonviolent teachings. And when I sat there I really feel you, you are the same age as my friends who are still in China. And I do want to do my speech, you know, without any paper, just like what I did in China, but because of my poor English, I should write down and read it.

To fight without fighting, that is the razor's edge of nonviolence. This is what I believe happened in the American civil rights movement. I am here to learn as well as to inform, so you must teach me. But I know that this definitely happened during the spring of 1989 in Beijing's Tiananmen Square.

My first encounter with the concept of nonviolence was in high school when I read about Martin Luther King and Mahatma Gandhi. At the time this method of nonviolence seemed, to my superficial understanding, extremely logical and beautiful. Here was a method which would clearly win in the end, no matter how long the struggle may last. Although the process may take longer, you get the true result—a real and lasting change—not a fake result.

At the time, Dr. King's ideas seemed very idealistic to me from my simple understanding of his principles, just like the sense of nonviolence which

Albert Einstein gave to me, which Gandhi gave to me. But that was the first step in my life, and that was the first step in the lives of many young Chinese seeking some beautiful way for China. We were exposed to the principles of nonviolence, and it gave us inspiration. It was something very pure, very idealistic in our minds.

There is one thing you must know, however, to understand China's nonviolent movement and the principle of nonviolence within the Chinese individual: China has suffered through more than four thousand years of violence and revolution. The Chinese people have suffered oppression and tyranny for over four thousand years. One dynasty after another was established and then violently destroyed. And always the people suffered. The most recent dynasty, with its most recent set of emperors, is the Communist Party. I say this without bitterness or ill will. It is a statement of fact. The Communist Party leaders have followed in the footsteps of all other violent, oppressive dynasties in China. And soon they too will fall.

This is where we took the second step towards nonviolence as we moved closer to the spring demonstrations. In the universities, the student organizations and salons studied and discussed the future of China—the culture, history, and psychology of the Chinese people. And we realized quite clearly that China cannot suffer any more. China cannot possibly live though any more violent revolutions or any more "national salvation." This myth of "national salvation" plays into the circle of dynasty after dynasty. Those who carried out the revolt knew only what they wanted to destroy, not what they wanted to achieve or build up. "Destroy the empire," they said, "and we will be saved." But saved from what? To what goal? The end result is violence and tyranny again, perhaps more terrible than the tyranny which was destroyed. Just look at Mao and the so-called Cultural Revolution, a grand name for the "national salvation" which jailed, persecuted, and terrorized a generation.

The "universal truth" for Chinese people is that government comes from a barrel of a gun. In the light of this Chinese reality, we had to find a good way for China, a good way to achieve true change. First of all, we came to the conclusion that individualism—the self-awareness which recognizes the value of every human life—this individualism was the only way for the Chinese to break out of the dynastic cycle. And I feel that these two are the same thing, nonviolence and individualism.

But this has also confused me. I'm still unclear. How can this nonviolence and this individualism come to some reality, to some practical skill or method in social revolution? It is still a question for the Chinese. Perhaps you can help me to understand this. So many nonviolent struggles succeed, like the civil rights movement and eastern Europe. But the question still remains for the

Chinese youth: How? It is a time for us to really learn and practice the principle, to learn from the examples of struggles like yours.

But personal learning, learning through experience, came to us through our third nonviolent step, the actual movement itself. We knew that the one thing necessary to achieve real democracy and human rights in China was peace. China could suffer no more violence. Peaceful revolution was the only answer. Early on, we leaders were approached by several high-ranking military generals. They stated that they would support us and stand with us against the other part of the army. We knew this would lead to civil war. We knew that, so we refused to even meet with them.

We did not want to give the government any excuse to crack down on the demonstrators. So we tried to prevent anything from confusing our principles or our goals. We prevented not only violence but even people saying some bad slogans against the Communist Party. We tried to prevent this to keep our goals and our principles very clear. Even if people wanted to support us and join us, we said, "Okay, you can stand beside us and support us and cheer and protect us, but you cannot join our march." We wanted to be sure that the people participating were those dedicated to our goals and nonviolent principles with full understanding. And those people were primarily the students from Beijing.

And the more strict we were in this path, the more support we received from the people until automatically almost four million people supported us. And they began to have their own demonstrations. The workers, the intellectuals, the journalists, even the peasants, held their own demonstrations. It was beautiful and moving.

Also, we were dedicated to making this demonstration absolutely peaceful. We controlled the traffic, policed the square and surrounding areas to be sure no violence or crime would happen. Actually, during those months, the crime rate in Beijing dropped tremendously because thieves declared something of a strike to support our movement. They didn't want to give the government any excuse to crack down either. . . .

[D]uring the small conflict before the massacre the students tried to persuade the citizens to hold back, to be peaceful. They shouted at the crowd, "Stop throwing stones, do not hurt the truck or the soldiers." And even during the night of the massacre, our students, the marshals, they tried to prevent people from hurting, from even killing the soldiers who shoot into the crowd, and protect the wounded soldiers and send them to the ambulance, send them to the hospital.

And at that time, I was in the Chang An Avenue, one mile west of the Tiananmen Square, in the most brutal killing field. And now the people in

Beijing they call that part of Chang An Avenue the Blood Alley. And at that time me and the other students, we tried to organize a line to prevent Beijing's people to throw stones, bottles into the trucks rushing through the avenue, Chang An Avenue. I felt at that time really angry because the people lost—out of control, they lost their ideas, their original principle of nonviolence. They are too angry, they lost their brothers, lost their friends, lost their neighbors to shooting without any reason, and dead. So I understand they are angry, but the more they fight back the more they got hunted.

So at the end me and other students went to the middle of the road and talked with the soldiers in the trucks and said, "Do you know where you are? You are in the Chang An Avenue. This means 'Avenue for Peace Forever.' Even in 1949, the year the so-called People's Republic of China [was] founded, there's no fight, no fire in the downtown Beijing. And our movement is peaceful. You're the army of the people, so don't shoot us." But at that time the officer of that truck hold his pistol, stand beside me and keep talking with one soldier who had seemed moved by her. But the officer shoot on, on her face and she died immediately.

And the most moving picture I have in my mind is that one of my schoolmates: He got a rifle, he held it in his hand and above his head, but the soldiers didn't listen to him. They hold billy club, begin to beat him. But my schoolmate, he kneeled on the ground, still holding the gun above his head till the death. All this memory shows me that once you practice nonviolence it becomes rooted in your heart.

I do not fully understand the theory of this nonviolence principle. But I feel I know its spirit. I know that it is the only way for China and the only way for the world if we are to survive. Our various communities struggle to achieve justice and equality, freedom and human rights. We must join our hands and stand as one. As Dr. King once said, "Injustice anywhere is a threat to justice everywhere. Whatever affects one directly affects all indirectly."

We must learn from each other. All our communities must learn peace from each other. And there is much, so much, I must learn from you and from Dr. King. Please help China and the Chinese people find that crystal way which will lead to the crystal goal. And together, as one movement for human rights and peace worldwide, we will be able to look at the tyrants and oppressors of history and say to them, in Dr. King's words, "We have matched your capacity to inflict suffering with our capacity to endure suffering. We have matched your physical force with soul force. We are free."

Thank you.

President George Bush Announces the Allied Air Attack on Saddam Hussein's Forces in Iraq and Kuwait.

The specter of Vietnam loomed ominously over the Bush administration in the winter of 1990 and 1991 after Iraqi leader Saddam Hussein, once an American ally, ordered the invasion of neighboring Kuwait in August 1990. In response, President Bush orchestrated the largest multinational military force since the D-Day invasion of World War II—Operation Desert Shield. (The U.S. presence alone was almost as massive as it had been during the height of the Vietnam War.) The uncertainties were daunting: If Hussein used chemical weapons, if other Arab nations broke from the coalition and joined with Iraq, or if the Iraqi military, the fourth-largest standing army in the world, overwhelmed U.S. troops, the war in the Gulf could result in tens of thousands of American casualties, if not more. But despite the risks—and after months of sanctions against Iraq—Bush decided it was time to attack. On the evening of January 16, 1991, as the first wave of air assaults began, the president explained to the nation why the full-scale military response of Desert Storm was required to eject Hussein's troops from Kuwait.

Just two hours ago, allied air forces began an attack on military targets in Iraq and Kuwait. These attacks continue as I speak. Ground forces are not engaged.

This conflict started August second when the dictator of Iraq invaded a small and helpless neighbor. Kuwait—a member of the Arab league and a member of the United Nations—was crushed, its people brutalized. Five months ago, Saddam Hussein started this cruel war against Kuwait. Tonight, the battle has been joined. . . .

As I report to you, air attacks are underway against military targets in Iraq. We are determined to knock out Saddam Hussein's nuclear bomb potential. We will also destroy his chemical weapons facilities. Much of Saddam's artillery and tanks will be destroyed. Our operations are designed to best protect the lives of all the coalition forces by targeting Saddam's vast military arsenal. Initial reports from General Schwarzkopf are that our operations are proceeding according to plan.

Our objectives are clear: Saddam Hussein's forces will leave Kuwait. The legitimate government of Kuwait will be restored to its rightful place, and Kuwait will once again be free. Iraq will eventually comply with all relevant United Nations resolutions, and then, when peace is restored, it is our hope that Iraq will live as a peaceful and cooperative member of the family of nations, thus enhancing the security and stability of the Gulf.

Some may ask, Why act now? Why not wait? The answer is clear: The world could wait no longer. Sanctions, though having some effect, showed no signs of accomplishing their objective. Sanctions were tried for well over five months, and we and our allies concluded that sanctions alone would not force Saddam from Kuwait.

While the world waited, Saddam Hussein systematically raped, pillaged, and plundered a tiny nation, no threat to his own. He subjected the people of Kuwait to unspeakable atrocities—and among those maimed and murdered, innocent children.

While the world waited, Saddam sought to add to the chemical arsenal he now possesses an infinitely more dangerous weapon of mass destruction—a nuclear weapon. And while the world waited, while the world talked peace and withdrawal, Saddam Hussein dug in and moved massive forces into Kuwait.

While the world waited, while Saddam stalled, more damage was being done to the fragile economies of the Third World, emerging democracies of eastern Europe, to the entire world, including to our own economy.

The United States, together with the United Nations, exhausted every means at our disposal to bring this crisis to a peaceful end. However, Saddam clearly felt that by stalling and threatening and defying the United Nations, he would weaken the forces against him.

While the world waited, Saddam Hussein met every overture of peace with open contempt. While the world prayed for peace, Saddam prepared for war. I had hoped that when the United States Congress, in historic debate, took its resolute action, Saddam would realize he could not prevail and would move out of Kuwait in accord with the United Nation resolution. He did not do that. Instead, he remained intransigent, certain that time was on his side.

Saddam was warned over and over again to comply with the will of the United Nations: Leave Kuwait, or be driven out. Saddam has arrogantly rejected all warnings. Instead, he tried to make this a dispute between Iraq and the United States of America.

Well, he failed. Tonight, twenty-eight nations—countries from five continents, Europe and Asia and Africa and the Arab League—have forces in the Gulf area standing shoulder to shoulder against Saddam Hussein. These countries had hoped the use of force could be avoided. Regrettably, we now believe that only force will make him leave.

Prior to our ordering our forces into battle, I instructed our military commanders to take every necessary step to prevail as quickly as possible and with the greatest degree of protection possible for American and allied service men and women. I've told the American people before that this will not become another Vietnam, and I repeat this here tonight. Our troops will have the best possible support in the entire world, and they will not be asked to fight with one hand tied behind their back. I'm hopeful that this fighting will not go on for long and that casualties will be held to an absolute minimum.

This is an historic moment. We have in this past year made great progress in ending the long era of conflict and Cold War. We have before us the opportunity to forge for ourselves and for future generations a New World Order—a world where the rule of law, not the law of the jungle, governs the conduct of nations. When we are successful—and we will be—we have a real chance at this New World Order, an order in which a credible United Nations can use its peacekeeping role to fulfill the promise and vision of the U.N.'s founders.

We have no argument with the people of Iraq. Indeed, for the innocents caught in this conflict, I pray for their safety. Our goal is not the conquest of Iraq. It is the liberation of Kuwait. It is my hope that somehow the Iraqi people can, even now, convince their dictator that he must lay down his arms, leave Kuwait, and let Iraq itself rejoin the family of peace-loving nations.

Thomas Paine wrote many years ago: "These are the times that try men's souls." Those well-known words are so very true today. But even as planes of the multinational forces attack Iraq, I prefer to think of peace, not war. I am convinced not only that we will prevail but that out of the horror of combat will come the recognition that no nation can stand against a world united, no nation will be permitted to brutally assault its neighbor. . . .

Tonight, as our forces fight, they and their families are in our prayers. May God bless each and every one of them and the coalition forces at our side in the Gulf, and may He continue to bless our nation, the United States of America.

After a monthlong pummeling from the sky, the ground assault commenced on February 24. It was over in 100 hours, and Kuwait was liberated. The number of Americans killed in action was fewer than 150, lower than even the military's most optimistic predictions.

Judge Clarence Thomas Vehemently Denies Charges of Sexual Harassment Made by Former Employee Anita Hill
&
Anita Hill Describes Judge Thomas's Sexual Advances Towards Her in Lurid Detail.

Not since the debate on explicit music lyrics in 1985 had the nation listened to congressional testimony as lurid as the October 1991 Clarence Thomas–Anita Hill hearings. (The Starr referral on President Clinton was still seven years away.) Thomas, a former Reagan appointee who had recently been nominated by President Bush to re-place Thurgood Marshall on the Supreme Court, immediately earned the scorn of lib-erals who felt his conservative beliefs and scant qualifications were an insult to Marshall's legacy. (Civil rights leaders were particularly appalled by Thomas's denun-ciation of Brown v. Board of Education, considered one of the Court's greatest decisions this century, as "dubious social engineering.") Thomas's confirmation was nevertheless expected to sail through the Senate Judiciary Committee and then the full Senate. But in early October there was a startling development: Thomas was accused of having sex-ually harassed a former employee named Anita Hill. Like Thomas, Hill was born into a poor African American family, worked hard to gain an education, attended Yale Law School, held conservative beliefs, and was deeply religious. Hill's charges were especially explosive because Thomas's inappropriate behavior was said to have occurred when he was chairman of the Equal Employment Opportunity Council (EEOC), the very agency that supposedly protects workers from sexual harassment. After Hill's allega-tions were made public, the Capitol was deluged with phone calls and letters primarily from women furious that Hill's charges weren't being taken more seriously. In response, the Judiciary Committee began televised proceedings on October 11. Thomas, who was asked to speak first, could barely contain his fury at the position in which he had been placed.

Mr. Chairman, Senator [Strom] Thurmond, members of the committee: As excrutiatingly difficult as the last two weeks have been, I welcome the op-portunity to clear my name today. No one other than my wife and Senator [John] Danforth, to whom I read this statement at 6:30 A.M., has seen or heard the statement—no handlers, no advisers.

The first I learned of the allegations by Professor Anita Hill was on Sep-tember 25, 1991, when the FBI came to my home to investigate her allega-tions. When informed by the FBI agent of the nature of the allegations and the person making them, I was shocked, surprised, hurt, and enormously sad-dened.

I have not been the same since that day. For almost a decade my respon-sibilities included enforcing the rights of victims of sexual harassment. As a boss, as a friend, and as a human being I was proud that I have never had such an allegation leveled against me, even as I sought to promote women and mi-norities into nontraditional jobs.

In addition, several of my friends, who are women, have confided in me about the horror of harassment on the job, or elsewhere. I thought I really understood the anguish, the fears, the doubts, the seriousness of the matter. But since September 25, I have suffered immensely as these very serious charges were leveled against me.

I have been racking my brains and eating my insides out trying to think of what I could have said or done to Anita Hill to lead her to allege that I was interested in her in more than a professional way, and that I talked with her about pornographic or X-rated films.

Contrary to some press reports, I categorically denied all of the allegations and denied that I ever attempted to date Anita Hill when first interviewed by the FBI. I strongly reaffirm that denial. . . .

Though I am by no means a perfect person—no means—I have not done what she has alleged, and I still do not know what I could possibly have done to cause her to make these allegations.

When I stood next to the president in Kennebunkport, being nominated to the Supreme Court of the United States, that was a high honor. But as I sit here before you 103 days later, that honor has been crushed. From the very beginning charges were leveled against me from the shadows—charges of drug abuse, anti-Semitism, wife beating, drug use by family members, that I was a quota appointment, confirmation conversion, and much, much more. And now this.

I have complied with the rules. I responded to a document request that produced over 30,000 pages of documents. And I have testified for five full days under oath. I have endured this ordeal for 103 days. Reporters sneaking into my garage to examine books I read. Reporters and interest groups swarming over divorce papers, looking for dirt. Unnamed people starting preposterous and damaging rumors. Calls all over the country specifically requesting dirt. This is not American. This is Kafkaesque. It has got to stop. It must stop for the benefit of future nominees and our country. Enough is enough.

I am not going to allow myself to be further humiliated in order to be confirmed. I am here specifically to respond to allegations of sex harassment in the workplace. I am not here to be further humiliated by this committee or anyone else, or to put my private life on display for a prurient interest or other reasons. I will not allow this committee or anyone else to probe into my private life. This is not what America is all about. To ask me to do that would be to ask me to go beyond fundamental fairness. Yesterday, I called my mother. She was confined to her bed, unable to work and unable to stop crying. Enough is enough.

Mr. Chairman, in my forty-three years on this Earth, I have been able, with the help of others and with the help of God, to defy poverty, avoid prison, overcome segregation, bigotry, racism, and obtain one of the finest educations available in this country. But I have not been able to overcome this process. This is worse than any obstacle or anything that I have ever faced. Throughout my life I have been energized by the expectation and the hope that in this country I would be treated fairly in all endeavors. When there was segregation, I hoped there would be fairness one day or some day. When there was bigotry and prejudice, I hoped that there would be tolerance and understanding some day.

Mr. Chairman, I am proud of my life, proud of what I have done and what I have accomplished, proud of my family. And this process, this process is trying to destroy it all. No job is worth what I have been through—no job. No horror in my life has been so debilitating. Confirm me if you want, don't confirm me if you are so led, but let this process end. Let me and my family regain our lives. I never asked to be nominated. It was an honor. Little did I know the price, but it is too high. . . .

Mr. Chairman, I am a victim of this process and my name has been harmed, my integrity has been harmed, my character has been harmed, my family has been harmed, my friends have been harmed. There is nothing this committee, this body, or this country can do to give me my good name back—nothing.

I will not provide the rope for my own lynching or for further humiliation. I am not going to engage in discussions, nor will I submit to roving questions of what goes on in the most intimate parts of my private life or the sanctity of my bedroom. They are the most intimate parts of my privacy, and they will remain just that—private.

Hill's statement would prove equally as compelling.

Mr. Chairman, Senator Thurmond, members of the committee, my name is Anita F. Hill, and I am a professor of law at the University of Oklahoma. . . .

In 1981, I was introduced to now Judge Thomas by a mutual friend. Judge Thomas told me that he was anticipating a political appointment and asked if I would be interested in working with him. He was, in fact, appointed as assistant secretary of education for civil rights. After he had taken that post, he asked if I would become his assistant, and I accepted that position.

In my early period there, I had two major projects. First was an article I wrote for Judge Thomas's signature on the education of minority students. The second was the organization of a seminar on high-risk students, which was abandoned because Judge Thomas transferred to the EEOC, where he became the chairman of that office.

During this period at the Department of Education, my working relationship with Judge Thomas was positive. I had a good deal of responsibility and independence. I thought he respected my work and that he trusted my judgment.

After approximately three months of working there, he asked me to go out socially with him. What happened next and telling the world about it are the two most difficult things, experiences of my life. It is only after a great deal of agonizing consideration and a number of sleepless nights that I am able to talk of these unpleasant matters to anyone but my close friends.

I declined the invitation to go out socially with him, and explained to him that I thought it would jeopardize what at the time I considered to be a very good working relationship. I had a normal social life with other men outside the office. I believed then, as now, that having a social relationship with a person who was supervising my work would be ill advised. I was very uncomfortable with the idea and told him so.

I thought that by saying "no" and explaining my reasons, my employer would abandon his social suggestions. However, to my regret, in the following few weeks he continued to ask me out on several occasions. He pressed me to justify my reasons for saying "no" to him. These incidents took place in his office or mine. They were in the form of private conversations which would not have been overheard by anyone else.

My working relationship became even more strained when Judge Thomas began to use work situations to discuss sex. On these occasions, he would call me into his office for reports on education issues and projects, or he might suggest that because of the time pressures of his schedule we go to lunch to a government cafeteria. After a brief discussion of work, he would turn the conversation to a discussion of sexual matters. His conversations were very vivid.

He spoke about acts that he had seen in pornographic films involving such matters as women having sex with animals, and films showing group sex or rape scenes. He talked about pornographic materials depicting individuals with large penises or large breasts involved in various sex acts.

On several occasions Thomas told me graphically of his own sexual prowess. Because I was extremely uncomfortable talking about sex with him at all, and particularly in such a graphic way, I told him that I did not want to talk about these subjects. I would also try to change the subject to education matters or to nonsexual personal matters, such as his background or his beliefs. My efforts to change the subject were rarely successful. . . .

When Judge Thomas was made chair of the EEOC, I needed to face the question of whether to go with him. I was asked to do so, and I did. The work itself was interesting, and at that time it appeared that the sexual overtones which had so troubled me had ended.

I also faced the realistic fact that I had no alternative job. While I might have gone back to private practice, perhaps in my old firm or another, I was dedicated to civil rights work and my first choice was to be in that field. Moreover, at that time the Department of Education itself was a dubious venture. President Reagan was seeking to abolish the entire department.

For my first months at the EEOC, where I continued to be an assistant to Judge Thomas, there were no sexual conversations or overtures. However, during the fall and winter of 1982, these began again. The comments were random and ranged from pressing me about why I didn't go out with him, to remarks about my personal appearance. I remember him saying that someday I would have to tell him the real reason that I wouldn't go out with him.

He began to show displeasure in his tone and voice and his demeanor in his continued pressure for an explanation. He commented on what I was wearing in terms of whether it made me more or less sexually attractive. The incidents occurred in his inner office at the EEOC.

One of the oddest episodes I remember was an occasion in which Thomas was drinking a Coke in his office. He got up from the table at which we were working, went over to his desk to get the Coke, looked at the can and asked, "Who has put pubic hair in my Coke?"

On other occasions he referred to the size of his own penis as being larger than normal, and he also spoke on some occasions of the pleasures he had given to women with oral sex. At this point, late 1982, I began to feel severe stress on the job. I began to be concerned that Clarence Thomas might take out his anger with me by degrading me or not giving me important assignments. I also thought that he might find an excuse for dismissing me.

In January 1983, I began looking for another job. I was handicapped because I feared that if he found out he might make it difficult for me to find other employment, and I might be dismissed from the job I had. . . .

In the spring of 1983, an opportunity to teach at Oral Roberts University opened up. I participated in a seminar, taught an afternoon session in a seminar at Oral Roberts University. The dean of the university saw me teaching and inquired as to whether I would be interested in pursuing a career in teaching, beginning at Oral Roberts University. I agreed to take the job, in large part because of my desire to escape the pressures I felt at the EEOC due to Judge Thomas. . . .

On, as I recall, the last day of my employment at the EEOC in the summer of 1983, I did have dinner with Clarence Thomas. We went directly from work to a restaurant near the office. We talked about the work that I had done both at Education and at the EEOC. He told me that he was pleased with all of it except for an article and speech that I had done for him while we were at the Office for Civil Rights. Finally he made a comment that I will vividly remember. He said that if I ever told anyone of his behavior that it would ruin his career. This was not an apology, nor was it an explanation. That was his last remark about the possibility of our going out, or reference to his behavior. . . .

From 1983 until today I have seen Judge Thomas only twice. On one occasion I needed to get a reference from him, and on another he made a public appearance at Tulsa. On one occasion he called me at home and we had an inconsequential conversation. On one occasion he called me without reaching me and I returned the call without reaching him and nothing came of it. I have, at least on three occasions, been asked to act as a conduit to him for others. . . .

It is only after a great deal of agonizing consideration that I am able to talk of these unpleasant matters to anyone except my closest friends, as I have said before. These last few days have been very trying and very hard for me, and it hasn't just been the last few days this week. It has actually been over a month now that I have been under the strain of this issue. Telling the world is the most difficult experience that occasioned this meeting. I may have used poor judgment early on in my relationship with this issue. I was aware, however, that telling at any point in my career could adversely affect my future career. And I did not want, early on, to burn all the bridges to the EEOC.

As I said, I may have used poor judgment. Perhaps I should have taken angry or even militant steps, both when I was in the agency or after I had left it, but I must confess to the world that the course that I took seemed the better, as well as the easier, approach.

I declined any comment to newspapers, but later when Senate staff asked me about these matters, I felt that I had a duty to report. I have no personal vendetta against Clarence Thomas. I seek only to provide the committee with information which it may regard as relevant.

It would have been more comfortable to remain silent. I took no initiative to inform anyone. But when I was asked by a representative of this committee to report my experience, I felt that I had to tell the truth. I could not keep silent.

After a relentless grilling by the Judiciary Committee, Hill's credibility became more suspect in the eyes of many. Thomas would go on to be confirmed 52 to 48 by the Senate—the slimmest number of votes any Supreme Court justice had ever received. Women, however, did not forget the all-male Judiciary Committee's interrogation of Hill and in November 1992, voted in an unprecedented number of female senators and representatives to Congress.

The Reverend Cecil L. Murray, During the L. A. Riots, Implores His Parishioners to Find Faith and Refrain from Violence.

What began as a traffic stop for speeding in the early morning hours of March 3, 1991, escalated into the most savage act of police brutality ever caught on videotape. Within *a period of only eighty seconds a small cluster of Los Angeles police officers clubbed a twenty-five-year-old African American man named Rodney King fifty-six times to the head, chest, arms, and legs. The guilt of the four officers—Laurence Powell, Theodore Briseno, Timothy Wind, and Stacey Koon—seemed incontrovertible. But when a Simi Valley jury found the officers not guilty on April 29, 1992, Los Angeles erupted. Shootings, arson, mass looting, and other acts of violence left fifty-four people dead and over $900 million worth of property destroyed. Not since the Watts riot of 1965—which was also sparked by the arrest of a young African American and reportedly drunk driver—had domestic turmoil turned so murderous. Church and community leaders pleaded for restraint, and one of the most impassioned calls came from the Reverend Cecil L. Murray of the First AME Church, the oldest black church in Los Angeles. Speaking on May 3, Reverend Murray inveighed against the conditions that ignited the riot, but also against those who took part in the frenzy.*

"Jesus, why did you come to Los Angeles?"

"I have come that you might have life."

"But Jesus we already have life. Jesus, we've got day life, night life, morning life, afternoon life. We already have life."

"Yes, I see you people are very lively. As a matter of fact, you might say you are incendiary. I spent a few hours in the Simi Valley. Oh, you have life! And I was down to Parker Center. You have life all right, but I have come that you might have a different kind of life."

The good shepherd always sentences you to life. The bad shepherd always sentences you to death. And the good sheep always know the difference. . . .

Some shepherds create chaos, and some sheep capitalize on chaos. It's bad enough when the bad shepherd mistreats the black sheep. It's even worse when the black sheep mistreat each other. Now, black sheep, you didn't start all of those fires. Every four minutes a fire? My goodness, fires don't move on CPT. (Our precious non-black brothers and sisters, CPT stands for Colored People's Time.) Little black sheep didn't start all of those fires. For the first news reports the northern boundary was Florence Avenue. Then we come up to Slauson Avenue. Then we are at Vernon Avenue. Then we are at Wilshire Avenue. Then we are at Melrose Avenue. Then we are at Sunset Boulevard. And we don't live up there. We work up there.

We didn't set all of those fires. When the record is cleared, maybe it will show we didn't set most of those fires. But we do have to confess that we set some of those fires.

To our shame, because now our mothers are crying in the ghetto. Because Boys Market had built stores in the ghetto, and Boys Market came in along with a few other markets when nobody would return after the 1965 riots. Fifteen of the stores burned down can never open up again because they'll have to build new; that yesterday three representatives of Boys Market came and we sat together in the office and we talked together in the office, and we had prayer together in the office. I felt their pain. How could you treat us in the same category as your enemies? How could you treat your friends and enemies alike? And I have to say we understand that Ted Watkins of Watts Labor Action Committee in South Central has served his own black folks for a generation. They burned his office down. Golden Bird Chicken is Black Bird Chicken. They burned his office down. The truth of the matter is, we have no excuse for going around setting fires, for now we have no place where mothers can buy milk for their children. It is in our communities that we have no means, and somebody is gonna have to get a bus transfer and go way up in another section of town, leaving our wealth in that section of town and coming back with nothing but a bag full of nothingness to show for it.

We are not proud that we set those fires, but we'd like to make a distinction to America this morning: the difference between setting a fire and starting a fire. We set some of those fires, but we didn't start any of those fires. Those fires were started when some men of influence decided that this nation can indeed exist half-slave and half-free. Those fires were started when somebody decided that the very pioneers who started this city should not have freedom and justice under law in this city. Those fires were started when somebody poured gasoline on the criminal court and the civil court, when somebody took word and truth and poured gasoline on it and burned the whole structure down. But it is not to our credit that in a flicker of those fires we were found looting and robbing and pillaging and stealing, for that is not us, dear hearts. We are noble people. I know a mother can say, "I was stealing milk for my baby." I understand, but why didn't you come to the church? I understand what you were doing, but I can't condone it. . . .

Well I'm coming on home now. I just want to tell you about our friend who says, "I'm for real." He says, "I know my sheep. My sheep know me and my good sheep follow me and my sick sheep will follow anybody." My good sheep, let me tell you this morning, we've got to clean up the town. We've got to clean up the air. And as you clean up, smoke gets in your eyes. But don't you worry about that. Weep a little bit and keep on walking. Blink a little bit because you cannot see through teardrops. You cannot see through the occlusion of hatred and anger and violence and you'll lump all white folks together. You'll lump all Korean folks together. You'll lump all black folks together. Weep a little bit, but keep on working, and when the smoke gets too thick for you sit down by the side of the road and have a little talk with Jesus. Tell him all about your troubles. Then remember: Jesus, you brought me all the way. You are such a wonderful Savior. I have never known you to fail me. Jesus, you brought me all the way.

Then you get up and you start walking, walking up the King's highway. And before you know it, there's a warm hand in your hand. There is your Friend who defended you when you couldn't afford an attorney. There is your Friend who helped you build a house when the bank redlined your district. There is a Friend. Walk on with Him. Walk on by faith. Clean up. The smoke is passing over. Walk on by faith and you'll never walk alone. *Walk on in the name of Jesus!*

Senator Daniel Inouye Pays Tribute to the Courage and Patriotism of the Highly Decorated 442nd Regiment of Japanese American Soldiers.

Several months after the Japanese attack at Pearl Harbor on December 7, 1941, more than 120,000 men, women, and children of Japanese ancestry—many of them Americans by birth—were forced to leave their homes and live in internment camps situated throughout the United States for the duration of the war. Despite the flagrant offensiveness and unconstitutionality of the policy, more than 33,000 Japanese American men were determined to prove their loyalty to the United States and volunteered to serve in the U.S. Armed Forces. Not only did they fight valiantly, one of the regiments—the 442nd—went on to become one of the most decorated units in American military history. On the fiftieth anniversary of the founding of the 442nd, the unit's most esteemed member, Senator Daniel Inouye (D–HI), reflected on the harrowing moments they faced both at home and abroad, as well as the courage the 442nd demonstrated throughout the war.

This gathering is an important one. It will be a gathering of nostaligia, a gathering of of sad memories, a gathering of laughter and fun, a gathering of good-byes, for this may be our last roll call of the regiment.

We have traveled vast distances—from every state and from many foreign lands—to be together in Honolulu. We have traveled a lifetime together for this meeting in Honolulu. When did this journey to Honolulu begin?

Although this is our fiftieth reunion, our journey began before that date. Our fate was decided fifty-two years, three months, and two weeks ago on that tragic Sunday in December. Our journey began on December 7, 1941.

Soon after that tragic Sunday morning, we who were of Japanese ancestry were considered by our nation to be citizens without a country. I am certain all of us remember that the Selective Service system of our country designated us to be unfit for military services because we were "enemy aliens." Soon after that, on February 19, 1942, the White House issued an extraordinary executive order, Executive Order 9066. This dreaded executive order forcibly uprooted our mainland brothers and their families and their loved ones from their homes with only those possessions that they were able to carry themselves and were granted forty-eight hours to carry out this order.

Our mainland brothers were not charged or indicted or convicted for the commission of any crime, because no crime was committed. Their only crime, if any, was that they were born of Japanese parents, and for that crime they were incarcerated in internment camps surrounded by barbed-wire fences, guarded by machine-gun towers. They were sent to strange places with strange names—Zanar, Tule Lake, Rohwer, Gila, Topaz. Although a few members of Hawaii's Japanese community were interned in Honolulu—a rather well-kept secret—very few if any of us in Hawaii were aware of the mass internment of our mainland brothers and their families.

Although we were separated by a vast ocean and mountain ranges, we from the mainland and Hawaii shared one deep-seated desire: to rid ourselves of that insulting and degrading designation, "enemy alien." We wanted to serve our country. We wanted to demonstrate our love for our country.

After many months of petitions and letters, another executive order was issued with the declaration that "Americanism is a matter of mind and heart; Americanism is not, and never was, a matter of race or ancestry." By this executive order, the formation of the special combat team made up of Japanese Americans was authorized.

More than the anticipated numbers volunteered; in fact, in Hawaii, about 85 percent of the eligible men of Japanese Americans volunteered. Those who were selected assembled in Schofield Barracks to prepare for our departure from Hawaii. That was fifty years ago. . . .

There are too many battles to recall—from Belvedere to Bruyeres, from Hill 140 to the Po Valley. But there is one we will never forget and one hopefully that our nation will always remember—the Battle of the Lost Battalion.

This battle began during the last week of October 1944. The members of the First Battalion of the 141st Infantry Regiment of the 36th Texas Division found themselves surrounded by a large number of enemy troops. This "lost battalion" was ordered to fight its way back, but could not do so. The Second and Third Battalions of the Texas Regiment were ordered to break through but they were thrown back, and so on October 26, the 442nd was ordered to go into the lines to rescue the "lost battalion." On November 15, the rescue was successfully concluded.

Two days later, we were ordered to assemble in formal retreat parade formation to personally receive the commendation of the 36th Division from the commanding general of the Texas unit. The men of the regiment assembled in a vast field of a French farm. I can still hear the company commanders making their reports: A Company, all present and accounted for; B Company, all present and accounted for; E Company, all present and accounted for. It was an eerie scene. It has been reported that General Dahlquist, who had ordered this formation, was at first angered by the small attendance and reprimanded our commander, who in reply is reported to have said, "Sir, this is the regiment." As a result of the Battle of the Lost Battalion, two thousand men were in hospitals and over three hundred had died. The price was heavy. Although we did not whimper or complain, we were sensitive to the fact that the rescuers of the Texas Battalion were not members of the Texas Division. They were Japanese Americans from Hawaii and from mainland internment camps. They were "enemy aliens."

I can still hear the proud and defiant voices of the company commanders as they made their reports. I can still see the company commander of E Company making his report. E Company had forty-two men, and though we were less than a quarter of the authorized company strength, E Company was the largest company at that retreat parade. K Company was made up of twelve men. When I heard the last commander shout out his report, "All present and accounted for," like many of you, I could almost feel the insulting, degrading designation that was placed on our shoulders long ago in December 1941—the designation of "enemy alien"—fall crashing to the ground in that faraway French farm. And we knew that from that moment on, no one could ever, ever question our loyalty and our love for our country. The insulting stigma was finally taken away.

Years later, the United States Army called upon a special commission of military historians, analysts, and strategists to select the ten most important battles of the U.S. Army Infantry from the Revolutionary War to the Korean War. The Battle of the Lost Battalion was selected as one of the honored ten. Our battle is listed together with our nation's most glorious and historic battles, such as the Battle of Vicksburg during the Civil War, the Battle at Meuse–Argonne in France during World War I, and the Battle of Leyte in the Philippines during World War II. Today, specially commissioned paintings of these ten most important battles are proudly displayed in the Pentagon.

Over the years, many have asked us, Why? Why did you fight and serve so well? My son, like your sons and daughters, has asked the same question: Why? Why were you willing and ready to give your life? We have tried to provide answers to these questions, and I hope that my answer to my son made sense.

I told my son it was a matter of honor. I told him about my father's farewell message when I left home to put on the uniform of my country. My father was not a man of eloquence, but he said, "Whatever you do, do not dishonor the family and do not dishonor the country." I told my son that for many of us, to have done any less than what we had done in battle would have dishonored our families and our country.

Second, I told my son that there is an often-used Japanese phrase, *Kodomo no tame ni* [for the children]. Though most of us who went into battle were young and single, we wanted to leave a legacy of honor and pride and the promise of a good life for our yet-to-be-born children and their children.

My brothers, I believe we can assure ourselves that we did succeed in upholding our honor and that of our families and our nation. And I respectfully and humbly believe that our service and the sacrifices of those who gave their all on the battlefield ensure a better life for our children and their children.

Yes, I believe we can stand tall this evening in knowing that our journey together, a journey that began on that tragic Sunday morning, was not in vain. And so tonight, let us embrace with our hearts and minds the memory of those brothers who are not with us this evening, and let us do so with all of our affection and gratitude. Let us embrace with deep love our loved ones for having stood with us and walked with us on our journey. Let us embrace with everlasting gratitude and Aloha those many friends and neighbors who supported us throughout our journey. Let us embrace with everlasting love our great nation.

And finally, let us embrace our sons and daughters with full pride and with the restful assurance that the story of our journey of honor will live on for generations to come.

And so, my brothers, let us this evening, in the spirit of our regiment, stand tall with pride, have fun, and let's "Go For Broke."

President Bill Clinton Addresses a Predominantly Black Church on What Dr. Martin Luther King Jr. Would Say If He Were Alive Today.

"When I was about nine years old," President Bill Clinton joked before an audience in Memphis on November 13, 1993, "my beloved and now departed grandmother, who was a very wise woman, looked at me and she said, 'You know, I believe you could be a preacher—if you were just a little better boy.'" President Clinton was standing in the very spot from which Dr. Martin Luther King Jr. had delivered his last speech the night before he was assassinated, and the audience of 5,000 mostly African American ministers listened in rapt attention as Clinton disregarded his notes and launched into a mesmerizing, podium-pounding speech on Dr. King and how enraged he would be if he saw the violence now tearing apart America's communities.

The proverb says, "A happy heart doeth good like medicine, but a broken spirit dryeth the bone." This is a happy place, and I'm happy to be here. I thank you for your spirit.

By the grace of God and your help, last year I was elected president of this great country. I never dreamed that I would ever have a chance to come to this hallowed place where Martin Luther King gave his last sermon. I ask you to think today about the purpose for which I ran and the purpose for which so many of you worked to put me in this great office. I have worked hard to keep faith with our common efforts: to restore the economy; to reverse the politics of helping only those at the top of our totem pole and not the hard-working middle class or the poor; to bring our people together across racial and regional and political lines; to make a strength out of our diversity instead of letting it tear us apart; to reward work and family and community and try to move us forward into the twenty-first century. I have tried to keep faith. . . .

If Martin Luther King, who said, "Like Moses, I am on the mountaintop and I can see the promised land, but I'm not going to be able to get there with you, but we will get there"—if he were to reappear by my side today and give us a report card on the last twenty-five years, what would he say? You did a good job, he would say, voting and electing people who formerly were not electable because of the color of their skin. You have more political power, and that is good. You did a good job, he would say, letting people who have the ability to do so live wherever they want to live, go wherever they want to go in this great country. You did a good job, he would say, elevating people of color into the ranks of the United States Armed Forces to the very top, or into the very top of our government. You did a very good job, he would say. He would say, you did a good job creating a black middle class of people who really are doing well; and the middle class is growing more among African Americans than among non–African Americans. You did a good job. You did a good job in opening opportunity.

But, he would say, I did not live and die to see the American family destroyed. I did not live and die to see thirteen-year-old boys get automatic weapons and gun down nine-year-olds just for the kick of it. I did not live and die to see young people destroy their own lives with drugs and then build fortunes destroying the lives of others. That is not what I came here to do.

I fought for freedom, he would say, but not for the freedom of people to kill each other with reckless abandon; not for the freedom of children to have children and the fathers of the children walk away from them and abandon them as if they don't amount to anything. I fought for people to have the right to work, but not to have whole communities and people abandoned. This is not what I lived and died for.

My fellow Americans, he would say, I fought to stop white people from being so filled with hate that they would wreak violence on black people. I did not fight for the right of black people to murder other black people with reckless abandon.

The other day the mayor of Baltimore, a dear friend of mine, told me a story of visiting the family of a young man who had been killed—eighteen years old—on Halloween. He always went out with little bitty kids so they could trick-or-treat safely. And across the street from where they were walking on Halloween, a fourteen-year-old boy gave a thirteen-year-old boy a gun and dared him to shoot the eighteen-year-old boy, and he shot him dead. And the mayor had to visit the family.

In Washington, D.C., where I live, your nation's capital, the symbol of freedom throughout the world—look how that freedom is being exercised. The other night a man came along the street and grabbed a one-year-old child and put the child in his car. The child may have been the child of the man. And two people were after him and they chased him in the car, and they just kept shooting with reckless abandon, knowing that baby was in the car. And they shot the man dead, and a bullet went through his body into the baby's body and blew the little bootie off the child's foot.

The other day on the front page of our paper, the nation's capital, are we talking about world peace or world conflict? No, big article on the front page of the *Washington Post* about an eleven-year-old child planning her funeral: "These are the hymns I want sung. This is the dress I want to wear. I know I'm not going to live very long." That is not the freedom—the freedom to die before you're a teenager is not what Martin Luther King lived and died for.

More than 37,000 people die from gunshot wounds in this country every year. Gunfire is the leading cause of death in young men. And now that we've all gotten so cool that everybody can get a semiautomatic weapon, a person shot now is three times more likely to die than fifteen years ago, because they're likely to have three bullets in them. One hundred and sixty thousand children stay home from school every day because they are scared they will be hurt in their school.

The famous African American sociologist William Julius Wilson has written a stunning book called *The Truly Disadvantaged,* in which he chronicles in breathtaking terms how the inner cities of our country have crumbled as work has disappeared. And we must find a way, through public and private sources, to enhance the attractiveness of the American people who live there to get investment there. We cannot, I submit to you, repair the American community and restore the American family until we provide the structure, the value, the discipline, and the reward that work gives.

I read a wonderful speech the other day given at Howard University in a lecture series funded by Bill and Camille Cosby, in which the speaker said, "I grew up in Anacostia years ago. Even then it was all black and it was a very poor neighborhood. But you know, when I was a child in Anacostia, 100 percent African American neighborhood, a very poor neighborhood, we had a crime rate that was lower than the average of the crime rate of our city. Why? Because we had coherent families. We had coherent communities. The people who filled the church on Sunday lived in the same place they went to church. The guy that owned the drugstore lived down the street. The person that owned the grocery store lived in our community. We were whole."

And I say to you, we have to make our people whole again. This church has stood for that. Why do you think you have five million members in this country? Because people know you are filled with the spirit of God to do the right thing in this life by them.

So I say to you, we have to make a partnership—all the government agencies, all the business folks. But where there are no families, where there is no order, where there is no hope, where we are reducing the size of our armed services because we have won the Cold War—who will be there to give structure, discipline, and love to these children? You must do that. And we must help you.

Scripture says you are the salt of the Earth and the light of the world, that if your light shines before men they will give glory to the Father in heaven. That is what we must do. How would we explain it to Martin Luther King if he showed up today and said: Yes, we won the Cold War. Yes, the biggest threat that all of us grew up under—communism and nuclear war—communism gone, nuclear war receding. Yes, we developed all these miraculous technologies. Yes, we all have got a VCR in our home. It's interesting. Yes, we get fifty channels on the cable. Yes, without regard to race, if you work hard and play by the rules, you can get into a service academy or a good college, you'll do just great.

How would we explain to him all these kids getting killed and killing each other? How would we justify the things that we permit that no other country in the world would permit? How could we explain that we gave people the freedom to succeed and we created conditions in which millions abuse that freedom to destroy the things that make life worth living and life itself? We cannot.

And so I say to you today, my fellow Americans, you gave me this job. And we're making progress on the things you hired me to do. But unless we deal with the ravages of crime and drugs and violence, and unless we recognize that it's due to the breakdown of the family, the community and the disappearance of jobs, and unless we say some of this cannot be done by government because we have to reach deep inside to the values, the spirit, the soul and the truth of human nature, none of the other things we seek to do will ever take us where we need to go.

So in this pulpit, on this day, let me ask all of you in your heart to say we will honor the life and the work of Martin Luther King. We will honor the meaning of our church. We will somehow, by God's grace, we will turn this around. We will give these children a future. We will take away their guns and give them books. We will take away their despair and give them hope. We will rebuild the families and the neighborhoods and the communities. We won't make all the work that has gone on here benefit just a few. We will do it together by the grace of God.

Barbra Streisand Defends the Role of the Arts— and Actors as Activists—in American Society and Politics.

Led by a brash, staunchly conservative congressman from Georgia named Newt Gingrich, Republicans swept the House of Representatives in 1994 and gained control of the House for the first time in four decades. Although liberals throughout the country watched Gingrich's ascension to Speaker of the House with trepidation, one rather well-known citizen —Barbra Streisand—was especially horrified. An Oscar-, Emmy-, Tony-, and Grammy-winning actor, producer, director, and singer, Streisand remains one of the most talented performers in America. An unabashed liberal with strong views on a host of issues, Streisand was offered an opportunity to voice her opinions, particularly in relation to the arts, on February 3, 1995, at the John F. Kennedy School of Government of Harvard University. The following text is an excerpt from her speech.

The subject of my talk is the artist as citizen. I guess I can call myself an artist, although after thirty years, the word still feels a bit pretentious. But I am, first and foremost, a citizen: a tax-paying, voting, concerned American citizen who happens to have opinions—a lot of them—which seems to bother some people. So I'm going to try to say something about those two roles. This is an important moment to deal with this subject because so much of what the artist needs to flourish and survive is at risk now.

When I was asked to speak here a year ago, I was much more optimistic. We had seven women in the Senate, bringing the hope of full representation for more than half the population. And we had a president who judged our ethnic, cultural, and artistic diversity as a source of strength rather than weakness.

Then came the election of 1994, and suddenly the progress of the recent past seemed threatened by those who hunger for the "good old days" when women and minorities knew their place. In this resurgent reactionary mood, artists, derided as the "cultural elite," are convenient objects of scorn. And those institutions which have given Americans access to artistic works—such as the National Endowment for the Arts and the Corporation for Public Broadcasting—are in danger of being abolished.

From my point of view, this is part of the profound conflict between those who would widen freedom and those who would narrow it; between those who defend tolerance and those who view it as a threat.

All great civilizations have supported the arts. However, the new Speaker of the House, citing the need to balance the budget, insists that the arts programs should be the first to go. But the government's contribution to the NEA and PBS is actually quite meager. To put it in perspective, the entire budget of the NEA is equal to one F-22 fighter jet—a plane that some experts say may not even be necessary. And the Pentagon is planning to buy 442 of them. One less plane and we've got the whole arts budget! Seventy-two billion dollars for those planes. Now that's real money. On the other hand, PBS costs each taxpayer less than one dollar a year and National Public Radio costs them 29 cents.

So maybe it's not about balancing the budget. Maybe it's about shutting the minds and mouths of artists who might have something thought-provoking to say. William Bennett, in calling recently for the elimination of the arts agencies, charged that they were corrupt for supporting artists whose work undermines "mainstream American values." Well, art does not exist only to entertain—but also to challenge one to think, to provoke, even to disturb, in a constant search for the truth. To deny artists, or any of us, for that matter, free expression and free thought—or worse, to force us to conform to some rigid notion of "mainstream American values"—is to weaken the very foundation of our democracy.

The far right is waging a war for the soul of America by making art a partisan issue. And by trying to cut these arts programs, which bring culture, education, and joy into the lives of ordinary Americans, they are hurting the people they claim to represent.

The persistent drumbeat of cynicism on the talk shows and in the new Congress reeks of disrespect for the arts and artists. But what else is new? Even Plato said that artists were nothing but troublemakers and he wanted to ban poets from his perfect Republic. In Victorian times, there were signs requiring actors and dogs to eat in the kitchen. As recently as last year, artists who have spoken out politically have been derided as airheads, bubbleheads, and nitwits. And this is not just by someone like Rush Limbaugh, who has called people in my industry the "spaced-out Hollywood left." This is also the rhetoric of respectable publications.

Imagine talking about the leaders of any other group in our society this way—say, leaders of the steelworkers union, agribusiness, or chief executives of the automobile industry. Imagine having this kind of contempt for an industry that is second only to aerospace in export earnings abroad. According to Business Week, Americans spent 340 billion dollars on entertainment in 1993. Maybe policy makers could learn something from an industry that makes billions while the government owes trillions.

The presumption is that people in my profession are too insulated, too freethinking, too subversive. One can almost hear the question—are you now or have you ever been a member of the Screen Actors Guild? Never mind that the former president of our guild did become President of the United States. The Hollywood smear only seems to apply to liberals.

With no special interest and serving no personal or financial agenda, artists make moral commitments to many issues that plague our society. Indeed, this participation often makes artists vulnerable professionally. They take the risk of offending part of their audience or their government. As the record of the Hollywood blacklist demonstrates, they can even pay the price of serving time in jail, having their works banned, or being prevented from practicing their craft. . . .

[W]e, as people, are more than what we do—as performers, professors, or plumbers—we also are, we also should be: participants in the larger life of society.

In the old days of the dominant movie studios, an artist wasn't allowed to express political opinions. But with the breakup of the studio system, creative people gained independence. And with the rise of the women's, environmental, and gay rights movements, there has been an increase in artists who support liberal causes. Why is that?

Well, most artists turn up on the humanist, compassionate side of public debate because this is consistent with the work we do. The basic task of the artist is to explore the human condition. In order to do what we do well, the writer, the director, the actor has to inhabit other people's psyches, understand other people's problems. We have to walk in other people's shoes and live in other people's skins. This does tend to make us more sympathetic to politics that are more tolerant. In our work, in our preparation, and in our research, we are continuously trying to educate ourselves. And with learning comes compassion. Education is the enemy of bigotry and hate. It's hard to hate someone you truly understand.

I'm not here to defend everything that comes out of the entertainment industry. A lot of junk is produced—gratuitously violent, sexist, exploitative, and debasing of the human spirit. I don't like it, and I won't defend it. This is a profit-driven industry that produces the best and the worst in its attempt to find a market. If you notice, the far right rarely attacks the violent movies—in fact, their candidates campaign alongside of the major practitioners of this so-called art form.

Art is the signature of a generation. Artists have a way of defining the times. Marion Anderson singing on the steps of the Lincoln Memorial because as a black woman she was forbidden to sing at Constitution Hall forced Americans to confront the outrageousness of segregation. Art can illuminate, enlighten, inspire. Art finds a way to be constructive. It becomes heat in cold places. It becomes light in dark places.

When there was chaos in the Sixties, Bob Dylan said it was like "Blowin' in the Wind." During the riots of the Sixties, when people tried to explain the inexplicable, Aretha Franklin sang, simply what was being asked for, "R-E-S-P-E-C-T."

Then there are the movies that spoke for their times. The movie version of John Steinbeck's *Grapes of Wrath* brought the sad reality of the Depression home to those who wanted to ignore it. In the 1940s, a movie called *Gentleman's Agreement* raised the issue of anti-Semitism in America. *In the Heat of the Night* was named Best Picture of 1967, and is remembered for its unsparing look at the issue of race. *Mr. Smith Goes to Washington* focused on buying votes and favors, a problem we still haven't solved. A generation ago, *Inherit the Wind* took on the Scopes trial and the subordination of science to one narrow religious view, and the movie is powerfully relevant today in light of the Christian Coalition's efforts to reintroduce creationism into the public school curriculum.

Just last year, we saw a motion picture called *Schindler's List* bring the subject of the Holocaust to millions of people around the world. Steven Spielberg rescued it from fading newsreels and recast it in black-and-white film, which makes it vivid and real—and yes, undeniable.

Moviemakers can be late to a subject, or afraid, but often they are brave and ahead of their time. Artists were criticized for their involvement in the civil rights struggle and their early opposition to the Vietnam War. In those cases at least, I would suggest that the painters and performers were wiser than most pundits and politicians.

I'm not suggesting that actors run the country. We've already tried that. But I am suggesting, for example, that on the issue of AIDS, I would rather have America listen to Elizabeth Taylor, who had the courage to sponsor the first major fund-raiser against this dreaded disease, than to Jesse Helms, who has consistently fought legislation that would fund AIDS research.

Our role as artist is more controversial now because there are those, claiming the absolute authority of religion, who detest much of our work as much as they detest most of our politics. Instead of rationally debating subjects like abortion or gay rights, they condemn as immoral those who favor choice and tolerance. They disown their own dark side and magnify everyone else's until, at the extreme, doctors are murdered in the name of protecting life. I wonder, who is this God they invoke, who is so petty and mean? Is God really against gun control and food stamps for poor children?

All people need spiritual values in their lives, but we can't reduce the quest for eternal meaning to a right-wing political agenda. What is dangerous about the far right is not that it takes religion seriously—most of us do—but rather that it condemns all other spiritual choices—the Buddhist, the Jew, the Muslim, and many others who consider themselves to be good Christians. The wall of separation between church and state is needed precisely because religion, like art, is too important a part of the human experience to be choked by the hands of censors.

Artists have long felt the stranglehold of censorship by officially established religions. A sixteenth-century pope ordered loincloths painted on the figures in Michelangelo's *Last Judgment*; nineteenth-century clerics damned Walt Whitman; Tolstoy was viewed as a heretic; and today, Islamic extremists, sanctioned by governments, are still hunting down Salman Rushdie.

It's interesting that Americans applaud artists in *other* parts of the world for speaking out—in China, for example. It's very often the artist who gives a voice to the voiceless by speaking up when no one else will. The playwright Václav Havel went to jail because of that. Now he's the president of his country.

I know that I can speak more eloquently through my work than through any speech I might give. So, as an artist, I've chosen to make films about subjects and social issues I care about, whether it's dealing with the inequality of women in *Yentl,* or producing a film about Colonel Grethe Cammermeyer, who was discharged from the army for telling the truth about her sexuality. Her story reminded me of a line from George Bernard Shaw's *St. Joan* that said, "He who tells too much truth shall surely be hanged."

I promised myself I wouldn't get too partisan here. Some of my best customers are Republicans. When I sang in Washington, D.C., I asked the audience for a show of party allegiance, and a majority turned out to be Republican. I should have known—who else could afford those ticket prices?

Fortunately, there are reasonable Republicans. But I am worried about the direction in which the new Congress now seeks to take the country. I'm worried about the name calling, the stereotypical labeling. I want to believe that these people have good intentions, but I think it was dangerous when Newt Gingrich developed a strategy in the last campaign of pitting President Clinton against so-called "normal Americans." Just last week, the Speaker attacked again when he said, and I quote, "I fully expect Hollywood to have almost no concept of either normal American behavior, in terms of healthy families, healthy structures, religious institutions, conservative politics, the free enterprise system.". . .

I'm also very proud to be a liberal. Why is that so terrible these days? The liberals were liberators. They fought slavery, fought for women to have the right to vote, fought against Hitler, Stalin, fought to end segregation, fought to end apartheid. Thanks to liberals we have Social Security, public education, consumer and environmental protection, Medicare and Medicaid, the minimum wage law, unemployment compensation. Liberals put an end to child labor and they even gave us the five-day workweek! What's to be ashamed of? Such a record should be worn as a badge of honor!

Liberals have also always believed in public support for the arts. At the height of the Depression, Franklin Delano Roosevelt created the Works Progress Administration, which helped struggling artists. Willem de Kooning, Jackson Pollack, and John Cage were among those who benefited from the support of the WPA.

Art was a way out for me. I represent a generation of kids who happened to benefit from government support of the arts in public schools. I was a member of the choral club at Erasmus Hall High School in Brooklyn. Sadly, this current generation of young people does not have the same opportunities.

How can we accept a situation in which there are no longer orchestras, choruses, libraries, or art classes to nourish our children? We need *more* support for the arts, not less—particularly to make this rich world available to young people whose vision is choked by a stark reality. How many children, who have no other outlet in their lives for their grief, have found solace in an instrument to play or a canvas to paint on? When you take into consideration the development of the human heart, soul, and imagination, don't the arts take on just as much importance as math or science?

What can I say? I have opinions. No one has to agree. I just like being involved. After many years of self-scrutiny, I've realized that the most satisfying feelings come from things outside myself.

Most artists are not experts, but all of us *are* something more. As President Carter said in 1980, "In a few days, I will lay down my official responsibilities in this office, to take up once more the only title in our democracy superior to that of president: the title of citizen."

We also need to keep in mind some words spoken by the man for whom this school of government is named. President Kennedy said he valued so much what artists could give because they "knew the midnight as well as the high noon [and] understood the ordeal as well as the triumph of the human spirit." He also said, "In serving his vision of the truth, the artist best serves his nation." By the way, President Kennedy was the first to suggest the creation of the National Endowment for the Arts. Well aware that art can be controversial, he concluded, the artist "must often sail against the currents of his time. This is not a popular role."

But in 1995, I continue to believe it is an indispensable one: that artists, especially those who have had success and have won popularity in their work, not only have the right, but the responsibility, to risk the unpopularity of being committed and active. We receive so much from our country. We can and should give something back.

So, until women are treated equally with men, until gays and minorities are not discriminated against, and until children have their full rights, artists must continue to speak out. I will be one of them. Sorry, Rush, Newt, and Jesse, but the artist as citizen is here to stay.

The Reverend Billy Graham, After the Oklahoma City Bombing, Offers a Sermon on the "Mystery of Evil."

It was the worst domestic act of terrorism in our nation's history. At 9:03 A.M. on April 19, 1995, a bomb exploded in front of the Alfred P. Murrah Federal Building in Oklahoma City, shearing off the front half of the nine-story building instantaneously. The fireball was so immense it could be seen over 30 miles away, and 167 innocent people, including 19 children, were killed. Although initial reports implicated a militant Islamic group (like the one that had set off a bomb in New York's World Trade Center two years earlier), the culprit was in fact a twenty-seven-year-old Gulf War veteran named Timothy McVeigh. McVeigh was purportedly outraged by the FBI's attack on the Branch Davidians in Waco, Texas, on April 19, 1993, and swore retaliation against the federal government. Whatever McVeigh's motivations, the question of why anyone would commit such a vicious act was incomprehensible to many Americans, especially the citizens of Oklahoma City. During a prayer service for the victims on April 24, the Reverend Billy Graham spoke movingly on God's power and purpose in a world in which evil often thrives.

We come together here today not only to pray and forgive and love, but to say to those who masterminded this cruel plot and to those who carried it out that the spirit of this city and this nation will not be defeated. Someday the wounds will heal, and someday those who thought they could sow chaos and discord will be brought to justice, as President Clinton has so eloquently promised. The wounds of this tragedy are deep, but the courage and the faith and determination of the people of Oklahoma City are even deeper. . . .

Since I have been here I have been asked the question several times, many times: Why does a God of love and mercy that we read about and hear about allow such terrible things to happen?

Over 3,000 years ago, there was a man named Job who struggled with the same question. He asked why because he was a good man and yet disaster struck him suddenly and swiftly. He lost seven sons, three daughters. He lost all his possessions. He even lost his health. Even his wife and friends turned against him. His wife and friends said: Curse God and die. And in the midst of his suffering he asked this question: Why? Job didn't know. "Why did I not perish at birth?" he cried.

Perhaps this is the way you feel. And I want to assure you that God understands those feelings. The Bible says in Isaiah 43:2, "When you pass through the waters, I will be with you. And when you walk through the fire, you will not be burned. The flames will not set you ablaze." And yet Job found there were lessons to be learned from his suffering even if he didn't fully understand it. And that is true for all of us as well.

What are some of the lessons that we can learn from what has happened? First, there's a mystery to it. I've been asked why God allows it. I don't know. I can't give a direct answer. I have to confess that I never fully understand even for my own satisfaction. I have to accept by faith that God is a God of love and mercy and compassion even in the midst of suffering. I can remember many years ago lying on a dirt floor in a field hospital in Korea and looking up into the face of a soldier suspended in a frame, who was horribly wounded, and the doctor said, "He'll never walk again." And I asked myself, Why. I can recall standing at the bedside of children who were dying, and I've asked myself, "Lord, why?" I recall walking through the devastation left by hurricanes in Florida and South Carolina and typhoons in India and earthquakes in Guatemala and California, and I've asked myself, Why.

The Bible says God is not the author of evil, and it speaks of evil in First Thessalonians as a mystery. There's something about evil we will never fully understand this side of eternity. But the Bible says two other things that we sometimes attempt to forget. It tells us that there is a devil, that Satan is very real and he has great power. It also tells us that evil is real and that the human heart is capable of almost limitless evil when it is cut off from God and from the moral law. But Father Jeremiah said the heart is deceitful above all things and desperately wicked. Who can know it? That's your heart and my heart without God. That's one reason we each need God in our lives. For only He can change our hearts and give us the desire and the power to do what is right and keep us from wrong.

Times like this will do one of two things: they will either make us hard and bitter and angry at God, or they will make us tender and open and help us to reach out in trust and faith. And I think that's what the people of Oklahoma are doing that I have met since I've been here these past two days. I pray that you will not let bitterness and poison creep into your souls, but you will turn in faith and trust in God even if we cannot understand. It is better to face something like this with God than without Him.

The lesson of this event has not only been about mystery; we've already heard it's a lesson of a community coming together and what an example Oklahoma City and the people of Oklahoma have given to the world. . . . The forces of hate and violence must not be allowed to gain their victory, not just in our society but in our hearts. We must not respond to hate with more hate. This is a time of coming together, and we've seen that already and have been inspired by it. This tragedy also gives us a lesson in comfort and compassion. We've seen an outpouring of sympathy and help not only in Oklahoma City and Oklahoma but throughout the United States and throughout the world. We've been reminded that a cruel event like this which so vividly demonstrates the depths of human evil also brings out the best of us, brings out the best of the human spirit, the human compassion and sympathy and sacrifice. But this can also teach us about God's comfort and compassion.

Some of you today are going through heartache and grief so intense that you wonder if it'll ever go away. I've had the privilege of meeting some of you and talking to you, but I want to tell you that our God cares for you and for your family and for your city. Jesus said, "Blessed are they that mourn, for they shall be comforted." I pray that every one of you will experience God's comfort during these days as you turn to him, for God loves you, and He shares in your suffering.

Difficult as it may be for us to see right now, this event gives us, as we've heard from the archbishop, a message of hope. Yes, there is hope. There is hope for the present because I believe the stage has already been set for the restoration and renewal of the spirit of this city. You're a city that will always survive, and you'll never give up. Today it's my prayer that all Americans will rededicate ourselves to a new spirit of brotherhood and compassion, working together to solve the problems and barriers that would tear us apart. . . .

My prayer for you today is that you will feel the loving arms of God wrapped around you and will know in your heart that He will never forsake you as you trust him. God bless Oklahoma.

Elizabeth Birch Appeals to Members of the Christian Coalition to Find "Common Ground" with Gays and Lesbians.

In September 1995 the Christian Coalition, which describes itself as "the largest and most effective grassroots political movement of Christian activists in the [nation's] his-

tory," held a conference in the Hilton hotel in Washington, D.C. The coalition's executive director, Ralph Reed, was asked by Elizabeth Birch, director of a national nonprofit organization called the Human Rights Campaign (HRC), if she could speak before the coalition's members. Reed's office promptly denied the request, which came as no surprise to Birch; the Christian Coalition, which was founded by Pat Robertson, considers homosexuality a sin, and Birch's HRC is one of the country's most powerful gay rights organizations. (Birch herself is a lesbian.) Birch nevertheless went to the Hilton, reserved one of the banquet rooms, and proceeded to give a speech (attended mostly by the media and a handful of curious Christian Coalition members) in which she sought not to attack Reed, but to establish the common ground Birch believed existed between their two organizations.

Dear Members of the Christian Coalition:

An open letter was not my first choice as a way of reaching you. I would have preferred speaking to all of you directly, and in a setting where you would be most comfortable.

That was my motivation some weeks ago when I asked your executive director, Ralph Reed, for the opportunity to address the Christian Coalition's "Road to Victory" conference. It is still my motivation today. And it is supported by a single, strong belief that the time has come for us to speak to each other rather than past each other.

It took Mr. Reed very little time to reject my request. Perhaps he misunderstood my motivation. But I can assure you that what has driven my request is this: I believe in the power of the word and the value of honest communication. During my years of work as a litigator at a major corporation, I was often amazed at what simple, fresh, and truthful conversation could accomplish. And what is true in the corporate setting is also true, I'm convinced, in our communities. If we could learn to speak and listen to each other with integrity, the consequences might shock us.

Although your podium was not available to me, I am grateful for those who have come today and will give me the benefit of the doubt and be willing to consider what I have to say. I will be pleased if you are able to hear me without prejudging either the message or the messenger. And I will be hopeful, most of all, if you respond by joining me in finding new ways to speak with honesty not only *about* one another, but also *to* one another.

If I am confident in anything at all, it is this: Our communities have more in common than we care to imagine. This is not to deny the many differences. But out of our sheer humanity comes some common ground. Although the stereotype would have us believe otherwise, there are many conservative Americans within the nation's gay and lesbian communities. What's more, there are hundreds of thousands of Christians among us—

Christians of all traditions, including those represented in the Christian Coalition. And, like it or not, we are part of your family. And you are part of our community. We are neighbors and colleagues, business associates and friends. More intimately still, you are fathers of sons who are gay and mothers of daughters who are lesbians. I know many of your children very, very well. I work with them. I worry with them. And I rejoice that they are part of our community.

Part of what I want you to know is that many of your children who are gay and lesbian are gifted and strong. Some are famous. Most of them are not. But many are heroic in the way they have conquered barriers to their own self-respect and the courage with which they've set out to serve a higher good. All were created by God. And you have every right to be proud of each of them.

I begin by noting the worthiness of the gays and lesbians in your family and our community for a reason: It's hard to communicate with people we do not respect. And the character of prejudice, of stereotype, of demogoguery, is to tear down the respect others might otherwise enjoy in public, even the respect they would hold for themselves in private. By taking away respectability, rhetorically as well as legally, we justify the belief that they are not quite human, not quite worthy, not quite deserving of our time, of our attention, of our concern.

And that is, sadly, what many of your children and colleagues and neighbors who are gay and lesbian have feared is the intent of the Christian Coalition. If it were true, of course, it would be not only regrettable, but terribly hypocritical. It would not be worthy of the true ideals and values based in love at the core of what we call Christian.

The reason I have launched this conversation is to ask you to join me in a common demonstration that this is not true. I make my appeal as an individual, Elizabeth Birch, and also as the executive director of the Human Rights Campaign Fund, America's largest policy organization for gay men and lesbian women.

This is such a basic appeal to human communication and common decency that I do not even know how to distinguish between what is personal and what is professional. But my appeal is sincere. I am convinced that if we cannot find ways to respect one another as human beings, and therefore to respect one another's rights, we will do great damage not only to each other, but also to those we say we represent.

I recognize that it is not easy for us to speak charitably to each other. I have read fund-raising letters in which people like me are assigned labels which summon up the ugliest of dehumanizing stereotypes. Anonymous writers have hidden under the title of "Concerned Christian" to condemn me with the fires of God and to call on all of you to deny me an equal opportunity to participate in the whole range of American life. I have heard of political agendas calling not merely for the defeat of those I represent, but for our eradication.

Such expressions of hatred do not—cannot—beget a spirit of trust. Nor do they pass the test of either truthfulness or courage. They bear false witness in boldface type. And I believe that they must embarrass those who, like me, heard of another gospel—even the simple Gospel taught me as a child in Sunday School.

I would not ask that you, as members of a Christian group, or as supporters of a conservative political cause, to set aside either your basic beliefs or your historic commitments. The churches which many of you represent—Baptist, for example, and Pentecostal—were also the churches I attended as a young woman. In those days, I heard sermons about justice and sang songs about forgiveness. My greatest hope is not that you will give up your faith, but that it will work among all of us.

Neither of us should forsake our fundamental convictions. But we could hold those convictions with a humility that allows room for the lives of others. Neither of us may be the sole possessors of truth on every given issue. And we could express our convictions in words that are—if not affectionate, and if not even kind—then at least decent, civil, humane. We need not demonize each other simply because we disagree.

I came to my task in the campaign for human rights with this conviction: If we, in the name of civil rights, slander you, we have failed our own ideals as surely as any Christian who slanders us in the name of God has failed the ideals of Scripture. . . .

Many of us in this community have a long history with the church. Gay men I have loved deeply and lesbians I've known well have talked long into the night about their love for God and for God's church. For some of them, the church had provided the one message of hope they knew as children. The promise of good news was seized gladly by adolescents who did not understand why they were different, or what that difference would mean.

For some, the deepest agony of life is not that they risk physical abuse or that they will never gain their civil rights, but that they have felt the judgment of an institution on which they have staked their lives: the church. What they long for most is what they once believed was theirs as a birthright: the knowledge that they are God's children, and that they can come home.

And it is not only those of us who are gay or lesbian who have suffered on the doorstep of some congregations. Parents, fearing what others at church might whisper, choose to deny the reality that their son is gay or their daughter is a lesbian. Brothers and sisters suffer an unhealthy, and unwarranted, and un-Christian shame. They bear a burden that cripples their faith, based on a fear that cripples us all.

This means, I think, that we are still a long way from realizing the ideal of America as a land of hope and promise, from achieving the goal of religion as a healing force that unites us, from discovering that human beings are, simply by virtue of being human beings, deserving of respect and common decency.

And so, I have come today—in person, bearing this letter, and in writing, to those who will only receive it—to make three simple, sincere appeals to those of you who are members of the Christian Coalition.

The first appeal is this: Please make integrity a watchword for the campaigns you launch. We all struggle to be people of integrity, especially when we campaign for funds. But the fact that we are tempted by money is no excuse. We need to commit ourselves to a higher moral ground.

I do not know when the first direct-mail letter was issued in your name that defamed gay men and abused gay women, that described us as less than human and certainly unworthy of trust. Neither do I know when people discovered that the richest return came from letters that depicted gays and lesbians with intentionally dishonest images. But I do know—and I must believe that you know too—that this is dishonest, this is wrong.

I can hardly imagine that a money machine is being operated in your name, spinning your exaggerations as if they were truths, and that you do not see it. But perhaps you do not. In which case, I ask that you hear my second appeal: I ask that, as individuals, you talk to those of us who are gay or lesbian, rather than succumb to the temptation to either avoid us at all cost, as if we are not a part of your community, or to rant at us, as if we are not worthy of quiet conversation.

We are, all of us and those we represent, human beings. As Americans, you will have your political candidates; we will have ours. But we could, both of us, ask that our candidates speak the truth to establish their right to leadership, rather than abuse the truth in the interest of one evening's headline. We may work for different outcomes in the elections, but we can engage in an ethic of basic respect and decency.

Finally, I appeal to you as people who passionately uphold the value of the family. You have brothers and sons who have not heard a word of family affection since the day they summoned the courage to tell the simple truth. You have sisters and daughters who have given up believing that you mean it when you say, "The family is the basic unit of society," or even, "God loves you, and so do I."

Above all the other hopes with which I've come to you hovers this one: that some member of the Christian Coalition will call some member of the

Human Rights Campaign Fund and say, "It's been a long time, son," or "I'm missing you, my daughter," and before the conversation ends, someone will hear the heartfelt words, "Come home. Let's talk to each other."

In that hope, I appeal to each of you.

***

Defense Attorney Johnnie Cochran Enumerates the Reasons Why O.J. Simpson Must Be Found "Not Guilty."

The evidence could not have seemed more overwhelming: Blood found at the scene of the crime matched the defendant's DNA. Footprints at the scene of the murders matched the defendant's. The bloodied gloves used in the crime were identical to ones the defendant is known to have owned. The defendant's alibi was conflicting—in one report he said he was sleeping, in another he was outside his house chipping golf shots. And the defendant had a long history of physically abusing his wife, who was one of the victims. But what seemed an open-and-shut case against football legend O. J. Simpson for the June 1994 murder of Nicole Brown Simpson and Ronald Goldman dissolved into a media circus and legal free-for-all. Simpson's "dream team" of lawyers, led by attorney Johnnie Cochran, wove ingenious alternative scenarios involving either racist police officers intent on framing Simpson or anonymous drug dealers who confused Nicole with a close friend of hers who owed them money. On September 28, 1995, Cochran made his final summation to the jury.

It has been a long, long, long road to get to this point. It has been kind of like a relay race, hasn't it been, in many respects, in this journey toward justice? The prosecution was first running with it. We then took the baton and we started running with it. We have run almost up to the jury box and soon we are going to pass the baton to you. This is how our system works. This is what makes it so great. We pass the baton to you and we will be glad. . . . I know that you will stay the course, keep your eye on the prize, and do the right thing. . . .

As you have been told many, many times, these are very heavy burdens placed upon the people, and for good reason, to prove this case beyond a reasonable doubt.

As such it is, [prosecuting attorney Marcia] Clark's duty is to answer for you as best she can any legitimate questions arising from the evidence, which we believe casts doubt upon Mr. Simpson's guilt. There may be 1,000 such questions in a case like this which could be put to her, but we intend no such exercise. I do think, after careful deliberation, that it might be fair to suggest fifteen questions, just fifteen questions which literally hang in the air in this courtroom at this moment. And as the time approaches for you to decide this case, for us to hand the baton to you, I offer these questions now as a most important challenge to the prosecution, the prosecution which claims that it has met its burden in this case. If that burden has in fact been met, you will be given logical, sensible, credible satisfying answers to each of these fifteen questions. If the questions are overwhelming and unanswerable, they will be ignored or you will be told that the prosecution has no obligation to answer the questions. If you are given anything less than a complete, sensible, and satisfactory response, satisfying you beyond a reasonable doubt to these fifteen questions, you will quickly realize that the case really is transparent and you will think about the scenario that I just went through for you and that—the term smoke and mirrors that you heard about doesn't apply to the defense. We proved real hard things for you, things that you can see, things you could take back into that jury room. And accordingly, you would have to find Mr. Simpson not guilty.

When I'm concluded, for Miss Clark's convenience, should she decide to deal with these very troublesome questions, I'm going to leave her a written list of these questions here when I conclude.

Let me go over these fifteen questions with you just briefly.

One. Why, there on the monitor, did the blood show up on the sock almost two months after a careful search for evidence? And why, as demonstrated by Dr. Lee and Professor MacDonnell, was the blood applied when there was no foot in it? Do you think that is a fair question in this case? Let's see if she can answer that question.

Two. What was Mark Fuhrman, a detective who had been pushed off the case, a person who went by himself to the Bronco over the fence to interrogate Kato [Kaelin, who lived on Simpson's estate] to discover the glove and the thump, thump, thump area?

Three. Why was the glove still moist when Fuhrman found it if Mr. Simpson had dropped it seven hours earlier? As Agent Bodziak told you, as Herb MacDonell has told you, blood dries very rapidly.

Four. If Mark Fuhrman, who speaks so openly about his intense genocidal racism to a relative stranger such as Kathleen Bell, how many of his coworkers, the other detectives in this case, were also aware that he lied when he denied using the N-word yet failed to come forward? Part of [fellow defense attorney] Barry Sheck's fourth C of "continuing cover-up."

Five. Why did the prosecution not call a single police officer to rebut police photographer Rokahr's testimony that Detective Fuhrman was pointing at the glove, before, before Fuhrman went to Rockingham? That is around 4:30 in the morning.

Six. If the glove had been dropped on the walkway at Rockingham ten minutes after the murder, why is there no blood or fiber on that south walkway or on the leaves the glove was resting on? Why is there no blood in the 150 feet of narrow walkway or on the stucco wall abutting it? And you've been back there.

Seven. For what purpose was [detective Philip] Vannatter carrying Mr. Simpson's blood in his pocket for three hours and a distance of twenty-five miles instead of booking it down the hall at Parker Center?

Eight. Why did Deputy District Attorney Hank Goldberg, in a desperate effort to cover up for the missing 1.5 milliliters of Mr. Simpson's blood, secretly go out to the home of police nurse Thano Peratis without notice to the defense and get him to contradict his previous sworn testimony at both the grand jury and the preliminary hearing? Peratis was never sworn. We were never given notice.

Nine. Why, if according to Miss Clark [Simpson] walked into his own house wearing the murder clothes and shoes, there is not any soil or so much as a smear or drop of blood associated with the victims on the floor, the white carpeting, the doorknobs, the light switches, and his bedding?

Ten. If Mr. Simpson had just killed Mr. Goldman in a bloody battle involving more than two dozen knife wounds where Mr. Goldman remains standing and struggling for several minutes, how come there is less than seven-tenths of one drop of blood consistent with Mr. Goldman found in the Bronco?

Eleven. Why, following a bitter struggle allegedly with Mr. Goldman, were there no bruises or marks on O. J. Simpson's body? And you will have those photographs back in the jury room.

Twelve. Why do bloodstains with the most DNA not show up until weeks after the murder, those on the socks, those on the back gate those on—those are the two major areas.

Thirteen. Why did Mark Fuhrman lie to us?

Fourteen. Why did Phil Vannatter lie to us?

And finally, fifteen. Given Professor MacDonnell's testimony that the gloves would not have shrunk no matter how much blood was smeared on them, and given that they never shrank from June 21, 1994, until now, despite having been repeatedly frozen and thawed, how come the gloves just don't fit?

I'm going to leave those questions for Miss Clark and we'll see what she chooses to do with and about them. That will be her choice. But I think you have a right to demand answers. If you are going to do your job in this case, it seems to me you will need to have answers to those questions. Now, there are many, many, many more, but as with everything in this case, there comes a time when you can only do so much. We took fifteen as representatives, but I can tell you we had more than fifty questions, but fifteen will be enough, don't you think? I think so.

In this case, when we started out a long time ago, we talked a lot about truth. And I always like, in a circular fashion, that you kind of end up where you started out. The truth is a wonderful commodity in this society. Some people can't stand the truth. But you know what? That notwithstanding, we still have to deal with truth in this society.

[Scottish writer and historian Thomas] Carlyle said that no lie can live forever. We have seen a number of big lies in this case, in this so-called rush to judgment. We have seen lie after lie, so much so that at least two of the major witnesses, Vannatter and—strike that—and Fuhrman, their testimony by you may be totally disregarded, further dismantling the people's case. You have that right, you know, in this search for truth.

In times like these we often turn to the Bible for some answers to try to figure out when you've got situations like this and you want to get an answer and you want to try to understand. I happen to really like the book of Proverbs and in Proverbs, it talks a lot about false witnesses. It says that a false witness shall not be unpunished and he that speaketh lies shall not escape. That meant a lot to me in this case because there was Mark Fuhrman acting like a choirboy, making you believe he was the best witness that walked in here, generally applauded for his wonderful performance.

It turns out he was the biggest liar in the courtroom during this process, for the Bible had already told us the answer, that a false witness shall not be unpunished and he that speaketh lies shall not escape. In that same book it tells us that a faithful witness will not lie, but a false witness will utter lies. Finally, in Proverbs it says that he that speaketh the truth showeth the forthrightfulness but a false witness shows deceit.

So when we are talking about truth, we are talking about truth and lies and conspiracies and cover-ups, I always think about one of my favorite poems, which I think is so very appropriate for this case. You know when things are at the darkest there is always light the next day. In your life, in all of our lives, you have the capacity to transform Mr. O. J. Simpson's dark yesterday into bright tomorrow. You have that capacity, you have that power in your hand. And James Russell Lowell said it best about wrong and evil. He said that truth forever on the scaffold, wrong forever on the throne, yet that scaffold sways the future and beyond the dim unknown standeth God within the shadows, keeping watch above his own.

You walk with that every day, you carry that with you and things will come to you and you will be able to reveal people who come to you in uniforms and high positions who lie and are corrupt. That is what happened in this case and so the truth is now out. It is now up to you. We are going to pass this baton to you soon. You will do the right thing. You have made a commitment for justice. You will do the right thing.

I will some day go on to other cases, no doubt as will Miss Clark and Mr. Darden. Judge Ito will try another case someday, I hope, but this is O. J. Simpson's one day in court. By your decision you control his very life in your hands. Treat it carefully. Treat it fairly. Be fair. Don't be part of this continuing cover-up. Do the right thing remembering that if it doesn't fit, you must acquit, that if these messengers have lied to you, you can't trust their message, that this has been a search for truth. That no matter how bad it looks, if truth is out there on a scaffold and wrong is in here on the throne, when that scaffold sways the future and beyond the dim unknown standeth the same God for all people keeping watch above His own.

He watches all of us and He will watch you in your decision.

Thank you for your attention.

God bless you.

Marcia Clark did in fact respond to Cochran's questions, as well as to many others. But it made no difference. The jury took less than four hours to deliberate Simpson's fate, and the verdict was "not guilty." The decision left the majority of white Americans dumbfounded, while a majority of blacks felt it was justified. Two years later, after Simpson was found responsible for wrongful death in a civil case, polls would show less of a discrepancy.

Handgun Control Activist (and Registered Republican) Sarah Brady Speaks to the Democratic National Convention on Gun Violence in America
&
Famed Actor and NRA Leader Charlton Heston Lashes Out at Those Who Attempt to "Undermine the Second Amendment."

Caught in the path of a bullet meant for President Ronald Reagan, press secretary Jim Brady became the worst casualty of John Hinckley's failed March 30, 1981 assassination attempt. Although Brady was shot directly in the head and miraculously survived, he is paralyzed on the left side of his body and suffers from chronic pain to this day. Sarah Brady, Jim's wife, initiated a campaign to impose a five-day waiting period and other restrictions on handgun purchases, and although both Jim and Sarah are registered Republicans, they were invited to address the 1996 Democratic National Convention. (President Clinton signed the Brady Bill into law after his election after George Bush, despite the urging of both Nancy and Ronald Reagan, refused to do so during his presidency.)

Jim, we must have made a wrong turn—this isn't San Diego.

[Jim Brady:] "I told you Sarah, this is the Democrats' convention."

Fifteen years ago, Jim was White House press secretary. Our son Scott was just two years old. All our dreams had come true.

But then one rainy afternoon in March our dreams were shattered by an assassination attempt on Ronald Reagan. President Reagan was shot. And so was Jim. We almost lost Jim that day. And we almost lost the president. But thanks to the heroism of the Secret Service and the determination of the physicians and staff at George Washington Hospital, Jim lived and so did the president. Thank God. But our lives would never be quite the same. All it took was one gun, one bullet and one man who should never have owned a gun.

Every year in this country, nearly 40,000 Americans are killed with a firearm. More than 100,000 more are wounded. Every two hours another child is killed with a gun. And with each death and each wound, another American dream, another American family, is shattered. This must stop.

Jim and I decided that we should do something about it—not as Republicans, but as Americans. I became chair of Handgun Control and Jim and I joined together in speaking out against gun violence. We have traveled from coast to coast during the past ten years. We've met thousands of gun violence victims and their families. Their stories continue to break our hearts. Especially those involving children. That's why we supported legislation that would require a waiting period for the purchase of a handgun. The idea was simple: establish a cooling-off period and give police the time they need to conduct a background check with the buyer.

Introduced in 1987, the Brady Bill was an overnight success. Every major national law enforcement group endorsed it. So did former Presidents Reagan, Carter, Ford, and Nixon. In fact, nine out of ten Americans supported a waiting period. It just made sense. But the gun lobby defeated the Brady Bill.

The National Rifle Association said that seven days, or even seven hours, was just too long to wait to buy a handgun. It was an inconvenience. Well, our family can tell the gun lobby a little something about the inconvenience, the despair, and the pain that can result from a gunshot wound. But don't take our word for it. Ask anyone whose life has been touched by gun violence.

In 1991, both Houses of Congress passed the Brady Bill. Jim and I were elated. But the gun lobby and the threat of a presidential veto killed the Brady Bill once again. It was then that we learned the value of having a president who is really committed to putting an end to gun violence. And four years ago, the American people elected just such a president. President Bill Clinton, in his first state of the union address, told Congress, "If you pass the Brady Bill, I'll sure sign it." After seven long years, Congress finally passed the Brady Bill and President Clinton kept his promise: He signed it into law.

Thank you, Mr. President. That moment was the proudest moment of our lives. And let me tell you why. Since the Brady law went into effect on February 28, 1994, the Brady law has stopped more than 100,000 convicted felons and other prohibited purchasers from buying a handgun. Today, and every day, the Brady law is stopping an estimated eighty-five felons from buying a handgun.

But we need to do more. We should, as President Clinton proposed today, stop people convicted of domestic violence from buying a handgun. Jim and I join with you tonight in saluting the great job that President Clinton has done in fighting crime and gun violence. He's a hunter and a sportsman, but he understands the difference between a Remington rifle and an AK-47. And he knows that you don't go hunting with an UZI. Mr. President, you deserve our thanks.

[Jim Brady:] "And a big 'Bear' thumbs up."

But gun violence is not a Democratic or a Republican problem. It's a problem that affects each and every one of us. It was a Democratic Congress which passed the Brady Bill and a Democratic president who signed it, but we could never have passed the Brady Bill without the support of a lot of Republicans, including former President Ronald Reagan. And we could never have passed it without the support of law enforcement officials.

But now we need your help. This battle is not about guns. It's about families. It's about children. It's about our future. You can't have stronger families without safer children.

The gun lobby likes to say that Jim and I are trying to take guns away from hunters and sportsmen. The gun lobby is wrong. To the hunters and sportsmen of America we say: Keep your guns. Just give us the laws that we need to keep guns out of the hands of criminals and out of the hands of our children.

In 1968, Senator Robert Kennedy expressed great optimism about ending gun violence in America. He told a crowd of supporters in Los Angeles that "we are a great country, an unselfish country, and a compassionate country." Moments later an assassin's bullet took his life. He was right then, and he is right now. We are a great country, we are a compassionate country.

Jim and I are full of hope. With all of us working together, we can restore peace in our neighborhoods, we can eliminate random violence, and we can preserve the American dream for all of us. Don't do it for Sarah and Jim Brady.

[Jim Brady:] "Do it for all of our children."

Established in 1871, the National Rifle Association—Sarah Brady's most formidable foe—opposes virtually every proposed restriction on gun owners, including waiting periods, the production and sale of Teflon-coated bullets (which can pierce bullet-proof vests), and semi-automatic weapons. Although many Americans consider the organization's positions extreme, famed actor Charlton Heston spoke at the National Press Club on September 11, 1997 to defend his and the NRA's unwavering belief in the Second Amendment to the Constitution (which states in its entirety, "A well regulated Militia, being necessary to the security of a free State, the right of the people to keep and bear Arms shall not be infringed").

Today I want to talk to you about guns: why we have them, why the Bill of Rights guarantees that we can have them, and why my right to have a gun is more important than your right to rail against it in the press.

I believe every good journalist needs to know why the Second Amendment must be considered more essential than the First Amendment. This may be a bitter pill to swallow, but the right to keep and bear arms is not archaic. It's not an outdated, dusty idea some old dead white guys dreamed up in fear of the redcoats. No, it is just as essential to liberty today as it was in 1776. These words may not play well at the Press Club, but it's still the gospel down at the corner bar and grill.

And your efforts to undermine the Second Amendment, to deride it and degrade it, to readily accept diluting it and eagerly promote redefining it, threaten not only the physical well-being of millions of Americans but also the core concept of individual liberty our founding fathers struggled to perfect and protect.

So now you know what doubtless does not surprise you: I believe strongly in the right of every law-abiding citizen to keep and bear arms, and for what I think are good reasons.

The original amendments we refer to as the Bill of Rights contain ten of what the constitutional Framers termed unalienable rights. These rights are ranked in random order and are linked by their essential equality. The Bill of Rights came to us with blinders on. It doesn't recognize color, or class, or wealth. It protects not just the rights of actors, or editors, or reporters, but extends even to those we love to hate.

That's why the most heinous criminals have rights until they are convicted of a crime. The beauty of the Constitution can be found in the way it takes human nature into consideration. We are not a docile species capable of coexisting within a perfect society under everlasting benevolent rule. We are what we are: egotistical, corruptible, vengeful, sometimes even a bit power mad. The Bill of Rights recognizes this and builds the barricades that need to be in place to protect the individual.

You, of course, remain zealous in your belief that a free nation must have a free press and free speech to battle injustice, unmask corruption, and provide a voice for those in need of a fair and impartial forum. I agree wholeheartedly—a free press is vital to a free society. But I wonder: How many of you will agree with me that the right to keep and bear arms is not just equally vital but the most vital to protect all the other rights we enjoy?

I say that the Second Amendment is, in order of importance, the first amendment. It is America's first freedom, the one right that protects all the others. Among freedom of speech, of the press, of religion, of assembly, of redress of grievances, it is the first among equals. It alone offers the absolute capacity to live without fear. The right to keep and bear arms is the one right that allows rights to exist at all.

Either you believe that, or you don't, and you must decide. Because there is no such thing as a free nation where police and military are allowed the force of arms but individual citizens are not. That's a "Big Brother knows best" theater of the absurd that has never boded well for the peasant class, the working class—or even for reporters.

Yes, our Constitution provides the doorway for your news and commentary to pass through free and unfettered. But that doorway to freedom is framed by the muskets that stood between a vision of liberty and absolute anarchy at a place called Concord Bridge. Our Revolution began when the British sent redcoats door to door to confiscate the people's guns. They didn't succeed: The muskets went out the back door with their owners.

Emerson said it best:

By the rude bridge that arched the flood,
Their flag to April's breeze unfurled,
Here once the embattled farmers stood,
And fired the shot heard round the world.

King George called us "rabble in arms." But with God's grace, George Washington and many brave men gave us our country. Soon after, God's grace and a few great men gave us our Constitution. It's been said that the creation of the United States is the greatest political act in history. I'll sign that.

In the next two centuries, though, freedom did not flourish. The next revolution, the French, collapsed in the bloody terror, then Napoleon's tyranny. There's been no shortage of dictators since, in many countries. Hitler, Mussolini, Stalin, Mao, Idi Amin, Castro, Pol Pot—all these monsters began by confiscating private arms, then literally soaking the earth with the blood of tens and tens of millions of their people. Ah, the joys of gun control.

Now, I doubt any of you would prefer a rolled up newspaper as a weapon against a dictator or a criminal intruder. Yet in essence that is what you have asked our loved ones to do through an ill-contrived and totally naive campaign against the Second Amendment.

Besides, how can we entrust to you the Second Amendment, when you are so stingy with your own First Amendment? I say this because of the way, in recent days, you have treated your own—those journalists you consider the least among you. How quick you've been to finger the paparazzi with blame and to eye the tabloids with disdain. How eager you've been to draw a line where there is none, to demand some distinction within the First Amendment that sneers, "They are not one of us." How readily you let your lesser brethren take the fall, as if their rights were not as worthy, and their purpose not as pure, and their freedom not as sacred as yours.

So now, as politicians consider new laws to shackle and gag paparazzi, who among you will speak up? Who here will stand and defend them? If you won't, I will. Because you do not define the First Amendment. It defines you. And it is bigger than you—big enough to embrace all of you, plus all those you would exclude. That's how freedom works.

It also demands you do your homework. Again and again I hear gun owners say, How can we believe anything the anti-gun media says when they can't even get the facts right? For too long you have swallowed manufactured statistics and fabricated technical support from anti-gun organizations that wouldn't know a semi-auto from a sharp stick. And it shows. You fall for it every time.

That's why you have very little credibility among 70 million gun owners and 20 million hunters and millions of veterans who learned the hard way which end the bullet comes out. And while you attacked the amendment that defends your homes and protects your spouses and children, you have denied those of us who defend all the Bill of Rights a fair hearing or the courtesy of an honest debate.

If the NRA attempts to challenge your assertions, we are ignored. And if we try to buy advertising time or space to answer your charges, more often than not we are denied. How's that for First Amendment freedom?

Clearly, too many have used freedom of the press as a weapon not only to strangle our free speech, but to erode and ultimately destroy the right to keep and bear arms as well. In doing so you promoted your profession to that of constitutional judge and jury, more powerful even than our Supreme Court, more prejudiced than the Inquisition's tribunals. It is a frightening misuse of constitutional privilege, and I pray that you will come to your senses and see that these abuses are curbed.

As a veteran of World War II, as a freedom marcher who stood with Dr. Martin Luther King long before it was fashionable, and as a grandfather who wants the coming century to be free and full of promise for my grandchildren, I am troubled.

The right to keep and bear arms is threatened by political theatrics, piecemeal lawmaking, talk show psychology, extreme bad taste in the entertainment industry, an ever-widening educational chasm in our schools, and a conniving media, that all add up to cultural warfare against the idea that guns ever had, or should now have, an honorable and proud place in our society.

But all of our rights must be delivered into the twenty-first century as pure and complete as they came to us at the beginning of this century. Traditionally the passing of that torch is from a gnarled old hand down to an eager young one. So now, at seventy-two, I offer my gnarled old hand.

I have accepted a call from the National Rifle Association of America to help protect the Second Amendment. I feel it is my duty to do that. My mission and vision can be summarized in three simple parts.

First, before we enter the next century, I expect to see a pro–Second Amendment president in the White House.

Second, I expect to build an NRA with the political muscle and clout to keep a pro–Second Amendment Congress in place.

Third is a promise to the next generation of free Americans. I hope to help raise a hundred million dollars for NRA programs and education before the year 2000. At least half of that sum will go to teach American kids what the right to keep and bear arms means to their culture and country.

We have raised a generation of young people who think that the Bill of Rights comes with their cable TV. Leave them to their channel surfing and they'll remain oblivious to history and heritage that truly matter. Think about it: What else must young Americans think when the White House proclaims, as it did, that "a firearm in the hands of youth is a crime or an accident waiting to happen"? No, it is time they learned that firearm ownership is constitutional, not criminal. In fact, few pursuits can teach a young person more about responsibility, safety, conservation, their history, and their heritage all at once.

It is time they found out that the politically correct doctrine of today has misled them. And that when they reach legal age, if they do not break our laws, they have a right to choose to own a gun—a handgun, a long gun, a small gun, a large gun, a black gun, a purple gun, a pretty gun, an ugly gun— and to use that gun to defend themselves and their loved ones or to engage in any lawful purpose they desire without apology or explanation to anyone, ever.

This is their first freedom. If you say it's outdated, then you haven't read your own headlines. If you say guns create only carnage, I would answer that you know better. Declining morals, disintegrating families, vacillating political leadership, an eroding criminal justice system, and social mores that blur right and wrong are more to blame—certainly more than any legally owned firearm.

I want to rescue the Second Amendment from an opportunistic president and from a press that apparently can't comprehend that attacks on the Second Amendment set the stage for assaults on the First.

I want to save the Second Amendment from all these nitpicking little wars of attrition: fights over alleged "Saturday-night specials," plastic guns, cop-killer bullets, and so many other made-for-prime-time non-issues invented by some press agent over at gun control headquarters that you guys buy time and again.

I simply cannot stand by and watch a right guaranteed by the Constitution of the United States come under attack from those who either can't understand it, don't like the sound of it, or find themselves too philosophically squeamish to see why it remains the first among equals: Because it is the right we turn to when all else fails. That's why the Second Amendment is America's first freedom.

Please, go forth and tell the truth. There can be no free speech, no freedom of the press, no freedom to protest, no freedom to worship your god, no freedom to speak your mind, no freedom from fear, no freedom for your children and for theirs, for anybody anywhere without the Second Amendment freedom to fight for it.

If you don't believe me, just turn on the news tonight. Civilization's veneer is wearing thinner all the time.

Thank you.

Heston was elected president of the NRA in June 1998.

Bill Henderson Laments Society's Increasing Dependence on Computers and Technology.

Every revolutionary invention of the twentieth century—including the airplane in the early 1900s, television in the 1920s, the computer and the transistor in the 1940s, and the personal computer in the 1980s—has transformed the life of all Americans and, indeed, virtually every person in the world for better and for worse. Through inventions in medicine and science, technology has saved untold millions. But through the invention of atomic bombs and other more "advanced" forms of weaponry, technology has also killed untold millions. Time-saving devices have freed us from mundane and tedious chores. But these same gadgets—from faxes and voice mail to cell phones and e-mail—also have the potential to make our lives more harried and stressed. Few peo-

ple have voiced concern over society's increasing dependence on technology more pas-
sionately than author Bill Henderson, founder of a national nonprofit organization
called the Lead Pencil Club. Speaking before an audience in Barnesville, Ohio, in
April 1996, Henderson described the emotional poverty and social bleakness of a world
dehumanized by the ubiquity of technology.

Is the Lead Pencil Club a put-on? Are these people serious? Isn't this just
some exercise in nostalgia? There's no stopping technology, right?

Our club is not only serious, it's also practical. We are not romantics, we
are pragmatists. And we don't lack a sense of humor. But what computers are
doing to us, our society, and our children is a disaster. We are fed up with the
electronic industry's hype of convenience and speed. From the Internet to
television to voice mail to faxes to e-mail to the World Wide Web, we have
had it. This nonsense has got to stop. . . .

We have been informed by the industry that the march of computers and
assorted gadgetry into every home, business, school, library, and pocket is "inevitable." Microsoft's Bill Gates and his pals tell us we can't fight back because in
the very near future everything will be digital. If you aren't hooked up now,
your children will be illiterate and your business will be bankrupt. Worse yet,
you will be cut off from the Internet and therefore from the rest of the world.
In short, you will be branded a PONA—Person Of No Account, in cyberspeak.

Since the victory of gadgetry is "inevitable," you might as well come
along quietly and let us smother you in speed and convenience, says the digital mafia.

This is propaganda of the most insidious sort, threatening those of us
who don't want and don't need contraptions in our lives. If you are the parent of a young child, as I am, you are assaulted with a constant advertising and
media onslaught that makes you feel both guilty and terrified if you do not
spring for a computer immediately. Every time your child comes home with
tales of new computers and software on the desks of neighborhood kids, you
imagine yourself to be both a cheapskate and crank for insisting on paper,
pencil, and a mind free from machine programming.

You worry that maybe all of this *is* inevitable. The stock market is in an
electronic feeding frenzy. Microsoft made Bill Gates the richest man in the
United States in just a few years. Steven Jobs collected a billion dollars
overnight on the stock offering of his Pixar cartoon computer animation device. Businesses are desperate to stake a claim on a World Wide Web site. Millions of ordinary folk tap into the Internet for sex, info, and chat. The New
York Public Library warns of a "new Dark Ages in literacy" if it can't raise the
funds for computers. School boards trim teachers' salaries and slash programs
so they can afford new and better computer labs. Teachers worry about the

day when they will be terminated so a computer can teach and entertain the kids. No big business today will answer the phone without voice mail or do without e-mail. No letter can simply be mailed: It must be faxed or we are convinced it will be ignored as unimportant.

The electronic wizards tell us we can't balance our checkbooks without Quicken, research a simple fact without a CD-ROM, and we shouldn't even attempt our own handwriting—there is a software program with computer fonts that duplicate handwriting fast and neatly for a mere $39.95. Soon, so Bill Gates envisions in his instant best-seller *The Road Ahead,* we won't dare to stroll the street without a pocket PC that will be combination fax, stock market monitor, digital cash dispenser, e-mail receiver and sender, storer of our kids' photos, and—get this—a Global Positioning System that will let you know within 300 feet exactly where you are on the globe. You didn't know you needed this? Well, you do, and it's "inevitable!" The info highway is paving us over.

But it gets worse. As if we needed any more proof that near absolute power corrupts nearly absolutely, the cyberspace cadets have concocted a new religion complete with a passel of techno-evangelists and their own secret lingo—plus of course, the Apocalypse right around the corner.

According to these techno-evangelists, the digital revolution is the most stunning advance in evolution since the capture of fire. They preach that nothing will be the same by the millennium. Their gospel rejoices that we are witnessing the end of the human race. We will soon be replaced by an electronic superbeing. . . .

We PONAs of the Lead Pencil Club say, "Enough!" We want no part of your new apocalyptic religion, your demigods of speed and convenience. As to your ubiquitous proclamation of the forthcoming information age, you must be daft. We are drowning in information right now.

We encourage you to resist this gizmo juggernaut and revel in your PONA status. It's just fine to be meat—cyberslang for a living being. RL (real life) beats VL (virtual life) any day, and the techies need a moral reeducation. . . .

We suggest that when you destroy our ideas of who we are you cancel our future. Each time you give a machine a job to do you can do yourself, you give away a part of yourself to the machine. That's not practical. If you drive instead of walk, if you use a calculator instead of your mind, you have disabled a portion of yourself. On the other hand, every time you remove a technology from your life, you discover a gift.

Of course Gates and Company proclaim from their silicon mountain that their tools will benefit us immeasurably—that we will be elevated by their machines, not enervated. And no doubt, particularly in medical technology, they are correct.

But let's think for a second about instant information access, the center-piece of their wizardry. As Neil Postman points out, we are already stuffed like geese with 260,000 billboards, 11,520 newspapers, 11,556 periodicals, 27,500 outlets for video rentals, 500 million radios, 100 million computers, 40,000 new books a year, and 60 million pieces of junk mail annually. Plus 98 percent of our homes have TVs—and many more than one. We need more information? Get a life!

Yes, but what of the Internet's World Wide Web—doesn't the Library of Congress have a site there? Can't I download all their books on my magic toy? No, you can't, and for most books you never will. You can window-shop through library listings, but most of the books you want stay in the library and you will have to go get them.

The Lead Pencil Club declares that the World Wide Web is a duck primed for slaughter. Soon, with every individual, organization, and company owning a site, the World Wide Web will resemble the World Wide Yellow Pages, and you know how much fun it is to flip through the phone book. . . .

So what can you do against the reign of Gates and the gospel according to *Wired*? Lots, it turns out. . . .

Personally, you can adopt Sven Birkerts's motto about electronic technology: "Refuse it." At home, hang up on voice mail and unplug the TV. Persuade your children that they would be better off without a computer. Sit around the fire in the evening—a real fire in the fireplace—and read to them, or let them read to you. Play games that use the brain, not pickle it. After years of lobbying for a computer, my own daughter recently announced she'd prefer a clarinet for Christmas. For me this was a terrific personal victory. She had played the CD-ROMs of her friends and opted instead for music she could play with her mind and spirit. Now of an evening, I play my trumpet, and she the clarinet. The TV is dark.

At work, eschew e-mail. Fax not. Pencil and paper will produce a better response. A trip to the water cooler evokes more interesting office chatter. Haste makes waste. What's your hurry? Not so fast. Speed kills.

If you still feel lonely and cut off from Web sites and Internet sex and chat, try communicating again with your wife or husband or real-life lover. Read a book. . . .

Take out a stack of poetry from your library, and while you are there inquire about what they did with the card catalogue. Maybe it's in the basement and they could bring it back upstairs. Here's a poem by T. S. Eliot that might offer solace for your lonely unwired self.

> *The endless cycle of ideas and action,*
> *Endless innovation, endless experiment*

Brings knowledge of motion but not of stillness;
Knowledge of speech but not of silence;
Knowledge of words and ignorance of the word.
All our knowledge brings us nearer to our ignorance—
Where is the life we have lost in living?
Where is the Wisdom we have lost in knowledge?
Where is the Knowledge we have lost in information?
The cycles of heaven in twenty centuries bring us farther from God
And nearer to the dust.

The Original Draft of President Bill Clinton's Apology to the American People for His "Improper Relationship" with Monica Lewinsky & The Speech He Ultimately Gave.

After years of exhaustive probes on the Whitewater land deal and other purported misdeeds going back to the 1970s, Independent Counsel Kenneth Starr was nearing the end of his investigations by late 1997, having found nothing concrete on President Bill Clinton or First Lady Hillary Rodham Clinton. And then, in January 1998, Starr's office was suddenly revitalized: A government worker named Linda Tripp had secretly taped her conversations with a former White House intern named Monica Lewinsky, who claimed to have had a sexual relationship with the president. Although the revelation had nothing to do with the original inquiry, Starr convinced Attorney General Janet Reno to let him look into the matter further. For the president, the scandal lurched from the personally embarrassing to the politically and legally perilous when there was speculation he had lied about the Lewinsky affair during a deposition for a sexual harassment suit brought against him by Paula Corbin Jones. Under threat of subpoena, Clinton appeared before Starr's grand jury (via closed circuit from the White House) on August 17, 1998, and was specifically asked whether he had or had not committed perjury during the Jones deposition. Clinton denied that he had lied under oath, but he did confess to having had an "inappropriate sexual relationship" with Lewinsky. Knowing the admission would leak to the public, Clinton decided to tell the nation that despite previous denials, he and Lewinsky had had a sexual relationship. What follows is the original draft of that speech, which the president was to deliver at 9 P.M. on the evening of August 17.

My fellow Americans:

No one who is not in my position can understand the remorse I feel today. Since I was very young, I have had a profound reverence for this office I hold. I've been honored that you, the people, have entrusted it to me. I am proud of what we have accomplished together.

But in this case, I have fallen short of what you should expect from a president. I have failed my own religious faith and values. I have let too many people down. I take full responsibility for my actions—for hurting my wife and daughter, for hurting Monica Lewinsky and her family, for hurting friends and staff, and for hurting the country I love. None of this ever should have happened.

I never should have had any sexual contact with Monica Lewinsky, but I did. I should have acknowledged that I was wrong months ago, but I didn't. I thought I was shielding my family, but I know in the end, for Hillary and Chelsea, delay has only brought more pain. Their forgiveness and love, expressed so often as we sat alone together this weekend, means more than I can ever say.

What I did was wrong—and there is no excuse for it. I do want to assure you, as I told the Grand Jury under oath, that I did nothing to obstruct this investigation.

Finally, I also want to apologize to all of you, my fellow citizens. I hope you can find it in your heart to accept that apology. I pledge to you that I will make every effort of mind and spirit to earn your confidence again, to be worthy of this office, and to finish the work on which we have made such remarkable progress in the past six years.

God bless you, and good night.

This speech, however, was replaced by one that was less contrite and sterner in tone. Sixty-seven million Americans tuned in to hear the president explain his actions and express remorse for what he had done, and this is what they ultimately heard.

Good evening.

This afternoon in this room, from this chair, I testified before the Office of Independent Counsel and the grand jury. I answered their questions truthfully, including questions about my private life—questions no American citizen would ever want to answer. Still, I must take complete responsibility for all my actions, both public and private. And that is why I am speaking to you tonight.

As you know, in a deposition in January, I was asked questions about my relationship with Monica Lewinsky. While my answers were legally accurate, I did not volunteer information. Indeed, I did have a relationship with Ms. Lewinsky that was not appropriate. In fact, it was wrong. It constituted a critical lapse in judgment and a personal failure on my part for which I am solely and completely responsible. But I told the grand jury today—and I say to you now—that at no time did I ask anyone to lie, to hide or destroy evidence, or to take any other unlawful action.

I know that my public comments and my silence about this matter gave a false impression. I misled people, including even my wife. I deeply regret that. I can only tell you I was motivated by many factors. First, by a desire to protect myself from the embarrassment of my own conduct.

I was also very concerned about protecting my family. The fact that these questions were being asked in a politically inspired lawsuit, which has since been dismissed, was a consideration, too.

In addition, I had real and serious concerns about an independent counsel investigation that began with private business dealings twenty years ago—dealings, I might add, about which an independent federal agency found no evidence of any wrongdoing by me or my wife over two years ago. The independent counsel investigation moved on to my staff and friends, then into my private life. And now the investigation itself is under investigation.

This has gone on too long, cost too much, and hurt too many innocent people. Now, this matter is between me, the two people I love most—my wife and our daughter—and our God.

I must put it right, and I am prepared to do whatever it takes to do so. Nothing is more important to me personally. But it is private, and I intend to reclaim my family life for my family. It's nobody's business but ours. Even presidents have private lives. It is time to stop the pursuit of personal destruction and the prying into private lives and get on with our national life.

Our country has been distracted by this matter for too long, and I take my responsibility for my part in all of this. That is all I can do. Now it is time—in fact, it is past time—to move on. We have important work to do, real opportunities to seize, real problems to solve, real security matters to face.

And so tonight, I ask you to turn away from the spectacle of the past seven months, to repair the fabric of our national discourse, and to return our attention to all the challenges and all the promise of the next American century.

Thank you for watching, and good night.

President Clinton read from the latter speech for several reasons. First, and unbeknownst to even many of his closest advisers, the president was planning a military strike against terrorist leader Osama bin Laden for his role in the embassy bombings in Africa, and the president did not want either the United States or himself to appear weak before conducting the attack. (The strikes were carried out on August 21.) The president also chose the second, less contrite speech for personal reasons. After his grand jury testimony before Ken Starr and his team of prosecutors, the president was seething with anger at the indignity of the process and the nature of their questions. Much to the shock of his political enemies, the president's popularity grew in the wake of the scandal. During the 1998 congressional elections, Republicans unexpectedly lost seats in the Congress. Speaker of the House Newt Gingrich, who had orchestrated a last-minute attack on the president during the election, was roundly criticized by his party for mishandling the affair. He announced his retirement from Congress the day after the elections. The House of Representatives impeached President Clinton—only the second president in history, after Andrew Johnson, to be impeached—but the president was acquitted by the Senate in February 1999.

Journalist Tom Brokaw Looks Back on the Triumphs and Turmoils of the Twentieth Century—and Looks Ahead to the Challenges and Possibilities of the Century to Come.

Walking along the beaches of Normandy, France, with American veterans during the fortieth anniversary of the D-Day invasion, news anchor Tom Brokaw underwent what he would later describe as a "life-changing" experience. "I began to reflect on the wonders of these ordinary people," Brokaw remarked of the generation that fought World War II. "At every stage of their lives they were part of historic challenges and achievements of a magnitude the world had never before witnessed." Brokaw's realization evolved into a crusade to honor and remember the sacrifices made of this generation, culminating in a New York Times *best-seller,* The Greatest Generation. *Invited to address the graduating class of Santa Fe College on May 15, 1999, Brokaw used the opportunity not merely to wax nostalgic about a time gone by, but to summon a new generation of leaders to recognize and confront the problems they would face in the coming millennium.*

One hundred years ago, another class of '99 was anticipating a new century, rich with the possibility of new technologies—electricity, the automobile, the first tentative steps toward flight. The men who controlled the railroads and steel and oil were amassing great fortunes and making America the new industrial and financial capital of the world. The labor leaders who aroused armies of workers to claim their fair share.

As it turns out, all of that exciting and empowering new technology was in its seminal stages, primitive, really, compared to what was to come—the splitting of the atom, jet travel and the space age, the mapping of the body's molecular structure, the expansive new universe of cyber-technology.

God, the possibilities for advancing the human condition and expanding the cosmos of intellectual understanding! In fact, giant steps were taken, great leaps well beyond what the most prescient member of the class of 1899 could have anticipated.

The twentieth century—what a triumph. And what an ugly scar on the face of history.

Two world wars with millions of casualties, holocausts in the heart of Western civilization, in Southeast Asia and in Africa, killing millions more. An ideology designed to empower the masses became one of the most ruthless instruments of oppression. Rival nations pointed at each other terrible weapons capable of destroying life on Earth as we know it.

In the closing days of this momentous time, in the American culture, maniacal homicide committed by schoolboys shocked the nation into a dialogue of ill-defined blame—while in Europe the most powerful political military alliance on the globe made a clumsy attempt to neutralize a murderous tyrant and in the execution of that attempt, set off a refugee crisis of historic proportions.

The short lesson: technology is not enough, not even when it comes with a generous package of stock options, sabbaticals, and leased time on a private plane.

The long lesson? It is not enough to wire the world if you short-circuit the soul. It is not enough to probe the hostile environments of distant galaxies if we fail to resolve the climate of mindless violence, ethnic and racial hate here in the bosom of Mother Earth. It is not enough to identify the gene that predetermines the prospect of Alzheimer's disease if we go through the prime of life with a closed mind.

I am incapable of helping you advance your knowledge in the matters that brought you to this institution. Frankly, I still don't understand how the picture gets from where I work to your television set. I call it a miracle and leave it at that.

So I am all the more in awe of your capacity to change the gears on all the machinery of the world, broadly speaking. But I have learned something of the political and social possibilities—and failings—of mankind in my thirty-seven years as a journalist.

First, for all of its shocking and brutal stretches of oppression and extermination, the most powerful idea of the twentieth century is freedom. There is so much more political and individual freedom at the end of the twentieth century than at the beginning, and that is a tribute to the enduring and inherent instinct for self-determination, even in the darkest shadows of tyrannical control.

If we fail to first recognize then deal with these societal cancers in our system we will have squandered a priceless legacy left to us by what I have come to call the Greatest Generation. Some of them are here today, although they would not have you know it for they are characteristically modest. They prefer to let their lives and sacrifices speak for them.

They are the men and women who came of age in the Great Depression, when economic despair was on the land like a plague. There were great bands of migrant workers, drifting across the American landscape, looking for enough of a wage to get through the next day. In families youngsters quit school to go to work—not to buy a car for themselves or a new video game. They quit to earn enough to help their family get through another week.

Then, just as the economic gloom was beginning to lift, World War. Two powerful and ruthless regimes, one east, the other west, were determined to choke off the idea of political freedom, political and ethnic pluralism—and to impose their twisted ideology on vast areas of the globe with brutal military might.

Here, the young men and women who had just been tested by the Great Depression were to be tested again—in the battlefields thousands of miles across the Atlantic or thousands of miles across the Pacific. In bitter European cold and the suffocating heat of the jungle. In the air and on the seas, they fought—often hand to hand—for more than three years, day in and day out. More than twelve million in uniform, millions more at home on the assembly lines, converting the American economy into a war machine overnight. Women went to work where only men had prevailed—in the cabs of trucks, in research labs, in shipbuilding yards.

It was a tense, dangerous, and vibrant time. The world was at stake—and at a time in their lives when their days should have been filled with the rewards of starting careers and families, their nights filled with love and innocent adventure, this generation was fighting for survival—theirs and the world's.

They prevailed through extraordinary acts of courage and heroism by ordinary people from the farms and the small towns, from the pavement of big cities, from the bucolic and privileged surroundings of great universities.

They saved the world. Nothing less.

Then, they came rushing home to go to college in record numbers; married in record numbers; gave us new art and breakthroughs in science and industry; and expanded political freedoms and, always, a sense of the possible. They rebuilt their enemies and drew the line against a new form of oppression rising like a dark cloud out of Moscow.

They weren't perfect: they were slow to recognize the equal place of women—and racial minorities, especially black and Asian Americans. But those women and black and Asian Americans were part of the tensile strength of this generation, for they never gave up.

They all recognized that for all of the genius of the American political system and the framework of laws, beginning with the Constitution, the enduring strength of this immigrant nation has been its common ground, wide enough and strong enough to accommodate all races and beliefs.

Now great fault lines run through that common ground. We have allowed it to be so fractured we are in danger of becoming less than the sum of our parts. We have become the culture of cheap confrontation rather than resolution.

We have political leaders too eager to divide for their selfish aims rather than unify for the common good. And, yes, we have a mass media much too inclined to exploit these instincts. The quick hit has become a suitable substitute for thoughtful dialogue in both the political and journalistic arena.

In the business arena, we celebrate the astonishing good fortune of those at the top without raising enough questions about the economic opportunity of those at the bottom.

I wonder, is this what the Greatest Generation made all those sacrifices for? Did we win the war—then—and the Cold War later to lose our way?

Francis Fukuyama, the provocative student of social and historical trends, has given voice to the concerns of many, most recently in a long article in *The Atlantic Monthly*. He concludes that in this postindustrial information age, the old conceit that social order has come from a centralized, rational, bureaucratic hierarchy is outdated. Instead, he argues that in the twenty-first century, societies and corporations will decentralize and devolve power and rely on people to be self-organizing, using the new tools of this age.

Social order norms have been disrupted by new technologies before. The shift from rural agrarian to urban industrial economies representing only the most recent example—the impact of freeways and jet travel—in establishing new living patterns.

So now, in this new age of spellbinding possibilities for communication, information retrieval, marketing, and proselytizing, we are undergoing another major shift in the norms of how society is organized for everyday life, work, and play.

It is wildly exciting to be on the frontier of such an empowering era.

But no piece of software, no server or search engine will offer you the irreplaceable rewards of a loving personal relationship, the strength and comfort of a real community of shared values and common dreams, the moral underpinning of a life lived well, whatever the financial scorecard. Nor will this new technology by itself make you more racially tolerant—more sensitive to the plight of the disenfranchised—more courageous to take a firm stand for what you know is right.

These are mere tools in your hands. Your hands are an extension not only of your mind, but also of your heart and soul.

Taken altogether they're a powerful combination.

Use them well.

Take care of your Mother, Mother Earth.

Become color-blind.
Hate hate.
Fight violence.
And take care of each other.

You have a whole new century to shape. I envy you, but I want to stand aside now because you have work to do.

PERMISSIONS

ADDITIONAL SOURCES

James R. Andrews and David Zarefsky, eds., *Contemporary American Voices: Significant Speeches in American History, 1945–Present* (New York: Longman, 1987); Eliot Asinof, *Eight Men Out: The Black Sox and the 1919 World Series* (New York: Holt, 1963); Douglas Brinkley, *History of the United States* (New York: Viking, 1998); George Bush, *Public Papers of the Presidents of the United States* (Washington: USGPO, 1992); Gregory Bush, *Campaign Speeches of American Presidential Candidates* (New York: Ungar, 1985); Robert C. Byrd, *The Senate: Addresses on the History of the United States Senate* (Washington: USGPO, 1991); Karlyn Kohrs Campbell, *Man Cannot Speak for Her* (New York: Praeger, 1989); Harvey Cantil, *Invasion from Mars* (Princeton, NJ: Princeton University Press, 1940); Jimmy Carter, *Public Papers of the Presidents of the United States* (Washington: USGPO, 1978); Anne Charters, *The Portable Kerouac* (New York: Viking, 1995); Samuel Langhorne Clemens, *Mark Twain Speaking* (Iowa City: University of Iowa Press, 1976); William J. Clinton, *Public Papers of the Presidents of the United States* (Washington: USGPO, 1995); Robert E. Conot, *Justice at Nuremburg* (New York: Harper & Row, 1983); Lewis Copeland and Lawrence W. Lamm, eds., *The World's Great Speeches* (New York: Dover, 1973); John R. Coyne, *The Impudent Snobs: Agnew vs. the Intellectual Establishment* (New Rochelle, NY: Arlington House, 1972); Carlo D'Este, *A Genius for War* (New York: HarperCollins, 1995); Dwight D. Eisenhower, *Public Papers of the Presidents of the United States* (Washington: USGPO, 1962); Harold Evans, *The American Century* (New York: Random House, 1998); Philip S. Foner, ed., *Helen Keller: Her Socialist Years* (New York: International Publishers, 1967); Philip S. Foner, ed., *The Voice of Black America: Major Speeches by Negroes in the United States, 1797–1971* (New York: Simon & Schuster, 1972); Henry Ford, *The Ford Plan, A Human Document: Testimony to the Committee on Industrial Relations* (1915); Betty Friedan, *"It Changed My Life": Writings on the Women's Movement* (Cambridge, MA: Harvard University Press, 1998); Steven Gragertt, ed., *Radio Broadcasts of Will Rogers* (Stillwater: Oklahoma State University Press, 1983); John Graham, ed., *Great American Speeches, 1898–1963: Texts and Studies* (New York: Appleton-Century-Crofts, 1970); Robert Hall, *Marcus Garvey and the Universal Negro Improvement Association Papers* (Berkeley: University of California Press, 1983); Richard D. Heffner, *A Documentary History of the United States* (New York: Mentor, 1991); Homer Hickham, *Rocket Boys* (New York: Delacorte, 1998); Charles Hurd, *A Treasury of Great American Speeches* (New York: Hawthorn, 1959); Steve Israel and Seth Forman, eds., *Great Jewish Speeches Throughout History* (Northvale, NJ: Aronson, 1992); Peter Jennings and Todd Brewster, *The Century* (New York: Doubleday, 1998); Lyndon B. Johnson, *Public Papers of the Presidents of the United States* (Washington: US-GPO, 1968–69); Walter Johnson, ed., *The Papers of Adlai Stevenson* (Boston: Little, Brown, 1972); John F. Kennedy, *Public Papers of the Presidents of the United States* (Washington: USGPO, 1961–64); Philip Kurland, ed., *Landmark Briefs and Arguments Before the Supreme Court of the United States* (Chicago: University Press of America, 1975); Tom Kuntz, ed., *The Titanic Disaster Hearings* (New York: Dove, 1998); Linda Lear, *Lost Woods: The Discovered Writing of Rachel Carson* (Boston: Beacon, 1998); Arthur Link, ed., *The Papers of Woodrow Wilson* (Princeton, NJ: Princeton University Press, 1986); Brian MacArthur, *The Penguin Book of Twentieth-Century Speeches* (New York: Penguin, 1992); Brian MacArthur, *The Penguin Book of Historic Speeches* (New York: Penguin, 1996); Richard M. Nixon, *Public Papers of the Presidents of the United States* (Washington: USGPO, 1975); Sheldon Novick, *The Collected Works of Justice Holmes* (Chicago: University of Chicago Press, 1995); Donald R. McCoy and Raymond G. O'Connor, *Readings in Twentieth-Century American History* (New York: Macmillan, 1963); Michael O'Brien, *Vince: A Personal Biography of Vince Lombardi* (New York: Morrow, 1987); Doreen Rappaport, *American Women: Their Lives and Their Words* (New York: HarperCollins, 1990); Ronald W. Reagan, *Public Papers of the Presidents of the United States* (Washington: USGPO, 1984, 1987, 1989); William L. Riordon, *Plunkitt of Tammany Hall: A Series of Very Plain Talks on Very Practical Politics* (New York: Dutton, 1963); Lloyd Rohler and Roger Cook, *Great Speeches for Criticism and Analysis* (Greenwood, IN: Alistair Press, 1993); Franklin D. Roosevelt, *Public Papers of the Presidents of the United States* (Washington: USGPO, 1941); Theodore Roosevelt, *Presidential Addresses and State Papers of Theodore Roosevelt* (New York: Collier, 1905); Halford Ross Ryan, *American Rhetoric from Roosevelt to Reagan* (Prospect Heights, IL: Waveland, 1987); William Safire, *Lend Me Your Ears* (New York: Morrow, 1992); Warren Choate Shaw, ed., *History of American Oratory* (Indianapolis: Bobbs-Merrill, 1928); Deborah Gillian Straub, *Voices of Multicultural America* (Detroit: Gale Research, 1995); Billy Sunday, *"Billy" Sunday: The Man and His Message with His Own Words Which Have Won Thousands for Christ* (Philadelphia: Winston, 1914); Harry S. Truman, *Public Papers of the Presidents of the United States* (Washington: USGPO, 1946); Mark Tucker, *The Duke Ellington Reader* (New York: Oxford, 1993); U.S. Congress, House of Representatives, 81st Congress, First Session, Committee on Un-American Activities, *Hearings Regarding Communist Infiltration of Minority Groups—Part 1* (Washington: USGPO, 1949); U.S. Congress, House of Representatives, Committee on Internal Security, 92nd Congress, Second Session, *Hearings Regarding HR 16742: Restraints on Travel to Hostile Areas* (Washington: US-

GPO, 1972); U.S. Congress, Select Committee on Secret Military Assistance to Iran and Select Committee to Investigate Covert Arms Transactions with Iran, 100th Congress, First Session, *Iran–Contra Investigation* (Washington: US-GPO, 1988); U.S. Congress, Senate, Committee on the Judiciary, *Nomination of Judge Clarence Thomas to Be Associate Justice of the Supreme Court of the United States* (Washington: USGPO, 1993); Robbie Jean Walker, *The Rhetoric of Struggle: Public Address by African American Women* (New York: Garland, 1992); James M. Washington, ed., *I Have a Dream: Writings and Speeches That Changed the World* (New York: HarperCollins, 1992); Malcolm X, *Malcolm X Speaks* (New York: Pathfinder Press, 1965); Winthrop Yinger, *Cesar Chavez: The Rhetoric of Nonviolence* (Hicksville, NY: Exposition Press, 1975).